The Journals of Each Provincial Congress Of Massachusetts

In 1774 And 1775, And Of The
Committee Of Safety, With An Appendix,
Containing The Proceedings Of The
County Conventions--Narratives Of The
Events Of The Nineteenth Of April, 1775-
-Papers Relating To Ticonderoga And
Crown Point, And Other Documents,
Illustrative Of The Early History Of The
American Revolution

William Lincoln

Alpha Editions

This Edition Published in 2020

ISBN: 9789354211492

Design and Setting By
Alpha Editions
www.alphaedis.com
Email – info@alphaedis.com

INTRODUCTION.

By a resolve of the legislature of the Commonwealth, approved March 10, 1837, the governor was authorized to procure the publication of the Journals of each Provincial Congress of Massachusetts, and of such papers connected with those records, as would illustrate the patriotic exertions of the people of the state in the revolutionary contest. The subscriber had the honor of being appointed to carry this resolve into effect, by His Excellency Edward Everett, at whose suggestion measures were first adopted for perpetuating and multiplying copies of these memorials of the history of that period when the authority of the crown had been overthrown, and the powers of government were exercised by the people in their primary assemblies.

The journal of the first Provincial Congress, formed at Salem, on the seventh of October, 1774, and dissolved on the tenth day of December following, was recorded by Benjamin Lincoln, Esq., the clerk, afterwards distinguished by civic and military honors. The brave and wise men uniting in that assembly, might have foreseen through the gloomy shadow of impending war, the im-

A

portance of the consequences to result from their acts, but they could not realize the value the gratitude of posterity would attach to the memorials of their doings. The legislature had been driven from its ancient seat, and the depositaries of the public records were in the hands of an armed enemy. The documents relating to the proceedings of the first Congress, entrusted to the custody of members, whose minds were devoted to the great political events of the day, and who soon engaged in the active duties of the field, were dispersed and have perished. Returns had been procured of the militia, munitions of war, manufactures, and resources of the towns. Letters, petitions, and other communications were received, showing the spirit of the times, and the progress of the preparations for resistance of usurpation. All these have been lost, and no papers from the files, once so rich, have been preserved. It is not improbable, that in the confusion occasioned by the sudden march of the British troops to Concord, the documents exhibiting the weakness of the province in martial stores, as well as the strength of its patriotism, were destroyed.

The journal of the Second Provincial Congress, which met at Cambridge, February 1, 1775, kept in part by the same careful clerk, and partly by SAMUEL FREEMAN, Esq., suffered mutilation before it was placed in the archives of the Commonwealth. The official records of this assembly, from May 21, 1775, to its dissolution, are not known to exist, and but few of the reports, and little of the evidence, on which its proceedings were founded, have been retained.

The Third Provincial Congress convened on the thirty-first day of May, 1775, and SAMUEL FREEMAN, Esq. was elected secretary. The labors of the recording officer of a body exercising the legislative and executive powers of government, in that stormy period, called hour by hour to issue orders to the army and the towns, must have been oppressive. From that part of the original records which has been preserved, it is apparent, that the memoranda taken amid the heavy pressure of engagements, and filled with references to reports and documents afterwards to be inserted, were designed to be perfected by future revision. The time which elapsed before they were transcribed in the fair volume now in the archives of the state, prevented the omissions from being fully supplied.

Long after the two earliest assemblies had separated, copies of their journals were prepared with extraordinary neatness. The waste of years was irreparable, and the beauty of the transcript gives slight consolation for the imperfection of its contents.

So far as was possible, the fulness of the original journals has been restored in this edition : many resolutions and papers have been recovered and restored from contemporary newspapers and publications, and from other authentic sources.

The text of the original journals has been carefully preserved, and the variations introduced by later writers, except such as were too inconsiderable to be matter of importance or curiosity, have been indicated.

Documents elucidating the subjects of action or debate, have been placed in connection with the proceedings of each Congress, and some brief explanatory notes occasionally added.

Preparations for defence, and the execution of important measures pointed out by each Congress, were confided to the committees of safety and of supplies. The proceedings of these bodies while their sessions were held in union, and of the former, after the increasing weight of labor and responsibility rendered a division of duties necessary, were closely connected with the acts of the assemblies conferring the powers exercised for the common good. The journals, preserved with many imperfections, have been inserted in this volume.

The resolutions of the conventions held in the several counties, were of deep interest, and it is hoped, will be deemed appropriate additions to those of the representatives of the state. The whole journal of the local assembly held in Worcester, redeemed from the destruction which has overwhelmed so many of the memorials of the revolution, has been printed with the notices of the acts of the other communities, unfortunately less full, but the most complete which could be obtained.

The records of the towns of Massachusetts, from the first practical attempt to separate the power of taxation and the right of representation, to the termination of the war of independence, are filled with papers breathing an ardent spirit of patriotism. On their pages are eloquent vindications of the principles of civil liberty, able expositions of chartered privileges, and bold appeals against the encroachments of the crown. They bring to us the thoughts and words of the fathers of the revolution as vividly as they rose on the minds or came from the lips of the authors of the heroic resolutions. Desirable as it was to embody these representations of the virtues of the patriots of former time, it was found that the doings of each of the municipal republics, formed connected series of noble acts and exertions, spreading through many years, and that a mere selection from among the documents, made at the risk of unjust preference, would impair the value by separation, and possibly prevent the collection and publication of all of these honorable relics.

Soon after the nineteenth of April, 1775, a narrative of the events of that memorable day was prepared, substantiated by numerous depositions of witnesses of the ravages of the British during their excursion from Boston. They were transmitted to England and to the Continental Congress, and widely circulated, as the justification to the nation and the world, for the appeal to arms. These have been placed in the Appendix.

Frequent references in the journals to the letters of Arnold, and to communications relating to the capture of the fortresses at Ticonderoga and Crown Point, rendered the correspondence with Congress and the committees, a necessary supplement to the volume.

Some extracts have been made from the journals of the Continental Congress, detailing proceedings connected with the acts of the provincial assemblies. A few papers of interesting character, copied from the files, have been added.

A copious table of the principal subjects, and a full index, will afford the means of ready access to the facts spread through the pages of the work, and will render the use more easy.

Such are the contents of this volume. It was conceived to be the primary purpose of the resolve authorizing the publication, to *perpetuate materials* for the history of a glorious era in our national existence. Within the restrictions imposed by its terms, efforts have been made to give to the records the best form which could be bestowed. It was not the object of the legislature to provide for the preparation of a new narrative of the revolution, but to preserve the remains of the past. Had it been permitted, it would have been a pleasant labor to have drawn from the journals illustrations of the virtues of our ancestors, and of their devotion to liberty: the humbler duty of arranging some testimonials of their worth, it is hoped, will be found to have been executed with diligence and fidelity.

WILLIAM LINCOLN.

EXPLANATIONS OF THE REFERENCES.

|| || Words in the original journals which have been omitted from the copy in the archives of the Commonwealth, and words different in the original from those in that copy, have been enclosed by parallels : the reading of the original has been followed in this volume ; that of the copy is placed at the foot of the page with appropriate references.

||a|| The words added to the original journals in the copy before described, have been placed in the margin, and the place they occupied in the public transcript indicated by a letter of reference between parallels.

[ ] Words and passages neither in the original nor copy, inserted in the text of this edition, are enclosed between brackets.

[a] A letter of reference enclosed by brackets, points to some word removed from the text to the margin as being superfluous. Words clearly erroneous in the original or copy have been changed, and those substituted have been enclosed by the same marks, while suitable reference points to the words first used.

CONTENTS.

FIRST PROVINCIAL CONGRESS OF MASSACHUSETTS.

B

SECOND PROVINCIAL CONGRESS OF MASSACHUSETTS.

1775.

CONTENTS.

CONTENTS.

c

THIRD PROVINCIAL CONGRESS OF MASSACHUSETTS.

CONTENTS.

E

CONTENTS.

CONTENTS.

F

THE COMMITTEE OF SAFETY AND THE COMMITTEE OF SUPPLIES OF THE PROVINCIAL CONGRESS.

1774.

xliv CONTENTS.

G

CONTENTS.

CONTENTS.

CONTENTS.

CONVENTIONS OF THE PEOPLE IN THE COUNTIES OF MASSA-CHUSETTS.

Convention of Suffolk County.

Convention of Middlesex County.

Convention of Essex County.

CONTENTS.

NARRATIVES OF THE EXCURSION OF THE KING'S TROOPS,
April 19, 1775.

PAPERS RELATING TO TICONDEROGA AND CROWN POINT.

1775.

Doings of the Continental Congress.

EXTRACTS FROM THE JOURNALS OF THE CONTINENTAL CONGRESS RELATING TO MASSACHUSETTS.

1774.

MISCELLANEOUS PAPERS.

JOURNAL

OF THE

FIRST PROVINCIAL CONGRESS

OF

𝕸𝖆𝖘𝖘𝖆𝖈𝖍𝖚𝖘𝖊𝖙𝖙𝖘,

Convened at Salem, Friday, October 7, 1774.—Adjourned on the same day.
Convened at Concord, Tuesday, October 11.—Adjourned Friday, October 14.
Convened at Cambridge, Monday, October 17.—Adjourned Saturday, October 29.
Convened at Cambridge, Wednesday, November 23.—Dissolved Saturday, Dec. 10.

FIRST MEETING OF THE MEMBERS

OF THE

PROVINCIAL CONGRESS.

===

On the first day of September, 1774, his excellency Thomas Gage, governor of Massachusetts Bay, sent out precepts to the several towns and districts of the province, commanding the inhabitants to return representatives to the great and general court, ordered to be convened at Salem, on the fifth day of October then next. Alarmed by the preparations for resisting usurpations of chartered rights, by the bold spirit of the county resolves, and the patriotic instructions of the people to their delegates, it was determined by the royal council to countermand the summons for the meeting of the assembly, and to postpone its session. The following proclamation was issued, on the twenty-eighth day of September, by Governor Gage, announcing his view of the inexpediency of the meeting of the legislature at the time appointed, discharging the members from attendance, and declaring his intention not to be present at Salem.

Province of Massachusetts Bay.

By the Governor.

A PROCLAMATION.

Whereas, on the first day of September instant, I thought fit to issue writs for calling a great and general court, or assembly, to be convened and held at Salem, in the county of Essex, on the fifth day of October next; and whereas, from the many tumults and disorders which have since taken place, the extraordinary resolves which have been passed in many of the counties, the instructions given by the town of Boston, and some other towns, to their representatives, and the present disordered and unhappy state of the province, it appears to me highly inexpedient that a great and general court should be convened at the time aforesaid; but that a session at some more distant day will best tend to promote his majesty's service and the good of the province; I have, therefore, thought fit to declare my intention not to meet the said general court, at Salem, on the said fifth day of October next. And I do hereby excuse and discharge all such persons as have been, or may be elected and deputed representatives to serve at the same, from giving their attendance: any thing in the aforesaid writs contained to the contrary notwithstanding: whereof all concerned are to take notice and govern themselves accordingly.

And the sheriffs of the several counties, their under sheriffs, or deputies, and the constables of the several towns within the same, are commanded to cause this proclamation to be forthwith published and posted within their precincts.

Given at Boston, the twenty-eighth day of September, 1774, in the fourteenth year of the reign of our sovereign lord, George the third, by the grace of God, of Great Britain, France and Ireland, king, defender of the faith, &c.

THOMAS GAGE.

By His Excellency's command.

THOMAS FLUCKER, Secretary.

GOD SAVE THE KING.

Notwithstanding the executive prohibition, ninety[1] of the representatives elected in pursuance of the writs for calling the general assembly, met at Salem, on Wednesday, October, 5, 1774. With cautious courtesy they awaited during that day the attendance of the governor, or other constitutional officer, to administer the usual oaths. When it had become certain, by the lapse of time, that the presence of the chief magistrate could no longer be expected, a convention was organized, on Thursday. The Hon. John Hancock was chosen chairman, and Benjamin Lincoln, Esq., clerk. A committee was appointed to consider the proclamation, and consult on the measures proper to be adopted. Their report was presented on Friday, and the following resolutions submitted, which were accepted, and afterwards published in the newspapers of the time.

(1.) The number of those in attendance is thus stated by Gordon, *History of the American Revolution*, vol. 1, page 280; and in the *Essex Gazette, Massachusetts Spy, Boston Gazette, Boston Evening Post*, and other cotemporary prints. Some historians have supposed the members were 208 or 288; probably counting those who met at *Concord*, instead of those who assembled at *Salem*. Many of the towns refused to obey the governor's precept, and declined electing representatives to the general court, but sent delegates to the Provincial Congress.

PROVINCE OF THE MASSACHUSETTS BAY.

In the Court House at Salem, October 7, 1774.

WHEREAS, his excellency Thomas Gage, Esq., did issue writs bearing date the first of September last, for the election of members to serve as representatives in a great and general court, which he did "think fit and appoint" to be convened and holden the fifth day of October instant, at the court house in this place : And whereas, a majority of members duly elected in consequence of said writs, did attend at said court house the time appointed, there to be qualified according to charter for taking seats and acting as representatives in said great and general court ; but were not met by the governor, or other constitutional officer or officers by him appointed for administering the usual oaths, and qualifying them thereto : And whereas, a proclamation, bearing date the 28th day of September last, and published in sundry newspapers, with the signature of his excellency, contains many reflections on this province, as being in a tumultuous and disorderly state ; and appears to have been considered by his excellency as a constitutional discharge of all such persons as have been elected in consequence of his excellency's said writs: The members aforesaid so attending, having considered the measures which his excellency has been pleased to take by his said proclamation, and finding them to be unconstitutional, unjust, and disrespectful to the province, think it their duty to pass the following resolves :

Therefore, *Resolved,* as the opinion of said members :

1st. That by the royal charter of the province, the governor, for the time being, is expressly obliged to convene, "upon every last Wednesday in the month of May, every year forever, and at such other times as he shall think fit, and appoint a great and general court." And, therefore, that as his excellency had thought fit, and by his writ appointed a great and general court to be convened on the fifth day of October instant, his conduct in preventing the same is against the express words, as well as true sense and meaning of the charter, and unconstitutional ; more especially as, by charter, his excellency's power "to adjourn, prorogue and dissolve all great and general courts," doth not take place after said courts shall be appointed, until they have first "met and convened."

2dly. That the constitutional government of the inhabitants of this province, being, by a considerable military force at this time attempted to be superseded and annulled ; and the people, under the most alarming and just apprehensions of slavery, having, in their laudable endeavors to preserve themselves therefrom, discovered, upon all occasions, the greatest aversion to disorder and tumult, it must be evident to all attending to his excellency's said proclamation, that his representations of the province as being in a tumultuous and disordered state, are reflections the inhabitants have by no means merited; and, therefore, that they are highly injurious and unkind.

3dly. That, as the pretended cause of his excellency's proclamation for discharging the members elected by the province in pursuance of his writs, has for a considerable time existed, his excellency's conduct in choosing to issue said proclamation, (had it been in other respects unexceptionable,) but a few days before the court was to have been convened, and thereby unavoidably putting to unnecessary expense and trouble a great majority of members from the extremities of the province, is a measure by no means consistent with the dignity of the province; and, therefore, it ought to be considered as a disrespectful treatment of the province, and as an opposition to that reconciliation between Great Britain and the colonies so ardently wished for by all the friends of both.

4thly. That some of the causes assigned as aforesaid for this unconstitutional and wanton prevention of the general court, have, in all good governments, been considered among the greatest reasons for convening a parliament or assembly; and, therefore, the proclamation is considered as a further proof, not only of his excellency's disaffection towards the province, but of the necessity of its most vigorous and immediate exertions for preserving the freedom and constitution thereof.

Upon a motion made and seconded,

Voted, That the members aforesaid do now resolve themselves into a Provincial Congress, to be joined by such other persons as have been or shall be chosen for that purpose, to take into consideration the dangerous and alarming situation of public affairs in this province, and to consult and determine on such measures as they shall judge will tend to promote the true interest of his majesty, and the peace, welfare and prosperity of the province.

BENJAMIN LINCOLN, *Clerk.*

The subsequent proceedings of the Congress thus formed are detailed in the following journal.

JOURNAL.

||ᵃMɪɴᴜᴛᴇs of the proceedings of a Provincial Congress of Deputies of|| the several towns and districts in the Province of the Massachusetts Bay, in New England, convened at Salem, on Friday the seventh day of October, A. D., 1774; with a list of persons chosen to represent them in the same.

¹COUNTY OF SUFFOLK.

Boston.—Hon. Thomas Cushing, Esq., Mr. Samuel Adams, Hon. John Hancock, Esq., Doct. Joseph Warren, Doct. Benjamin Church, Mr. Nathaniel Appleton.

Roxbury.—Capt. William Heath, Mr. Aaron Davis.

Dorchester.—Capt. ||ᵇLemuel|| Robinson.

Milton.—Capt. David Rawson, Mr. James Boice.

Braintree.—Ebenezer Thayer, Esq., Mr. Joseph Palmer, John Adams, Esq.

Weymouth.—Mr. Nathaniel Bailey.

Hingham.—Benjamin Lincoln, Esq.

Cohasset.—Mr. Isaac Lincoln.

Dedham.—Hon. Samuel Dexter, Esq., Mr. Abner Ellis.

Medfield.—Mr. Moses Bullen, Capt. Seth Clark.

Wrentham.—Mr. Jabez Fisher, Mr. Lemuel Kollock.

Brookline.—Capt. Benjamin White, William Thompson, Esq., Mr. John Goddard.

Stoughton and ²Stoughtonham.—Mr. Thomas Crane, Mr. John Withington, Mr. Job Swift.

---

a ||At a Congress of Delegates from.|| b ||Samuel.||

(1.) The southern part of the county of Worcester and the whole of the county of Norfolk were originally included within the territorial limits of Suffolk. The former was separated by the act of incorporation, passed April 2, 1731. By the statute of March 26, 1793, all the towns mentioned in the text as belonging to the county of Suffolk, except Boston and Chelsea, were united to form the county of Norfolk. This act was repealed June 20, 1793, so far as it related to Hingham and Hull, which were annexed to the county of Plymouth, June 18, 1803.

(2.) The name of Stoughtonham was changed to Sharon, by the Legislature, February 25, 1783.

Walpole.—Mr. Enoch Ellis.
Medway.—Capt. Jonathan Adams.
Needham.—Capt. Eleazer Kingsbury.
Bellingham.—Mr. Luke Holbrook.
Hull.—[None.]
Chelsea.—Mr. Samuel Watts.

COUNTY OF ESSEX.

Salem.—Mr. John Pickering, Jun., Mr. Jonathan Ropes, Jun.
Danvers.—Doct. Samuel Holten.
Ipswich.—Capt. Michael Farley, Mr. Daniel Noyes.
Newbury.—Hon. Joseph Gerrish, Esq.
Newburyport.—Capt. Jonathan Greenleaf.
Marblehead.—Jeremiah Lee, Esq., Azor Orne, Esq., Mr. Elbridge Gerry.
Lynn.—Ebenezer Burrill, Esq., Capt. John Mansfield.
Andover.—Mr. Moody Bridges.
Beverly.—Capt. Josiah Batchelder.
Rowley.—Mr. Nathaniel Mighill.
Salisbury.—Mr. Samuel Smith.
Haverhill.—Samuel White, Esq., Mr. Joseph Haynes.
Gloucester.—Capt. Peter Coffin.
Topsfield.—Capt. Samuel Smith.
Boxford.—Aaron Wood, Esq.
Amesbury.—Isaac Merrill, Esq.
Bradford.—Capt. Daniel Thurston.
Wenham.—Mr. Benjamin Fairfield.
Manchester.—Mr. Andrew Woodbury.
Methuen.—Mr. James Ingles.
Middleton.—Capt. Archelaus Fuller.

COUNTY OF MIDDLESEX.

Cambridge.—Hon. John Winthrop, Esq., Capt. Thomas Gardner, Mr. Abraham Watson, [Mr. Francis Dana.]
Charlestown.—Mr. Nathaniel Gorham, Mr. Richard Devens, Doct. Isaac Foster, David Cheever, Esq.
Watertown.—Capt. Jonathan Brown, Mr. John Remington, Mr. Samuel Fisk.
Woburn.—Mr. Samuel Wyman.

Concord.—Capt. James Barrett, Mr. Samuel Whitney, Mr. Ephraim Wood, Jun.

Newton.—Abraham Fuller, Esq., Mr. John Pigeon, Mr. Edward Durant.

Reading.—Mr. John Temple, Mr. Benjamin Brown.

Marlborough.—Mr. Peter Bent, Mr. Edward Barnes, Mr. George Brigham.

Billerica.—William Stickney, Esq., Mr. Ebenezer Bridge.

Framingham.—Joseph Haven, Esq., Mr. [William] Brown, Capt. Josiah Stone.

Lexington.—Mr. Jonas Stone.

Chelmsford.—Mr. Simeon Spaulding, Mr. Jonathan Williams Austin, Mr. Samuel Perham.

Sherburne.—Capt. Samuel Bullard, Mr. Jonathan Leland.

Sudbury.—Mr. Thomas Plimpton, Capt. Richard Heard, Mr. James Mosman.

Malden.—Capt. Ebenezer Harnden, Capt. John Dexter.

Medford.—Mr. Benjamin Hall.

Weston.—Samuel P. Savage, Esq., Capt. Braddyl Smith, Mr. Josiah Smith.

Hopkinton.—Capt. Thomas Mellen, Capt. Roger Dench, Mr. James Mellen.

Waltham.—Mr. Jacob Bigelow.

Groton.—James Prescot, Esq.

Shirley.—Capt. Francis Harris.

Pepperell.—Capt. William Prescot.

Stow.—Henry Gardner, Esq.

Townshend.—Mr. Jonathan Stow, Capt. Daniel Taylor.

Ashby.—Mr. Jonathan Locke, Capt. [Samuel] Stone.

Stoneham.—Capt. Samuel Sprague.

Wilmington.—Mr. Timothy Walker.

Natick.—Mr. Hezekiah Broad.

Dracut.—Mr. William Hildreth.

Bedford.—Deac. Joseph Ballard, John Read, Esq.

Holliston.—Capt. Abner Perry.

Tewksbury.—Mr. Jonathan Brown.

Acton.—Mr. Josiah Hayward, Mr. Francis Faulkner, Mr. Ephraim Hapgood.

Westford.—[Capt.] Joseph Reed, Mr. Zaccheus Wright.

Littleton.—Mr. Abel Jewett, Mr. Robert Harris.

Dunstable.—John Tyng, Esq., James Tyng, Esq.

Lincoln.—Capt. Eleazer Brooks, Mr. Samuel Farrar, Capt. Abijah Pierce.

¹COUNTY OF HAMPSHIRE.

Springfield.—Doct. Charles Pynchon, Capt. George Pynchon, Mr. Jonathan Hale, Jun.

Wilbraham.—Mr. John Bliss.

Ludlow.—Mr. Joseph Miller.

West Springfield.—Mr. Benjamin Ely, Doct. Chauncy Brewer.

Northampton.—Seth Pomeroy, Esq., Hon. Joseph Hawley, Esq.

Southampton.—Mr. Elias Lyman.

Hadley.—Mr. Josiah Pierce.

South Hadley.—Mr. Noah Goodman.

Amherst.—Mr. Nathaniel Dickerson, Jun.

Granby.—Mr. Phineas Smith.

Hatfield.—Mr. John Dickerson.

Whateley.—[Mr. Oliver Graves.]

Williamsburgh.—[None.]

Deerfield.—Mr. Samuel Barnard, Jun.

Greenfield.—Mr. Daniel Nash.

Shelburne.—Mr. John Taylor.

Conway.—Mr. Thomas French.

Westfield and Southwick.—Capt. John Mosely, Mr. Elisha Parks.

Sunderland.—Mr. Israel Hubbard.

Montague.—Deac. Moses Gunn.

Brimfield.—Mr. Timothy Danielson.

South Brimfield.—Mr. Daniel Winchester.

(1) The county of Hampshire, as established May 7, 1662, comprehended the western towns of Massachusetts. A small portion of the ancient county was separated when Worcester was established, April 2, 1731. Another partition took place on the incorporation of Berkshire county, by the act of the great and general court of the province, in May 1761. The old county of Hampshire was subdivided by the statute of June 24, 1811, setting off the northern part into the county of Franklin, which included Whateley, Deerfield, Greenfield, Shelburne, Conway, Sunderland, Montague, Northfield, New Salem, Colrain, Warwick, Charlemont, Ashfield, Shutesbury, Leverett and Bernardston, named in the text, and Buckland incorporated in 1779, Wendell incorporated in 1781, Orange incorporated in 1783, Rowe and Heath both incorporated in 1785, Hawley incorporated in 1792, Gill incorporated in 1793, and Leyden incorporated in 1809. The county of Hampden was formed from the southern towns of Hampshire, by the statute passed February 25, 1812. Within its boundaries were united, Springfield, Wilbraham, Ludlow, West Springfield, Westfield, Southwick, Brimfield, South Brimfield, Monson, Granville, Murraysfield and Palmer, mentioned in the text, with Blanford incorporated in 1741, Montgomery incorporated in 1792, Tolland incorporated in 1796, and Holland incorporated in 1810. The name of Murraysfield was altered to Chester, February 21, 1783: and that of South Brimfield changed to Wales, February 20, 1828. The other towns and districts enumerated in the text, situated around the central part of the Old County, are within the present county of Hampshire; as are Pelham incorporated April 21, 1742, and Westhampton incorporated September 29, 1772, and omitted in the list of municipal corporations existing in 1774.

Monson.—Mr. Abel Goodale.
Northfield.—Mr. Phineas Wright.
Granville.—Timothy Robinson, Esq.
New Salem.—Mr. William Page, Jun.
Colrain.—Capt. Thomas McGee.
Belchertown.—Capt. Samuel Howe.
Ware.—Mr. Joseph Foster.
Murraysfield.—[None.]
Warwick.—Capt. Samuel Williams.
Charlemont.—Mr. Hugh Maxwell.
Ashfield.—[None.]
Worthington.—Capt. Nahum Eager.
Greenwich.—Mr. John Rea.
Shutesbury.—[None.]
Chesterfield.—[None.]
Norwich.—Mr. Ebenezer Meacham.
[1]*Edgecomb.*—[None.]
Leverett.—[None.]
Palmer.—Mr. David Spear.

COUNTY OF PLYMOUTH.

Plymouth.—Hon. James Warren, Esq., Mr. Isaac Lothrop.
Scituate.—Nathan Cushing, Esq., Mr. Gideon Vinal, Mr. Barnabas Little.
Marshfield.—Mr. Nehemiah Thomas.
Middleborough.—Capt. Ebenezer Sprout.
Hanover.—Capt. Joseph Cushing.
Rochester.—Capt. Ebenezer White.
Plympton.—Mr. Samuel Lucas.
Pembroke.—Mr. John Turner, Capt. Seth Hatch.
Abington.—Capt. Woodbridge Brown, Doct. David Jones.
Bridgewater.—Capt. Edward Mitchel, Doct. Richard Perkins.
Kingston.—John Thomas, Esq.
Duxbury.—Mr. George Partridge.
Halifax.—[None.]
Wareham.—[None.]

(1) Edgecomb was probably inadvertently placed among the towns of Hampshire, instead of those of Lincoln county, in Maine.

[1]COUNTY OF BARNSTABLE.

Barnstable.—Daniel Davis, Esq.
Sandwich.—Mr. Stephen Nye.
Yarmouth.—Capt. Elisha Bassett.
Eastham and Welfleet.—Mr. Naaman Holbrook.
Harwich.—Mr. Benjamin Freeman.
Falmouth.—Mr. Moses Swift.
Chatham.—Capt. Joseph Doane.
Truro.—Mr. Benjamin Atkins.

COUNTY OF BRISTOL.

Taunton.—Robert Treat Paine, Esq., Doct. David Cobb.
Rehoboth.—Capt. Thomas Carpenter, Timothy Walker, Esq.
Swansey and [2]Shawamet.—Col. [Andrew] Cole, Capt. Levi Whea-
ton, [Col. Jerathmiel Bowers.]
Dartmouth.—Benjamin Aikin, Esq.
Norton and Mansfield.—Mr. Eleazer Clap,
Attleborough.—Mr. Ebenezer Lane, Capt. John Daggett.
Dighton.—Elnathan Walker, Esq., Doct. William Baylies.
Freetown.—[None.]
Easton.—Mr. Eliphalet Leonard, Capt. Zephaniah Keith.
Raynham.—Mr. Benjamin King.
Berkley.—[None.]

COUNTY OF YORK.

York.—Capt. Daniel Bragdon.
Kittery.—Charles Chauncey, Esq., Edward Cutt, Esq.
Wells.—Mr. Ebenezer Sayer.
Berwick.—Capt. William Gerrish.
Biddeford.—Mr. [James] Sullivan.
[3]*Pepperrellborough.*—[None.]
Lebanon.—[None.]
Sandford.—[None.]
Buxton.—[None.][4]

(1) Provincetown, incorporated June 14, 1727, belonged to Barnstable county in 1774.

(2) That part of Swansey known as "the Shawamet purchase," became the town of Somerset February 20, 1790.

(3) The name of Saco was adopted instead of Pepperrellborough, February 25, 1805.

(4) Another town had been established in York county, previous to the session of the Provincial Congress, called Cape Porpoise in 1753, Arundel from June 5, 1718, and Kennebunk Port after 1820. The northern part of the counties of York and Cumberland, uninhabited in 1774, was incorporated as the county of Oxford, March 4, 1805.

COUNTY OF DUKES.

Edgarton.—[None.]
Chilmark.—Joseph Mayhew, Esq.
Tisbury.—Mr. Ranford Smith.

COUNTY OF NANTUCKET.

[1]*Sherburn.*—[None.]

COUNTY OF WORCESTER.

Worcester.—Mr. Joshua Bigelow, Mr. Timothy Bigelow.

Lancaster.—Capt. Asa Whitcomb, Doct. William Dunsmore.

Mendon.—Joseph Dorr, Esq., Mr. Edward Rawson.

Brookfield.—Jedediah Foster, Esq., Capt. Jeduthan Baldwin, Capt. Phinehas Upham.

Oxford.—Capt. Ebenezer Learned, Doct. Alexander Campbell.

Charlton.—Capt. Jonathan Tucker.

Sutton.—Capt. Henry King, Mr. Edward Putnam.

Leicester, Spencer and Paxton.—[2]Col. Thomas Denny, Capt. Joseph Henshaw.

Rutland.—Mr. Daniel Clap.

Rutland District.[3]—Mr. John Mason.

(1) This town received the name of Nantucket June 8, 1795.

(2) Col. Denny was early compelled by fatal sickness to leave his seat in Congress, and return to Leicester, where he died October 23, 1774, at the age of 49 years. The vacancy in the delegation occasioned by his retirement was supplied by the election of Capt. Henshaw, October 20, 1774.

(3) Rutland District had been made a town in June, 1774. The act of incorporation, as it went from the representative branch of the legislature, conferred municipal powers, but bestowed no corporate name. When the parchment reached the council chamber, the blank was filled by the executive, and the unwelcome designation of Hutchinson imposed on the patriotic citizens. The measures taken to remedy such heavy civic calamity, are recited in the following remarkable preamble of the statute, passed at the May session of the general court, in 1776, strongly expressing the popular sentiment of the time: " Whereas, the inhabitants of the town of Hutchinson have, by their petition, represented to this court, that in June, 1774, when the said town was incorporated, General Gage, then governor, gave it the name of Hutchinson, in honor to, and to perpetuate the memory of Thomas Hutchinson, his immediate predecessor in the chair of government, whom they justly style the well known enemy of the natural and stipulated rights of America ; that, at a town meeting, notified for that purpose, they voted, unanimously, to petition, and accordingly have petitioned the general court, that the name of the said town might be altered [to Wilkes,] and that it might no longer bear the disgraceful name of Hutchinson: And, whereas, there is a moral fitness that traitors and parricides, especially such as have remarkably distinguished themselves in that odious character, and have long labored to deprive their native country of its most valuable rights and privileges, and to destroy every constitutional guard against the evils of an all enslaving despotism, should be held up to public view in their true characters, to be execrated by mankind, and that there should remain no other memorials of them, than such as will transmit their names with infamy to posterity : And, whereas, the said Thomas Hutchinson, contrary to every obligation of duty and gratitude to this his native country which raised him from private life to the highest and most lucrative offices in the government, has acted toward her the part of a traitor and parricide as above described, which has been clearly manifested to the world by his letters lately published,

Oakham.—Mr. Jonathan Bullard.

Hubbardston.—Mr. John Clark.

Westborough.—Capt. Stephen Maynard, Doct. James Hawse.

Northborough.—Mr. Levi Brigham.

Shrewsbury.—Hon. Artemas Ward, Esq., Mr. Phineas Hayward.

Lunenburgh and Fitchburgh.—Capt. George ||ªKimball,|| Capt. Abijah Stearns, Capt. David Goodridge.

Uxbridge.—Capt. Joseph Reed.

Harvard.—Mr. Joseph Wheeler.

Bolton.—Capt. Samuel Baker, Mr. Ephraim Fairbanks.

Petersham.—Capt. Ephraim Doolittle.

Southborough.—Capt. Jonathan Ward.

Hardwick.—Capt. Paul Mandell, Mr. Stephen Rice.

¹*Western.*—Mr. Gershom Makepeace.

Sturbridge.—Capt. Timothy Parker.

Leominster.—Thomas Legate, Esq., Mr. Israel Nichols

Dudley.—Thomas Cheney, Esq.

Upton.—Mr. Abiel Sadler.

New Braintree.—Capt. James Wood.

Holden—Mr. John Child.

Douglass.—Mr. Samuel Jennison.

Grafton.—Capt. John Goulding.

Royalston.—Mr. Henry Bond.

Westminster.—Mr. Nathan Wood, Mr. Abner Holden.

Templeton.—Mr. Jonathan Baldwin.

Athol.—Mr. William Bigelow.

Princeton.—Mr. Moses Gill, Capt. Benjamin Holden.

Ashburnham.—Mr. Jonathan Taylor.

Winchendon.—Mr. Moses Hale.

²*Woodstock.*—[None.]

Northbridge.—Mr. Samuel Baldwin.

COUNTY OF CUMBERLAND.

Falmouth and Cape Elizabeth.—Enoch Freeman, Esq.

---

a ||Campbell.||

and by his having thus acted, it has become fit and just that every honorable memorial of him should be obliterated and cease:" Therefore, it was enacted, that the town of Hutchinson should no longer bear that name, but thenceforth should be called Barre.

(1) The name of Western was altered to Warren, March 13, 1834.

(2) Woodstock is erroneously inserted in the text. The inhabitants of that town, settled in 1686, long attached to Suffolk, afterwards connected with Worcester county, seceded from the jurisdiction of Massachusetts, in 1747; in 1752 they were admitted to the privileges and protection of Connecticut, and on the settlement of their boundary line, became, and have remained citizens of that state.

Scarborough.—Mr. Samuel March.
North Yarmouth.—Mr. John Lewis.
Gorham.—Solomon Lombard, Esq.
Brunswick and Harpswell.—Mr. Samuel Thompson.

¹COUNTY OF LINCOLN.—[None.]

²COUNTY OF BERKSHIRE.

Sheffield, Great Barrington, Egremont and Alford.—John Fellows, Esq., Doct William Whiting.
Stockbridge and West Stockbridge.—Mr. Thomas Williams.
Tyringham.—Capt. Giles Jackson.
Pittsfield.—John Brown, Esq.
Richmond.—[None.]
Lenox.—Mr. John Patterson.
Becket.—Mr. Jonathan Wadsworth.

The Congress proceeded to the choice of a Chairman, when the Hon. John Hancock, Esq., was elected.

Benjamin Lincoln, Esq. was chosen clerk.

Upon a motion, *Voted,* That the Congress be adjourned to the ||ᵃcourt house in|| Concord, ||there to meet on Tuesday next, at ten o'clock in the forenoon.³||

TUESDAY, October 11, 1774, A. M.

The Congress met according to adjournment.

Upon a motion ||*Resolved,* That the Congress be adjourned to the meeting house in Concord: Being met there, upon a motion|| the

a ||Meeting house at.||

(1) This county, established in 1760, extended at the period of the entries in the journal over the vast territory of Maine, where the counties of Lincoln, Hancock, Waldo, Washington, Kennebeck, Somerset and Penobscot have risen. The figures prefixed to the names of the towns existing in 1774, indicate the date of incorporation of each: 1716, Georgetown; 1753, Newcastle; 1759, Woolwich; 1760, Pownalsborough, changed to Wiscasset, June 10, 1802; 1762, Bowdoinham; 1764, Boothbay, Topsham; 1765, Bristol; 1771, Hallowell, Winthrop, Vassalborough, Winslow; 1773, Waldoborough, Belfast; 1774, Edgecomb; Gardnerstown received the name of Pittston, February 4, 1773.

(2) In Berkshire were the following towns, in addition to those enumerated in the text, incorporated prior to 1774, in the year annexed to each name; Partridgefield, 1771, named Peru, June 19, 1806; New Marlborough, 1759; Lanesborough, 1765; Sandisfield, 1762; Williamstown, 1765; Gageborough, 1771, called Winsor, 1778; Otis, 1773.

(3) Conventions of delegates in the several counties had appointed the second Tuesday of October and the town of Concord, as the time and place for the meeting of the Congress of the province, long before writs were issued by the governor for convening the general court. The adjournment was in conformity with the resolutions of the local assemblies.

"The meeting was first held in the old court house, but that being too small to convene so large an assembly, it was adjourned to the meeting house. Two sessions, one at nine, and the other at three o'clock, were held each day."——*Shattuck's Concord,* 91.

question was put, whether they would reconsider their vote relative to the appointing a chairman, and then proceed to the choice of a president, by written votes, and passed in the affirmative.

Upon a motion, *Ordered*, That Capt. Heath, Hon. Mr. Dexter, and Hon. Col. Ward, be a committee to count and sort the votes for a president.

The Congress proceeded to bring in their votes for a president, and the committee having counted and sorted the same, reported that the Hon. John Hancock, Esq., was chosen.

The Congress then appointed Benjamin Lincoln, Esq., secretary.

Upon a motion, *Ordered*, That Capt. Barrett, Doct. Warren, and Hon. Col. Ward, be a committee to wait on the Rev. Mr. Emerson, and desire his attendance on the Congress, that the business might be opened with prayer.

The committee appointed to wait on the Rev. Mr. Emerson, reported that they had attended [to] that service, and that the Rev. Mr. Emerson would soon attend on the Congress agreeable to their desire.

Adjourned to three o'clock this afternoon.

Three o'clock, P. M.—The Congress is further adjourned to half after eight o'clock to-morrow morning.

WEDNESDAY, October 12, 1774, A. M.

‖ᵃ‖ Upon a motion, *Ordered*, That Major Fuller, Col. Prescot, Doct. Warren, and Doct. Holten, be appointed to return the Congress when necessary, in order the more easily to ascertain a vote, and that they observe the following divisions, viz : The wall pews on the right of the desk for one division; [those] on the left for another; the men's seats and the pews adjoining them, a third; and the women's seats and the pews adjoining them, the fourth.

Upon a motion, the question was put whether the several resolutions entered into by the counties respectively, be now read, and passed in the affirmative.   They were read accordingly.[1]

Resolved, That a doorkeeper be appointed.

Resolved, That Capt. Barrett be desired to appoint some suitable person for a doorkeeper; he appointed accordingly, Mr. Jeremiah Hunt for that purpose.

Ordered, That the Hon. John Hancock, Esq., Hon. Joseph Hawley, Esq., Doct. Warren, Hon. Samuel Dexter, Esq., Hon. Col. Ward, Hon.

a ‖Congress met agreeably to adjournment.‖

(1) The records of the county conventions so far as they can be recovered will be found in the Appendix.

Col. Warren, Capt. Heath, Col. Lee, Doct. Church, Doct. Holten, Mr. Gerry, Col. Tyng, Capt. Roberson, Major Foster, and Mr. Gorham, be a committee to take into consideration the state of the province, and report as soon as may be.

||Then the Congress|| adjourned to three o'clock this afternoon.

Afternoon.

Adjourned to nine o'clock to-morrow morning.

THURSDAY, October 13, 1774, A. M.

||ᵃ||Adjourned to three o'clock this afternoon.

Afternoon.

The committee on the state of the province, reported the following message to his excellency. The same was considered and accepted by the Congress with one ||ᵇdissentient|| only, and the president was ||ᶜordered|| to attest the same.

May it please your Excellency :

The delegates from the several towns in the province of the Massachusetts Bay, having convened in general Congress, beg leave to address your excellency. The distressed and miserable state of the province, occasioned by the intolerable grievances and oppressions to which the people are subjected, and the danger and destruction to which they are exposed, of which your excellency must be sensible, and the want of a general assembly, have rendered it indispensably necessary to collect the wisdom of the province by their delegates in this Congress, to concert some adequate remedy for preventing impending ruin, and providing for the public safety.

It is with the utmost concern we see your hostile preparations, which have spread such alarm throughout this province and the whole continent, as threatens to involve us in all the confusion and horrors of a civil war ; and while we contemplate an event so deeply to be regretted by every good man, it must occasion the surprise and astonishment of all mankind, that such measures are pursued against a people whose love of order, attachment to Britain, and loyalty to their prince, have ever been truly exemplary. Your excellency must be sensible that the sole end of government is the protection and security of the people. Whenever, therefore, that power, which was originally instituted to effect these important and valuable purposes, is employed to harass, distress, or enslave the people, in this case it becomes a curse rather than a blessing.

a||Congress met agreeably to adjournment.|| b ||dissentient voice.|| c ||requested.||

The most painful apprehensions are excited in our minds by the measures now pursuing. The rigorous execution of the Port Bill, with [ᵃincreased] severity, must eventually reduce the capital and its numerous dependencies to a state of poverty and ruin. The acts for altering the charter and the administration of justice in the colony, are manifestly designed to abridge this people of their rights, and to license murders; and, if carried into execution, will reduce them to a state of slavery. The number of troops in the capital, increased by daily accessions drawn from the whole continent, together with the formidable and hostile preparations which you are now making on Boston Neck, in our opinion, greatly endanger the lives, liberties and properties, not only of our brethren in the town of Boston, but of this province in general. Permit us to ask your excellency, whether an inattentive and unconcerned acquiescence [ᵇin] such alarming, such menacing measures, would not evidence a state of insanity; or, whether the delaying to take every possible precaution for the security of the province, would not be the most criminal neglect in a people heretofore rigidly and justly tenacious of their ||ᶜconstitutional|| rights?

Penetrated with the most poignant concern, and ardently solicitous to preserve union and harmony between Great Britain and the Colonies, so indispensably necessary to the well being of both, we entreat your excellency to remove that brand of contention, the fortress at the entrance of Boston. We are much concerned that you should have been induced to construct it, and thereby causelessly excite such a spirit of resentment and indignation as now generally prevails.

We assure you, sir, that the good people of this colony never have had the least intention to do any injury to his majesty's troops; but, on the contrary, most earnestly desire that every obstacle to treating them as fellow-subjects may be immediately removed; [ᵈand we] are constrained to tell your excellency, that the minds of the people will never be relieved till those hostile works are demolished; and we request you, as you regard his majesty's honor and interest, the dignity and happiness of the empire, and the peace and welfare of this province, that you immediately desist from the fortress now constructing at the south entrance into the town of Boston, and restore the pass to its natural state.

Upon a motion,

Ordered, That a fair copy of the foregoing report be taken and presented to his excellency Thomas Gage, Esq., and that a committee be

---

a [improved.]   b [to]   c ||constituted.|| d [but.]

appointed to wait upon him early to-morrow morning with the same. Accordingly, Col. Lee, Hon. Col. Ward, Col. Orne, Capt. Gardner, Henry Gardner, Esq., Mr. Devens, Mr. Gorham, Capt. Brown, Col. Pomeroy, Hon. Col. Prescot, Col. Thayer, Mr. Williams, Capt. Heath, Capt. Upham, Mr. Barnes, Capt. Doolittle, Mr. Lothrop, Major Thompson, Mr. Palmer, Mr. Pickering, and Capt. Thompson, were appointed.

Resolved, That when this Congress shall adjourn over the sabbath, that it be adjourned to the court house in Cambridge.

Then the Congress adjourned till to-morrow morning, nine o'clock.

FRIDAY, October 14, 1774, A. M.

Resolved, That the message to his excellency be printed in the Boston newspapers.

Adjourned to three o'clock this afternoon.

Afternoon.

The committee on the state of the province reported the following resolve, which was read, considered and accepted, and *ordered* that it be printed in the Boston newspapers, and attested by the secretary.

Resolved, That the several constables and collectors of taxes throughout the province, who have or shall have any moneys in their hands collected on province assessments, be advised not to pay the same, or any part thereof, to the Hon. Harrison Gray, Esq., but that such constables and collectors, as also such constables and collectors as have or shall have any county moneys in their hands, take and observe such orders and directions touching the same, as shall be given them by the several towns and districts by whom they were chosen. And that the sheriffs and deputy sheriffs of the several counties in the province, who have in their hands any province moneys, be also advised not to pay the same to the said Harrison Gray, Esq., but that they retain the same in their hands respectively, until the further advice of a Provincial Congress, or order from a constitutional assembly of this province. And that the present assessors of the several towns and districts in the province, be advised to proceed to make assessments of the tax granted by the great and general court of the province at their last May session, and that such assessments be duly paid by the persons assessed, to such person or persons as shall be ordered by the said towns and districts respectively. And the Congress strongly recommend the payment of the tax accordingly.

The Congress then adjourned to the court house in Cambridge, there to meet on Monday next, at ten o'clock in the forenoon.

||CAMBRIDGE,|| Monday, October 17, 1774, A. M.

The Congress met according to adjournment, and adjourned to the meeting house in Cambridge.

Upon a motion,

Ordered, That Capt. Gardner, Mr Watson, and Mr. Cheever, be a committee to wait on the Rev. Doct. Appleton, and desire that he would attend the Congress and open the meeting with prayer.

The committee reported, that they had waited on the Rev. Doct. Appleton, and delivered the message, and that he would wait on the Congress immediately.

Upon a motion, the question was put, whether application be made to the governor of the college, for leave for the Congress to sit in the new chapel, and passed in the negative.

Resolved, That the seats now chosen by the members in Congress, and those which may be chosen by them in future upon their first coming into the same, be their seats during the session thereof.

Resolved, That the Congress be returned in divisions as agreed on at Concord.

Mr. President informed the Congress that he had in his hand his excellency's answer to our message to him of the thirteenth instant, directed to Col. Lee, ||and others which he read and is as followeth :||

To Col. Lee, Hon. Col. Ward, Col. Orne, Capt. Gardner, Henry Gardner, Esq., Mr. Devens, Mr. Gorham, Capt. Brown, Col. Pomeroy, Hon. Col. Prescot, Col. Thayer, Mr. Williams, Capt. Heath, Capt. Upham, Mr. Barnes, Capt. Doolittle, Mr. Lothrop, Major Thompson, Mr. Palmer, Mr. Pickering, and Capt. Thompson, said to be a committee to wait on his excellency with a message.

GENTLEMEN : The previous menaces daily thrown out, and the unusual warlike preparations throughout the country, made it an act of duty in me to pursue the measures I have taken in constructing what you call a fortress, which, unless annoyed, will annoy nobody.

It is surely highly exasperating, as well as ungenerous, even to hint that the lives, liberties, or properties of any persons, except avowed enemies, are in danger from Britons; Britain can never harbor the black design of wantonly destroying, or enslaving, any people on earth. And notwithstanding the enmity shewn the king's troops, by withholding from them almost every necessary for their preservation, they have not, as yet, discovered the resentment which might justly be expected to arise from such hostile treatment.

No person can be more solicitous than myself to procure union and harmony between Great Britain and her colonies, and I ardently wish to contribute to the completion of a work so salutary to both countries. But an open and avowed disobedience to all her authority, is only bidding defiance to the mother country, and gives little hopes of bringing a spirited nation to that favorable disposition, which a more decent and dutiful conduct might effect.

Whilst you complain of acts of parliament that make alterations in your charter, and put you in some degree on the same footing with many other provinces, you will not forget that by your assembling, you are yourselves subverting that charter, and now acting in ||direct|| violation of your own constitution.

It is my duty, therefore, however irregular your application is, to warn you of the rock you are upon, and to require you to desist from such illegal and unconstitutional proceedings.

THOMAS GAGE.

PROVINCE HOUSE, October 17, 1774.

Resolved, That his excellency's answer be committed to the committee on the state of the province.

Ordered, That the letters on his honor's table, said to be wrote by the Rev. Mr. Peters,[1] be committed to the committee on the state of the province.

Adjourned to three o'clock this afternoon.

(1) Rev. Samuel Peters, born at Hebron, in Connecticut, December 12, 1735, of Yale College 1757, took orders and assumed the charge of the churches of his native town and of Hartford in 1762. He resided in Hebron until 1774. In that year, public indignation was strongly roused by communications to the royalist newspapers attributed to his pen. His house was often visited by committees from the patriotic inhabitants, his papers searched, and his person sometimes treated with severity. The letters mentioned in the text were sent from Boston, where he had taken refuge, to his friends and relatives: they were intercepted, and submitted to the Congress.

On the 28th of September, he writes to his mother: "I should be happy if my friends and relations at Hebron were provided for at these bad times when things are growing worse. Six regiments are coming over from England and sundry men of war. So soon as they come HANGING WORK will go on, and DESTRUCTION will attend first the sea port towns. The lintel sprinkled on the sidepost will preserve the faithful."

In a letter to Dr. Auchmuty, at New York, dated at Boston, October 1, 1774, he writes:

"The riots and mobs that have attended me and my house, set on by the Governor of Connecticut, have compelled me to take up my abode here; and the clergy of Connecticut must fall a sacrifice with the several churches, very soon, to the rage of the puritan mobility, if the old serpent, that dragon, is not bound."...."Judge Auchmuty will do all that is reasonable for the neighboring charter. Necessity calls for such friendship, as the head is sick and heart faint, and spiritual iniquity rides in high places, with halberts, pistols, and swords. See the proclamation I sent you by my nephew, on their pious sabbath day, the 4th of last month, when the preachers and magistrates left the pulpits, &c., for the gun and drum and set off for Boston, cursing the King and Lord North, General Gage, the bishops and their cursed curates, and the church of England. And for my telling the church people not to take up arms, &c., it being high treason, &c., the sons of liberty have almost killed one of my church, tarred and feathered two, abused others, and on the 6th day destroyed my windows, and rent my clothes, even my gown, &c., crying out, down with the church,

Afternoon.

Resolved, That in the absence of the president, the secretary have power to adjourn the Congress.

Ordered, That the committee appointed to wait on the Rev. Doct. Appleton this morning to desire his attendance on the Congress, and [that he would] open the meeting with prayer, again wait on him, and return him the thanks of this Congress for his attendance ||on|| and prayer with them this morning; and desire that he would officiate as their chaplain during their session here.

Adj urned till to-morrow morning, nine o'clock.

TUESDAY, October 18, 1774, A. M.

||ᵃ||*Ordered*, That the galleries be now cleared, and that the doors of the house be kept shut, during the debates of the Congress, until the further order thereof.

Resolved, That a doorkeeper be appointed; and that the members of the town of Cambridge appoint some suitable person for that purpose.   Mr. ||William|| Darling was appointed accordingly.

Adjourned to three o'clock this afternoon.

Afternoon.

Moved, That the Congress now determine whether they will, or will not, reply to his excellency's answer.

After some debate thereon, the question was put, whether the Congress will make a reply to his excellency's answer, and it passed in the affirmative.

||Then the Congress|| adjourned till to-morrow morning, ten o'clock.

WEDNESDAY, October 19, 1774, A. M.

Ordered, That the doorkeeper see that the galleries be now cleared.

The committee on the state of the province reported a reply to his excellency's message.   The same was read and ordered to be recommitted.

Ordered, That Capt. Heath, Major Fellows, Col. Thomas, Capt. Gardner, and Col. Pomeroy, be a committee to make as minute an inquiry into the present state and operations of the army as may be, and report.

a ||Congress met pursuant to adjournment.||

the rags of popery, &c.   Their rebellion is obvious, and treason is common, and robbery is the daily devotion.   The Lord deliver us from anarchy.   The bounds of New York may directly extend to Connecticut river; Boston meet them; New Hampshire, take the province of Maine; and Rhode Island be swallowed up as Dathan.   Pray lose no time, nor fear worse times than attend us."

Mr. Peters went to England in the autumn of 1774: published a history of Connecticut in 1781, which has not been considered a work of good authority: returned to America in 1805: went to the falls of St. Anthony claiming a large territory under Carver, in 1817 and 1818: and died in New York, April 19, 1826, aged 90.

Ordered, That no members be called out.

The committee on the state of the province reported an answer to his excellency's message; which, having been read and considered, in ||^aparagraphs, and so passed|| was ordered to lie on the table.

Adjourned till to-morrow morning, nine o'clock.

THURSDAY, October 20, 1774, A. M.

The committee appointed to make inquiry into the state and operations of the army reported. The report, after being read, was ordered to lie on the table.

Afternoon.

Resolved, That a committee be appointed to consider what is necessary to be now done for the defence and safety of the province.

Resolved, That the committee consist of thirteen, viz: two in the county of Suffolk, and one in each other county [^bwhich has] returned members to this Congress.

Resolved, That each county appoint its own member.

The members of the several counties retired, soon returned, and reported that they had made choice of the following gentlemen respectively, viz:

Suffolk.—Hon. Samuel Dexter, Esq., and Capt. Heath. *Middlesex.*— Capt. Gardner. *Essex.*—Col. Orne. *Hampshire.*—Major Hawley. *Plymouth.*—Col. Thomas. *Barnstable.*—Daniel Davis, Esq. *Bristol.*—Col. Walker. *York.*—Edward Cutt, Esq. *Dukes.*—Mr. Smith. *Worcester.*—Hon. Col. Ward. *Cumberland.*—Major Freeman. *Berkshire.*—Major Fellows.

Upon a motion, *Ordered,* That the gentlemen appointed by the several counties respectively be a committee for the purpose aforesaid.

The committee on the state of the province reported a resolve relative to the payment and collecting of the outstanding rates and taxes; the same ||^cwas|| read, and ordered to be recommitted.

Upon a motion, *Ordered,* That the answer to his excellency's message remain on the table.

Then adjourned till nine o'clock to-morrow morning.

FRIDAY, October 21, 1774, A. M.

Ordered, That Mr. Gerry, Col. Warren, and Col. Lee, be a committee to report a letter to the selectmen, overseers of the poor, committee of correspondence, and committee of donations, for the town of

---

a ||paragraph by paragraph.|| b [who have.]   c ||being.||

Boston, desiring their attendance at this Congress, to consult ||ᵃmeans|| for the preservation of the town of Boston at this alarming crisis.

Upon a motion, the question was put, whether the Congress will now assign a time when they will take into consideration the propriety of recommending a day of public thanksgiving throughout this province, and passed in the affirmative; accordingly three o'clock this afternoon was ||ᵇassigned|| for that purpose.

||Upon a motion the question was put, whether the Congress will now assign a time when they will take into consideration the propriety of recommending a day of fasting and prayer throughout this province, and it passed in the affirmative. Accordingly, four o'clock this afternoon is assigned for that purpose.||

Upon a motion, the question was put whether a time be now assigned to take into consideration the propriety of appointing an agent or agents, to repair to the government of Canada, in order to consult with the inhabitants thereof, and settle a friendly correspondence and agreement with them, and passed in the affirmative; accordingly, five o'clock this afternoon was appointed for that purpose.

The committee appointed to report a letter to the selectmen of the town of Boston, and others, reported a letter accordingly, which was read and accepted, and the president ||ᶜordered|| to sign the same.

Ordered, That the gentlemen wrote to and expected from Boston, [be requested to] bring with them six or eight of Rivington's late newspapers.

The committee on the state of the province, reported several resolves relative to the counsellors and others who have acted in obedience to the late act of parliament for altering the civil constitution of this government, and are now in Boston. The same being read and considered, were ordered to be recommitted for amendments; which were accordingly recommitted, amended, reported, accepted, and ordered to be printed in all the Boston newspapers, and are as follow, viz:

Whereas, sundry persons now in Boston, have as mandamus counsellors, or in other capacities, accepted or acted under commissions or authority derived from the act of parliament passed last session, for changing the form of government and violating the charter of this province; and by such disgraceful, such detestable conduct, have counteracted not only the sense of this province, but of the United American Colonies, in Grand Congress expressed:

Therefore, *Resolved,* That the persons aforesaid who shall not give satisfaction to this injured province and continent, within ten days from the publication of this resolve, by causing to be published in all the Boston newspapers, acknowledgments of their former misconduct, and renunciations of the commissions and authority mentioned, ought to be considered as infamous betrayers of their country; and that a committee of Congress be ordered to cause their names to be published repeatedly, that the inhabitants of this province, by having them entered on the records of each town, as rebels against the state, may send them down to posterity with the infamy they deserve; and that other parts of America may have an opportunity of stigmatizing them in such way as shall effectually answer a similar purpose.

Resolved, That it be and hereby is recommended to the good people of this province, so far to forgive such of the obnoxious persons aforesaid, who shall have given the satisfaction required in the preceding resolve, as not to molest them for their past misconduct.

Ordered, That Major Thompson, Mr Devens, and Mr. Watson, be a committee to cause the names of sundry persons now in Boston, having as mandamus counsellors, or in other capacities, accepted or acted under commission or authority derived from the act of parliament passed last session, for changing the form of government and violating the charter of this province, to be published repeatedly, in case they shall not, within ten days, give satisfaction to this injured province, by causing to be published in all the Boston newspapers, acknowledgments of their misconduct, and renunciations of the commissions and authority aforesaid.

Ordered, That Mr. Appleton, Mr. Gill, Mr. Pickering, Mr. Legate, and Major Thompson, be a committee to report a non consumption agreement relative to British and India goods.

Ordered, That Mr. Palmer, Capt. Doolittle, Capt. Greenleaf, Doct. Foster, and Col. Danielson, be a committee to report a resolve recommending the total disuse of India teas.

Then adjourned till three o'clock this afternoon.

Afternoon.

Mr. President informed the Congress that he had in his hands a number of Rivington's newspapers; Whereupon

Ordered, That Mr. Gerry, Capt. Farley, and Doct. Church, be a committee to look over the same; and if any thing therein should appear to have been written with a design to injure this province, that they report it to the Congress.[1]

(1) *Rivington's New York Gazateer, or the Connecticut, Hudson's River, New Jersey, and Quebec Weekly Advertiser*, was published in the city of New York. It commenced April 22, 1773;

Ordered, That Mr. Gill, Major Fuller, Col. Prescott, Mr. Hall, Mr. Gardner of Stow, Mr. Davis, and Capt. Upham, be a committee to wait on the gentlemen selectmen, and others, expected from Boston, and conduct them to this body.

The gentlemen selectmen, overseers of the poor, committee of correspondence, and committee of donations, being introduced, a free conversation was had with them on means for preserving the town of Boston at this alarming crisis.

The committee appointed to bring in a resolve recommending the total disuse of India teas in this province, reported. The report was read and accepted, and is as follows:

Whereas, the unnecessary and extravagant consumption of East India teas in time past, has much contributed to the political destruction of this province; and as tea has been the mean by which a corrupt administration have attempted to tax, enslave, and ruin us: Therefore,

Resolved, That this Congress do earnestly recommend to the people of this province an abhorrence and detestation of all kinds of East India teas, as the baneful vehicle of a corrupt and venal administration, for the purpose of introducing despotism and slavery into this once happy country; and that every individual in this province ought totally to disuse the same. And it is also recommended, that every town and district, appoint a committee to post up in some public place the names of all such in their respective towns and districts, who shall sell or consume so extravagant and unnecessary an article of luxury.

The committee appointed to consider what is necessary to be done for the defence and safety of this province, reported. The report was read, and ordered that the consideration thereof be referred till to-morrow morning.

||The Congress then|| adjourned till to-morrow morning nine o'clock.

was devoted to the support of the principles of the British administration; had extensive circulation among the royalists of the principal towns of the colonies; and received the patronage of government. It was continued until November 27, 1775, when a troop of armed men from Connecticut surrounded the printing house, broke the press, destroyed the cases, scattered the forms, and carried away a large quantity of type to melt into bullets.

James Rivington, the publisher, born in London, arrived in America in 1760, and commenced business as a bookseller in Philadelphia. He pursued the same trade in Boston and in New York, without success, and in 1773 became printer. After the disaster which terminated the existence of the Gazateer, he procured new apparatus, was appointed the king's printer for New York, and reestablished his newspaper. His editorial labors ceased in 1783. He resumed the occupation of bookseller, and died in July, 1802, aged seventy-eight years.—*See Thomas's History of Printing,* vol. II, pages 111, 312.

The newspapers exhibited to the Congress, had a decided tone of loyal sentiment, but contained no reflections peculiarly injurious to the character or feelings of the people of the province.

SATURDAY, October 22, 1774, A. M.

The Congress resumed the consideration of the report of the committee appointed to consider what is necessary to be done for the defence and safety of this province; and ordered the same to be recommitted for amendments.

Ordered, That the Hon. John Winthrop, Esq., Mr. Wheeler, and Mr. Lombard, be a committee to bring in a resolve recommending to the people of this province that they observe a day of public thanksgiving throughout the same; and that they sit immediately.

Resolved, That the consideration of the propriety of sending agents to Canada be referred to the next meeting of this Congress.

Ordered, That Mr. Cushing, of Scituate, Capt. Doolittle, Mr. Williams, and Mr. Palmer, be joined to the committee appointed to prepare a non-consumption agreement relative to British and India goods; and that the committee sit forthwith.

Moved, That a committee be appointed to bring in a resolve relative to the king's troops providing themselves with straw. After a long debate had ||ᵃupon the matter|| the question was ordered to subside.

The committee appointed to bring in a resolve recommending to the people of this province to observe a day of public thanksgiving throughout the same, reported; which report was read, amended, and accepted, and is as followeth, viz:

From a consideration of the continuance of the gospel among us, and the smiles of Divine Providence upon us with regard to the seasons of the year, and the general health which has been enjoyed; and in particular, from a consideration of the union which so remarkably prevails, not only in this province, but throughout the continent, at this alarming crisis, it is resolved, as the sense of this Congress, that it is highly proper that a day of public thanksgiving should be observed throughout this province; and it is accordingly recommended to the several religious assemblies in the province, that Thursday, the fifteenth day of December next, be observed as a day of thanksgiving, to render thanks to Almighty God for all the blessings we enjoy; and, at the same time, we think it incumbent on this people to humble themselves before God, on account of their sins, for which he hath been pleased, in his righteous judgment, to suffer so great a calamity to befall us as the present controversy between Great Britain and the colonies; as also to implore the Divine blessing upon us, that, by the assistance of his grace, we may be enabled to reform whatever is amiss among us; that so God may be pleased to continue to us the blessings we enjoy,

a ||thereon.||

and remove the tokens of his displeasure, by causing harmony and union to be restored between Great Britain and these colonies, that we may again rejoice in the smiles of our sovereign, and in possession of those privileges which have been transmitted to us, and have the hopeful prospect that they shall be handed down ||entire|| to posterity under the protestant succession in the illustrious house of Hanover.

Afternoon.

The report of the committee appointed to consider what is necessary to be done for the defence and safety of the province, being amended, was again read, and ordered to be recommitted for further amendment; and was committed accordingly.

Resolved, That the ||*resolve|| recommending that a day of thanksgiving be observed throughout this province, be printed, and a copy thereof sent to all the religious assemblies in this province; and that the president sign the same.

Ordered, That Mr. Appleton, Doct. Foster, and Mr. Devens, be a committee to agree with Messrs. Edes and Gill, to print the resolve entered into by this Congress, recommending to the inhabitants of this province to observe a day of public thanksgiving; and that they send a copy thereof to all the religious assemblies therein.

||Then the Congress adjourned till Monday next, [at] ten o'clock in the forenoon.

MONDAY, October 24, 1774, A. M.

The report of the committee appointed to consider what is necessary to be done for the defence and safety of the province, being amended, was taken into consideration, and a long debate had thereon.

||The Congress|| adjourned till three o'clock, P. M.

Afternoon.

||b|| *Ordered,* That Col. Lee, Mr. Palmer, Capt. Batchelder, Capt. Keith, and Col. Orne, be a committee to consider of and report to this Congress the most proper time for this province to provide a stock of powder, ordnance, and ordnance stores; and that they sit forthwith.

Ordered, That the committee appointed to bring in a non consumption agreement, ||°sit|| forthwith.

Resolved, That the debates had in Congress this afternoon, and that all those which may be had ||therein|| in future, be kept secret by the members thereof, until leave shall be had from the Congress to disclose the same.

a ||order.|| b ||Congress met pursuant to adjournment.|| c ||report.||

Ordered, That Mr. Bliss wait upon the committee appointed to consider of the most proper time for this province to provide themselves with powder, ordnance, &c. He waited on the committee accordingly, and reported that they would ||ᵃbe in|| Congress in a few minutes. The committee came in accordingly, and reported, as their opinion, that *now* was the proper time for the province to procure a stock of powder, ordnance, and ordnance stores.

||ᵀhen|| *Ordered,* That Col. Lee, Mr. Palmer, Capt. Batchelder, Capt. Keith, Col. Orne, Capt. Gardner, Capt. Heath, Col. Warren, and Col. Pomeroy, be a committee to take into consideration and determine what number of ordnance, [and] what quantity of powder, and ordnance stores will be now necessary for the province stock, and estimate the expense thereof.

The Congress resumed the consideration of the report of the committee appointed to consider what is necessary to be done for the defence and safety of the province, and ordered it to be recommitted for further amendments, and that Capt. Roberson, Major Foster, Capt. Bragdon and Mr. Gerry, be added to the committee.

||Then the Congress|| adjourned till nine o'clock to-morrow morning.

TUESDAY, October 25, 1774, A M.

||ᵇ||*Ordered,* That the committee appointed to report a non consumption agreement, sit forthwith.

Mr. Wheeler brought into Congress a letter directed to Doct. Appleton, purporting the propriety, that while we are attempting to free ourselves from our present embarrassments, and preserve ourselves from slavery, that we also take into consideration the state and circumstances of the negro slaves in this province. The same was read, and it was moved that a committee be appointed to take the same into consideration. After some debate thereon, the question was put, whether the matter now subside, and it passed in the affirmative.

Ordered, That Mr. Patterson, Mr. Devens and Doct. Holten be a committee to inquire into the state of all the stores in the commissary general's office.

Upon a motion, the question was put, whether a committee be appointed to take into consideration the propriety of having the donations which shall be made to the poor of the town of Boston, stored in the country, and passed in the negative.

Resolved, That four o'clock this afternoon be assigned to take into

a ||attend on the.|| b ||Congress met agreeably to adjournment.||

consideration the state of the executive courts throughout this province.

Ordered, That the committee appointed to inquire into the state of all the stores in the commissary general's office, ||*sit|| forthwith.

Afternoon.

Ordered, That the doorkeeper be directed to call in the members.

The committee appointed to take into consideration what number of ordnance, [and] what quantity of powder and ordnance stores are now necessary for the province stock, and estimate the expense thereof, reported. The report was read, considered and accepted; which is as followeth:

The committee appointed to take into consideration and determine what number of ordnance, [and what] quantity of powder and ordnance stores will be necessary for the province stock at this time, and estimate the expense, beg leave to report the following schedule of articles as necessary to be procured at this time, in addition to what we are already possessed of, with the estimate of expenses attendant, amounting in the whole to ten thousand seven hundred and thirty-seven pounds, viz:

16 field pieces, 3 pounders, with carriages, irons, &c.;
wheels for ditto, irons, sponges, ladles, &c., a £30,   .   £480 0 0
 4 ditto, 6 pounders, with ditto, a £38,   .   .   .   152 0 0
 Carriages, irons, &c., for 12 battering cannon, a £30,   360 0 0
 4 mortars, and appurtenances, viz: 2 8-inch and 2 13-
inch, a £20, ...   80 0 0
 20 tons grape and round shot, from 3 to 24 lb., a £15,   300 0 0
 10 tons bomb-shells, a £20, ...   200 0 0
 5 tons lead balls, a £33, ...   165 0 0
 1,000 barrels of powder, a £8,   .   .   .   8,000 0 0
 Contingent charges, ...   1,000 0 0
            ————
           £10,737 0 0

In addition to the above estimate,

Ordered, That there be procured 5,000 arms and bayonets, a £2, ...   10,000 0 0
 And 75,000 flints, ...   100 0 0
            ————
  ||In the whole|| £20,837 0 0

Ordered, That all the matters which shall come under consideration before this Congress, be kept secret, and that they be not disclosed to any but the members thereof, until the further order of this body.

a ||report.||

The committee appointed to consider what is necessary to be done for the defence and safety of the government, reported. The report was read.

||Then the Congress|| adjourned till eight o'clock to-morrow morning.

WEDNESDAY, October 26, 1774, A. M.

||ᵃ|| The Congress resumed the consideration of the report of the committee appointed to consider what is necessary to be done for the defence and safety of the province, and ordered that it be read and considered ||ᵇin|| paragraphs.

||Then|| adjourned to three o'clock this afternoon.

Afternoon.

Ordered, That the doorkeeper be directed to call in the members.

The Congress then resumed the consideration of the above report, relative to what is necessary to be done for the defence and safety of the province, and ordered that it be recommitted for amendments; which was amended, read and accepted, almost unanimously, and is as followeth, viz :

Whereas, in consequence of the present unhappy disputes between Great Britain and the colonies, a formidable body of troops, with warlike preparations of every sort, are already arrived at, and others destined for the metropolis of this province; and the express design of their being sent, is to execute acts of the British parliament utterly subversive of the constitution of the province : and whereas, his excellency General Gage has attempted, by his troops, to disperse the inhabitants of Salem, whilst assembled to consult measures for preserving their freedom, and to subjugate the province to arbitrary government; and proceeding to still more unjustifiable and alarming lengths, has fortified against the country the capital of the province, and thus greatly endangered the lives, liberties and properties of its oppressed citizens; invaded private property, by unlawfully seizing and retaining large quantities of ammunition in the arsenal at Boston, and sundry pieces of ordnance ||in the same town; committed to the custody of his troops, the arms, ammunition, ordnance,|| and warlike stores of all sorts, provided at the public expense for the use of the province; and by all possible means endeavored to place the province entirely in a defenceless state; at the same time having neglected and altogether disregarded the assurances from this Congress of the pacific disposition of the inhabitants of the province, and entreaties that he would cease from

a ||Congress met pursuant to adjournment.|| b ||by.||

measures which tended to prevent a restoration of harmony between Great Britain and the colonies :

Wherefore, it is the opinion of this Congress, that notwithstanding nothing but slavery ought more to be deprecated than hostilities with Great Britain; notwithstanding the province has not the most distant design of attacking, annoying or molesting his majesty's troops aforesaid; but, on the other hand, will consider and treat every attempt of the kind, as well as all measures tending to prevent a reconciliation between ||*Britain|| and the colonies, as the highest degree of enmity to the province; nevertheless, there is great reason, from the consideration aforesaid, to be apprehensive of the most fatal consequences, and that the province may be in some degree provided against the same; and under full persuasion that the measures expressed in the following resolves are perfectly consistent with such resolves of the Continental Congress as have been communicated to us.

Resolved, That . . . . be a committee of safety, to continue in office until the further order of this or some other Congress or house of representatives of the province; whose business it shall be, most carefully and diligently to inspect and observe all and every such person and persons as shall, at any time, attempt or enterprise the destruction, invasion, detriment or annoyance of this province, &c.; which said committee, or any five of them, (provided always, that not more than one of the said five shall be an inhabitant of the town of Boston,) shall have power, and they are hereby directed, whenever they shall judge it necessary for the safety and defence of the inhabitants of this province, and their property, against such person or persons as aforesaid, to alarm, muster and cause to be assembled, with the utmost expedition, and completely armed, accoutred, and supplied with provisions sufficient for their support in their march to the place of rendezvous, such and so many of the militia of this province, as they shall judge necessary for the ends aforesaid, and at such place or places as they shall judge proper, and them to discharge as soon as the safety of the province shall permit. And this body do most earnestly recommend to all the officers and soldiers of the militia in this province, who shall, from time to time, during the commission of the said committee, receive any call or order from the said committee, to pay the strictest obedience thereto, as they regard the liberties and lives of themselves and the people of this province.

Also, *Resolved*, That . . . .
or the major part of them, be a committee, in case of any such muster
and assembling of the militia as aforesaid, to make such provision as
shall be necessary for their reception and support, until they shall be
discharged by order of the said committee of safety; and also sufficient provisions to support them in their return to their respective
homes; and shall also, without delay, purchase and provide, upon the
credit of the moneys already granted by the province, not paid into the
treasury, so many pieces of cannon and carriages for the same, small
arms, such quantities of ammunition [and] ordnance stores as they
shall judge necessary, not exceeding the value of twenty thousand
eight hundred and thirty-seven pounds, to be deposited in such secure
places as the said committee of safety shall direct.

Also, *Resolved*, That . . . .
be and they hereby are appointed officers to command, lead and conduct such of the militia as shall be mustered and assembled by order
of the said committee of safety, in manner and for the purposes aforesaid, so long as they shall be retained by the said committee of safety,
and no longer, who shall, while in the said service, command in the
order in which they are above named.

Also, *Resolved*, That all the said officers and soldiers who may be
mustered and retained in service by the above said committee of safety, for the purposes aforesaid, shall be entitled to such an allowance
from this province, as shall be adequate to their services from the time
that they shall march from their respective places of abode, until they
shall be discharged from the said service, and reasonable time for their
return home.

Also, *Resolved*, That it be recommended to the several companies
of militia in this province, who have not already chosen and appointed
officers, that they meet forthwith and elect officers to command their
respective companies; and that the officers so chosen assemble as soon
as may be; and where the said officers shall judge the limits of the
present regiments too extensive, that they divide them, and settle and
determine their limits, and proceed to elect field officers to command
the respective regiments so formed; and that the field officers so elected, forthwith endeavor to enlist one quarter, at the least, of the number
of the respective companies, and form them into companies of fifty privates, at the least, who shall equip and hold themselves in readiness, on
the shortest notice from the said committee of safety, to march to the
place of rendezvous; and that each and every company so formed
choose a captain and two lieutenants to command them on any such

emergent and necessary service as they may be called to by the committee of safety aforesaid; and that the said captains and subalterns so elected, form the said companies into battalions, to consist of nine companies each; and that the said captains and subalterns of each battalion so formed, proceed to elect field officers to command the same. And this Congress doth most earnestly recommend that all the aforesaid elections be proceeded in and made with due deliberation and ||*generous|| regard for the public service.

Also, *Resolved*, That, as the security of the lives, liberties, and properties of the inhabitants of this province, depends, under Providence, on their knowledge and skill in the art military, and in their being properly and effectually armed and equipped, it is therefore recommended, that they immediately provide themselves therewith; that they use their utmost diligence to perfect themselves in military skill; and that, if any of the inhabitants are not provided with arms and ammunition according to law, and that, if any town or district within the province, is not provided with the full town stock of arms and ammunition, according to law, that the selectmen of such town or district take effectual care, without delay, to provide the same.

Resolved, That the blanks in the foregoing report be filled up tomorrow morning, at ten o'clock; and that the committees and officers therein recommended be chosen by ballot.

Resolved, That a committee be appointed to prepare, in the recess of this Congress, a well digested plan for the regulating and disciplining the militia, placing them in every respect on such a permanent footing as shall render them effectual for the preservation and defence of the good people of this province.

Ordered, That Capt. Heath, Capt. Gardner, Mr. Bigelow, Col. Orne, and Col. Thayer, be a committee to take into consideration what exercise will be best for the people of this province at this time to adopt, and report [thereon.]

Adjourned to nine o'clock to-morrow morning.

THURSDAY, October 27, 1774, A. M.

The order of the day was moved for.

||*Ordered*, That the doorkeeper be directed to call in the members.||

Ordered, That Col. Warren, Doct. Holten, and Col. Lee, be a committee to count and sort the votes for the committees and officers this day to be elected.

a ||patriotic.||

Resolved, That the Congress will proceed to the choice of the committee of safety, which is to consist of nine members, viz: three in the town of Boston, and six in the country, in the manner following, viz: they will give their votes first, for the three members of the town of Boston, and then for the six in the country.

The Congress accordingly proceeded to bring in their votes for the three members of the town of Boston, and the committee appointed to count and sort the votes, reported, that the following gentlemen were chosen, viz: Hon. John Hancock, Esq., Doct. Warren, and Doct. Church.

The Congress then proceeded to bring in their votes for six gentlemen of the country; after sorting and counting the same, the committee reported, that the following were chosen, viz: Mr. Devens, Capt. White of Brookline, Mr. Palmer, Norton Quincy, Esq., Mr. Watson, and Col. Orne.

Afternoon.

The Congress then proceeded to bring in their votes for five commissaries; and the committee having sorted and counted the votes, reported that the following gentlemen were chosen, viz: Mr. Cheever, Mr. Gill, Col. Lee, Mr. Greenleaf, Col. Warren.

Upon a motion made by Col. Warren, that he might be excused from serving on the committee for supplies, and having offered his reasons therefor, the question was put, whether he be excused from serving on said committee, and passed in the affirmative.

The Congress then proceeded to bring in their votes for a person to serve in the place of Col. Warren, who hath been excused, and after sorting and counting the same, they reported that Col. Lincoln was chosen.

It was then moved, that the Congress proceed to the choice of three general officers; and, *Resolved*, That they would first make choice of the gentleman who should have the chief command; and the committee having sorted and counted the votes, reported that the Hon. Jedediah Preble, Esq., was chosen.

The Congress then proceeded to bring in their votes for the second in command, and the committee having sorted and counted the votes, reported that the Hon. Artemas Ward, Esq., was chosen.

The Congress then proceeded to bring in their votes for the third in command, and the committee having sorted and counted the votes, reported that Col. Pomeroy was chosen.

The Congress then proceeded to bring in their votes for a committee to sit in the recess of this Congress, agreeable to the resolve of yesterday, and the committee having sorted and counted the votes, reported that the following gentlemen were chosen, viz:

The Hon. Joseph Hawley, Esq., Hon. John Hancock, Esq., Hon. Samuel Dexter, Esq., Mr. ||Elbridge|| Gerry, Capt. Heath, Major Foster, Hon. James Warren, Esq.

Resolved, That to-morrow morning, nine o'clock, the Congress will take into consideration the propriety of appointing a receiver general.

Ordered, That the members be enjoined to attend, and that they do not absent themselves for any cause saving that of absolute necessity.

Resolved, That the replication to his excellency's answer, which was ordered to lie on the table for the members to revise, be now taken up and recommitted for some amendments.

Upon a motion, the question was put, whether the Hon. Samuel Danforth, Esq.,[1] be desired to attend this Congress upon the adjournment, and passed in the negative.

Upon a motion, the question was put, severally, whether the Hon. James Pitts, Esq., Hon. Artemas Ward, Esq., Hon. Benjamin Green-

(1) Twenty-eight counsellors had been chosen, May 25, 1774, at the annual meeting of the general court, agreeably to the provisions of the charter of William and Mary:

For the territory formerly the colony of Massachusetts Bay, eighteen: Samuel Danforth, John Erving, *James Bowdoin*, James Pitts, *Samuel Dexter*, Artemas Ward, Benjamin Greenleaf, Caleb Cushing, Samuel Phillips, *John Winthrop*, *Timothy Danielson*, *Benjamin Austin*, Richard Derby, Jun., *William Phillips*, *Michael Farley*, James Prescot, *John Adams*, *Norton Quincy*:

For the territory formerly the colony of New Plymouth, four: James Otis, William Seaver, Walter Spooner, *Jerathmiel Bowers*.

For the territory formerly the province of Maine, extending from Piscataqua to Kennebeck, three: Jeremiah Powell, Jedediah Preble, *Enoch Freeman*:

For Sagadahock, including that part of the present state of Maine between Kennebeck and New Brunswick, one: Benjamin Chadburn:

For the province at large, two: George Leonard, Jun., *Jedediah Foster*.

When the list was presented to the governor for his approbation, Gen. Gage exercised the prerogative of negative reserved by the charter, and rejected thirteen of the counsellors elect. The names of the gentlemen distinguished by executive disapprobation are printed above in italics.

By the act of Parliament "for the better regulating the government of the province of the Massachusetts Bay," great alterations were made in the charter. The number of counsellors was increased to thirty-six: the right of choosing these officers was taken away from the representatives of the people, and the power of selection vested in the crown, after the first day of August, 1774. The gentlemen named below were appointed by the king to be counsellors by writ of mandamus:

Thomas Oliver, *Thomas Flucker*, *Peter Oliver*, *Foster Hutchinson*, Thomas Hutchinson, Jun., *Harrison Gray*, Samuel Danforth, John Erving, James Russell, *Timothy Ruggles*, Joseph Lee, Isaac Winslow, Israel Williams, George Watson, *Nathaniel Ray Thomas*, Timothy Woodbridge, William Vassall, *William Brown*, Joseph Green, *James Boutineau*, Andrew Oliver, *Josiah Edson*, *Richard Lechmere*, *Joshua Loring*, John Worthington, Timothy Paine, *William Pepperrell*, Jeremiah Powell, Jonathan Simpson, John Murray, *Daniel Leonard*, Thomas Palmer, Isaac Royall, Robert Hooper, Abijah Willard, *John Erving*, *Jun.*

The people assembled in large bodies and compelled many of the mandamus counsellors to resign the obnoxious office. The names of those who resisted popular sentiment, by accepting and retaining the appointment, are in italics in the list above.

The Hon. Samuel Danforth had been sworn, although he publicly declared his determination not to act under his commission.

leaf, Esq., Hon. Caleb Cushing, Esq., Hon. Samuel Phillips, Esq., Hon. Richard Derby, Esq., Hon. James Otis, Esq., Hon. William Seaver, Esq., Hon. Walter Spooner, Esq., Hon. Benjamin Chadburn, Esq., Hon. Jedediah Preble, Esq., and the Hon. George Leonard, Esq., be desired to attend this Congress at the next meeting upon the adjournment, and passed in the affirmative.

The question was then put, whether the Hon. John Erving, Esq., and the Hon. Jeremiah Powell, Esq., be desired also to attend this Congress, upon its being evident that they had not accepted, and upon their having given full assurances that they would not accept, of their commissions as mandamus counsellors, and it passed in the affirmative.

Ordered, That Mr. Cushing, Col. Prescot, and Capt. Greenleaf, be a committee to bring in a resolve inviting the counsellors aforesaid to attend accordingly.||ᵃ||

FRIDAY, October 28, 1774, A. M.

The order of the day was moved for.

Resolved, That the Congress now proceed to the choice of a receiver general.

Ordered, That Col. Warren, Doct. Holten, and Col. Lee, be a committee to count and sort the votes for a receiver general.

The Congress then proceeded to bring in their votes for a receiver general; the committee having counted and sorted the same, reported that the Hon. Samuel Dexter, Esq., was chosen. But upon a motion by him made, that he might be excused from serving in that office, and having offered his reasons for his motion, the question was put, whether he be excused accordingly, and it passed in the affirmative.

Resolved, That the choice of a receiver general be put off till three o'clock this afternoon.

The committee on the state of the province reported a resolve, relative to the removal of the inhabitants of the town of Boston from thence, which was read.

Afternoon.

Upon a motion made by Mr. Greenleaf, one of the committee for providing stores, that he might be excused from serving in that office, and having offered his reasons for his motion, the question was put, whether he be excused accordingly, and it passed in the affirmative.

The Congress resumed the consideration of the report of the committee recommending the removal of the inhabitants of the town of Boston from thence. *Ordered* to be recommitted and that the committee sit forthwith.

a ||Adjourned till to-morrow morning, nine o'clock.||

Resolved, That the Congress now proceed to the choice of a receiver general.   The votes being carried in, and the committee having sorted and counted the same, reported that Henry Gardner, Esq., was chosen.

Resolved, That the Congress now proceed, according to their order in the forenoon, to bring in their votes for the choice of a person to fill up the committee for providing stores, in the place of Mr. Greenleaf, who was excused.   The committee having counted and sorted the same, reported that Mr. Benjamin Hall was chosen.

The committee on the state of the province reported a resolve relative to the collecting and paying the outstanding taxes, which was read and accepted; but, upon a motion, the above vote was reconsidered, and the report was committed to Major Hawley, Mr. Gerry, and Major Foster, for amendments, which ||ᵃbeing|| done, was again considered and accepted, and is as followeth, viz :

Whereas, the moneys heretofore granted and ordered to be assessed by the general court of this province, and not paid into the province treasury, will be immediately wanted to supply the unexpected and pressing ||ᵇexigencies|| of this province, in its present distressed circumstances, and it having been recommended by this Congress that the same should not be paid to the Hon. Harrison Gray, Esq., for reasons most obvious ; Therefore,

Resolved, That Henry Gardner, Esq., be, and he hereby is, appointed receiver general until the further order of this or some other Congress, or house of representatives of this province, whose business it shall be to receive all such moneys as shall be offered to be paid into his hands to the use of the province by the several constables, collectors, or other persons, by order of the several towns or districts, and to give his receipts for the same ; and the same moneys to pay out to the committee of supplies, or a major part of them, already appointed by this Congress, or the order of said committee, or the major part of them, for the payment of such disbursements as they shall find to be necessary for the immediate defence of the inhabitants of this province.   And it is hereby recommended to the several towns and districts within this province, that they immediately call town and district meetings, and give directions to all constables, collectors, and other persons who may have any part of the province ||ᶜtaxes|| of such towns or districts in their respective hands or possession, in consequence of any late order and directions of any towns or districts, that he or they immediately pay the same to the said Henry Gardner, Esq., for the purpose aforesaid.

a ||was.|| b ||demands.|| c ||money collected by taxes.||

And it is also recommended, that the several towns and districts in said directions, signify and expressly engage, to such constables, collectors, or other persons, who shall have their said moneys in their hands, that their paying the same in manner as aforesaid, and producing a receipt therefor, shall ever hereafter operate as an effectual discharge to such persons for the same. And it is hereby recommended, that the like order be observed respecting the tax ordered by the great and general court at their last May session.

And it is hereby further recommended, to all sheriffs who may have in their hands any moneys belonging to the province, that they immediately pay the same to the said receiver general, for the purposes aforesaid, taking his receipt therefor.

And the said Henry Gardner, Esq., the receiver general, shall be accountable to this or some other Congress or house of representatives of this province, for whatever he shall do touching the premises. And to the end that all the moneys heretofore assessed in pursuance of any former grants and orders of the great and general court or assembly of this province, and hitherto uncollected by the several constables and collectors, to whom the several lists of assessments thereof were committed, may be effectually levied and collected, and also to the end, that all the moneys granted, and ordered to be assessed by the general court at their session in May last, which have been assessed, or which may be assessed, may be also speedily and punctually collected, it is earnestly recommended by this body, to the several constables and collectors respectively, who have such assessments in their hands, or to whom any assessments yet to be made, may be committed by the assessors of any towns or districts, that in the levying and collecting the respective part or proportion of the total of such assessments, therein set down to the several persons named therein, they should act and proceed in the same ||way and|| manner as is expressed and prescribed in the form of a warrant given and contained in an act or law of this province, entitled "an act prescribing the form of a warrant for collecting of town assessments," &c. And it is also hereby strongly recommended to all the inhabitants of the several towns and districts in this province, that they, without fail, do afford to their respective constables and collectors all that aid and assistance which shall be necessary to enable them in that manner to levy the contents of such assessments, and that they do oblige and compel the said constables and collectors to comply with and execute the directions of this resolve, inasmuch as the present most alarming situation and circumstances of this province do make it absolutely necessary for the safety thereof.

Ordered, That Mr. Appleton, Mr. Cushing, and Mr. Palmer be a committee to bring in a resolve relative to a non consumption agree-ment.

Ordered, That Major Hawley, Mr. Cushing, and Mr. Gerry, be a committee to prepare and bring in a resolve relative to an equal repre-sentation of the province in Congress at the next meeting thereof.

The committee appointed to bring in a resolve inviting the constitu-tional counsellors of this province to attend this Congress at the next meeting thereof upon adjournment, reported; which report was read and accepted, and is as followeth, viz :

Resolved, That the Hon. John Erving, Esq., Hon. ||ªJames|| Pitts, Esq., Hon. Artemas Ward, Esq., Hon. Benjamin Greenleaf, Esq., Hon. Caleb Cushing, Esq., Hon. Samuel Phillips, Esq., Hon. Richard Derby, Esq., Hon. James Otis, Esq., Hon. William Seaver, Esq., Hon. Walter Spooner, Esq., Hon. Jeremiah Powell, Esq., Hon. Benjamin Chadburn, Esq., Hon. Jedediah Preble, Esq., and Hon. George Leo-nard, Esq., constitutional members of his majesty's council of this colony, by the royal charter, chosen to said office last May session, be desired to give their attendance at the next meeting of this Congress upon adjournment, that this body may have the benefit of their advice upon the important matters that may then come under consideration And the secretary of this Congress is hereby directed to transmit to those gentlemen severally a copy of this resolve.

The committee appointed to bring in a resolve relative to a non-consumption agreement, reported. The report was read and ordered to be committed for amendments. It was accordingly amended, read again, and accepted, and is as followeth, viz :

Whereas, ||the people of|| this province have not, as yet, received from the Continental Congress such explicit directions respecting non-importation and non consumption agreements as are expected; and whereas, the greatest part of the inhabitants of this colony have lately entered into non importation and non consumption agreements, the good effects of which are very conspicuous: Therefore,

Resolved, That this Congress approve of the said agreements, and earnestly recommend to all the inhabitants of this colony, strictly to conform to the same, until the further sense of the continental or the pro-vincial Congress is made public. And further, this Congress highly applaud the conduct of those patriotic merchants, who have generously refrained from importing British goods since the commencement of the cruel Boston port bill; at the same time reflect with pain on the conduct of those who have sordidly preferred their private interest to the salvation of their suffering country, by continuing to import as usual; and recommend it to the inhabitants of the province, that they discourage the conduct of said importers by refusing to purchase any articles whatever of them.

[*Ordered*, That the foregoing report] be published.

The committee appointed to inquire into the state of the warlike stores in the commissary general's office, reported; and it was thereupon *Ordered*, That Capt. Heath, Doct. Warren, and Doct. Church, be a committee to take care of, and lodge in some safe place in the country, the warlike stores now in the commissary general's office, and that the matter be conducted with the greatest secrecy.

Resolved, That the committee of correspondence of the town of Worcester be desired to take proper care that the bayonets, the property of this province, now in the hands of Col. Chandler, be removed to some safe place at a distance from his house.

||The Congress then|| adjourned till to-morrow morning nine o'clock.

SATURDAY, October 29, 1774, A. M.

The committee appointed to take into consideration what military exercise is best for the people of this province now to adopt, reported; the report was read and accepted, and

Ordered, That Major Foster bring in a resolve accordingly; who, in obedience to the above order, reported the following resolve, which was read and accepted, and ordered to be published in the Boston newspapers.

Resolved, That it be recommended to the inhabitants of this province, that in order to their perfecting themselves in the military art, they proceed in the method ordered by his majesty in the year 1764, it being, in the opinion of this Congress, best calculated for appearance and defence.

Upon a motion, the question was put, whether the Congress will now go into the consideration of the propriety of keeping the records of the county of Suffolk in the town of Boston, and passed in the affirmative.

After a very considerable debate on the question, it was ordered that the matter now subside.

Resolved, That the consideration of the state of the executive courts in the province be referred to the next meeting of this Congress.

Ordered, That Capt. Gardner, Mr. Wheeler, and Mr. Watson, be a

6

committee to wait on the Rev. Doct. Appleton, with the thanks of this body for his constant attendance on, and praying with them, during their session in the town of Cambridge.

Ordered, That the payment of several expenses of this Congress be referred until the next meeting thereof.

Resolved, That the committee of safety be desired to write to the Continental Congress, showing them the grounds and reasons of our proceedings, and enclose them a copy of our votes and resolutions.

Ordered, That Major Foster, Doct. Holten, and Mr. Appleton, be a committee to look over the resolves and orders of this Congress, and point out what is necessary now to be made public.

The Committee appointed to wait on the Rev. Doct. Appleton, with the thanks of this Congress, reported that they had attended to that service, and that the Doct. informed them that the Congress were welcome to his services, and that he wished them the blessing of heaven.

Resolved, That when this Congress shall adjourn that it be adjourned to the 23d day of November next, at ten o'clock in the forenoon, then to meet at this place.

The committee on the state of the province having amended the replication to his excellency's answer to our message to him, the same being read, was accepted unanimously.

Ordered, That Capt. Heath, Capt. White, Capt. Gardner, Mr. Cheever, and Mr. Devens, be a committee to wait upon his excellency with the following replication to his excellency's [answer.]

May it please your Excellency :

The province having been repeatedly alarmed by your excellency's unusual and warlike preparations since your arrival into it, and having, by this Congress, expressed a reasonable expectation that you would desist from, and demolish your fortifications on Boston neck, it must afford matter of astonishment not only to the province, but the whole continent, that you should treat our importunate applications with manifest insensibility and disregard.

The Congress are possessed of a writing with your signature, which purports itself to be a message to this body, although addressed to sundry gentlemen by name, who, officiating as our committee, presented an address to your excellency. We are surprised at your saying, that "what we call a fortress, unless annoyed, will annoy nobody ;" when, from your acquaintance with the constitution of Britain, and of the province over which you have been by his majesty commissioned to preside, you must know, that barely keeping a standing army in the province, in time of peace, without consent of the representatives, is against law, and must be considered as a great grievance to the subject—a grievance which this people could not, with a due regard to their freedom, endure, was there not reason to hope that his majesty, upon ||ᵃbeing|| undeceived, would order redress. Is it not astonishing then, sir, that you should have ventured to assert that a " fortress," by whatever name your excellency is pleased to call it, which puts it in the power of the standing army which you command to cut off communication between the country and the capital of this province; to imprison the many thousand inhabitants of the town of Boston; to insult and destroy them upon the least, or even without any provocation, and which is evidently a continual annoyance to that oppressed community, " unless annoyed, will annoy nobody ?"

A retrospect of your excellency's conduct, since your late residence in this province, we conclude, will convince you of that truth, the mere hinting of which, you tell us, " is highly exasperating as well as ungenerous." We presume your excellency will not deny that you have exerted yourself to execute the acts made to subvert the constitution of the province, although your excellency's connections with a ministry inimical to the province, and your being surrounded by men of the worst political principles, preclude a prospect of your fully exercising towards this province your wonted benevolence and humanity; yet, sir, we pray you to indulge your social virtues so far as to consider the necessary feelings of this people under the hand of oppression. Have not invasions of private property, by your excellency, been repeatedly made at Boston? Have not the inhabitants of Salem, whilst peaceably assembled for concerting measures to preserve their freedom, and unprepared to defend themselves, been in imminent danger from your troops? Have you not, by removing the ammunition of the province, and by all other means in your power, endeavored to put it in a state utterly defenceless? Have you not expressly declared that " resentment might justly be expected" from your troops, merely in consequence of a refusal of some inhabitants of the province to supply them with property undeniably their own? Surely these are questions founded on incontestible facts, which, we think, must prove that while the " avowed enemies" of Great Britain and the colonies, are protected by your excellency, the lives, liberties, and properties of the inhabitants of the province, who are real friends to the British constitution, are greatly endangered, whilst under the control of your standing army.

a ||his being.||

It must be matter of grief to every true Briton, that the honor of British troops is sullied by the infamous errand on which they are sent to America; and whilst, in the unjust cause, on which you are engaged, menaces will never produce submission from the people of this province, your excellency, as well as the army, can only preserve your honor by refusing to submit to the most disgraceful prostitution of subserving plans so injurious, [and] so notoriously iniquitous and cruel to this people.

Your excellency professes to be solicitous for "preserving union and harmony between Great Britain and the colonies;" and we sincerely hope that you will distinguish yourself by exertions for this purpose; for, should you be an instrument of involving in a civil war this oppressed and injured land, it must forever deprive you of that tranquillity which finally bids adieu to those whose hands have been polluted with innocent blood.

Your excellency reminds us of the spirit of the British nation; we partake, we rejoice in her honors, and especially revere her for her great national virtues; we hope she never will veil her glory, or hazard success by exerting that spirit in support of tyranny.

Your excellency's strange misconception of facts, is not less conspicuous in the close of your message than in many other parts of it. You have suggested that the conduct of the province, for supporting the constitution, is an instance of its violation. To declare the truth, relative to this matter, must be a full vindication of our conduct therein.

The powers placed in your excellency, for the good of the province, to convene, adjourn, prorogue, and dissolve the general court, have been perverted to ruin and enslave the province, while our constituents, the loyal subjects of his majesty, have been compelled, for the laudable purposes of preserving the constitution, and therein their freedom, to obtain the wisdom of the province in a way which is not only justifiable by reason, but, under the present exigencies of the state, directed by the principles of the constitution itself; warranted by the most approved precedent and examples, and ||ᵃsanctioned|| by the British nation, at the revolution; upon the strength and validity of which precedent the whole British constitution now stands, his present majesty wears his crown, and all subordinate officers hold their places. And although we are willing to put the most favorable construction on the warning you have been pleased to give us of the " rock on which

a ||sanctified.||

we are," we beg leave to inform you that our constituents do not expect, that, in the execution of that important trust which they have reposed in us, we should be wholly guided by your advice. We trust, sir, that we shall not fail in our duty to our country and loyalty to our king, or in a proper respect to your excellency.

Resolved, That the foregoing replication to his excellency's answer be published in the newspapers.

Ordered, That Major Hawley, Col. Lee, and Mr. Gerry, be a committee to extract such parts of the resolves which passed in this Congress, the 26th and 28th current, and are necessary now to be published; who reported as followeth:

Whereas, it has been recommended by this Congress, that the moneys heretofore granted and ordered to be assessed by the general court of this province, and not paid into the province treasury, should not be paid to the Hon. Harrison Gray, Esq., for reasons most obvious:

Therefore, *Resolved*, That Henry Gardner, Esq., of Stow, be, and hereby is, appointed receiver general until the further order of this or some other Congress or house of representatives of this province, whose business it shall be to receive all such moneys as shall be offered to be paid into his hands to the use of the province, by the several constables, collectors, or other persons, by order of the several towns or districts, and to give his receipt for the same. And it is hereby recommended to the several towns and districts, within this province, that they immediately call town and district meetings, and give directions to all constables, collectors, and other persons who may have any part of the province tax of such town or district in their respective hands or possession, in consequence of any late order and directions of any town or district, that he or they immediately pay the same to the said Henry Gardner, Esq., for the purposes aforesaid. And it is also recommended that the several towns and districts, in said directions, signify and expressly engage to such constable, collector, or other persons as shall have their said moneys in their hands, that their paying the same to Henry Gardner, Esq., aforesaid, and producing his receipt therefor, shall ever hereafter operate as an effectual discharge to such persons for the same. And it is hereby recommended, that the like order be observed respecting the tax ordered by the great and general court at their last May session. And it is further recommended to all sheriffs or deputy sheriffs, or coroners, who may have in their hands any moneys belonging to the province, that they immediately pay the same to the said receiver general, taking his receipt therefor. And the said Henry Gardner, Esq., the receiver general, shall be accountable to this or some other Congress or house of representatives of this province.

And to the end that all the moneys heretofore assessed in pursuance of any former grants and orders of the great and general court or assembly of this province, and hitherto uncollected by the several constables and collectors to whom the several lists of assessment thereof were committed, may be effectually levied and collected; and also to the end that all the moneys granted and ordered to be assessed by the general court at their session in May last, which have been assessed, or which may be assessed, may be also speedily and punctually collected, it is earnestly recommended by this body to the several constables and collectors, respectively, who have such assessments in their hands, or to whom any assessments yet to be made may be committed by the assessors of any towns or districts, that, in levying and collecting the respective part or proportion of the total of such assessments therein set down to the several persons named therein, they should act and proceed in the same way and manner as is expressed and provided in the form of a warrant, given and contained in ||ᵃan|| act or law of this province, entitled " an act prescribing the form of a warrant for collecting of town assessments," &c.

And it is hereby strongly recommended to all the inhabitants of the several towns and districts in this province, that they, without fail, do afford to their respective constables and collectors all that aid and assistance which shall be necessary to enable them in that manner to levy the contents of such assessments; and that they do oblige and compel the said constables and collectors to comply with and execute the directions of this resolve, inasmuch as the present most alarming situation and circumstances of this province do make it absolutely necessary for the safety thereof.

Whereas, in consequence of the present unhappy disputes between Great Britain and the colonies, a formidable body of troops, with warlike preparations of every sort, are already arrived at, and others destined for the metropolis of this province; and the ||ᵇexpressed|| design of their being sent, is to execute acts of the British parliament utterly subversive of the constitution of the province; and whereas, his excellency General Gage has attempted by his troops to disperse the inhabitants of Salem, whilst assembled to consult measures for preserving their freedom, and to subjugate the province to arbitrary government; and, proceeding to still more unjustifiable and alarming lengths, has fortified against the country the capital of the province, and thus

a ||one.|| b ||express.||

greatly endangered the lives, liberties and properties of its oppressed citizens; invaded private property by unlawfully seizing and retaining large quantities of ammunition in the arsenal at Boston, and sundry pieces of ordnance in the same town; committed to the custody of his troops, the arms, ammunition, ordnance, and warlike stores of all sorts, provided at the public expense, for the use of the province; and by all possible means endeavored to place the province entirely in a defenceless state; at the same time having neglected and altogether disregarded assurances from this Congress of the pacific dispositions of the inhabitants of the province, and entreaties that he would cease from measures which tended to prevent a restoration of harmony between Great Britain and the colonies:

Wherefore it is the opinion of this Congress, that notwithstanding nothing but slavery ought more to be deprecated than hostilities with Great Britain, notwithstanding the province has not the most distant design of attacking, annoying, or molesting his majesty's troops, aforesaid, but, on the other hand, will consider and treat every attempt of the kind, as well as all measures tending to prevent a reconciliation between Great Britain and the colonies as the highest degree of enmity to the province, nevertheless, there is great reason, from the considerations aforesaid, to be apprehensive of the most fatal consequences; and that the province may be in some degree provided against the same, and under full persuasion that the measures expressed in the following resolves are perfectly consistent with such resolves of the Continental Congress as have been communicated to us, it is

Resolved, and hereby recommended to the several companies of militia in this province, who have not already chosen and appointed officers, that they meet forthwith, and elect officers to command their respective companies; and that the officers so chosen assemble as soon as may be; and where the said officers shall judge the limits of the present regiments too extensive that they divide them, and settle and determine their limits, and proceed to elect field officers to command their respective regiments ||so formed;|| and that the field officers, so elected, forthwith endeavor to enlist one quarter, at least, of the number of the respective companies, and form them into companies of fifty privates, at the least, who shall equip and hold themselves in readiness to march at the shortest notice; and that each and every company, so formed, choose a captain and two lieutenants to command them on any necessary and emergent service, and that the said captains and subalterns, so elected, form the said companies into battalions, to consist of nine companies each, and that the captains and subalterns of each battalion, so formed, proceed to elect field officers to command the same. And the Congress doth most earnestly recommend that all the aforesaid elections be proceeded in and made with due deliberation and ||a|| generous regard to the public service.

Also *Resolved*, That the security of the lives, liberties, and properties of the inhabitants of this province depends, under Providence, on their knowledge and skill in the art military, and in their being properly and effectually armed and equipped; if any of said inhabitants are not provided with arms and ammunition, according to law, that they immediately provide themselves therewith, and that they use their utmost diligence to perfect themselves in military skill; and that if any town or district within the province is not provided with the full town stock of arms and ammunition, according to law, the selectmen of such town or district take effectual care, without delay, to provide the same.

The committee on the state of the province, reported a resolve relative to the removal of the inhabitants of the town of Boston. After the same was read and some debate had thereon, the question (upon a motion made) was put, whether the matter now subside, and it passed in the affirmative.

Resolved, As the opinion of this Congress, that Cambridge is the most eligible place for the committee of safety, at present, to sit in.

Resolved, That two gentlemen be added to the committee of safety.

Ordered, That Col. Prescot, Doct. Holten, and Mr. Gill, be a committee to count and sort the votes for two gentlemen to be added to the committee of safety.

The Congress then proceeded to bring in their votes. After counting and sorting the same, the committee reported that Mr. Pigeon and Capt. Heath were chosen.

Resolved, That the extract of the resolves, relative to the militia, which passed this day be printed, and a copy thereof sent to all the towns and districts in this province.

The Congress adjourned till the 23d day of November next, at ten o'clock in the forenoon, then to meet in this place.

WEDNESDAY, November 23, 1774, A. M.

The Congress met according to adjournment, and then adjourned till half past two o'clock this afternoon.

Afternoon.

The Congress being apprehensive that the Hon. Walter Spooner, Esq., had not received the resolve passed by them, inviting the members of his majesty's constitutional council to attend the Congress on this day, *Resolved* that he be again wrote to, desiring his attendance here immediately, and that a messenger be despatched therewith without delay.

Resolved, That the gentlemen who were members of the late Continental, and are of this Provincial Congress, be joined to the committee on the state of the province.[1]

Resolved, That John Adams, Esq., be desired to favor this Congress with his presence, as soon as may be.

Resolved, That Robert Treat Paine, Esq., be desired to attend this Congress, as soon as possible.

Then the Congress adjourned till to-morrow morning, ten o'clock.

THURSDAY, November 24, 1774, A. M.

Resolved, That the chairman of the committee from this province who were members of the continental Congress, be desired to report the proceedings of said Congress.

Ordered, That Capt. Gardner, Col. Prescot, and Doct. Holten, be a committee to wait on the Rev. Doct. Appleton, and desire that he would officiate as chaplain to this Congress, during their session in this town.

The committee waited on the Rev. Doct. Appleton accordingly, and reported that they had delivered the message, and that the Doctor would officiate as chaplain, agreeably to the desire of the Congress.

The chairman of the committee appointed by this province to meet in Continental Congress, reported, that they had attended that service; that the Congress had taken into consideration the state of the colonies, [and] that he had a journal of their whole proceedings, which he would lay on the table.[2]

Resolved, That the doings of the Continental Congress be now read, which were read accordingly.

Resolved, That the state of rights, state of grievances, and the as-

(1) Hon. James Bowdoin, Hon. Thomas Cushing, Mr. Samuel Adams, John Adams, Esq., and Robert Treat Paine, Esq., were elected by the house of representatives of Massachusetts, June 17, 1774, delegates to the Continental Congress, which convened at Philadelphia, September 5th, and was dissolved October 26, 1774. These gentlemen, with the exception of James Bowdoin, were returned as members of the Provincial Congress.

(2) The journal of the proceedings of the Continental Congress was printed immediately after the dissolution of that body, in October, 1774, by William and Thomas Bradford, at Philadelphia, in an octavo pamphlet of 132 pages.

sociation, as stated by the Continental Congress, be committed.[1]   The same was accordingly committed to the Hon. Major Hawley, Hon. Mr. Dexter, Doct. Warren, Col. Lee, Mr. Gerry, Col. Warren, and Doct. Church, who are to consider thereof and report.

Adjourned to three o'clock this afternoon.

Afternoon.

The petition from the officers of the minute men, in the northwest part of the county of Worcester, [was] read and committed to the committee on the state of the province.[2]

Ordered, That the committee appointed to sit in the recess to prepare a plan for the defence and safety of the government, be directed to sit forthwith.

Ordered, That the committee appointed to publish the names of the mandamus counsellors, and others, now in the town of Boston, be directed to sit forthwith and prepare a report.

Adjourned till to-morrow morning, ten o'clock.

FRIDAY, November 25, 1774, A. M.

Ordered, That Doct. Holten, Col. Foster, and Col. Roberson, be a committee to inquire what number of the constitutional counsellors are now in town.

Resolved, That the members from the town of Worcester apply to Col. Chandler, and receive from him the bayonets he has in his hands and is now ready to deliver ;[3] and inquire what sum or sums of money have been paid to him by the treasurer, for the purpose of procuring bayonets ; how many were procured by him, and to whom they were delivered, and the state of his account relative to the money by him received for the purpose aforesaid.

Ordered, That a copy of this resolve be given to the members aforesaid.

Resolved, That Doct. Holten, Col. Foster, Col. Roberson, Capt. Baldwin, and Mr. Cushing, be a committee to wait on such gentlemen of his majesty's constitutional council of this province, who are now in town at the request of this Congress, and acquaint them that this

(1) The declaration of rights and statement of grievances, were adopted by the Continental Congress, October 14, 1774 : the plan of an association for carrying into effect the non consumption, non importation, and non exportation agreements, having been reported and considered, was accepted and subscribed by the members, October 20, 1774.

(2) The militia of Worcester county requested that the Congress would establish the military drill called the *Norfolk exercise*, instead of that system prescribed for the discipline of his majesty's troops in 1764.

(3) About one hundred bayonets were in the keeping of Col. Chandler.

Congress respectfully acknowledge their cheerful attendance, but will not be ready to offer any matters for their advice, until a quorum of that honorable board shall appear, and which is soon expected ; and that in the mean time a seat is provided for them in this house, if they shall see cause to be present.

Resolved, That it be the rule of this Congress at present, that they sit in the forepart of the day, and that they adjourn over the afternoon, in order to give time for the committees to sit and perfect the business with which they are severally charged.

Ordered, That Col. Thomas, Capt. Gardner, and Mr. Watson, be a committee to inquire whether a more convenient place than that in which the Congress now sits, can be procured for them to meet in.

Resolved, That every member of this Congress be enjoined to give constant attendance during the session thereof ; and in case any should be under a necessity of absence, that they signify the same to the Congress, in order to their obtaining leave to withdraw.

Adjourned till ten o clock to-morrow morning.

SATURDAY, November 26, 1774, A. M.

The committee appointed to wait on the members of his majesty's council now in town, reported, that they had attended that service ; had seen the Hon. Mr. Cushing, and the Hon. Mr. Seaver, and had delivered to them the message with which they were charged ; they being the only members in town.

Ordered, That the same committee wait on the other gentlemen of his majesty's council, invited by this Congress to attend here, as they come into town, and inform them of the resolve of this Congress.

Ordered, That Capt. Heath, Mr. Adams, Col. Doolittle, Col. Pomeroy, and Hon. Mr. Dexter, be a committee to devise some means of keeping up a correspondence between this province, Montreal and Quebec, and of gaining very frequent intelligence from thence of their movements.

The committee appointed yesterday to see if some more convenient place could be procured for the Congress, than that in which they now sit, reported, that the new chapel can be had, and that it is the most convenient place that they can obtain.

Ordered, That this matter now subside.

Ordered, That Mr. Sullivan, Hon. Major Hawley, and the Hon. Mr. Cushing, be a committee to draw the form of an order with respect to the treasurer's giving bonds, and report.

Ordered, That Mr. Wheeler, Mr. Adams, Hon. Mr. Cushing, and

Doct. Church, be added to the committee appointed to publish the names of the mandamus counsellors, and others, now in Boston.

Adjourned till Monday morning, ten o'clock.

MONDAY, November 28, 1774, A. M.

Ordered, That Mr. Palmer, Mr. Cushing, Col. Gerish, Mr. Bigelow, Major Fuller, Mr. Pickering, and Col. Pomeroy, be a committee to take into consideration the state of the manufactures, and how they may be improved in this province.

||Congress|| adjourned till to-morrow morning, ten o'clock.

TUESDAY, November 29, 1774, A. M.

Ordered, That Col. Henshaw, Mr. Palmer, Mr. Gorham, Mr. Lothrop, and Mr. Pigeon, be a committee to make as just an estimate as may be of the loss and damage of every kind ||*accrued|| to the province by the operation of the Boston port bill and the act for altering the civil government, from their commencement to this time.

Ordered, That Doct. Foster, Mr. Gorham, and Col. Orne, be a committee to state the amount of the sums which have been extorted from us since the year 1763, by the operation of certain acts of the British parliament.

Resolved, That a messenger be despatched to the town of Salem, in order to gain what intelligence can be had by the last vessels from London, and that the messenger bring with him the Essex paper to this Congress; and that Mr. Bigelow be desired to take upon him the above service.

Resolved, That Mr. Devens be desired to go to Boston and inquire what advice came by the last vessels from London.

Resolved, That when this Congress shall adjourn, that it be adjourned to three o'clock this afternoon, ||^bwhich was then adjourned accordingly.||

Afternoon.

Mr. Devens reported that, in obedience to the order of the Congress, he had been to the town of Boston; that the letters from London by the last ships had not come to hand; that Doct. Church was in Boston, and would bring them to the Congress as soon as they should arrive.

Resolved, That to-morrow, at eleven o'clock, the Congress will take into consideration the expediency of appointing members to attend a

a ||occasioned.|| b ||Adjourned to three o'clock this afternoon.||

Continental Congress, to be held at Philadelphia, agreeably to the recommendation of the last Continental Congress.

Adjourned to ten o'clock to-morrow morning.

WEDNESDAY, November 30, 1774, A. M.

The order of the day was moved for.

The expediency of appointing members to attend a Continental Congress, was considered: Thereupon,

Resolved, unanimously, as the opinion of this body, that members be appointed to attend a Continental Congress, proposed to be held at Philadelphia, on the tenth day of May next, agreeably to the recommendation of the late Continental Congress.

Resolved, That five members be appointed.

Resolved, That to-morrow, at three o'clock in the afternoon, be assigned to come to the choice of delegates to attend the Continental Congress, proposed to be held at Philadelphia, on the 10th day of May next.

Ordered, That the Hon. Mr. Winthrop, Mr. Sullivan, and Doct. Foster, bring in a resolve expressing the thanks of this body to the other colonies, for their generous donations to the inhabitants of the town of Boston, now laboring under the oppression of certain acts of the British parliament.

‖*Resolved*, That the same committee prepare a brief, to be circulated throughout the several towns in this province, to promote donations for the persons suffering, in the towns of Boston and Charlestown, under the operation of certain acts of the British parliament.‖

Adjourned till three o'clock this afternoon.

Afternoon.

Resolved, That the letters from Doct. Franklin to Mr. Cushing, which have been now read, be committed to the provincial committee of correspondence.[1]

‖Then the Congress‖ adjourned till to-morrow morning, ten o'clock.

(1) Letters addressed by Doct. Franklin to the Hon. Thomas Cushing, bearing date, December 2, 1772; January 5, March 9, April 3, May 6, June 2, June 4, July 7, July 25, August 24, September 12, November 1, 1773; and January 5, 1774; have been published in the collections of the writings of the patriot and philosopher. As none of the communications preserved by the editors of Franklin's writings, correspond with the time when those mentioned in the text were laid before Congress, it is probable that the letters entrusted to the committee of correspondence have perished with the other papers on their files.

THURSDAY, December 1, 1774, A. M.

The committee appointed to bring in a resolve expressing the thanks of this body to the other colonies, for their generous donations to the inhabitants of the town of Boston, reported. The report was recommitted for amendments.

The same committee reported a brief to be circulated through the several towns, to promote donations to the towns of Boston and Charlestown; also recommitted for amendments.

The committee appointed to take into consideration the state of rights, the state of grievances, and the association, as stated by the Continental Congress, reported. The report was then taken into consideration, [and] the further consideration thereof [was] referred to three o'clock this afternoon.

||*Resolved*, That the choice of delegates, which was to have been at three o'clock this afternoon, be deferred till three o'clock to-morrow afternoon.||

||Then adjourned till three o'clock this afternoon.||

Afternoon.

The Congress resumed the consideration of the report of the committee, agreeably to their resolve in the forenoon; after some debate thereon, it was ordered to be recommitted for an amendment.

The resolve expressing the thanks of this body to the other colonies, for their donations to the town of Boston, &c., as amended, was read and accepted, and is as followeth:

Whereas, by the rigorous operation of the Boston Port Bill, the metropolis of this province, and the neighboring town of Charlestown, have been brought into the most distressful state, many of the inhabitants being deprived of the means of procuring their subsistence, and reduced to the cruel alternative of quitting their habitations, or of perishing in them by famine, if they had not been supported by the free and generous contributions of our sister colonies, even from the remotest part of this continent:

Resolved, That the grateful acknowledgments of this Congress be returned to the several colonies, for having so deeply interested themselves in behalf of said towns, under their present sufferings in the common cause; and that the Congress consider these donations, not merely as unexampled acts of benevolence to this province in general, which has also greatly suffered, and of charity to those towns in particular, but as convincing proofs of the firm attachment of all the colonies to the glorious cause of American liberty, and of their fixed determination to support them in the noble stand they are now making for the liberties of themselves and of all America.

The committee appointed to prepare a brief, reported their draught, amended: *Ordered*, to be recommitted for a revision, and for such further amendments as they shall think proper.

Ordered, That Mr. Devens apply to the secretary for a list of counsellors appointed by mandamus; and in case he should be refused such list, he is desired to take with him a notary public, and in his presence again desire the same and tender the secretary his fee.

||Then|| adjourned till to-morrow morning, ten o'clock.

FRIDAY, December 2, 1774, A. M.

The doorkeeper [was] directed to call in the members, and to call none out till the further order of this Congress.

The committee on the state of the province reported. The report [was] taken into consideration.

Ordered, That the further consideration thereof be referred till four o'clock this afternoon.||*||

Afternoon.

The order of the day [was] moved for.

Ordered, That Doct. Holten, Capt. Cushing, and Doct. Church, be a committee to sort and count the votes for five members to be chosen to represent this province at an American Congress, to be held at Philadelphia, at or before the tenth day of May next.

The Congress then proceeded to bring in their votes for five gentlemen to be delegated for the purpose aforesaid. The committee having counted and sorted the same, reported that the Hon. John Hancock, Hon. Thomas Cushing, Esq., Mr. Samuel Adams, John Adams, and Robert Treat Paine, Esquires, were chosen.

The consideration of the report of the committee made in the forenoon, [was] resumed: some time [was] spent thereon, then, *ordered*, that the further consideration thereof be referred till nine o'clock to-morrow morning.

Ordered, That the vote which passed yesterday, expressing the thanks of this body to the other colonies for their donations made to the towns of Boston and Charlestown, be published in all the Boston newspapers: and that it be attested by the president.

Resolved, That the committee appointed to publish the names of the mandamus counsellors who have been sworn and have not resigned,

a ||*To which time this Congress stands adjourned.||

be desired to send a messenger to Mr. Hall, printer, in Salem, and inquire of him whether he hath a list of the counsellors appointed by mandamus, which he received from the secretary's office; and if he hath a list so received, to desire him to favor this Congress therewith.

The report of the committee appointed to take into consideration the state of rights, the state of grievances, and the association, as stated by the Continental Congress, being amended, was read, and a consideration thereof went into.

Ordered, That the further consideration thereof be referred till tomorrow morning, ten o'clock.

||Then the Congress|| adjourned till nine o'clock to-morrow morning.

SATURDAY, December 3, 1774, A. M.

The Congress then went into the consideration of the report of the committee on the state of the province, agreeably to their order of yesterday. After a long debate thereon, it was ordered to lie on the table, and that the committee have leave to sit again.

||Then the Congress|| adjourned till Monday next, at ten o'clock in the forenoon.

MONDAY, December 5, 1774, A. M.

Ordered, That Doct. Winthrop, Mr. Sullivan, Mr Pickering, Mr. Bridge, and Mr. Cheever, be a committee to prepare an address to the clergy of this province, desiring them to exhort their people to carry into execution the resolves of the Continental Congress.

||Then the Congress|| adjourned till three o'clock this afternoon.

Afternoon.

The Congress resumed the consideration of the report of the committee appointed to take into consideration the state of rights, state of grievances, and the association, as stated by the Continental Congress, and it was accepted, and is as followeth:

Resolved, That the proceedings of the American Continental Congress, held at Philadelphia on the fifth of September last, and reported by the honorable delegates from this colony, have, with the deliberation due to their high importance, been considered by us; and the American bill of rights therein contained, appears to be formed with the greatest ability and judgment; to be founded on the immutable laws of nature and reason, the principles of the English constitution, and the respective charters and constitutions of the colonies; and to be worthy of their most vigorous support, as essentially necessary to liberty: likewise the ruinous and iniquitous measures, which, in violation of their rights, at present convulse and threaten destruction to America, ||ᵃ|| appear to be clearly pointed out, and judicious plans adopted for defeating them.

Resolved, That the most grateful acknowledgments are due to the truly honorable and patriotic members of the Continental Congress, for their wise and able exertions in the cause of American liberty; and this Congress, in their own names, and in behalf of this colony, do hereby, with the utmost sincerity, express the same.

Resolved, That the Hon. John Hancock, Hon. Thomas Cushing, Esqrs., Mr. Samuel Adams, John Adams, and Robert Treat Paine, Esqrs., or any three of them, be, and they hereby are appointed and authorized to represent this colony on the tenth of May next, or sooner, if necessary, at the American Congress to be held at Philadelphia, with full power, with the delegates from the other American colonies, to concert, direct, and order such further measures as shall to them appear to be best calculated for the recovery and establishment of American rights and liberties, and for restoring harmony between Great Britain and the colonies.

And whereas, it is of the utmost importance that the salutary association of the Continental Congress be effectually executed, and the plans of foes to America defeated; who, aided by tyrannical power, intend to import goods, wares, and merchandize prohibited by the association, which may clandestinely be vended, as goods imported before the first of December instant, by assistance of such merchants and traders as to this intent shall basely prostitute themselves; and it will be extremely difficult to distinguish between goods imported before the said first of December, and such as after said day shall, in violation of the association, be imported and secretly dispersed throughout the colony: and whereas, it is expressly recommended by the Continental Congress " to the Provincial Conventions, and to the committees in the respective colonies, to establish such further regulations as they may think proper, for carrying into execution the association;".

Resolved, That from and after the tenth day of October next, it will be indispensably necessary, that all goods, wares, or merchandize, directly or indirectly imported from Great Britain or Ireland; molasses, syrups, paneles, coffee, or pimento, from the British plantations, or from Dominica; wines from Madeira or the Western Islands, and foreign indigo, should cease to be sold or purchased in this colony, notwithstanding they shall have been imported before the first of December aforesaid, unless the acts and parts of acts of parliament, (partic-

a ||and.||

8

ularly enumerated in a paragraph of the American Congress's Association, subsequent to the fourteenth article,) shall be then repealed: and it is hereby strongly recommended to the inhabitants of the towns and districts in this colony, that from and after the said tenth of October, they cease to sell or purchase, and prevent from being exposed to sale within their respective limits, any goods, wares, or merchandize, &c., above enumerated, which shall at any time have been imported into America, whether before or after the first of December aforesaid, unless said acts of parliament shall then be repealed. And it is likewise strongly recommended to the committee of inspection, (which ought immediately to be chosen, agreeably to the said association, by each town and district in the colony not having already appointed such committees,) that they exert themselves in causing the association, as thereby directed, to be ||ªstrictly|| executed; and that after the said tenth day of October, (unless the acts of parliament aforesaid are repealed,) they apply to all the merchants and traders in their respective towns and districts, and take a full inventory of all goods, wares, and merchandize aforesaid in their possession, whether they shall have been imported before or after the first of December aforesaid, requiring them to.offer no more for sale, until said acts ||ᵇ|| shall be repealed. And if any merchants, traders, or others, shall refuse to have an inventory taken, or shall offer for sale after the said tenth of October, any such goods, wares, or merchandize, it is expressly recommended to the committees aforesaid, that they take the goods into their possession, to be stored at the risk of the proper owners, until the repeal of the acts aforesaid, and publish the names of such refractory merchants, traders, or purchasers, that they may meet with the merits of enemies to their country. And the towns and districts throughout the province are also advised that they by no means fail vigorously to assist and support their committees in discharging this as well as other duties of their offices, and to cause this resolution to be executed by every measure which they shall think necessary.

Resolved, That John Adams, Esq. be joined to the committee on the state of the province.

Resolved, That the above report made by the committee appointed to take into consideration the state of rights, &c., as reported by the Continental Congress, be published in all the newspapers in the province, and that it be signed by the president and attested by the secretary; and also, that copies thereof be sent to all the towns and districts in the province.

a ||fully.|| b ||of parliament.||

Resolved, That the vote relating to a brief be reconsidered, and that it be in order to be revised.

‖Then the Congress‖ adjourned till to-morrow morning, nine o'clock.

TUESDAY, December 6, 1774, A. M.

The committee appointed to take into consideration the state of the manufactures in this province, reported; the report was recommitted for some additions.

The committee appointed to devise means of keeping up a correspondence between this province, Montreal and Quebec, and of gaining frequent intelligence from thence of their movements, reported, that a committee be appointed to correspond with the inhabitants of Canada. Accordingly, the Hon. Major Hawley, Col. Pomeroy, Mr. Brown, Mr. Samuel Adams, Doct. Warren, Hon. Mr. Hancock, and Doct. Church, were appointed a committee for that purpose.

The committee appointed to prepare a brief to be circulated through the several towns in this province, to promote donations for the persons suffering in the towns of Boston and Charlestown, under the operation of certain acts of the British parliament, having amended the same, reported; the report was read and accepted, and is as followeth:

The operation of the cruel and iniquitous Boston port bill, that instrument of ministerial vengeance, having reduced our once happy capital and the neighboring town of Charlestown, from affluence and ease to extreme distress; many of their inhabitants being deprived of even the means of procuring the necessaries of life; from all which they have most nobly refused to purchase an exemption, by surrendering the rights of Americans; and although the charitable donations from the other colonies and several towns in this province, have, in a good measure, relieved their immediate necessities, while their approbation has animated them to persevere in patient suffering for the public good, yet as the severity of winter is now approaching, which must add greatly to their misery; and there has been no general collection for them in this colony, we hold ourselves obliged, in justice, to contribute to their support; while they, under such a weight of oppression, are supporting our rights and privileges.

It is therefore *Resolved,* That it be recommended to our constituents, the inhabitants of the other towns, districts, and parishes, within this province, that they further contribute liberally to alleviate the burden of those persons, who are the more immediate objects of ministerial resentment, and are suffering in the common cause of their country; seriously considering how much the liberty, and consequently the happiness, of ourselves and posterity depend, under God, on the firmness and resolution of those worthy patriots.

And it is *Ordered*, That Doct. Foster, Mr. Devens, and Mr. Cheever, be a committee to transmit printed copies of the above resolve to the ministers of the gospel in the several towns, districts, and parishes, in this province, who are desired to read the same to their several congregations, in order that their contributions of such necessaries of life as they can spare, may be forwarded as soon as possible.

The committee appointed to prepare an address to the clergy, having amended the same, again reported; the report was read and accepted, and ordered that copies thereof be sent to all the ministers of the gospel in the province; ||which|| is as followeth:

Reverend Sirs:—When we contemplate the friendship and assistance our ancestors, the first settlers of this province, (while overwhelmed with distress) received from the pious pastors of the churches of Christ, who, to enjoy the rights of conscience, fled with them into this land, then a savage wilderness, we find ourselves filled with the most grateful sensations. And we cannot but acknowledge the goodness of heaven in constantly supplying us with preachers of the gospel, whose concern has been the temporal and spiritual happiness of this people.

In a day like this, when all the friends of civil and religious liberty are exerting themselves to deliver this country from its present calamities, we cannot but place great hopes in an order of men who have ever distinguished themselves in their country's cause; and do therefore recommend to the ministers of the gospel in the several towns and other places in this colony, that they assist us in avoiding that dreadful slavery with which we are now threatened, by advising the people of their several congregations, as they wish their prosperity, to abide by, and strictly adhere to, the resolutions of the Continental Congress, as the most peaceable and probable method of preventing confusion and bloodshed, and of restoring that harmony between Great Britain and these colonies, on which we wish might be established, not only the rights and liberties of America, but the opulence and lasting happiness of the whole British empire.

Resolved, That the foregoing address be presented to all the ministers of the gospel in the province.

||The Congress then|| adjourned to three o'clock, P. M.

Afternoon.

Resolved, That the names of the following persons be published repeatedly, they having been appointed counsellors of this province by mandamus, and have not published a renunciation of their commission, viz : Thomas Flucker, Foster Hutchinson, Harrison Gray, William Browne, James Bouteneau, Joshua Loring, William Pepperrell, John Erving, Jr., Peter Oliver, Richard Lechmere, Josiah Edson, Nathaniel Ray Thomas, Timothy Ruggles, John Murray, and Daniel Leonard, Esquires.

Adjourned to nine o'clock to-morrow morning.

WEDNESDAY, December 7, 1774, A. M.

Ordered, That Capt. Barrett, Mr. Bridge, and Major Fuller, be a committee to collect the several expenses that have accrued to the Congress in this and the former session thereof, and they are directed to sit forthwith.

Ordered, That Mr. Sullivan, Doct. Holten, Mr. Palmer, Col. Lee, and the Hon. Col. Ward, be a committee to take into consideration and determine what recompense the delegates, who, from this province attended the Continental Congress at Philadelphia, in September last, shall be allowed for their services and expenses.

Ordered, That Col. Orne, Hon. Mr. Cushing, and Hon. Major Hawley, be a committee to bring in a resolve, directing the Hon. James Russell, Esq., impost officer, to pay the moneys now in his hands to Henry Gardner, Esq., ||and not to Harrison Gray, Esq. ;|| the committee are directed to sit immediately.

Ordered, That John Adams, Esq., Mr. Samuel Adams, and Col. Danielson, be a committee to bring in a resolve, relative to the taking the number of inhabitants, and the quantity of exports and imports of merchandize and of the manufactures of all kinds in this colony ; and the committee was directed to sit immediately. The ||above|| committee having attended that service, reported as followeth, viz :

Resolved, That a committee be appointed, consisting of one gentleman from each county, and one from each maritime town of this colony, to prepare from the best authentic evidence which can be procured, a true state of the number of the inhabitants, and of the quantities of exports and imports of goods, wares, and merchandize, and of the manufactures of all kinds, within the colony, [to] be used by our delegates ||ªat|| the Continental Congress, to be held at Philadelphia, on or before the tenth day of May next, as they shall think proper. And the members of this committee for each county be nominated by the members of this Congress for said county, and the mem-

a ||in.||

ber for each maritime town be nominated by the representatives of such town.

Ordered, That the several counties be ready to report their nominations at three o'clock this afternoon.

Resolved, That Mr. Sullivan be desired to forward to the Hon. Jedediah Preble, Esq., a resolve of this Congress appointing him a general officer.||ᵃ||

Afternoon.

The several counties and maritime towns nominated their members for the committee according to the resolve in the forenoon, who were accepted by the Congress, and are as follow, viz:

COUNTY OF SUFFOLK, Mr. Palmer; *Boston*, Doct. Warren; ESSEX, Col. Gerrish; *Lynn*, Capt. Mansfield; *Marblehead*, Col. Orne; *Salem*, Hon. Mr. Derby; *Beverly*, Capt. Batchelder; *Manchester*, Mr. Woodbury; *Gloucester*, Capt. Coffin; *Ipswich*, Capt. Farley; *Newburyport*, Capt. Greenleaf; *Haverhill*, Samuel White, Esq.; *Danvers*, Doct. Holten; MIDDLESEX, Col. Prescot; *Charlestown*, Mr. Gorham; *Medford*, Mr. Hall; HAMPSHIRE, Hon. Major Hawley; PLYMOUTH, Doct. Perkins; *Town of Plymouth*, Mr. Lothrop; *Kingston*, Col. Thomas; *Duxbury*, Mr. Partridge; *Scituate*, Nathan Cushing, Esq.; BARNSTABLE, Daniel Davis, Esq.; *Sandwich*, Capt. Nye; *Eastham*, Mr. Holbrook; BRISTOL, Doct. Cobb; *Dartmouth*, Benjamin Aiken, Esq.; *Freetown*, Mr. Durfee; YORK, Mr. Sullivan; *Kittery*, Charles Chauncy, Esq.;[1] [*Wells*, Mr. Ebenezer Sayer; DUKES COUNTY, Joseph Mayhew, Esq.; *Tisbury*, Mr. Ranford Smith; WORCESTER, Jedediah Foster, Esq.; CUMBERLAND, Enoch Freeman, Esq.; *Scarborough*, Mr. Samuel March; *North Yarmouth*, Mr. John Lewis; *Harpswell*, Mr. Samuel Thompson; BERKSHIRE, John Fellows, Esq.; LINCOLN, Mr. Langdon.]

[THURSDAY, December, 8, 1774, A. M.]

[The report of the committee appointed to take into consideration the state of the manufactures of the province being amended, was read, accepted, and is as follows:]

[As the happiness of particular families arises in a great degree, from their being more or less dependent upon others; and as the less occasion they have for any article belonging to others, the more independent, and consequently the happier they are; so the happiness of

a ||Adjourned to three o'clock this afternoon.||

(1) A leaf has, unhappily, been lost from the original journal of the Provincial Congress. The defective list of members of the committee has been partially restored from the fragment of a memorandum in the hand writing of Hon. Jedediah Foster. The report, to the fourth resolution, is supplied from the Massachusetts Spy, December 22, 1774.

every political body of men upon earth is to be estimated, in a great measure, upon their greater or less dependence upon any other political bodies; and from hence arises a forcible argument, why every state ought to regulate their internal policy in such a manner as to furnish themselves, within their own body, with every necessary article for subsistence and defence, otherwise their political existence will depend upon others who may take advantage of such weakness and reduce them to the lowest state of vassalage and slavery. For preventing so great an evil, more to be dreaded than death itself, it must be the wisdom of this colony at all times, more especially at this time, when the hand of power is lashing us with the scorpions of despotism, to encourage agriculture, manufactures, and economy, so as to render this state as independent of every other state as the nature of our country will admit; from the consideration thereof, and trusting that the virtue of the people of this colony is such, that the following resolutions of this Congress, which must be productive of the greatest good, will by them be effectually carried into execution, and it is therefore *Resolved:*]

[1st. That we do recommend to the people the improvement of their breed of sheep, and the greatest possible increase of the same; and also the preferable use of our own woollen manufactures; and to manufacturers that they ask only reasonable prices for their goods; and especially a very careful sorting of the wool, so that it may be manufactured to the greatest advantage, and as much as may be into the best goods.]

[2d. We do also recommend to the people the raising of hemp and flax; and as large quantities of flaxseed, more than may be wanted for sowing, may be produced, we would also farther recommend the manufacturing the same into oil.]

[3d. We do likewise recommend the making of nails, which we apprehend must meet with the strongest encouragement from the public, and be of lasting benefit both to the manufacturer and the public.]

4th. The making of steel, and the preferable use of the same, we do also recommend to the inhabitants of this colony.

5th. We do in like manner recommend the making tin plate, as an article well worth the attention of this people.

6th. As fire arms have been manufactured in several parts of this colony, we do recommend the use of such in preference to any imported; and we do recommend the making gun-locks, and furniture, and other locks, with other articles in the iron way.

7th. We do also earnestly recommend the making of saltpetre, as an article of vast importance, to be encouraged as may be directed hereafter.

8th. That gun powder is also an article of such importance, that every man among us who loves his country, must wish the establishment of manufactories for that purpose; and as there are the ruins of several powder mills, and sundry persons among us who are acquainted with that business, we do heartily recommend its encouragement by repairing one or more of said mills, or erecting others, and renewing said business as soon as possible.

9th. That as several paper mills are now usefully employed, we do likewise recommend a preferable use of our own manufactures in this way; and a careful saving and collecting of rags, &c. And, also, that the manufacturers give a generous price for such rags, &c.

10th. That it will be the interest as well as the duty of this body, or of such as may succeed us, to make such effectual provision for the further manufacturing of the several sorts of glass, as that the same may be carried on to the mutual benefit of the undertaker and the public, and firmly established in this colony.

11th. Whereas buttons, of excellent qualities, and of various sorts, are manufactured among us, we do earnestly recommend the general use of the same, so that the manufactories may be extended to the advantage of the people and the manufacturers.

12th. And whereas salt is an article of vast consumption within this colony, and in its fisheries, we do heartily recommend the making the same in the several ways wherein it is made in several parts of Europe, especially in the method used in that part of France where they make bay salt.

13th. We do likewise recommend an encouragement of horn smiths in all their various branches, as what will be of public utility.

14th. We do also recommend the establishment of one or more manufactories for making wool-combers' combs, as an article necessary in our woollen manufactures.

15th. We do in like manner heartily recommend the preferable use of the stockings and other hosiery ||ᵃwove|| among ourselves, so as to enlarge the manufactories thereof, in such a manner as to encourage the manufacturers and serve the country.

16th. As madder is an article of great importance in the dyer's business, and which may be easily raised and cured among ourselves, we do therefore earnestly recommend the raising and curing the same.

a ||worn-||

17th. In order the more effectually to carry these resolutions into effect, we do earnestly recommend that a society or societies be established for the purposes of introducing and establishing such arts and manufactures as may be useful to this people, and are not yet introduced, and the more effectually establishing such as we already have among us.

18th. We do recommend to the inhabitants of this province to make use of our own manufactures, and those of our sister colonies, in preference to all other manufactures.

Afternoon.

The order of the day was moved for.

Resolved, That Doct. Church, Mr. Wheeler, and Doct. Holten, be a committee to count and sort the votes for two general officers, and that the Congress vote for the officers separately.

The Congress then proceeded to bring in their votes for a general officer; the committee having sorted and counted the same, reported that Col. Thomas was chosen.

The Congress then proceeded to bring in their votes for one other general officer; the committee having counted and sorted the same, reported that Col. William Heath was chosen.

||Then the|| Congress adjourned till to-morrow morning, ten o'clock.

FRIDAY, December 9, 1774, A. M.

The committee appointed to inquire into the sufficiency of the bondmen procured by the receiver general, reported that they had attended [to] that service, and that the gentlemen he had engaged as his ||ᵃbondmen were in their opinion a very ample security|| for the sum mentioned.

Ordered, That Mr. Sullivan, Mr. Pickering, and Mr. Sayer, be a committee to bring in a resolve relating to an address from the Baptists to this Congress.

Ordered, [That] the report of the committee relative to the public moneys, now in the hands of the constables and others, which was ordered to lie on the table, be now taken up; which was taken up accordingly, and passed, and is as followeth, viz:

Whereas, this Congress, at their session in October last, taking into consideration the alarming state of this colony, were, upon the most mature deliberation, fully convinced, that to provide against the danger to which it was then exposed by a standing army illegally posted in Boston, and from time to time reinforced for the purposes of subverting our ancient constitution and the liberties of all North America, it

a ||security were amply sufficient.||

was indispensably necessary that a considerable sum of money should
be immediately laid out for the just defence of this people ; and whereas, by a resolve of the Congress, bearing date the 28th of said October, and published in the newspapers, it was, among other things, earnestly recommended to the several towns and districts, that they would
cause to be paid into the hands of Henry Gardner, Esq., all the province moneys due from them respectively, to supply the said pressing
exigencies of the colony; and whereas, the danger ||ᵃwhich|| then
threatened the province is still continued and daily increasing :

It is *Resolved*, and hereby most earnestly recommended to all
the inhabitants of the towns and districts aforesaid, as they regard
their own safety and the preservation of their inestimable rights and
liberties, that they cause the moneys aforesaid to be paid forthwith to
the said Henry Gardner, Esq., who has given bonds with sufficient
sureties, to the satisfaction of this Congress ; and that they cause their
respective proportion of the tax granted by the general court in June
last, and all other the province moneys due from them respectively, to
be supplied in some way that shall be more expeditious than the usual
mode of collecting the taxes, in order to prevent any delay in providing against the imminent dangers above mentioned.   And the members
of the Congress are hereby desired to ||ᵇuse|| their utmost industry for
having this resolve speedily and punctually complied with ; and the
sheriffs and deputy sheriffs of the several counties, to pay the province
moneys in their respective hands as has been already recommended.

Ordered, That Col. Orne, Mr. Pickering, and Col. Cushing, be a
committee to bring in a resolve purporting the sense of this Congress
of the Continental Congress's association, as now voted, relative to
goods, wares, and merchandize, landed in England and Ireland, as well
as those which are manufactured in England and Ireland ; who reported as followeth ; which was read and accepted, and ordered to be sent to
the committee at Marblehead, and published in the newspapers :

Resolved, That it is the clear opinion of this Congress, that the first
article in the association of the Continental Congress, extends to all
goods, wares, and merchandize, of the growth, production, or manufacture, of any part of Europe, or any other part of the world, imported from Great Britain or Ireland, in case they have been entered and
cleared in any part of either of those kingdoms, as fully as to goods,
wares, and merchandize, of the growth, production and manufacture of
Great Britain or Ireland, and that the said first article ought to be so

a ||that.|| b ||exert.||

:

construed by all concerned, and in that universal sense carried strictly
into execution.

Ordered, That Col. Heath, Col. Gerrish, Col. Gardner, Capt. Fuller,
Col. Thomas, Col. Orne, and Col. Barnes, be a committee to take into
consideration a plan of military exercise, proposed by Capt. Timothy Pickering.

Ordered, That the petition of the officers in the northwesterly part
of the county of Worcester, be committed to the same committee, ||to||
report.

Afternoon.

The committee appointed to bring in a resolve, relative to the petition of Rev. Mr. Backus, in behalf of the Baptists, reported; which
was read and accepted, and the secretary directed to send him a copy
of the resolve, which [is] as followeth, viz :

On reading the memorial of the Rev. Isaac Backus, agent to the
Baptist churches in this government, *Resolved*, That the establishment
of civil and religious liberty, to each denomination in the province, is
the sincere wish of this Congress; but being by no means vested with
powers of civil government, whereby they can redress the grievances
of any person whatsoever, they therefore recommend to the Baptist
churches, that, when a general assembly shall be convened in this colony, they lay the real grievances of said churches before the same, when
and where their petition will most certainly meet with all that attention
due to the memorial of a denomination of christians so well disposed
to the public weal of their country.

Ordered, That Mr. Stickney, Col. Gardner, Col. Pomeroy, Col.
Thayer, and Mr. Wheeler, be a committee to wait on the Rev. Doct.
Appleton, and return him the thanks of this Congress for his services
as chaplain during this session.

Ordered, That Major Fuller, Capt. Brown, and Mr. Pigeon, be a
committee to wait on the proprietors of the meeting-house and return
them the thanks of the Congress for the use thereof.

The Congress then adjourned for half an hour.

Being met upon the adjournment, Mr. President brought into Con-
gress a letter from the committee of correspondence of the town of
Hardwick, with a number of papers enclosed, which were read; the
Congress then ordered that Mr. Sullivan, Mr. Pickering, Col. Gardner,
Col. Mandell, and Col. Danielson, be a committee to take the same into
consideration and report in the morning.

||Then the Congress|| adjourned till nine o'clock to-morrow morning.

SATURDAY, December 10, 1774, A. M.

The committee ||appointed|| to take into consideration the letter and papers enclosed, received from the committee of correspondence of the town of Hardwick, reported; which was read and accepted, and ordered to be published in the public papers, and also the papers on which the said report is founded. The report is as followeth, viz:

Whereas, it appears to this Congress, that one or more members of the lately appointed unconstitutional council in this province, now residing in Boston, has sent to the town of Hardwick, a paper purporting [to be] an association to be entered into by those persons who falsely assume the name of friends to government;[1] calculated to coun-

(1) The following is the form of the association, intended for the signature of the royalists, prepared, and sent by the Hon. Timothy Ruggles to the town of Hardwick, where he had resided until his acceptance of the appointment of mandamus counsellor compelled him to seek refuge from public indignation in Boston:

" We, the subscribers, being fully sensible of the blessings of good government on the one hand, and convinced, on the other hand, of the evils and calamities attending on tyranny in all shapes, whether exercised by one or many, and having lately seen, with great grief and concern, the distressing efforts for a dissolution of all government, whereby our lives, liberties, and properties, are rendered precarious, and no longer under the protection of the law: and apprehending it to be our indispensable duty, to use all lawful means in our power for the defence of our persons and property against all riotous and lawless violence and to recover, and secure the advantages which we are entitled to have, from the good and wholesome laws of the government, do hereby associate, and mutually covenant, and engage to and with each other, as follows, viz:

" 1. That we will, on all occasions, with our lives, and fortunes, stand by and assist each other in the defence of life, liberty, and property, whenever the same shall be attacked or endangered by any bodies of men, riotously assembled, upon any pretence or under any authority not warranted by the laws of the land."

" 2. That we will, upon all occasions, mutually support each other in the free exercise and enjoyment of our undoubted right to liberty, in eating, drinking, buying, selling, communing and acting, what, with whom, and as we please, consistent with the laws of God, and of the King."

" 3. That we will not acknowledge, or submit to the pretended authority of any Congresses, committees of correspondence, or other unconstitutional assemblies of men: but will, at the risk of our lives, if need be, oppose the forcible exercise of all such authority."

" 4. That we will, to the utmost of our power, promote, encourage, and, when called to it, enforce obedience to the rightful authority of our most gracious sovereign, King George the Third, and of his laws."

" 5. That when the person or property of any one of us shall be invaded or threatened by any committees, mobs, or unlawful assemblies, the others of us, will, upon notice received, forthwith repair, properly armed, to the person whom, or place where such invasion or threatening shall be, and will, to the utmost of our power, defend such person and his property, and, if need be, will oppose and repel force with force."

" 6. That if any one of us shall unjustly and unlawfully be injured in his person or property, by any such assemblies as before mentioned, the others of us will, unitedly, demand, and, if in our power, compel the offenders, if known, to make full reparation and satisfaction for such injury: and if all other means of security fail we will have recourse to the natural law of retaliation."

" In witness of all which we hereto subscribe our names."

As the order of the Congress for the publication of these resolutions was not immediately executed, a copy was sent by the writer himself, to the printer of the Boston Evening Post, and inserted in that paper, December 26, 1774, with a letter from General Ruggles, in which he writes thus: " As many of the people for some time past have been arming themselves, it may not be amiss to let them know, that their number will not appear in the field so large as was imagined before it was known that *independence was in contemplation*; since which, many have associated in divers parts of the province to preserve their freedom and support government."

teract the salutary designs of the Continental and Provincial Congresses, to deceive the people into agreements contrary to the welfare of this country, and tending in its consequences to hinder an amicable accommodation with our mother country, the sole end of those Congresses, and the ardent wish of every friend to America : it is therefore recommended by this Congress to the several committees of correspondence in this colony, that they give notice to the Provincial Congress, that shall meet in this province on the first day of February next, and the earliest notice to the public, of all such combinations, and of the persons signing the same, if any should be enticed thereto, that their names may be published to the world, their persons treated with that neglect, and their memories transmitted to posterity with that ignominy, which such unnatural conduct must deserve.

The committee on the state of the province reported an address to the inhabitants of Massachusetts Bay ; the report was considered in paragraphs, and so passed, and was ordered to be printed in all the Boston newspapers, and also in handbills, and a copy thereof sent to all the towns and districts in the province, and is as followeth, viz :

To the Freeholders and other Inhabitants of the Towns and Districts of Massachusetts Bay.

FRIENDS AND BRETHREN : At a time when the good people of this colony were deprived of their laws, and the administration of justice, civil and criminal ; when the cruel oppressions brought on their capital had stagnated almost all their commerce ; when a standing army was illegally posted among us for the express purpose of enforcing submission to a system of tyranny ; and when the general court was, with the same design, prohibited to sit ; we were chosen and empowered by you to assemble and consult upon measures necessary for our common safety and defence.

With much anxiety for the common welfare, we have attended this service, and upon the coolest deliberation have adopted the measures recommended to you.

We have still confidence in the wisdom, justice, and goodness of our sovereign, as well as the integrity, humanity and good sense of the nation ; and if we had a reasonable expectation that the truth of facts would be made known in England, we should entertain the most pleasing hopes that the measures concerted by the colonies jointly and severally, would procure a full redress of our grievances ; but we are constrained in justice to you, to ourselves, and posterity, to say, that the incessant and unrelenting malice of our enemies has been so successful as to fill the court and kingdom of Great Britain with falsehoods and calumnies concerning us, and to excite the most bitter and groundless prejudices against us; that the sudden dissolution of parliament, and the hasty summons for a new election, gives us reason to apprehend that a majority of the house of commons will be again elected under the influence of an arbitrary ministry; and that the general tenor of our intelligence from Great Britain, with the frequent reinforcements of the army and navy at Boston, excites the strongest jealousy that the system of colony administration, so unfriendly to the protestant religion, and destructive of American liberty, is still to be pursued and attempted with force to be carried into execution.

You are placed by Providence in [the] post of honor, because it is the post of danger: and while struggling for the noblest objects, the liberties of your country, the happiness of posterity, and [the] rights of human nature, the eyes not only of North America and the whole British empire, but of all Europe, are upon you. Let us be therefore altogether solicitous, that no disorderly behavior, nothing unbecoming our characters as Americans, as citizens, and christians, be justly chargeable to us.

Whoever, with a small degree of attention, contemplates the commerce between Great Britain and America, will be convinced that a total stoppage thereof, will soon produce in Great Britain such dangerous effects, as cannot fail to convince the ministry, the parliament, and people, that it is their interest and duty to grant us relief. Whoever considers the number of brave men inhabiting North America, will know, that a general attention to military discipline must so establish their rights and liberties, as, under God, to render it impossible for an arbitrary ministry of Britain to destroy them. These are facts which our enemies are apprized of, and if they will not be influenced by principles of justice, to alter their cruel measures towards America, these ought to lead them thereto. They, however, hope to effect by stratagem what they may not obtain by power, and are using arts, by the assistance of base scribblers, who undoubtedly receive their bribes, and by many other means, to raise doubts and divisions throughout the colonies.

To defeat their ||ᵃiniquitous|| designs, we think it necessary for each town to be particularly careful, strictly to execute the plans of the Continental and Provincial Congresses; and while it censures its own individuals, counteracting those plans, that it be not deceived or diverted from its duty by rumors, should any take place, to the prejudice of

a ||wicked.||

other communities. Your Provincial Congresses, we have reason to hope, will hold up the towns, if any should be so lost as not to act their parts, and none can doubt that the Continental Congresses will rectify errors should any take place in any colony through the subtilty of our enemies. Surely no arguments can be necessary to excite you to the most strict adherence to the American association, since the minutest deviation in one colony, especially in this, will probably be misrepresented in the others, to discourage their general zeal and perseverance, which, however, we assure ourselves cannot be effected.

While the British ministry are suffered with so high a hand to tyrannize over America, no part of it, we presume, can be negligent in guarding against the ravages threatened by the standing army now in Boston ; these troops will undoubtedly be employed in attempts to defeat the association, which our enemies cannot but fear will eventually defeat them ; and so sanguinary are those our enemies, as we have reason to think, so thirsty for the blood of this innocent people, who are only contending for their rights, that we should be guilty of the most unpardonable neglect should we not apprize you of your danger, which appears to us imminently great, and ought attentively to be guarded against. The improvement of the militia in general in the art military has been therefore thought necessary, and strongly recommended by this Congress. We now think that particular care should be taken by the towns and districts in this colony, that each of the minute men, not already provided therewith, should be immediately equipped with an effective fire arm, bayonet, pouch, knapsack, thirty rounds of cartridges and balls, and that they be disciplined three times a week, and oftener, as opportunity may offer. To encourage these, our worthy countrymen, to obtain the skill of complete soldiers, we recommend it to the towns and districts forthwith to pay their own minute men a reasonable consideration for their services : and in case of a general muster, their further services must be recompensed by the province. An attention to discipline the militia in general is, however, by no means to be neglected.

With the utmost cheerfulness we assure you of our determination to stand or fall with the liberties of America ; and while we humbly implore the Sovereign Disposer of all things, to whose divine providence the rights of his creatures cannot be indifferent, to correct the errors, and alter the measures of an infatuated ministry, we cannot doubt of his support even in the extreme difficulties which we all may have to encounter. May all means devised for our safety by the General Congress of America, and assemblies or conventions of the colonies, be resolutely executed, and happily succeeded; and may this injured people be reinstated in the full exercise of their rights without the evils and devastations of a civil war.

Ordered, That the members of the town of Boston, with the secretary, be a committee to revise the doings of this Congress, and cause such parts thereof, as they think fit should be published, to be printed in a pamphlet, and a copy thereof be sent to every town and district in this province.

The report of the committee on the state of the province, relative to assuming civil government, [was] taken up, and ordered further to lie on the table.

Ordered, That the members be enjoined to attend in the afternoon.

||Then the Congress|| adjourned to three o'clock this afternoon.

Afternoon.

The committee appointed to collect the several expenses which have accrued to the Congress in this and a former session thereof, reported; which report was read and accepted, and the receiver general ordered to pay and discharge the several demands therein mentioned.

Ordered, That the secretary be directed to furnish the committee of safety with a number of attested copies of their appointment to that trust.

Resolved, That a gentleman be appointed in each county, to apply to the field officers of the regiments within the same, for the list of the names of the field officers of each regiment, the number of other officers, and the number of the men therein, as well the minute men as the common militia, and return the same unto Mr. Abraham Watson, of Cambridge.

Accordingly, the following gentlemen were appointed: For the COUNTY OF SUFFOLK, Col. Heath; ESSEX, Capt. Farley; MIDDLESEX, Col. Smith; HAMPSHIRE, Col. Pomeroy; PLYMOUTH, Col. Warren; BARNSTABLE, Daniel Davis, Esq.; BRISTOL, Major Keith; YORK, Mr. Sullivan; WORCESTER, Capt. Bigelow; CUMBERLAND, Mr. March; BERKSHIRE, Doct. Whiting; LINCOLN, Capt. Thompson; DUKES COUNTY, Joseph Mayhew, Esq.

The committee on the state of the province reported: which report was read and accepted; and *Ordered,* That printed copies be sent to the several committees of correspondence, and where there is no such committee, to the selectmen in each town and district in the province; and that the same order be observed relative to the address to the inhabitants of Massachusetts Bay, and that the members of the town of

Boston, and the secretary, disperse the same.   The report is as followeth, viz :

Inasmuch as many states have been taught by fatal experience, that
powers delegated by the people for long periods have been abused to
the endangering the public rights and liberties, and this Congress having just reason to suppose that their constituents, the good people of
this province, when they appointed their present delegates, were not
apprehensive that the business necessary to be done would require their
attendance for any long time,

Resolved, That the adjournment of this Congress on the twenty-
ninth day of October last, was ordered and made from a due consideration of the present exigencies of the public affairs, and the evident
necessity of farther deliberation thereon.   And, whereas, for the reason
first mentioned, it is not expedient that there should be a further adjournment of this Congress; therefore, *Resolved*, that after the business necessary to be immediately despatched shall be finished, the Congress be dissolved.

And this Congress being deeply impressed with a sense of the increasing dangers which threaten the rights and liberties of the people
of this province with total ruin ; our adversaries being still indefatigable in their attempts to carry into execution their deep laid plans for
that wicked purpose : and considering the indispensable necessity that
an assembly of the province should be very frequently sitting to con-
sult and devise ||ᵃmeasures|| for their common safety ; therefore *Resolv-
ed*, That it be, and it is hereby earnestly recommended to the several
towns and districts in this province, that they each of them do forthwith, elect and depute as many members as to them shall seem necessary and expedient, to represent them in a Provincial Congress, to be
held at Cambridge, on the first day of February next ensuing ; to be
chosen by such only as are qualified by law to vote for representatives
in the general assembly, and to be continued by adjournment, as they
shall see cause, until the Tuesday next preceding the last Wednesday
of May next, and no longer ; to consult, deliberate and resolve upon such
farther measures as, under God, shall be effectual to save this people
from impending ruin, and to secure those inestimable liberties derived
to us from our ancestors, and which it is our duty to preserve for posterity.

And considering the great uncertainty of the present times, and that
unexpected important events may take place, from whence it may be absolutely necessary that the delegates who may be elected as above propos-

ed should meet sooner than the day before mentioned, it is recommended to the several towns and districts, that they instruct and authorize their said delegates, to assemble at Cambridge aforesaid, or any other place, upon notice given them of the necessity thereof, by the delegates that may be chosen by the towns of Charlestown, Cambridge, Brookline, Roxbury and Dorchester, or the majority of them, in such way as they shall judge proper.

And it is further recommended to the delegates to be elected, that they conform themselves to such instructions.

Ordered, That the further consideration of the report of the committee appointed to take into consideration what allowance should be made the delegates who attend the Continental Congress from this province, be referred to the sitting of the next Provincial Congress.

The committee appointed to take into consideration a plan of military exercise, proposed by Capt. Pickering, and also the petition of the officers of the northwest part of the county of Worcester, reported; the report was read and accepted.

Ordered, That the expense of transmitting the address to the Canadians be paid by this government.

The business necessary to be immediately transacted, being finished, and the Congress having returned their thanks to the Hon. John Hancock, Esq., for his constant attendance and faithful services as president during their session, dissolved.||ᵃ||

a ||the same to convene again the first day of February next, conformably to the preceding resolve.||

JOURNAL

OF THE

SECOND PROVINCIAL CONGRESS

OF

𝕸𝖆𝖘𝖘𝖆𝖈𝖍𝖚𝖘𝖊𝖙𝖙𝖘,

Convened at Cambridge, Wednesday, Feb. 1, 1775.—Adjourned Thursday, Feb. 16.
Convened at Concord, Tuesday, March 22.—Adjourned Saturday, April 15.
Convened at Concord, Saturday, April 22.—Adjourned to Watertown.
Convened at Watertown, Saturday, April 22.—Dissolved May 29, 1775.

JOURNAL.

RECORD of the proceedings of a Provincial Congress of deputies of the several towns and districts in the province of the Massachusetts Bay, in New England, convened at Cambridge, on Wednesday, the first day of February, A. D. 1775; with a list of the persons chosen to represent them in the same.

COUNTY OF SUFFOLK.

Boston.—Hon. Thomas Cushing, Esq., Mr. Samuel Adams, Hon. John Hancock, Esq., Doct. Joseph Warren, Doct. Benjamin Church, Mr. Oliver Wendall, Mr. John Pitts.

Roxbury.—Col. William Heath, Capt. Aaron Davis.

Dorchester.—Capt. Ebenezer Withington.

Milton.—Capt. David Rawson.

Braintree.—Col. Joseph Palmer.

Weymouth.—Mr. Nathaniel Bailey.

Hingham and Cohasset.—Benjamin Lincoln, Esq.

Dedham.—Hon. Samuel Dexter, Esq., Mr. Abner Ellis.

Medfield.—Mr. Moses Bullen.

Wrentham.—Mr. Jabez Fisher, [Mr. Lemuel Kollock, Mr. Samuel Lethbridge.]

Brookline.—Capt. Benjamin White.

Needham.—Capt. Eleazer Kingsbury.

Stoughton.—Mr. Thomas Crane.

Stoughtonham.—Mr. Job Swift.

Medway.—Capt. Jonathan Adams.

Bellingham.—[Mr. Stephen Metcalf.]

Hull.—[None.]

Walpole.—Mr. Enoch Ellis.

Chelsea.—Mr. Samuel Watts.

COUNTY OF ESSEX.

Salem.—Mr. John Pickering, Mr. Richard Manning, [Mr. Jonathan Ropes, Jun.]

Danvers.—Doct. Samuel Holten.

Ipswich.—Col. Michael Farley.

Newburyport.—Capt. Jonathan Greenleaf, Mr. Stephen Cross, Tristram Dalton, Esq.

Newbury.—Joseph Gerrish, Esq.

Marblehead.—Jeremiah Lee, Esq., Col. Azor Orne, Mr. Elbridge Gerry.

Lynn.—Col. John Mansfield.

Andover.—Mr. Samuel Osgood, Jun.

Beverly.—Capt. Josiah Batchelder.

Rowley.—Mr. Nathaniel Mighill.

Salisbury.—Mr. Samuel Smith.

Gloucester.—Capt. Peter Coffin, Mr. Samuel Whittemore.

Topsfield.—Capt. Samuel Smith.

Boxford.—Major Asa Perley.

Amesbury.—Isaac Merrill, Esq.

Bradford.—Col. Daniel Thurston.

Haverhill.—Nathaniel Peaslee Sargent, Esq., Mr. Jonathan Webster, Jun.

Wenham.—Mr. Benjamin Fairfield.

Middleton.—Capt. Archelaus Fuller.

Manchester.—[None.]

Methuen.—Mr. John Bodwell.

COUNTY OF MIDDLESEX.

Cambridge.—Col. Thomas Gardner, Mr. Abraham Watson, Jun.

Charlestown.—Mr. Nathaniel Gorham, Mr. Richard Devens, David Cheever, Esq.

Watertown.—Capt. Jonathan Browne.

Woburn.—Mr. Samuel Wyman.

Concord.—Col. James Barrett.

Newton.—Abraham Fuller, Esq , Mr. Edward Durant.

Reading.—Mr. John Temple.

Malborough.—Mr. Peter Bent.

Billerica.—William Stickney, Esq.

Framingham.—Capt. Josiah Stone.

Lexington.—Mr. Jonas Stone.

Chelmsford.—Mr. Simeon Spaulding.

Sherburne.—Mr. Benjamin Fasset, Mr. Richard Sanger.

Sudbury.—Mr. Thomas Plympton.

Malden.—Capt. Ebenezer Harnden, Capt. John Dexter.

Weston.—Col. Braddyl Smith.

Medford.—Mr. Benjamin Hall, Mr. Stephen Hall, 3d.
Littleton.—Mr. Abel Jewett.
Hopkinton.—[None.]
Westford.—Capt. Joseph Reed.
Waltham.—Jonas Dix, Esq.
Stow.—Henry Gardner, Esq.
Groton.—Col. James Prescot.
Shirley.—Capt. Francis Harris.
Pepperel.—Capt. Edmund Bancroft.
Townshend.—Mr. Israel Hobart.
Ashby.—[None.]
Stoneham.—Capt. Samuel Sprague.
Wilmington.—Mr. Timothy Walker.
Natick.—[None.]
Dracut.—Mr. Peter Coburn.
Bedford.—John Reed, Esq.
Holliston.—Col. Abner Perry.
Tewkesbury.—Mr. Jonathan Browne.
Dunstable.—John Tyng, Esq., James Tyng, Esq.
Acton.—Mr. Josiah Hayward.
Lincoln.—Major Eleazer Brooks.

COUNTY OF HAMPSHIRE.

Springfield.—Mr. William Pynchon, Jun., [Mr. John Hale, Mr. Moses Field.]
Wilbraham.—Major John Bliss.
West Springfield.—Mr. Jonathan White, Doct. Chauncy Brewer.
Northampton.—Hon. Joseph Hawley, Esq., Col. Seth Pomeroy.
Southampton.—Major Elias Lyman.
Hadley.—[None.]
South Hadley.—Mr. Noah Goodman.
Amherst.—Mr. Nathaniel Dickerson, Jun.
Williamsburgh.—Mr. Russell Kellogg.
Granby.—[None.]
Hatfield.—Mr. John Dickerson, Mr. Perez Graves.
Westfield.—Col. John Moseley, Col. Elisha Parks.
Deerfield.—[Mr. David Field, Mr. David Welles.]
Greenfield.—Mr. Samuel Hinsdale.
Shelburne.—[None.]
Conway.—[Mr. Daniel Denham.]
Sunderland.—[None.]

Montague.—[None.]
Northfield.—Mr. Ebenezer Jones.
Brimfield, [*South Brimfield and Monson.*—Col. Timothy Danielson.]
Pelham.—[None.]
Greenwich.—[None.]
Blanford.—[None.]
Palmer.—[None.]
Granville.—[None.]
New Salem.—Mr. William Page, Jun.
Belchertown.—Col. Samuel Howe.
Colrain.—Mr. Thomas Bell.
Ware.—[None.]
Warwick.—Capt. Samuel Williams.
Bernardston.—[None.]
Murraysfield.—Capt. Malcom Henry.
Charlemont.—Mr. Samuel Taylor.
Shutesbury.—[None.]
Chesterfield.—Mr. Benjamin Mills, Major Ezra May.
Ashfield.—[None.]
Worthington.—[None.]
Ludlow.—Capt. Joseph Miller.
[*Whately.*—Mr. Elisha Tracy.]

COUNTY OF PLYMOUTH.

Plymouth.—Hon. James Warren, Esq., Mr. Isaac Lothrop.
Scituate.—Nathan Cushing, Esq., Mr. Barnabas Little.
Duxbury.—Mr. George Partridge.
Marshfield.—[Mr. Benjamin White.]
Bridgewater.—Col. Edward Mitchell, Major Richard Perkins.
Middleborough.—Mr. Joshua White.
Rochester.—[None.]
Plympton.—[Deac. Samuel Lucas.]
Pembroke.—Major Jeremiah Hall.
Kingston.—John Thomas, Esq.
Hanover.—Col. Joseph Cushing.
Abington.—Capt. Woodbridge Browne.
Halifax.—Mr. Ebenezer Tomson.

COUNTY OF BARNSTABLE.

Barnstable.—Daniel Davis, Esq.

Sandwich.—[None.]
Yarmouth.—Capt. Elijah Basset.
Eastham.—Mr. Naaman Holbrook.
Wellfleet.—[None.]
Harwich.—Mr. Benjamin Freeman.
Falmouth.—[None.]
Chatham.—[None.]
Truro.—Mr. Benjamin Atkins.
Provincetown.—[None.]

COUNTY OF BRISTOL.

Taunton.—Robert Treat Paine, Esq.
Rehoboth.—Major Timothy Walker, Capt. Thomas Carpenter.
Swansey.—Jerathmiel Bowers, Esq.
Dighton.—Elnathan Walker, Esq., Doct. William Baylies.
Dartmouth.—Benjamin Aiken, Esq.
Norton and Mansfield.—Capt. William Holmes.
Attleborough.—Col. John Daggett.
Freetown.—Mr. Thomas Durfee.
Raynham.—Mr. Benjamin King.
Easton.—Capt. Eliphalet Leonard.
Berkley.—[None.]

COUNTY OF YORK.

York.—Capt. Daniel Bragdon.
Kittery.—Edward Cutt, Esq., Charles Chauncy, Esq.
Wells.—Mr. Ebenezer Sayer.
Berwick.—Mr. Ichabod Goodwin, Jun.
Arundel.—Mr. John Hovey.
Biddeford.—James Sullivan, Esq.
Pepperrellborough.—[None.]

DUKES COUNTY.

Edgarton.—[None.]
Chilmark.—[None.]
Tisbury.—[None.]

[COUNTY OF] NANTUCKET.

Sherburne.—[None.]

COUNTY OF WORCESTER.

Worcester.—Capt. Timothy Bigelow.
Lancaster.—Col. Asa Whitcomb, Doct. William Dunsmore.
Mendon.—Doct. William Jennison, Mr. Edward Rawson.
Woodstock.—[None.]
Brookfield.—Jedediah Foster, Esq.
Oxford.—Col. Ebenezer Learned.
Charlton.—Capt. Jonathan Tucker.
Sutton.—Capt. Henry King, Mr. Amos Singletary.
Leicester and Spencer.—Col. Joseph Henshaw.
Paxton.—[None.]
Rutland.—Mr. Jonas Howe.
Hutchinson.—Mr. John Mason.
Oakham.—Capt. Isaac Stone.
Hubbardston.—Capt. John Clark.
New Braintree.—Capt. James Wood.
Southborough.—Capt. Josiah Fay.
Westborough.—Capt. Stephen Maynard, Doct. James Hawse.
Northborough.—Mr. Levi Brigham.
Shrewsbury.—Hon. Artemas Ward, Esq.
Lunenburgh.—Doct. John Taylor.
Fitchburgh.—Capt. David Goodridge.
Uxbridge.—Mr. Benjamin Green.
Harvard.—Mr. Oliver Whitney.
Dudley.—[None.]
Bolton.—Capt. Samuel Baker.
Upton.—Mr. Abiel Sadler.
Sturbridge.—Capt. Timothy Parker.
Leominster.—Mr. Israel Nichols.
Hardwick.—Col. Paul Mandel.
Holden.—Mr. John Child.
Douglas.—Mr. Samuel Jennison.
Grafton.—Mr. John Sherman.
Petersham.—Col. Jonathan Grout.
Royalston.—Mr. Nahum Green.
Westminster.—Mr. Nathan Wood.
Athol.—Mr. William Bigelow.
Templeton.—Mr. Jonathan Baldwin.
Princeton.—Mr. Moses Gill.
Ashburnham.—[None.]
Winchendon.—[None.]
Western.—Simeon Dwight, Esq.

COUNTY OF CUMBERLAND.

Falmouth and Cape Elizabeth.—Mr. Samuel Freeman.
North Yarmouth.—[None.]
Scarborough.—Mr. Samuel March.
Brunswick and Harpswell.—Col. Samuel Thompson.
Gorham.—Capt. Bryant Morton.
Windham—[None.]
Persontown.—[None.]

COUNTY OF LINCOLN.

Pownalsborough.—[None.]
Georgetown.—Capt. Samuel McCobb.
Newcastle.—[None.]
Topsham.—Mr. John Merril.
Bowdoinham.—Capt. Samuel Harnden.
Woolwich.—[None.]
Gardnerston.—Mr. Joseph North.
Vassalborough.—Mr. Remington Hobby.
Hallowell.—[None.]
Winslow.—[None.]
Winthrop.—Mr. Ichabod How.

COUNTY OF BERKSHIRE.

Sheffield and Great Barrington.—Col. John Fellows.
Egremont and Alford.—Doct. William Whiting.
Stockbridge.—Mr. Samuel Browne.
New Malborough.—Doct. Ephraim Guiteau.
Richmond.—Capt. Elijah Browne.
Lenox.—John Paterson, Esq.
Pittsfield and Partridgefield.—John Browne, Esq.
Tyringham.—[None.]
Lanesborough.—[None.]
Sandisfield.—Mr. David Deming.
Williamstown.—Mr. Samuel Kellog.
Becket.—[None.]
Gageborough.—Capt. William Clark.

Moved, That a president be appointed.

Ordered, That Doct. Holten, Mr. Cushing, and Doct. Baylies be a committee to count and sort the votes for a president. The Congress then proceeded to bring in their votes for a president; and the committee having counted the same, reported that the Hon. John Hancock, Esq. was unanimously chosen.

Benjamin Lincoln was appointed secretary.

Ordered, That Hon. John Hancock, Esq., Major Hawley, Hon. Mr. Cushing, [of Boston,] Mr. Adams, Col. Warren, Mr. Paine, Mr. Pitts, Doct. Holten, Col. Heath, Col. Gerrish, Mr. Cushing of Scituate, Hon. Col. Ward, and Col. Gardner, be a committee to take into consideration the state and circumstances of the province.

Adjourned till ten o'clock to-morrow morning.

THURSDAY, February 2, 1775, A. M.

Ordered, That Col. Lee, Col. Orne, Col. Palmer, Mr. Gerry, Col. Foster, and Col. Bowers, be joined to the committee on the state of the province.

Ordered, That Col. Gardner, Col. Palmer, and Mr. Watson, be a committee to wait on the Rev. Doct. Appleton, and desire his attendance on this Congress, and [that he would] officiate as ||their|| chaplain during the session thereof.

The committee appointed to wait on the Rev. Doct. Appleton and desire that he would officiate as chaplain to this Congress, reported that they had attended that service, and that the Doctor would officiate as chaplain agreeably to the desire of this Congress.

Ordered, That Mr. Aiken, Col. Gerrish, Major Fuller, and Doct. Holten, be monitors to this Congress.

Ordered, That, in returning the Congress, the monitors observe the following divisions, viz: That the pews on the right of the desk be one division; on the left, another; the men's body seats, and the pews adjoining, a third; the women's body seats, and the pews adjoining, the other.

Then adjourned to three o'clock in the afternoon.

Afternoon.

Met and adjourned till to-morrow morning, ten o'clock.

FRIDAY, [a] February 3, 1775, A. M.

Ordered, That Mr. Pickering, Capt. Greenleaf, and Mr. Lothrop, be a committee to inspect the journals of the last Congress, and ||[b]extract|| therefrom what relates to the public taxes and the militia, and cause the same to be printed in a pamphlet, and a copy thereof to be sent to each town and district in the province.

a [morning.]   b ||abstract.||

A ||ᵃvote|| from the committee of correspondence for the town of Boston and other committees from a large number of towns in the vicinity thereof, setting forth that several inhabitants of the town of Boston and several other towns in this province, are constantly employed in diverse kinds of works for the army now in Boston, and in supplying them with lumber, &c., and every other article of field equipage, to qualify them to take the field in the spring, &c.;

Read, and *Ordered*, that Col. Prescot, Capt. Carpenter, Col. Cushing, Mr. Fisher, Mr. Partridge, Col. Thomas, and Doct. Taylor, be a committee to take the said vote into consideration and report thereon.

Then Congress adjourned till to-morrow morning ten o'clock.

SATURDAY, February 4, 1775, A. M.

Resolved, That all the debates and resolutions of this Congress be kept as an entire secret, unless ||their|| special leave be first ||ᵇhad|| for disclosing the same.

Resolved, That the vote of yesterday, relative to publishing in a pamphlet some of the doings of the late Provincial Congress, be reconsidered, so far as it relates to publishing the resolve respecting the militia.

Ordered, That Mr. Sullivan, Mr. Partridge, Daniel Davis, Esq., and Mr. Sayer, be added to the committee appointed to publish in a pamphlet some of the doings of the late Congress, and that the same committee prepare an address to the inhabitants of this province, recommending to them immediately to pay all their province tax to Henry Gardner, Esq., and to carry the resolves of the late Congress relative to the militia into execution.

Upon a motion *Ordered*, that the secretary be directed to write to Col. Roberson, desiring him to deliver the four brass field pieces, and the two brass mortars now in his hands, the property of the province, to the order of the committee of safety.

The committee appointed to take into consideration the vote from the committee of correspondence of the town of Boston and others in the vicinity, &c., reported; the consideration of the report referred till to-morrow morning, ten o'clock.

||Then the Congress|| adjourned till next Monday morning, ten o'clock.

MONDAY, February 6, 1775, A. M.

Order of the day moved for.

The report of the committee on the vote from the committee of

a ||resolve.|| b ||obtained.||

correspondence of the town of Boston, &c., read; after some debate thereon, *Ordered*, that it be recommitted for amendments.

Resolved, That the Hon. John Hancock, and Thomas Cushing, Esq., Mr. Samuel Adams, John Adams, Robert Treat Paine, Esq., appointed by the late Provincial Congress, to represent this colony, on the 10th of May next, or sooner if necessary, at the American Congress to be held at Philadelphia, be, and they hereby are authorized and empowered, with the delegates from the other American Colonies, to adjourn from time to time, and place to place, as they shall judge necessary; and to continue in being as delegates for this colony, until the thirty-first day of December next ensuing, and no longer.

A petition of Abijah Browne and others, setting forth the irregularity of the choice of Jonas Dix, Esq., to represent the town of Waltham in this Congress, with a counter petition signed by Leonard Williams and others, were read: whereupon, it was *Resolved*, that in case the averments in Browne's petition mentioned [*were] true, [they] are not sufficient to disqualify Jonas Dix, Esq., member from Waltham, from having a seat in this Congress.

A petition of John Sawyer and others of Rowley, in the county of Essex, setting forth that they have raised a troop of horse, praying the aid of this Congress that they may be established, &c., [was] read and committed to Mr. Sullivan, Col. Grout, and Major Fuller, to consider of and report thereon.

Afternoon.

Resolved, That the secretary have power to adjourn this Congress in the absence of the president.

||Then the Congress|| was adjourned till to-morrow morning, ten o'clock.

TUESDAY, February 7, 1775, A. M.

The committee on the vote of the committee of correspondence of the town of Boston and others, having amended their report, again reported, which was considered and accepted, and is as followeth:

Whereas, it appears to this Congress, that certain persons are employed in diverse kinds of works for the army now stationed in Boston, for the purpose of carrying into execution the late acts of parliament, and in supplying them with iron for waggons, canvas, tent poles, and other articles of field equipage, whereby said army may be enabled to take the field and distress the inhabitants of this country,

Therefore, *Resolved*, as the opinion of this Congress, and it is accordingly strongly recommended to the inhabitants of the several towns

a [if.]

and districts of this province, that, should any person or persons presume to supply the troops now stationed at Boston or elsewhere in said province, with timber, boards, spars, pickets, tentpoles, canvas, bricks, iron, waggons, carts, carriages, entrenching tools, or any materials for making any of the carriages or implements aforesaid; with horses or oxen for draught; or any other materials whatever, which may enable them to annoy, or in any manner distress said inhabitants, he or they ||so offending|| shall be held in the highest detestation, and deemed inveterate enemies to America, and ought to be prevented and opposed by all reasonable means whatever.

And whereas, it appears to this Congress, that large quantities of straw will be wanted by the inhabitants of this province, in case we should be driven to the hard necessity of taking up arms in our own defence, therefore, *Resolved*, That no person or persons ought to sell or dispose of any straw, which he or they may have on hand, except to the inhabitants of this province for their own private use, or the use of said province.

And it is strongly recommended by this Congress, to the committees of correspondence and inspection in the several towns and districts in this province to see that the above resolves be strictly and faithfully adhered to, till otherwise ordered by this or some other Provincial Congress, or house of representatives.

Ordered, That the above resolves be published in all the newspapers in this province, and that [ªthey] be attested by the secretary.

Ordered, That Mr. Fisher, Doct. Church, Mr. Bailey, Doct. Warren, and Col. Thomas, be a committee to take into consideration the account of the late delegates from this province who attended the Continental Congress, and report what they be allowed for their expenses, and for their time while absent on the business of the province; and also [to] devise some method how the money shall be procured to discharge the same; and also how the money shall be procured to enable our present delegates appointed to attend the American Congress to refund their expenses.

The committee appointed to draught an address to the inhabitants of this province, accompanying the resolve which is ordered to be published relative to the province taxes being paid to Henry Gardner, Esq., reported; read and considered in paragraphs; *Ordered* to be recommitted for amendments, and that Doct. Church, and Doct. Warren, be added to the committee.

||Then the Congress|| adjourned till three o'clock, P. M.

a [it.]

In consideration of the coldness of the season, and that the Congress sit in a house without fire, *Resolved,* That all those members who incline thereto may sit with their hats on while in Congress.

The committee on the state of the province reported an addition to the report of the late Provincial Congress, relative to the power of the committee of safety, and general officers ; after some debate thereon it was referred for farther consideration till to-morrow morning, ten o'clock.

Resolved, That at ten o'clock to-morrow morning, the Congress will come to the choice of some person to serve on the committee of safety, instead of Norton Quincy, Esq., who declined accepting that trust.

||Then the Congress|| adjourned till to-morrow morning, nine o'clock.

WEDNESDAY, February 8, 1775, A. M.

The committee appointed to prepare an address to the inhabitants of this province, having amended, again reported the same ; after some consideration thereon, it was ordered to be recommitted for further amendments.

Upon a motion made by Mr. Hall, that he might be excused from serving any longer on the committee of supplies, in consideration of his ill state of health, the question was put whether he be excused for the reason mentioned, and passed in the affirmative.

Resolved, That at three o'clock this afternoon, the Congress will come to the choice of some person to serve on the committee of supplies instead of Mr. Hall, excused.

The order of the day was moved for; accordingly, the Congress resumed the consideration of the report of the committee, relative to the power of the committee of safety, and the power of the general officers ; after some debate thereon, it was referred for farther consideration, to the afternoon.

Afternoon.

The Congress resumed the consideration of the same report, which was recommitted for amendments proposed.

Ordered, That, as Doct. Warren, and Doct. Church are absent, that Col. Dwight, and Col. Coffin be added to the committee, on the account of the late delegates from this province to the Continental Congress.

The committee appointed to report an address to the inhabitants of this province, having amended their draught, reported; which was again ordered to be recommitted for amendments.

A petition of Boice and Clark, praying that this Congress will take some step for the encouragement of collecting of linen rags in their respective towns [was] read and *Ordered*, that Mr. Gorham, Mr. Bigelow, and Mr. Freeman, be a committee to bring in a resolve recommending the saving of linen rags, according to the prayer of the petition.

Resolved, That the Congress will now proceed to the choice of some person to serve on the committee of safety, in the place of Norton Quincy, Esq., who declined serving thereon.

Ordered, That Mr. Pitts, Major Fuller, and Doct. Holten, be a committee to count and sort the votes for a person to serve on the committee of safety, in the stead of Norton Quincy, Esq., who declined serving thereon.

The Congress then proceeded to bring in their votes for a person to serve on the committee of safety: the committee having sorted and counted the same, reported that Mr. Jabez Fisher was chosen.

Resolved, That to-morrow morning at ten o'clock, the Congress will come to the choice of some person to serve on the committee of supplies, instead of Mr. Hall, who hath been excused.

||The Congress then|| adjourned till to-morrow morning, nine o'clock.

THURSDAY, February 9, 1775, A. M.

The report of the committee relative to the power of the committee of safety, and the power of the general officers, being amended, was accepted, and is as followeth, viz :

Resolved, That the Hon. John Hancock, Esq., Doct. Joseph Warren, Doct. Benjamin Church, Jun., Mr. Richard Devens, Capt. Benjamin White, Col. Joseph Palmer, Mr. Abraham Watson, Col. Azor Orne, Mr. John Pigeon, Col. William Heath, and Mr. Jabez Fisher, be and hereby are appointed a committee of safety, to continue until the farther order of this or some other Congress, or house of representatives of this province; whose business and duty it shall be, most carefully and diligently to inspect and observe all and every such person or persons as shall at any time attempt to carry into execution by force, an act of the British parliament, entitled "an act for the better regulating the government of the province of the Massachusetts Bay, in New England;" or who shall attempt to carry into execution by force, another act of the British parliament, entitled "an act for the impartial administration of justice, in the cases of persons questioned for an act done by them in the execution of the law, or for the suppression of riots and tumults, in the province of the Massachusetts Bay:" which said committee, or any five of them, provided always

12

that not more than one of the said five shall be an inhabitant of the town of Boston, shall have power, and they are hereby empowered and directed, when they shall judge that such attempt or attempts are made, to alarm, muster, and cause to be assembled with the utmost expedition, and completely armed, accoutred and supplied with provisions sufficient for their support in their march to the place of rendezvous, such and so many of the militia of this province, as they shall judge necessary for the end and purpose of opposing such attempt or attempts, and at such place or places as they shall judge proper; and them to discharge as the safety of the province shall permit.

And this Congress doth most earnestly recommend to all the officers and soldiers of the militia in this province, who shall from time to time during the commission of the said committee, receive any call or order from the said committee, to pay the strictest obedience thereto, as they ||ᵃ|| regard the liberties and lives of themselves and the people of this province—any order or orders of any former Congress varying therefrom notwithstanding.

Resolved, That the Hon. Jedediah Prebble, Esq., Hon. Artemas Ward, Esq., Col. Seth Pomeroy, Col. John Thomas, and Col. William Heath, be and they hereby are appointed general officers; whose business and duty it shall be, with such and so many of the militia of this province, as shall be assembled by order of the committee of safety, effectually to oppose and resist such attempt or attempts as shall be made for carrying into execution by force, an act of the British Parliament, entitled " an act for the better regulating the government of the province of the Massachusetts Bay in New England," or who shall attempt the carrying into execution by force, another act of the British parliament, entitled " an act for the more impartial administration of justice in the cases of persons questioned for any act done by them in the execution of the law, or for the suppression of riots and tumults, in the province of the Massachusetts Bay," so long as the said militia shall be retained by the committee of safety and no longer; and the said general officers shall, while in the said service, command, lead and conduct, in such opposition, in the order in which they are above named, any order or orders of any former Congress varying therefrom, notwithstanding.

The order of the day was moved for.

Upon a motion, *Ordered*, That a committee be appointed to count and sort the votes for the choice of a person to serve on the committee of supplies in the place of Mr. Hall, who hath been excused; ac-

ᵃ ||shall.||

cordingly Mr. Sayer, Mr. Lothrop, and Capt. Greenleaf, were appointed.

The Congress then proceeded to bring in their votes for a person to serve on the committee of supplies; after counting and sorting the same, the committee reported that Mr. Manning was chosen. Upon a motion made by Mr. Manning, the question was put whether he be excused from serving on the committee of supplies, and passed in the affirmative. The Congress then proceeded to bring in their votes for a person to serve in his place, and, after counting and sorting the same, the committee reported that Mr. Elbridge Gerry was chosen.

Ordered, That during the debates of the Congress, the members thereof be seated in their proper places.

A number of letters, said to be from gentlemen in England, were read; upon a motion, *Ordered,* that they be committed to the committee on the state of the province, to take them into consideration and report.

The committee appointed to prepare an address to the inhabitants of this province, having amended their report, the same was read, considered and accepted, and ordered to be attested and added to the pamphlet directed to be printed by this Congress, and is as followeth, viz:

To the Inhabitants of the Massachusetts Bay.

FRIENDS AND FELLOW SUFFERERS :—When a people entitled to that freedom, which your ancestors have nobly preserved, as the richest inheritance of their children, are invaded by the hand of oppression, and trampled on by the merciless feet of tyranny, resistance is so far from being criminal, that it becomes the christian and social duty of each individual.

While you see the lives of your fellow men, in other nations, sported with and destroyed, and their estates confiscated by their prince, only to gratify the caprice, ambition, or avarice of a tyrant, you ought to entertain and cultivate in your minds, the highest gratitude to the Supreme Being, for his having placed you under such a form of government, as, when duly administered, gives the meanest peasant the same security in his life and property, as his sovereign has in his crown.

This constitution of government secures to each one subject thereto, such an entire property in his inheritance and the fruit of his industry, that they cannot be taken from him without his personal or representative consent; and as the evidence of entire property arises from the uncontrollable power of disposing, when your estates shall be brought into such a situation, or under such a form of government, as that they can be disposed of or granted by persons who are by no means accountable to you therefor, you cease to have any thing more than a licensed and precarious property in them.

Notwithstanding these principles have been warmly contended for and nobly defended at the expense of much blood and treasure, by your British ancestors, who have ever been seriously alarmed at the least infringement on this branch of their happy privileges, the house of commons there, over whom you have not the least control, and in whose election you have no voice, have claimed and exercised the power of granting your money without your consent; and what renders the same more aggravated, is, that the money extorted from you, is applied to the vile purpose of maintaining a set of men, who, through depravity of mind, and cruelty of disposition, have been, and still are, endeavoring to enforce certain acts of parliament, made with express purpose to take from you your charter rights, and reduce you to a state of misery, equal to that ever attendant on those, whose prince has the sole disposal of their lives and properties.

Fleets, troops, and every implement of war, are sent into the province, with apparent design to wrest from you that freedom which it is your duty, even at the risk of your lives, to hand inviolate to posterity.

Those strides of tyranny have fixed the united attention of all America; and, being greatly and justly alarmed, the wisdom of the whole continent has been collected in that Congress, whose salutary resolutions have pointed you to effectual means of redress, and the execution of the plan projected by that honorable assembly, has been warmly recommended to you by your former Provincial Congress.

The transactions of your former Congress, with regard to placing the militia on such a footing as may serve to defend you from each act of hostility that may be offered, have been carefully transmitted to you, and we rejoice to hear, that you have cheerfully paid the strictest attention to them, and ardently wish that the same martial spirit which so remarkably prevails among you may be encouraged and increased.

Though we deprecate a rupture with the mother state, yet we must still urge you to every preparation for your necessary defence; for, unless you exhibit to your enemies such a firmness as shall convince them that you are worthy of that freedom your ancestors fled here to enjoy, you have nothing to expect but the vilest and most abject slavery.

The foregoing sheets contain the resolutions of your former Congress, respecting the improvement of your public monies at this critical juncture of your public affairs. Such is the alarming state of the

province, that the necessity of punctually complying with these resolves can, by no means, need any further argument to stimulate thereto, than what naturally arises from facts under your constant observation; but as necessary preparations for your defence require immediate supplies of money, duty and faithfulness to you, compel us to take
leave to hint, that, should you be so unhappy as to be driven to un-
sheath the sword, in defence of your lives and properties, the having
proper magazines duly prepared, may give that success which cannot
be expected without them.

Subjects generally pay obedience to the laws of the land, to avoid
the penalty that accrues on breach of them; and on the same principles we are assured, that, as you hitherto have, you will continue still
strictly to adhere to the resolutions of your several congresses; for
we can conceive of no greater punishment for the breach of human
laws, than the misery that must inevitably follow your disregarding the
plans, that have, by your authority, with that of the whole continent,
been projected.

Your conduct hitherto, under the severest trials, has been worthy of
you as men and christians, and, notwithstanding the pains that have
been taken by your enemies, to inculcate the doctrines of non-resist-
ance and passive obedience, and, by every art, to delude and terrify
you, the whole continent of America has, this day, cause to rejoice in
your firmness. We trust you will still continue steadfast, and having
regard to the dignity of your characters as freemen, and those generous sentiments resulting from your natural and political connections,
you will never submit your necks to the galling yoke of despotism
prepared for you; but with a proper sense of your dependance on
God, nobly defend those rights which Heaven gave, and no man ought
to take from us.

An address from the committee of correspondence of the town of
Scituate and others, showing that a number of his majesty's troops
are now stationed in the town of Marshfield, &c. ||ᵃwas|| read :

Ordered, That Doct. Warren, Doct. Taylor, Col. Henshaw, Mr.
Watson, and Mr. Gill, be a committee to take the same into consideration, and the papers accompanying it, and report.

Ordered, That Mr. Sullivan Mr. Pickering, and Capt. Greenleaf, be
a committee to bring in a resolve, empowering the committee of safety
to take into their hands the warlike stores, the property of the province.

Ordered, That Col. Thomas, Col. Heath, Hon. Col. Ward, Col.

a ||being.||

Pomeroy, and Col. Gardner, be a committee to bring in a resolve, directing how the ordnance in the province shall be used.

Afternoon.

The committee on the petition of John Sawyer and others, reported by way of resolve, which report was ordered to lie on the table.

Ordered, That the several members who were appointed to make return of the officers and number of the militia, and minute men, in the several counties, be directed to comply with the said order as soon as possible.

Upon a motion, *Ordered,* That Col. Paterson, Mr. Browne, of Pittsfield, and Major Bliss, be a committee to report a resolve for the publication of the names of those who have been appointed counsellors by mandamus, and have refused to resign their appointments.

The committee on the accounts of the delegates from this province to the Continental Congress, reported, which was accepted; and thereupon *Ordered,* That Mr. Sullivan, Mr. Devens, and Mr. Gorham, be a committee to report a resolve agreeably to the same.

The committee on the petition of Boice and Clark, reported, by way of resolve, which was read and accepted, and is as followeth, viz :

Whereas, the encouragement of the manufactories of this country will, at all times, and more especially at this, be attended with the most beneficial effects, and Messrs. Boice and Clark, having represented to this Congress, that they have, at a very considerable expense, erected works at Milton, in this province, for the making paper, and have not heretofore been able to obtain a sufficiency of rags to answer their purpose, and in order to procure a larger quantity of that article, have raised the price thereof;

Therefore, *Resolved,* That it be recommended, and it is by this Congress accordingly recommended, to every family in this province, to preserve all their linen, and cotton and linen rags, in order that a ||ᵃmanufacture|| so useful and advantageous to this country, may be suitably encouraged: and it is also recommended to our several towns, to take such farther measures for the encouragement of the manufacture aforesaid, as they shall think proper.

||Then the Congress|| adjourned till to-morrow morning, 9 o'clock.

FRIDAY, February 10, 1775, A. M.

Ordered, That Mr. Devens, Mr. Watson, Col. Gardner, Col. Howe, and Capt. Batchelder, be a committee to observe the motion of the troops said to be on their road to this town.

a ||manufactory.||

An application from Thomas Legate, Esq. was read. *Ordered,* That it be committed : Accordingly *Ordered,* That Mr. Pickering, Col. Cushing, and Col. Farley, be a committee to take the same into consideration.

Ordered, That Col. Palmer, Col. Cushing, and Mr. Cushing of Scituate, be a committee to sit in the recess of this Congress, to prepare all such rules and regulations, for the officers and men of the constitutional army which may be raised in this province, as shall be necessary for the good order thereof.

The committee appointed by the late Provincial Congress, to estimate the loss and damage which hath accrued to the province by the operation of the Boston port bill and the act for altering the civil government of this province, reported ; the report ordered to be filed.

||The committee appointed to take into consideration how the ordnance should be disposed of, are directed to make report to the committee of safety.[1]||

The committee appointed to bring in a resolve relative to the payment of the late delegates to the Continental Congress, reported ; the report was accepted, and is as followeth, viz :

Whereas, the account of expenses incurred by the Hon. Thomas Cushing, Mr. Samuel Adams, John Adams, and Robert Treat Paine, Esquires, in the execution of the trust reposed in them as representatives of this province at the grand Continental Congress, held at Philadelphia, in the months of September and October last, has been exhibited to, and approved of, by this Congress, and there appears to be due to the said delegates the sum of nine pounds, seventeen shillings, and ten pence, lawful money, in order to discharge their said expenses, and this Congress have voted, that the sum of fifty-six pounds [be paid] to each of the aforesaid delegates, in order to compensate them for their time spent in said service ;

Therefore, *Resolved,* That Henry Gardner, Esq., receiver general of this province, be directed, and he is hereby accordingly directed, to pay to the Hon. Thomas Cushing, Esq., the above sum of nine pounds, seventeen shillings, and ten pence, for expenses, and the sum of fifty-six pounds for his time spent in the service aforesaid; and to Mr. Samuel Adams, John Adams and Robert Treat Paine, Esquires, each, the sum of fifty-six pounds, as a recompense for their time spent in said service.

The same committee reported the following resolve, which was accepted, viz :

(1) This order is inserted in the copy of the journal among the proceedings of the afternoon session.

Whereas, the Hon. John Hancock, Hon. Thomas Cushing, Mr. Samuel Adams, John Adams and Robert Treat Paine, Esquires, were, by a former Provincial Congress, chosen and appointed a committee of delegates, to meet the delegates from the other American colonies, at Philadelphia, on the tenth day of May next, or sooner, if necessary; and whereas, it is ordered by this Congress, that the sum of one hundred pounds be allowed and paid each of them, to enable them to perform said journey; therefore, ||*Resolved*, That Henry Gardner, Esq. receiver general of this province, be, and hereby is ordered and directed, to pay each of the said committee of delegates of this province, the sum of one hundred pounds, for which they are to be accountable to some future Congress, or house of representatives of this colony.||

Resolved, That Henry Gardner, Esq., receiver general of th · province, be and hereby is ordered and directed, to pay, unto Robert Treat Paine, Esq., the sum of forty-six pounds, lawful money, in consideration of the same sum being by him accidentally lost out of his pocket while on his journey to Philadelphia in the service of this government.

Afternoon.

Ordered, That Mr. Sullivan, Col. Paterson, and Col. Thomas, be a committee to revise the commission of the committee of safety, and the commission of the committee of supplies, and point out what amendments, if any, are necessary.

Upon a motion made, the question was put, whether the vote relative to committing the petition of Thomas Legate, Esq., be reconsidered, and the petitioner have leave to withdraw his petition, and passed in the affirmative.

Ordered, That the secretary be directed to publish the names of the mandamus counsellors now in Boston, in all the newspapers of the province, agreeably to the [order of the] late Provincial Congress.

A petition from the delegates of the several towns and districts in the counties of Hampshire and Berkshire was read; thereupon, *Ordered*, That the same be committed to the committee on the state of the province, and that the committee make the petition public if they think proper.

||Then the Congress|| adjourned till to-morrow morning, nine o'clock.

Saturday, February 11, 1775, A. M.

The committee appointed to revise the commission of the committee of safety and the committee of supplies, &c., reported by way of resolve, which was considered and accepted, and is as followeth, viz:

Whereas, several resolves have been passed by this and the former Provincial Congress, authorizing and directing the committee of safety, in case of necessity, in the defence of the province, to call together, arm, accoutre, and equip, the inhabitants thereof: and, whereas, by resolves of the same Congress, a committee of supplies is appointed, to provide ordnance, stores, provisions, and arms, and to place them where the said committee of safety shall order ; but there is no provision made by whom, to whom, or in what manner and quantities, the supplies provided by said committee of supplies shall be delivered ;

It is ||therefore|| *Resolved*, That the said committee of safety, or the major part of them, shall be, and hereby [are,] empowered to appoint one of their number, a commissary, whose business it shall be to deliver all such stores, ordnance, arms, and provisions, as shall be, by the committee of supplies provided, as the said committee of safety shall order and direct, until the constitutional army shall take the field; when, and during all the time said army shall be in the field, until they are discharged by the committee of safety, the commissary appointed by the committee of safety shall deliver the said warlike stores to the order of the commanding officers of said army.

The committee appointed to bring in a resolve relative to the disposal of some bayonets, &c., reported the following resolve, which was accepted :

Whereas, there are a number of bayonets and other implements of war, purchased at the expense of the province, that are not now in the hands of the committee of safety, as they ought to be, it is therefore *Resolved*, as the opinion of this Congress, that the committee of safety ought to possess themselves of all the same bayonets and implements of war, as soon as they conveniently can ; and that they ought to dispose of the same, for the use of the province, to such persons, and on such conditions, as they shall think proper.

The committee on the state of the province, reported a resolve recommending that a day of fasting and prayer be kept throughout the province, which was considered and *Ordered* to lie on the table.

Ordered, That Mr. Sullivan, Mr. Stickney, and Col. Cushing, be a committee to bring in a resolve, empowering the committee of safety to direct the committee of supplies, to make such further provision for the defence of the province as may be necessary.

Resolved, That all the members of the Congress be enjoined to attend, and that none depart without special leave be first obtained.

Ordered, That Col. Tyng, Mr. Adams, Doct. Warren, Major Hawley, Col. Ward, Hon. Mr. Hancock, and Mr. Paine, be a committee to

13

report a resolve, purporting the determination of this people, coolly and resolutely, to support their rights and privileges, at all hazards.

The committee appointed to take into consideration the address from the committee of correspondence, for the town of Scituate, and others, reported; the report was ||ᵃ|| ordered to be recommitted for amendments.

||Then the Congress|| adjourned till Monday next, ten o'clock in the forenoon.

MONDAY, February 13, 1775, A. M.

The committee on the state of the province, reported the form of a receipt, two of the same tenor and date to be signed by the receiver general, one of which to be lodged with the town or district treasurer, and the other to be kept by the constable, or other officer, who shall pay the money to him. *Ordered*, that the report be recommitted for amendments.

Then the Congress adjourned till three o'clock in the afternoon.

Afternoon.

Ordered, That Mr. Sullivan, Col. Paterson, Mr. Fisher, Mr. Hobby, and Mr. Freeman, be a committee to bring in a resolve for inquiring into the state of the militia, their numbers and equipments, and recommending to the selectmen of the several towns and districts in this province, to make return of their town and district stock of ammunition and warlike stores to this Congress.

Ordered, That Mr. Stephen Hall, Doct. Warren, and Mr. Browne of Abington, be a committee to take into consideration and report what is necessary for this Congress to do for the encouragement of making saltpetre.

Ordered, That Col. Paterson bring in a resolve appointing an agent for and in behalf of this province, to repair to the province of Quebec, and there establish a correspondence, to collect and transmit to us the best and earliest intelligence that can be obtained, of the sentiments and determination of the inhabitants of that province, with regard to the late acts of parliament, or any other important matters that do or may affect the colonies in their present dispute with Great Britain.

||Then the Congress|| adjourned till to-morrow morning, ten o'clock.

TUESDAY, February 14, 1775, A. M.

The committee appointed to bring in a resolve relative to an inqui-

a ||read and.||

ry into the state of the militia, town stocks, &c., reported; the report was recommitted for amendments.

Afternoon.

The committee appointed to bring in a resolve relative to inquiring into the state of the militia, &c., having amended their report, again reported, which [report] was read and accepted, and *Ordered*, that it be printed, and a copy thereof, attested by the president, sent to each town and district in this province : and is as followeth, viz :

Whereas, it appears necessary for the defence of the lives, liberties, and properties of the inhabitants of this province, that this Congress, on the first day of their next session, should be made fully acquainted with the number and military equipments of the militia and minute men in this province, as also the town stock of ammunition in each town and district :

It is therefore, *Resolved*, That it be and hereby is recommended to the commanding officers of each regiment of minute men that now is or shall be formed in this province, that they review the several companies in their respective regiments, or cause them to be reviewed, and take an exact state of their numbers and equipments : and where there is any company that is not incorporated into a regiment, the commanding officer thereof shall review the several companies, or cause them to be reviewed, and take a like state of their numbers and equipment : and it is also recommended to the colonels or commanding officers of each regiment of militia in this province, that they review the several companies in their respective regiments, or cause them to be reviewed, and take a state of their numbers and accoutrements, which said state of the minute men and militia, shall be, by said officers, returned, in writing, to this Congress on the first day of their next session after the adjournment.

And it is further *Resolved*, That it be recommended to the selectmen of each town and district in the province, that on the same day they make return in writing, of the state of the town and district stock of ammunition and warlike stores to this Congress.

Mr. Paterson reported a resolve relative to appointing an agent for and in behalf of this province, to repair to the province of Quebec, &c., which was recommitted; and he, with Mr. Bigelow and Col. Henshaw, are directed to bring in a resolve, directing and empowering the committee of correspondence for the town of Boston, to establish an intimate correspondence with the inhabitants of the province of Quebec, &c.

||Then the Congress|| adjourned till ten o'clock to-morrow morning.

WEDNESDAY, February 15, 1775, A. M.

Resolved, That at three o'clock this afternoon, the Congress will come to the choice of a general officer in addition to those already appointed.

The committee appointed to bring in a resolve empowering the committee of safety to give orders to the committee of supplies, to make such further provision for the defence of the government as they shall think necessary, reported; *Ordered*, that the consideration of this report be referred to the next session of this Congress.

The committee appointed to bring in a resolve empowering the committee of correspondence of the town of Boston, to correspond with Quebec, &c., for and in behalf of this province, reported; the report was read and accepted, and is as followeth, viz. :

Whereas, it appears the manifest design of administration, to engage and secure the Canadians and remote tribes of Indians, for the purpose of harassing and distressing these colonies, and reducing them to a state of absolute slavery : and, whereas, the safety and security of said colonies depend in a great measure, under God, on their firmness, unanimity, and friendship ;

Therefore, *Resolved*, That the committee of correspondence for the town of Boston, be and they are hereby directed and empowered, in such way and manner as they shall think proper, to open and establish an intimate correspondence and connection with the inhabitants of the province of Quebec, and that they endeavor to put the same immediately into execution.

The committee appointed to take into consideration what is necessary for this Congress to do for the encouragement of the making of saltpetre, reported; the report was read and accepted, (excepting that part thereof which relates to assay masters, which part was referred for further consideration to the next meeting of this Congress,) and is as followeth, viz. :

Resolved, [1st] That this Congress do now appoint a committee to draw up directions, in an easy and familiar style, for the manufacturing of saltpetre, and that the same be printed, and sent to every town and district in the province, at the public expense.

2d. That for the encouragement of such as are disposed to set up the manufacture of saltpetre, this Congress do engage to purchase the whole quantity that shall be manufactured in this province, within twelve months from this date, at the rate of fourteen pounds, &c., [for each hundred pounds weight.]

3d. That a proper assay master be appointed in every county, to receive and pay for the saltpetre which shall be brought to him with a satisfactory certificate that the same was actually manufactured in this province.

The committee on the state of the province reported again the form of a receipt, two of the same tenor and date to be signed by the receiver general; one of which is to be lodged with the town or district treasurer or clerk, who shall send their money, and the other to be kept by the constable, collector, or other officer, who shall pay the same to him; which was read and accepted, and is as followeth:

Resolved, That [it] is proper and expedient, that Henry Gardner, Esq., receiver general of this province, should, for the greater security of the province, give two several receipts for all such sums of money as he ||ᵃfor the future may receive|| for the use of the province; and for the greater satisfaction of all such persons as shall make payments to the said receiver general, it is hereby recommended to the said Henry [Gardner,] or his successor in office, that he make both such receipts as near as ||ᵇmay be|| to the form following, to wit:

——— ——— 177—, Received of A——— B———, the sum of ————————— being part ||or the whole|| of the province tax set on the town of C——— by the general court in the year 17—, for which sum, I have given the said A— B— another receipt of the same tenor and date with this.

One of which receipts, the person paying the said money, is requested to lodge with the treasurer or clerk of the town or district on whose account the money shall be paid, or such other person as the inhabitants of such town or district shall appoint.

Ordered, That Mr. Adams, Major Hawley, Mr. Gerry, Hon. Mr. Cushing, Mr. Paine, Col. Palmer, and Mr. Freeman, be a committee to bring in a ||ᶜresolve|| holding up to the people of this province, the imminent danger they are in, from the present disposition of the British ministry and parliament, and that there is reason to fear that they will attempt our sudden destruction: and the importance it is to the inhabitants of this colony to prepare themselves for the last event.

The committee on the state of the province, reported a resolve relative to pedlers, &c., which was read, considered, and accepted; and ordered to be published in all the newspapers, and is as followeth, viz.:

Whereas, the practice of pedlers and petty chapmen, in going from town to town, selling East India goods and teas, and various sorts of European manufactures, in direct opposition to the good and wholesome laws of this province, whereby they are liable to the forfeiture of all their goods, besides being subject to the penalty of twenty pounds,

a ||shall for the future receive.|| b ||possible.|| c ||bill.||

does manifestly tend to interrupt and defeat the measures necessary to recover and secure the rights and liberties of the inhabitants of these colonies : and whereas, the law relating to pedlers and petty chapmen, cannot, at present, be effectually carried into execution :

It is therefore hereby earnestly recommended to the committees of inspection of the several towns and districts in this province, that they be very vigilant and industrious to discover and find out, when any pedlers and petty chapmen shall come into their respective towns and districts ; and that the said committees, whenever they shall find out that any pedler or petty chapman shall be in the town or district for which such committee is appointed, that such committee, without fail, make a thorough and careful search and examination of the packs, baggage, and all the goods, wares, and merchandize of such pedler and petty chapman, and in case such committee shall find any India teas or European manufactures, in the possession of such pedler or petty chapman, it is further recommended to such committee to prevent, by all reasonable means, such pedler and petty chapman, from vending any such teas and manufactures ; and it is hereby recommended to the inhabitants of this province, not to trade with such pedlers and petty chapmen for any article whatever.

Ordered, That Major Fuller, Mr. Browne, and Mr. Bigelow, be a committee to direct and forward the pamphlets printed by order of Congress to the several towns and districts in the province.

The order of the day was moved for.

Ordered, That Mr. Gill, Mr. Pitts, and Col. Mansfield, be a committee to count and sort the votes for a general officer in addition to those already appointed.

The Congress then proceeded to bring in their votes for a general officer. The committee having counted and sorted the same, reported, that the Hon. John Whitcomb, Esq., was chosen.

Ordered, That the member from the town of ||ᵃBolton|| be desired to wait on the Hon. John Whitcomb, Esq., with a copy of ||ᵇhis being elected|| a general officer, and ||ᶜdesire|| his answer, whether he will accept that trust, as soon as may be.

||ᵈThe committee appointed in the morning to bring in a resolve holding up to the people the imminent danger they are in, &c., reported : the report was read,|| accepted, and ordered to be printed in all the newspapers, and is as followeth, viz :

---

a ||Boston.|| b ||the resolve electing him.|| c ||request.||

d ||*Ordered*, That the report of the committee appointed to bring in a resolve, holding up to the people the imminent danger they were in, &c., be now read ; which was done accordingly, and||

Whereas, it appears to this Congress, from the present disposition of the British ministry and parliament, that there is real cause to fear that the most reasonable and just applications of this continent to Great Britain, for " peace, liberty, and safety," will not meet with a favorable reception; but, on the contrary, from the large reenforcements of troops expected in this colony, the tenor of intelligence from Great Britain, and general appearances, we have reason to apprehend that the sudden destruction of this colony in particular is intended, ||ᵃ|| for refusing, with the other American colonies, tamely to submit to the most ignominious slavery;

Therefore, *Resolved*, That the great law of self-preservation, calls upon the inhabitants of this colony, immediately to prepare against every attempt that may be made to attack them by surprise; and it is, upon serious deliberation, most earnestly recommended to the militia in general, as well as the detached part of it in minute men, that they spare neither time, pains, nor expense, at so critical a juncture, in perfecting themselves forthwith in military discipline, and that skillful instructors be provided for those companies which may not already be provided therewith: and it is recommended to the towns and districts in this colony, that they encourage such persons as are skilled in the manufacturing of firearms and bayonets, diligently to apply themselves thereto, for supplying such of the inhabitants as may still be deficient.

And for the encouragement of American ||ᵇmanufacturers|| of fire arms and bayonets, it is further *Resolved*, that this Congress will give the preference to, and purchase from them, so many effective arms and bayonets as can be delivered in a reasonable time, upon notice given to this Congress at its next session.

The committee appointed to take into consideration the address from the committee of correspondence of the town of Scituate, and other towns in that vicinity, reported: their report was read and accepted, and *Ordered*, that it be published in the newspapers, and is as followeth, viz:

Voted, That the Congress do highly approve of the vigilance and activity of the selectmen and the committees of correspondence of the several towns of Plymouth, Kingston, Duxbury, Pembroke, Hanover, and Scituate, in detecting the falsehoods and malicious artifices of certain persons belonging to Marshfield and Scituate, not respectable either in their numbers or their characters, who are, with great reason, supposed to have been the persons who prevailed upon General Gage to take the imprudent step, of sending a number of the king's troops

a ||merely.|| b ||manufactures.||

into Marshfield, under pretence of protecting them : whereby great
and just offence has been given to the good people of this province, as
very fatal consequences must have arisen therefrom, if the same malevolent spirit which seems to have influenced them, had actuated the
inhabitants of the neighboring towns; or if the same indiscretion
which betrayed the general into the unwarrantable measure of sending
the troops, had led this people to destroy them.

Voted, That the Congress do earnestly recommend it to the selectmen and committees of correspondence in the several towns of Plymouth, Kingston, Duxbury, Pembroke, Hanover, and Scituate, steadi-
ly to persevere in the same line of conduct which has, in this instance,
so justly entitled them to the esteem of their fellow countrymen, and
to keep a watchful eye upon the behavior of those who are aiming at
the destruction of our liberties.[1]

(1) The petition, upon which the votes of Congress were founded, has not been preserved. An
address from the same towns, to General Gage, probably contains the substance of the memorial
presented to the assembly of delegates. It is copied from the Boston Evening Post, February
27, 1775.

" *To his excellency Thomas Gage, Esq : may it please your excellency :—*

" We, his majesty's loyal subjects, selectmen of the several towns of Plymouth, Kingston,
Duxbury, Pembroke, Hanover, and Scituate, deeply affected with a sense of the increasing dangers
and calamities which menace one of the most promising countries upon earth with political exci-
sion, cannot but lament, that, while we are endeavoring to preserve peace and maintain the authority of the laws, at a period when the bonds of government are relaxed, by violent infractions on the
charter of the province, our enemies are practising every insidious stratagem to seduce the people
into acts of violence and outrage."

" We beg leave to address your excellency, on a subject which excites our apprehensions extremely : and, in the representation of facts, we promise to pay that sacred regard to truth, which,
had our adversaries observed, we flatter ourselves, it would have precluded the necessity of our
addressing your excellency, on this occasion."

" We are informed, from good authority, that a number of people from Marshfield and Scituate,
have made application to your excellency, soliciting the aid of a detachment of his majesty's
troops, for the security and protection of themselves and properties. That their fears and intimidation were entirely groundless, that no design or plan of molestation, was formed against them,
or existed but in their own imaginations, their own declarations, and their actions, which have a
more striking language, abundantly demonstrate. Several men of unquestionable veracity, residing in the town of Marshfield, have solemnly called God to witness, before one of his majesty's
justices of the peace, that they not only never heard of any intention to disturb the complainants,
but repeatedly saw them after they pretended to be under apprehensions of danger, attending to
their private affairs, without arms, and even after they had lodged their arms a few miles from
their respective houses. They frequently declared, in conversation with the deponents, that they
were not apprehensive of receiving any injury in their persons or properties, and one of them, who
is a minor, as many of them are, being persuaded to save his life by adjoining himself to the petitioners, but afterwards abandoning them by the request of his father, deposeth, in like solemn manner, that he was under no intimidation himself, nor did he ever hear any one of them say that he
was. It appears as evident, as if written with a sunbeam, from the general tenor of the testimony,
which we are willing to lay before your excellency if desired, that their expressions of fear, were
a fallacious pretext, dictated by the inveterate enemies of our constitution, to induce your excellency to send troops into the country, to augment the difficulties of our situation, already very distressing ; and, what confirms this truth, if it needs any confirmation, is, the assiduity and pains

Ordered, That Mr. Adams, Mr. Gerry, Hon. Mr. Cushing, Mr. Paine, Hon. Col. Ward, Col. Prescot, and Major Holten, be a committee to wait on the Hon. Col. Williams, and [Nathaniel] Wales, Esq., and inform them that the Congress have had notice of their being in town as a committee from Connecticut, in order to have a conference with us; and that we are ready to confer with them by a committee, at such time and place as shall be most agreeable to them.

Ordered, That no member of this Congress depart therefrom until the conference with the committee from Connecticut is over.

The committee appointed to wait upon the gentlemen from Connecticut, reported, that they had attended that service, and delivered the message with which they were charged; and that the gentlemen propose this evening to meet the committee from this Congress at such place as you shall appoint.

Ordered, That the committee on the state of the province be the committee from this Congress, to meet the gentlemen from Connecticut, this evening, at Capt. Stedman's, for the proposed conference.

||The Congress then|| adjourned till to-morrow morning, nine o'clock.

THURSDAY, February 16, 1775, A. M.

Adjourned to twelve o'clock, at noon.

Met ||*upon the|| adjournment.

Ordered, That Mr. Pickering, Doct. Warren, and Mr. Lothrop, be a committee to bring in a resolve purporting the business and duty of a committee to be appointed to correspond with the House of Assembly of Connecticut; and, if necessary, with the other neighboring colonies.

Resolved, That at three o'clock this afternoon the Congress will come to the choice, by ballot, of a committee to correspond with the neighboring governments.

Afternoon.

Ordered, That Mr. Pitts, Mr. Gill, and Major Fuller, be a commit-

---

a ||agreeably to.||

which we have taken to investigate it. We have industriously scrutinized into the cause of this alarm, and cannot find that it has the least foundation in reality."

" All that we have in view in this address is, to lay before your excellency a true state of facts, and to remove that opprobrium, which this movement of the military reflects on this country : and as a spirit of enmity and falsehood is prevalent in the country, and as every thing which comes from a gentleman of your excellency's exalted station naturally acquires great weight and importance, we earnestly entreat your excellency to search into the grounds of every report, previous to giving your assent to it."

The troops stationed at Marshfield were detached from the British regiments in Boston, January 23, 1775.

14.

tee to count and sort the votes for the committee to correspond with the neighboring governments.

Ordered, That Major Hawley, Mr. Browne, and Col. Paterson, be a committee to bring in a resolve relative to the adjournment, and empowering the members of Charlestown and others, to call the Congress together at an earlier day than [that] to which it may be adjourned.

Ordered, That Col. Gardner, Major Holten and Capt. Batchelder, be a committee to wait on the Rev. Doct. Appleton, and return him the thanks of this Congress for his services as their chaplain during this session.

The Congress then proceeded to bring in their votes for a committee to correspond with the neighboring governments: after sorting and counting the same, the committee reported, that the Hon. John Hancock, Esq., Hon. Thomas Cushing, Esq., [Mr.] Samuel Adams, Doct. Joseph Warren, Mr. Elbridge Gerry and Col. William Heath, [were elected.]

Upon a motion, the question was put, whether the vote in the morning, relative to the choice of a committee to correspond with the neighboring governments, by ballot, be so far reconsidered, as that the three persons now to be appointed thereon, be chosen by hand vote, and that Mr. Richard Devens, Col. Joseph Palmer, and Mr. Moses Gill, be of the committee, and passed in the affirmative.

Resolved, That Henry Gardner, Esq., receiver general, be and he hereby is directed to pay into the hands of the committee of correspondence of the town of Boston, the sum of twenty pounds, lawful money, to enable the said committee to correspond with the inhabitants of Canada, they to be accountable for said sum to this or some other congress.

The committee appointed to bring in a resolve setting forth the business and duty of the committee appointed to correspond with the neighboring governments, reported; [which report was] read and accepted, and is as followeth, viz:

While the iron hand of power is stretched out against these American colonies, and the abettors of tyranny and oppression are practising every art to sow the seeds of jealousy and discord among the several parts of this country, it is incumbent on us to take every step in our power to counteract them in their wicked designs; and, as we are convinced, that the union now established throughout the several colonies can never be maintained without frequent communication of sentiments between them, nor can any plan formed for their common benefit [be] carried into execution without a previous knowledge of the general disposition of the colonies;[1]

Resolved, That the Hon. John Hancock, Esq., Hon. Mr. Cushing, Mr. Adams, Mr. Gerry, Doct. Warren, Col. Heath, Mr. Devens, Col. Palmer and Mr. Gill, or the majority of them, be and are hereby appointed to act as a committee of correspondence with the other colonies on this continent during the recess of this Congress; and they are hereby empowered and directed, to consult with, and make proposals to such committees as now are or shall hereafter be appointed as committees of correspondence in the several American colonies, and to make report of their doings to this Congress at their next sessions.

The report of the committee recommending a day of fasting and prayer to be kept throughout this province, which was ordered to lie on the table, [was] now taken up, considered, and accepted, and is as followeth, viz :

Whereas, it has pleased Almighty God, the just and good governor of the world, to permit so great a calamity to befal us as the present controversy between Great Britain and these colonies, and which threatens us with the evils of war;

And whereas, it has been the annual and laudable custom of this colony, at the opening of the spring, to observe a day of fasting and prayer, to humble themselves before God for their sins, and to implore his forgiveness and blessing;

It is, therefore, *Resolved,* as the sense of this Congress, that it is highly and peculiarly proper, and a duty incumbent upon this people more especially at a time of such general distress, that a day of public fasting and prayer should be observed and kept throughout this colony, not only on account of the present calamity, but also in conformity to the laudable custom of our ancestors; and it is accordingly recommended to the several religious assemblies in the same, that Thursday, the sixteenth day of March next, be observed as a day of fasting and prayer to humble ourselves before God, on account of our sins; to implore his forgiveness; to beg his blessing upon the labors of the field, upon our merchandize, fishery and manufactures, and upon the various means used to recover and preserve our just rights and liberties; and also, that his blessing may rest upon all the British empire, upon George the Third, our rightful king, and upon all the royal family, that they may all be great and lasting blessings to the world; to implore the outpourings of his spirit, to enable us to bear

---

(1) In the copy of the journal the preamble is placed after the resolution.

and suffer whatever his holy and righteous Providence may see fit to lay upon us; and also humbly to supplicate his direction and assistance, to discover and reform whatever is amiss, that so he may be pleased to remove these heavy afflictions, those tokens of his displeasure, and may cause harmony and union to be restored between Great Britain and these colonies, and that we may again rejoice in the free and undisturbed exercise of all those rights and privileges, for the enjoyment of which, our pious and virtuous ancestors braved every danger, and transmitted the fair possession down to their children, to be by them handed down entire to the latest posterity.

Ordered, That Mr. Devens, Mr. Gorham and Mr. Watson, be a committee to direct the [printed copies of the] resolve recommending a day of fasting and prayer, and send them to the several religious assemblies in this province.

Upon a motion made, the question was put, whether the injunction of secrecy now on the members of this Congress be taken off, and that they disclose such parts of their doings as shall appear to them to have a tendency to promote the public interest, and passed in the affirmative.

Ordered, That Col. Gardner, Mr. Watson, and Mr. Osgood, be a committee, to return the thanks of this body to the proprietors of the meeting-house in Cambridge, for their favors in indulging the Congress with the use thereof during their session.

Ordered, That Henry Gardner, Esq., receiver general of this province, be and he is hereby directed, to pay unto Mr. William Darling, the sum of two pounds and sixteen shillings, lawful money, in full for his services as doorkeeper.

The committee appointed to bring in a resolve relative to the adjournment of this Congress, and empowering the members from Charlestown, and others, to call the Congress together sooner than the day to which it may be adjourned, reported; the report was read and accepted, and is as followeth, viz. :

Resolved, That this Congress be adjourned from this day to the twenty-second day of March next, at nine o'clock in the forenoon, to meet at Concord, in the county of Middlesex; and considering the great uncertainty of the present times, and that important unforeseen events may take place, from whence it may be absolutely necessary that this Congress should meet sooner than the day abovesaid, notwithstanding the adjournment aforesaid :

It is farther *Resolved*, That the members of this Congress for the towns of Charlestown, Cambridge, Brookline, Roxbury and Dorchester, or the majority of them, be and [they] are hereby authorized, in case they shall judge it necessary, to give notice to the several members of this Congress, in such way as they shall think proper, to meet at Concord, aforesaid, at any ||ªearlier day|| than the abovesaid twenty-second day of March next, which shall be by them appointed ; and it is further recommended to the members of this Congress that they conform themselves to said notice.

The president then declared the Congress adjourned accordingly.

WEDNESDAY, March 22, 1775, A. M.

Congress met ||ᵇaccording|| to adjournment.

Ordered, That Col. Barrett, Hon. Mr. Dexter and Mr. Stickney, be a committee, to wait on the Rev. Mr. Emerson, and desire his attendance on the Congress, and [that he would] open the same with prayer, at three o'clock this afternoon.||ᶜ||

Afternoon.

Ordered, That Col. Barrett, Hon. Mr. Dexter, and Mr. Stickney, be a committee to wait again on the Rev. Mr. Emerson, and desire him, if his circumstances will admit of it, to attend daily on the Congress, and officiate as their chaplain.

Ordered, That all the debates and resolutions of this Congress be kept an entire secret, until the farther order thereof.

Ordered, That Col. Danielson, Col. Henshaw, Major Fuller, Col. Prescot and Col. Farley, be a committee to receive the returns of the several officers of militia, of their numbers and ||ᵈequipments,|| and the returns from the several towns of their town stock of ammunition.

Ordered, That Mr. Lothrop and the Hon. Col. Dexter, be added to the committee on the state of the province.

||The Congress then|| adjourned till to-morrow morning at nine o'clock.

THURSDAY, March 23, 1775, A. M.

The committee appointed to wait on the Rev. Mr. Emerson, and desire that he would officiate as chaplain to this Congress, during their present session, in the town of Concord, reported, that they had attended that service, and delivered the message, and that Mr. Emerson would officiate accordingly.

Ordered, That Mr. Gerry, Mr. Paine and Mr. Adams, be a committee to bring in a resolve, expressing the sense of this Congress, that for this people to relax in their preparations to defend themselves, &c., would be attended with the most dangerous consequences.

Ordered, That information be given by the members, to the committee on the state of the province, of the number of field pieces, whether the property of the province, towns, or private persons, which have fallen within their knowledge ; as also what number of men [there are] in the province acquainted with the business of making firearms.

Adjourned to three o'clock [this afternoon.]

Afternoon.

||Congress|| adjourned till to-morrow morning, ten o'clock.

FRIDAY, March 24, 1775, A. M.

Adjourned to three o'clock [this afternoon.]

Afternoon.

The committee appointed to bring in a resolve, expressing the danger there would be in relaxing from the present preparations for defence, &c., reported. The report [was] accepted, and *Ordered*, that it be attested and published in all the Boston newspapers.

[Whereas, it is indispensably necessary, for the safety of a free people and the preservation of their liberties, that they, at all times, keep themselves in a state of actual defence against every invasion or depredation ; and this country being still threatened by a powerful army posted in its capital, with a professed design of executing certain acts of the British parliament, calculated to destroy our invaluable rights and liberties and the government of this colony, as by charter and law established therein :]

[Therefore, *Resolved*, That the measures which have heretofore been recommended by this and the former Provincial Congress, for the purpose of putting this colony into a complete state of defence, be still most vigorously pursued, by the several towns, as well as individual inhabitants, and that any relaxation would be attended with the utmost danger to the liberties of this colony and of all America ; especially, as by the latest advices from Great Britain, we have undoubted reasons for jealousy, that our implacable enemies are unremitting in their endeavors, by fraud and artifice as well as by open force, to subjugate this people ; which is an additional motive to the inhabitants of this colony to persevere in the line of conduct recommended by the Congress, and to be ready to oppose, with firmness and resolution, at the utmost hazard, every attempt for that purpose.[1]]

Adjourned till ten o'clock to-morrow morning.

(1) This resolution, omitted in the original record and the copy of the journal, has been restored from the publication in the newspapers.

SATURDAY, March 25, 1775, A. M.

Ordered, That when this Congress ||ᵃadjqurn,|| it be adjourned to Monday next, at three o'clock in the afternoon.

Ordered, That the members be enjoined to attend punctually at the adjournment.

MONDAY, March 27, 1775, P. M.

The committee appointed to prepare a state of the imports, exports, &c., reported: *Ordered*, that the further consideration thereof be referred to Wednesday next, [at] three o'clock in the afternoon.

The committee appointed to prepare some rules, &c. for a constitutional army, reported; the report [was] read: *Ordered*, that the farther consideration of the report be ||ᵇon the morrow|| four o'clock, P. M., and that the committee make such additions thereto as they shall think necessary.

Adjourned to ten o'clock to-morrow morning.

[The several] committees [were] enjoined to sit.

TUESDAY, March 28, 1775, A. M.

The several committees [were] enjoined to sit.

Adjourned to three o'clock [this afternoon.]

Afternoon.

According to the order of the day, [the Congress] went into the consideration of the report of the committee appointed to prepare rules and regulations for a constitutional army, &c.

||ᶜThe above report|| was recommitted for amendments.

Adjourned to nine o'clock to-morrow morning.

WEDNESDAY, March 29, [1775,] A. M.

||ᵈResumed|| the consideration of the report of the committee, relative to rules, &c.; considered the same in paragraphs, [and] passed [the same] in part.

Adjourned to three o'clock [this afternoon.]

Afternoon.

The ||ᵉabove report|| relative to rules, &c., passed in whole, but [was] ordered to be recommitted for ||some|| additions.

Ordered, That Capt. Osgood, Col. Thompson and Capt. Greenleaf, be a committee to bring in a resolve, introductory to the publishing the names of the mandamus counsellors.

The vote of Tuesday relative to information being given to the

a ||shall adjourn that.|| b ||postponed until to-morrow.|| e ||which was.||
d ||revised.|| e ||report of the committee.||

committee on the state of the province, ||*was|| so far reconsidered as that the information be given to the committee appointed to receive the returns from the colonels.

Adjourned to ten o'clock to-morrow morning.

THURSDAY, March 30, 1775, A. M.

The doorkeeper [was] directed to call in the members : they [were] enjoined to attend. The committee on the state of the province reported a resolve, relative to what movements of the troops should make it fit to call the militia together, to act on the defensive ; report read and considered in paragraphs, and passed unanimously in the affirmative.

Upon a motion made and seconded, *Resolved,* that immediately, when notice shall be given for the assembling the forces of this colony, the members of this Congress repair, without delay, to the place to which they shall be adjourned.

Adjourned to three o'clock [this afternoon.]

Afternoon.

The committee appointed yesterday to draw an introduction to publishing the names of the mandamus counsellors, reported ; [the report was] recommitted, and the committee [were] directed to bring in a report by way of order, &c.

The committee appointed to receive the [returns of] exports and imports, &c., in the colony, reported ; [the report was] referred to Wednesday next at three o'clock.

Several committees [were] enjoined to sit and perfect their reports without delay, in order, if possible, that the Congress may rise to-morrow.

Adjourned to nine o'clock to-morrow morning.

FRIDAY, March 31, 1775, A. M.

The committee appointed to bring in a resolve as introductory to publishing the names of the mandamus counsellors, [reported a resolve, which] being amended, was read and accepted, and is as follows :

IN PROVINCIAL CONGRESS, *Concord,* March 31, 1775.

Resolved, That the names of the following persons be published in all the Boston newspapers, who, having been appointed counsellors by his majesty's mandamus, and having accepted, and acted under said commissions, have proved themselves implacable enemies to the liber-

a ||be.||

ties of their country, by refusing to publish a renunciation of their commissions, agreeably to a resolve of a former Provincial Congress: that the secretary be directed to transmit authenticated copies of this resolve, with the names annexed, to all the printers in Boston, and that they be desired to insert the same in their papers, that every town may be possessed of a copy of their names, which are to be entered upon the town and district records, that they may be sent down to posterity, if possible, with the infamy they deserve: [They are as follow :]

Thomas Flucker, Foster Hutchinson, Harrison Gray, William Brown, James Boutineau, Joshua Loring, William Pepperell, John Erving, Jun., Peter Oliver, Richard Lechmere, Josiah Edson, Nathaniel Ray Thomas, Timothy Ruggles, John Murray, and Daniel Leonard, Esquires.

The committee appointed to receive the returns from the several ||ᵃcolonels;|| &c., reported; the report was recommitted to be completed.

A memorial from the selectmen of the town of Billerica, [was] read, and committed to Mr. Marcy, Capt. Batchelder, Capt. Osgood, Capt. Manning and Mr. Freeman.

Ordered, That the receiver general be directed to lay a state of the treasury before this Congress.

The members [were] enjoined to attend until the farther order of this Congress.

Adjourned to three o'clock [this afternoon.]

Afternoon.

The committee on the state of the province reported a resolve relative to the payment of the public monies immediately to Mr. Gardner: read and accepted, and *Ordered*, that it be printed in hand bills, and a copy thereof sent to each town, directed to the committee of correspondence, if any; if not, to the selectmen; to be laid before the several towns.

IN PROVINCIAL CONGRESS, Concord, March 31, 1775.

Whereas, this Congress is informed that many collectors and constables, having in their hands considerable sums of the public moneys of this colony, have hitherto neglected to pay the same to Henry Gardner, Esq., of Stow; and the Congress, earnestly attentive to the ease of the inhabitants of the colony, are desirous of completing the preparations so essentially necessary to the public safety, without calling on them for other moneys, than such as are now due to the colony.

a ||colonies.||

It is, therefore, *Resolved,* That the constables and collectors aforesaid, ought, by no means, to be longer indulged in their unreasonable neglect of complying with the most important plans of this colony; and it is hereby strongly recommended, to the several towns and districts of the same, that they oblige said constables and collectors forthwith to pay the balances aforesaid, due from them respectively, to the receiver general; and it is also most earnestly recommended to those towns and districts, having any public moneys belonging to the colony yet uncollected, that they do not fail to hire and pay the same to the said Henry Gardner, Esq., without delay; and that they vigorously exert themselves to suppress every opposition to measures recommended by the Continental and Provincial Congresses, as they regard the freedom and happiness of themselves and future generations.

Ordered, That Mr. Gorham, Mr. Devens and Mr. Watson, be a committee to forward the hand bills to the several towns, &c.

Resolved, That each member be desired to urge the town, of which he is a representative, if they have not paid their money to Henry Gardner, that they would immediately pay it; and if it cannot be soon collected, that they be desired to borrow it; and if there is any town which does not incline to pay their public moneys to Mr. Gardner, they are desired to give their reasons for such refusal to this Congress, at the next session thereof.

Adjourned to nine o'clock to-morrow morning.

SATURDAY, April 1, 1775, A. M.

The committee appointed to report rules, &c., for the provincial army, having made the additions directed, the same were read and put in whole and passed; they were then ordered to be recommitted, for the bringing a form of oaths, and a resolve relative to witnesses.

The committee on the state of the province reported a resolve relative to furnishing the indians with blankets who have enlisted as minute men, &c., and an address to them; it passed, and is as follows:

IN PROVINCIAL CONGRESS, *Concord,* April 1, 1775.

Whereas, a number of indians, natives of the town of Stockbridge, have enlisted as minute men—*Resolved,* that, for their encouragement, the following address to said indians be presented to them, by Col. John Paterson and Capt. William Goodridge, and that Henry Gardner, Esq., the receiver general, be, and hereby is directed, to pay the sum of twenty-three pounds, lawful money, into the hands of Col. John Paterson and Capt. William Goodridge, to be employed in purchasing a number of blankets and some ribbons, which they are to present to the indians enlisted as aforesaid, viz : one blanket and one yard of ribbon to each person, that is or may be enlisted; and in case the whole of the money should not be employed, in the purchase aforesaid, they are to be accountable for the residue.

To Johoiakin Mothksin, and the rest of our brethren, the indians, natives of Stockbridge :

GOOD BROTHERS—It affords us great pleasure and satisfaction, to hear by Col. Paterson and Capt. Goodridge, that our brothers, the natives of Stockbridge, are ready and willing to take up the hatchet in the cause of liberty and their country. We find you have not been inattentive to the unhappy controversy we are engaged in with our mother country, by reason of sundry acts the British parliament have passed, by which, our rights and privileges have been invaded, and our property taken from us without our consent. We have frequently petitioned the king for redress of our grievances, and the restoration of our rights; but, instead of granting us relief, the king's ministers have sent a large fleet, and posted a great army in the town of Boston, who are daily abusing and •insulting the inhabitants, in order to enforce obedience to these acts. The whole continent, from Nova Scotia to Georgia, by their delegates, have lately presented a petition to the king, praying for relief, to which we hope we shall receive a gracious answer. We wish the fire of friendship may be again kindled between both countries; but in case our petition should not be attended to, and the ministry should determine to deprive us of our rights and property by a military force, we hold ourselves obliged to defend them at the point of the sword. This is a common cause ; a cause you are equally engaged in with ourselves; we are all brothers, and if the parliament of Great Britain takes from us our property, and our lands, without our consent, they will do the same by you ; your property, your lands will be insecure; in short, we shall not any of us have any thing we can call our own. Your engaging in this cause, discovers not only your attachment to your liberties, but furnishes us with an evidence of your gratitude to this province for their past favors. They have frequently, at your request, made laws and regulations for your protection and defence against the ravages and frauds of deceitful and designing men. They have constantly and cheerfully afforded you aid and assistance, because you have given them abundant proof of your fidelity. We have directed Col. Paterson and Capt. Goodridge to present each of you, that have enlisted in the service, with a blanket and a ribbon, as a testimony of our affection, and shall depend upon your firm and steady attachment to the cause you have engaged in.

Ordered, That Mr. Adams, Mr. Cushing, and Col. Paterson, be a committee to draught a letter to the Rev. Mr. Kirkland, and an address to the chief of the Mohawk indian tribes.

Moved, That the Congress now go into consideration of what ought to be the conduct of the several towns, in case general Gage should send out his precepts for convening a new assembly, on the last Wednesday of May next, and what ought to be their conduct in case he should not send out his writs.

Resolved, That it is the opinion of this Congress, that in case writs, in the form the law directs, should be issued, they ought to be obeyed.

Resolved, That, in case writs should not be issued forth, that a Congress be called, on the last Wednesday of May next; and in case general Gage should not issue precepts for calling an assembly, as the law directs, the members of the towns of Charlestown, Cambridge, Brookline, Roxbury, and Dorchester, be desired to publish this resolve and appoint a place where they shall assemble.

Ordered, That Col. Warren, Mr. Adams, and Mr. Gill, be a committee to reduce the several resolutions of this day, relative to calling a new Congress, into form, and bring in a resolve accordingly. The committee reported; [ªthe report was] read, accepted, and is as follows:

IN PROVINCIAL CONGRESS, April 1, 1775.

||*Resolved*, As the sense of this Congress, that if writs should be issued, in form as the law directs, for calling a general assembly, to be held on the last Wednesday of May next, that the several towns in this colony ought to obey such precepts, and choose their members as usual; and instruct them to transact no business with the council, appointed by mandamus; and if they should be dissolved, to meet in a Provincial Congress, for the purpose of considering and transacting the affairs of this colony.||

IN PROVINCIAL CONGRESS, April 1, 1775.

Resolved, That in case writs are not issued according to law, for calling a general assembly, on the last Wednesday of May next, it be recommended to the several towns and districts in this colony, to choose delegates for a Provincial Congress, to meet on the said last Wednesday of May next, at such place as the present members of the towns of Charlestown, Cambridge, Brookline, Roxbury, and Dorches-

a ||which was.||

ter, shall appoint; who are desired to cause this resolution to be published in the several newspapers, as soon as it can be ascertained that writs are not issued for calling an assembly.

An application from the committee of correspondence of the town of Boston, and others, was read; *Ordered*, that the consideration ||thereof|| be referred to three o'clock this afternoon.

Afternoon.

The Congress proceeded to consider the application from the committee of correspondence of Boston, &c., agreeably to the order of the forenoon; *Ordered*, that it be committed to Col. Danielson, Mr. Gerry, Col. Foster, Major Fuller of Middleton, and Col. Warren, to consider of, and report thereon.

The members enjoined to attend at the adjournment [a of this Congress.]

||The Congress adjourned to Monday morning, nine o'clock.||

MONDAY, April 3, 1775, A. M.

Resolved, That the committee on the state of the province be desired to collect all the late intelligence from Great Britain relative to their sending a reenforcement to General Gage, and on other matters which relate to this and the other colonies, and report to the Congress what is best to be done.

Ordered, That Doct. Church, Col. Pomeroy, and Doct. Warren, be a committee to bring in a resolve to be inserted in the Salem papers, requiring the attendance of all the absent members, and a recommendation to the several towns and districts, who have not yet sent members to the Provincial Congress, that they elect them, and direct their immediate attendance.

Ordered, That Major Bliss, Mr. Freeman, and Capt. Osgood, be a committee to bring in a resolve, to be forwarded by an express, to call in the absent members from the counties of Hampshire, Berkshire, Worcester, and Bristol.

Adjourned to three o'clock [this afternoon.]

Afternoon.

Ordered, That the committee on the memorial of the town of Billerica, be joined to the committee appointed to take into consideration the memorial from the town of Boston and others.

Ordered, That the committee be enjoined to sit immediately.

a ||which will be at 9 o'clock A. M., Monday next.||

Ordered, That Col. Foster be excused from [serving on the] last mentioned committee.

||ᵃ*Ordered*, That|| Col. Cushing be added to them.

||Congress|| adjourned till to-morrow morning, nine o'clock.

TUESDAY, April 4, 1775, A. M.

Upon a motion made that Capt. Goodridge have liberty to augment his company to one hundred men, and that they be considered as rangers; thereupon, *Ordered*, that Capt. Goodridge apply to Col. Paterson on this affair, who will have an opportunity to consult the field officers of those regiments of the militia, from which said company is to be enlisted, and that this matter be settled as they shall think best.

The committee appointed to prepare an address to the Mohawks, and a letter to the Rev. Mr. Kirkland, reported; [the report was] read, and *Ordered* that the address be recommitted for amendments.

||Congress|| adjourned to three o'clock [this afternoon.]

Afternoon.

A letter to the Rev. Mr. Kirkland, and an address to the Mohawks, amended, [were] reported, and passed, and are as follow:

CONCORD, April 4, 1775.

REV. SIR: The Provincial Congress have thought it necessary to address the sachem of the Mohawk tribe, with the rest of the five nations, upon the subject of the controversy between Great Britain and the American colonies. We were induced to take this measure, as we have been informed that those, who are inimical to us in Canada, have been tampering with those nations, and endeavoring to attach them to the interest of those, who are attempting to deprive us of our inestimable rights and privileges, and to subjugate the colonies to arbitrary power. From a confidence in your attachment to the cause of liberty, and your country, we now transmit to you the enclosed address, and desire you would deliver it to the sachem of the Mohawk tribe, to be communicated to the rest of the five nations, and that you would use your influence with them, to join with us in the defence of our rights; but if you cannot prevail with them to take an active part in this glorious cause, that you would, at least, engage them to stand neuter, and not, by any means, to aid and assist our enemies—and as we are at a loss for the name of the sachem of the Mohawk tribe, we have left it to you to direct the address to him, in such way as you may think proper.

a ||and that.||

BROTHERS :—We, the delegates of the inhabitants of the province of the Massachusetts Bay, being come together, to consider what may be best for you and ourselves to do in order to get ourselves rid of those hardships which we feel and fear, have thought it our duty to tell you, our good brothers, what our fathers in Great Britain have done and threaten to do with us.

Brothers:—you have heard how our fathers were obliged, by the cruelty of their brethren, to leave their country; how they crossed the great lake and came here; how they purchased this land with their own money, and how, since that time, they, and we, their sons and grandsons, have built our houses, and cut down the trees, and cleared and improved the land, at their and our own expense; how we have fought for them, and conquered Canada and a great many other places, which they have had, and have not paid us for; after all which, and many other troubles, we thought we had reason to hope, that they would be kind to us, and allow us to enjoy ourselves, and sit in our own houses, and eat our own victuals in peace and quiet; but, alas! our brothers, we are greatly distressed, and we will tell you our grief, for you, as well as we, are in great danger.

Brothers:—our fathers in Great Britain tell us, our land, and houses, and cattle, and money, are not our own; that we, ourselves, are not our own men, but their servants; they have endeavored to take away our money without our leave, and have sent their great vessels and a great many warriors for that purpose.

Brothers:—we used to send our vessels on the great lake, whereby we were able to get clothes and what we needed for ourselves and you; but such has lately been their conduct, that we cannot; they have told us, we shall have no more guns, no powder to use and kill our wolves and other game, nor to send to you, for you to kill your victuals with, and to get skins to trade with us, to buy you blankets, and what you want. How can you live without powder and guns? But we hope to supply you soon with both of our own making.

Brothers:—they have made a law to establish the religion of the pope in Canada, which lies so near you. We much fear some of your children may be induced, instead of worshipping the only true God, to pay *his* due to images made with their own hands.

Brothers:—these and many other hardships we are threatened with, which, no doubt, in the end, will equally affect you; for the same reason they would get our lands, they will take away yours. All we want is, that we and you may enjoy that liberty and security, which we have a right to enjoy, and that we may not lose that good land which enables us to feed our wives and children ; we think it our duty to inform you of our danger, and desire you to give notice to all your kindred ; and as we ||much|| fear they will attempt to cut our throats, and if you should allow them to do that, there will nobody remain to keep them from you, we therefore earnestly desire you to whet your hatchet and be prepared with us to defend our liberties and lives.

Brothers :—we humbly beseech that God, who lives above and does what is right here below, to enlighten your minds to see that you ought ||to endeavor|| to prevent our fathers from bringing those miseries upon us, and to his good providence we commend you.

The committee appointed to draught rules for the army, &c., again reported ; recommitted to bring in the form of two oaths.

Adjourned to ten o'clock to-morrow morning.

WEDNESDAY, April 5, 1775, A. M.

The committee appointed to prepare rules and regulations for the Massachusetts army, having brought in the form of two oaths as direct-ed, the report in whole [was read] and passed, and is as followeth :

||IN PROVINCIAL CONGRESS, *Concord,* April 5, 1775.||

Whereas, the lust of power, which of old oppressed, persecuted, and exiled our pious and virtuous ancestors from their fair possessions in Britain, now pursues with ten fold severity, us, their guiltless children, who are unjustly and wickedly charged with licentiousness, sedition, treason, and rebellion ; and being deeply impressed with a sense of the almost incredible fatigues and hardships our venerable progenitors en-countered, who fled from oppression for the sake of civil and religious liberty, for themselves and their offspring, and began a settlement here *on bare creation,* at their own expense ; and having seriously consider-ed the duty we owe to God, to the memory of such invincible worthies, to the king, to Great Britain, our country, ourselves, and posterity, do think it our indispensable duty, by all lawful ways and means, in our power, to recover, maintain, defend, and preserve, the free exercise of all those civil and religious rights and liberties, for which many of our forefathers fought, bled, and died, and to hand them down en-tire, for the free enjoyment of the latest posterity ; and whereas, the keeping a standing army in any of these colonies in times of peace, without the consent of the legislature of that colony in which such army is kept, is against law ; and whereas, such an army, with a large naval force, is now placed in the town and harbor of Boston, for the purpose of subjecting us to the power of the British parliament : and, whereas, we are frequently told by the tools of administration, dupes to ministerial usurpation, that Great Britain will not, in any degree, relax in her measures, until we acknowledge her " right of making laws binding upon us in all cases whatever;" and that, if we refuse by our denial of her claim, the dispute must be decided by arms; in which, it is said by our enemies, " we shall have no chance, being undisciplined, cowards, disobedient, impatient. of command, and possessed of that spirit of ||ᵃlevelling|| which admits of no order, subordination, rule or government; and, whereas, ||from|| the ministerial army and fleet now at Boston, the large reenforcement of troops expected, the late circular letters to the governors upon the continent, the general tenor of intelligence from Great Britain, and the hostile preparations making here; as also, from the threats and repeated insults of our enemies, in the capital town, we have reason to apprehend, that the sudden destruction of this province is in contemplation, if not determined upon;

And, whereas, the great law of self-preservation may suddenly require our raising and keeping an army of observation and defence, in order to prevent or repel any further attempts to ||ᵇenforce|| the late cruel and oppressive acts of the British parliament, which are evidently designed to subject us and the whole continent to the most ignominious slavery; and, whereas, in case of raising and keeping such an army, it will be necessary that the officers and soldiers in the same, be fully acquainted with their duty, and that the articles, rules, and regulations thereof, be made as plain as possible; and having great confidence in the honor and public virtue of the inhabitants of this colony, that they will readily obey the officers, chosen by themselves, and will cheerfully do their duty when known, without any such severe articles and rules, (except in capital cases,) and cruel punishments as are usually practised in standing armies; and will submit to all such rules and regulations as are founded in reason, honor and virtue: it is therefore, *Resolved*, that the following articles, rules, and regulations for the army, that may be raised for the defence and security of our lives, liberties, and estates, be, and hereby are, earnestly recommended to be strictly adhered to by all officers, soldiers, and others concerned, as they regard their own honor and the public good.

ART. 1. All officers and soldiers, not having just impediment, shall diligently frequent divine service and sermon, in the places appointed for the assembling of the regiment, troop, or company, to which

a ||revelling.|| b ||force.||

they belong, and such as wilfully absent themselves, or, being present, behave indecently or irreverently, shall, if commissioned officers, [be] brought before a regimental court martial, there to be publicly and severely reprimanded by the president; if non commissioned officers or soldiers, every person so offending shall, for his first offence, forfeit one shilling, to be deducted out of his wages; for the second offence, he shall not only forfeit one shilling, but be confined twenty-four hours; and for every like offence [after,] shall suffer and pay in like manner; which money so forfeited, shall be applied to the use of the sick soldiers of the troop or company to which the offender belongs.

ART. 2. Whatsoever non commissioned officer or soldier shall use any unlawful oath or execration, shall incur the penalties expressed in the ||*first|| article; and if a commissioned officer be thus guilty of profane cursing and swearing, he shall forfeit and pay for each and every such offence four shillings, lawful money.

ART. 3. Any officer or soldier who shall behave himself with contempt or disrespect toward the general or generals, or commanders in chief of the Massachusetts forces, or shall speak words tending to his or their hurt or dishonor, shall be punished, according to the nature of his offence, by the judgment of a general court martial.[1]

ART. 4. Any officer or soldier, who shall begin, excite, cause, ||ᵇor join in any|| mutiny or sedition, in the regiment, troop, or company, to which he belongs, or in any other regiment, troop, or company of the Massachusetts forces, either by land or sea, or in any party, post, detachment, or guard, on any pretence whatever, shall suffer such punishment as by a general court martial shall be ordered.

ART. 5. Any officer, non commissioned officer, or soldier, who, being present at any mutiny or sedition, does not use his utmost endeavors to suppress the same, or, coming to the knowledge of any mutiny, does not, without delay, give information thereof to his commanding officer, shall be punished by order of a general court martial, according to the nature of his offence.

ART. 6. Any officer or soldier, who shall strike his superior officer, or draw, or offer to draw, [his sword,] or shall lift up any weapon, or offer any violence against him, being in the execution of his office, on any pretence whatever, or shall disobey any lawful commands of his superior officer, shall suffer such punishment, as shall, according to the nature of his offence, be ordered by the sentence of a general court martial.

a ||preceding.|| b ||any mutiny, or sedition, or join in such.||

(1) In the copy, the third article is numbered fourth, and the fourth article inserted in the place of the third.

ART. 7. Any non commissioned officer or soldier, who shall desert, or without leave from his commanding officer, absent himself, from the troop or company to which he belongs, or from any detachment of the same, shall, upon being convicted thereof, be punished, according to the nature of his offence, at the discretion of a general court martial .

ART. 8. Whatever officer or soldier shall be convicted of having advised, or persuaded any other officer or soldier to desert, shall suffer such punishment as shall be ordered by the sentence of a general court martial.

ART. 9. All officers, of what condition soever, shall have power to part and quell all quarrels, frays, and disorders, though the persons concerned should belong to another regiment, troop, or company, and order officers to be arrested, or non commissioned officers or soldiers to be confined, and imprisoned, till their proper superior officers can be made acquainted therewith; and whoever shall refuse to obey such officer, though of an inferior rank, or shall draw his sword upon him, shall be punished at the discretion of a general court martial.

ART. 10. No officer or soldier shall use any reproachful or provoking speeches or gestures; nor shall presume to send a challenge to any person to fight a duel; ||ᵃ||and whoever shall knowingly and willingly suffer any person whatsoever, to go forth to fight a duel; ||ᵇor shall second, promote, or carry any challenge,|| shall be deemed as a principal; and whatsoever officer or soldier shall upbraid another for refusing a challenge, shall be considered as a challenger; and all such offenders in any of these or the like cases, shall be punished at the discretion of a general court martial.

ART. 11. Every officer, commanding in quarters or on a march, shall keep good order, and, to the utmost of his power, redress all such abuses or disorders, which may be committed to any officer or soldier under his command; if, upon any complaint made to him of officers or soldiers ||ᶜbeating|| or otherwise ill treating any person, or of committing any kind of riots, to the disquieting of the inhabitants of this continent, he, the said commander, shall refuse or omit to see justice done to the offender or offenders, and reparation made to the party or parties injured, as soon as the offender's wages shall enable him or them, [he] shall, upon due proof thereof, be punished, as ordered by a general court martial, in such manner, as if he himself had committed the crimes or disorders complained of.

ART. 12. If any officer should think himself to be wronged by his colonel or the commanding officer of the regiment, and shall, upon due application made to him, be refused to be redressed, he may complain to the general or commander in chief of the Massachusetts forces, in order to obtain justice, who is hereby required to examine into the complaint and see that justice be done.

ART. 13. If any inferior officer or soldier shall think himself wronged by his captain or other officer commanding the troop or company to which he belongs, he is to complain thereof to the commanding officer of the regiment, who is hereby required to summon a regimental court martial for the doing justice to the ||ᵃcomplainant;|| from which regimental court martial, either party may, if he thinks himself still aggrieved, appeal to a general court martial; but if, upon a second hearing, the appeal shall appear to be vexatious and groundless, the person so appealing shall be punished at the discretion of a general court martial.

ART 14. Whatsoever non commissioned officer or soldier shall be convicted at a regimental court martial, of having sold, or designedly, or through neglect, wasted the ammunition, arms, or provisions, or other military stores delivered out to him to be employed in the service of this colony, shall, if an officer, be reduced to a private sentinel, and, if a private soldier, shall suffer such punishment as shall be ordered by a regimental court martial.

ART. 15. All non commissioned officers or soldiers, who shall be found one mile from the camp, without leave in writing from their commanding officer, shall suffer such punishment as shall be inflicted on him or them, by the sentence of a regimental court martial.

ART. 16. No officer or soldier shall ||ᵇlie|| out of his quarters, or camp, without leave from the commanding officer of the regiment, upon penalty of being punished, according to the nature of his offence, by order of a regimental court martial.

ART. 17. Every non commissioned officer and soldier shall retire to his quarters, or tent, at the beating the retreat; in default of which, he shall be punished, according to the nature of his offence, by order of the commanding officer.

ART. 18. No officer, non commissioned officer, or soldier, shall fail of repairing, at the time fixed, to the place of parade, of exercise, or other rendezvous, appointed by the commanding officer, if not prevented by sickness or some other evident necessity; or shall go from the said place of rendezvous, or from his guard, without leave from his commanding officer, before he shall be regularly dismissed, or relieved,

a ||complaint.|| b ||be.||

on penalty of being punished, according to the nature of his offence, by the sentence of a regimental court martial.

ART. 19. Whatsoever commissioned officer shall be found drunk upon his guard, party, or other duty under arms, shall be cashiered for it; any non commissioned officer or soldier so offending, shall suffer such punishment as shall be ordered by the sentence of a regimental court martial.

ART. 20. Whatever sentinel shall be found sleeping upon his post, or shall leave it before he shall be regularly relieved, shall suffer such punishment as shall be ordered by the sentence of a general court martial.

ART. 21. Any person belonging to the Massachusetts army, who, by discharging of fire-arms, beating of drums, or by any other means whatever, shall occasion false alarms in camp or in quarters, shall suffer such punishment as shall be ordered by the sentence of a general court martial.

ART. 22. Any officer or soldier who shall, without urgent necessity, or without leave of his superior officer, quit his platoon or division, shall be punished, according to the nature of his offence, by the sentence of a regimental court martial.

ART. 23. No officer or soldier shall do violence, or offer any insult or abuse, to any person who shall bring provisions or other necessaries to the camp or quarters, of the Massachusetts army; any officer or soldier so offending, shall, upon complaint being made to the commanding officer, suffer such punishment as shall be ordered by a regimental court martial.

ART. 24. Whatever officer or soldier shall shamefully abandon any post committed to his charge, or shall speak words inducing others to do the like, in time of an engagement, shall suffer death immediately.

ART. 25. Any person belonging to the Massachusetts army, who shall make known the watchword to any person, who is not entitled to receive it according to the rules and discipline of war, or shall presume to give a parol or watchword different from what he received, shall suffer death, or such other punishment as shall be ordered by a general court martial.

ART. 26. Whosoever, belonging to the Massachusetts army, shall relieve the enemy with money, victuals, or ammunition, or shall knowingly harbor and protect an enemy, shall suffer such punishment, as, by a general court martial, shall be ordered.

ART. 27. Whosoever, belonging to the Massachusetts army, shall be convicted of holding correspondence with, or giving intelligence to the enemy, either directly or indirectly, shall suffer such punishment as, by a general court martial, shall be ordered.

ART. 28. All public stores, taken in the enemy's camp, whether of artillery, ammunition, clothing, or provisions, shall be secured for the use of the Massachusetts colony.

ART. 29. If any officer or soldier shall leave his post or colors, in time of an engagement, to go in search of plunder, he shall, upon being convicted thereof before a general court martial, suffer such punishment as, by said court martial, shall be ordered.

ART. 30. If any commander of any post, entrenchment or fortress, shall be compelled, by the officers or soldiers under his command, to give it up to the enemy, or to abandon it, the commissioned officers or soldiers, who shall be convicted of having so offended, shall suffer death, or such other punishment as may be inflicted upon them by the sentence of a general court martial.

ART. 31. All ||ᵃsutlers|| and retailers to a camp, and all persons whatsoever serving with the Massachusetts army, in the field, though not ||ᵇenlisted|| soldiers, are to be subject to the articles, rules and regulations of the Massachusetts army.

ART. 32. No general court martial shall consist of a less number than thirteen, none of which shall be under the degree of a field officer; and the president of each and every court martial, whether general or regimental, shall have power to administer an oath to every witness in order to the trial of offenders; and the members of all courts martial shall be duly sworn by the president; and the next in rank on the court martial, shall administer the oath to the president.

ART. 33. The members both of general and regimental courts martial shall, when belonging to different corps, take the same rank which they hold in the army; but when courts martial shall be composed of officers of one corps, they shall take ||ᶜtheir ranks|| according to their commissions, by which they are mustered in the said corps.

ART. 34. All the members of a court martial are to behave with calmness, decency and impartiality; and in the giving of their votes, are to begin with the youngest, or lowest in commission.

ART. 35. No field officer shall be tried by any person under the degree of a captain; nor shall any proceeding or trial be carried on, excepting between the hours of eight in the morning and three in the afternoon, except in cases which require an immediate example.

ART. 36. The commissioned officers of every regiment may, by the appointment of their colonel or commanding officer, hold regimental

a ||sellers.|| b ||entitled.|| c ||rank.||

courts martial for the inquiring into such disputes or criminal matters as may come before them, and for the inflicting corporal punishment for small offences, and shall give judgment by the majority of voices; but no sentence shall be executed, till the commanding officer, not being a member of the court martial, shall have confirmed the same.

ART. 37. No regimental court martial shall consist of less than five officers, excepting in cases when that number cannot be conveniently assembled, when three may be sufficient: who are likewise to determine upon the sentence, by the majority of voices; which sentence is to be confirmed by the commanding officer, not being a member of the court martial.

ART. 38. Any officer commanding in forts, castles, or barracks, or elsewhere, where the corps under his command consists of detachments from different regiments, or of independent companies, may assemble courts martial, for the trial of offenders in the same manner, as if they were regimental; whose sentence is not to be executed till it shall be confirmed by the said commanding officer.

ART. 39. No person whatsoever shall use menacing words, signs, or gestures in the presence of a court martial, then sitting, or shall cause any disorder or riot, so as to disturb their proceeding, on penalty of being punished at the discretion of said court martial.

ART. 40. To the end that offenders may be brought to justice, whenever any officer or soldier shall commit a crime deserving punishment, he shall, by his commanding officer, if an officer, be put in arrest; if a non commissioned officer or soldier, be imprisoned; till he shall be either tried by a court martial, or shall be lawfully discharged by proper authority.

ART. 41. No officer or soldier who shall be put in arrest or imprisonment, shall continue in his confinement more than eight days, or till such time as a court martial can be conveniently assembled.

ART. 42. No officer commanding a guard, or provost martial, shall refuse to receive or keep any prisoner committed to his charge by any officer belonging to the Massachusetts forces; which officer shall, [with the prisoner] at the same time, deliver an account in writing, signed by himself, of the crimes with which the said prisoner is charged.

ART. 43. No officer commanding a guard, or provost martial, shall presume to release any prisoner committed to his charge, without proper authority for so doing; nor shall he suffer any prisoner to escape, on the penalty of being punished for it, by the sentence of a general court martial.

ART. 44. Every officer or provost martial, to whose charge prisoners shall be committed, is hereby required, within twenty-four hours of such confinement, or as soon as he shall be ||ᵃrelieved|| from his guard, to give in writing, to ||ᵇthe|| colonel of the regiment, to whom the prisoner belongs, where the prisoner is confined upon the guard belonging to the said regiment, and [ᶜwhere] his offence only relates to the neglect of duty in his own corps : or, to the commander in chief, their names, their crimes, and the names of the officers, who committed them, on the penalty of his being punished for his disobedience or neglect at the discretion of a general court martial.

ART. 45. And if any officer under arrest shall leave his confinement before he is set at liberty by the officer who confined him, or by a superior power, he shall be cashiered for it.

ART. 46. Whatsoever commissioned officer shall be convicted before a general court martial, of behaving in a scandalous, infamous manner, such as is unbecoming an officer and a gentleman, shall be discharged from the service.

ART. 47. All officers, conductors, gunners, matrosses, drivers, or any other persons whatever, receiving pay or hire in the service of the Massachusetts artillery, shall be governed by the aforesaid rules and articles, and shall be subject to be tried by courts martial in like manner with the officers and soldiers of the Massachusetts troops.

ART. 48. For differences arising amongst themselves, or in matters relating solely to their own corps, the courts martial may be composed of their own officers; but where a number sufficient cannot be assembled, or in matters wherein other corps are interested, the officers of artillery shall sit in courts martial with the officers of the other corps.

ART. 49. All crimes not capital, and all disorders and neglects, which officers and soldiers may be guilty of, to the prejudice of good order and military discipline, though not mentioned in the articles of war, are to be taken cognizance of by a general or regimental court martial, according to the nature and degree of the offence, and be punished at their discretion.

ART. 50. No court martial shall order any offender to be whipped or receive more than thirty-nine stripes for any one offence.

ART. 51. The field officers of each and every regiment, are to appoint some suitable person belonging to such regiment, to receive all such fines as may arise within the same, for any breach of any of the foregoing articles, and shall direct the same to be carefully and properly applied to the relief of such sick, wounded, or necessitous soldiers as belong to such regiment, and such person shall account with such officer for all fines received and the application thereof.

ART. 52. All members sitting in courts martial, shall be sworn by the president of said courts, which president shall himself be sworn by the officer in said court next in rank; the oaths to be administered previous to their proceeding to the trial of any offender, [to be] in form following :—You A B swear, that you will well and truly try and impartially determine the cause of the prisoner now to be tried, according to the rules for regulating the Massachusetts army. So help you God.

ART. 53. All persons, called to give evidence in any case before a court martial, who shall refuse to give evidence, shall be punished for such refusal, at the discretion of such court martial. The oath to be administered in the form following :—You swear, the evidence you shall give, in the case in hearing, shall be the truth, the whole truth, and nothing but the truth. So help you God.

Resolved, That the inhabitants of the town of Northfield be desired, in consideration of the bodily indisposition of their present member, Mr. Ebenezer Jones, which prevents his attendance, to add one other member to him, in order that their town may be represented in Congress, who are very desirous that the wisdom of the province may be collected at this critical juncture of our public affairs.

The committee, appointed to take into consideration the application of the committee from Boston, and others, reported that the papers lie on the table for farther consideration at some future day.

Adjourned to three o'clock in the afternoon.

Afternoon.

Ordered, That the committee on the state of the province be directed to sit.

Congress adjourned till to-morrow morning, ten o'clock.

THURSDAY, April 6, 1775, A. M.

[On] an application from the committees of inspection of Taunton, and all the other towns in the county of Bristol, setting forth that General Gage had applied to five justices in said county, to provide quarters for two hundred of his majesty's troops, which may be sent to the town of Freetown: ||ᵃ|| *Ordered*, That Mr. Murray, Doct. Gunn, Col.

a ||thereupon.||

17

Pomeroy, Col. Cushing, Mr. Freeman, Capt. Holmes and Mr. Watson, be a committee to take the said application into consideration and report thereon.

||Congress|| adjourned till twelve o'clock at noon.

Met and adjourned to four o'clock, P. M.

Afternoon.

The committee appointed to take into consideration the application [from] all the towns in the county of Bristol, reported; [the report was] amended and passed unanimously, and is as followeth:

GENTLEMEN :—Your very interesting letter of the fourth instant, directed to the president, has been early laid before us. Heartily affected with the matters it contains, this Congress resolved on the immediate consideration of it. The part acted by Col. Gilbert respecting the common cause of America, since the commencement of its public troubles, is sufficiently consonant to the tenor of his ordinary conduct, so far as it has been the object of public observation; and leaves no American room to hesitate in pronouncing him an inveterate enemy to his country, to reason, justice, and the common rights of mankind; and, therefore, whoever has knowingly espoused his cause, or taken up arms for its support, does, in common with himself, deserve to be instantly cut off from the benefit of commerce with, or countenance of, any friend of virtue, America, or the human race.

This Congress cannot but rejoice in the satisfactory evidence they have of the patriotism and public spirit of the county of Bristol, and the vigilance of its inhabitants over the manœuvres of the incendiaries among them; we are much pleased with their joint readiness, for their most vigorous exertions in their country's cause, and earnestly hope that their preparations will be pursued with unabated zeal, as the known resolutions of our public enemies, have, at last, necessitated the contemplation of a plan of general defence, in support of which, the spirit and prowess of the county of Bristol may very soon be called up to the view of mankind.

We earnestly recommend it to you, gentlemen, as guardians of the public interest, to exert yourselves, that the militia, and especially the minute men of your county, be found in the best posture of defence; whenever any exigence may require this aid; but the plans laid for the general good oblige us to request that whatever patience and forbearance it may require for the present, you would act on the defensive only, until the further direction of this Congress.

And, therefore, though we could wish that a particular account of the conduct of Col. Gilbert and his adherents, as well as of the king's troops, whilst stationed among you, might be taken on sufficient evidence in *perpetuam rei memoriam*, yet we could not advise to any measures, either with respect to said Gilbert and his banditti, or the king's troops, that our enemies might plausibly interpret as a commencement of hostilities.

This Congress, however, are clearly of opinion, that, whatever justice of the peace, or other person in the county of Bristol, shall be active in providing quarters, or other supplies, for the said troops, or any others sent in like manner, will be considered by all America as aiding and assisting in the execution of the [acts of the] British parliament, against which, as fundamentally destructive of the most invaluable rights and privileges of the colonies, America has unitedly remonstrated.

IN PROVINCIAL CONGRESS, Concord, April 6, 1775.

Resolved, That the foregoing be signed by the president, in behalf of the Congress, and sent to the committees of inspection of the county of Bristol.

Ordered, That the application from the selectmen of Billerica, and the application from the committee of correspondence of the town of Boston and others,[1] be again committed to the committee, who had them under consideration, and reported that they lie on the table. The committee was ordered to sit immediately.

Adjourned to ten o'clock to-morrow morning.

---

(1) These applications related to an outrage on a citizen of Billerica, named Thomas Ditson, Jun. The story of his wrongs, which created great sensation, is told in the following narrative copied from the Massachusetts Spy, March 10, 1775.

"*The act of tarring and feathering not repealed.*"—"Last Thursday morning, a countryman was tarred and feathered, and carried through some of the streets, in this town, by a party of soldiers, attended by some officers. The following is the man's own deposition relative to that affair, sworn to before a magistrate ; upon which we shall make no remarks, but leave the public to judge of the conduct of some of those who are said to have been sent among us to preserve peace and good order, and to prevent mobs, tumults and other unlawful assemblies."

"I, Thomas Ditson, Jun., of Billerica, husbandman, testify and declare, that, while walking in Fore street, on the 8th of March, in the afternoon, I inquired of some towosmen, who had any guns to sell? one whom I did not know, replied, he had a very fine gun to sell. The man appeared to be a soldier, and I went with him to a house where one was, whom the soldier called sergeant, and seeing some old clothes about the house, I asked whether they sold such things ; the sergeant replied that they did frequently. I then asked his price for an old red coat ript to pieces ; he asked 8s. 6d. sterling ; but I refused to give it. Then one M'Clinchy, the soldier I met with at first in the street, said he had some old clothes to sell, and sent his wife out after them to a man he called a sergeant, and she soon brought an old coat and an old jacket. I then asked him if he had any right to sell them, and the sergeant said that they frequently sold them, and he would give a writing if I desired it, but said there was no occasion. I then bought the coat and jacket, and gave two pistareens, and then put the clothes in a bag, which I left behind ; after which I went to M'Clinchy to see his gun, which he said was a very fine piece. I asked him if he had any right to sell it. He replied he had, and that the gun was his to dispose of at any time. I then asked him whether he thought the sentry would not take it from me at the ferry, as I had heard that some persons had

FRIDAY, April 7, 1775, A. M.

Ordered, That Doct. Warren and Doct. Church be added to the committee on the state of the province.

had their guns taken from them, but never thought there was any law against trading with a soldier. He then told me he had stood sentry, and that they frequently let them pass. He then asked me what I would give him for the gun? I told him I would give four dollars, if there was no risk in carrying it over the ferry. He said there was not, and that I might rely on his word. I then agreed to give four dollars for his gun, but did not take it nor pay the money; coming away, he follows me down stairs, and says, that there was a sergeant had an old rusty piece, that he would sell cheap. I asked him his price; he said he would sell it for one dollar and a half, if I would pay the money down, and he urged me to take it. I then agreed to give him said sum. His wife, as he called her, then came down, and said, M'Clenchy, what are you going to do, to bring the man into a scrape? I then told them, that if there was any difficulty, to give me my money again, but he refused, and replied his wife made an oration for nothing, and that he had a right to sell his gun to any body. I was afraid from her speaking that there was something not right in it, and left the gun, and coming away, he followed me, and urged the guns upon me; I told him I had rather not take them for fear of what his wife had said; he then declared there was no danger, for he had spoken to the officer or sentry, who said he had a right to dispose of them, and urged me to pay the four dollars I had offered for the guns, which I then refused, and desired I might have the one and half dollar back which I had paid for the gun. He refused, saying there was no danger, and damned me for a fool. I then paid him the four dollars for the good gun, but did not receive any one of them. After I had paid the money, he then said, take care of yourself, and the first thing I saw was some men coming up. I stept off to go after my great coat, but they followed and seized me, and carried me to the guard-house upon Foster's wharf. This was about six or seven o'clock in the evening. When I came into the guard-house, they read me a law which I never before saw or heard of. I was detained till about seven in the morning, when I expected I should have been obliged to pay the £5 mentioned in the law read to me, and hired a regular to carry a letter to some friends over the ferry, which was to desire them to come to me as quick as possible with money to pay my fine. Soon after, the sergeant came in, and ordered me to strip. I then asked him what he was going to do with me. He said, damn you, I am going to serve you as you have served our men. Then came in a soldier with a bucket of tar and a pillow bier of feathers. I was then made to strip, which I did to my breeches. They then tarred and feathered me, and while they were doing it, an officer who stood at the door said, tar and feather his breeches, which they accordingly did, and I was then tarred and feathered from head to foot, and had a paper read to me which was then tied round my neck, but afterwards turned behind me, with the following words wrote upon it, to the best of my remembrance: "American liberty or democracy exemplified, in a villain who attempted to entice one of the soldiers of his majesty's 47th regiment to desert and take up arms with rebels against his king and country." I was then ordered to walk out, and get into a chair fastened upon trucks, which I did, when a number of the king's soldiers, as I imagined about forty or fifty, armed with guns and fixed bayonets, surrounded the trucks, and they marched with a number of officers before them, one of whom, I am told, was the colonel of the 47th regiment, who I have since heard was named Nesbit, together with a number of drums and fifes, from the wharf up King street and down Fore street, and then through the Main street, passing the governor's house, until they came to liberty tree; then they turned up Frog lane and made a halt, and a sergeant, as I took him to be, said get down: I then asked where I should go, and he said where you please. Near the governor's house the inhabitants pressed in upon the soldiers; the latter appeared to me to be angry, and I was afraid they would have fired, they being ordered to load their muskets, which they did.   THOMAS DITSON, Jun."

This narrative was verified by the oath of the deponent, March 9, 1775, before Edmund Quincy, Esq.

The selectmen of Billerica presented the following spirited protest against the cruel outrage of the soldiers, to general Gage.

" *May it please your excellency :—*

"We, the selectmen of the town of Billerica, beg leave to remonstrate to your excellency, that on the eighth day of this instant March, one Thomas Ditson, an inhabitant of said town of Bille-

. Mr. Crane laid on the table a number of letters, which were sent to him from Stoughton, and said to be from Col. Gilbert and others.

Ordered, That Col. Thomas, Mr. Devens, Mr. Gardner, Doct. Perkins and Mr. Crane, be a committee to take them into consideration and report ; they reported ||ᵃ|| that they be read.

Ordered, That the committee on the state of the province be directed to wait on the Hon. governor Hopkins and the Hon. governor Sessions, and congratulate them on their arrival to this town, and hold a conference with them on the present state of our public affairs.

The committee appointed to consider on the application from Billerica, &c. reported ; the report [was] amended, accepted and is as follows :

IN PROVINCIAL CONGRESS, ||*Concord*,|| April 7, 1775.

Resolved, That the following letter be signed by the president, and directed to the selectmen of Billerica :

GENTLEMEN :—This Congress, deeply sensible of the high-handed insult offered the town of Billerica, the colony of the Massachusetts Bay, and this continent in general, in the vile and ignoble assault in the person of Thomas Ditson, by a party of the king's troops under

rica, was tarred and feathered, and very much abused, by a party of his majesty's 47th regiment, under the command of lieutenant colonel Nesbit. As guardians for said town, and from a regard to the liberties and properties of its inhabitants, we cannot but resent this procedure. Your excellency must be sensible, that this act is a high infraction of that personal security, which every Englishman is entitled to, and without which his boasted constitution is but a name."

" It is sufficiently unhappy for us, that we find troops quartered among us for the purpose of enforcing obedience to acts of parliament of Great Britain, in the highest sense iniquitous, cruel and unjust. It is still more unhappy, if these troops, instead of preserving the character which British troops once had, should pour in additional insult, and be guilty of the most brutal outrages. We hope your excellency will take some proper steps for accommodating this affair : for, we assure you, we cannot, consistent with our duty, pass this matter over. We have been told by your excellency, that you never meant to disturb the intercourse between the town and country. Confiding in this, we have passed and repassed in our usual manner. We, therefore, hope your excellency will make it evident by your conduct that you are determined the intercourse shall be preserved, and we be not buoyed up with promises, which, in the end, we unhappily find, are not to be depended upon. Lieutenant colonel Nesbit is an officer under your excellency's command. Of *you*, therefore, *we demand satisfaction* for the insult committed by him. We think it is in your power. We beg, your excellency, that the breach, now too wide between Great Britain and this province, may not, by the brutality of the troops, still be increased. We assure you, sir, it always has been, and still is our sentiment and prayer, that harmony may be restored, and that we may not be driven to the last distress of nations. But, may it please your excellency, we must tell you, that we are determined, if the innocent inhabitants of our country towns, for we must think this man innocent in this affair, must be interrupted by soldiers in their lawful intercourse with the town of Boston, and treated with the most brutal ferocity, we shall, hereafter, use a different style from that of petition and complaint."

" If the grand bulwarks of our constitution are thus violently torn away, and the powers on earth prove unfriendly to the cause of virtue, liberty and humanity, we are still happy that we can appeal to *Him* who judgeth righteously, and to *Him* we cheerfully leave the event."

a ||as expedient.||

general Gage's command, do highly approve of the manly and resolute conduct of the town of Billerica, by their manifesting a due resentment to the general, and demanding a constitutional satisfaction.

Notwithstanding you have not received that satisfaction from the general which you had a just right to expect, yet this Congress humbly hope, under Providence, that the time is fast approaching, when this colony and continent will have justice done them, in a way consistent with the dignity of freemen, on such wicked destroyers of the natural and constitutional rights of Americans. Gentlemen, we are confident that the town of Billerica will still continue in that candid pursuit of peace and good order, which manifestly appears in their late conduct.

Ordered, That the letters which have been received or laid on the table by Mr. Crane, be sent to the committee on the state of the province.||ᵃ||

Afternoon.

The committee appointed to take into consideration the application from the committee of correspondence of Boston and others, reported; the report [was] read and accepted, and is as follows:

GENTLEMEN :—Your petition and memorial of the 31st of March we have received; since which, intelligence of the most extraordinary nature from Great Britain has come to hand. We are, gentlemen, much pleased with the spirit and sentiment of your memorial: but, as ||ᵇmatters of the greatest importance|| now demand our immediate attention, and the consideration of them will take up the most important matters in your petition; we, therefore, most earnestly recommend to you, gentlemen, as guardians of the public interest, to exert yourselves that the militia and minute men of your counties, be found in the best posture of defence, whenever any exigence may require their aid; but as the plans laying for the general good oblige us to request, that, whatever patience and forbearance it may require, you would act only on the defensive, until the farther order of this Congress.

And, therefore, though we could wish a particular account of the ministers' troops, while stationed among you, might be taken on sufficient evidence, yet we could not advise to any measures, respecting them, that our enemies might plausibly interpret as a commencement of hostilities: but, on the contrary, let your characteristic be, as it always has been, ||ᶜregard|| of peace and good order, and the just rights of mankind.

<hr>

a ||Adjourned till three o'clock this afternoon.||

b ||the greatest and most important matters.|| c ||conservators.||

We most earnestly wish that the blessing of Heaven may accompany your laudable endeavors to preserve the public weal of this province.

We remain, [&c.]

IN PROVINCIAL CONGRESS, *Concord*, April 7, 1775.

Resolved, That the foregoing letter be signed by the president, in behalf of this Congress, and sent to the committees of correspondence of the towns of Boston, Milton, Roxbury, Dorchester, Cambridge, Newton, Watertown, Lynn, Malden, Woburn, Charlestown and Marlborough, directed to William Cooper, clerk of said committees of correspondence.

Ordered, That Capt. Osgood, Major Fuller of Middleton, and Mr. Webster, be added to the committee appointed to disperse the handbills, &c.

‖The Congress‖ adjourned till to-morrow morning, at nine o'clock.

SATURDAY, April 8, 1775, A. M.

[The] doorkeeper [was] directed to call in the members, and to call none out till the farther order of this Congress.

The committee on the state of the province reported a resolve relative to raising and establishing an army, and that committees be appointed forthwith to repair to Connecticut, Rhode Island and New-Hampshire, to inform them of our resolution, and desire their co-operation, &c.

Resolved, That the report be considered in paragraphs: *Ordered*, that the members be enjoined to attend.

Adjourned to three o'clock in the afternoon.

Afternoon.

The Congress resumed the consideration of the report made in the forenoon, which passed: present 103 [members:] in favor 96—[which report] is as follows:

IN PROVINCIAL CONGRESS, *Concord*, April 8, 1775.

Resolved, That the present dangerous and alarming situation of our public affairs, renders it necessary for this colony to make preparations for their security and defence, by raising and establishing an army, and that delegates be appointed forthwith to repair to Connecticut, Rhode Island and New-Hampshire, informing them that we are contemplating upon, and are determined to take effectual measures for that purpose; and for the more effectual security of the New England colonies and the continent, to request them to co-operate with us, by furnishing their respective quotas for general defence.

Resolved, That there be sent two delegates to each New England colony with the above resolve.

Resolved, That the Congress choose in the first place delegates to repair to Connecticut : accordingly chose Col. Foster and Mr. Bliss.

Resolved, That they choose in the second place delegates to repair to Rhode Island : accordingly chose Col. Timothy Walker and Doct. Perkins.

Resolved, That in the third place the Congress choose delegates to repair to New Hampshire : accordingly chose Mr. Freeman and Capt. Osgood.

Ordered, That Mr. Gerry, Mr. Adams and Capt. Osgood draught a letter to each of the colonies, viz. : Connecticut, Rhode Island and New Hampshire.

Resolved, That the committee on the state of the province take into consideration what number of men, in their opinion, will be necessary to be raised by the four New England governments for their general defence, and report.

Adjourned to Monday next, nine o'clock in the forenoon.

Monday, April 10, 1775, A. M.

The committee appointed to draught a letter to the colonies of Connecticut, Rhode Island and New Hampshire, reported ; the report [was] read and accepted, and is as follows :

In Provincial Congress, *Concord*, April 10, ||ᵃ1775.||

Sir, or Gentlemen :—In consideration of the measures that have been taken by the British administration, to subjugate the North American colonies ; the rapidity with which their plans have been hitherto executed ; the late very alarming intelligence from Great Britain ; the false and inflammatory accounts that have been laid before our sovereign and his parliament, to induce them to consider this colony as in a state of rebellion, and our sister colonies as countenancing us therein, and the violent measures that are ordered, in consequence thereof, together with the daily and hourly preparations there are making by the troops under the command of general Gage, in Boston ; this Congress have come to a full conclusion, that very little, if any expectation of the redress of our common and intolerable grievances is to be had from the humble and dutiful petition and other wise measures of the late honorable Continental Congress ; and therefore have come into certain resolutions to be communicated to you by delegates, appointed for that purpose, in which they are earnestly desirous of the concurrence of your colony.

Wishing that the American colonies may, at this important crisis, be under the direction of Heaven, I am, in the name and by order of the Congress, [&c.]

Ordered, That the foregoing be signed by the president, in the name and behalf of this Congress.

Ordered, That the committee on the state of the province take into consideration, and report, what number of men, in their opinion, will be necessary for the army [ªproposed] to be raised.

Resolved, That there be ||ᵇan addition of three|| to the delegates appointed to repair to the neighboring governments, and that this Congress ||ᶜcome to the choice of them|| at three o'clock this afternoon, by ballot.

Adjourned to three o'clock this afternoon.

Afternoon.

The order of the day [was] moved for.

Ordered, That Major Fuller, Capt. Greenleaf and Mr. Ellis, be a committee to count and sort the votes for the gentlemen to be added to the delegates appointed to repair to Connecticut, Rhode Island and New Hampshire, and that they bring in their votes for a gentleman to repair to Connecticut.

Having ||counted and|| sorted the votes, [the committee] reported that the Hon. Timothy Danielson, Esq. was chosen.

Ordered, That votes be brought in for a gentleman to be added to the delegates appointed to repair to Rhode Island.

After counting and sorting the votes, [the committee] reported that the Hon. James Warren, Esq. was chosen.

Ordered, That votes be brought in for a gentleman to be added to the delegates appointed to repair to New Hampshire.

After counting and sorting the votes, [the committee] reported that Mr. Elbridge Gerry was chosen.

Ordered, That the committee on the state of the province be directed to draught such instructions as they shall think necessary to be given to the delegates appointed to repair to the neighboring governments, and report.

The committee on the state of the province reported a resolve, relative to exercising the minute men in battalions, and that they be paid

a [prepared.]   b ||three added.|| c ||choose them.||

out of the public treasury, &c. : *Ordered*, that the consideration of this report be deferred till to-morrow morning, ten o'clock.

||Congress|| adjourned till to-morrow morning, nine o'clock.

TUESDAY, April 11, 1775, A. M.

The committee on the state of the province reported instructions to the delegates appointed to repair to Connecticut, &c.; [which report was] read and accepted, and *Ordered*, that it be signed by the president, and is as follows :

IN PROVINCIAL CONGRESS, *Concord*, April 11, 1775.

GENTLEMEN :—The thorough knowledge you have of our public affairs, and the distressed circumstances of this devoted province, makes it unnecessary to be particular in any instructions with regard to the important trust committed to your care.

We would, notwithstanding, in general, give you some hints, which may serve to cement and continue that union which has so happily taken place in this continent. In order to effect these desirable ends, [we instruct you] that, ||as|| soon as may be, you repair to Connecticut, and endeavor to obtain such an early conference with the governor and company of that colony as the pressing exigencies of our affairs may demand : and as an immediate exertion of our united efforts to recover and maintain those invaluable blessings of liberty, which are, in part, wrested from us by the hands of arbitrary power, and of which we have no other prospect of a restoration, under God, but by the firm and unshaken resolutions and conduct of America; and as ministerial vengeance appears to be levelled at the north east colonies in particular, it is of the utmost importance, that immediate measures, such as are consonant with the union of all the colonies, be pursued for their mutual defence; and that you would endeavor to obtain an explicit and full answer, so that we may unitedly exert our strength in the common cause for the salvation of our country; and to this end we would recommend your continuance there until this important purpose may be effected, which we presume will be as soon as circumstances will admit; you will, however, govern yourselves with respect to time and conferences, as to you, in your wisdom, shall seem meet; and may God bless your endeavors for the common good.

Ordered, That the letter to New Hampshire be directed to the Hon. John Wentworth, Esq.

A letter from Mr. Barber [was] read ; thereupon *Ordered*, that it be committed to Doct. Holten, Mr. Sargeant and Col. Pomeroy, to consider thereof and report. The committee thereon reported verbally, that Col. Thompson be desired immediately to repair to Brunswick, Casco Bay, Woolwich, Georgetown, and other places, and take the most effectual measures to acquaint the people that one Mr. Perry is in the eastern part of the country, endeavoring to supply our enemies with masts, spars and timber, and to make use of all proper and effectual measures to prevent their aiding him in procuring said articles.

Moved, That the propriety of this Congress advising the inhabitants of the town of Boston to be moved from thence, be now taken into consideration. After a long debate thereon, *Resolved*, that a committee be appointed to take into consideration the particular state of the town of Boston, and report. Accordingly, Mr. Sargent, Mr. Murray, Col. Henshaw, Capt. Stone, Mr. Cross, Major Fuller of Middleton, Doct. Taylor and Col. Prescott were chosen.

Ordered, That [Mr.] Murray be joined to the committee on the state of the province.

Adjourned till ten o'clock to-morrow morning.

WEDNESDAY, April 12, 1775, A. M.

The committee on the state of the province reported a resolve, relative to appointing county committees to receive returns from the committees of correspondence, of the state of their towns, &c., [which was] read and accepted, and is as follows:

IN PROVINCIAL CONGRESS, *Concord*, April 12, 1775.

Whereas, the preservation of our county from slavery depends, under God, on an effectual execution of the continental and provincial measures for that purpose:

Resolved, That there be now appointed for each county in this colony, a committee, consisting of five persons, any three of whom to be a quorum, whose business it shall be to receive from the committees of correspondence in their respective towns, a state of the conduct of the towns and districts with respect to their having executed the continental and provincial plans, as aforesaid; and it shall be the duty of said committees to meet on the first Wednesdays of May, July, September, November, January and March, and prepare a report of the same, to be laid before the Congress at its then next session, that any neglect of such towns and districts in executing such plans may be speedily and effectually remedied.

Also, *Resolved*, That it be, and it hereby is strongly recommended to the committees of correspondence in the several towns and districts in this colony, sometime before the first Wednesdays in May, July, September, November, January and March aforesaid, to render to any one of the members of their county aforesaid, a true state of the conduct of their respective towns and districts, with respect to their having used each plan, recommended by the Continental and Provincial Congresses, and to use their utmost diligence for this important purpose.

And, whereas, some towns and districts in this colony may be destitute of so excellent an institution as committees of correspondence:

Resolved, That it be and it hereby is strongly recommended to such towns and districts forthwith to choose the committees of correspondence, and to afford them assistance, at all times, in effectually suppressing the efforts of the enemies of America whenever they shall make them.

||ᵃAlso,|| *Resolved,* That the county committees are hereby required to render their account quarterly, to this Congress, that they may receive an order therefor on the public treasury of the colony.

Resolved, That at three o'clock this afternoon the Congress will come to the choice of the county committees.

Resolved, That the members from each county be together, and agree on gentlemen to constitute their county committee.

The Congress renewed the consideration of the report of the committee on the state of the province, relative to exercising the minute men in battalions, and paying them for the time they spend in that service. After a long debate the question was put, whether the report be accepted; it passed in the negative.

Adjourned to three o'clock this afternoon.

Afternoon.

The order of the day [was] moved for.

The county of Suffolk having nominated, the Congress chose Mr. John Pitts, Mr. Nathaniel ||ᵇBailey,|| Col. Aaron Davis, Mr. Moses Bullen and Mr. Abner Ellis.

Essex.—Joseph Gerrish, Esq., Col. Michael Farley, Major Samuel Holten, Capt. Samuel Osgood, Capt. Josiah Batchelder.

Middlesex.—James Prescot, Esq., Major Eleazer Brooks, Mr. Richard Devens, Col. Simeon Spaulding, Capt. Jonathan Brown.

Worcester.—Col. Jedediah Foster, Esq., Capt. Timothy Bigelow, Mr. Edward Rawson, Capt. Samuel Brooks, Col. Jonathan Grout.

a ||It is further.|| b ||Baylies.||

BRISTOL.—Doct. David Cobb, Benjamin ||ᵃAikin,|| Esq., Doct. William Baylies, Capt. William Holmes, Capt. Thomas Carpenter.

BARNSTABLE.—Daniel Davis, Esq., Capt. Stephen Nye, Mr. Moses Swift, Mr. Benjamin Freeman and Mr. Naaman Holbrook.

BERKSHIRE.—Mr. Samuel Brown, Mark Hopkins, Esq., Capt. Charles Goodridge, Major Jonathan Smith, Capt. Caleb Hyde.

PLYMOUTH.—Hon. James Warren, Esq., Col. Edward Mitchel, Capt. Joshua White, Doct. Jeremiah Hall, Mr. Ebenezer White.

LINCOLN.—James Howard, Esq., Mr. Timothy Langdon, Mr. Dummer Sewall, Mr. [Samuel] Cobb, Mr. Joseph Waldo.

NANTUCKET.—Josiah Coffin, Esq., Grafton Gardner, Esq., Mr. Josiah Barker, Timothy Folger, Esq., Mr. Stephen Hussey.

DUKES COUNTY.—Joseph Mayhew, Esq., John Summer, Esq., Col. Beriah Norton, Shubael Cottle, Esq., Mr. Ranford Smith.

CUMBERLAND.—Solomon Lombard, Esq., Mr. Samuel Freeman, Mr. John Lewis, Col. Samuel Thompson, Mr. Timothy McDaniel.

YORK.—Charles Chauncy, Esq., Capt. Daniel Bragdon, Mr. Ebenezer Sawyer, James Sullivan, Esq., Major Ichabod Goodwin.

HAMPSHIRE.—Major [Joseph] Hawley, Col. Timothy Danielson, Mr. Noah ||ᵇGoodman,|| Col. Elisha Porter, Col. John Mosley.

Resolved, That the resolve recommending the aforesaid committees, be printed in hand bills, and sent to all the towns and districts.

Ordered, That Mr. Devens, Capt. Rawson and Col. Davis, be a committee to ||ᶜdisperse|| the hand bills. *Ordered*, that the committee be enjoined to sit and ||ᵈperfect this.||

An application from the plantation of New Providence [was] read; committed to Col. Dwight, Capt. Goodridge, Col. Pomeroy, Col. Paterson and Mr. Crane.

Adjourned till nine o'clock to-morrow morning.

THURSDAY, April 13, 1775, [A. M.]

Ordered, That the last resolve in the report, which was last night ordered to be published, be not printed.

The committee on the state of the province reported a resolve, [for] engaging six companies of the train, and keeping them constantly in exercise, and paying them, &c., [which was] read, considered and accepted, and is as follows:

IN PROVINCIAL CONGRESS, *Concord*, April 13, 1775.

Resolved, That the committee of safety be directed to engage a

a ||Atkin.|| b ||Goodwin.|| c ||distribute.|| d ||complete the business.||

suitable number of persons, and form six companies of the train for the artillery already provided by this colony, to immediately enter on discipline, and constantly be in readiness to enter the service of the colony, when an army shall be raised; and that the committee be, and they are hereby empowered, to draw on the public treasury for paying said companies a suitable consideration for their services.

The committee appointed to take into consideration the propriety of removing the inhabitants from the town of Boston, reported.

The consideration thereof [was] deferred till three o'clock this afternoon.

Afternoon.

The Congress resumed the consideration of the report deferred; after a long debate thereon, *Ordered*, that it be recommitted.||ᵃ||

FRIDAY, April 14, 1775, A. M.

The committee appointed to take into consideration the petition from the plantation called New Providence, reported: the report was read and accepted, and is as followeth:

IN PROVINCIAL CONGRESS, April 14, 1775.

Resolved, That Major Joseph Bennet, be advised to pay Henry Gardner, Esq. the full sum assessed on the plantation of New Providence for the year 1774, taking a proper and suitable receipt of said Henry Gardner, for the collector appointed by the town of Lanesborough to collect said sum, and that said collector be advised to discharge the several persons' proportion of said tax, in said plantation, and collect the same.

Per order of committee: SIMEON DWIGHT, *Chairman*.

The [report of the] committee appointed to take into consideration the removal of the inhabitants of the town of Boston, was ||ᵇread and accepted,|| and is as follows:

IN PROVINCIAL CONGRESS, *Concord*, April 14, 1775.

Whereas, the late accounts of the hostile intentions of the British parliament towards this colony, have so greatly agitated the minds and raised the fears of many good people in the town of Boston, as to induce many of those, who are able, to remove with their effects into the country; which in the opinion of this Congress is a prudent step; and as there is no prospect of the repeal of the cruel port bill, where-

a ||Adjourned to nine o'clock to-morrow morning.|| b ||reported, which report was accepted.||

by many poor, industrious persons, if continued in that place, must be still great sufferers, notwithstanding the generous donations; and as the season of the year is now approaching, in which they may be, in some measure, serviceable to themselves and families in such parts of the country as can find them employment in their several occupations:

It is therefore recommended to the committee of donations, that they afford to such poor persons, who are anxious to remove themselves and families into the country, such assistance as may enable them to do it.

Voted, That the members of the town of Boston be desired to communicate this recommendation, with the schedule, to the committee of donations.

The committee on the state of the province reported a resolve, relative to appointing a committee to apply to a suitable number of persons to be in readiness to enter the service of this colony, as officers, when an army shall be raised.

Ordered, That the consideration thereof be referred to three o'clock, P. M.

Ordered, That at four o'clock, P: M. the Congress will come to the choice, by ballot, of a person to serve on the committee of safety, instead of Doct. Fisher, who was excused.

||The Congress|| adjourned to three o'clock, P. M.

Afternoon.

The Congress resumed the consideration of the report referred, agreeable to the order of the day: after some debate thereon, it passed, and is as follows:

In Provincial Congress, *Concord*, April 14, 1775.

Resolved, That a committee be now appointed to apply to a suitable number of persons, to be in readiness to enter the service of this colony, to act as field officers: such field officers, in conjunction with the committee, to apply to proper persons as captains, and they to determine on such subaltern officers, as may be necessary for each regiment, when an army shall be raised; the committee and officers *cæteris paribus*, to give the preference to persons who have been chosen officers in the regiments of minute men.

Ordered, That the committee of safety be the committee to apply to a suitable number of persons to act as officers, as recommended in the foregoing resolve.

Ordered, That the Congress now proceed to the choice of a gentleman to serve on the committee of safety in the place of Mr. Fisher.

Ordered, That Mr. Cushing, Col. Palmer, and Mr. Bigelow, be a committee to count and sort the votes : [which committee] reported, that Col. Thomas Gardner was chosen.

Ordered, That the committee on the state of the province take the late newspapers from England into consideration, and report what there is relating to this province.

Ordered, That the Rev. Mr. Murray, Mr. Mayhew, and Col. Pomeroy, be a committee to bring in a resolve recommending a day of fasting and prayer.

Congress adjourned to ten o'clock to-morrow morning.

SATURDAY, April 15, 1775, A. M.

The committee appointed to bring in a resolve recommending a day of fasting and prayer, reported, [which report was] amended and accepted, and is as follows :

Whereas, it hath pleased the Righteous Sovereign of the universe, in just indignation against the sins of a people long blessed with inestimable privileges, civil and religious, to suffer the plots of wicked men, on both sides of the Atlantic, who, for many years, have incessantly labored to sap the foundation of our public liberties, so far to succeed, that we see the New England colonies reduced to the ungrateful alternative of a tame submission to a state of absolute vassalage to the will of a despotic minister, or of preparing themselves speedily to defend, at the hazard of ||ᵃlife,|| the unalienable rights of themselves and posterity against the avowed hostilities of their parent state, who openly threaten to wrest them from their hands, by fire and sword ;

In circumstances dark as these, it becomes us, as men and christians, to reflect, that whilst every prudent measure should be taken to ward off the impending judgments, or prepare to act a proper part under them when they come; at the same time, all confidence must be withheld from the means we use, and reposed only on that God, who rules in the armies of heaven, and without whose blessing, the best human councils are but foolishness, and all created power vanity.

It is the happiness of ||ᵇhis|| church, that when the powers of earth and hell combine against it, and those who should be nursing fathers become its persecutors, then the throne of grace is of the easiest access, and its appeal thither is graciously invited by that Father of mercies, who has assured it that when his children ask bread he will not give them a stone :

Therefore, in compliance with the laudable practice of the people of

a ||their lives.|| b ||this.||

God in all ages, with the humble regard to the steps of Divine Providence towards this oppressed, threatened, and endangered people, and especially in obedience to the command of Heaven, that ||ᵃbids|| us to call on him in the day of trouble.

Resolved, That it be, and hereby is, recommended to the good people of this colony, of all denominations, that Thursday, the eleventh day of May next, be set apart as a day of public humiliation, fasting, and prayer; that a total abstinence from servile labor and recreation be observed, and all the religious assemblies solemnly convened, to humble themselves before God, under the heavy judgments felt and feared, to confess the sins that have deserved them; to implore the forgiveness of all our transgressions, a spirit of repentance and reformation, and a blessing on the husbandry, manufactures, and other lawful employments of this people; and especially, that the union of the American colonies in defence of their rights, for which, hitherto, we desire to thank Almighty God, may be preserved and confirmed; that the Provincial, and especially the Continental Congress, may be directed to such measures as God will countenance: that the people of Great Britain and their rulers may have their eyes open to discern the things that shall make for the peace of the nation and all its connections: and that America may soon behold a gracious interposition of Heaven, for the redress of her many grievances, the restoration of all her invaded liberties, and their security to the latest generations.

Ordered, That ||ᵇit|| be copied, authenticated, and sent to all the religious assemblies in this colony.

Ordered, That Mr. Devens, Mr. Cheever, and Mr. Stephen Hall, be a committee to get the resolves printed and dispersed.

Adjourned to three o'clock [in the afternoon.]

Afternoon.

In Provincial Congress, *Concord*, April 15, 1775.

Resolved, That Henry Gardner, Esq., receiver general of the province of the Massachusetts Bay, be, and hereby is, directed to pay to Messrs. Edes and Gill, printers, the sum of thirty-six pounds, six shillings, and ninepence, lawful money, for printing for said province, to the twenty-seventh of March last.

In Provincial Congress, *Concord*, April 15, 1775.

Resolved, That Henry Gardner, Esq., receiver general of the province of the Massachusetts Bay, be, and is hereby directed, to pay to Richard Devens, the sum of eleven pounds, nineteen shillings, and six-

a ||binds.|| b ||the foregoing.||

pence half penny, for sundry accounts by him paid and discharged for services done for the said province.

IN PROVINCIAL CONGRESS, *Concord*, April 15, 1775.

Resolved, That Henry Gardner, Esq., receiver general of the province of the Massachusetts Bay, be, and hereby is, directed, to pay unto Jeremiah Hunt, the sum of four pounds, four shillings, for his attendance as doorkeeper, for paper and quills, ||ᵃfor|| the Congress.

Ordered, That Henry Gardner, Esq., Col. Barrett, and Col. Henshaw, be a committee to wait on the Rev. Mr. Emerson, and return him the thanks of this Congress for his faithful attendance on and ||ᵇ|| officiating as their chaplain during this session.

Ordered, That the same committee be directed to wait on the committee of the proprietors of this house, and return them the thanks of this Congress for the use thereof.

Ordered, That, on the return of the members to their respective towns, they use their interest with the inhabitants thereof, that they immediately pay their public moneys to Henry Gardner, Esq., receiver general of this colony.

Ordered, That the members use their interest to promote the military discipline.

Resolve for adjournment passed, and is as follows:

Resolved, That this Congress be adjourned from this day, to Wednesday, the tenth day of May next, at ten o'clock in the forenoon, to meet at Concord, in the county of Middlesex; and, considering the great uncertainty of the present times, and that important unforeseen events may take place, from whence it may be absolutely necessary that this Congress should meet sooner than the day abovesaid, notwithstanding the adjournment aforesaid;

It is farther *Resolved*, That the members of this Congress for the towns of Charlestown, Cambridge, Brookline, Roxbury, and Dorchester, or the majority of them, be, and they are hereby authorized, in case they should judge it necessary, to give notice to the several members of this Congress, in such way as they shall think proper, to meet at Concord aforesaid, at any earlier day than the abovesaid tenth day of May, which shall be by them appointed; and it is further recommended to the members of this Congress, that they conform themselves to such notice.

Ordered, That the thanks of this Congress be ||ᶜgiven to the presi-

---

a ||by him furnished for the use of.|| b ||especially for.||

c ||presented to the Hon. John Hancock, Esq.||

dent|| for his constant attendance ||on|| and faithful discharge of his duty as president during the several sessions hereof.

The business being finished, the president declared the Congress adjourned according ||*to the resolve.||

CONCORD, [SATURDAY,] April 22, 1775.[1]

Mr. Richard Devens ||was chosen|| chairman, [and] Mr. John Murray clerk.

Mr. Gerry represented to Congress, that a letter from Mr. Quincy to Mr. Adams,[2] had been delivered to him, with a desire that it might be opened by Congress in Mr. Adams's absence: after some debate, *Ordered*, That the members present belonging to the committee on the state of the province retire, open, and peruse the said letter, and report to Congress what parts they think proper: the committee returned, and desired that the whole be read in Congress; which being done, *Ordered*, That the same be sent to Doct. Warren, to be used at his discretion.

Adjourned to Watertown, at 4 o'clock, P. M.

WATERTOWN, [April 22,] 1775, 4 o'clock, P. M.

Congress met according to adjournment.

Ordered, That Mr. Watson notify the committee of safety,[3] of the time and place of our adjournment, and request their attendance, with whatever plans they may have in readiness for us, and also notify the

---

a ||until Wednesday, the tenth day of May next, conformably to the preceding resolve.||

(1) Two days only elapsed after the Provincial Congress had adjourned, and the members, returning to their respective homes, were widely separated, before apprehensions of immediate danger arose, and, on the 18th of April, grew so intense, that the committee constituted from Charlestown, Cambridge, Brookline, Roxbury, and Dorchester, met, and issued the following summons to recall each delegate:

"Sir: Having received certain intelligence of the sailing of a number of troops to reenforce the army under general Gage; this, with the industrious preparations making in Boston for a speedy march into the country, impresses us with the absolute necessity of convening the Provincial Congress at Concord, as soon as may be, agreeably to a vote of Congress, at the last session. You are therefore requested immediately to repair to Concord, as the closest deliberation, and the collected wisdom of the people, at this alarming crisis, are indispensably necessary for the salvation of the country."   RICHARD DEVENS, per order.

The notice, although circulated with the utmost speed of express messengers, could not have reached many of the members before the march of the British troops to Concord had roused the land to arms.

The adjournment of Congress from Concord to Watertown, was undoubtedly made, from the great necessity, that the body holding the executive and legislative powers of government, should be near to the army of the people, already in the field.

(2) The letter of Mr. Quincy has not been recovered, nor does any paper on the files of the Congress indicate its contents.

(3) The committee of safety had been in constant session during the preceding day and night in Cambridge.

absent members that are at Cambridge, and request their punctual attendance.

Ordered, That Mr. Sullivan, Col. Cushing, and Mr. Crane, be a committee to wait on the selectmen, for liberty ||of the use|| of the meeting-house during the session of Congress here : they returned, and reported that the selectmen readily granted their request.

Ordered, That Mr. Gerry, Col. Cushing, Col. Barrett, Capt. Stone, Doct. Taylor, Mr. Sullivan, Mr. Freeman, Mr. Watson, and Esquire Dix, be a committee to take depositions, *in perpetuam,* from which a full account of the transactions of the troops, under general Gage, in their route to and from Concord, &c., on Wednesday last, may be collected, to be sent to England, by the first ship from Salem.

Adjourned to this place, to-morrow, at 7 o'clock, A. M.

[SUNDAY,] April 23, 1775, [A. M.]

Congress met ||ªaccording|| to adjournment, and adjourned to the school-house.

Upon a letter from Gen. Ward[1] respecting the New Hampshire troops, *Resolved,* unanimously, that it is necessary for the defence of the colony, that an army of 30,000 men be immediately raised and established.

Resolved, That 13,600 men be raised immediately by this province.

Resolved, That the committee of safety be a committee to bring in a plan for the establishment of the officers and soldiers necessary for the army to be ||ᵇimmediately raised,|| and [that they] sit immediately.

Voted, That Col. Cushing, Mr. Sullivan, Col. Whitcomb, and Mr. Durant, be added to the committee of safety.

a ||conformably.|| b ||raised at this time.||

(1) This letter of Gen. Ward, which is lost, probably related to a communication from Col. Greenleaf, dated at Newburyport, April 21, stating, that "we have sent forward the bearer to have your orders, with all possible despatch, by his return, whether the forces that are coming from the province of New Hampshire and from the eastern parts of our province should be sent back, especially those that live near the sea shore. We are well informed that numbers passed our river yesterday at the upper ferry : besides, four companies went through this town on their way to you. We have a party of men from this town, upwards of one hundred upon their march to you : if they are not wanted, and you think proper, you can order our express to turn them back. We sent off last evening two field pieces to you : if not wanted, they may be of some use here."

A letter from Gen. Ward, of the date mentioned in the text, is preserved ; it states ; " My situation is such that, if I have not enlisting orders immediately, I shall be left all alone : it is impossible to keep the men here, excepting something be done :" and implores immediate action on the measures necessary for the organization of an army.

The committee of safety write thus to the Provincial Congress of New Hampshire : " Our friends from New Hampshire having shown their readiness to assist us in this day of distress, we therefore thought it best to give orders for enlisting such as were present in the service of this colony, as many desired something may be done to hold them together, until the resolve of your Congress is known, when we are ready and desirous that they should be discharged from us and put under such command as you shall direct."

Resolved, That Mr. Sullivan be a committee to wait on the New Hampshire Congress, at Exeter, to inform them of our resolutions, and request their concurrence, [and that] Major Bliss [go] to Connecticut, and Deacon Rawson to Rhode Island, for the same purpose.

Ordered, That Mr. Sullivan be a committee to inform the committee from the Congress of New Hampshire, now waiting, of our resolutions immediately.

Resolved, That Mr. Murray, Mr. Gill, and Capt. Stone, be a committee to draught a letter to each of the colonels, to be sent by ||ᵃthe expresses.||

Adjourned to this place, at two o'clock, P. M.

[Afternoon]

Two o'clock. Congress met according to adjournment, and adjourned to the meeting-house.

Being there met, the committee appointed to draught a letter [to the colonels, reported; the report was read,] which was accepted, and ordered to be copied by Capt. Stone.

Mr. Gerry read in his place a letter from Marblehead, reporting that [the British man of war Lively was lying off the harbor of that town; representing, that their means of defence were inadequate to repel attack; and asking direction and aid:] upon which, *Resolved,* that the matter subside till further information.

Doct. Warren read a letter from the committee of correspondence of Connecticut;[1] *Ordered,* that Mr. Gerry, Mr. Gill, and Doct. Taylor, be a committee to draught an answer, and report immediately.

Ordered, That Col. Orne, Major Fuller [of Newton,] and Major Fuller [of Middleton,] be a committee to count and sort votes for a president pro tempore.

The committee reported, that the vote was full for Doct. Warren. Col. Palmer was chosen secretary pro tempore.

||ᵇThe report of the committee|| for an establishment for the army, ||ᶜwas read.||

a ||express.|| b ||the committee reported a resolve.||

c ||which being read was referred for further consideration.||

(1) They wrote thus : "Every preparation is making to support your province. We have many reports of what is doing with you: the particulars we cannot yet get with precision: the ardor of our people is such that they cannot be kept back. The colonels are to forward a part of the best men and most ready, as fast as possible : the remainder to be ready at a moment's warning." The principal object of the letter, which was sent from Lebanon, and subscribed by William Williams, Nathaniel Wales, Jun., and Joseph Trumbull, was, to request correct information of the movements of the British troops, and of the condition of the colony of Massachusetts, "that we may know how to concert the measures proper for us to take." The answer contained a narrative of the expedition to Concord.

A report was made of a draught of an answer to the committee of Connecticut, which, after amendment, was accepted.

Voted, That a committee be appointed to draw up a narrative of the massacre on Wednesday last.

[*Ordered*, That] Doct. Church, Mr. Gerry, Mr. Cushing, be that committee.

Adjourned to eight o'clock to-morrow morning, [to meet] in this place.

WATERTOWN, [MONDAY,] April 24, 1775, A. M.

Met according to adjournment.

Rev. Mr. Murray [was] appointed president pro tempore, and Ichabod Goodwin secretary pro tempore: Jonas Dix, Esq., was appointed monitor.

Ordered, That Mr. Gerry give the express going to the press, his orders for the enlisting papers.

Ordered, That the enlisting paper going to the press, shall be authenticated by the secretary pro tempore.

Resolved, That six hundred of these papers be printed, and that the ||ªexpress|| wait for two hundred of them.

Resolved, That the committee of safety, or committee of supplies, be empowered to impress horses or teams, and direct the owners of them to send their accounts to the committee of supplies: also to empower other persons to impress on special occasions.

Resolved, That the [resolves for the] establishment of the army be printed in handbills, and that a copy of them be sent by the express who is going for the enlisting papers, and that three hundred of them be printed immediately.

Moved, That a member from each county be appointed to attend the committee of safety, and let them know the names of the officers in said counties belonging to the minute men, and such as are most suitable for officers in the army now raising.

Ordered, That [the following gentlemen be the committee:] Col. Lincoln, for the county of Suffolk: Major Fuller, for Essex: Col. Prescot, for Middlesex: Col. Pomeroy, for Hampshire: Nathan Cushing, Esq., for Plymouth: Daniel Davis, Esq., for Barnstable: Col. Dagget, for Bristol: Ichabod Goodwin, Esq., for York: Joseph Mayhew, Esq., for Dukes County: Major Bigelow, for Worcester: Mr. Samuel Freeman, for Cumberland: Rev. Mr. John Murray, for Lincoln: Col. John Patterson, for Berkshire, and [Stephen] Hussey, Esq., for Nantucket.

a ||Congress.||

Ordered, That each of these members attend the service according to their appointment, or write to the committee.

Ordered, That Major Fuller of Middletown, give a list of the names of these members to the committee of safety.

Resolved, That when this Congress do adjourn, that they adjourn to three o'clock this afternoon, and the members are enjoined to attend punctually at that time.

Adjourned accordingly to three o'clock.

Afternoon, April 24, 1775.

Letters from Hartford,[1] directed to the president of this Congress, laid on the table, were ordered to be read, and, after reading, were ordered to be immediately forwarded to the committee of safety, then sitting at Cambridge.

Moved, That a committee be now appointed to examine the records and report such matters contained therein, as may be made public, and such as shall remain secret at present.

Ordered, That Major Brooks, Deacon Fisher, and Mr. Freeman, be a committee for that purpose.

||Then the|| Congress adjourned till eight o'clock next morning, at this place.

||Tuesday, April 25, 1775.||

Eight o'clock, A. M. According to adjournment [the Congress] then met.

Ordered, That the treasurer be inquired of ||by this Congress|| respecting the state of the treasury.

Answered by said treasurer in a general way, that, for the year 1773, it was supposed that about £20,000 was due, and that he had received about £5,000.

Moved, That a committee be appointed to bring in a resolve, how we may ||ªget the knowledge|| of the towns and districts, who are delinquent; ||but|| passed in the negative.

Moved, for a reconsideration, and passed negatively.

The committee appointed to bring in a report of what they thought might be made public of the resolves, reported, that nothing relative to our proceeding with the indian nations be known, and that other matters be left at discretion with each member.

Moved, That this matter subside for the present.

a ||ascertain the number.||

(1) These letters, repeating the assurances given by the committee of correspondence, of the readiness of the men of Connecticut to support their brethren of Massachusetts, and desired the direction of Congress, as to the number of troops to be sent to Cambridge.

Leave of absence is granted [to Jerathmiel] Bowers, Esq., to return home.

||Then|| adjourned to three o'clock, afternoon.

[Afternoon.]

Three o'clock.   According to adjournment met.

The letter from Haverhill[1] committed.

Ordered, That Mr. Gill, Col. Gerrish, and Major Fuller of Middleton, be a committee for that purpose, and to sit forthwith.

Moved, by the committee of safety, for two gentlemen as engineers, and an establishment for them.

Ordered, That Mr. Gill, [Jonas] Dix, Esq., and Henry Gardner, Esq., be a committee for that purpose to bring in a resolve.

Ordered, That a resolve should be ||ᵃbrought in|| by the committee of safety to reduce the regiments.

Moved, That the companies in each regiment be reduced from one hundred men each to fifty-nine, including three officers; one captain, two subalterns; and passed unanimously in the affirmative.

Moved, That each regiment be reduced to ten of these companies, and passed in the affirmative.

Ordered, That Col. Orne, Col. Palmer and [Henry] Gardner, Esq., be a committee for regulating the regiments of the army, and to sit forthwith.

A letter from Salem [was] read, setting forth the expediency [that] the depositions we are now taking be forwarded as fast as possible; the same [was] ordered to be sent to the committee, for that purpose, at Lexington, immediately.

Ordered, That the memorial from Marblehead,[2] with the debate thereon, subside for the present.

||Then|| adjourned till eight o'clock next day.

a ||submitted.||

(1) The answer prepared by the committee, addressed to the town clerk of Haverhill, will explain the contents of the letter received by the Congress.

" Sir: The Congress have this day received a letter from Nathaniel Peaslee Sargeant, Esq., and Jonathan Webster, Esq., acquainting them that the late dreadful fire in Haverhill, together with some public disturbances in said town, make it necessary that they should be at home at this time. The Congress apprehend that the important business of the colonies requires that every town should be now represented; and therefore desire that if neither of those gentlemen can attend, others should be elected in their room, that the wisdom of the whole colony may be collected at our hour of need."

(2) Many memorials, of similar purport, were presented to the Congress from the maritime towns, representing that the long line of sea coast was without adequate defence; that armed vessels were hovering about the ports, ready to turn their cannon upon the villages of the shore; that the people were exhausted by strenuous exertions in the common cause; and praying for reenforcements of men, and supplies of arms and ammunition.

WEDNESDAY, April 26, 8 o'clock, A. M.

Then met according to adjournment.

Ordered, That Mr. President, Doct. Taylor, Mr. Freeman, [Henry] Gardner, Esq. and Col. Stone, be a committee to draught a letter to our agent in Great Britain.

||*Resolved,*|| That William Burbeck be, and he is hereby appointed an engineer of the forces now raising in this colony for the defence of the rights and liberties of the American continent, and that there be paid to the said William Burbeck, out of the public treasury of this colony, during his continuance in that service, at the rate of one hundred and fifty pounds, lawful money, per annum. And it is further *Resolved,* that from and after the time when the said forces shall be disbanded, during the life of the said Burbeck, there be paid to him out of said treasury, the sum of ninety-seven pounds six shillings and eight pence, lawful money, annually.

Ordered, That Col. Gerrish, Deacon Fisher, Col. Orne, Mr. Batchelder and Capt. Brown, be a committee to take into consideration the letter laid on the table by the committee of safety from James Sullivan,[1] Esq., and the committee to sit forthwith.

Ordered, That the letter drawn by the committee, to send to Doct. Franklin, as agent, be copied, and authenticated by the president pro tempore. [The letter is as follows:]

[IN PROVINCIAL CONGRESS, *Watertown*, April 26, 1775.]

[*To the Hon. Benjamin Franklin, Esq., at London.*]

[SIR:—From the entire confidence we repose in your faithfulness and abilities, we consider it the happiness of this colony, that the important trust of agency for it, in this day of unequalled distress, is devolved on your hands, and we doubt not, your attachment to the cause and liberties of mankind, will make every possible exertion in our behalf a pleasure to you; although our circumstances will compel us often to interrupt your repose, by matters that will surely give you pain. A singular instance hereof, is the occasion of the present letter. The contents of this packet will be our apology for troubling you with it. From these, you will see, how and by whom we are at last plunged into the horrors of a most unnatural war.]

[Our enemies, we are told, have despatched to Great Britain a falla-

a ||Ordered.||

(1) One letter of Mr. Sullivan was written to ask immediate attention to the relief of the eastern towns, the subject of a subsequent resolve.

cious account of the tragedy they have begun; to prevent the operation of which to the public injury, we have engaged the vessel that conveys this to you, as a packet in the service of this colony; and we request your assistance in supplying Capt. Derby, who commands her, with such necessaries as he shall want, on the credit of your constituents in Massachusetts Bay.]

[But we most ardently wish, that the several papers herewith enclosed, may be immediately printed, and dispersed through every town in England, and especially communicated to the lord mayor, aldermen and council of the city of London, that they may take such order thereon as they may think proper; and we are confident your fidelity will make such improvement of them as shall convince all, who are not determined to be in everlasting blindness, that it is the united efforts of both Englands that can save either. But that whatever price our brethren in the one, may be pleased to put on their constitutional liberties, we are authorized to assure you, that the inhabitants of the other, with the greatest unanimity, are inflexibly resolved to sell theirs only at the price of their lives.]

[The following address to the people of Great Britain, reported by a committee, was adopted.]

[In Provincial Congress, *Watertown*, April 26, 1775.]

[To the Inhabitants of Great Britain.]

[Friends and Fellow Subjects :—Hostilities are at length commenced in this colony by the troops under the command of general Gage, and it being of the greatest importance, that an early, true and authentic account of this inhuman proceeding should be known to you, the Congress of this colony have transmitted the same, and from want of a session of the honorable Continental Congress, think it proper to address you on this alarming occasion.]

[By the clearest depositions relative to this transaction, it will appear, that on the night preceding the nineteenth of April instant, a body of the king's troops, under the command of Col. Smith, were secretly landed at Cambridge, with an apparent design to take or destroy the military and other stores provided for the defence of this colony and deposited at Concord : that some inhabitants of the colony, on the night aforesaid, whilst travelling peaceably on the road between Boston and Concord, were seized and greatly abused by armed men, who appeared to be officers of general Gage's army : that the town of

Lexington, by these means, was alarmed, and a company of the inhabitants mustered on the occasion : that the regular troops, on their way to Concord, marched into the said town of Lexington, and the said company, on their approach, began to disperse : that notwithstanding this, the regulars rushed on with great violence ; and first began hostilities, by firing on said Lexington company, whereby they killed eight and wounded several others : that the regulars continued their fire, until those of said company, who were neither killed nor wounded, had made their escape : that Col. Smith, with the detachment, then marched to Concord, where a number of provincials were again fired on by the troops, and two of them killed and several wounded, before the provincials fired on them: and that these hostile measures of the troops, produced an engagement that lasted through the day, in which many of the provincials, and more of the regular troops, were killed and wounded.]

[To give a particular account of the ravages of the troops, as they retreated from Concord to Charlestown, would be very difficult, if not impracticable.   Let it suffice to say, that a great number of the houses on the road were plundered and rendered unfit for use ; several were burnt ; women in childbed were driven, by the soldiery, naked into the streets : old men, peaceably in their houses, were shot dead, and such scenes exhibited as would disgrace the annals of the most uncivilized nation.]

[These, brethren, are marks of ministerial vengeance against this colony, for refusing, with her sister colonies, submission to slavery : but they have not yet detached us from our royal sovereign. We profess to be his loyal and dutiful subjects, and so hardly dealt with as we have been, are still ready, with our lives and fortunes, to defend his person, family, crown and dignity. Nevertheless, to the persecution and tyranny of his cruel ministry, we will not tamely submit. Appealing to Heaven for the justice of our cause, we determine to die or be free.]

[We cannot think that the honor, wisdom and valor of Britons, will suffer them to be longer inactive spectators of measures, in which they themselves are so deeply interested : measures pursued in opposition to the solemn protests of many noble lords, and the expressed sense of conspicuous commoners, whose knowledge and virtue have long characterized them as some of the greatest men in the nation : measures executing contrary to the interest, petitions and resolves of many large, respectable and opulent counties, cities and boroughs in Great Britain : measures highly incompatible with justice, but still pursued with a specious pretence of easing the nation of its burthens : measures which, if successful, must end in the ruin and slavery of Britain as well as the persecuted American colonies.]

[We sincerely hope, that the Great Sovereign of the Universe, who hath so often appeared for the English nation, will support you in every rational and manly exertion with these colonies, for saving it from ruin, and that, in a constitutional connection with the mother country, we shall be altogether a free and happy people.][1]

The depositions taken by the committee for that purpose, were laid on the table, and ordered to be read.[2]

Ordered, That the committee make duplicates of the same, and Capt. Stone, [Jonas] Dix, Esq., Col. Tyng, Col. Dwight, Capt. Whittemore, Major Fuller and Mr. Freeman assist as scribes in that business.

And then adjourned till three o'clock.

Afternoon.

||Three o'clock, afternoon.   Met according to adjournment.||

Ordered, That the letters and papers just now received from Rhode Island[3] by Doct. Perkins, be sent to the committee of safety, now sitting in Cambridge, by him, and that he have leave to go home a few days.

(1) The letter to Doct. Franklin, and the address to the inhabitants of Great Britain, have been restored to their places in the journal of the Provincial Congress, from the copies preserved in the records of the Continental Congress, May 11, 1775.

(2) These depositions, with the narrative prepared by order of the Congress, will be found in the Appendix.

(3) The letters covered the following resolution of the general assembly of Rhode Island, adopted April 25, 1775.

" At this very dangerous crisis of American affairs : at a time when we are surrounded with fleets and armies, that threaten our immediate destruction ; at a time when the fears and anxieties of the people throw them into the utmost distress, and totally prevent them from attending to the common occupations of life : to prevent the mischievous consequences that must attend such a disordered state, and to restore peace to the minds of the good people of this colony, it is thought absolutely necessary, that a number of men be raised and embodied, properly armed and disciplined, to continue in this colony as an army of observation, to repel any insult or violence that may be offered to the inhabitants ; and also, if it be necessary for the safety and preservation of any of the colonies, that they be ordered to march out of this colony, and join and co-operate with the forces of our neighboring colonies."

" It is *Voted* and *Resolved,* that fifteen hundred men be enlisted, raised and embodied, as aforesaid, with all the expedition and despatch that the nature of the thing will admit of."

In the house of magistrates, on the passage of this resolution, the following protest was entered by the governor, deputy governor and two of the assistants.

" We, the subscribers, professing true allegiance to his majesty, king George the Third, beg leave to dissent from the vote of the house of magistrates for enlisting, raising and embodying an army of observation of fifteen hundred men, to repel any insults or violences that may be offered to the inhabitants : and also, if it be necessary for the safety and preservation of any of the colonies, to march them out of this colony, to join and co-operate with the forces of our neighboring colo-

Resolved, That Richard Gridley, Esq. be, and he hereby is appointed chief engineer of the forces now raising in this colony, for the defence of the rights and liberties of the American continent ; and that there be paid to the said Richard Gridley, out of the public treasury of this colony, during his continuance in that service, at the rate of one hundred and seventy pounds, lawful money, per annum. And it is further *Resolved*, that from and after the time when the said forces shall be disbanded, during the life of the said Gridley, there be paid to him, out of the said treasury, the sum of one hundred and twenty-three pounds, lawful money, per annum.

Ordered, That the duplicates lay on the table till the narrative comes in.

Ordered, That Mr. Freeman, Doct. Taylor, Deacon Cheever, Doct. Baylies and Col. Farley, be a committee to consider the state of the eastern parts of this province at large, in regard to supplying them with ammunition, and to sit forthwith.   [The committee presented the following report, which was accepted.]

[In PROVINCIAL CONGRESS, *Watertown*, April 26, 1775.]

[Whereas, representation has been made to this Congress, that several of the towns in the eastern parts of the colony are deficient in such supply of ammunition, as it is necessary that they should, at this day, be furnished with, for the safety and defence of the colony in general and that part of it in particular :]

[Therefore, *Resolved*, That the committee of supplies be, and they are hereby directed, forthwith, to take some effectual measures to procure such a quantity of powder and ball as will appear to them to be necessary for the use of this colony, under the present alarming situation of our public affairs ; and, in particular, that they immediately send to the colonies of Connecticut and Rhode Island for so much powder as they shall think necessary, and when procured, to deliver so much of it, to the order of the selectmen of such deficient towns, and in such

nies : because, we are of opinion, that such a measure will be attended with the most fatal consequences to our charter privileges, involve this colony in all the horrors of a civil war, and, as we conceive, be an open violation of the oath of allegiance, which we have severally taken upon our admission into the respective offices we hold in the colony."

"JOSEPH J. WANTON,   THOMAS WICKES,
DARIUS SESSIONS,   WILLIAM POTTER."

Michael Bowler, Esq., speaker of the house, writes thus : " Notwithstanding an exception of a few individuals, you may be assured that the colony are firm and determined, and greater unanimity scarce ever prevailed in the lower house than was found on the great questions before them.   We pray to God that he would be graciously pleased to bring to nothing the councils and designs of wicked men against our lives and liberties, and grant his blessing upon our righteous contest."

quantities as they may think will be proportional to the exigencies of
each town respectively, and to the safety and defence of the colony in
general : such towns to pay for the supplies which they may receive of
said committee, according to the net expense of procuring the same.][1]

Ordered, That Col. Cutts, Ichabod Goodwin and Deacon Fisher, be
appointed to proportion the powder that is recommended to be sold to
the towns of York, Welles, Biddeford, Boothbay and Sandford, and to
sit forthwith. [The committee reported the following resolve which
was accepted :]

[Whereas, the towns of York, Welles, Boothbay and Biddeford
have applied to this Congress, setting forth the dangerous situation
they are in, being sea ports, and thereby exposed to the ravages of
the enemy, although but a small force should be sent to attack them by
sea; and likewise shewing that they have not ammunition sufficient
wherewith to make defence should they be thus attacked; and considering them as they ought to be, part of the whole, and should they suffer that the whole must be affected :]

[Therefore, *Resolved*, That it be, and it hereby is recommended to
the selectmen of the towns of Marblehead, Salem and Newburyport,
that they forthwith sell out of their town stock four half barrels of
powder each, to said towns of York, Welles, Biddeford and Boothbay,
to put the inhabitants thereof in some tolerable state of defence ; and
should the towns of Marblehead, Salem and Newburyport be under
the necessity of having the quantities which they have delivered to the
said towns of York, Welles, Boothbay and Biddeford replaced, in that
case, the Congress will give orders for the same as soon as may be :
the powder to be apportioned according to the number of inhabitants
in the said towns : as also to Sandford, said town having made application for supplies of the same kind.]

Ordered, That Rev. J. Murray, Major Fuller and Jonas Dix,
Esq., be a committee to return the thanks of this Congress to the reverend ministers, who have generously offered to supply the army as
chaplains each a month in rotation.

Ordered, That three o'clock to-morrow [ᵃbe assigned] to take into
consideration some effectual method of supplying the treasury.

a [this Congress will take.]

(1) This resolve, and that which immediately follows, are copied from the original papers in the
office of the secretary of the Commonwealth.

Ordered, That Deacon How have leave to return home, but ||he is to|| return to his duty immediately.

Ordered, That copies of the order to Hon. Richard Derby, Esq., for fitting out his vessel as a packet, be taken and authenticated by the president pro tempore.[1]

Ordered, That the Hon Richard Derby, Esq.'s order to the treasury, be also authenticated by the president pro tempore.

Ordered, That the committee of supplies [be directed] to [cause the] draught of the letter to our agent in Great Britain ||*to be sent,|| with the papers now preparing for that purpose.

Ordered, That Doct. Holten, Doct. Baylies, Capt. Whittemore, Col. Dwight and Mr. Kollock, be a committee to take the recommendation of the committee of safety into consideration, with respect ||to armourers for|| the army now forming.

Moved, That when this Congress do adjourn, that they adjourn till seven o'clock to-morrow morning.

||And then|| adjourned accordingly.

THURSDAY, April 27, [1775, A. M.]

Seven o'clock—met according to adjournment.

Ordered, That Capt. Goodman inquire of the committee of safety, whether any provision is made for a post or posts to ride from the army to Worcester, agreeably to a request from the selectmen of that town, and also to procure a writ for calling a general assembly in May next, issued from general Gage for that purpose.

Ordered, That the secretary pro tempore take extracts from the minutes of the resolves of this Congress, and authenticate the same, and deliver them to the men now in waiting from York and Welles, for the purpose of obtaining some powder.

Ordered, That Mr. Gerry have leave to bring in a resolve with regard to the sea ports in the county of Essex.

[Whereupon, Mr. Gerry offered the following :]

[Whereas, hostilities have been commenced in this colony by Great Britain, and the sword may remain unsheathed for a considerable time:

a ||and be requested to send the same.||

(1) The order to Richard Derby, Esq. was as follows :

IN COMMITTEE OF SAFETY, April 27, 1775.

Resolved, That Capt. Derby be directed, and he hereby is directed, to make for Dublin, or any other good port in Ireland, and from thence to cross to Scotland or England, and hasten to London. This direction is given, that so he may escape all cruisers that may be in the chops of the channel, to stop the communication of the provincial intelligence to the agent. He will forthwith deliver his papers to the agent on reaching London.   J. WARREN, *Chairman*.

P. S.—You are to keep this order a profound secret from every person on earth.

Resolved, That it be, and it hereby is earnestly recommended to the committees of the sea port towns in the county of Essex, that they use their utmost endeavors to have all the effects of the inhabitants of their respective towns removed as soon as possible : that the Congress highly approves of the conduct of said towns in wearing a pacific appearance until their effects shall be secured : that the Congress consider it as absolutely necessary for said inhabitants to be in readiness to go into the country on the shortest notice, and to avoid mixing with our enemies, as thereby their own lives will ever be in imminent danger when the colony and the continent shall attack such enemies. And it is also recommended to them that their application to Congress for advice, and this resolve in consequence thereof, be kept a secret, that their effects may more easily be removed.][1]

Ordered, That three o'clock next Tuesday be assigned to take up the matter in the resolve brought in by Mr. Gerry.

Ordered, That Mr. President, Col. Orne, Doct. Taylor, Major Fuller of Middleton, and Capt. Goodman, be a committee to confer with the officers of the army, relative to the reduction of their pay.

Col. Dwight [was] appointed to wait on the committee of safety, and acquaint them with the names of the officers in the regiments of minute men in Worcester county.

Mr. Hale ||is|| appointed to the same business ||for|| the county of Hampshire.

Then adjourned till three o'clock.

[Afternoon.]

||Afternoon, three o'clock—met according to adjournment.||

Ordered, That Capt. Kingsbury, Doct. Holten and Deacon Stone, are appointed to enquire, and endeavor to get an exact account of the men killed, and wounded, and murdered, in the late scene on the 19th instant.

The order of the day was moved for, to take up the matter of supplying the treasury.

Ordered, That a committee be appointed for that purpose, to consist of five, and to be chosen by written votes.

Ordered, That two be added to this committee.

Ordered, That Doct. Holten, Mr. Bullen and Capt. Batchelder be appointed to count and sort the votes.

Ordered, That nine o'clock be assigned for that purpose.

Ordered, That Mr. Partridge, Capt. Greenleaf and Doct. Baker, be appointed to consider the petition from Gorham, and to sit forthwith.

(1) Mr. Gerry's resolution is transcribed from the original on the files of Congress.

Ordered, That Capt. Whittemore, Mr. Freeman and Doct. Baylies, assist as scribes, the committees in taking fair copies of the depositions in order for the press; and to sit forthwith.

Ordered, That Jonas Dix, Esq., [William] Stickney, Esq. and Deacon Stone, be appointed to take true copies of the depositions, and have them signed by the deponents, and authenticated by the justices and a notary public.

Ordered, That Mr. Hubbart have leave to go home a few days.

Then adjourned till nine o'clock [to-morrow morning.]

[FRIDAY, April 28, 1775, A. M.]

Nine o'clock—met ||ᵃaccording|| to adjournment.

Ordered, [That] Mr. President, Col. Gerrish, Mr. Gerry, Doct. Holten and Mr. Gill, be appointed to confer with the gentlemen from New Hampshire, and are desired to lay the letters just received from New York, before them.[1]

Ordered, At the desire of the secretary pro tempore, that he be excused from that service after another is appointed in that place.

Accordingly Mr. [Samuel] Freeman was appointed to that office pro tempore.

IN PROVINCIAL CONGRESS, *Watertown*, April 28, 1775.

Resolved, That the committee appointed to confer with the committee who this day arrived here from the colony of New Hampshire, have leave to report to this Congress a draught of a letter, which they have prepared as an answer to one received from the convention of the said colony of New Hampshire, dated 26th instant. The said draught was accordingly reported, read and unanimously accepted, and ordered to be authenticated by the president, and delivered to Col. Nathaniel Folsom, Col. Josiah Bartlet and Major Samuel Hobart, Esq., the committee from the said convention of New Hampshire, and is as follows, viz. :

"GENTLEMEN :—It is with pleasure we have received your letter abovementioned, and by a committee of this Congress, have had a conference with your respectable committee.

We find the fullest conviction in the minds of the inhabitants of

---

a ||conformably ||

(1) The letters from New York enclosed communications from London, containing intelligence of the proceedings of parliament, information of the designs of the ministry, and exhortations to union and firmness in resistance.

our sister colonies, as well as of this, that by their immediate and most vigorous exertions, there is the greatest prospect of establishing their liberties and saving their country; and that without such exertions all must be lost.

It is the opinion of this Congress, as already communicated, that a powerful army on our side, must, at once, cut out such a work for a tyrannical administration, as, under the great opposition which they meet with in England, they cannot accomplish; and that their system of despotism must soon be shaken to the foundation: but should they still pursue their sanguinary measures, that the colonies will then be able to make a successful stand.

We have the utmost confidence in your patriotic colony, whose inhabitants have signalized themselves in joining their brethren in this; and hope to see New Hampshire, and every other government which has been exposed to the corruption of a British ministry, soon placed upon such a footing as will be best calculated to promote the true interest of the same, and to prevent in future such unhappy disputes as have taken place with the mother country.

We have just received an agreeable account of the conduct of our brethren in New York, and have delivered a copy of the letter to your committee.

We sincerely thank you for your ||late|| measures taken ||ᵃby your|| convention at Exeter, and are fully persuaded that the Congress of your colony, which is to meet on the 17th May, will take such effectual steps as the present exigency of public affairs requires, and the continent of America must necessarily approve.

Ordered, That the secretary authenticate a copy of the letter this day received from governor Hopkins of Rhode Island, and deliver the same to the abovementioned committee from New Hampshire.

Ordered, That Mr. Dickenson, Doct. Holten and Col. Gerrish, be a committee to wait upon the committee from New Hampshire to the committee of safety of this colony, now sitting at Cambridge, to consult with them respecting the New Hampshire forces now at Cambridge.

Ordered, That the president, Mr. Gerry and Mr. Gardner, be a committee to take into consideration a letter this day received from the Hon. Stephen Hopkins, Esq., dated Providence, April 27th, 1775.[1]

a ||in.||

(1) This letter cannot be recovered: it related to the capture of Mr. John Brown: the substance is stated in the note to the journal of April 29.

Ordered, That Mr. Crane, Mr. Grout and Mr. Fisher, be a committee to take into consideration the expediency of establishing post riders between the Massachusetts forces and the town of Worcester.

Ordered, That Mr. Crane, Mr. Grout and Mr. Fisher, be a committee to take into consideration the propriety of recommending to the several towns and districts in this colony, that they take no notice of the precepts lately issued by general Gage, for calling a general assembly.

Ordered, That Major Fuller of Newton, Mr. Goodman, Doct. Taylor, Doct. Baylies and Major Brooks, be a committee to prepare a form of a commission for the several officers of the army now forming in this province.

Adjourned to three o'clock this afternoon.

Afternoon.

Ordered, That Mr. Fisher, Doct. Taylor and [Benjamin] Aikin, Esq., be a committee to prepare a draught of rules and regulations to be in future observed by the several members of this Congress.

The committee appointed in the forenoon to take into consideration a letter received from the Hon. Stephen Hopkins, Esq., reported.

The report [was] accepted, and ordered to lie on the table for the present.

Ordered, That the committee appointed to introduce the honorable delegates from the convention at Exeter, in New Hampshire, to the committee of safety, apply to said committee for an authentic account of what transactions have certainly taken place, with respect to the liberation of our friends in Boston, and report as soon as may be.

Ordered, That Col. Dexter, Major Brooks, Doct. Taylor, Capt. Batchelder and Capt. Greenleaf, be a committee to bring in a resolve empowering the committee of supplies to procure such provisions, military stores, and other stores, as they shall judge necessary for the army, now forming in this colony, during its establishment.

It was *Moved*, That the sense of this Congress be taken, whether it would be expedient to reduce the pay of the field officers of the army ||now forming in this colony :|| after much debate the question was put, and it passed in the affirmative by a large majority. Whereupon, it was determined, that the pay of the chief colonel be reduced from £15 to £12 : and that the lieutenant colonels and majors be reduced in the same proportion ; ||accordingly,|| *Ordered*, that Major Fuller ||of Newton,|| Col. Dexter and Capt. Little, be a committee to bring in a resolve for that purpose.

||This Congress was then|| adjourned till to-morrow morning, eight o'clock.

SATURDAY, April 29, [1775, A. M.]

The committee appointed to wait on the New Hampshire committee to the committee of safety, at Cambridge, and to make inquiry respecting the liberation of the inhabitants of Boston, reported, that they had attended that business, and had brought from the committee of safety a number of papers, which contain the proceedings of the town of Boston with general Gage, in respect to moving the inhabitants and their effects;

And that the committee of safety, having taken the substance of them into consideration, desired that [the papers] might be returned to them, and that the Congress would not pass any resolve respecting them, till they had come to some resolve concerning ||the subject of|| them;

Therefore, *Ordered,* That the subject matter of the said papers be referred to the consideration of the said committee of safety, they to make report to this Congress as soon as may be.

On a motion made, ||ᵃ *Voted,*|| That the day appointed for the first meeting of the county committees, which was the first Wednesday in May next, be postponed to the fourth Wednesday in May next.

The committee appointed to prepare a draught of rules and regulations to be observed by this Congress, reported. The rules were read and severally accepted, and are as follow, viz. :

1. No member shall speak out of his place, nor without standing up, and applying to the president for leave, and shall sit down as soon as he is done speaking.

2. No member, speaking by leave of the president, shall be interrupted by another, but by rising up to speak to order.

3. No member shall speak more than twice to one question, without first obtaining leave of Congress; nor more than once until others have spoken that shall desire it.

4. Whenever any member shall have liberty from the president to make a motion, and such motion shall be seconded by another, the same shall be received and considered by the Congress, and not otherwise.

5. No member shall declare, or question, whether it be a vote or not.

6. No grant for money or other thing shall be made, unless there be a time before assigned for that purpose.

7. No vote shall be reconsidered when a less number is present in Congress than there was when it passed.

8. No member shall nominate more than one person for a committee, provided the person so nominated be chosen.

a ||Ordered.||

9. No member shall be obliged to be upon more than two committees at [the same] time, nor chairman of more than one.

10. That no member be permitted to stand up to the interruption of another, while such other member is speaking.

Ordered, That the monitors of this Congress be, and they are hereby directed, to see that the foregoing rules are observed by the several members of this Congress.

Ordered, The letter and resolve prepared to be sent to the Hon. Stephen Hopkins, Esq., of Rhode Island, be recommitted for a suitable addition, and the committee to sit forthwith.

Ordered, That the Hon. Mr. Dexter be a committee to bring in a resolve expressive of the vote of this Congress for altering the first meeting of the county committees.

The committee ||who were|| appointed to bring [in] a resolve empowering the committee of supplies to procure provisions and military stores, reported. The report was read and accepted, and is as follows:

In Provincial Congress, *Watertown,* April 29, 1775.

Resolved, That the committee of supplies be, and they hereby are empowered to purchase every kind of military stores, provisions, and all other supplies which they shall judge necessary for the use of the forces of this colony, during the establishment of an army for its defence, or until it shall be otherwise ordered by this or some future congress, or house of representatives, on the credit of the colony; and ||ᵃmake drafts of|| suitable sums, from the treasury, for payment for the same: also to deposit the said stores in such ||suitable|| places as they, in consultation with the generals of the colony, shall judge proper; and to deliver such, and so many of said stores, to the commissary general, from time to time, as he shall ||ᵇhave demand for|| to supply the army. Likewise, said committee of supplies are hereby empowered to employ such and so many assistants, as they shall judge necessary, to be paid as aforesaid; said committee of supplies to be accountable, when called upon, for their doings, to this or some future congress, or house of representatives of this colony.

The committee appointed to prepare an addition to a letter to the Hon. Stephen Hopkins, Esq., reported the following, which was read and accepted:

In Provincial Congress, *Watertown,* April 28, 1775.

It is with the deepest concern that we find Mr. Brown, that valuable friend to the cause of America, betrayed into the hands of our com-

a ||draw.||　　　　　　　　b ||shall judge needful.||

mon enemies, and every measure for his release, that can be pursued by us, shall most earnestly be adopted. We have ordered Samuel Murray, son of a mandamus counsellor, and such officers of general Gage's army as are prisoners of war and not disabled from travelling, to be immediately sent, with sufficient guards, to Providence, and think it best that Murray and the officers should write to their friends in Boston, acquainting them that Mr. Brown's friends have the same advantage over them as general Gage hath over Mr. Brown.

We beg leave to suggest to you the critical situation of this colony at the present time, which disables this Congress from immediately seizing every crown officer in the government. Boston is closed, and its numerous inhabitants, so obnoxious to our enemies, are imprisoned therein. Several of our sea ports are [ᵃblockaded] with ships, and threatened destruction if they join the army. Under this situation, the inhabitants of the places most in danger are, day and night, removing their furniture and effects, and we hope soon to see it generally done. Should we, therefore, seize the crown officers as proposed, it may hurl on our numerous sea ports sudden destruction, before they have had opportunity of saving themselves. We had it in contemplation to send a letter to the general, acquainting him that we should treat the crown officers with severity, if Mr. Brown should be so treated by him. But we are apprehensive that it would rather produce an unhappy than good effect, as he has a greater number of our valuable friends than we can shew of his. We desire you to give us your further sentiments in the matter, and if any other way is best wherein the Congress can save Mr. Brown, it shall be readily pursued.

We are, &c.

To the Hon. Stephen Hopkins, Esq.

In Provincial Congress, *Watertown*, April 28, 1775.

Whereas, a worthy friend to the liberties of America, Mr. John Brown, of Providence, hath been lately seized, and with two other persons, carried on board a British ship of war at Newport: *Ordered*, that Samuel Murray, and such officers of general Gage's army as are prisoners of war, and not disabled from travelling on account of their wounds, be immediately sent, under a sufficient guard, to Providence, and delivered to the Hon. Stephen Hopkins, Esq., or other friend of said Mr. Brown, to be made such use of as they shall think proper for obtaining the liberty of the said Mr. Brown.

a [blocked.]

In Provincial Congress, *Watertown*, April 29, 1775.

Sir :—The above is a copy of an order and letter which passed this Congress yesterday, since which we have received from Boston copies of sundry votes of that town to general Gage, upon the subject of a license [for the inhabitants] to remove, with their effects, into the country; and by his answers it appears, that he has consented to suffer such inhabitants as have inclination therefor, to leave the place, with all their effects, excepting fire arms, which are to be delivered at Faneuil hall to the selectmen of the town, and the names of the owners to be placed on them; and the general expects, on the other hand, a proclamation from Congress, giving liberty to all inhabitants of the colony, having inclination therefor, to remove, with their effects, into Boston. Some of the inhabitants have already left the town, by permission of the general; ||and under these circumstances,|| should we issue the order which has passed in Congress, it may put a stop to this unexpected favorable event, and prevent the emancipation of many thousands of friends to America. We, nevertheless, purpose to detain the prisoners of war; and if the general should not forfeit his plighted faith, to use all expedition in getting out families and the effects of our friends from Boston, that we may be at liberty to use our prisoners, and every other means in our power, for the release of Mr. Brown, as was intended.

P. S.—We have just heard the passages from Boston are again stopped, but the occasion of this extraordinary manœuvre we cannot yet learn.

To the Hon. Stephen Hopkins, Esq., ||of Providence.||

Ordered, That a postscript be added to the letter just prepared to be sent to the Hon. Stephen Hopkins, Esq., purporting that we have just received intelligence that the passages to and from Boston are stopped; the reason of which extraordinary manœuvre we are not yet acquainted with.

Adjourned to three o'clock [this afternoon.]

[Afternoon.]

The committee appointed to bring in a resolve with respect to reducing the pay of the field officers, reported the following, which was read and accepted, and ordered to be signed by the secretary, and transmitted to the committee of safety.

In Provincial Congress, *Watertown*, April 29, 1775.

Whereas, the reducing of the several regiments to be raised in the provincial service, from one thousand men in a regiment to five hundred and ninety, makes the service of the said field officers of said regiments less burdensome; therefore, *Resolved*, that the pay of said field officers be reduced one fifth part from the first establishment, and that said field officers' pay, in said service of this province, to the last day of December next, unless dismissed before, shall be as follows, viz.: a colonel's pay, twelve pounds per month: a lieutenant colonel's pay, nine pounds twelve shillings per month: a major's pay, eight pounds per month.

Ordered, That Mr. Rawson, Doct. Dunsmore and Col. Davis, be a committee to wait on the committee of safety now sitting at Cambridge, to inform them of the deep concern this Congress feel, on account of the state and situation of the cannon, and desire information respecting the disposition of them—and that this committee forthwith proceed on this business.

Resolved, That this Congress will now proceed to choose a committee, to consider some method of supplying the treasury.

Ordered, That Esquire Greenleaf, Mr. Hall, (in the room of Doct. Holten,) and Mr. Batchelder, be of the committee to count and sort the votes.

The absent members were ordered to be called in.

The Hon. Mr. Dexter, who was appointed to bring in a resolve expressive of the vote of this Congress for altering the first meeting of the county committees, reported; which report being read and amended, was accepted, and is as follows:

Whereas, this Congress, on the 12th day of this instant April, appointed a committee for each county, to receive from the committees of correspondence in such counties, a state of the conduct of the towns and districts, with respect to their having executed the continental and provincial measures for the preservation of this country from slavery. And, whereas, the distressed circumstances of the colony may probably render it very inconvenient that so great a number of members should be absent from the Congress on the first Wednesday of May next, the day mentioned for their first meeting;

Therefore, *Resolved*, That the first meeting of said committees be postponed to the fourth Wednesday in said month; and it is recommended to the several committees of correspondence to render a true state of the conduct of their respective towns and districts on the said fourth Wednesday of May accordingly; and especially with respect to their outstanding province rates, any thing contained in the former resolve of this Congress differing herefrom notwithstanding.

Ordered, That the several county committees be, and they hereby are directed to inform the committees of correspondence of the several ||*towns in their respective counties|| of the purport of the foregoing resolve.

Ordered, That the secretary be, and he hereby is directed to notify the chairman of each of the said county committees, of the purport of the said resolve.

The committee appointed to count and sort the votes for a committee to consider on some method for supplying the treasury, reported that the following gentlemen were chosen, viz.: Rev. Mr. Murray, Col. Dexter, Col. Gerrish, Mr. Gill, Mr. Gerry, Capt. Stone ||of Framingham|| and Capt. Greenleaf.

On a motion made by Rev. Mr. Murray, that he might be excused from serving on the above committee, and having offered his reasons therefor, the question was put, whether he be excused agreeably to his request, from serving on said committee, and it passed in the affirmative.

The Congress then made choice of Doct. Taylor to serve on said committee, in the room of Mr. Murray, who hath been excused.

IN PROVINCIAL CONGRESS, ||*Watertown*,|| April 29, 1775.

The president having received a letter from Messrs. Nicholas Brown and Joseph Brown, dated Providence, April 27th, 1775, desiring that this Congress would observe secrecy in respect to the capture of their brother, John Brown, at Newport, on the 26th instant, and also another, from the Hon. Stephen Hopkins, Esq., dated Providence, April 27th, 1775,[1] presented the same to this Congress: which being read—

a ||counties.||

(1) These letters are not preserved on the books or files of Congress; the information contained in that written by Honorable Stephen Hopkins is repeated in a communication on the following day, addressed to the president.

PROVIDENCE, April 28, 1775.

GENTLEMEN:—Mr. Joseph Brown and Mr. Moses Brown, of this place, principal merchants, and gentlemen of distinction and probity, will wait upon you with this letter. Their brother, Mr. John Brown, of this town, merchant, was, two days ago, forcibly taken at Newport in a packet, as he was coming from thence with a quantity of flour, which he had purchased there. He was carried on board a ship of war and confined. We have since heard that ho is sent round to Boston with the flour. I request you to give the bearers any aid and assistance in your power, for procuring the relief and discharge of their brother. In my letter of yesterday to the Congress, the measure of reprisal [by holding the British prisoners of war as hostages] was recommended: and if it may be, I wish it may be pursued.

I am your friend and humble servant,

STEPHEN HOPKINS.

The embarrassment created by the capture of the small quantity of stores seized by the British man of war, appears from the following letter addressed to the president of Congress.

PROVIDENCE, April 28, 1775.

SIR:—At the request of his honor the deputy governor, [Hon. Darius Sessions,] I have under-

Ordered, That Mr. Gerry, Col. Gerrish and Doct. Taylor be, and hereby are appointed a committee to confer with the abovesaid Joseph Brown, who now waits the further advice of this Congress.

Ordered, That said committee be, and they are hereby authorized to consider what is proper to be done; to sit forthwith, and make report ||ᵃas soon as may be.||

The president, ||ᵇlikewise,|| received a letter from Worcester,[1] in-

a ||forthwith.|| b ||also.||

taken to answer yours of the 26th instant; we, sir, sensibly feel the distresses of our brethren in the Massachusetts Bay, and can only say, that, as brigadier of the three battalions under my command, in the county of Providence, I will furnish you, upon any alarm, with six hundred men; but the situation of matters is such, occasioned partly by our assembly's not appointing officers for the fifteen hundred men, which they ordered to be raised for your assistance; and partly by the seizure made by the man of war, at Newport, of three hundred barrels of flour, bought by this colony for supplying our army, that it will be impossible for our forces immediately to proceed to join your army, unless they go destitute of provision, which we imagine here would rather be a burden than a help to our friends; however, men are enlisting very fast, and, when our assembly meets here, which will be next week, you may rely on it, that our forces will, as fast and as soon as possible, march to your assistance.

I am, Sir, your most obedient humble servant,

JAMES ANGELL.

(1) Information of the arrival of intelligence from Europe, was contained in a most interesting letter from the Hon. John Hancock, who, on his way to attend the Continental Congress, remained at Worcester two days, waiting for suitable escort, and for the coming of his colleagues.

WORCESTER, 24th April, 1775, Monday Evening.

" GENTLEMEN :—Mr. S. Adams and myself, just arrived here, find no intelligence from you and no guard. We just hear an express has just passed through this place to you from New York, informing that administration is bent upon pushing matters; and that four regiments are expected there. How are we to proceed? Where are our brethren? Surely we ought to be supported. I had rather be with you; and, at present, am fully determined to be with you before I proceed. I beg, by the return of this express, to hear from you; and pray furnish us with depositions of the conduct of the troops, the certainty of their firing first, and every circumstance relative to the conduct of the troops, from the 19th instant to this time, that we may be able to give some account of matters as we proceed, and especially at Philadelphia. Also I beg you would order your secretary to make out an account of your proceedings since what has taken place; what your plan is; what prisoners we have, and what they have of ours; who of note was killed on both sides; who commands our forces, &c."

" Are our men in good spirits? For God's sake, do not suffer the spirit to subside until they have perfected the reduction of our enemies. Boston *must* be entered; the troops *must* be sent away, or [blank] Our friends are valuable, but our country must be saved. I have an interest in that town: what can be the enjoyment of that to me, if I am obliged to hold it at the will of general Gage, or any one else? I doubt not your vigilance, your fortitude and resolution. Do let us know how you proceed. We must have the castle. The ships must be [blank] Stop up the harbor against large vessels coming. You know better what to do than I can point out. Where is Mr. Cushing? Are Mr. Paine and Mr. John Adams to be with us? What are we to depend upon? We travel rather as deserters, which I will not submit to. I will return and join you, if I cannot travel in reputation. I wish to hear from you. Pray spend a thought upon our situation. I will not detain this man, as I want much to hear from you. How goes on the Congress? Who is your president? Are the members hearty? Pray remember Mr. S. Adams and myself to all friends. God be with you.

I am, gentlemen, your faithful and hearty countryman,

JOHN HANCOCK."

To the gentlemen committee of safety.

closing one from New York, which gave information of the arrival of a packet there, with despatches for general Gage, and recommended that care be taken to intercept the same.

Ordered, That Col. Grout be directed to carry the letter last mentioned to the committee of safety, now sitting at Cambridge.

||The Congress then|| adjourned till to-morrow morning, seven o'clock.

SUNDAY, April 30, 1775, A. M.

The committee appointed yesterday to wait on the committee of safety, reported, that they had attended the business to which they were appointed, and brought from said committee the following account.

IN COMMITTEE OF SAFETY, *Cambridge*, April 29, 1775.

Agreeably to the order of the Provincial Congress, this committee have inquired into the state and situation of the cannon and ordnance stores, with the provision made for the companies of artillery, and beg leave to report as follows, viz. :

In Cambridge.—Six three pounders complete, with ammunition, and one six pounder.

In Watertown.—Sixteen pieces of artillery of different sizes; the said six pounder, and sixteen pieces, will be taken out of the way; and the first mentioned six pieces will be used in a proper way of defence.

Capt. Foster is appointed to command one of the companies of artillery, and ordered to enlist said company.

Capt. William Lee, of Marblehead, [has been] sent for, to take the command of another, and several other persons [have been] sent for, to take the command of other companies.

JOSEPH WARREN, *Chairman.*

Ordered, That Col. Grout be directed to request of the committee of safety a report, respecting the inhabitants of Boston.

A motion was made for an addition to the committee of safety, and, after some debate, the matter was ordered to subside.

The Congress then adjourned to twelve o'clock this day.

[Noon.]

The Congress ||ᵃmet at twelve o'clock, and then adjourned|| to half an hour after one.

a ||then adjourned after meeting according to adjournment.||

||ªAt half an hour after one, the Congress met again,|| and adjourned to half an hour after three : at which time the Congress met again

Ordered, That another express be immediately sent to the committee of safety, to procure their result with respect to moving out the inhabitants of Boston.

Ordered, That Col. Mosely be directed to repair forthwith to Cambridge on this errand.

The president was then desired to write a short letter to said committee on this important purpose. The letter is as follows :

IN PROVINCIAL CONGRESS, April 30, 1775.

SIR :—I am directed to inform you, that it is with regret, this Congress find themselves obliged to send to the committee of safety a third messenger, to request their immediate report on the subject of the removal of the poor inhabitants of Boston.

To wait for that report, the Congress have suspended all proceedings on that matter, and sat in almost impatient expectation, by several adjournments, since seven o'clock this morning. I am obliged to request your answer by this express, without loss of time, that the Congress may then see what it is their duty to conclude on.

I have the honor to be, with great respect, Sir,

Your most obedient humble servant,

JOHN MURRAY.

To Joseph Warren, Esq.,
  Chairman of the Committee of Safety :

Ordered, That Esquire Dix, Doct. Taylor and Mr. Bullen, be a committee to inquire into the conduct of the several towns relative to the prisoners of war.

Ordered, That the resolve relative to altering the time ||of the first meeting of the|| county committees, be printed in the Salem Gazette and in the Massachusetts Spy.

A committee from the committee of safety offered to this Congress a resolve, respecting the liberation of the inhabitants of Boston, which being read and amended, was accepted, and is as follows :

IN PROVINCIAL CONGRESS, *Watertown,* April 30, 1775.

Whereas, an agreement has been made between general Gage and

a ||Congress met pursuant to adjournment.||

the inhabitants of the city of Boston, for ||the|| removal of the persons and effects of such of the inhabitants of the town of Boston as may be so disposed, excepting their fire arms and ammunition, into the country :

Resolved, That any of the inhabitants of this colony, who may incline to go into the town of Boston with their effects, fire arms and ammunition excepted, have toleration for that purpose; and that they be protected from any injury and insult whatsoever in their removal to Boston, and that this resolve be immediately published.

P. S.—Officers are appointed for giving permits for the above purposes; one, at the sign of the Sun, at Charlestown; and another, at the house of Mr. John Greaton, Jun., at Roxbury.

Ordered, That attested copies of the foregoing resolve be forthwith posted up at Roxbury, Charlestown and Cambridge.

Resolved, That the resolution of Congress, relative to the removal of the inhabitants of Boston, be authenticated, and sent to the selectmen of Boston, immediately, to be communicated to general Gage, and also be published in the Worcester and Salem papers.

Ordered, That Doct. Taylor, Mr. Bailey, Mr. Lothrop, Mr. Holmes and Col. Farley, be a committee to consider what steps are necessary to be taken for the assisting the poor of Boston in moving out with their effects : to bring in a resolve for that purpose ; and to sit forthwith.

||Then|| adjourned till to-morrow morning, seven o'clock.

[MONDAY,] May 1, 1775, [A. M.]

The committee who were appointed to consider what steps are necessary to be taken with respect to assisting the poor of Boston in moving out with their effects, reported. The report was recommitted for amendment, and Capt. Smith, of Granby, Col. Mosely, Capt. Goodridge and Major Smith were added to the committee.

Ordered, That Mr. Patridge, Doct. Baylies and Mr. Greenleaf, be a committee to inspect the papers of this Congress, and consider what would be proper to furnish the printer with for publication, and make report.

The committee appointed to inspect the papers of the Congress, reported several extracts of letters for publication, which are ordered to be delivered to Mr. Hall, of Salem, for that purpose.[1]

(1) The letters published by Mr. Hall, appear to have been intercepted communications from soldiers, in Boston, relating to the incidents of the march to Concord. They will be annexed to the narrative of that excursion, in the Appendix.

On a motion made, that the sense of the Congress be taken on this question, viz. : whether the commissions to be given for the officers of the army now forming in this colony, shall be signed by the president of the Congress : the question was put, and it passed in the affirmative.

The Congress then adjourned to three o'clock this afternoon.

Afternoon.

A letter brought from North Hampton, by express, from Major Hawley, respecting the bearer of despatches from general Gage, was read : on which, *Ordered*, that Col. Gerrish, Esquire Gardner and Major Gooding, be a committee to take the same into consideration, and report.

The committee appointed to consider the letter from Major Hawley, reported, that the most likely way of detecting the bearer of the despatches to general Gage, was, to forward the said letter by Major Gooding to the committee of safety, at Cambridge, that they may take order thereon ; which report was accepted, and the said letter, together with two anonymous letters from London, were ordered to be sent to the said committee of safety.

Moved, That William Reed, Esq. be admitted in this house, to represent to this Congress the sufferings he met with on the 19th April, at Lexington. The question being put, after debate had thereon, it passed in the negative.

Ordered, That Capt. Bragdon, Capt. Dix and Mr. Gill, be a committee to confer with the abovenamed Esquire Reed, and to make report of their conference.

Resolved, That Mr. Gerry have leave to bring in an order of this house, for leave to the several members of this Congress to pass the guards of the colony army without molestation.

Mr. Gerry accordingly brought in an order for this purpose, and after debates had thereon it was ordered to be recommitted.

The committee appointed to prepare the form of a commission for the officers of the colony army, reported. The form which they reported was read and accepted, and is as follows :

THE CONGRESS OF THE COLONY OF THE MASSACHUSETTS BAY.
To   *Greeting :*
We, reposing especial trust and confidence in your courage and good conduct, do, by these presents, constitute and appoint you, the said   to be   of the regiment of foot   raised by the Congress aforesaid for the defence of said colony.

You are, therefore, carefully and diligently to discharge the duty ot a   in leading, ordering and exercising the said   in arms, both inferior officers and soldiers, and to keep them in good order and discipline; and they are hereby commanded to obey you as their   ; and you are yourself to observe and follow such orders and instructions as you shall, from time to time, receive from the general and commander in chief of the forces raised in the colony aforesaid, for the defence of the same, or any other your superior officers, according to the military rules and discipline in war, in pursuance of the trust reposed in you.

By order of the Congress,

, the   of   A. D. 1775.

President pro tempore.

Secretary pro tempore.

Ordered, That a fair copy of the foregoing form of a commission be taken, and transmitted to the press, and that one thousand copies thereof be printed.

Mr. Gerry again reported the form of a pass for the use of the members of this Congress, which was accepted, and six hundred of them ordered to be printed. It is as follows:

To the Guards of the Colony Army.

Pursuant to a resolve of the Provincial Congress, you are hereby ordered to permit   a member of said Congress, to pass and repass at all times.

Secretary.

In Provincial Congress, ||*Watertown,*|| May 1, 1775.

Resolved, That the general officer of the army of this colony be, and he hereby is directed to sign a sufficient number of blank passes for members of this Congress, and to deliver the same to the secretary ||of Congress.||

The committee who were appointed to consider of measures for assisting the poor of Boston to move out of said town, having amended their report, again reported: which report being read ||and amended,|| was accepted, and one hundred and fifty copies thereof ordered to be printed, and a copy ||thereof|| forthwith transmitted to the committee of donations, in Boston, and that Mr. Gill take the charge of transmitting the same. The report is as follows, viz.:

IN PROVINCIAL CONGRESS, ||*Watertown*,|| May 1, 1775.

Whereas, the inhabitants of the town of Boston have been detained by general Gage, but at length, by agreement, are permitted to remove, with their effects, into the country, and as it has been represented to this Congress that about five thousand of said inhabitants are indigent, and unable to be at the expense of removing themselves:

Therefore, *Resolved*, That it be, and it is hereby recommended to all the good people of this colony, and especially to the selectmen, and committee of correspondence most convenient to Boston, that they aid and assist such poor inhabitants ||of said town|| (with teams, waggons, &c.,) as shall procure a certificate from the committee of donations, that they are unable to remove themselves; and it is further recommended to the selectmen of the several towns specified in the schedule annexed, to provide for said inhabitants in the best and most prudent way ||and manner,|| until this, or some future congress, shall take further order thereon, and that the said selectmen receive, support and employ their proportion of said inhabitants assigned them in said schedule, and no other; and render their accounts to this, or some future congress, or house of representatives, for allowance, which reasonable accounts shall be paid out of the public treasury: and it is further recommended, to the committee of donations, to apply said donations for the removal of said inhabitants, and for their support whilst removing; and in case that is insufficient, it is further recommended to said committee of donations, that they make up said deficiency, and lay their accounts before the Congress for allowance, which reasonable expense shall be paid out of the public treasury of the colony: and it is further *Resolved*, that the inhabitants of Boston thus removed shall not, in future, be considered as the poor of said town into which they remove; and it is to be understood, that if the number of the poor who shall be removed in consequence hereof, should surpass, or fall short of the number herein calculated, the distribution of them shall be increased or diminished, in proportion ||according|| to this regulation:

County of Suffolk.—Wrentham, 89 persons; Stoughtonham, 32; Medway, 38; Bellingham, 25; Walpole, 31;   .   215

Middlesex.—Concord, 66; Marlborough, 80; Billerica, 54; Framingham, 63; Chelmsford, 49; Sherburne, 31; Sudbury, 85; Weston, 41; Westford, 45; Littleton, 41; Hopkinton, 42; Stow, 36; Groton, 61; Pepperel, 34; Townsend, 26; Natick, 20; Dracut, 35; Bedford, 29; Holliston, 34;

Tewksbury, 28; Acton, 32; Dunstable, 30; Lincoln, 29; Wilmington, 25;   1016

Plymouth.—Bridgewater, 81; Abington, 22; Halifax, 12; .   115

Bristol.—Taunton, 103; Rehoboth, 129; Dartmouth, 113; Norton, 47; Mansfield, 30; Attleborough, 75; Raynham, 31; Easton, 35; Berkley, 25;   .   .   .   588

Berkshire.—Sheffield, 54; Great Barrington, 24; Stockbridge, 25; Pittsfield, 31; New Marlborough, 30; Egremont, 13; Richmond, 23; Lenox, 16; Tyringham, 13; Lanesborough, 32; Sandisfield, 23; Williamstown, 20; East Hoosock, 10;   314

Hampshire.—Springfield, 68; Wilbraham, 31; Northampton, 70; Southampton, 25; Hadley, 30; South Hadley, 23; Amherst, 34; Granby, 17; Hatfield, 35; Whately, 13; Williamsburg, 9; Westfield, 50; Deerfield, 36; Greenfield, 24; Shelburne, 14; Conway, 17; Sunderland, 19; Montague, 18; Northfield, 26; Brimfield, 44; South Brimfield, 26; Monson, 23; Pelham, 25; Greenwich, 24; Blandford, 19; Leverett, 4; Palmer, 25; Granville, 44; New Salem, 22; Belchertown, 28; Colrain, 17; Ware, 13; Warwick, 10; Bernardston, 14; Murraysfield, 17; Charlemont, 12; Worthington, 6; Shutesbury, 14; Chesterfield, 22; Southwick, 19; West Springfield, 72; Ludlow, 10;   .   .   .   .   .   .   [788]

Worcester.—Worcester, 82; Lancaster, 103; Mendon, 76; Brookfield, 99; Oxford, 35; Charlton, 35; Sutton, 98; Leicester, 36; Spencer, 31; Paxton, 20; Rutland, 48; Oakham, 14; Hutchinson, 42; Hubbardston, 9; New Braintree, 32; Southborough, 36; Westborough, 38; Northborough, 25; Shrewsbury, 32; Lunenburg, 51; Fitchburg, 19; Uxbridge, 36; Harvard, 50; Dudley, 32; Bolton, 48; Upton, 20; Sturbridge, 45; Leominster, 38; Hardwick, 55; Holden, 26; Weston, 35; Douglass, 22; Grafton, 38; Petersham, 38; Royalston, 8; Westminster, 31; Athol, 20; Templeton, 25; Princeton, 24; Ashburnham, 12; Winchendon, 9; Northbridge, 13;   .   .   [539]

Whole amount, ...   4903

23

Ordered, That Mr. Partridge, Mr. Lothrop and Doct. Baylies, be directed to assist the secretary in copying the foregoing report.

The committee appointed to confer with William Reed, Esq., reported the following [statements of losses sustained by each from the British troops,] presented to them by William Reed, Esq., of Lexington, in behalf of Joseph Loring, Joseph Loring, Jun., Widow Mulliken and Joseph Pond, viz. :[1]

Whereupon, *Ordered,* That the committee of supplies be, and they are hereby directed to deliver to said William Reed, Esq., or to his order, for the use of the said Joseph Loring, Joseph Loring, Jun., Widow Mulliken and Joseph Pond, one barrel of pork.

Ordered, That Mr. Hollock, Col. Howe and Capt. White, be a committee to consider what is proper to be done with respect to furnishing the army with some present necessaries.

All [the] committees [were] enjoined to sit.

Adjourned to nine o'clock to-morrow morning.

[Tuesday,] May 2, [1775, A. M.]

Resolved, That another president be chosen pro tempore, and that he be chosen by nomination.

Col. Warren was then nominated and chosen.

Ordered, That Mr. Partridge, Doct. Taylor and Mr. ||ªDix,|| be a committee to wait on Col. Warren, and inform him of said choice.

Col. Warren accordingly attended, and, after offering his reasons for excuse, *Moved,* that a committee be appointed to wait on Doct. Joseph Warren, informing him of the absence of the Rev. Mr. Murray, who has lately officiated as president ||of this Congress,|| and to know ||of Doct. Warren|| if he can now attend the Congress in that station. Whereupon, *Ordered,* that Doct. Dunsmore be a committee for that purpose.[2]

Ordered, That Col. Gerrish, Col. Warren, Hon. Mr. Dexter, Mr.

a ||Dicks.||

(1) These statements have shared the fate of many of the most interesting documents of the time, and are not on the files. From some representations subsequently made, it appears, that the loss sustained by Deacon Joseph Loring, was estimated to be £720; that of Mrs. Lydia Mulliken, £431; including buildings, household furniture and wearing apparel. The house of Deacon Loring, near the spot where the brigade of Lord Percy joined the retreating detachment under Lieut. Col. Smith, is stated by himself to have been the first destroyed by the troops, in Lexington, on the memorable 19th of April. From the nature of the relief granted by Congress, it may be presumed, that some of the petitioners had suffered so severely as to be without the means of providing food.

(2) The reply to the invitation of Congress is brief:

"Doct. Warren presents his respects to the honorable Provincial Congress: informs them that he will obey their order, and attend his duty in Congress in the afternoon."

Cambridge, May 2, 1775.

Gill, and Capt. Brown of Abington, be a committee to consider the propriety of taking measures for securing the records of those counties which are more immediately exposed in this day of danger.

Ordered, That the Hon. Mr. Dexter, Col. Warren and Mr. Gill, be a committee to prepare a draught of a letter to the delegates of Congress, now in Connecticut, giving them instructions with respect to the arrival at this colony of two gentlemen from the assembly of Connecticut, with an address to general Gage, and a commission to treat with him respecting a cessation of hostilities, &c.

Ordered, That Capt. Stone of Oakham, Deacon Rawson and Major Fuller of Newton, be a committee to draw up the form of an oath to be taken by the officers and soldiers of the army now forming in this colony.

The committee ||who were|| appointed to consider what ||ªis|| proper to be done with respect to furnishing the army with some present necessaries, reported: the report was read, and ordered to lie on the table for the present.

A letter from Manchester to Doct. Taylor, respecting a computation of the taxes paid by Great Britain and America, &c., was read:

Whereupon, *Ordered*, That Mr. Webster, Deacon Cheever, and Capt. Stone ||of Framingham,|| be a committee to take the said letter into consideration, and make report.

The committee who were appointed to prepare a letter to the delegates of this Congress at Connecticut, reported: which report being read, was unanimously accepted, and is as follows, viz.:

GENTLEMEN:—Although this Congress entertain the highest opinion of the virtue and public spirit of the colony of Connecticut, and have not the smallest doubt of the attachment of the general assembly of that colony to the glorious cause of freedom, now threatened with total destruction by a corrupt ministry; yet, the arrival of two gentlemen of the first character from that colony, with an address to general Gage, and a commission to treat with him on the subject of American grievances; and to propose, as we are informed, a cessation of hostilities, at a time when that gentleman can be considered in no other light than as an instrument in the hands, and under the absolute direction of administration, to subjugate, and, for that detestable purpose, to spread slaughter and ||ᵇdesolation|| among his majesty's loyal subjects; of his disposition to do which, he has recently given a flagrant proof, in massacring a number of innocent people, who were in the peace

a ||might be.|| b ||destruction.||

of God and the king; and by other acts of injustice and cruelty; we cannot but be greatly alarmed for the consequences. Any interruptions of that happy union of the colonies which has taken place, would prove of the most fatal tendency, and we cannot but view every kind of negociation between any colony and the chief instrument of ministerial vengeance here, as being likely to operate towards such an interruption. We apprehend that things are now reduced to such a state, that nothing but an immediate recourse to arms, and a steady and persevering exertion in military operations, can possibly prevent our destruction, and that a recourse to any other method is, at best, nugatory and vain. Any proposals, either to parliament, to the ministry, or to their agents here, made separately by a single colony, may produce most tremendous events with regard to America; and we apprehend nothing could be more pleasing to our enemies than the making such proposals. We are so deeply impressed with the sense of the importance and absolute necessity of a thorough union of the colonies, and particularly with respect to the raising and supporting an army, to act with the utmost vigor at this alarming crisis; and so fearful of any measures taking place, whereby the common cause may be endangered, that we have unanimously concluded it necessary to suggest to you our fears respecting the effects of this embassy from Connecticut to [general] Gage; and we expect ||that|| you will make a proper representation of the sentiments of this Congress to their assembly, in hopes that you will receive such an explanation of their motives, and such assurances of their intention immediately to co-operate with this colony, as may remove every gloomy apprehension, and confirm us in that high estimation in which we have ever held the respectable colony of Connecticut.

P. S.—If the assembly should be dissolved, it is expected that you will tarry to treat with the next assembly.[1]

To Jedediah Foster, Timothy Danielson and John Bliss, Esquires.

(1) Doct. Samuel Johnson and Col. Oliver Wolcot were commissioned to deliver the following letter from the governor, in behalf of the general assembly of Connecticut, to general Gage.

HARTFORD, April 28, 1775.

To his excellency Thomas Gage:

" SIR :—The alarming situation of public affairs in this country, and the late unfortunate transactions in the province of the Massachusetts Bay, have induced the general assembly of this colony, now sitting in this place, to appoint a committee of their body to wait upon your excellency, and to desire me, in their name, to write to you relative to these very interesting matters."

" The inhabitants of this colony are intimately connected with the people of your province, and esteem themselves bound, by the strongest ties of friendship, as well as of common interest, to regard whatever concerns them. You will not, therefore, be surprised, that your first arrival in Boston, with a body of his majesty's troops, for the declared purpose of carrying into execution certain

On a motion made, *Ordered*, That, at three o'clock this afternoon, this Congress do take into consideration the precepts issued by general Gage for calling a general assembly.

acts of parliament, which, in their apprehension, were unconstitutional and oppressive, should have given the good people of this colony a very just and general alarm; your subsequent proceedings in fortifying the town of Boston, and other military preparations, greatly increased the apprehensions for the safety of their friends and brethren; they could not be unconcerned spectators of their sufferings, in that which they esteemed the common cause of their country; but the late hostile and secret inroads of some of the troops under your command into the heart of the country, and the violences they have committed, have driven them almost into a state of desperation. They feel now, not only for their friends, but for themselves, and their dearest interests and connections. We wish not to exaggerate; we are not sure of every part of our information; but, by the best intelligence that we have yet been able to obtain, the late transaction was a most unprovoked attack upon the lives and property of his majesty's subjects, and it has been represented to us, that such outrages have been committed as would disgrace even barbarians, and much more Britons, so highly famed for humanity as well as bravery. It is feared, therefore, that we are devoted to destruction, and that you have it in command and intention to ravage and desolate the country. If this is not the case, permit us to ask, why have these outrages been committed? Why is the town of Boston now shut up? and to what end are all the hostile preparations that are daily making, and why do we continually hear of fresh destinations of troops for this country? The people of this colony, you may rely upon it, abhor the idea of taking arms against the troops of their sovereign, and dread nothing so much as the horrors of civil war; but, at the same time, we beg leave to assure your excellency, that as they apprehended themselves justified by the principle of self-defence, so they are most firmly resolved to defend their rights and privileges to the last extremity; nor will they be restrained from giving aid to their brethren if any unjustifiable attack is made upon them. Be so good, therefore, as to explain yourself upon this most important subject, as far as is consistent with your duty to our common sovereign. Is there no way to prevent this unhappy dispute from coming to extremities? Is there no alternative but absolute submission, or the desolations of war? By that humanity which constitutes so amiable a part of your character, for the honor of our sovereign, and by the glory of the British empire, we entreat you, to prevent it, if it be possible: surely it is to be hoped that the temperate wisdom of the empire might, even yet, find expedients to restore peace, that so all parts of the empire may enjoy their particular rights, honors and immunities. Certainly, this is an event most devoutly to be wished for, and will it not be consistent with your duty to suspend the operations of war on your part, and enable us on ours to quiet the minds of the people, at least till the result of some further deliberations may be known? The importance of the occasion will, we doubt not, sufficiently apologise for the earnestness with which we address you, and any seeming impropriety which may attend it, as well as induce you to give us the most explicit and favorable answer in your power.

I am, with great esteem and respect, in behalf of the general assembly, Sir, &c.,

JONATHAN TRUMBULL."

The reply of general Gage, a dignified and able paper, follows:

BOSTON, 3d May, 1775.

"SIR:—I am to acknowledge the receipt of your letter of the 28th April last, in behalf of the general assembly of your colony, relative to the alarming situation of public affairs in this country, and the late transactions in this province. That this situation is greatly alarming, and that these transactions are truly unfortunate, are truths to be regretted by every friend to America, and by every well wisher for the peace, prosperity and happiness of this province. The intimate connection and strong ties of friendship between the inhabitants of your colony and the deluded people of this province, cannot fail of inducing the former to interpose their good offices, to convince the latter of the impropriety of their past conduct, and to persuade them to return to their allegiance, and to seek redress of any supposed grievances, in those decent and constitutional methods, in which alone they can hope to be successful."

"That troops should be employed for the purpose of protecting the magistrates in the execution of their duty, when opposed with violence, is not a new thing in the English, or any other government. That any acts of the British parliament are unconstitutional or oppressive, I am not to sup-

Resolved, That Capt. Goodman be ||ªdesired|| to take the charge of transmitting, forthwith, the letter to the delegates of this colony now in Connecticut.

pose; if any such there are, in the apprehension of the people of this province, it had been happy for them if they had sought relief, only the in way which the constitution, their reason and their interest pointed out."

" You cannot wonder at my fortifying the town of Boston, or making any other military preparations, when you are assured, that, previous to my taking these steps, such were the open threats, and such the warlike preparations throughout this province, as rendered it my indispensable duty to take every precaution in my power, for the protection of his majesty's troops under my command, against all hostile attempts."

" The intelligence you seem to have received, relative to the late excursion of a body of troops into the country, is altogether injurious, and contrary to the true state of facts. The troops disclaim, with indignation, the barbarous outrages of which they are accused, so contrary to their known humanity. I have taken the greatest pains to discover if any were committed, and have found examples of their tenderness, both to the young and the old, but no vestige of cruelty or barbarity. It is very possible, that in firing into houses, from whence they were fired upon, that old people, women or children may have suffered; but if any such thing has happened, it was in their defence and undesigned. I have no command to ravage and desolate the country; and were it my intention, I have had pretence to begin it, upon the sea ports, who are at the mercy of the fleet. For your better information I enclose you a narrative of that affair, taken from gentlemen of indisputable honor and veracity who were eye witnesses of all the transactions of that day. The leaders here have taken pains to prevent any account of this affair getting abroad, but such as they have thought proper to publish themselves; and, to that end, the post has been stopped, the mails broke open, and letters taken out; and, by these means, the most injurious and inflammatory accounts have been spread throughout the continent, which have served to deceive and inflame the minds of the people."

" When the resolves of the Provincial Congress breathed nothing but war, when those two great and essential prerogatives of the king, the levying of troops and disposing of the public moneys, were wrested from him, and when magazines were forming, by an assembly of men, unknown to the constitution, for the declared purpose of levying war against the king, you must acknowledge it was my duty, as it was the dictate of humanity, to prevent, if possible, the calamities of a civil war, by destroying such magazines. This, and this alone, I attempted."

" You ask, why is the town of Boston now shut up; I can only refer you, for an answer, to those bodies of armed men who now surround the town, and prevent all access to it. The hostile preparations you mention, are such as the conduct of the people of this province have rendered it prudent to make, for the defence of those under my command. You assure me, the people of your colony abhor the idea of taking up arms against the troops of their sovereign; I wish the people of this province, for their own sakes, could make the same declaration."

" You enquire, is there no way to prevent this unhappy dispute from coming to extremities? is there no alternative but absolute submission or the desolations of war? I answer I hope there is. The king and parliament seem to hold out terms of reconciliation, consistent with the honor and interest of Great Britain, and the rights and privileges of the colonies. They have mutually declared their readiness to attend to any real grievances of the colonies, and to afford them every just and reasonable indulgence, which shall, in a dutiful and constitutional manner, be laid before them; and his majesty adds, it is his ardent wish, that this disposition may have a happy effect on the temper and conduct of his subjects in America. I must add, likewise, the resolution of the 27th February, on the grand dispute of taxation and revenue; leaving it to the colonies to tax themselves, under certain conditions. Here is surely a foundation for an accommodation, to people who wish a reconciliation, rather than a destructive war, between countries so nearly connected by the ties of blood and interest; but I fear that the leaders of this province have been, and still are, intent only on shedding blood."

" I am much obliged by your favorable sentiments of my personal character; and assure you, as it has been my constant wish and endeavor hitherto, so I shall continue to exert my utmost efforts to

a ||directed.||

Ordered, That a postscript be added to said letter, instructing said delegates, that if their assembly should be dissolved, they tarry there, to treat with the new assembly.

The ||Congress then|| adjourned to three o'clock this afternoon.

Afternoon.

A letter was presented to this Congress by Esquire Aikin, from Mr. Lemuel Williams, dated Dartmouth, May 1, 1775,[1] to said Aikin, which was read: whereupon, *Ordered,* that Mr. Batchelder, Esquire Dix, Col. Farley, Mr. Greenleaf and Mr. Bent, be a committee to take the said letter into consideration, and report as soon as may be, and that Esquire Aikin be desired to attend on said committee.

The order of the day [was] moved for.

Resolved, That the further consideration of the precepts for calling a general assembly, be referred to Thursday next, ten o'clock, A. M.

Ordered, That Deacon Cheever, Col. Warren, Mr. Gill, Hon. Mr. Dexter, and the president, be a committee to bring in a resolve for the purpose of granting liberty to such persons in Boston as incline to send into the country for their effects, that so another obstacle may be removed to the liberating of the inhabitants of Boston.

||The committee on the letter from Lemuel Williams to Esquire Aikin, reported verbally. The matter was ordered to subside.||

Ordered, That Mr. Gerry, President Warren, Hon. Mr. Dexter, Col. Warren and Col. Gerrish, be a committee to forward an express to the Hon. Continental Congress, with authenticated copies of the depositions, and address to the inhabitants of Great Britain, and letter to Mr. Franklin, lately sent to Great Britain, per Capt. Derby of Salem; also to send another original set of said papers, by said express, to be forwarded by the vessel in the southern colonies to London, and

protect all his majesty's liege subjects under my care, in their persons and property. You ask, whether it will not be consistent with my duty to suspend the operations of war on my part, &c.? I have commenced no operations of war but defensive; such you cannot wish me to suspend, while I am surrounded by an armed country, who have already begun, and threaten farther to prosecute an offensive war; and are now violently depriving me, the king's troops, and many others of the king's subjects under my immediate protection, of all the conveniences and necessaries of life, with which the country abounds. But it must quiet the minds of all reasonable people, when I assure you, that I have no disposition to injure or molest quiet and peaceable subjects; but, on the contrary, shall esteem it my greatest happiness, to defend and protect them against every species of violence and oppression.

I am, with great regard and esteem, Sir, your most obedient humble servant,

THOMAS GAGE."

The Hon. Gov. Trumbull.

(1) The enquiry was proposed by Mr. Williams, whether it would be proper for the merchants of Dartmouth to send their vessels to sea. The opinion expressed by the committee was, that they should be restrained in port.

to report an application to be sent by said express to the Continental Congress.

Col. Learned *Moved*, That the sense of this Congress might be taken, whether the regiment he is now raising may be a regiment of grenadiers : the matter was ordered to subside.

A motion was made and seconded, that a committee be appointed, to take into consideration the expediency of drafting a certain proportion of the town's stock of powder, &c., from such towns as they shall think proper, for the present supply of the army now establishing in this colony. The matter was ordered to subside, till the Congress had passed upon a report for giving license to such persons, in Boston, as incline to, send into the country for their effects : which report was read, amended and accepted, and is as follows, viz. :

[IN PROVINCIAL CONGRESS, *Watertown*, May 2, 1775.]

[*Resolved*, That such inhabitants of this colony, as have repaired to the town of Boston, there to take up their residence, and have effects in the other towns of this government, be permitted, each of them, to send out a servant, or other person, without arms, to put up and transport, into the said town of Boston, any such goods or effects, excepting arms and ammunition ; and that the officers appointed for granting permits, at Roxbury and Charlestown, be, and hereby are, directed to provide a suitable attendant to each person so sent out, whose business it shall be to continue with him till he returns, and that permits, agreeable to the intention of this resolve, be granted.][1]

The committee appointed to devise ways and means for supplying the treasury, reported as to the first step, and asked leave to sit again.

Ordered, That Mr. Freeman, Doct. Taylor, Mr. Lewis, Col. Dwight and Esquire Gardner, be a committee to consider what measures are proper to be taken for liberating those persons who were taken prisoners by the troops under the command of general Gage, on the 19th [of April last.]

All the committees ||of the Congress were|| enjoined to sit, ||and then the Congress|| adjourned till to-morrow morning, nine o'clock.

[WEDNESDAY,] May 3, 1775, [A. M.]

Ordered, That Deacon Cheever be desired to make application to the Rev. Doct. Cooper, to request that he would officiate as chaplain for this Congress during its session in this place.

(1) This resolve is restored to the journal from a copy made by Mr. Secretary Freeman.

Ordered, That Doct, Taylor, Mr. Lothrop and Mr. Paine, be a committee to forward the proclamations, for a fast, into the country, as soon as possible.

Resolved, That this last mentioned order be reconsidered; and thereupon, *Ordered,* that the committee who were appointed at Concord for dispersing the proclamations, be required to perform their duty with all possible expedition.

On the application from the committee of safety, relative to supplying Col. Arnold with one hundred pounds [lawful money,] and sundry warlike stores;

Ordered, That Mr. Greenleaf, Mr. Gill and Mr. Partridge, be a committee to take said application into consideration, and report.

The committee on the application from the committee of safety, reported: [the report was] read and accepted, and is as followeth:

IN PROVINCIAL CONGRESS, *Watertown,* May 3, 1775.

Resolved, That the within request of the committee of safety be granted, and that the committee of supplies be, and they hereby are directed, to furnish Col. Benedict Arnold with ten horses, two hundred pounds of gunpowder, two hundred pounds of lead balls, and one thousand flints, at the expense of the colony, and that said committee draw upon Henry Gardner, Esq., receiver general, for one hundred pounds, [lawful money,] in favor of said Arnold, and take his receipt for the whole—said Arnold to be accountable therefor to this or some other congress, or future house of representatives.

Ordered, That Col. Warren, Doct. Holten, Mr. Dix, Col. Farley and Doct. Taylor, be a committee to ||*overlook the commission of the committee of safety, and the commission of the committee of supplies,|| and to see whether it be necessary that they be invested with other powers than they now have.

The committee [appointed] to bring in the form of a resolve, empowering the treasurer to borrow a certain sum of money, and the form of a note, to be by him given to the lender, &c., reported; the report [was] amended, read and accepted, and is as followeth:

Resolved, That the receiver general be, and hereby is empowered and directed, to borrow the sum of one hundred thousand pounds, lawful money, and issue colony securities for the same, payable with annual interest, at six per cent., June 1, 1777, and that the Continental Congress be desired to recommend to the several colonies to give a currency to such securities.

a ||ascertain the power of the committees of supplies and of safety.||

Resolved, That the securities given by the receiver general for the moneys borrowed by him, in pursuance of the aforegoing resolve, be in the form following, viz :

No.   The   day of   A. D. 177 .

Borrowed and received of A. B. the sum of   pounds, lawful money, for the use and service of the colony of the Massachusetts Bay; and in behalf of said colony, I do hereby promise and oblige myself, and my successors in the office of treasurer or receiver general, to repay to the said A. B., or to his order, on the first day of June, 1777, the aforesaid sum of   pounds, lawful money, in Spanish milled dollars, at six shillings each, or in the several species of coined silver and gold, enumerated in an act ||made and passed in the twenty-second year of his late majesty king George the Second, entitled an act|| for ascertaining the rates at which coined silver and gold, English half-pence and farthings, may pass within this government, and according to the rates therein mentioned, with interest, to be paid annually, at six per cent.

A. B.⎫
C. D.⎬ £   *Witness my hand,*
E. F.⎭
                                            H. G.

The committee on the letter from Mr. Lee to Doct. Taylor, reported verbally, that a copy of said letter be forwarded to our members of the Continental Congress : upon a motion, the question was put, whether the above report be accepted, and passed in the negative.

Resolved, That in all orders for impressing horses and carriages, the horses and carriages of the members of this Congress be excepted, and that a copy of this resolve be sent to the committee of safety and committee of supplies.

Ordered, That at three o'clock this afternoon, the Congress will take into consideration the propriety of establishing pay for a brigade major.

Ordered, That at five o'clock this afternoon, the Congress will come to the choice of a committee of three [persons,] by ballot, to procure a copper plate for printing the colony notes, and to countersign them.

Ordered, That the committee who reported a resolve relative to borrowing money, &c., bring in a resolve that no note be given by the receiver general for a less sum than four pounds.

Adjourned till three o'clock, P. M.

                                            Afternoon.

The committee appointed to bring in a resolve that no note be given by the receiver general for any sum less than four pounds, reported; and the report was amended and accepted, and is as follows:

Whereas, inconveniences may arise by the receiver general's issuing notes for small sums: therefore, *Resolved*, that the receiver general be, and he hereby is directed, not to issue any notes for a less sum than four pounds, lawful money.

The report of the committee appointed to take into consideration the advance pay to the soldiers, was taken up and read; but as part of the report is superseded by a resolve in the morning, therefore, *Ordered*, that the report be recommitted, and that part thereof which hath been superseded be left out, and that each soldier be allowed twenty shillings, lawful money, in advance.

The order of the day [was] moved for.

Resolved, That Capt. Parker, Col. How and Col. Farley, be a committee to take into consideration the propriety of establishing pay for a brigade major.

The above vote was reconsidered.

The committee appointed to report the form of an oath, reported: the report was read, and recommitted.

Ordered, That Major Fuller, ||Capt. Brown|| and Capt. Brown of Watertown, be a committee to count and sort the votes for a committee to procure a copperplate for printing the colony notes, and to countersign them. The committee having attended that service, reported, that the Hon. Samuel Dexter, Esq., Doct. Joseph Warren and Mr. Moses Gill, were chosen.

Mr. Cheever, who was appointed to wait on the Rev. Doct. Cooper, and desire his attendance on this Congress, to officiate as their chaplain, reported, that he had attended the service assigned him, and that the state of the Doctor's affairs was such, that he could not attend according to the desire of the Congress.

The committee appointed to report a letter to the Continental Congress, reported. The report was read and accepted, and ordered to be copied, and forwarded as soon as may be, and is as follows, viz.:

To the Honorable American Continental Congress, to be convened at Philadelphia, on the tenth of May instant:

MAY IT PLEASE YOUR HONORS :—The Congress of this colony, impressed with the deepest concern for their country, under the present critical and alarming state of its public affairs, beg leave, with the most respectful submission, whilst acting in support of the cause of America, to request the direction and assistance of your respectable assembly.

The enclosed packet, containing the copies of depositions which we have despatched for London, also an address to the inhabitants of Great Britain, and a letter to our colony agent, Benjamin Franklin, Esq., are humbly submitted to your consideration.

The sanguinary zeal of the ministerial army, to ruin and destroy the inhabitants of this colony, in the opinion of this Congress hath rendered the establishment of an army indispensably necessary. We have accordingly passed an unanimous resolve for thirteen thousand six hundred men, to be forthwith raised by this colony; and proposals are made by us to the congress of New Hampshire, and governments of Rhode Island and Connecticut colonies, for furnishing men in the same proportion. The sudden exigency of our public affairs precluded the possibility of waiting for your direction in these important measures; more especially, as a considerable reenforcement from Great Britain is daily expected in this colony, and we are now reduced to the sad alternative of defending by arms, or submitting to be slaughtered.

With the greatest deference, we beg leave to suggest, that a powerful army, on the side of America, hath been considered by this Congress as the only mean left to stem ||ᵃ|| the rapid progress of a tyrannical ministry. Without a force superior to our enemies, we must reasonably expect to become the victims of their relentless fury: with such a force, we may still have hopes of seeing an immediate end put to the inhuman ravages of mercenary troops in America, and the wicked authors of our miseries brought to condign punishment, by the just indignation of our brethren in Great Britain.

We hope that this colony will, at all times, be ready to spend, and be spent, in the cause of America. It is, nevertheless, a misfortune, greatly operating to its disadvantage, that it has a great number of sea port towns exposed to the approach of the enemy by sea, from many of which the inhabitants have removed, and are now removing their families and effects, to avoid destruction from ships of war: these, we apprehend, will be generally distressed from want of subsistence, and disabled from contributing aid for supporting the forces of the colony; but we have the greatest confidence in the wisdom and ability of the continent to support us, so far as it shall appear necessary for supporting the common cause of the American colonies.

We also enclose several resolves for empowering and directing our receiver general to borrow the sum of £100,000, lawful money, and

a ||the torrent and.||

to issue his notes for the same; it being the only measure which we could have recourse to for supporting our forces; and we request your assistance, in rendering our measures effectual, by giving our notes currency through the continent.

Ordered, That Col. Davis be desired to wait on the Rev. Mr. Gordon, and desire that he would attend on this Congress, and officiate as their chaplain, during their session in the town of Watertown.

The committee who were appointed to take under consideration the advance pay to the soldiers, reported. The report was recommitted, and Capt. Stone ||of Framingham|| and Doct. Taylor, added to the committee.

[The committee who were appointed to consider what measures are proper to be taken for liberating those persons who were taken prisoners by the troops, under general Gage, on the 19th of April, reported a resolve, which was read and accepted, and *Ordered*, that any member who desires a copy may have one. The resolve is as follows :]

IN PROVINCIAL CONGRESS, *Watertown*, May 3, 1775.

[Whereas, a number of the inhabitants of this colony were taken prisoners by the troops, under the command of general Gage, on the 19th of April last, and are by him so held :]

[*Resolved*, That it is the opinion of this Congress that an application be sent to general Gage, signed by the wives or nearest relations of such prisoners, and the selectmen of the towns to which they respectively belong, desiring that he would discharge their friends from their said imprisonment; and they are empowered hereby to offer to send in to the general an equal number of his troops, now in the hands of this people, who were taken prisoners on the aforesaid 19th of April, upon his liberating their friends as aforesaid.]

||The Congress|| then adjourned to nine o'clock to-morrow morning.

[THURSDAY,] May 4, [1775, A. M.]

Col. Davis, who was appointed to wait upon the Rev. Mr. Gordon, to desire that he would officiate as chaplain to this Congress, reported, that he had waited upon Mr. Gordon, and that Mr. Gordon informed him he would attend accordingly.

The committee who were appointed to take into consideration the advance pay to the soldiers, again reported; which report was read, amended and accepted, and ordered to be authenticated, and sent forthwith to head quarters. It is as follows :

Whereas, the distressed state of this colony, at this alarming crisis, calls for its utmost exertions, that the army now to be raised be forthwith completed : therefore, *Resolved*, that each non commissioned officer and private soldier, who has, or shall, enlist himself into the service of this colony, shall have twenty shillings paid him out of the receiver general's office, as advance ||pay ;|| and that the commanding officer of each regiment who shall be, ||and hereby is,|| empowered to act as muster master for his said regiment, shall draw from the receiver general's office the sum of twenty shillings, for each non commissioned officer and private soldier in his said regiment, and pay the same, according to the tenor of this resolve, as soon as said men shall have enlisted themselves, and be duly sworn, and give his bond, with sufficient surety, to the receiver general, therefor ; said bond to be discharged by a receipt produced, by said officer, from each non commissioned officer and private soldier, that he has received the same.

On an application made to this Congress, for an order on the committee of supplies, for one barrel of powder, for the use of the inhabitants of Falmouth, in Casco Bay ; *Ordered*, that this matter be referred to the said committee of supplies, they to act thereon as they think best.

The order of the day [was] moved for.

The absent members were ordered to be called in.

On a motion made, that a committee be appointed to bring in a resolve containing a reconsideration of a resolve, passed by this Congress, at Concord, the first of April last, giving it as their opinion, that "if writs should be issued for calling a general assembly, to be held on the last Wednesday of May next, that the several towns in this colony ought to obey such precepts, and to bring in a resolve recommending to the several towns and districts in this colony not to obey such precepts,"—after a long and serious debate, the question was put, and it passed in the affirmative : for the question, 94 : the whole number of the house, 107.

Col. Warren, Mr. Gerry, Col. Gerrish, Doct. Holten and Col. Mandell, were accordingly appointed for this purpose.

Ordered, That Capt. Stone of Framingham, Mr. Bent and Major Fuller, be a committee to examine the returns of the several town and district stocks of powder, and to bring in a resolve recommending to such towns as they think proper, which are not immediately exposed, to furnish the towns of Falmouth and Arundel with one barrel of powder each.

Then adjourned to three o'clock this afternoon.

Resolved, That Gen. Putnam and Col. Porter, who were, with other of the committee of safety, appointed by the said committee of safety, and the council of war, to lay some special matters before this Congress, be admitted into this house, and that Col. Warren, Mr. Devens and Col. Gerrish, be a committee to introduce them ||accordingly.||

The left hand front pew was assigned them to sit in.

The absent members were directed to attend.

The said committee having accordingly attended this Congress, they informed the Congress, that the gentlemen delegated by the assembly of Connecticut, to execute an embassy to general Gage, had come out of Boston, with letters from him to the assembly of Connecticut, of which they thought it proper to inform this Congress, that they might take order thereon, if they thought fit: whereupon, *Ordered*, that the president, Col. Warren, Doct. Holten, Col. Gerrish, Col. Palmer, Doct. Baylies, Doct. Taylor, Mr. Gardner, Mr. Partridge, Mr. Gerry and Mr. Mills, together with the committee from the committee of safety, and council of war, be a committee to hold a conference with the said Connecticut delegates, and to attend forthwith.

The committee appointed to enquire into the conduct of the several towns, relative to the prisoners of war, reported: whereupon, *Ordered*, that Mr. Wyman apply to the committee of safety, desiring that they would take such measures with respect to the colony stores, and two regular officers, with their waiters, now at Woburn, as will remove the necessity of keeping so large a guard as is now placed there to guard the same.

The committee appointed to confer with the Connecticut delegates, reported, that they had conferred with them on the subject of their embassy, and of the letter to their assembly from general Gage, but that they thought it inconsistent with their honor, and the interest of the colonies, to open it; but that they would use their influence, when they returned, to have the contents of it communicated to this colony

Moved, That the delegates from Connecticut be desired to attend this Congress: after debate the matter was ordered to subside.

Ordered, That the president, Col. Warren, Col. Dwight, Mr. Gerry and Col. Holten, be a committee to return the compliments to the gentlemen from Connecticut, for their patient attendance to the inquiry made of them by this Congress, respecting their embassy to general Gage.

Moved, That the resolve passed yesterday, respecting advance pay for the soldiers, be reconsidered, so far as it respects muster masters, and that two muster masters be appointed by this Congress. After debate [the matter was] ordered to subside.

Ordered, That the president, Mr. Gerry and Col. Warren, be a committee to prepare a letter to the assembly of Connecticut, respecting their late application to general Gage.

Ordered, That Capt. Stone, Mr. Mills, Capt. McCobb, Doct. Perkins, Col. Grout and Mr. Kollock, be directed to copy the depositions of the late hostile proceedings of general Gage's troops, to be transmitted to Connecticut.

Then adjourned to to-morrow morning, nine o'clock.

[FRIDAY,] May 5, 1775, [A. M.]

Ordered, That Deacon Stickney and Mr. Webster be added to the committee who were appointed to examine the returns, and districts' stock of powder, &c., May 4th, A. M.

Ordered, That Doct. Taylor, Mr. Batchelder and Doct. Holten, be a committee to bring in a resolve relative to an obstruction to the removing the inhabitants of Boston, as expressed in a letter to this Congress from the selectmen of Boston, and other papers: and that said resolve, when passed, together with the resolve which passed this Congress the 2d instant, giving license to those persons in Boston, who incline, to send a servant out for their effects, be authenticated, and transmitted to Gen. Ward.

The committee who were appointed to bring in two resolves respecting general Gage's writs for calling an assembly, reported: both of which were read and accepted, and are as follow, viz.:

Whereas, this Congress did, at their session at Concord, on the first day of April last, resolve, as their opinion, that if writs be issued in form as the law directs, for calling a general assembly, to be held on the last Wednesday of May next, that such writs should be obeyed, &c.; and whereas, many reasons now prevail to convince us that consequences of a dangerous nature would result from the operation of that resolution : therefore, *Resolved,* that the said vote and resolution be reconsidered, and it is hereby reconsidered, and declared null and void.

Whereas, his excellency general Gage, since his arrival into this colony, hath conducted as an instrument in the hands of an arbitrary ministry to enslave this people, and a detachment ||of the troops,|| under his command, have, of late, been ||by him|| ordered to the town of Concord, to destroy the public stores deposited in that place for the use of the colony : and, whereas, by this clandestine and perfidious measure, a number of respectable inhabitants of the colony, without any provocation ||given by them,|| have been illegally, wantonly and inhumanly slaughtered by the troops: therefore, *Resolved*, that the said general Gage hath, by these means, and many others, utterly disqualified himself to serve this colony as a governor, and in every other capacity, and that no obedience ought, in future, to be paid by the several towns and districts in this colony, to his writs for calling an assembly, or to his proclamations, or any other of his acts or doings; but that, on the other hand, he ought to be considered and guarded against, as an unnatural and inveterate enemy to this country.

Ordered, That Mr. Gardner, Col. Dwight and Col. Warren, be a committee to bring in a resolve, recommending to the several towns and districts in this colony, to choose delegates for a new Provincial Congress, to be held on the last Wednesday of the present month.

The committee who were appointed to prepare the form of an oath, to be taken by the officers and soldiers of the army now raising in this colony, reported: which report was ordered for the present to subside.

The committee who were this day appointed to bring in a resolve for the purpose of removing an obstruction to the liberating the inhabitants of Boston, reported: which report was ordered to be recommitted, and that Mr. Gill and Mr. Partridge be added to the committee.

The committee who were yesterday appointed to prepare a letter to the assembly of Connecticut, reported a letter, which was read, amended and accepted, and is as follows:

To the Honorable, the Governor and Company of the ||ᵃColony|| of Connecticut:

GENTLEMEN:—The delegates appointed by your ||ᵇrespectable|| assembly, to treat with general Gage on the late unhappy events which have occured in this colony, have favored us with a conference, and communicated the substance of their interview with him. We are greatly alarmed at the unparalleled wickedness of our unnatural enemies, in endeavoring to persuade our sister colony, that the inhabitants of this, first commenced hostilities; a suggestion which, we cannot but think, will appear absurd, when the great inequality of the Lexington company and the detachment of regular troops, which attacked them, is coolly considered.

But to put this matter in the clearest light, we beg leave to enclose you the copies of depositions, taken by order of this Congress, and

a ||State.|| b ||respectful.||

25

despatched for London, containing the most incontestable evidence, that the king's troops first fired upon, and killed, several of the inhabitants of this colony, before any injury was offered to them. We also enclose you the copies of an address to the inhabitants of Great Britain, and of a letter to our colony agent, and think it expedient to suspend the publication of the address and letter, until they shall have had their effect in England.

The experience which we have had of general Gage, hath fully convinced us, that but little dependence can be placed in his professions. Whilst he has been collecting his forces, fortifying our capital, and in every other respect preparing for war, we have been amused with his pretensions to benevolence and kindness, evidently calculated to retard the measures which we were necessarily pursuing for self defence. And we are constrained to declare, that should he be, at any future time, possessed of forces superior to those raised for opposing him, we should, from his past conduct, have no hopes ||left|| of escaping the heaviest vengeance which ministerial tyranny can devise, assisted by the most inveterate enemies to mankind in general, and of this their native country in particular. On the exertions of the colonies, and blessings of heaven, we alone can depend for safety and support. And it is clearly the opinion of this Congress, that the establishment of a powerful army, is the best and only measure left, to bring the present disputes to a happy issue. It is evidently the business of the general, to subjugate these and the other colonies; and, we think, there are the most convincing proofs that, in order to effect it, he is constantly aiming to suspend their ||ᵃpreparations|| for defence, until his reenforcements shall arrive; but, although we have been under great apprehensions with respect to the advantages which the conference of Connecticut, with general Gage, ||ᵇmight|| give our enemies, yet, we have the greatest confidence in the wisdom and vigilance of your respectable assembly and colony, as well as of our other sister colonies; and have reason to hope, that, while he fails in his intentions to lull and deceive this continent, he can never accomplish his designs to conquer it.

Ordered, That the foregoing letter be fairly ||ᶜtranscribed|| and authenticated, and committed to the care of Col. Dwight, together with a copy of the depositions respecting the late hostile proceedings of general Gage's troops, attested by the secretary, to be delivered by Col. Dwight to the governor and company of Connecticut as soon as may be.

Adjourned to three o'clock, P. M.

a ||operations.|| b ||may.|| c ||copied.||

[Afternoon]

The committee who were to bring in a resolve for the purpose of removing an obstruction to the liberating the inhabitants of Boston, again reported: which report, being read and accepted, it was *Ordered*, that Mr. Partridge carry the same immediately to ||*Gen.|| Ward. It is as follows, viz. :

Resolved, That the following letter be sent to Gen. Ward, and a copy of the same to the selectmen of Boston.

Sir :—By the enclosed papers you will see, that the liberation of our good friends in Boston is greatly obstructed : therefore, Sir, you are directed to examine into the matter, and give such orders as shall be effectual, for the future, strictly to execute the resolutions of this Congress, respecting permits into the country, and protection of all persons thus permitted; and also communicate your doing hereon to the selectmen of Boston, with all possible despatch, that our friends may not be detained any longer : and also, that you give directions to your officers carefully to execute the resolves of Congress, in all matters in which they are to act, without any levity, or indecency of expression or behavior.

To the Hon. Artemas Ward, Esq. :

P. S.—The pass given by the selectmen must be in strict conformity to the resolve of Congress, viz. : that the bearer is sent out, to put up and transport into the town of Boston, the goods and effects of such persons as have repaired to Boston, there to take up their residence.

On a petition from Charles Glidden and others, for a supply of powder, &c. : *Ordered*, that Doct. Taylor inform said Glidden, now in waiting, that this Congress would gladly comply with their request, did not the present exigencies of the colony make it necessary that all their stock of ammunition be retained in the colony magazine.

The committee who were appointed to bring in a resolve recommending the choice of delegates for a new Provincial Congress, reported the following : which was read and accepted, and is as follows, viz. :

Whereas, the term for which this present Congress was chosen, expires on the 30th instant, and the exigencies of our public affairs render it absolutely necessary, for the safety of this colony, that a new Congress be elected and convened, to consider of, and transact, the public affairs thereof: *Resolved*, that it be, and it is hereby recommended to the several towns and districts in this colony, that they each

a ||Mr.||

of them do, forthwith, elect and depute as many members as to them shall seem necessary and expedient, to represent them in a Provincial Congress, to be held at the meeting-house in Watertown, on the 31st day of May instant, to be chosen by such only as are qualified by law to vote for representatives in the general assembly, and to be continued by adjournment, ||ᵃ|| as they shall see cause, until the expiration of six months from their being first convened on the 31st of this instant May, and no longer; and consult, deliberate and resolve upon such further measures, as, under God, shall be effectual to save this people from impending ruin, and to secure those inestimable liberties derived to us from our ancestors, and which it is our duty to preserve for posterity.

Ordered, That this last mentioned resolve, together with the resolve passed in the forenoon, respecting general Gage's precepts, be printed in hand bills; and that Major Fuller, Capt. Batchelder and Esquire Dix, be a committee to get the same printed, and dispersed to the several towns and districts in this colony.

The gentlemen who were appointed delegates for this colony to the colony of Connecticut, reported, that they had attended the business to which they were appointed, and had brought a letter from the speaker of the Connecticut assembly, which they laid before this Congress.[1]

Resolved, That the vote which passed in Congress this day, respecting a petition made by Charles Glidden and others, for powder and ball, be reconsidered, and that the committee of supplies be, and hereby are ||ᵇdirected,|| to furnish the said Charles ||Glidden,|| for the use of the subscribers to said petition, one half barrel of powder, and such a quantity of lead as will be proper and proportional thereto.

Resolved, That the assembly of Connecticut be supplied with the rules and regulations which have been recommended to be observed by the army now raising in this colony.

---

a ||from day to day.|| b ||desired.||

(1) Governor Jonathan Trumbull replies to the letter of the Provincial Congress, from Hartford, May 4, 1775, in behalf of the colony of Connecticut:.

"Your letter of the second of May instant," he writes, "is received. You need not fear our firmness, deliberation and unanimity, to pursue the measures which appear best for our common defence and safety, and in no degree to relax our vigilant preparations for that end, and to act in union and concert with our sister colonies. We shall be cautious of trusting promises which it may be in the power of any one to evade. We hope no ill consequences will attend our embassy to general Gage. We should be glad to be furnished with the evidence, duly authenticated, concerning the attack, on the 19th of April last, at Lexington, which it is presumed you have taken. Although we are at a distance from the most distressing scenes before your eyes, yet we are most sensibly affected with the alarming relations of them."

The letter from the speaker stated, that preparations were made for raising an army of fifteen hundred men, in the colony of Connecticut.

On a motion made by Capt. McCobb, that some measures might be taken to preserve a number of large masts, plank, &c., now lying in Kennebeck river, and to prevent their being carried to Halifax, where they might be ||ªappropriated|| to the injury of this country : *Ordered*, that the consideration thereof be referred to the committee of safety, and that Capt. McCobb be desired to attend the said committee, and give them all the information he can relative thereto.

A resolution of the committee of safety, giving it as their opinion, that government, in full form, ought to be taken up immediately, was read : whereupon, *Ordered*, that the consideration of this matter be referred to Tuesday next, at three o'clock, P. M.

||Then|| adjourned till to-morrow morning, nine o'clock.

[SATURDAY,] May 6, 1775, A. M.

Resolved, That the committee of ||ᵇsupplies|| be, and they are hereby empowered, to procure powder, in such quantities as they shall think necessary, not only at Connecticut and Rhode Island, but at New York, or any other colony on the continent.

Ordered, That Mr. Sawyer, Capt. Stone and Doct. Taylor, be a committee to bring in a resolve for the purpose of appointing two officers, one in each camp of the colony army, whose business it shall be to pass muster on the soldiers, and draw for them, out of the treasury, their half month's pay.

Ordered, That the president, Col. Dexter, Col. Warren, Doct. Holten and Mr. Mills, be a committee to take ||ᶜunder|| consideration the letter received yesterday from the speaker of the general assembly of Connecticut.

A form of a pass, and resolve thereon, brought in by Col. Warren, was accepted, and is as follows, viz. :

To the Guards of the Colony Army :

Pursuant to a resolve of the Provincial Congress, you are hereby ordered to permit   a member of said Congress, to pass and repass, with his company, at all times.

President pro tempore.

May   1775.

Resolved, That the general officer of the army of this colony be, and hereby is directed to give orders to his officers, to pay obedience to all permits of the foregoing form, signed by the president of this Congress.

a ||used.|| b ||safety.|| c ||into.||

Resolved, That Col. Dwight proceed with the letters and depositions as ordered by this Congress, with all possible speed, to Hartford, there to tarry, if at his discretion he thinks necessary, till he receives an answer to said letter, and a copy of the letter sent by general Gage to the assembly at Connecticut; and to inform the said assembly of the alteration made by this Congress in the pay of the field officers of the army now raising in this colony.

Ordered, That Mr. Whiting, Major Fuller, Col. Thurston, Doct. Taylor, Col. Field, Doct. Sawyer and Col. Warren, be a committee, to bring in a resolve containing a reconsideration of the resolve passed yesterday, respecting the choice of delegates for a new Congress, so far as to determine what towns should send members, and how many members each town and district ought to send. This last order reconsidered : whereupon, *Ordered,* that Mr. Rawson of Mendon, Col. Gardner, Mr. Thurston, Esquire Davis and Mr. Sawyer, be a committee to take into consideration an equal representation of this colony, and report thereon.

Ordered, That Col. Thurston, Esquire Dix and Mr. Lothrop, be a committee to take into consideration the form of an establishment for the train, and report a resolve thereon.

The committee appointed to bring in a resolve for the appointment of muster masters, reported.

Resolved, That three o'clock this afternoon be assigned for choosing two muster masters, and that they be chosen by ballot.

Col. Lincoln brought in a resolve, empowering the committee of supplies to import military stores from such place, and in such ||ᵃ|| quantities as they shall judge proper : which was read and accepted, and is as follows, viz. :

Whereas, in the course of the present disputes with Great Britain, it may be necessary to import, on the risque of the colony, many kinds of military and other stores :

Resolved, That the committee of supplies be, and they hereby are empowered and directed, to import, or cause to be imported, from any place whatever, such and so many stores aforesaid, as they shall judge necessary for the defence of the colony, and the same to risk, at their discretion, with or without making insurance on the vessels and cargoes which may be so ||employed,|| sent out, or imported.

Ordered, That this resolve be kept an absolute and entire secret by every member of this Congress.

Resolved, That four o'clock this afternoon be assigned to consider

a ||manner and.||

if any method can be taken for settling the appointment of the field officers.

||Then|| adjourned to three o'clock, P. M.

[Afternoon]

The order of the day [was] read.

Ordered, That Mr. Dix, Mr. Gill and Doct. Sawyer, be a committee to sort and count the votes for two muster masters.

||*The committee appointed to sort and count the votes for two muster masters,|| reported, that Gen. John Whitcomb and Col. Benjamin Lincoln, were unanimously chosen.

The report of the committee respecting the appointment of muster masters was accepted, and is as follows, viz. :

Resolved, That Gen. John Whitcomb and Col. Benjamin ||Lincoln,|| be, and hereby are appointed muster masters in the Massachusetts army, whose business it shall be to pass muster on every soldier that [shall] be enlisted into said army, and by no means to accept of any but such as are able bodied, effective men ; and also to examine if their arms and accoutrements are in proper order : and said muster masters are hereby directed and empowered to receive from Henry Gardner, Esq., receiver general, or his successor in office, twenty shillings, lawful money, for each and every non commissioned officer and private soldier thus mustered and sworn, who shall appear with their arms and accoutrements ; and shall give bonds to said receiver general, with sufficient surety, for such monies drawn out of the treasury ; and shall forthwith pay out said sum of twenty shillings, as advance pay, to each and every non commissioned officer and private soldier, and on producing receipts from them to said receiver general, said bonds shall be cancelled.

Resolved, That the consideration of the pay of the muster masters be referred to some future time.

Ordered, That Col. Thurston and Mr. Sawyer be a committee to apply to the committee of safety for a list of all such persons to whom they have given encouragement to receive commissions as field officers of the army now raising in this colony ; and they are directed to inquire of said committee of safety, what field officers they expect will be most likely to succeed in filling up their regiments.

Ordered, That Esquire Rawson, Mr. Partridge, Major Brooks, Mr. Webster, Col. Mosely, Mr. Bliss and Capt. Stone ||of Oakham,|| be a committee to inquire what number of province arms there are in the province, and in what place ; and, in particular, that they apply to the committee of supplies, to know what number of fire arms they have procured, and how they have disposed of them.

The committee who were appointed to consider the form of an establishment for the train, reported verbally, that the pay was in their opinion reasonable, but, as to the number of matrosses, they were not proper judges. The establishment was accepted, and is as follows, viz. :

An establishment for the company of the train, as fixed upon by the committee of safety :

1 captain, ...	£6 10s	per month.
2 lieutenants, each, ...	4 10	"
1 lieutenant fire worker, . . .	3 10	"
4 serjeants, each, ...	2 10	"
4 corporals, each, . . .	2 6	"
32 matrosses, each, ...	2 3	"
1 drummer, ...	2 6	"
1 fifer, ...	2 6	"

46 men, officers included, in each company of matrosses; a blanket and coat, as for the rest of the army.

WILLIAM COOPER, *Secretary*.

||The Congress then|| adjourned to to-morrow morning, eight o'clock.

SUNDAY, May 7, 1775, A. M.

Resolved, That the committee of supplies be, and they are hereby empowered and directed, to procure at Connecticut, Rhode Island, New York, or any other colony on the continent, such a number of fire arms and bayonets, for the use of this colony, as they shall think necessary.

The committee appointed to make application to the committee of supplies, to know what number of fire arms they had procured, reported verbally, that they had not procured any.

On an application made to this Congress, by Capt. Benjamin Dunning, of Harpswell, for powder, this Congress passed the following resolve, viz. :

Whereas, the district of Harpswell, in the county of Cumberland, lies exposed to the ravages of the enemies, and is unprovided with a supply of powder : therefore, *Resolved*, that it be recommended, ||and it is hereby accordingly recommended,|| to the selectmen of the town of Haverhill, that they deliver to Capt Nehemiah Curtis and Mr. Benjamin Dunning, for the use of the said district of Harpswell, one half barrel of powder, they paying for the same : which shall be replaced, if needed, as soon as the colony magazine can be supplied.

Adjourned to twelve o'clock this day.

[Noon.]

Met at twelve o'clock, and adjourned to four o'clock, P. M.

[Afternoon.]

Met at four o'clock, and adjourned to to-morrow morning, nine o'clock.

MONDAY, May 8, 1775, A. M.

Ordered, That Mr. Lothrop, Mr. Partridge, Mr. Mills, Mr. Whiting, Capt. Stone, Col. Howe, Col. Mandell, Col. Mosely, Col. ||*Pierce|| and Col. Thurston, be a committee to transcribe the narrative of the proceedings of the king's troops, on the 19th ult., together with depositions thereof accompanying, to be transmitted to Mr. Thomas for immediate publication.

A letter from a number of the inhabitants of the town of Hopkinton, was read : whereupon, *Ordered,* that Doct. Church, Col. Foster and Deacon Rawson, be a committee to prepare an answer to the selectmen of that town, giving the opinion of the Congress on the subject thereof.

The form of an oath, to be administered to the officers and private soldiers of the army now raising ||bin|| this colony, was read and accepted, and is as follows, viz. :

Resolved, That all officers and soldiers of the Massachusetts army now raising for the defence and security of the rights and liberties of this and our sister colonies in America, shall each and every of them, excepting only the general officers, repeat and take the following oath, viz. :

I, A. B., swear, I will truly and faithfully serve in the Massachusetts army, to which I belong, for the defence and security of the estates, lives and liberties of the good people of this and the sister colonies in America, in opposition to ministerial tyranny, by which they are or may be oppressed, and to all other enemies and opposers whatsoever; that I will adhere to the rules and regulations of said army ; observe and obey the generals and other officers set over me ; and disclose and make known to said officers all traitorous conspiracies, attempts and designs whatsoever, which I shall know to be made against said army, or any of the English American colonies. So help me God.

Ordered, That Col. Warren, Col. Gerrish and Col. Foster, be a committee to prepare the form of an oath to be administered to the general officers.

Ordered, That Col. Warren, Esquire Dix and Col. Foster, be a committee to draw up a resolve, recommending to the committees of correspondence of the several towns and districts in this colony, and to the selectmen of towns and districts who have no such committees, to take effectual care to ||*disarm|| all such persons, in their respective towns, who will not give them an assurance of their good intentions and regard to the interest of this country ; and also to recommend to the people of this colony to take effectual measures to oblige all who are liable by law to appear in arms in the militia, to appear, when properly called upon by their officers.

Resolved, That the muster masters be, and hereby are empowered and directed, to administer the oath to the officers and private soldiers of the army now raising in this colony, agreeably to the form prescribed by this Congress,

The committee who were appointed to prepare a letter to the selectmen of the town of Hopkinton, reported the following, which was read and accepted, and ordered to be dated, signed, and delivered to the messenger in waiting :

" GENTLEMEN :—Your favor of the 7th instant was duly considered in Congress. We cannot but regret that any persons, who have heretofore evidenced their attachment to the rights and liberties of their country, should, in this day of trial and hazard, be so far influenced by an inordinate attachment to their personal safety, or the security of their property, as to desert the common interest, and basely refuse to contribute of their wealth, or assist, personally, in that struggle, which they are conscientiously led to approve. Nevertheless, gentlemen, such is the peculiar delicacy of our situation, that true policy suggests we should act with extreme caution respecting these fugitives. A violation of the natural right of an individual to remove his person and effects wherever he pleases, ||we apprehend|| would ill become those who are contending for the unalienable right of every man to his own property, and to dispose of it as he pleases. We would likewise suggest, that, should we restrain any inhabitant from conveying his goods to Philadelphia, our brethren there might justly arraign us of selfishness in such a transaction, and it would evidence such a distinction of interests in the two colonies, as might have a tendency to disunite us, at a time when the safety of the whole must ultimately depend upon

a ||discover.||

the firmest confederacy. We are ||thoroughly|| aware of the mischiefs too general a removal might produce ; but we have so much confidence in the disinterested virtue of our countrymen, as to indulge hopes that Mr. Barrett's example will not become infectious. We highly approve the steady patriotism and manly jealousy of our brethren in Hopkinton, and are, with much esteem,

Gentlemen, yours, &c.

Ordered, That the president pro tempore, Doct. Church, Doct. Taylor, Doct. Holten and Doct. Dunsmore, be a committee to examine such persons as are, or may be, recommended for surgeons for the army now forming in this colony.

Resolved, That the persons recommended by the commanding officers of the several regiments, be appointed as surgeons to their respective regiments, provided they appear to be duly qualified upon examination.

A letter from the committee of correspondence, in Portsmouth, was received by a messenger, express. The messenger was admitted on the floor.[1]

Ordered, That said letter be committed, for an answer, to Doct. Church, the president and Capt. Foster.

A letter from Gen. Ward was read ; whereupon,

Ordered, That Col. Danielson, Doct. Church, Col. Foster, Mr. Bliss and Mr. Rawson, be a committee to take the subject thereof into consideration, and report.

Leave of absence was ||ªgiven|| to Mr. Partridge.

The committee on the letter from Portsmouth, in New Hampshire, reported the following answer, which was read and accepted, and ordered to be copied and sent :

a ||grantod.||

(1) The letter was addressed to the president of Congress, and is as follows :

PORTSMOUTH, May 6, 1775.

SIR :—We have received intelligence, that Mr. Edward Parry, of this town, together with Mr. John Barnard and Mr. Wilson, are now confined in irons, in the county of Lincoln ; for what cause we have not been able to explore.

But, from the past conduct of Mr. Parry, in this town, we are convinced he never merited such treatment ; and, that it cannot but meet with the disapprobation of your Congress, which have constantly manifested, in all their proceedings, a contrary temper.

We trust the Congress will exert their influence to procure the immediate release of that gentleman, and wish that humanity and candor may distinguish all our noble struggles in the cause of liberty.

By order of the committee.

I am your most obedient servant,

WILLIAM WHIPPLE.

GENTLEMEN :—The Congress have considered the subject of your express; are surprised that a gentleman, of the character you have mentioned, should have such just reason to complain of unmerited severity, from any of our brethren in this colony. From a regard to justice, as well as to your recommendation, gentlemen, we shall not fail to make immediate inquiry into this transaction; and if any outrage has been offered to innocent persons, the perpetrators, you may be assured, will be properly censured, and the sufferers meet with all that redress which it may be in the power of this Congress to obtain. Be assured, gentlemen, we shall be studious to maintain that character for humanity, which, we would wish, may ever be the characteristic of Americans; and [we] cannot but applaud those generous and benevolent sentiments, which influenced you in your application.

We are, &c.

The committee who were appointed to prepare the form of an oath, to be taken by the general officers, reported: the consideration whereof was referred to some future time.

Ordered, That Col. Mosely and Major Bliss be, and are hereby empowered and directed, to collect all the province arms which are in the county of Hampshire; and that Doct. William Whiting be empowered and directed to collect all the province arms which are in the county of Berkshire.

Adjourned to three o'clock, P. M.

[Afternoon.]

Resolved, That Capt. Trueman Wheeler, of Great Barrington, be desired to assist Doct. Whiting in collecting the province arms which are in the county of Berkshire.

Mr. Sawyer informed the Congress, that Gen. [John] Whitcomb, on account of his various avocations, could not acccept of the office of muster master to which he had been appointed. Whereupon,

Resolved, That this Congress will now proceed to the choice of another person, by ballot, in his room; and that Mr. Sawyer, Esquire Dix and Major Fuller, be a committee to sort and count the votes.

On a motion made, *Resolved*, that this last resolve be reconsidered, and that to-morrow morning, eleven o'clock, be assigned for the choice of a muster master, in the room of Gen. [John] Whitcomb, who declines that trust.

Ordered, That Major Bliss, Deacon Whitney and Col. Patterson, be a committee to give notice to such members of this Congress as are now at Cambridge and Roxbury, and other absent members whom they can notify, that a matter of the greatest importance is to be taken into consideration, at three o'clock, to-morrow afternoon, and to direct their attendance at that time.

The committee who were appointed to bring in a resolve recommending the disarming certain persons in the colony, reported ; which report was read, amended and accepted, and is as follows, viz. :

" Whereas, there are divers persons now in this colony, who have, by their conduct, discovered themselves to be enemies to the rights of mankind, and the interest of America ; and whereas, our very peculiar situation renders it absolutely necessary, not only to discriminate them from those who have shewn a disposition to be friendly to their country, but ||ᵃlikewise|| to put it out of their power to join with the open and avowed enemies of America, in their endeavors to ||injure, and|| subjugate their countrymen to the full operations of the tyrannical system of the British administration, and the ruin and destruction concerted by the British parliament against the secolonies : therefore,

Resolved, That it be, and hereby is recommended, to the several committees of correspondence, in the several towns and districts where such committees ||ᵇhave been appointed,|| and to the selectmen of such towns and districts as have not appointed them, to inquire into the principles and conduct of such suspected persons, and that they cause all such to be disarmed, who do not give them full and ample assurances, in which they can with safety confide, of their readiness to join their countrymen, on all occasions, in defence of the rights and liberties of America ; and likewise, that they take effectual steps to put it out of the power of such persons to obstruct, by any means whatever, the measures which shall be taken for the common defence ; and it is also hereby recommended, to the good people of this colony, that they take effectual care to secure obedience to the several resolves of Congress for the regulation of the militia, and cause a due regard to be paid to the orders of the several military officers, who have been elected by the suffrages of the several companies and regiments, agreeably to the resolves of Congress.

Ordered, That Major Fuller, Doct. Taylor and Mr. Webster, be a committee to get the resolve last mentioned printed, and dispersed through the several towns and districts in this colony.

Ordered, That the committee who were appointed to take into consideration the subject matter of the letter from Gen. Ward, now send a written message, by the messenger in waiting, to the general, inform-

a ||also.|| b ||reside.||

ing him that they are considering the same, and will make report as soon as possible.

Ordered, That said committee sit forthwith.

Ordered, That Mr. Fisher be added to said committee, in the room of Mr. Bliss, who is going to Cambridge on other business of the Congress.

Ordered, That Mr. Lothrop, Doct. Taylor and Mr. Webster, be a committee to bring in a resolve, recommending to the inhabitants of this province to save their straw.

Ordered, That Col. Mosely, Esquire Davis, Col. Walker, Deacon Hovey, Mr. Lewis, Capt. McCobb and Major Smith, be a committee to confer with the committee of safety, with respect to settling the appointment of field officers, and to sit forthwith.

Mr. Gerry, by leave of Congress, brought in a resolve, empowering the committee of supplies to furnish commissaries ||with necessaries|| for the army, &c., which was recommitted.

The committee appointed to consider the letter from Gen. Ward, reported an answer thereto, which was amended and accepted, and is as follows :

Sir :—This Congress received your letter of this day, and the complaint enclosed, informing that several persons, falsely pretending to have your order to search for fire-arms, have committed robbery on private property ; we have taken the matter ||ªinto|| consideration, and are of opinion that such criminals ought to meet with condign punishment.   The persons suspected to be the offenders are one Saunders, Samuel Mallows, Jacob Whittemore, Edward Bugby and Ebenezer Smith, all of Roxbury, with two other persons unknown.   Therefore, Sir, you are directed to apprehend the abovesaid persons, by a number of men under your command, and cause them to be carried before the committee of safety, who are hereby empowered and directed to examine them touching their offence, and search for, and, if possible, to find the goods, and direct that they are immediately replaced from whence they were taken.   And if, on examination, the said persons are found guilty of the said robbery, the committee of safety are hereby directed to imprison them till the further order of Congress.

Ordered, That the committee just now appointed to confer with the committee of safety, respecting the appointment of field officers, be instructed to inquire into the state of the army at Cambridge and Roxbury, and if they find the numbers ||thereof|| reduced, as is reported to

a ||seriously into.||

this Congress, that they advise the committee of safety to send out immediately for reenforcements.

Resolved, That the consideration of the expediency of assuming government, which was to have been entered upon to-morrow afternoon, be postponed to Friday next, at three o'clock, P. M., and that the committee who were just now appointed to confer with the committee of safety, be directed to give notice hereof to the several members of this Congress who are now at Cambridge and Roxbury.

||Then|| adjourned to nine o'clock to-morrow morning.

[TUESDAY,] May 9, 1775, A. M.

Resolved, That the receiver general be, and he is hereby directed, to give public notice of the resolve, lately passed by this Congress, for borrowing money on the credit of the colony, and assign certain time and place when he will attend that business.

The Congress granted permission to Col. Trumbull, to have a copy of the resolve of this Congress, relative to the [ªinhabitants] moving out of Boston.

Henry Gardner, Esq., receiver general, requested that this Congress would excuse him from serving any longer in that office; the consideration thereof was ordered to subside for the present.

Mr. Gerry brought in again a resolve respecting the supply of the soldiers, which was accepted, and is as follows, viz. :

Whereas, it hath frequently happened, that sutlers, whilst permitted to supply soldiers in the service of this colony, have vended their goods at extravagant rates, and thereby, in a great measure, deprived the families of such soldiers of the benefit of their wages; therefore,

Resolved, That the committee of supplies be, and they hereby are directed and empowered, to purchase and supply the commissary, for the time being, with such goods, wares and merchandize as they shall, at any time, judge necessary for supplying the colony forces, and to draw on the public treasury therefor. And the commissary aforesaid, as also his deputies, who shall be accountable to him, are hereby directed and empowered to supply, at the first cost, the soldiers who shall belong to the regiments in which they shall be stationed, with such articles as their respective captains shall, at any time, order ; and to keep and render to the captains aforesaid, true and exact accounts thereof, any time before the making up of the muster rolls. And the said captains are hereby directed to give orders for such articles only as they judge ||requisite and|| necessary for their respective soldiers,

ª [troops.]

not exceeding one half of the wages that shall, at any time, be due to them, and to cause the same to be deducted from their wages, on making up the muster rolls.

Ordered, That Doct. Church, the president, Col. Dexter, Col. Warren and Mr. Gerry, be a committee to prepare a spirited application to general Gage, respecting his treatment of the inhabitants of Boston.

Ordered, That the same gentlemen be a committee, to consider what provision shall be made for furnishing such enlisted soldiers, as are unprovided with fire arms, with such effective fire arms as are necessary for them to carry into the field.

Ordered, That Col. Barrett, Doct. Holten and Col. Danielson, be a committee to take into consideration a printed false account of the late excursion of the king's troops to Concord.

The order of the day [was] moved for.

Ordered, That Col. Farley, Doct. Holten and Col. Danielson, be a committee to sort and count the votes for a muster master.

The committee appointed to sort and count the votes for a muster master, in the room of Col. John Whitcomb, who declined accepting that trust, reported, that Col. Asa Whitcomb was chosen.

A motion was made and seconded, that a committee be appointed to take into consideration the expediency of restraining the people of this colony from supplying the inhabitants of Boston with provisions. After debate, the question was put, and it passed in the negative.

Adjourned to three o'clock, P. M.

[Afternoon.]

On a motion made, that the resolve passed yesterday, assigning Friday next, three o'clock, P. M., for the consideration of the expediency of assuming government, [be reconsidered,] and that an earlier day be assigned for that purpose. The question was put, and it passed in the negative.

Ordered, That Mr. Pickering be added to the committee appointed to take into consideration an equal representation of this colony, in the room of Mr. Rawson, absent.

Ordered, That Mr. Sawyer, Col. Foster and Mr. Dix, be a committee to take into consideration the expediency of establishing post offices and riders in this colony.

The committee who were appointed to prepare a remonstrance to general Gage, reported. The report was ordered to lie on the table till the further orders of this Congress.

The same committee, agreeably to their appointment, reported a resolve, relative to furnishing those enlisted soldiers with fire arms who are unequipt therewith; which, after debate, was ordered to be recommitted.

Ordered, That Capt. Stone ||of Framingham,|| be added to the committee who were appointed to consider of some measures to be taken with respect to the county records, in the room of Mr. Brown, of Abington, now absent.

The committee appointed to consider the expediency of establishing post offices and riders, in this colony, reported: whereupon, ||*Ordered*,|| that the further consideration thereof be referred to to-morrow morning, ten o'clock.

The committee appointed to consider the false account of the late excursion of the king's troops, reported; which report being read, amended and completed, was accepted, and is as follows, viz. :

Whereas, a printed paper, said to be a circumstantial account of an attack, which happened on the 19th of April, 1775, on his majesty's troops, by a number of the people of the province of the Massachusetts Bay, has been read in this Congress, which contains, among many falsehoods, the following paragraph, viz. :

"When Capt. Parsons returned with the three companies over the bridge, at Concord, they observed three soldiers on the ground, one of them scalped, his head much mangled, and his ears cut off, though not quite dead."

Resolved, That Col. Barrett be, and hereby is directed, to make strict inquiry of the persons who saw the three soldiers aforementioned lying at the said bridge, and also of those who buried them, and take their depositions, that so the truth or falsity of the aforesaid assertion may be ascertained.

The committee appointed to consider of some method for furnishing those soldiers with fire arms, who are not therewith equipt, again reported; the report was read ||and accepted,|| and is as follows, viz. :

Whereas, a few of the inhabitants of this colony, who are enlisted into its service, are destitute of fire arms, bayonets, and other accoutrements;

Resolved, That the selectmen of the several towns and districts in this colony be, and hereby are, directed and empowered to examine into the state of the equipment of such inhabitants of their respective towns and districts as are, or may be, enlisted into the service of this colony, and where any are deficient in arms or accoutrements, as aforesaid, it is recommended to the selectmen to supply them out of the town stock, and in case of a deficiency there, to apply to such inhabi-

a ||resolved.||

27

tants of their respective towns and districts as, in their opinions, can best spare their arms or accoutrements, and to borrow or purchase the same for the use of said inhabitants so enlisted: and the selectmen are also directed to take a bill from such persons as shall sell their arms and accoutrements, in the name of this colony, and receipts from the soldiers to whom they shall cause them to be delivered, and render the same to the committee of supplies for this colony: and each soldier, so supplied, shall pay for the use of such arms and accoutrements, out of his wages, the sum of six shillings: and if he does not return the said arms and accoutrements, there shall be deducted from his wages, at the time of making up the muster roll, the full value of said arms and accoutrements, as appraised by the selectmen, at the time of borrowing or purchasing the same; and it is strongly recommended to such inhabitants of the colony as the selectmen, as aforesaid, shall apply to for arms or accoutrements, that they supply the colony with the same.   And, as many arms in this colony which are now useless may, by small repairs, be rendered fit for service, *Resolved*, that a sufficient number of armourers, not exceeding twenty, be appointed by the committee of safety, to mend and repair such arms as shall be brought to them by the soldiers enlisted into the Massachusetts army.

Ordered, That Mr. Webster, Major Fuller and Mr. Batchelder, be a committee to get this resolve published and dispersed.

Adjourned till to-morrow morning, nine o'clock.

WEDNESDAY, May 10, 1775, A. M.

Ordered, That the committee appointed to confer with the committee of safety, upon the general state of the army, be directed particularly to confer with them on the propriety of removing the whole or part of the cannon and stores, now at Cambridge, further back into the country.

Resolved, That the general officers be, and are hereby directed, forthwith to call in all the soldiers who are already enlisted in the service of this colony, and that they give immediate orders to all the enlisted soldiers, and all others now in the camp at Cambridge and Roxbury, that they do not depart till the further orders of this Congress.

A petition from the committees of correspondence, and the committees of inspection, for the town of Pownalborough, was preferred by Joseph Tinkham:

Ordered, That this petition lie on the table.

Ordered, That the resolve passed by this Congress the 23d ultimo, recommending to the selectmen of the several towns in this colony, to furnish each non commissioned officer and ||ᵃsoldier|| with a blanket, be fairly copied by the secretary, and printed in a hand bill, and sent to the selectmen of the several towns and districts in the colony.

Ordered, That the petition from Pownalborough, just now read, be delivered to Mr. Joseph Tinkham, agreeable to his request.

Ordered, That Mr. Lothrop, Doct. Taylor and Doct. Holten, be a committee to take into consideration the proceedings of the town of Bristol, presented to this Congress by Mr. Thomas Bracket, in behalf of said town.

The committee appointed to bring in a resolve, recommending to the inhabitants of this colony to save their straw, reported; which report was read and accepted, and ordered to be copied, and sent to the printer of the Cambridge newspaper, and to the printer of the Worcester newspaper, for publication. ||ᵇIt|| is as follows, viz. :

Whereas, it will be indispensably necessary that large quantities of straw be provided for the use of the army now forming for the defence and protection of this colony;

Therefore, *Resolved*, and it is hereby strongly recommended to all such inhabitants of this colony as have, or may have, of that article by them, that, as they regard the lives and health of their brethren, who engage in the service abovesaid, they take immediate care the same be preserved for the purpose above mentioned.

Ordered, That Capt. Foster, Mr. Lothrop and Mr. Pickering, be a committee to transcribe the depositions taken by a committee of this Congress, of the proceedings of the troops, under command of general Gage, the 19th ultimo, and that they transmit them to Mr. Hall, at Cambridge, to be published in a pamphlet, and that said committee agree with him for the expense of publication.

Ordered, That Col. Barrett attend the business to which he was yesday appointed, of inquiring into the truth or falsity of a paragraph, taken from a printed account of the action of the king's troops, on the 19th instant.

The committee appointed to consider some measures for securing the county records, reported; the report was read and accepted, and is as follows, viz. :

Resolved, That the committee appointed for each county, on the 12th of April last, be instructed to take proper measures for securing the records of their several counties where they are exposed.

The order of the day was moved for.

a ||private soldier.|| b ||and.||

The committee appointed to consider on the expediency of establishing post offices, &c., reported; the report was recommitted, for the purpose of settling the rates of postage, and taking into consideration some method of establishing post offices. Mr. Hall, of Medford, and Mr. Cross, were added to the committee; also Mr. Batchelder, in the room of Mr. Dix.

Resolved, That the resolve for accepting the establishment for the train, which passed this Congress the 6th instant, be reconsidered, and that Col. Mandell, Capt. Baker, Doct. Taylor, Major Perley and Col. Coffin, be a committee to take into consideration the propriety of establishing a regiment of the train, and that they sit forthwith.

Ordered, That Col. Warren, Mr. Gerry and Col. Foster, be a committee to take into consideration a resolve of the committee of safety, recommending to this Congress to establish a court of inquiry.

Ordered, That Col. Richard Gridley be, and hereby is directed, forthwith to recommend to the committee of safety, for officers of the train of artillery, such persons as he thinks are qualified for that appointment.

On a complaint of the selectmen of the town of Worcester, against Samuel Paine and William Campbell, prisoners from that town, *Ordered*, that said prisoners be committed to the care of Capt. Brown, or such persons as he shall appoint, to be kept in custody till the further orders of this Congress.

Ordered, That the committee appointed to transcribe the depositions of the late proceedings of the king's troops, be directed to prepare a narrative thereof, as an introduction to the said depositions, which are ordered to be printed.

Adjourned to three o'clock, P. M.

[Afternoon.]

Ordered, That Mr. Gill, Col. Warren, Col. Gerrish, Mr. Dix and Doct. Perkins, be a committee to inquire into the complaint made by the selectmen of the town of Worcester, against Samuel Paine and William Campbell, and report to this Congress.

The consideration of the remonstrance to general Gage was resumed: and [the same was] accepted, and ordered to be authenticated, and sent forward. It is as follows, viz. :

To His Excellency Gen. Gage:

SIR :—This Congress have received frequent intelligence, that their brethren, the inhabitants of the town of Boston, have to contend, in their removal therefrom, with numerous delays and embarrassments, contrary to the stipulation proposed and agreed to between your excellency and the selectmen of that town.

We think it our duty to remonstrate to your excellency, that, from the papers communicated to us by the said selectmen, it appeared, that the inhabitants were promised, upon surrendering their arms, that they should be permitted to leave the town, and carry with them their effects. The condition was immediately complied with, on the part of the people; since which, though a number of days have elapsed, but a very small proportion of the inhabitants have been allowed to take the benefit of your covenant.

We would not affront your excellency by the most distant insinuation, that you intended to deceive and disarm the people, by a cruel act of perfidy. A regard to your own character, as well as the fatal consequences which will necessarily result from the violation of your solemn treaties, must ||*suggest|| sufficient reasons, to deter a gentleman of your rank and station from so injurious a design. But your excellency must be sensible, that a delay of justice is a denial of it, and extremely oppressive to the people now held in duress.

This Congress, though not the original party in the treaty, have taken every step in their power to facilitate the measure, and, in the whole of their conduct, have endeavored to evidence a disposition to act upon the principles of humanity and good faith, and still indulge hopes, that the confidence of the inhabitants of Boston, in your excellency's honor and faithfulness, is not misplaced; and that, notwithstanding any disagreeable occurrences, naturally resulting from the confused state of the colony, which this Congress have discountenanced, and endeavored to rectify, your excellency will no longer suffer your treaty with a distressed people, who ought by no means to be affected thereby, to be further violated.

The committee appointed to take into consideration the expediency of establishing ||a regiment|| of the train, reported.

Part of the establishment reported was accepted; the consideration of the residue was referred to a future time.

Resolved, That the resolve which this Congress passed at Concord, the 13th ultimo, directing the committee of safety to engage a suitable number of persons, for forming six companies of the train, be so far reconsidered, as that it be, and hereby is *Resolved,* that the committee of safety be directed to engage a suitable number of persons, and form ten companies of the train, for the artillery already provided by this colony, to enter immediately on constant discipline, and be in readiness to enter the service of the colony; and that said committee be, and they are hereby empowered, to draw on the public treasury, for said companies, a suitable consideration for their services.

The petition of Timothy Langdon[1] was read, and ordered to lie on the table till some of the eastern members should be present.

Ordered, That the secretary be directed, pursuant to a request of the committee of safety, to furnish them with copies of all such resolves as have passed the Congress in any ways relative to the duty enjoined them.

The secretary pro tempore represented to the Congress, that the multiplicity of the business of his office was such, as made it necessary that he should have some assistance; whereupon, *Ordered*, that Capt. Stone, of Oakham, assist him in that service.

The committee appointed to inquire into the state of the army, and to settle the appointment of the field officers, reported a letter from head quarters.

The committee appointed to inquire into the complaint of the selectmen of the town of Worcester, against Samuel Paine and William Campbell, reported; which report was accepted, and ordered to be transcribed, and delivered to Capt. Jonas Hubbard and Mr. Edward Crafts, who exhibited the above complaint, together with a printed resolve of Congress, lately passed, for disarming the disaffected inhabitants of the colony. The report is as follows, viz.:

The committee appointed to hear the complaints, exhibited by the selectmen of Worcester, against William Campbell and Samuel Paine, have attended that service, heard the parties, and beg leave to report, that we find the charges against them proved by depositions, and conceded by them; and that William Campbell has been guilty of leaving the town of Worcester without a permit from the selectmen, contrary to his own engagements: and that the said Samuel Paine has, in one instance, propagated reports with regard to our Massachusetts soldiers' rifling the house of Mr. Bradish, instead of the regular troops, and that those which were quartered in the colleges were lousy, and desert-

---

(1) This petition represented, that the committee of safety, formed from ten towns in the county of Lincoln, after consultation, came to the determination, that the king's masts, in the dock yard at Georgetown, should not be removed or fitted for use, and received assurances from Edward Parry, Esq., who had procured the timber, that it should remain: that when the result of the deliberations of the committee were known, Col. Samuel Thompson of Brunswick, with twenty armed men, seized Mr. Parry, and compelled him to give bonds, with the penalty of £2000, to abide in the town until the pleasure of Congress could be known, and exacted money for the refreshment of the captors: and prayed that the bonds might be cancelled, and Mr. Parry discharged from false imprisonment.

ed in great numbers; which, however indiscreet, does not appear to us to be done with any bad design, and that he ought to be dismissed immediately; and that the said Campbell may be returned to the town of Worcester, to be dealt with, by the committee of correspondence of that town, agreeably to a resolve of this Congress, passed the 8th instant. The matter, however, we think not important enough to be brought before this Congress.

The consideration of the petition of Timothy Langdon was again resumed, and ordered to lie on the table.

Ordered, That Capt. McCobb, Mr. Lewis and Doct. Perkins, be a committee to take under consideration the several applications made to this Congress, from the eastern parts of the province, for arms and ammunition.

Adjourned till to-morrow morning, eight o'clock.

THURSDAY, May 11, 1775, A. M.

The petition of James Cargill, of Newcastle, committed to the committee who were appointed to consider the ||several|| applications to this Congress for ammunition, &c.

The committee appointed to take into consideration the several applications to this Congress for a supply of ammunition, &c., reported : the report was recommitted, and the committee directed to inspect the list of returns of the town's stock of powder, &c., that it may be known whether this Congress can, with prudence, recommend to any town which may be stocked therewith, to supply those towns which are destitute.

Adjourned to twelve o'clock this day.

[Noon]

The Congress met at twelve o'clock, ||ᵃaccording|| to adjournment.

The committee appointed to consider the several applications made to this Congress for ammunition, and to inspect the list of returns, &c., reported. The report was read and accepted, and is as follows, viz. :

Whereas, the towns of Falmouth and Arundel, and the district of Cape Elizabeth, being sea port places, and much exposed to the rage of our enemies, and not having a sufficient quantity of gunpowder to defend themselves in case of any long attack ; and the town of Andover being well stocked with gunpowder, and not so much exposed ;

Therefore, *Resolved*, and it is hereby recommended to the selectmen of the town of Andover, that they deliver to Mr. Joseph McLellan, of Falmouth, two half barrels of gunpowder, for the use of the town of Fal-

a ||agreeably.||

mouth, in the county of Cumberland ; also to deliver to Mr. Zebulon Trickey, of Cape Elizabeth, one half barrel of gunpowder, for the use of Cape Elizabeth ; also to deliver to Mr. John Hovey, of Arundel, two half barrels of gunpowder, for the use of said Arundel, they paying them for said powder, which shall be replaced, if needed, as soon as the colony magazine can be supplied.

Whereas, the towns of Brunswick, Pownalborough, Bristol and Newcastle, being sea port places, in the eastern parts of this colony, and much exposed to the rage and incursions of our unnatural enemies, and not having a sufficient quantity of gunpowder to defend themselves, in case of any attack ; and the towns of Marlborough, Sudbury and Framingham, being well stocked with gunpowder, and not so much exposed;

Therefore, *Resolved*, and it is hereby recommended to the selectmen of the above mentioned several towns, that they deliver as follows, viz. : the selectmen of Sudbury, one half barrel of gunpowder, to Nathaniel Larrabee, for the use of Brunswick : the selectmen of Marlborough, two half barrels of gunpowder, one to Joseph Tinkham, for the use of Pownalborough, the other to Lieut. John Farley, for the use of Newcastle : the selectmen of Framingham, one half barrel of gunpowder, to Thomas Bracket, for the use of Bristol : they paying them for said powder, which shall be replaced, if needed, as soon as the colony magazine can be supplied.

Ordered, That each person now in waiting, who has made application to this Congress for powder, be served with a copy thereof.

Information being made to this Congress, that two men of war, with troops, had sailed from Boston to New York, with a design, as is supposed, of frustrating a design of the inhabitants of that colony and Connecticut, to secure the arms and ammunition now in the fort at New York ;

Ordered, That Mr. Gerry, Col. Warren and Col. Lincoln, be a committee to prepare a letter to the committee of correspondence of New York, informing them of the sailing of said men of war, and inserting such articles therein as will put the people upon their guard against any attempt that may be made against them by said ships.

Ordered, That this committee prepare said letter, and forward it forthwith, without waiting to report to this Congress, said committee laying before this Congress, as soon as may be, a copy of said letter.[1]

Adjourned to four o'clock, P. M.

(1) The following letter was sent to the committee of inspection of New York, subscribed by Elbridge Gerry, James Warren and Benjamin Lincoln :

" GENTLEMEN :—We are directed by the Congress of this colony, who are just informed that

[Afternoon.]

Met at four o'clock, according to adjournment.
Adjourned to eight o'clock to-morrow morning.

FRIDAY, May 12, 1775, A. M.

Moved, That a committee be appointed to consider the expediency of recommending to the selectmen of the several towns in the colony, to furnish such as may enlist in their respective towns, with necessaries for their march to head quarters. The question was put, and it passed in the negative.

Ordered, That Capt. Stone, Col. Warren and Mr. Sullivan, be a committee, to take into consideration an extract of a letter from the Hon. Enoch Freeman, Esq., of Falmouth, to Samuel Freeman.[1]

two men of war, the Asia, and one other ship, with three or four companies of troops on board, sailed yesterday from Boston for your place, to give you the earliest notice thereof. It is supposed that they have orders to secure the ammunition and military stores in the fort of your city. Your noble exertions in the common cause, have given the Congress reason to think, that timely information, relative to this matter, would be important to you. The post is now waiting, which prevents us from indulging an inclination for enlarging.

We are, respectfully, gentlemen, yours, &c."

(1) The extracts which follow are from a letter of Hon. Enoch Freeman, dated Falmouth, May 5, 1775, probably relating to the subjects presented for the consideration of Congress:

" We have lately heard that the Penobscot indians are highly exasperated at Capt. Goldthwaite, for suffering the tender to dismantle the fort there, and carrying off the powder : and truck trade is stopped, as we are informed ; and that there were a number of men round about there, going to take Goldthwaite, for delivering up the fort, into their custody, but what they intend to do with him I dont hear. Perhaps it would be prudent for the Congress to send down there, and secure the indians in our interest, by keeping the truck trade open, supplying them powder, or any other method in their wisdom, upon mature consideration they may think best. A hint on this head is enough."

" The selectmen of this town have this moment agreed with one Jabez Matthews and one David Dinsmore, of New Gloucester, to go over to Quebec, to make discovery whether any Canadians are in motion to come on our back settlements, or to excite the indians to do it ; and I have wrote to Mr. Remington Holby, of Vassalborough, to procure one or two to go with them, as hunters ; and they are charged to be cautious not to let the Canadians have reason so much as to suspect their business, and they will depend on your endeavoring to get the Congress to order them adequate satisfaction out of the public fund. If they discover any evil designs, we shall be glad to know it, that we may prepare accordingly for our defence. If they find there is no design upon us, it will be a great satisfaction to this eastern country."

" I could write a good deal in favor of sending such an embassy, but as my time is almost wholly taken up on public matters, I have little time to spare."

References, in the journal, to original papers, too often lead to the repetition of the same sad tale of loss and destruction. The letter of the Hon. Enoch Freeman, mentioned on page 220, undoubtedly related to a transaction fully detailed in the following communication from Gen. Jedediah Preble, addressed to the president of the Provincial Congress.

FALMOUTH, May 14, 1775.

" HONORED SIR:—The committee of correspondence in this town, beg leave to inform you, that some time past, we received advices from Georgetown, that Col. Thompson was fitting two vessels there, with design to attempt the taking the king's ship Canceaux, stationed in this harbor, commanded by Capt. Mowat, a gentleman, whose conduct since he has been here, has given no grounds of suspicion he had any design to distress or injure us ; but, on the other hand, he has af-

Ordered, That Capt. Stone, Col. Warren and Mr. Sullivan, above mentioned, be a committee to take into consideration the expediency of taking measures for raising a company or two of indians.

Resolved, That to-morrow morning, at ten o'clock, be, and is now assigned, for the purpose of choosing some person to preach a sermon to the Congress, on the 31st May instant.

Resolved, That all persons who have the care of any prisoners detained at Concord, Lexington, or elsewhere, be, and hereby are directed, to give the Rev. Mr. Gordon free access to them, whenever he shall desire it; and it is recommended to all civil magistrates, and others, to be aiding and assisting him in examining, and taking depositions of them, and others, without exception.

Ordered, That the establishment for a train of artillery be recommitted.

Ordered, That Mr. Sullivan be added to the committee appointed for revising the [commissions of the] committee of safety and committee of supplies, in the room of Doct. Holten, absent.

forded his assistance to sundry vessels in distress. As we thought such an attempt had the appearance of laying a foundation for the destruction of this town, the committee of correspondence met, and wrote to the committee of correspondence at Georgetown, desiring they would prevent their coming; we also wrote to Col. Thompson, desiring him to desist from such an attempt, as it would throw this town into the greatest confusion imaginable; we sent an express, and received his answer that he had dropped the design of coming. But, on Monday night, [May 10,] he landed upwards of sixty men, on the back side of a neck of land joining to the town, who came there in a number of boats, and lay undiscovered till about the middle of the next day; at which time, Capt. Mowat, the doctor of the ship and parson Wiswall, were taking a walk on said neck, when a detachment of Col. Thompson's party rushed from their concealment, surrounded the gentlemen, and made them prisoners, and conducted them to the colonel, who was with the main body, on the back side of the neck. Capt. Hog, who now commanded the ship, immediately clapped springs on his cables, she lying within musket shot of the town, and swore if the gentlemen were not released by six o'clock, he would fire on the town. He fired two cannon, and, although there was no shot in them, it frightened the women and children to such a degree, that some crawled under wharves, some ran down cellar and some out of town. Such a shocking scene was never before presented to view here. The gentlemen who were in custody, were conducted to a public house, where Capt. Mowat declared, if he was not released, it would be the destruction of the town. Every gentleman present used his utmost endeavors to accommodate the matter. Col. Thompson consented that a committee should be chosen, consisting of officers from his party and gentlemen from the town, to consult in what manner the affair could be accommodated; but, as it was late, the committee chose to defer the consideration of it till next morning. Capt. Mowat then requested he might go on board his ship that night, and he would pawn his word and honor that he would return next morning, at what time and at what place should be appointed. Col. Thompson consented, provided Col. Freeman and Brigadier Preble would pass their words that the several gentlemen should return according to their promises, and also pawn their word and honor, if the gentlemen failed of coming, that they would deliver themselves up, and stand by the consequences, which was consented to. Capt. Mowat not coming according to his promise, which was to have been at nine o'clock the next morning, the sponsors appeared according to promise, and were confined. Capt. Mowat wrote to them, and let them know he had fully determined to have complied with his promise, but he had sent his man on shore, to carry some dirty linen to his washing-woman, and to bring off some clean: that said man made oath, that two of the body, under arms, one of which swore, by all that was sacred, the moment he come on shore he should have what was in his piece, and the other, that he

Resolved, That the several committees be enjoined to sit, and that this Congress be adjourned to this afternoon, three o'clock.

[Afternoon.]

The committee appointed to consider measures for establishing post offices and post ||*riders,|| reported. After some debate, the matter thereof was ordered for the present to subside.

The order of the day was moved for.

The absent members were ordered to be called in.

It was then *Moved*, That the sense of the Congress be taken on this question, viz. : Whether there is now existing in this colony a necessity of taking up, and exercising the powers of civil government, in all its parts.

After some debate, it was *Resolved*, that this Congress will now form itself into a committee of the whole house, for consideration of the question in debate.

The committee having considered thereon, the president, on a motion made, [ᵇresumed] the chair. The committee then, by the Hon. Joseph Warren, Esq., their chairman, reported, " that a committee be raised, for the purpose of reporting to the Congress an application to the Continental Congress, for obtaining their recommendation for this colony to take up and exercise civil government, as soon as may be, and that the committee be directed to ground the application on the necessity of the case ;" which report being read, was accepted, by a very large majority ; whereupon, *Ordered*, that the president, Doct.

should never return on board again with his life : and that two more of his men made oath, they heard several of the men under arms say, the moment he came on shore they would have his life ; this was what he wrote to plead an excuse for not complying with his promise. Col. Thompson told the two gentlemen under confinement, that he must have some provisions and refreshments for his men, which they procured, to the amount of thirteen or fourteen pounds, lawful money, on which they were dismissed. About ten o'clock, he sent an account to them for time and expense, amounting to £158 18s. lawful money, and gave them till next morning, nine o'clock, to return an answer, which they did in the negative ; he said he would have satisfaction before he left town. He then seized all the goods he could find, belonging to Capt. Coulson and William Tyng, Esq ; they also carried off one boat belonging to Coulson, and one other to Capt. Mowat ; they also obliged Capt. Pote to furnish them with some provisions, and a small matter of cash ; they also brought one man on his knees, for speaking disrespectfully of the colonel and his men. Col. Thompson, we doubt not, is a true friend to his country, and a man of courage and resolve ; but our town lies so much exposed to the navy that, had he succeeded in his attempt, which there was not the least probability of, it must have proved the destruction of this town, and the country back, who are now in the greatest distress for want of provisions. We have only related plain facts, that the honorable members of the Provincial Congress may not be imposed on with false accounts, to whom please to communicate this letter.

We are, with great esteem, gentlemen, your most obedient humble servants.

JEDEDIAH PREBLE, *Chairman*."

a ||roads.|| b [assumed.]

Church, Mr. Gerry, Col. Warren, Mr. Sullivan, Col. Danielson and Col. Lincoln, be a committee to prepare an application agreeably to said report.

A letter from Col. Quincy ||of Braintree,|| to the president, was read; whereupon, *Resolved*, that Gen. Ward be, and hereby is directed, to order four respectable officers to escort the president of this Congress to Col. Quincy, at Braintree, to-morrow morning.

Ordered, That Major Fuller, Mr. Goodwin and Deacon Whitney, be a committee to estimate the damages done at Concord, Lexington and Cambridge, by the king's troops, on the 19th ultimo, so far as respects private property only.

Ordered, That Mr. Sullivan, Doct. Taylor and Mr. Lewis, be a committee to take into consideration a letter from the Hon. Enoch Freeman, Esq., dated May 10, 1775, to his son, Mr. Samuel Freeman.[1]

Resolved, That the further consideration of the report of the committee who were appointed to bring in a resolve respecting the establishment of post offices and post riders, be resumed to-morrow morning, nine o'clock.

Resolved, That the establishment for a train of artillery, which has been accepted by this Congress, be reconsidered, and that the following report, for such an establishment, be accepted, viz.:

Resolved, That the following establishment be made for ten companies of matrosses:

Captain, ...	£6 10s. 0	per month.
Captain Lieutenant, ...	5 10 0	"
1st Lieutenant, ...	4 10 0	"
Two 2d Lieutenants, each	3 12 0	"
Serjeants, each	2 10 0	"
Corporals, each	2 6 0	"
6 Bombardiers, each	2 4 6	"
6 Gunners, each	2 4 0	"
32 Matrosses, each	2 3 0	"

Adjourned till to-morrow morning, eight o'clock.

[SATURDAY,] May 13, 1775, A. M.

Met according to adjournment.

The petition of the selectmen of the town of Topsham, in the county of Lincoln, respecting their being supplied with powder, [was] read, and *Ordered*, that the same be committed to Capt. McCobb, Mr. Lewis and Doct. Taylor.

(1) See the note to page 217 *ante*. The letter mentioned in the text is not on the files of Congress.

The order of the day, respecting the further consideration of the report of the committee appointed to bring in a resolve respecting the establishing post offices, &c., was taken up, and the blanks for post masters being filled up, ordered to subside till the report on the letter from Hon. Enoch Freeman, Esq. was read.

The committee appointed to take into consideration a letter from the Hon. Enoch Freeman, Esq., dated May 10, reported; and after a long debate thereon, [the report] was ordered to be recommitted for amendment.

Moved, That a committee be appointed to count and sort the votes, for a committee, to be chosen by ballot, to appoint post riders; [the] time assigned for that purpose [was] voted to be three o'clock, P. M.

The order of the day was moved for, to choose a gentleman to preach the sermon on the 31st May.

Moved, That a committee be chosen to count and sort the votes. Col. Warren, Capt. Jennison, Major Bliss, were chosen.

The committee chosen to count and sort the votes, reported that the Rev. Doct. Langdon was chosen.

Moved, That a committee of three persons be appointed, to wait on the Rev. Doct. Langdon, and acquaint him that this Congress have made choice of him to preach a sermon to the Congress of this colony on the 31st instant May, and desire his compliance therewith. Col. Gerrish, Mr. Pitts and Doct. Sawyer, were chosen accordingly.

The committee appointed to prepare a resolve respecting the taking a third set of the depositions relative to the battle of Lexington, reported, and [the report] was accepted, and is as follows, viz. :

Resolved, That William Reed, William Stickney, Thadeus Mason, Jonathan Hastings, Jonathan Cummings, Josiah Johnson, Duncan Ingraham, Jonas Dix and Simon Tufts, Esqs., be, and they hereby are required, to take a third set of the depositions relative to the battle of Lexington, similar to the two sets already by them taken ; and they are empowered to summon, or cause to be summoned, such inhabitants of this colony as they shall think proper, to attend them, at any time and place in this ||*county,|| which they shall direct, for the purposes mentioned ; and all such persons as shall be summoned by the justices aforesaid, are hereby directed punctually to obey their summons.

Ordered, That Mr. Pitts, Mr. Gill and Mr. Sawyer, be a committee to take into consideration a letter from Mr. John Peck, respecting his confinement, to the selectmen of Boston, and the said selectmen's letter to this Congress on the same subject.

The committee reported their amendment of the report on the Hon. Enoch Freeman's letter; referred to the afternoon.

Adjourned to three o'clock, P. M.

[Afternoon]

||The Congress met at three o'clock, P. M.||

The report of the committee respecting the Hon. Enoch Freeman, Esq.'s letter, [was] taken up, amended and [ᵃaccepted.]¹

The committee appointed to consider the petition of the selectmen of the town of Topsham, reported; the report was accepted, and is as follows, viz.:

Whereas, the town of Topsham being a sea port place, in the eastern part of the colony, and much exposed to the rage and excursions of our unnatural enemies, and not having a sufficient quantity of gunpowder to defend themselves, in case of an attack, and the town of Wrentham being well stocked therewith;

Therefore, *Resolved*, and it is hereby recommended to the selectmen of the abovesaid town of Wrentham, to deliver one half barrel of gunpowder to Mr. Prince Rose, for the use of the town of Topsham, he paying them for said powder, which shall be replaced, if needed, as soon as the colony magazine can be supplied.

||ᵇThe order of the day was called for,|| and Capt. Jonathan Brown, Jonas Dix, Esq. and Deacon Cheever, were chosen a committee to count and sort the votes for a committee to establish post riders; which committee was chosen; and the blanks in the resolve respecting post offices, being filled up with said committees' names, the resolve was accepted, and is as follows, viz.:

Resolved, as the opinion of this Congress, that post riders be immediately established to go from Cambridge, and to ride the following roads, viz.: to Georgetown in the county of Lincoln, to Haverhill, to Providence, to Woodstock by Worcester, and from Worcester to Great Barrington by Springfield, and to Falmouth in the county of Barnstable, and that post offices be kept as followeth, viz.: One at Cambridge; one at Salem; one at Ipswich; one at Haverhill; one at Newburyport; one at ||ᶜKennebunk|| or Welles; one at Falmouth in the county of Cumberland; one at Georgetown, in the county of Lincoln; one at Worcester; one at Springfield; one at Great Barrington; one

a [accepted, and is as follows:]

b ||*Resolved*, That the order of the day, on the subject of post riders, be now taken up.||

c ||Kennebeck.||

(1) The report, unfortunately omitted in the journal, is not preserved on the files.

at Plymouth; one at Sandwich; one at Falmouth, in the county of Barnstable.

And it is further *Resolved*, That Mr. James Winthrop be appointed post master for the town of Cambridge; Mr. Edward ||ᵃNorris|| for Salem; Mr. James Foster for Ipswich; Mr. ||ᵇSimon|| Greenough for Haverhill; Mr. Bulkley Emerson for Newburyport; Capt. Nathaniel Kimball for Kennebunk; Mr. Samuel Freeman for Falmouth, in Cumberland; Mr. John Wood for Georgetown; Mr. Isaiah Thomas for Worcester; Mr. Moses Church for Springfield; Doct. William Whiting for Great Barrington; Joseph Nye, 3d. for Sandwich; William Watson, Esq. for Plymouth; and Mr. Moses Swift for Falmouth, in Barnstable; and that Capt. Jonathan Brown, Jonas Dix, Esq. and David Cheever, Esq., be a committee to give directions for the setting off and returning of the posts in their several routes, and to appoint the number of riders, and agree with them, and to agree likewise with the post masters for their service; and that the rates of, and duties for postage of letters, &c., be as follow, viz. : for any distance not exceeding 60 miles, 5 1-4 pence; upwards of 60 miles, and not exceeding 100 miles, 8 pence; upwards of 100 miles, and not exceeding 200, 10 1-2 pence; upwards of 200, and not exceeding 300, 1 shilling 1 penny; upwards of 300, and not exceeding 400, 1 shilling 4 pence; upwards of 400, and not exceeding 500, 1 shilling 6 1-2 pence; upwards of 500, and not exceeding 600, 1 shilling 9 pence; upwards of 600, and not exceeding 700, 2 shillings; upwards of 700, and not exceeding 800, 2 shillings 2 1-2 pence; upwards of 800, and not exceeding 900, 2 shillings 5 pence; upwards of 900, and not exceeding 1000, 2 shillings 8 pence. The above rates to be paid in lawful money of this colony.

The above rates are for the postage of a single letter; they are to be doubled for all double letters; trebled for all treble letters; and for every ounce weight, four times as much to be charged as for a single letter; and that the post masters be accountable to the aforenamed committee for what they shall receive; and that the foregoing rules and orders continue, until the Continental Congress, or the congress, or future house of representatives of this colony, shall make some further order relative to the same.

The committee ||appointed|| to draw a resolve respecting a court of inquiry, reported; and *Ordered*, that Monday, three o'clock in the afternoon, be assigned for taking the same into consideration.

Adjourned till to-morrow morning, eight o'clock.

a ||Morris.|| b ||Simeon.||

SUNDAY, May 14, 1775, [A. M.]

Met, and adjourned to twelve o'clock.

[Noon.]

At twelve o'clock met, and adjourned to three o'clock.

[Afternoon.]

At three o'clock met again.

Moved, That a committee be appointed to apply to the committee of safety, for a list of such persons as they have given enlisting orders to, that this Congress may commission such as they think proper, without delay.

Resolved, That the further consideration of this matter be referred to to-morrow morning, nine o'clock.

[MONDAY,] May 15, 1775, A. M.

Resolved, That four o'clock in the afternoon of this day, be assigned for making choice of two persons, members of this Congress, to attend the Provincial Congress of New Hampshire, on Wednesday next.

The order of the day was moved for, and read.

Resolved, That David Cheever, Esq., for reasons by him offered, be excused from serving in the business, to which he was appointed, by a resolve of this Congress, passed the 12th instant, for establishing post offices and post riders; and that Mr. William Greenleaf, Joseph Greenleaf, Esq. and Mr. John Pitts, be added to the committee therein appointed.

Resolved, That five o'clock this afternoon be assigned for the choice of a person to serve on the committee of supplies, in the room of Col. Lee, deceased.

Ordered, That the committee appointed to prepare an application to the Continental Congress, be directed to insert a clause therein, desiring that the said congress would take some measures for directing and regulating the American forces.

The committee appointed to prepare an introduction to the depositions ['relating to] the late affair at Lexington, reported; the same was recommitted, for the purpose of examining it, to find if the narrative contained in the said introduction be supported by the depositions, and to add such other depositions as may be procured.

Ordered, That Mr. Fisher, Col. Field and Mr. Bullen, be a committee to examine the letters of Governor Hutchinson,[1] lately discovered,

a [of.]

(1) The following account of the discovery of the letter books of Governor Hutchinson, containing his correspondence with the ministry, and with private individuals, is copied from *Gordon's History of the American Revolution*, Vol. I., Page 356.

"When he [Governor Hutchinson,] quitted the province, all his furniture was left behind at his seat in Milton. After the Lexington engagement, the committee of the town removed and report to this Congress such letters, and extracts, as they think it will be proper to publish.

||*Ordered,* That the committee appointed to revise [the commission of] the committee of safety, sit forthwith.||

Ordered, That Col. Warren, Mr. Sawyer and Major Bliss, be a committee to take into consideration the subject of a letter, read in Congress, from William Watson, Esq. to Col. Warren and Mr. Lothrop.

Col. Barrett, who was appointed to take a deposition at Concord, reported; the deposition reported was ordered to be committed to the committee who were appointed to prepare an introduction to the depositions.

The committee appointed to take into consideration extracts of a letter from the Hon. Enoch Freeman, Esq., reported a letter to the eastern tribes of indians, which was accepted, and ordered to be authenticated, and sent to Mr. John Lane, to be communicated to them. It is as follows, viz. :

FRIENDS AND GOOD BROTHERS :—We, the delegates of the colony of the Massachusetts Bay, being come together in congress, to consider what may be best for you and ourselves to do, to get rid of the slavery designed to be brought upon us, have thought it our duty to write you the following letter.

BROTHERS : the great wickedness of such as should be our friends, but are our enemies, we mean the ministry of Great Britain, has laid deep plots to take away our liberty and your liberty ; they want to get all our money ; make us pay it to them, when they never earned it ; to make you and us their servants ; and let us have nothing to eat, drink, or wear, but what they say we shall ; and prevent us from having guns and powder to use, and kill our deer, and wolves, and other game, or to send to you, for you to kill your game with, and to get skins and fur to trade with us for what you want : but we hope soon

---

it, in order to save it from being totally ruined. Mr. Samuel Henshaw, desirous of seeing how the house looked when stript of all the furniture, repaired thither with the gentleman who had the key. He went, at length, up into a dark garret, where he discovered an old trunk, which, he was told, was left behind, as it contained nothing but a parcel of useless papers. Curiosity led him to examine them, when he soon discovered a letter book of Mr. Hutchinson's, which he secured, and then posted away to Doct. Warren, to whom he related what had happened: on which, an order was soon sent to Gen. Thomas, at Roxbury, to possess himself of the trunk. It was brought to his quarters : and there, through the imprudent exultations of some about the general, the contents were too often exposed to persons resorting thither, and some single letters conveyed away ; one [was suppressed] for the public good ; it being thought, that if the same was generally known, it might be of disservice in the present moment, as it had not a favorable aspect upon the staunch patriotism of Mr. Hancock. The letter books, and other papers, were afterwards taken proper care of.''

These interesting manuscripts were deposited, and are still retained, in the archives of the state.

to be able to supply you with both guns and powder, of our own making.

We have petitioned to England for you and us, and told them plainly we want nothing but our own, and do not want to hurt them; but they will not hear us, and have sent over great ships, and their men with guns, to make us give up, and kill us, and have killed some of our men; but we have driven them back and beat them, and killed a great many of their men.

The Englishmen of all the colonies, from Nova Scotia to Georgia, have firmly resolved to stand together and oppose them; our liberty and your liberty is the same; we are brothers, and what is for our good is for your good; and we, by standing together, shall make those wicked men afraid, and overcome them, and all be free men. Capt. Goldthwait has given up Fort Pownall into the hands of our enemies; we are angry at it, and we hear you are angry with him, and we do not wonder at it. We want to know what you, our good brothers, want from us of clothing, or warlike stores, and we will supply you as fast as we can. We will do all for you we can, and fight to save you, any time, and hope that none of your men, or the indians in Canada, will join with our enemies. You may have a great deal of ||good|| influence on them. Our good brothers, the indians at Stockbridge, all join with us, and some of their men have enlisted as soldiers, and we have given them that enlisted, each one, a blanket and a ribbon, and they will be paid when they are from home in the service; and if any of you are willing to enlist, we will do the same for you.

We have sent Capt. John Lane to you, [to consult with you] for that purpose, and he will show you his orders for raising one company of your men to join with us in the war with your and our enemies.

BROTHERS: we beseech that God who lives above, and that does what is right here below, to be your friend and bless you, [and] to prevent the designs of those wicked men from hurting you or us.

BROTHERS: if you will let Mr. John Preble know what things you want, he will take care to inform us, and we will do the best for you that we can.

The committee appointed to consider a letter from William Watson, Esq., of Plymouth, reported the following resolve, which was accepted, and ordered to be printed, and dispersed to the several towns in the colony, and is as follows, viz. :

Whereas, some of the inhabitants of this colony, and most of them such as have been inimical to the constitution and interest of the same, are now, after having united themselves with our enemies, in reducing us to the distresses and difficulties we are laboring under, taking steps to remove themselves and effects out of this colony, into the government of Nova Scotia, and elsewhere, in order to avoid their proportion of burdens necessarily incurred for our defence, to prevent which, it is *Resolved*, that no person be, from this time, permitted to move his goods and effects out of this colony, unless he shall obtain the permission of the committee of correspondence of the town he belongs to; or if no such committee be there appointed, of the selectmen, or the majority of them, under their hands, for that purpose, but by the leave of this or some future congress; and the several committees of correspondence, or selectmen, where there are no such committees, are hereby directed to be very vigilant in observing the motions of all such persons who they may have reason to suspect, and to see that this resolve be carried into full execution.

Then adjourned to three o'clock, P. M.

[Afternoon.]

The committee appointed to consider the extracts of a letter from the Hon. Enoch Freeman, Esq., reported a resolve respecting an embassy to Canada, which being read and amended, was accepted, a copy ordered to be authenticated, and sent to the selectmen of Falmouth, and is as follows, viz. :

Whereas, it is absolutely necessary for the interest and safety of this colony, in its present unhappy situation, that the most certain intelligence, from Canada, of the designs and manœuvres of the inhabitants of that colony should be obtained as ||ᵃfrequently|| as possible : and whereas, the selectmen of the town of Falmouth, having been alarmed by reports which had prevailed in the eastern parts of the colony, that the Canadians would soon attack them on their frontiers, and thereby bring not only themselves, but the whole colony, into a still more deplorable situation ; and judging it of the utmost importance, that the truth or falsity of such reports be known without delay, have employed Mr. Jabez Matthews and Mr. David Dinsmore, to go across the woods to Quebec, in order to observe the motions of the people there, and, as far as possible, to gain a knowledge of their intention ;

Therefore, *Resolved*, That this Congress do approve of the care and attention of the selectmen of Falmouth, to the general interest of the colony. And it is hereby recommended to the said selectmen, that they transmit the intelligence they may receive by them, together with the expenses of the said embassy, to this or some future congress of

a ||speedily.||

this colony, with all convenient speed, that the account of their expenses may be adjusted and allowed out of the treasury of the colony.

The order of the day [was] moved for.

The report of the committee appointed to bring in a resolve for establishing a court of inquiry, was read; after debate, the question was put, whether said report be accepted, and it passed in the negative.

Ordered, That the committee who reported a letter to the eastern tribes of indians, be directed to prepare instructions to Mr. John Lane, who is appointed to communicate the letter to them, and enlist a company of them in the service of the colony.

Ordered, That Mr. Gill, Mr. Bliss and Mr. How, be a committee to sort and count the votes for two persons, members of this Congress, to repair to the congress of the province of New Hampshire.

The committee last mentioned, reported, that the Hon. Joseph Gerrish, Esq. and Col. Ebenezer Sawyer, were chosen.

Ordered, That Col. Dexter, Col. Warren and Col. Foster, be a committee to bring in a resolve for supplying the soldiers with two twenty shilling bills each, for a month's advance pay, and they are directed to draw up a form for said bills, and employ an engraver to prepare a plate for [*printing] the same, without delay, and *Resolved*, that tomorrow morning, ten o'clock, be assigned for the consideration of the report of said committee thereon.

Ordered, That the committee appointed to prepare an application to the Continental Congress, sit forthwith.

Ordered, That Mr. Gill, Mr. Bliss and Mr. How, be a committee to sort and count the votes for a member of the committee of supplies, in the room of Col. Lee, deceased.

The committee last mentioned, reported, that Mr. John Pitts was chosen.

Ordered, That Col. Barrett, Esquire Rawson and Mr. Webster, be a committee to take into consideration a petition to this Congress, from Mr. Boice and Mr. McLean, of Milton.[1]

Ordered, That Mr. Lothrop, Col. Warren and Mr. Jennison, be a committee to draw up some instructions to the delegates appointed to go to the Congress of New Hampshire.

Adjourned to eight o'clock to-morrow morning.

a [engraving.]

(1) John Boice and Hugh McLean represented, that they were engaged in the business of manufacturing paper; that four apprentices, well skilled in the employment, had enlisted in the army; that their services were necessary for the operation of the mills; and prayed that these soldiers might be discharged from military service.

[TUESDAY,] May 16, 1775, A. M.

Ordered, That Doct. Taylor, Mr. Greenleaf and Capt. Dix, be a committee to apply to the committee of safety, for a list of such persons as they have given enlisting orders to; and, in particular, [for] a list of such as have completed, or nearly completed, their respective regiments; and as far as can be speedily obtained, the number of men each officer has enlisted, that this Congress may commission such persons as they think proper, without delay.

The committee appointed to consider a petition of Messrs. Boice and McLean, reported. A long debate was had thereon, and it was finally determined, that the petitioners have leave to withdraw their petition.

Ordered, That Mr. Sullivan, Capt. Stone, Col. Farley, Major Brooks and Doct. Rawson, be a committee to take into consideration a verbal information of the capture of three vessels, by a king's cutter, at Dartmouth, and the retaking two of them, and fifteen marines prisoners.

Adjourned to three o'clock, P. M.

[Afternoon.]

Henry Gardner, Esq. having renewed his request, that this Congress would excuse him from serving the colony in the office of receiver general, *Resolved,* that the determination of this matter be referred to to-morrow morning, ten o'clock; and if Mr. Gardner should then insist on being excused, that then the Congress will proceed to the choice of some other person to supply his place.

The committee appointed to prepare an application to the Continental Congress, reported the following, which was read paragraph by paragraph, and accepted, viz. :

Resolved, That Doct. Church be ordered to go immediately to Philadelphia, and deliver to the president of the honorable American Congress, there now sitting, the following application, to be by him communicated to the members thereof; and the said Church is also directed to confer with the said congress, respecting such other matters as may be necessary to the defence of this colony, and particularly [as to] the state of the army therein.

MAY IT PLEASE YOUR HONORS :—That system of colony administration which, in the most firm, dutiful and loyal manner, has been in vain remonstrated against, by the representative body of the united colonies, seems still, unless speedily and vigorously opposed, by the collected wisdom and force of all America, to threaten ruin and destruction to this continent.

For a long time past this colony has, by a corrupt administration in Great Britain and here, been deprived of the exercise of those powers of government, without which, a people can be neither rich, happy or secure. The whole continent saw the blow impending, which, if not warded off, must inevitably have subverted the freedom and happiness of each colony. The principles of self-defence, roused in the breasts of freemen by the dread of impending slavery, caused to be collected the wisdom of America, in a congress, composed of men who, through time, must, in every land of freedom, be revered, amongst the most faithful assertors of the essential rights of human nature.

This colony was then reduced to great difficulties, being denied the exercise of civil government, according to our charter, or the fundamental principles of the English constitution; and a formidable navy and army, not only inimical to our safety, but flattered with the prospect of enjoying the fruit of our industry, were stationed, for that purpose, in our metropolis. The prospect of deciding the question, between our mother country and us, by the sword, gave us the greatest pain and anxiety; but, we have made all the preparation for our necessary defence, that our confused state would admit of; and as the question equally affected our sister colonies and us, we have declined, though urged thereto by the most pressing necessity, to assume the reins of civil government, without their advice and consent: but have, hitherto, patiently borne the many difficulties and distressing embarrassments necessarily resulting from a want thereof. We are now compelled to raise an army, which, with the assistance of the other colonies, we hope, under the smiles of Heaven, will be able to defend us, and all America, from the further butcheries and devastations of our implacable enemies.

But, as the sword should, in all free states, be subservient to the civil powers, and as it is the duty of the magistrate to support it, for the people's necessary defence, we tremble at having an army, although consisting of our own countrymen, established here, without a civil power to provide for and control it.

We are happy in having an opportunity of laying our distressed state before the representative body of the continent, and humbly hope you will favor us with your most explicit advice, respecting the taking up and exercising the powers of civil government, which we think absolutely necessary for the salvation of our country; and we shall readily submit to such a general plan as you may direct for the colonies; or make it our great study to establish such a form of government here, as shall not only most promote our advantage, but the union and interest of all America.

As the army, collecting from different colonies, is for the general defence of the rights of America, we would beg leave to suggest to your consideration, the propriety of your taking the regulation and general direction of it, that the operations may more effectually answer the purposes designed.

The Committee appointed to prepare instructions to the delegates who are going to New Hampshire, reported the following, which was accepted, viz :

Resolved, That the Hon. Joseph Gerrish, Esq., and Col. Ebenezer Sawyer, who are by this Congress chosen a committee to wait on the delegates of the colony of New Hampshire, are hereby empowered and directed, to take such methods, and make such application to the said congress, as shall, in the judgment of said committee, appear most conducive to the union of the colonies, and the most direct way to induce said Congress of New Hampshire, to raise their proportion of men to defend the colonies. And it is also *Resolved,* That the said committee be furnished with a copy of the application of this Congress to the honorable members of the Continental Congress, which the said committee is directed to deliver the president of the congress of that colony, and to do all that they can to procure the approbation of that colony to our assuming government, and to communicate to said congress such of the proceedings of this Congress as they shall think conducive to the good of the whole.

Ordered, That the said delegates be furnished with a copy of the establishment for the Massachusetts army, and rules and regulations for the same, and form of the oath for the officers and soldiers.

A letter from Col. Thomas Legate, dated Cambridge, May 16, 1775,[1] was read, and committed to Col. Foster, Mr. Parker, and Mr. Bliss.

The Committee appointed to bring in a resolve for supplying the soldiers with two twenty shilling bills for a month's advance pay, again reported.

The order of the day [was] moved for.

Ordered, That Col. Foster, Major Bliss, and Mr. Bent, be a committee to sort and count the votes for a member of this Congress, to go to Philadelphia with the application of this Congress, to the Continental Congress.

(1) This related to the organization of the train of artillery in the provincial army.

The committee reported, that Doct. Benjamin Church was chosen.

The committee appointed to take under consideration the letter from Col. Legate reported; which report being read and amended, was accepted, and is as follows, viz :

Whereas, it is of the utmost importance, that the men who shall be enlisted into the artillery company should be well qualified for that employment, and it being impossible to enlist the men for the artillery at large, in the colony, so soon as the service requires, therefore, *Resolved*, That the officers of the artillery be allowed to enlist the men from the several regiments already engaged, when the men are willing to engage in that service, until the whole artillery establishment shall be completed, always provided, that such enlistments shall be no prejudice or hindrance to the officers with whom such men are already enlisted, in entitling them to their respective commissions ; and that not more than four men be taken from any one company : and the officers of the train of artillery are directed to use their endeavor, to enlist as many ||men,|| who are not under any previous engagement in the army, as they can, speedily ; and the officers, from whose regiment or company any person is enlisted into the train of artillery, are also directed to fill up their said regiment or companies with all convenient speed, by enlisting other soldiers in the place of those enlisted into the train of artillery.

Ordered, That Mr. Gerry, Mr. Pitts, Doct. Taylor, the President, and Mr. Batchelder, be a committee to consider what measures it would be expedient to take, relative to the prisoners in Boston, and the inhabitants which are there kept in duress.

The committee appointed to apply to the committee of safety for a list of officers, &c., reported, verbally, that they had no other list than what they had before sent to the congress : that they had received no returns, and knew not how many had enlisted, or whether any regiments were completed.

Ordered, That Col. Barrett, Doct. Taylor, and Mr. Fuller, be a committee to take into consideration a petition from the inhabitants of Canaan and Norridgewock, on Kennebeck river, and report.[1]

The committee who were appointed to consider the information from Dartmouth, reported ; the report was recommitted for further examination and inquiry into the affair.

Ordered, That Mr. Freeman and Doct. Holten be added to the committee appointed to examine Hutchinson's letters.

Adjourned till to-morrow morning, 9 o'clock.

(1) This petition, like most others from the eastern part of the province, appears to have been for supplies of arms, ammunition, and provisions.

[WEDNESDAY,] May 17, 1775, [A. M.]

A letter from [Edward] Mott to this Congress, dated May 11, 1775, giving an account of the taking of the fortress at Ticonderoga, was read, together with a letter from Ethan Allen; also an application from Col. Easton, and others: whereupon, *Ordered*, That Col. Foster, Mr. Sullivan, and Doct. Holten, be a committee to introduce Col. Easton to this house, to give a narrative of that transaction, and that each member have liberty to ask him any questions.[1]

Ordered, That Mr. President, Doct. Taylor, Col. Foster, Doct. Holten, and Mr. Cross, be a committee to take the same into consideration, and report.

A resolve from the committee of safety, relative to the seizing the servants and friends to government, improperly so called, was read, and ordered to lie on the table.

Resolved, That three o'clock, P. M., be assigned for the purpose of considering the expediency of making out a commission to Gen. Ward.

The Congress appointed two other monitors, viz.: Mr. John Hale and Capt. Woodbridge Brown.

The resolve, and form of an oath to be taken by the general officers, were read, amended and accepted, and are as follow, viz.:

Resolved, That the general officers of the Massachusetts army, now raising for the defence and security of the rights and liberties of this and our sister colonies in America, shall each and every of them repeat, take, and subscribe the following oath, to be administered by [blank] viz.:

I, A. B., do solemnly swear, that, as a general officer in the Massachusetts army, I will well and faithfully execute the office of a general, to which I have been appointed, according to my best abilities, in defence and for the security of the estates, lives, and liberties of the good people of this and the sister colonies in America, in opposition to ministerial tyranny, by which they are or may be oppressed, and to all other enemies and opposers whatsoever; that I will adhere to the rules and regulations of said army, established by the Congress of ||the colony of|| the Massachusetts Bay, observe and obey the resolutions and orders which are or shall be passed by said Congress, or any future congress, or house of representatives, or legislative body of said colony, and such committees as shall be by them authorized for that purpose; and that I will disclose and make known to the authority aforesaid, all traitorous conspiracies, attempts and designs whatsoever,

---

(1) The papers relating to Ticonderoga, will be found in the Appendix.

which I shall know to be made, or have reason to suspect are making, against the army, or any of the English American colonies.

Ordered, That Jonas Dix, Esq. be directed to take depositions relative to the destruction of private property, by the king's troops, on the 19th instant, and their driving women in childbed out of their houses, and killing old men unarmed.

Henry Gardner, Esq., informed the house, that he was willing to continue to serve this colony in the office of receiver general.

Ordered, That Mr. Kollock, Deacon Nichols and Mr. Rawson, be a committee to consider what steps are proper to be taken, for the relief of such of the inhabitants of Boston as come over to Charlestown, who are not able to take care of themselves.

The committee appointed to consider the account of taking the fortress of Ticonderoga, reported the following resolve, and letter to the assembly of Connecticut, which were accepted, and the letter ordered to be authenticated and sent forward :

GENTLEMEN :—We have the happiness of presenting our congratulations to you, on the reduction of that important fortress, Ticonderoga ; we applaud the conduct, both of the officers and soldiers, and are of opinion, that the advantageous situation of that fortress, makes it highly expedient, that it should be repaired and properly garrisoned. In the mean time, as we suppose that there is no necessity for keeping all the cannon there, we should be extremely glad, if all the battery cannon, especially brass cannon, which can be spared from that place, or procured from Crown Point, which, we hope, is, by this time, in the hands of our friends, may be forwarded this way, with all possible expedition, as we have here to contend with an army furnished with as fine a train of artillery as ever was seen in America; and we are in extreme want of a sufficient number of cannon to fortify those important passes, without which, we can neither annoy general Gage, if it should become necessary, nor defend ourselves against him; we, therefore, must, most earnestly, recommend this very important matter to your immediate consideration; and we would suggest it, as our opinion, that the appointing Col. Arnold to take charge of them, and bring them down with all possible haste, may be a means of settling any disputes which may have arisen between him and some other officers, which we are always desirous to avoid, and, more especially, at a time when our common danger ought to unite us in the strongest bonds of unity and affection.

We are, gentlemen, &c.

This Congress, having received authentic intelligence, that the fort at Ticonderoga, is surrendered into the hands of Col. Ethan Allen and others, together with the artillery, and artillery stores, ammunition, &c., thereunto belonging, for the benefit of these colonies, occasioned by the intrepid valor of a number of men under the command of the said Col. Allen, Col. Easton of the Massachusetts, and others, and by the advice and direction of the committee for that expedition, the said Col. Allen is to remain in possession of the same, and its dependencies, until further order:

Resolved, That this Congress do highly approve of the same, and the general assembly of the colony of Connecticut are hereby desired to give directions, relative to garrisoning and maintaining the same for the future, until the advice of the Continental Congress can be had in that behalf; and, as this colony is in want of some battering cannon for their defence, immediately, it is further *Resolved*, that the president of this Congress be desired to write to the general assembly of the colony of Connecticut, desiring that they would give orders for the immediate removal of some of those cannon to this colony, for the purpose aforesaid.

Adjourned to three o'clock, P. M.

[Afternoon.]

The committee appointed to consider the petition from the inhabitants of Canaan and Norridgewalk, reported; the question being put, whether the report shall be accepted, and it passed in the negative; thereupon, *Resolved*, that the petitioners have leave to withdraw their petition.

Ordered, [That] Col. Foster, Mr. Sullivan and Capt. Farley, be a committee to prepare a commission for Gen. Ward.

The committee appointed to consider of the verbal information from Dartmouth, reported verbally, that the inhabitants of Dartmouth be advised to conduct themselves, with respect to the prisoners they have taken, agreeably to the direction of the committee of inspection for that town. After a long debate, it was *Moved*, that the consideration of this matter should subside; and the question being put, it passed in the affirmative, and the matter accordingly subsided.

Ordered, That the secretary be directed to inform the gentlemen from Dartmouth of the determination of the Congress, respecting the information from Dartmouth, and the reason thereof.

Ordered, That the committee appointed to revise the commission of the committee of safety, sit forthwith, and report as soon as may be; that Mr. Sullivan be excused, and that Col. Foster and Deacon Fisher be added to this committee.

Resolved, That Doct. Church be allowed one servant to attend him in his journey to Philadelphia.

Ordered, That the letters relative to taking the fortress of Ticonderoga, be delivered to the committee of safety.

Ordered, That the committee appointed to prepare an establishment for post offices, &c., be directed to bring in a resolve, for the purpose of empowering the committee, who were appointed to agree with the post riders, &c., to take bonds of the post masters, and appoint oaths to be taken by the post masters and post riders; and that Col. Foster be excused, and Capt. Stone and Mr. Greenleaf be added to the committee.

Adjourned to nine o'clock to-morrow morning.

[THURSDAY,] May 18, 1775, A. M.

The committee who were appointed to revise the resolves respecting the committee of safety, reported; whereupon, *Resolved,* that three o'clock in the afternoon be assigned for the choice of a committee of safety, to consist of thirteen members, and for the further consideration of said report.

Ordered, That Capt. Rawson, Mr. Bullen and Col. Farley, be a committee to consider the practicability of employing chaplains for the army, out of the number of clergy of this colony.

Ordered, That Col. Warren, Mr. Gardner and Mr. Sullivan, be a committee to bring in a resolve, recommending it to the inhabitants of this colony, not to choose any person to represent them in Congress, who has a commission in the army.

Ordered, That Major Fuller ||of Middleton,|| Mr. Whittemore and Mr. Bliss, be a committee to wait upon the Hon. James Russell, Esq., impost master, to know if he has any public moneys now in his hands.

Ordered, That the president, Mr. Sullivan and Col. Warren, be a committee to bring in a resolve, recommending to the inhabitants of this colony to make no purchases, nor receive any conveyances of estates, from the mandamus counsellors, or other inveterate enemies to the rights of this country, and that they have no dealings of any kind with such persons.

Ordered, That Mr. Gardner, Doct. Taylor and Mr. Kollock, be a committee to consider and inquire into the subject matter of a resolve of the committee of safety, respecting Lady Frankland.[1]

Adjourned to three o'clock, P. M.

(1) Sir Henry Frankland was the proprietor of extensive estates in Hopkinton, where he had a country residence previous to the Revolution, and maintained the splendor of an English nobleman. On the commencement of hostilities, his lady became alarmed at the movements of the people, and asked and obtained leave to remove to Boston with a small portion of her effects.

[Afternoon.]

Ordered, That Mr. Sullivan, Col. Foster, Doct. Holten, Mr. Bragdon and Capt. Batchelder, be a committee to take into consideration a letter from the committee of correspondence for the town of Falmouth, and such parts of a letter from the Hon. Enoch Freeman, Esq., to the secretary, as he may communicate.[1]

(1) The committee of correspondence of Falmouth addressed the committee of safety of the Provincial Congress, on the 15th of May, as follows:

"*May it please your honors:*

We, the committee of correspondence in Falmouth, would beg leave to represent to your honors, the situation and circumstances of this town and county; and if there is any impropriety in our doing it, your candor will excuse it."

"The alarming attempt of Col. Thompson, to take the ship Canceaux, Capt. Henry Mowat, commander, now in this harbor, has occasioned very great uneasiness in this town, as it has a tendency to bring on us certain ruin, by the admiral's resenting it, in such a manner, as to block up our harbor before the time. We have no force to oppose or prevent it, no fortifications, no ammunition, no cannon, and, if provisions are stopped from coming in here, the town is ruined, as well as the country, which depends upon the town for supplies, of which, at present, there is a great scarcity. We think Col. Thompson's attempt was rash and injudicious, if not unjustifiable, as we cannot learn he had any authority from you or the Congress; we are sure it was contrary to the will, and without any orders from his superior officers in the militia, though solicited for by him, and the people here seemed to be laid under contribution to subsist his men. We hope care will be taken that every attack upon our enemies, through the province, shall be conducted by proper officers, orderly, regularly, and with proper authority, lest it should occasion a civil war among ourselves. It is true, in defending ourselves, which may be sudden, immediate and resolute opposition, in the best manner that can be suddenly thought of, should be adopted; but we are afraid, that if any number of men, at any time, and in any manner, may collect together, and attack any thing, or any person they please, every body may be in danger. *Sat verbum sapienti.*"

"We are also concerned, lest there should a good deal of confusion arise, from a number of our men in the country, possessing themselves of the enlisting papers, lately printed, some calling themselves colonels, some majors, appointing their own officers, adjutants, chaplains, chirurgeons, &c., &c., without having, as we can learn, any written orders for so doing: for they seem to contend, already, who shall be chief officers; and they are uncertain, whether the men they enlist are to be stationed here, for our defence, or march to the camp at Cambridge, to make up the standing army."

"Enlisting papers, we understand, were sent to Gen. Preble, but he, not having any written orders, did not act in the affair. If the army can be completed without drawing men from hence, as we have all along been made to understand was the case, we cannot help thinking it would be most prudent; however, we shall not be backward, if there is real occasion for our men; and, in that case, we humbly submit, whether it would not be best, that some person or persons should be appointed, to conduct the affair according to orders. We hope we shall be excused for thus troubling your honors, as we were solicited to do it by a number of gentlemen."

"We are, with great veneration, your honors' most obedient humble servants.

ENOCH FREEMAN, *per order.*"

The committee to whom the communications, in relation to Col. Thompson, were referred, reported the following letter to that gentleman, which, however, was not accepted.

"SIR:—This Congress have received information, that the committee of correspondence of the town of Falmouth, on hearing that you were about making an attack on the Canceaux, man of war, lying in the harbor of that town, desired you to forbear any proceedings of that kind, which you promised to do; but that you afterwards took the captain of said ship of war, and detained the Hon. Jedediah Preble and Enoch Freeman, Esquires, as hostages for the return of the said captain; and that you levied contributions of money, and other things, from the subjects there, and took a boat belonging to the said Canceaux."

"Though this Congress approves of your general zeal for this country, yet it appears that your

The order of the day was moved for.

Ordered, That Capt. Brown, Mr. Bayley and Mr. Baker, be a committee to sort and count the votes for a committee of safety.

The committee appointed to count and sort the votes for a committee of safety, reported, that the following gentlemen were chosen, viz. : Hon. John Hancock, Esq., Doct. Joseph Warren, Doct. Benjamin Church, Capt. Benjamin White, Col. Joseph Palmer, Mr. Richard Devens, Mr. Abraham Watson, Mr. John Pigeon, Col. Azor Orne, Hon. Benjamin Greenleaf, Esq., Mr. Nathan Cushing, Doct. Samuel Holten, Hon. Enoch Freeman, Esq.

The report was recommitted for filling up the blanks.

Ordered, That Mr. Kollock, Doct. Taylor and Col. Davis, be a committee to inquire where the treasurer may procure money for the muster masters to supply the soldiers with advance pay.

The committee who were appointed to consider the resolve of the committee of safety, respecting Lady Frankland, reported : whereupon *Resolved*, that Mr. ||Abner|| Craft be, and hereby is directed, forthwith to attend this Congress. Mr. Craft accordingly attended, and having heard the allegations against him, and having made his defence, withdrew. The Congress then *Resolved* that he should be gently admonished by the president, and be assured, that the Congress were determined to preserve their dignity and power over the military. Mr. Craft was again called in, and the president politely admonished him, agreeably to the resolve of Congress.[1]

Resolved, That Lady Frankland be permitted to go into Boston with the following articles, viz. : seven trunks ; all the beds, and furniture to them ; all the boxes and crates ; a basket of chickens and a bag of corn ; two barrels and a hamper ; two horses and two chaises, and all the articles in the chaise, excepting arms and ammunition ; one phaeton ; some tongues, hams and veal ; sundry small bundles. Which articles, having been examined by a committee from this Congress, she is permitted to have them carried in, without any further examination.

[Adjourned to nine o'clock to-morrow morning.]

conduct, in taking the captain of the ship, against your promise, and your levying money, or other things, of the people, is, by no means, justifiable : and it is therefore expected, that you attend the next congress that shall be held in this colony, and to do your character justice in this matter, and that you return said boat, and stay all further proceedings of this kind in the mean time."

(1) Notwithstanding the permission given by the committee to Lady Frankland, to carry with her the articles of property mentioned in one of the resolves, some excitement arose among the inhabitants of the vicinity, from the preparations made for her departure. An armed party arrested her journey, and detained her person and effects, until the action of Congress liberated them from captivity. The censure, so lightly inflicted, seems to have been incurred, for the indiscreet zeal, which interposed to prevent the enjoyment of the privileges granted by the resolve.

[FRIDAY,] May 19, 1775, A. M.

Resolved, That Col. Bond be, and hereby is directed, to appoint a guard of six men to escort Lady Frankland to Boston, with such of her effects as this Congress have permitted her to carry with her ; and Col. Bond is directed to wait on Gen. Thomas, with a copy of the resolves of this Congress respecting Lady Frankland.

Resolved, That Mr. Ezekiel Hall, of this town, be recommended to the generals of our colony army, in order to have such aid as they can afford him, in going into or out of Boston, or sending some suitable person there, which appears to be necessary, in order to save some of his valuable effects, which, there is reason to fear, were exposed by the late fire.

Ordered, That Col. Warren wait on Gen. Ward, directing him to attend this Congress forthwith, to receive his commission ; and also on the committee of safety, for a list of such colonels and other officers, as they shall report to be prepared for receiving their commissions.

A letter from the committee of correspondence ||of Connecticut|| was read, respecting the taking of Ticonderoga ; whereupon, *Ordered*, that Mr. Gerry prepare an answer thereto, informing them what steps this Congress have taken relative to that affair.[1]

(1) The committee of correspondence write from Hartford, May 16, 1775. The letter is subscribed by Erastus Wolcot, William Williams, Samuel Bishop and Samuel H. Parsons.

" GENTLEMEN :—We were yesterday informed of the success of an expedition, undertaken and set on foot by some individuals of this colony, in a secret manner, against Ticonderoga and Crown Point, the particular account of which you will have received before this comes to hand ; immediately on the receipt of this news, an express was despatched from hence to the Continental Congress, for their advice in this important matter ; posts were also sent to Albany, to the committee of correspondence for that city, requesting them to afford their aid in maintaining that pass, till the opinion of the colonies can be known. We understand an expedition against the same place hath been undertaken under the authority of your province ; but, the adventure being set on foot by some private gentlemen in this colony, and success having attended their enterprize before the forces from the Massachusetts Bay came up, some question arose about the right to command and hold this important pass. We consider all the colonies, and the New England colonies especially, as brethren, united together in one joint interest, and pursuing the same general design ; and that whatever expedition, in furtherance of the grand designs, may be undertaken by any one of the colonies, or body of men, in either of them, ought to be considered as undertaken for the joint benefit of the whole confederate colonies, and the expenses of the enterprize, and cost of maintaining and defending the same, are to be borne by all, in proportion to their abilities. This is not a time for the colonies to contend about precedence ; but we hope all will wish to put to a helping hand, and mutually afford each other all necessary assistance against our common enemy. Some parts of your province are conveniently situated to furnish men, &c., for maintaining our possession ; we doubt not you will exert yourselves to secure every advantage which may accrue from this successful attempt, in which we hope the city and county of Albany, and the colony of Connecticut, will cooperate with you ; but of this we cannot assure you, as our calls are very many, &c.

We are, gentlemen, your humble servants."

" We hope you will not omit any thing you can do, as it is uncertain what New York will undertake, without the advice of the general congress, &c."

Ordered, That Doct. Perkins and Capt. Baker be added to the committee, who were appointed to inquire where the treasurer can borrow money.

Resolved, That all persons who may have any goods or chattels, belonging to Lady Frankland, now in their custody, which are not mentioned in the resolve of this Congress for allowing her, with certain effects to go into Boston, be, and hereby are directed, to permit her to send them to Hopkinton, or dispose of them in any way agreeable to her, not inconsistent with the resolves of this Congress.

The committee appointed to consider what steps may be taken for the relief of such of the inhabitants of Boston as come over to Charlestown, &c., reported; whereupon, *Ordered*, that Deacon Cheever, Col. Davis and Capt. Withinton, be a committee to bring in a list of names of persons to fill up the blank in said report.

Mr. Gerry reported an answer to a letter from the committee of correspondence of Connecticut; which was [ᵃaccepted.][1]

Adjourned to three o'clock, P. M.

[Afternoon.]

Ordered, That Doct. Holten, Mr. Whittemore and Major Bliss, be a committee to take into consideration the representation made to this Congress by Col. Warren, by desire of Gen. Ward, of the necessity there is, that the army should be immediately supplied with iron pots, as well as an additional stock of powder, as also for providing a house for the abode of Joseph Trumbull, Esq., of Connecticut, and another for the chairman and the other members of the committee of safety.

The report of the committee for revising the commissions of [the committee of] safety, after being read paragraph by paragraph, was amended and accepted, and is as follows, viz. :

Whereas, the former Congresses of this colony have chosen, and by divers resolutions have empowered, John Hancock, Esq., Doct. Joseph Warren, Doct. Benjamin Church, Capt. Benjamin Church, Capt. Benjamin White, Col. Joseph Palmer, Mr. Richard Devens, Mr. Abraham Watson, Jr., Mr. John Pigeon, Col. Azor Orne, Nathan Cushing, Esq., Col. William Heath, Col. Thomas Gardner, Col. Asa Whitcomb, Mr. Edward Durant and Mr. James Sullivan, to be a committee of safety, and by virtue of the authority of that office, on certain occasions, to cause to be assembled the militia of this colony, for the defence of the inhabitants thereof; and which committee of safety are, by the resolu-

---

a [accepted, and is as follows, viz.]

(1) Mr. Gerry's draft of an answer, never entered on the record, is not retained on the files of Congress

tions of said congresses, empowered to do several other acts for the service of the colony, as by the journals and records of said congresses appear:

It is *Resolved*, That, whatever the said committee of safety, or any of them, have done pursuant to the said resolutions of said Congress, shall be held good and valid; and that the said inhabitants of said colony shall be held thereby, as well according to the true intent and meaning of said resolutions, as according to the strict letter thereof: and, whereas, there appears to be still a deficiency of power in said committee, considering the particular exigencies of the colony, and it being necessary to have their commission as concise and explicit as possible, which can be done only by consolidating the powers intended in the several resolutions of this, as well as the former congresses, to be given them. It is, therefore, *Resolved*, that all and every resolution now in force, respecting the said committee of safety, shall be, and hereby are, repealed, revoked, and rendered null and void.

And it is also *Resolved*,That [Hon. John Hancock, Esq., Doct. Joseph Warren, Doct. Benjamin Church, Capt. Benjamin White, Col. Joseph Palmer, Mr. Richard Devens, Mr. Abraham Watson, Mr. John Pigeon, Col. Azor Orne, Hon. Benjamin Greenleaf, Esq., Mr. Nathan Cushing, Doct. Samuel Holten, Hon. Enoch Freeman, Esq.,] be a committee of safety for this colony hereafter, until some further order of this, or some future congress or house of representatives of this colony shall revoke their, or either of their appointments.

And it is also *Resolved*, That the said committee of safety shall be, and hereby are empowered, when they shall think it necessary, in defence of the lives and properties of the inhabitants of this colony, to assemble such and so many of the militia thereof, and them to dispose and place where, and detain so long, as the said committee of safety shall judge necessary, and to discharge said militia when the safety of this colony will admit of it; and the officers of the said militia are hereby enjoined to pay strict obedience to the orders and directions of the said committee of safety.

And it is also *Resolved*, That the said committee of safety shall be, and hereby are empowered, to direct the army of this colony to be stationed where the said committee of safety shall judge most conducive to the defence and service of the colony; and the general, and other officers of the army, are required to render strict obedience to such orders of said committee: provided always, that it shall be in the power of this, or any future congress, to control any order of the said committee of safety, respecting this or any other matter.

31

And, whereas, the former committee of safety were, by a resolve of this Congress, empowered to nominate persons to this Congress, to be commissioned to be officers in the army now establishing for the defence of this colony, and said committee having already given orders to a number of persons, to enlist men for that purpose : *Resolved*, that the committee of safety now appointed, proceed in that matter, that such officers, where the regiments are completed, may be commissioned by this Congress; and if any regiments should be nearly completed, and the officers thereof ready to be commissioned, agreeably to the resolve of this Congress, during the time between the dissolution of this Congress and the meeting of the next, the said committee shall have power to fill up and deliver out commissions to them, and blank commissions, signed by the president of this Congress, and attested by the secretary, shall be delivered to the said committee for this purpose.

And it is also *Resolved*, That any five of the said committee be a quorum, with full power to transact any business which the committee, by the resolves above, are empowered and vested with authority to do.

Ordered, That letters be sent to the Hon. Benjamin Greenleaf, Esq. and the Hon. Enoch Freeman, Esq., informing them of their being chosen members of the committee of safety, and requesting their attendance as soon as possible.

Resolved, That Mr. John Pigeon be, and he hereby is appointed and empowered, as a commissary for the army of this ||ᵃcolony,|| to draw from the magazines, which are or may be provided for that purpose, such provisions and other stores as, from time to time, he shall find necessary for the army ; and he is further empowered, to recommend to the Congress such persons as shall be necessary, and as he shall think qualified, to serve as deputy commissioners ; and said deputy commissioners, when confirmed by the congress for the time being, shall have full power to act in said office, and are to be accountable to the commissary for their doings; also, said commissary is empowered to contract with, and employ, such other persons to assist him in executing his office, as shall be, by him, found necessary ; and his contracts, for necessaries to supply the army, during the late confused state of the colony, shall be allowed; and the committee of supplies are hereby directed to examine, and if they find them reasonable, considering the exigencies of the times, to draw on the treasury for payment of the same.

The form of a commission for Gen. Ward was read, amended and accepted, and is as follows :

a ||province.||

THE CONGRESS OF THE COLONY OF THE MASSACHUSETTS BAY.

To the Hon. Artemas Ward, Esq.—Greeting:

We, reposing especial trust and confidence in your courage and good conduct, do, by these presents, constitute and appoint you, the said Artemas Ward, to be general and commander in chief of all the forces raised by the congress aforesaid, for the defence of this, and the other American colonies. You are, therefore, carefully and diligently to discharge the duty of a general, in leading, ordering and exercising the said forces in arms, both inferior officers and soldiers; and to keep them in good order and discipline, and they are hereby commanded to obey you as their general; and you are yourself to observe and follow such orders and instructions as you shall, from time to time, receive from this, or any future congress or house of representatives of this colony, or the committee of safety, so far as the said committee is empowered, by their commission, to order and instruct you, for the defence of this, and the other colonies; and to demean yourself according to the military rules and discipline established by Congress, in pursuance of the trust reposed in you.

                , the   of   A. D., 1775.

By order of Congress.

President pro tempore.

Secretary pro tempore.

Ordered, That Col. Foster, Capt. Stone and Mr. Webster, be a committee to get the depositions, and narrative of the late excursion of the king's troops to Concord, printed in a pamphlet, on the best terms they can; and that they forward one pamphlet to each town and district in the colony.

Resolved, That there be a blank left in the commissions, to be given the officers of the several regiments of the colony army, for the rank of the regiment, and that   [blank]   be a committee to settle the ranks of the regiments, when the regiments are completed.

Resolved, That the same committee be directed to bring in a resolve, settling the rank or number of the regiments, according to the rank or age of the counties from whence the majority of the regiments shall come.

Resolved, That the rank of the regiments, where there are more than one in each county, be according to the rank which those regiments ||have|| formerly sustained in the old arrangement from which they are taken, provided that can be ascertained, and where that cannot be determined, the rank to be determined by lot.

Resolved, That the commissions be all of one date, and that the rank of the officers be determined by this Congress, or by a committee from this Congress, at some future time.

Resolved, That Col. Samuel Gerrish have a commission for a colonel in the army, and that the oath be administered to him by Mr. Gardner, the receiver general.

['Also, that commissions, as captains, issue for Richard Dodge, Jacob Gerrish, William Rogers,] to bear date the 19th of May.

Adjourned till to-morrow morning, nine o'clock.

[SATURDAY,] May 20, 1775, A. M.

Ordered, That Col. Foster, Doct. Holten and Major Brooks, be a committee to confer with Mr. Revere, respecting his proposal for an alteration in the value of the colony notes, which have been ordered to be struck off.

Ordered, That Col. Thurston, Esquire Aikin and Mr. Crane, be a committee to take into consideration a petition from a number of the inhabitants of Deer Island.[1]

The committee appointed to consider the case of the prisoners in Boston, and the inhabitants which are there kept in duress, reported ; the report was read and accepted, and is as follows, viz. :

Whereas, this Congress did, on the 30th of April last, pass a resolve for permitting such inhabitants of the colony to remove into Boston, with their effects, fire arms and ammunition excepted, as

---

a [Also that captain's commission for Richard Dodge ; do. Jacob Gerrish ; do. William Rogers ; commissions to bear date the 19th of May.]

(1) The petition of the inhabitants of Deer Island, corresponds in the representations of distress, with those coming from many of the towns of the eastern coast. It was subscribed by Nathan Dow, Robert Nason, Francis Haskell, Samuel Haynes, Courtney Babidge, Isaiah Crockett and Thomas Thompson, and is almost a solitary exception to the general correctness with which the memorials to the Provincial Congress were drawn. The inartificial construction and simplicity of language, render the description of want and embarrassment more vivid :

"DEER ISLAND, *in the county of Lincoln.*

" *To the honored gentlemen of the Provincial Congress:*

"SIRS :—We, who are the committee of this town, do desire to make our complaint unto you, and will inform you in what poor circumstances we are at this time : and would beg your assistance, as we are without powder and ball, and [have] no way to get any, as our wood and lumber will not sell at any price ; and, gentlemen, we are in great want for corn and pork, and shall suffer, unless we have help from you, and unless the ports are opened and trade goes on. And, gentlemen, if you will be so kind unto us as to help us, we will make you full satisfaction for the same, when we can sell our lumber. We would inform you, that there are on this island about three hundred souls, and we beg you would consider in what poor condition we must be. Gentlemen: we can't purchase corn nor pork at any rate whatsoever: and we hope, that your love and regard for your brethren and true sons of liberty, will send us speedy relief. And, gentlemen, in complying with the above, you will greatly oblige your humble servants."

May 11, 1775.

should incline thereto, it being in consequence of general Gage's promise to the inhabitants of Boston, that, upon resigning their arms and
ammunition, they should have liberty to remove from said town with
their effects : and, whereas, but a small proportion of the said inhabitants of Boston have been, hitherto, permitted to leave the town, and
those only to bring their clothing and household furniture, they being
constrained to leave their provisions and all their other effects; therefore,
Resolved, that Gen. Ward be, and he hereby is directed, to order the
guards, in future, not to suffer any provisions or effects, excepting furniture and clothing, to be carried into the town of Boston, so long as
the said general Gage shall suffer the persons or effects of the inhabitants of said town, contrary to his plighted faith, to be restrained.

The committee appointed to confer with Mr. Revere, brought in the
following resolves, which were accepted, and the secretary [was] directed to erase from the minutes the resolve which passed this Congress
for issuing colony notes of ten shillings each.

Whereas, this Congress did, on the fourth day of this instant May,
pass a resolve in the following form, viz. : *Resolved*, that each non-
commissioned officer and private soldier, who has, or shall enlist himself into the service of this colony, shall have twenty shillings paid
him, out of the receiver general's office, as advance pay; and that the
commanding officer of each regiment, who shall be, and hereby is, empowered to act as muster master to his said regiment, shall draw from
the receiver general's office the sum of twenty shillings, for each non-
commissioned officer and private soldier in his said regiment, and pay the
same according to the tenor of this resolve, as soon as said men have
enlisted themselves and been duly sworn, and give his bond, with sufficient sureties, to the receiver general therefor; said bond to be discharged by a receipt produced by said officer, from each non-commissioned officer and private soldier, that he has received the same :

And, whereas, this Congress have, by a subsequent resolve, superseded the appointment of the muster masters aforementioned, and directed that Col. Benjamin Lincoln and Col. Asa Whitcomb be appointed muster masters in the Massachusetts army, whose business it
shall be to pass muster on every soldier that should be enlisted into
the said army, and by no means to accept of any but such as are able
bodied and effective men, and also to examine their arms and accoutrements, &c., [to ascertain] that they are in proper order ; and said
muster masters are thereby directed and empowered to receive from
Henry Gardner, Esq., receiver general, twenty shillings, lawful money,
for each and every non-commissioned officer and private soldier then

mustered and sworn, as shall appear with arms, &c., and shall give bond to said receiver general, with sufficient sureties, for such moneys drawn out of the treasury, and shall forthwith pay out said sum of twenty shillings, advance pay, to each and every non-commissioned officer and private soldier, and on producing receipts from them to said receiver general, said bonds shall be cancelled : and, whereas, it is found that sufficient ready cash cannot be obtained so soon as it will be needed for the purpose aforesaid ;

Therefore, *Resolved*, That each non-commissioned officer and private soldier aforesaid, if he will accept the same, shall, instead of twenty shillings advance pay, upon the muster aforesaid, receive forty shillings advance pay, in three notes on interest, from the receiver general, to be paid in one year from the date of said notes ; and that for all such sums as the said Col. Lincoln and Col. Whitcomb shall receive of the receiver general, in notes aforesaid, they give bonds, and that such bonds be discharged by receipts, as in and by the last mentioned resolve is directed.

Ordered, That the president, Major Hawley, Gen. Whitcomb, Mr. Gerry, Col. Palmer, Col. Lincoln and Col. Foster, be a committee to consider what measures are proper to be taken for organizing the Massachusetts army in the most effectual and ready manner.

Resolved, That for the payment of advance pay to the Massachusetts army, there be issued by the receiver general, on the credit of this colony, a sum not exceeding twenty-six thousand pounds, lawful money, in notes of the following denominations, viz. : of twenty shillings, of eighteen, sixteen, fifteen, fourteen, twelve, ten, nine, and of six shillings : to be four thousand, three hundred, and thirty-three, of each denomination, and no more; and to be of the form following, viz.:

COLONY OF THE MASSACHUSETTS BAY.

No.   *May 25, 1775.*

The possessor of this note shall be entitled to receive, out of the public treasury of this colony, the sum of   shillings, lawful money, on the twenty-fifth day of May, A. D., 1776, with interest, at the rate of six per cent. per annum ; and this note shall be received in all payments at the treasury, at any time after the date hereof, for the principal sum, without interest, if so paid before the said 25th day of May, A. D., 1776.

Receiver General.

Which notes shall be received in all payments in this colony, and no discount or abatement shall be made thereon, in any payment, trade, or exchange whatsoever.

The committee appointed to consider the practicability of providing chaplains for the army, reported; the report was read, and recommitted.

The petition of Benjamin Thompson to the committee of safety, was read, and ordered to subside.[1]

Adjourned to three o'clock, P. M.

[Afternoon.]

The report of the committee appointed to consider the practicability of providing chaplains, was again read and accepted, and is as follows, viz. :

Whereas, it is necessary that chaplains should be appointed in the Massachusetts army, under the command of the Hon. Artemas Ward, Esq., which, if appointed, on the establishment made by this Congress, will greatly enhance the colony debt; and, whereas, it has been represented to this Congress, that several ministers of the religious assemblies within this colony, have expressed their willingness to attend the army aforesaid, in the capacity of chaplains, as they may be directed by this Congress; therefore, *Resolved*, that it be, and it is hereby recommended, to the ministers of the several religious assemblies within this colony, that, with the leave of their several congregations, they attend said army in their several ||ᵃturns,|| to the number of thirteen at one time, during the time the army shall be encamped, and that they make known their resolutions, to the Congress, thereon, or to the committee of safety, as soon as may be.

Resolved, unanimously, that the president be desired to deliver to Gen. Ward, the commission prepared for him by this Congress, as general and commander in chief of the Massachusetts forces.

Ordered, That Major Brooks, Col. Mitchell, Esquire Rawson, Esquire Dix and Major Bliss, be a committee to examine the prisoner at the door, brought from head quarters, and report some order to be taken thereon.

The president communicated to the Congress the request of the selectmen of Boston, that the Congress would permit Mr. Hall to carry

---

a ||towns.||

(1) Mr. Benjamin Thompson, of Concord, in New Hampshire, represented, that he had been arrested and confined in Woburn, upon suspicion of being inimical to the liberty of the country : that the committee of correspondence had made a public examination, but were not pleased to acquit or condemn him : that his personal safety and reputation depended on a thorough and impartial investigation of the charges against him : and prayed the committee of safety to take the subject into consideration, and afford him a full and fair trial, and an honorable discharge from confinement.

two loads of hay into Boston, one for himself and one for another person, (lieutenant governor Oliver;) whereupon, *Ordered*, that the messenger in waiting ||for an answer|| be dismissed.

Resolved, That only the colonels of each regiment should attend this Congress to receive their commissions, unless they should be indisposed, or otherwise necessarily prevented; in which case, the next field officer may apply for his commission, and commissions for the inferior officers in his regiment.

The Hon. Mr. Dexter having, by order of Congress, administered the oath to Gen. Ward, his commission was delivered to him by the president.

The following commissions were likewise delivered, viz.: to Thomas Cogswell, John Wood, captains, under the command of Col. Gerrish; Ephraim Doolittle, colonel; Ebenezer Learned, colonel; Joseph Reed, colonel; James Bricket, lieutenant colonel, under Col. James Fry; Calvin Smith, major, under Col. Joseph Reed; Danforth Keyes, lieutenant colonel, Jonathan Holman, major, under Col. Ebenezer Learned; Ebenezer Clap, lieutenant colonel, under Col. Joseph Reed.

Ordered, That commissions be delivered to the captains of Col. Fry's regiment, agreeably to a list exhibited.

Resolved, That nine o'clock, next Tuesday morning, be assigned for taking into consideration the expediency of giving lieutenants' commissions to the subaltern officers.

Resolved, That three o'clock, next Tuesday afternoon, be assigned to consider a motion made by Col. Doolittle, for appointing a muster master for the enlisted companies at Northfield.

Ordered, That Capt. Brown and Esquire Dix, be a committee to procure a guard over the prisoners ||brought|| from head quarters, and that the guard who conducted them from thence be now released.

Adjourned till to-morrow afternoon at four o'clock.

SUNDAY, May 21, 1775, A. M.

Met at four o'clock, and adjourned to to-morrow morning, eight o'clock.[1]

(1) From this date until the dissolution of the second Provincial Congress, no journal of the proceedings is preserved. The fragments on the following pages, have been gathered from the papers on the files, from the copies of resolves certified to be correct by Mr. Secretary Freeman, and from authorized publications in the prints of the times. These relics afford a very imperfect history of the doings of the Congress during the last eight days of its existence, and excite deep regret for the loss of the record, which, it is probable, from the evidence afforded by the volumes preserved, was never entered in regular form by the clerk.

Monday, May 22, 1775.

[The committee on the petition from the inhabitants of Deer Island, reported as follows, viz. :]

[The committee on the petition of a number of the inhabitants of Deer Island, so called, in the county of Lincoln, beg leave to report, that they have made inquiry of the bearer of the petition, Major Low, and find that the people there are greatly in want of provisions, and ought to be relieved : but whether it will be best to remove them from the island, or to supply them with 150 bushels of corn, 100 bushels of potatoes, 2 barrels of pork, 20 cod lines, with leads and hooks, and a small quantity of salt, we submit to the Congress.]

[*Ordered*, That the consideration of this report be deferred until there is a fuller house.]

[The committee appointed to consider what measures should be adopted in relation to the estates of persons unfriendly to the country, reported the following resolve, which was accepted, and ordered to be published in the newspapers printed in Cambridge and Salem :]

[Whereas, a number of men, some of whom have, in times past, by the good people of this province, been raised to the highest places of honor and trust, have become inimical to this colony ; and merely on principles of avarice have, in conjunction with the late Gov. Hutchinson, been trying to reduce all America to the most abject state of slavery : and as well to avoid the just indignation of the people, as to pursue their diabolical plans, have fled to Boston, and other places, for refuge :]

[Therefore, *Resolved*, That those persons, among whom are the mandamus counsellors, are guilty of such atrocious and unnatural crimes against their country, that every friend to mankind ought to forsake and detest them, until they shall give evidence of a sincere repentance, by actions worthy of men and christians ; and that no person within this colony shall take any deed, lease, or conveyance whatever, of the lands, houses, or estates of such persons. And it is hereby recommended to the committee of inspection, in every town in this colony, to see this resolve fully enforced, unless in such cases as the Congress shall otherwise direct.]

[A letter was received from Gen. Ward, recommending that the ordnance, arms and ammunition, mentioned in the following list, be immediately procured, and sent to head quarters, for the supply of the army of Massachusetts :]

[30 twenty-four pounders, and if that number of cannon cannot be

32

obtained, that the weight of metal be made up with eighteen pounders, double fortified: 10 twelve pounders: 18 nine pounders: 21,600 pounds of powder, and 80 balls for each gun: 1500 stands of arms: 20,000 pounds of musket powder: 40,000 pounds of lead: 1700 iron pots:]

[*Ordered*, That the letter be referred to the committee of safety.]

[The Congress having'requested the Rev. Doct. Langdon to deliver a sermon before the next Massachusetts Congress, at their meeting in Watertown, on the last Wednesday of this month, and he having signified that he will comply with such request:]

[*Resolved*, That it is the desire of this Congress, that the reverend ministers of the gospel in this colony, would assemble at that time, agreeably to their ancient custom, and hold a convention as usual, if they think proper: as, in the opinion of this Congress, the cause of religion, and the political interest of this colony, may be served by such meeting.]

[*Ordered*, That the secretary be directed to cause the foregoing resolution to be published in the newspapers, as soon as may be.]

[A letter was received from the committee of safety, inclosing a communication from Col. Benedict Arnold, giving information of the surrender of Ticonderoga.][1]

[*Ordered*, That the following letter to Col. Arnold, reported by a committee, be accepted, signed by the secretary, and forwarded in the name and behalf of this Congress, as soon as may be.]

[SIR:—This Congress have this day received your letter of the 11th instant, informing the committee of safety of the reduction of the fort at Ticonderoga, with its dependencies, which was laid before this Congress by said committee. We applaud the conduct of the troops, and esteem it a very valuable acquisition.]

[We thank you for your exertions in the cause, and considering the situation of this colony at this time, having a formidable army in the heart of it, whose motions must be constantly attended to; and as the affairs of that expedition began in the colony of Connecticut, and the cause being common to us all, we have already written to the general assembly of that colony, to take the whole matter respecting the same under their care and direction, until the advice of the Continental Congress can be had in that behalf, a copy of which letter we now enclose you.] .

[The president communicated the following letter from the Hon‧ James Russell, commissioner of imposts:]

(1) The letters of Col. Arnold will be found in the Appendix.

[CHARLESTOWN, *May 19th*, 1775.

To JOSEPH WARREN, ESQ., *President of the Provincial Congress.*

SIR :—I yesterday, by Major Fuller, Mr. Whittemore and Mr. Bliss, received a resolve of the Congress, appointing them a committee to call on me, to know whether I have any of the public moneys in my hands; in answer thereto, I would desire you, Sir, to inform the Provincial Congress, that the light money, for several years past, since the increase of light houses, and more especially since the obstructions of the last year upon our trade, has not been sufficient to defray the expense of said houses; and I have, consequently, been under a necessity to apply the money arising from the impost for that purpose. Ever since I received the favors of my country in being chosen to the impost office, I have done all in my power to discharge my duty therein, to their satisfaction. The means of procuring oil, by the unhappy and increasing troubles of our country, appearing very uncertain and precarious, I have endeavored to purchase as large a stock as I could ; and as the impost bill expired on the first of March last, the public moneys I have in my hands, will not be more than sufficient to enable me to pay for the oil contracted for, to complete the stock for the present year.

I am your most humble servant,

JAMES RUSSELL.]

[*Ordered*, That Doct. Taylor, Mr. Hale and Mr. Kollock, be a committee to take the foregoing letter into consideration, and, in particular, to inquire into Mr. Russell's right of making the contract therein mentioned, and the circumstances of it, and report as soon as may be.]

TUESDAY, May 23, 1775.

[The committee appointed to consider the letter from Brownfield, reported, that they find by the bearer of the letter, that the inhabitants have some arms, powder, &c , and are not in immediate danger, except from indians, who are friendly at present ; and the state of our affairs calls for such large supplies, that the consideration of their request should be deferred till the sitting of the next Congress.]

[The report was accepted, and Mr. Israel Hobart was directed to inform the bearer of the letter of the action of the Congress thereon.]

[The committee appointed to bring in a resolve respecting the depredations of the British troops on the islands and sea coasts, reported as follows :]

[Whereas, the forces under the command of general Gage and admiral Graves, are frequently plundering and making depredations on the islands and sea coasts of this province, from whence they plunder or purchase hay, cattle, sheep, and many other things, to the injury, not only of individuals but also to the great damage of the public, and thus strengthen the hands of our enemies :]

[Therefore, *Resolved*, That it be recommended to the several towns and districts on the sea coasts of this colony, and to all those persons living on the several islands on said coasts, that they remove their hay, cattle, sheep, &c., that are exposed to those ravages, and cannot be sufficiently guarded, so far into the country as to be out of the way of those implacable enemies to this people. Also, that it be recommended to the committees of correspondence in each town and district, and to the selectmen where no such committee is chosen, that they take effectual care that this resolve be immediately and strictly put into execution, and that all persons who refuse to comply with the aforegoing resolve, shall be held as incorrigible enemies to the rights and liberties of this country.]

[This report being read and amended, *Ordered*, That the further consideration thereof be referred to the next Provincial Congress.]

[Whereas, Edward How hath been brought before this Congress, and charged with crimes committed in the camp, and as this Congress do adjudge the head quarters of the army to be the most suitable and proper place to try the said Edward, and determine what is adequate to his demerits :]

[Therefore, *Resolved*, That the said Edward How, be sent under a guard to head quarters, and that he be there dealt with as the nature of his offence doth require.]

[*Ordered*, That Capt. Brown be directed to see that said How is sent to head quarters, with a copy of the foregoing resolve.]

[Whereas, Thomas Nichols, a negro man, hath been brought before this Congress, and there being no evidence to prove any matters or things alleged against him :]

[Therefore, *Resolved*, That the said Thomas be sent to the town or district where he belongs, and that the committee of correspondence, or selectmen of said town or district, take such care of the said Thomas, that he may be dealt with as they, in their judgment, shall think proper.]

[*Ordered*, That Capt. Kingsbury be directed to appoint some persons to conduct the abovementioned negro to Natick, agreeably to the foregoing resolve.]

[The committee appointed to consider what further measures are necessary to be taken for the organization of the army, presented their report, which was read, accepted, and is as follows:]

[The committee appointed on the 20th of May current, to consider what further orders are necessary to be taken and passed, that the army now raising by this province, for the necessary defence thereof, may be effectually officered and organized, have attended that service, and beg leave to report, that they are humbly of opinion, that, for the end aforesaid, it is necessary that, over and above the general already appointed for the said army, and commissioned by Congress, the following officers, not yet ordered by Congress, should be chosen and commissioned, to wit: one lieutenant general, two major generals, four brigadiers generals, two adjutants generals, and two quarter master generals; and that this Congress, before they shall rise, and as soon as shall be convenient, proceed to choose and commission such lieutenant general; but that the choice of the rest of the officers above specified, should be referred to the beginning of the first session of the next Congress; and they beg leave to subjoin, as their opinion, that it will be proper that such brigadiers general should be chosen and taken, of and from among the colonels, who may be commissioned by Congress.

All which is humbly submitted by your committee, who ask leave to sit again.

JOSEPH HAWLEY, per order.]

WEDNESDAY, May 24, 1775.

[Ebenezer Cutler, of Northborough, having been brought before this Congress, on complaint of sundry persons, for uttering sundry expressions against the liberties of the good people of this colony, and the same having been inquired of by a committee, who reported, among other matters, that all the expressions of which he is accused, were uttered some time ago, and that the said Ebenezer had requested that he might have the same privilege of going into the town of Boston, without his effects, as other persons have, by the order of Congress:]

[The report was accepted, and it was thereupon *Resolved*, that he have liberty for so doing.]

[Mr. Gerry, from the committee to consider the propriety of appointing some additional armourers, reported as follows, viz.:]

[*Resolved*, That the committee of supplies be empowered and directed to appoint such and so many armourers, in addition to those already appointed, as may be wanted by the army of this colony; provided the whole number, including those already appointed, shall not exceed fifteen, and that the said armourers, as also those already appointed by the committee of safety, shall each receive four pounds per month, and be entitled to billeting as soldiers, they providing their own tools; and the said armourers are hereby directed to keep true accounts of the expense of repairing the fire arms of the soldiers, to qualify them to pass muster. And the committee of supplies are hereby empowered and directed to discharge such armourers as are or may hereafter be appointed, when they shall think it for the interest of the colony so to do.]

[The report being read and amended, *Ordered*, that Mr. Whittemore, Capt. Dwight and Mr. Kollock, be a committee to bring in a resolve for the appointment of a number of armourers as aforesaid, and for the establishment of their pay.]

[It being made to appear to this Congress, that the major part of the committee, appointed to effect the removal of the poor of the town of Boston, to the place to which they are destined, are removed out of the towns of Charlestown and Roxbury to which they belonged; *Resolved*, that Messrs. Isaac Foster, Nathaniel Gorham, Edward Goodwin, John Frothingham, Joseph Hopkins, Col. Joseph Williams, Mr. Nathaniel Patten, Mr. Lewis Fay, Mr. James Bridge, Jr., Major Nathaniel Ruggles, Mr. Noah Brown, Mr. William Gridley, or any three of them, being present, be a committee for all the purposes, and with all the powers, to which the said committee were appointed.]

[And it being also made to appear, that said committee cannot proceed unless further provision be made in that behalf; therefore, *Resolved*, that said committee, or any three of them, shall have full power to procure, upon the credit of this colony, in the most frugal manner, as much provision as they shall find necessary to support those poor persons to the places of their destination; and the said committee are further empowered to procure teams to carry such persons and their effects to those places; and if such teams cannot be hired, to impress them for that service, and all the charges arising by the measures before directed, shall be paid out of the donations to the poor of said town of Boston, now in the hands of the committee who were appointed to receive and dispose thereof; and if that should be insufficient, the remainder shall be paid by this colony; and the committee hereby appointed to the service aforesaid, are hereby directed to lay before the next Congress, an account of the charges arising in pursuance of the above commission, that whatever shall appear to be reasonable and just, may be liquidated and allowed.]¹

[*Ordered*, That Col. Joseph Cushing, Mr. Ellis and Mr. Crane, be a committee to fill up and deliver to the colonels of each regiment, the commissions for the officers of their respective regiments, when said committee shall be notified, by the secretary of this Congress, that the Congress have approved of the persons to be commissioned; and that blank commissions be put in the hands of said committee, properly authenticated, for that purpose; and that when said commissions are filled up, they be delivered by said committee to the colonel, on his applying for the same, he engaging that he will not deliver such commissions to the respective officers, until they shall have taken the oath appointed to be taken by them, by order of this Congress; and that William Holden, Esq., be appointed to administer the oath to the officers stationed at Roxbury, and James Prescott, Esq., be appointed to administer the oath to the officers stationed at Cambridge.]

[The committee appointed to prepare an address to the inhabitants of the Massachusetts Bay, relative to an issue of notes by said colony, reported. The address was read and accepted, and is as follows, viz.:]

[*To the Inhabitants of the Massachusetts Bay :*]

[FRIENDS AND FELLOW COUNTRYMEN :—With great satisfaction we bear public testimony of your disposition to serve the glorious cause in which America is now engaged, evidenced by your readiness to supply, on the credit of the colony, many necessary articles for the use of the army, and in various other ways; by which you have given convincing proofs that you are heartily disposed to maintain the public liberty.]

[The cause, we have not the least doubt, if you continue to exert yourselves in conjunction with our sister colonies, will finally prevail.]

[This Congress have opened a subscription for one hundred thousand pounds, lawful money, for which the receiver general is directed to issue notes, on interest, at the rate of six per cent. per annum, payable in June, 1777; and as it is of the utmost importance that the money be immediately obtained, that the public credit may not suffer, we most earnestly recommend to such of you as have cash in your hands, which you can spare from the necessary supplies of your families, that you would lend the same to the colony, by which you will put it in

(1) On the sheet containing the foregoing resolves, are endorsed the following names: Mr. Fisher, Col. Barrett, Capt. Homes, Hon. Col. Bowers, Mr. Sawyer, Hon. Mr. Dexter, Col. Grout, Mr. Webster. Mr. Sayer was subsequently substituted for Mr. Dexter.

our power to carry into effect the measures undertaken for the salvation of the country.]

[That the army should be well supplied with every article necessary for the most effectual military operations, you must all be sensible; and that if we should fail herein, it may prove ruinous and destructive to the community, whose safety, under God, depends upon their vigorous exertions.]

[As you have already, in many instances, nobly exerted yourselves, this Congress have not the smallest doubt, but that you will, with great cheerfulness, crown all, with furnishing as much cash as will be necessary for the good purposes before mentioned, especially when it is considered, that there are now no ways of improving money in trade, and that there is the greatest probability, that the other colonies will give a ready currency to the notes, which will render them, in one respect at least, on a better footing than any notes heretofore issued in this colony. If you should furnish the money that is now needed, you will perform a meritorious service for your country, and prove yourselves sincerely attached to its interests; but, if an undue caution should prevent your doing this essential service to the colony, the total loss, both of your liberties and that very property which you, by retaining it, affect to save, may be the unhappy consequence; it being past all controversy that the destruction of individuals must be involved in that of the public.]

THURSDAY, May 25, 1775.

[The committee ordered to inspect the several towns and district stocks of powder, and consider what towns are well stocked, and what proportion they could spare for the public service, have attended that business, and beg leave to report the following proportion, viz. :]

[*Suffolk*—Roxbury 3 barrels, Medfield 1, Wrentham 4, Stoughton 1, Medway 1, Walpole 1. *Essex*—Marblehead 3, Newburyport 3, Newbury 1, Andover 2, Haverhill 2, Bradford 1-2, Boxford 1-2. *Middlesex*—Cambridge 3, Charlestown 3 3-4, Marlborough 3, Framingham 2, Littleton 1-2, Chelmsford 1 1-2, Sudbury 2, Weston 1, Westford 1-2, Groton 1, Townshend 1-2, Dracut 1, Stow 1-2. *Plymouth*—Bridgewater 4, Middleborough 1. *Worcester*—Worcester 1, Lancaster 1, Mendon 2 1-2, Brookfield 3, Oxford 1 1-2, Charlton 1-2, Sutton 2 1-2, Leicester 1, Westborough 1 1-2, Shrewsbury 2 1-2, Lunenburg 1, Bolton 1. *Total*—67 3-4 barrels.

DANIEL THURSTON, *per order*.]

[Upon the foregoing report, *Ordered*, that the committee who brought in said report, be directed to bring in a resolve in conformity thereto, and that it be inserted in the resolve, that the towns shall be respectively paid for what powder is drawn from their several towns stock, or have it replaced, and that each town be notified of the quantity respectively to be taken from its stock.]

[The committee reported a resolve as directed, which was read and accepted, and is as follows, viz.: *Resolved*, that there be drafted out of the town stocks of powder from each respective town aforesaid, the quantity of powder affixed to the name of the town, for the use of the army in the defence of the colony, and that it be replaced as soon as the state of the colony magazine will admit of it, or otherwise paid for in money, and that the selectmen of each town be forthwith served with an account of the draft made on their town, and that they immediately deliver it to the committee of supplies, or their order.]

[The committee of safety having represented to this Congress, that considerable difficulty exists in the adjustment of Gen. Ward's regiment, in consequence of the pretensions of Col. Joseph Henshaw and Col. Jonathan Ward to the post of lieutenant colonel in said regiment, it was *Ordered*, that said representation, as also the memorial of Col. Henshaw, setting forth his claims to said post, be referred to a committee. The committee having considered the matter, reported a resolve, which was accepted, and is as follows:]

[*Resolved*, as the opinion of this Congress, that Col. Ward is best entitled to receive the commission as lieutenant colonel of the regiment, which right was disputed by Lieut. Col. Henshaw.]

[*Ordered*, That the Hon. Mr. Dexter be desired to attend his duty on the committee for countersigning the treasurer's notes, immediately.]

[Mr. Dexter transmitted the following letter to the Congress, which was ordered to be read.]

[DEDHAM, *May* 25, 1775.

HONORED GENTLEMEN:—I was under the necessity to come home last evening. Had I been at Congress to-day, and been as unwell as I am at present, I should have very poorly performed my duty respecting the notes. I found myself so indisposed this morning, that I ventured to conclude to tarry till to-morrow morning at home, and sick or well, will endeavor to be early at Watertown for that purpose.

    With much regard, I am your very humble servant,

                                        S. DEXTER.]

[The committee appointed to take into consideration the petition of several persons at Roxbury, reported verbally, that it is the opinion

33

of the committee, that the said petition be sent to Gen. Thomas, and that he be directed to inquire into the causes of the complaint therein contained, and take proper measures for their redress.]

[The report was accepted.]

[The following letter was received from Gen. Thomas, and ordered to be read.]

[ROXBURY CAMP, *May* 25, 1775.

GENTLEMEN:—I have had the honor of being informed by your committee, that the honorable Congress have made choice of me as lieutenant general of the Massachusetts army, and to know whether I would accept that trust. I am sensible of the great importance of the office, and of my inability of discharging that duty, but since you have done me the honor of appointing me to that important office, shall accept of the same, and attend the Congress to-morrow.

I am, gentlemen, with the most profound respect,

Your most obedient humble servant,

JOHN THOMAS.

To the honorable Provincial Congress.]

[The committee to whom was referred an application from the officers of the army, respecting absconding soldiers, reported. The report was read, accepted, and is as follows, viz.: Whereas, application hath been made to this Congress, by some of the officers of the army, that some effectual method may be taken for the speedy return of absconding soldiers, or such as shall tarry beyond the time limited by furlough: therefore, *Resolved*, that it be, and it hereby is recommended, to the committees of correspondence in the several towns and districts in this colony, or to the selectmen, where no such committees are appointed, that they take effectual care that such absconding or delinquent soldiers be immediately sent back to their respective regiments.]

FRIDAY, May 26, 1775.

[The Hon. Joseph Hawley, from the committee to prepare a letter to the Provincial Congress of New York, now sitting in that colony, reported the following, which was accepted, and ordered to be forwarded.]

[WATERTOWN, *May* 26, 1775.

GENTLEMEN:—Enclosed are copies of a letter from Col. Arnold, and a list of military stores at Ticonderoga.[1] You cannot fail to ob-

(1) The letters of Col. Arnold, and the other documents relating to the capture of Ticonderoga, will be inserted in the Appendix.

serve, that Mr. Arnold, for the defence of this colony, is endeavoring that such ordnance as he judges can be spared from that quarter, should be transported to the army in this colony. This step is taken in consequence of orders given to him by our committee of safety. Perhaps this may appear to you extraordinary, but, we trust, you will candidly overlook such a mistake, if it be one, made in the hurry and confusion of war, and, we most solemnly declare to you, that this Congress, and the inhabitants of this colony, are at the utmost remove from any disposition or design to make any the least infraction upon, or usurpation of, the jurisdiction of any of our sister colonies; and if any of those cannon, &c., taken at the Lake Champlain, should happen, through the exertions of enterprising spirits, to be brought within the allowed limits of this colony, and come to our use, we shall hold ourselves accountable for them to the representatives of the continent, and whenever they shall inform us that they are needed for the general defence, at any other part of the continent, than, in this colony, we shall endeavor, that they be removed thither with the utmost despatch.]

[Gentlemen and brethren : could you have seen the horrid devastation and carnage in this colony, committed by ministerial troops, those sons of violence, who have got some footing in this colony, the breach of a most solemn treaty with respect to the inhabitants of Boston, when they had surrendered their arms, and put themselves wholly in the power of a military commander, relying upon his faith then pledged, that they should immediately depart from the town with their effects, as stipulated, which was no sooner done, than they were not only refused liberty to carry out the most valuable part of those effects, but their persons were detained under the most idle pretences, and suffered only to scatter from their prison, a few in a day, hardly to be seen or noticed; we say, gentlemen, could you see and realize these scenes of distress, you could not refrain one moment from doing every thing in your power to prevent the like distress from happening to your metropolis, and availing yourselves of every article which our enemies can improve with the least advantage to themselves for effecting the like desolation, horrors and insults, on the inhabitants of your city and colony, or which might enable you to make the most effectual defence.]

[Have you not, gentlemen, divers of those articles, as it were, under your hand? If you should delay securing them until they should be out of your power, and, within a few days, you should behold those very materials improved in murdering you, and yourselves perishing for the want of them, will not the chagrin and regret be intolerable?

Brethren, pardon our importunity. It is our own case. We behold Castle William, and realize the ample warlike provisions and apparatus therein, held by our enemies, to our infinite and inexpressible mortification. We wish to Heaven that you may be timely admonished by the consequences of our delay.

We are, &c.]

[The committee to whom was referred the letter of the Hon. James Russell, reported the following resolve, which was accepted.]

[*Resolved*, That the Hon. James Russell, Esq. be, and he hereby is directed, immediately to call in all the public moneys committed to his care as impost officer, and pay the same to Henry Gardner, Esq., receiver general of this province.]

[It having been represented to this Congress, that it would be agreeable to the inhabitants of the colony of New Hampshire, that the post rider on the road from Cambridge to Haverhill, should extend his route to the town of Exeter, to meet the post rider from Portsmouth to that place, and a post office having been appointed at Exeter, by the inhabitants of New Hampshire:]

[*Resolved*, That the route of the post rider from Cambridge be extended to said Exeter, so long as it shall be found to be expedient, or until the Massachusetts or New Hampshire Congress, or future house of representatives, shall otherwise order.]

[Whereas, it appears to this Congress, that although divers able bodied and effective men, who have enlisted into the Massachusetts army, are either not furnished with arms and accoutrements, or with such only as are insufficient for use, yet, that it will be for the public service that such men be accepted:]

[Therefore, *Resolved*, That the resolve of this Congress, passed on the 6th instant, be so far reconsidered, that the muster masters be, and they hereby are directed, to accept of all such able bodied and effective men, and muster them accordingly, any thing contained in the aforementioned resolve to the contrary notwithstanding; and that the several muster masters be, and hereby are directed, to make a return to this or some future congress, or house of representatives, of the names of such soldiers as shall be found deficient in arms and accoutrements, and also of the names of the towns to which they respectively belong.]

[Upon a representation of the committee of safety, that Mr. Jonathan Brewer, of Waltham, has, contrary to the orders of said committee, undertaken to enlist a company of rangers, has made use of artifices and impositions to obtain said enlistments, and that he has also seized and retained possession of horses and certain real estate, the private property of various individuals, and converted the same to his own use, whereby he has disqualified himself for the command of a regiment, it was *Ordered*, that the matter be referred to Doct. Perkins, Mr. Kollock and Mr. Bent.]

[The committee appointed to consider of the charges alleged against Mr. Jonathan Brewer, by the honorable committee of safety, having attended that service, beg leave to report the defence of said Brewer, viz.: that he, the said Brewer, absolutely denies the charge of seducing men, belonging to other corps, to enlist in his regiment, or any of the companies thereof. As to the taking the horses of Cols. Jones and Taylor, he acknowledges his thus doing, and thinks himself justified therein, by furthering the service of the province in which he was engaged, that he had used them some time past in that way, and on Saturday last past had returned Jones's horse.]

[He also owns the leasing part of said Jones's estate, and taking security; which security, he says, was in the keeping of one Capt. Butler; that he had proceeded in the affair merely from a principle of saving the improvement of one Mr. Jennison, (whose lands were contiguous to those of said Jones,) and which were exposed by a neglect of said Jones in keeping up sufficient fences. Said Jennison, (as Brewer says,) supposing, if he would thus dispose of the above leased land to him, he could fence and improve it without molestation. And that the committee can proceed no further, unless they are enabled, by hearing the full of the evidence supposed to support the complaint.

Per order :   RICHARD PERKINS, *Chairman*.]

SATURDAY, May 27, 1775.

[*Resolved*, That the committee of safety be directed to write to Col. Arnold, and inform him that it is his duty to conform himself to such advices and orders as he shall receive from this Congress.]

[Doct. Richard Perkins, from the committee appointed to examine into the complaint against lieutenant colonel Brown, setting forth that said Col. Brown has, at various times and places, used language disrespectful to the Congress, and tending to lessen and bring into contempt the power and authority of the Congress of this province, made the following report, which was accepted, viz. :]

[That after a full hearing of the allegations and proofs, for and against said Brown, on the complaint of some unknown person, through the selectmen of Waltham, to this honorable Congress, we are of the sentiment, that an unhappy controversy has existed in said town, relating to public affairs, in which said Brown had exerted himself very earnestly in favor of the cause of liberty, by which means he had disgusted several persons, who have since endeavored therefor to censure and stigmatize him as being an officious, busy, designing man; and, unhappily, it appears, that Mr. Brown has associated in taverns, indiscriminately, with many persons, in discourse with whom, he, at some times, had inadvertently expressed himself, which he would not strictly justify himself in. And that it is evident, those disaffected antagonists of Mr. Brown's, had taken the advantage of his halting, purely from revenge; and the committee adjudge, from the whole of the evidence for and against said Brown, that he is injuriously treated by the secret resentment of designing persons, and that he ought to be reinstated to the esteem and countenance of every friend to the liberties of this country.]

[Hon. Joseph Hawley, from the committee to bring in a resolve for the regular administration of justice, reported the following:]

[Whereas, it appears to this Congress, that a want of a due and regular execution of justice in this colony, has encouraged divers wicked and disorderly persons, not only to commit outrages and trespasses upon private property and private persons, but also to make the most daring attacks upon the constitution, and to unite in their endeavors to disturb the peace, and destroy the happiness and security of their country: and, whereas, this Congress conceive it to be their indispensable duty to take effectual measures to restrain all disorders, and promote the peace and happiness of this colony, by the execution of justice in criminal matters:]

[Therefore, *Resolved*, That a court of inquiry be immediately erected, consisting of seven persons, to be chosen by this Congress, whose business it shall be to hear all complaints against any person or persons, for treason against the constitution of their country, or other breaches of the public peace and security, and to determine and make up judgment thereon, according to the laws of this province, and those of reason and equity; no judgments to be made up, or punishments inflicted, in consequence of them, unless in such cases where five of the judges, so appointed, were agreed; any three of said judges to have power, upon complaint made, to cause any person or persons complained of, to be imprisoned, until the said court can be convened to hear the same, or for any further orders of Congress which may be thought necessary, five of said judges to be a quorum, and to be vested with the full powers of the court, and to meet and sit in such place or places as they shall agree on.]

[*Resolved,* That   [blank]   be, and hereby are appointed, as judges of the said court of inquiry, to execute the trust, agreeable to the above resolve.]

[This report having been read, after some debate, *Ordered,* that the further consideration thereof be referred to the next Congress.]

[The following letter, reported by a committee, to the governor and company of the colony of Connecticut, was accepted, and ordered to be forwarded :]

[WATERTOWN, *May* 27, 1775.

GENTLEMEN :—Enclosed are copies of a letter from Col. Arnold, and a list of military stores at Ticonderoga, &c. We have wrote you of the 17th instant, relative to that fortress, &c., and we are desirous that you would give such orders relative thereto, as to you should seem meet ; but, we are of opinion, that the advice of the Continental Congress should be had therein, as soon as may be, and also the particular advice of the Provincial Congress of New York, to each of whom we have wrote upon this matter : those fortresses being within the jurisdiction of the colony of New York, we are of opinion that it is necessary to consult them upon a matter in which they are so greatly interested.]

[We have appointed and directed Col. Joseph Henshaw to repair to you, and consult with you upon the affair of that fortress, the maintenance of which, we think of the utmost importance to the security of New York, and the New England colonies. His instructions will be laid before you, and, we have no doubt, you will take such measures relative thereto, as will promote the general safety of these colonies.

To the Hon. the Governor and Company of the
                    Colony of Connecticut.]

[The following letter to Col. Benedict Arnold, reported by a committee, was read, accepted, and ordered to be forwarded :]

[WATERTOWN, *May* 27, 1775.

SIR :—We have this day, with pleasure, received your letter to the committee of safety, of the 19th instant, by Capt. Brown, and return you our hearty thanks for your exertions in the public cause, and fully agree with you, that the interposition of Providence, in this, and many other instances, is apparent, for which we have the greatest cause of thankfulness.]

[We are clearly of opinion, that keeping Ticonderoga is a matter of great importance, and, we make no doubt, the honorable Continental

Congress will take that affair immediately under their wise consideration, and give all necessary orders therefor, as we have addressed them
most earnestly on the subject.]

[You inform us you have had intimation that some persons were determined to apply, in order to injure your character; if any such applications should be made here, you may be assured, we shall be so
candid as not to suffer any impressions to your disadvantage, until you
shall have opportunity to vindicate your conduct.]

[We enclose a resolve of this Congress, appointing and directing
Col. Joseph Henshaw to repair to Hartford, and consult with the general assembly there upon this important matter, by which you will see
the resolution this Congress has taken relative thereto.]

[We would just add, that the letter you refer to, of the 14th instant,
by Mr. Romans, has not come to hand, so that no order can be taken
thereon.

We are, &c.]

> To Col. Benedict Arnold,
> > Ticonderoga.

[*Resolved*, That Col. Joseph Henshaw, be appointed and directed to
repair to Hartford, and inquire whether provision is made, by the general assembly of the colony of Connecticut, for securing and maintaining the fortress at Ticonderoga, and the adjacent posts; and if that
assembly has made provision for that purpose, the said Col. Henshaw
proceed directly to Ticonderoga, and acquaint Col. Arnold that it is
the order of this Congress that he return, and render accounts of his
expenses in that expedition, in order that he may be honorably discharged; but if Col. Henshaw shall find that such provision is not
made, and the general assembly be not sitting, that he proceed to Ticonderoga, and inform Col. Arnold that it is the order of this Congress that he continue there, with such number of forces as said Col.
Henshaw shall judge necessary for the purpose. Nevertheless, if the
said Col. Henshaw shall find the general assembly sitting, and that
they have not made such provision, that he consult with them touching
this important matter, and take their proposals, and immediately make
report to the Congress of this colony.]

MONDAY, May 29, 1775.

[The committee appointed to prepare a letter to the Continental
Congress, upon the necessity of maintaining a fortress at Ticonderoga,
reported. The report being read, *Ordered*, that it be accepted, and a
copy of the same, fairly transcribed, be sent immediately to Philadelphia. It is as follows, viz. :]

[MAY IT PLEASE YOUR HONORS :—Enclosed are copies of a letter from Col. Arnold, and a list of military stores at Ticonderoga, &c.

It seems that the step Col. Arnold is taking, in transporting into this colony part of the ordnance taken at the Lake Champlain, is in consequence of directions given him in the haste and confusion of war; and if this Congress had considered the proposal in a calmer season, perhaps they might have thought it would have been proper, previously to have consulted our brethren of the colony of New York. Certain it is, that this colony is in the most pressing need of the ordnance which Col. Arnold is transporting hither. We beg leave, on this occasion, most solemnly to assure your honors, that nothing can be more abhorrent to the temper and spirit of this Congress, and the people of this colony, than any attempt to usurp on the jurisdiction of any of our sister colonies, which, upon the superficial consideration of this step, there may seem to be some appearance of. But we assure ourselves, that such is the candor and generous sentiments of our brethren of the colony of New York, as that we may rest secure that they will readily overlook this mistake, if it is one, committed in the haste of war, and which may be naturally attributed thereto. And if any of those cannon should arrive within the limits of this colony, we shall hold ourselves accountable for them, to your honors, or any succeeding representatives of the continent. Permit us to observe, that, in our opinion, nothing can be more obvious, than the infinite importance to the safety of the inhabitants of the colonies of New York, Massachusetts, New Hampshire, and even Connecticut, than the maintaining, holding, and effectually securing the post of Ticonderoga, or some spot near the southwest end of Lake Champlain; for if that post is abandoned, the whole Lake Champlain will be commanded by the government of Canada; and the command of that water will amazingly facilitate all such descents upon these colonies, whether greater or less, which administration shall see fit to order; but if that post should be held by the colonies, all such attempts, for the destruction of the colonies, may be vastly obstructed, if not wholly defeated. We have, therefore, the most full confidence, that your honors will immediately take these matters into your most serious consideration, and make such order thereon as will appear most fit and reasonable, and most conducive to the general safety.]

[We would further humbly suggest, that we stand in need of large quantities of gunpowder, and it is impossible to obtain that article from any quarter this way; we, therefore, most earnestly entreat your honors, that some effectual measures may be devised, that we may be

34

supplied with that most necessary means of defence; and we find that deficiency of that article prevails in all the colonies. We most earnestly press this matter, as the salvation of these colonies so much depends thereon. We would not presume to dictate to your honors, but would quere whether it would not be prudent, to advertise all nations of the opportunity they now have to dispose of that article in America at the best market. We have the strongest persuasion, that the settled plan of the British administration, is, to break the chain of union of the colonies at New York; and we are sure that the evidence of such design, and their machinations for that purpose, cannot escape your attention. We confide in the wisdom and vigilance of your honors to devise such measures as, under God, will effectually defeat a plan so fatal, and which, if effected, will be the destruction of all the colonies.]

[Hon. Joseph Hawley, from the committee appointed to prepare a letter to the governor of the colony of Connecticut, relative to the fortresses at Ticonderoga, Crown Point, &c., reported the following, which was read, accepted, and ordered to be sent, viz. :

[WATERTOWN, *May* 29, 1775.

MAY IT PLEASE YOUR HONOR :—Yesterday, about three of the clock, P. M., this Congress received your honor's most kind and friendly letter of the 25th instant, enclosing the resolution of the general Congress, of the 18th instant, relating to Ticonderoga, the order of the general committee of association of New York for executing the said resolution, the letter from the Connecticut delegates at New York, each of which contain articles of intelligence very important and interesting to all the New England governments. But while we are consoled and rejoiced to find that the general Congress is attentive to the safety and general interests of the colonies, we cannot conceal from the general assembly of your colony, that we should be to the last degree agitated, if we really supposed that the said resolution of general Congress, touching Ticonderoga and said posts on Lake Champlain, was their ultimatum, and that they would not reconsider that resolution. But as we cannot suffer ourselves to doubt of their best intentions, and great concern for the liberty and safety of all the colonies, we assure ourselves, that, upon better information, and knowledge more just, they will be fully convinced of the great impolicy of abandoning Lake Champlain, which we conceive they have, in effect, advised to; although we confess their expressions are not of the clearest; but we are confirmed in our construction of the said resolution, by the order taken by the general committee of New York, to execute the same.]

[May it please your honor: Permit us to acquaint you, that as soon as possible after we had received advice of the success of our people at Crown Point and St. Johns, and the taking of the armed sloop on that lake, by Col. Arnold's letter, a copy whereof we have sent you by Col. Henshaw, we sent an express to New York, and to the general Congress, signifying to the general Congress, and to the Congress of New York, in the strongest manner, our opinion of the absolute necessity, and great advantages, of maintaining the post of Ticonderoga: but, as we conceived the reasons and grounds of such an opinion were obvious, and generally known, we supposed that a detail of the arguments and proofs was altogether unnecessary. But, upon seeing the resolution of the general Congress, upon that important matter, we were much surprised and concerned, and in the little time we have had to deliberate on the subject, we have resolved to endeavor to suggest to your honor, and your assembly, the reasons which at present occur to us; which, we apprehend, make it evident, that the maintaining that post is not only practicable, and, under God, in the power of the colonies, but of inexpressible necessity for the defence of the colony of New York, and all the New England colonies; and having enumerated those reasons, as they occur, without consulting method, or any orderly arrangement, to submit them to your assembly; most importunately praying that if your honors approve them, you will, with the greatest despatch, communicate them, with many more observations, which your better knowledge of facts will suggest, to the general Congress; and, if you should judge it advisable, also to the Congress of New York, conceiving that, in several respects, they would go from you with more advantage, not only to New York but also to the general Congress, than from us. It seems natural to compare the two stations proposed to be maintained, namely, Ticonderoga and William Henry, in the following manner, that is to say: with regard to the benefits and advantages of the two stations, which will arise for the purposes of general defence, and annoyance of the Canada enemy, and with regard to the feasibility of maintaining each place. And, in the first place, as to the advantages of general defence, resulting from a post at Ticonderoga, beyond those of William Henry, they are so great and many, that they cannot be enumerated in an ordinary letter. In the view of a post of observation, we beg leave to observe, that all movements from Canada, intended against New England or New York, by the way of Lake Champlain, whether by scalping parties or large bodies, whether in the winter or open seasons of the year, may almost certainly be discovered, so seasonably, as that the blow may be generally warded off: whereas, if the post at William Henry be only kept, it is probable that three fourths of the attempts on the frontiers of New York and New England, by Champlain, will never be known until executed; as to enterprises, by any large bodies, by the way of Champlain, it is clear that they may be known much earlier from the former than the latter station; also, if it should become necessary and just that the united colonies should annoy the inhabitants of Canada, and cause them to feel the grievousness of war on their borders, as it most certainly will be felt, in case they engage in the war upon us, the two stations scarcely bear any comparison; for, if we abandon the post at Ticonderoga, the enemy will infallibly seize it, and, in that case, what annoyance can we give Canada, by the way of Champlain, by means of a fortified post at William Henry? If the enemy hold Ticonderoga, they will effectually command the whole of Lake Champlain; if the united colonies hold it, they will so far command that lake, as by the way of it, they will be able to make descents by small parties, upon great part of the country of Canada, and infinitely distress them: but from William Henry none can be made without vast difficulty and risk. As to the advantages of subsisting and defending a garrison, and maintaining a post against the efforts of Canada, either at Ticonderoga or fort William Henry, we conceive they are much in favor of the former. For us to supply victuals for a garrison or an army stationed at some one place or the other, we conceive, that on the whole, they may be more easily and certainly afforded to Ticonderoga than William Henry. We suppose that what should be sent from ports on the westerly side of Hudson's river, may almost as easily be transported to Ticonderoga or to William Henry; and as to such supplies as would go from all parts eastward of Hudson's river, they may be conveyed to the former place with much more facility than the latter. And as to the speed and certainty of marching succors, for the relief of a garrison at one place or the other, in case of an attack, we suppose the advantages of Ticonderoga are vastly superior to those of William Henry; for we cannot forbear observing, that our brethren of New York government, settled on the westerly side of Hudson's river, have been always rather slow in warlike efforts, and if the succors must go from Connecticut, Massachusetts, New Hampshire, or the northeasterly parts of New York governments, they may be mustered and marched much sooner to the former station than the latter. We have no doubt, but, on a pressing emergency, a large body of men might be marched from the middle of the county of Hampshire to Ticonderoga, in six days; but to gentlemen so well acquainted with the geography of the two places, we need not dwell on this part of the argument; and, in short, we have no idea of maintaining the one or the other of the two posts, in time of war with Canada, but either by constantly keeping an army on the spot, or making a fort of sufficient strength for a garrison, to hold out against an attack, until an army could be marched from New York or New England, sufficient to raise the seige; the latter method we suppose most politic, and quite practicable, with regard to Ticonderoga. But, at the same time, we beg leave just to hint, that a fortified station, on the easterly side of South Bay or Lake Champlain, opposite to Ticonderoga, Crown Point, or still further on, affords great advantages for the maintaining Ticonderoga, and defending the settlements on the eastwardly side of Lake Champlain; and there is artillery enough to spare, to other places; and if we abandon the land between the Lakes George and Champlain, we shall give the enemy an opportunity to build, at or near the points, and, by that means, we shall lose the whole of Lake Champlain, and the shipping we now have on that lake, by which we can command the whole of it, and keep the enemy at a distance of a hundred miles from our English settlements, near Otter Creek, &c.; but if that fortress should be maintained, we shall have those very settlements, with some aids from the old settlements, to support it, which will not be half the charge that it would be to maintain a sufficient number of soldiers, so far from their homes. We have there about four or five hundred hardy men, with many families, who, if those grounds should be abandoned, will be driven from their settlements, and leave the Massachusetts and New Hampshire people naked, without any barrier, and exposed to the Canadians and savages, who will have a place of retreat at the point, as they had almost the whole of the last war. By abandoning this ground, we give up an acquisition which cost immense sums of money, the loss of many lives, and five campaigns. As to the expenses of maintaining a fortress at Ticonderoga, this colony will not fail to exert themselves to the utmost of their power. We are under the greatest obligations to your honor, and the general assembly, for the intelligence you have given us, and you may depend, we shall not fail of continuing to communicate to you all important intelligence, with the utmost despatch. The interpositions of Divine Providence, in favor of America, are very obvious, which demand our utmost thankfulness. Enclosed is a brief narrative of some of them.

We are, &c.]

[The committee to whom were referred the papers relating to Jonathan Brewer, reported. The report was accepted, and is as follows, viz. :

[*Resolved,* That the papers respecting Jonathan Brewer, be transmitted by the secretary to the committee of safety, to be by them acted upon in such a manner as they think fit, so far as to determine on the expediency of recommending, or not recommending him, to this Congress, as an officer of the army now raising in this colony.]

[The committee appointed to draft a letter to the Provincial Congress of New Hampshire, reported the following, which was accepted, and ordered to be forwarded :]

[GENTLEMEN :—Enclosed are copies of governor Trumbull's letter to this Congress, enclosing a resolution of the Continental Congress, respecting the fortresses at Ticonderoga, Crown Point, &c., and the resolution of the general committee of association of New York thereon, and a letter from the Connecticut delegates at New York to their assembly.]

[The measure taken by the Continental Congress, if carried into execution, in our humble opinion, will affect those colonies east of Hudson's river in the highest degree; by that you will see that all the lands and waters between the south end of Lake George and Crown Point, together with all Lake Champlain, will be left open for Canadians and savages, if they should be so disposed, to range all that country east, and distress all our river settlements.]

[We have addressed the Continental Congress upon the necessity of keeping a fortress at or near Ticonderoga, and have also most pressingly desired the colony of Connecticut to exert themselves to effect the maintaining such a fortress. We have also written to New York upon the matter. We now lay the same advice before you, that you may have opportunity to take such measures as you shall think proper. As your colony is so deeply affected, you will, from a concern for that, and a generous regard to the common safety, which you have appeared at all times to have, we trust, take the matter up, and by decent and respectful addresses to the Continental Congress, endeavor to prevail with them to alter a measure so dangerous in its effects.

We are, &c.]

(1) During the sessions from the 23d of May until the dissolution of Congress, commissions were issued to officers in the regiments commanded by colonels Learned, Doolittle, Reed, Thomas, Walker, Whitcomb, Cotton, Ward, Prescott, Gerrish, Danielson, Mansfield, Bridges, Patterson, and Scammond, on the certificates of the committee of safety, that the several corps were filled with a proper complement of men.

JOURNAL

OF THE

THIRD PROVINCIAL CONGRESS

OF

Massachusetts,

Convened at Watertown, Wednesday, May 31, 1775....Dissolved Wednesday, July 19, 1775.

JOURNAL.

At a Congress of Delegates from the several towns and districts in the Colony of the Massachusetts Bay, began and held at the Meeting-house, in Watertown, the 31st of May, 1775.

Mr. Samuel Freeman was unanimously chosen Secretary, and the Hon. Joseph Warren, Esq., President.

Resolved, That the Congress will now proceed to hear the returns, and consider the qualifications of the members.

The returns being read, it appeared, that the following gentlemen were elected by the inhabitants of their respective towns, to represent them in this Congress, viz. :

COUNTY OF SUFFOLK.

Boston.—Hon. Thomas Cushing, Esq., Mr. Samuel Adams, Hon. John Hancock, Esq., Joseph Warren, Esq., Mr. John Pitts, Benjamin Church, Jr., Esq., Mr. Oliver Wendall.

Roxbury.—Capt. Aaron Davis.

Dorchester.—Col. [Lemuel] Robinson, Mr. James Robinson.

Milton.—Capt. Daniel Vose.

Braintree.—Col. Joseph Palmer.

Weymouth.—Deacon Nathaniel Bailey.

Hingham and Cohasset.—Benjamin Lincoln, Esq.

Dedham.—Hon. Samuel Dexter, Esq., Mr. Abner Ellis.

Medfield.—Mr. Daniel Perry.

Wrentham.—Mr. Jabez Fisher, Mr. Lemuel Kollock.

Brookline.—Capt. Benjamin White.

Stoughton.—Mr. Thomas Crane.

Medway.—Capt. Jonathan Adams, Mr. Moses Adams.

Needham.—Col. William McIntosh.

Walpole.—Mr. Enoch Ellis.

Bellingham.—Doct. John Corbet.

Chelsea.—Deacon John Sale.

COUNTY OF ESSEX.

Salem.—Hon. Richard Derby, Jr., Esq., Mr. John Pickering, Jr., Capt. Samuel Williams, Mr. Daniel Hopkins.

Danvers.—Doct. Samuel Holten, Capt. William Shillaber.

Ipswich.—Col. Michael Farley, Dummer Jewett, Esq.

Newbury.—Joseph Gerrish, Esq.

Newburyport.—Capt. Jonathan Greenleaf, Mr. Stephen Cross.

Marblehead.—Azor Orne, Esq., Mr. Elbridge Gerry, Capt. Jonathan Glover, Mr. Joshua Orne.

Lynn.—Mr. Edward Johnson.

Andover.—Mr. Samuel Phillips, Jr.

Beverly.—Capt. Josiah Batchelder, Jr.

Rowley.—Mr. Nathaniel Mighill.

Salisbury.—Major Nathaniel Currier.

Haverhill.—Mr. Jonathan Webster, Jr.

Gloucester.—Col. Peter Coffin, Major Samuel Whittemore.

Boxford.—Capt. Asa Perley.

Almsbury.—Capt. Caleb Pillsbury.

Wenham.—Mr. Benjamin Fairfield.

Topsfield.—Deacon John Gould.

Methuen.—Mr. James Ingalls.

Middleton.—Mr. Archelaus Fuller.

Bradford.—[Col. Daniel Thurston.]

Manchester.—[None.]

COUNTY OF MIDDLESEX.

Cambridge.—Mr. Abraham Watson, Jr., Capt. Samuel Thatcher.

Charlestown.—Mr. Richard Devens, David Cheever, Esq.

Watertown.—Capt. Jonathan Brown.

Woburn.—Josiah Johnson, Esq.

Concord.—Col. James Barrett.

Newton.—Abraham Fuller, Esq.

Reading.—Mr. John Temple.

Marlborough.—Mr. Peter Bent.

Billerica.—William Stickney, Esq.

Framingham.—Joseph Haven, Esq., Capt. Josiah Stone.

Lexington.—Deacon Jonas Stone.

Chelmsford.—Col. Simeon Spaulding.

Sudbury.—Deacon Thomas Plympton.

Malden.—Capt. Ebenezer Harnden.

Weston.—Col. Braddyl Smith.

Medford.—Mr. Benjamin Hall, Mr. Stephen Hall, 3d.

Hopkinton.—Capt. John Holmes.

Westford.—Capt. Joseph Read.

Groton.—Hon. James Prescott, Esq.

Pepperell.—Capt. Edmund Bancroft.

Waltham.—Mr. Jacob Bigelow.

Stow.—Henry Gardner, Esq.

Sherburne.—Mr. Daniel Whitney.

Littleton.—Mr. Abel Jewett.

Townshend.—Mr. Israel Hobart.

Stoneham.—Capt. Samuel Sprague.

Wilmington.—Capt. Timothy Walker.

Dracut.—Deacon Amos Bradley.

Holliston.—Col. Abner Perry.

Acton.—Mr. Josiah Hayward.

Tewkesbury.—Mr. Ezra Kendall.

Dunstable.[1]—John Tyng, Esq., James Tyng, Esq., Mr. Joel Parkhurst.

Lincoln.—Major Eleazer Brooks.

COUNTY OF HAMPSHIRE.

Springfield.—Mr. John Hale, Mr. Edward Chapin.

West Springfield.—Major Benjamin Ely, Doct. Chauncy Brewer.

Northampton.—Joseph Hawley, Esq., Mr. Elias Lyman.

Wilbraham.—Major John Bliss.

South Hadley and Granby.—Capt. Phinehas Smith, [Mr. Noah Goodman.]

Hatfield.—John Dickenson, John Hastings, Elihu White.

Westfield.—Col. John Mosely, Col. Elisha Parks.

Greenfield.—Mr. Samuel Hinsdale.

Hadley.—Col. Elisha Porter.

Sunderland and Montague.—Capt. Israel Hubbart, Doct. Moses Gunn.

Brimfield, Monson and South Brimfield.—Col. Timothy Danielson.

Northfield.—Mr. Phinehas Wright.

Blandford.—Deacon William Boies, Capt. William Knox.

Granville.—Timothy Robinson, Esq., Mr. Nathan Barlow.

---

(1) John Tyng, Esq. and James Tyng, Esq., were returned as delegates from Dunstable, May 25; as the health of the former was so much impaired as to prevent his attendance, and the multiplicity of engagements of public and private business compelled the latter to resign his seat, Mr. Joel Parkhurst was elected, to supply the vacancies thus occasioned, June 12, 1775.

Palmer.—Capt. David Spear.

New Salem.—Lieut. Amos Foster.

Belchertown.—Capt. Nathaniel Dwight.

Colraine.—Lieut. Hezekiah Smith.

Greenwich.—Mr. Joseph Hendrick.

Amherst.—Nathaniel Dickinson, Jr.

Chesterfield.—Capt. Benjamin Bonney.

Shutesbury.—Mr. John Hamilton.

Williamsburg.—Mr. Josiah Dwight.

Shelburne.—Deacon Samuel Fellows.

Ware.—Joseph Foster, Esq.

Ludlow.—Capt. Joseph Miller.

Worthington.—Doct. Moses Morse.

Whately.—Mr. Noah Wells, Mr. Salmon White.

Warwick.—Col. Samuel Williams.

COUNTY OF BERKSHIRE.

Sheffield, Great Barrington, Egremont and Alford.—Mr. William Whiting.

Tyringham.—Major Giles Jackson.

Stockbridge.—Timothy Edwards, Esq., [Jerathmiel] Woodbridge, Esq.

Lenox.—Capt. Caleb Hyde.

Williamstown.—Mr. Samuel Kellogg.

Richmond.—Capt. Elijah Brown.

Sandisfield.—Deacon Samuel Smith.

Tyringham.—Mr. Elijah Warren, John Chadwick, Esq.

Leverett.[1]—[None.]

COUNTY OF WORCESTER.

Worcester.—Mr. David Bancroft.

Lancaster.—Doct. William Dunsmore, Deacon Thomas Fairbanks.

Brookfield.—Jedediah Foster, Esq.

[*Mendon.*—Capt. Thomas Wiswall.]

Oxford.—Edward Davis, Esq.

Sutton.—Capt. Henry King, Mr. Amos Singletary.

Rutland.—Mr. John Fessenden.

(1) The town of Leverett considering " their circumstances as very young and weak," declined returning a member.

Hutchinson.—John Caldwell, Esq.

Oakham.—Capt. Isaac Stone.

Leicester and Spencer.—Deacon Oliver Watson.

Paxton.[1]—Rev. Alexander Thayer.

Westborough.—Capt. Stephen Maynard.

Shrewsbury.—Mr. Daniel Hemenway.

Lunenburg.—Doct. John Taylor.

Fitchburg.—Mr. Joseph Fox.

Uxbridge.—Mr. Abner Rawson.

Harvard.—Mr. Joseph Wheeler.

Bolton.—Capt. Samuel Baker.

Sturbridge.—Capt. Timothy Parker.

Hardwick.[2]—Capt. William Page.

Grafton.—Doct. Joseph Batchelder.

New Braintree.—Major James Woods.

Dudley.—Major William Learned.

Southborough.—Lieut. William Collins.

Upton.—Mr. Abiel Sadler.

Leominster.—Deacon Israel Nichols.

Holden.—Mr. John Child.

Western.—Simeon Dwight, Esq.

Douglas.—Deacon Jeremiah Whiting.

Athol.—Capt. John Haven.

Petersham.—Col. Jonathan Grout.

Westminster.—Deacon Nathan Wood.

Templeton.—Mr. Jonathan Baldwin.

Princeton.—Mr. Moses Gill.

Royalston.[3]—[None.]

Hubbardston.—Lieut. William Muzzy.

Charlton.—Rev. Caleb Curtis.

Northborough.—Mr. Levi Brigham.

(1) The district of Paxton, " to show their dislike of the extravagant wages of some of the officers in the army, in a time of general calamity," instructed their delegate, on his election, to use his influence, that no field officer should receive more than £6 per month, no captain more than £5, and no other person have compensation in a greater proportion.

(2) The inhabitants of Hardwick, on the 22d of May, elected Capt. William Page to represent them in Congress during June and July ; Capt. Stephen Rice to attend during August and September ; Col. Jonathan Warner to sit during October and November. The early dissolution of the session prevented the two last named gentlemen from taking their seats.

(3) The inhabitants of Royalston, May 25, 1775, considering the infancy of the town, the number of men absent in military service, and the inability of the people to maintain a representative, voted not to send a member of Congress at that time, but expressed readiness to comply with whatever the provincial assembly should recommend for the public good.

COUNTY OF PLYMOUTH.

Plymouth.—Hon. James Warren, Esq., Mr. Isaac Lothrop.

Scituate.—Nathan Cushing, Esq.

Duxbury.—Mr. George Partridge.

Marshfield.—Mr. Benjamin White.

Bridgewater.—Col. Edward Mitchell.

Middleborough.—Capt. Joshua White.

Rochester.—Major Ebenezer White.

Plympton.—Capt. Seth Cushing.

Pembroke.—Mr. John Turner, Mr. Jeremiah Hall, Mr. Edward Thomas.

Kingston.—Hon. William Seaver, Esq., Deacon Ebenezer Washburn.

Hanover.—Col. Joseph Cushing.

Abington.—Doct. David Jones.

Halifax.—Mr. Ebenezer Thompson.

COUNTY OF BARNSTABLE.

Barnstable.—Col. Joseph Otis, Daniel Davis, Esq.

Yarmouth.—Capt. Elisha Basset.

Sandwich.—Mr. Stephen Nye, Col. [Nathaniel] Freeman.

Eastham.—Mr. Amos Knowles.

Wellfleet.—Col. Elisha Cobb.

Harwich.—Mr. Joseph Nye.

Falmouth.—Mr. Moses Swift.

Chatham.—Col. Joseph Doan.

Truro.—Mr. Samuel Harding.

COUNTY OF BRISTOL.

Taunton.—Robert T. Paine, Esq., Col. George Williams, Capt. [Simeon] Williams.

Rehoboth.—Capt. Thompson Carpenter, Mr. [Ephraim] Starkweather.

Swanzey.—Col. [Jerathmiel] Bowers, Mr. Philip Slead.

Dartmouth.—Hon. Walter Spooner, Esq., Benjamin Aikin, Esq.

Attleborough.—Capt. John Stearns.

Dighton.—Ezra Richmond, Esq., Doct. William Baylies.

Freetown.—Mr. Thomas Durfee.

Norton and Mansfield.—Capt. William Homes.

Easton.—Mr. Benjamin Pettingil.

Raynham.—Mr. Benjamin King.
Berkley.—Mr. Samuel Tobey, Jr.

COUNTY OF YORK.

York.—Mr. Daniel Bragdon.
Kittery.—Edward Cutt, Esq.
Wells.—[None.]
Berwick.—Major Ichabod Goodwin.
Arundell.—Mr. John Hovey.
Biddeford.—James Sullivan, Esq.

COUNTY OF CUMBERLAND.

Falmouth and Cape Elizabeth.—Mr. Samuel Freeman.
Gorham.—Capt. Bryant Morton.
Brunswick.—Col. Samuel Thompson.
North Yarmouth.—David Mitchel, Esq.
[*Scarborough.*]¹—[None.]

COUNTY OF LINCOLN.

Pownalborough.—Mr. Timothy Langdon.
Georgetown and Woolwich.—Capt. Samuel McCobb.
Topsham.—[Mr. James Fulton.]
Gardinerston.—Mr. Joseph North.

DUKES COUNTY.

Chilmark.—[None.]
Tisbury.—James Athearn, Esq.
Edgarton.—Mr. Beriah Norton.

COUNTY OF NANTUCKET.

[*Sherburn.*]—[None.]

31st May, 1775. *Ordered,* That Doct. Holten, Mr. Watson and Col. Lincoln, be a committee to wait on the Rev. Doct. Langdon, and

---

(1) The inhabitants of Scarborough represented, that " they thought themselves not able to support the chaige of a member of Congress, said town having no money to pay any tax whatever: lumber was the chief trade; that being done, the crops having been very short, and no supplies coming from the southern colonies, they were in great distress for want both of money and provisions: but they were willing to exert themselves to the uttermost to support good government and defend just rights and privileges." They added their "prayers, that God might bless the counsels of Congress, and, in the end, confirm that liberty which our forefathers came into these regions to enjoy."

inform him that this Congress are now ready to attend divine service, and request his attendance.

Resolved, That four o'clock this afternoon be assigned for the consideration of the returns of members from Hardwick, Eastham,[1] and several other towns.

Ordered, That Mr. Brown, Doct. Taylor and Col. Sayer, be [a] committee to wait on the commanding officer of the militia of this town, to thank him for his polite offer to escort the Congress to the meeting-house, and to inform him, that, as this Congress are now sitting, the Congress think it needless to withdraw for that purpose : but will, with the reverend gentlemen of the clergy, attend them to Mrs. Coolidge's, if they please to escort them thither, when the Congress adjourns.

[Afternoon.]

Ordered, That Mr. Gill, Doct. Whiting, Mr. Pitts, Mr. Jewett and Col. Lincoln, be a committee to return the thanks of this Congress to the Rev. Doct. Langdon, for his excellent sermon delivered to the Congress in the forenoon, and to desire a copy of it for the press.[2]

Ordered, That Doct. Taylor, Mr. Pitts and Mr. Greenleaf, be a committee to consider some method for supplying the soldiers immediately with advance pay, and also to consider a letter from Gen. Thomas on that subject.

Resolved, That a copy of the resolve of the last Congress, relative to providing the army with chaplains, be laid before the reverend gentlemen of the clergy, now in convention, at Watertown.

The order of the day [was] moved for.

Ordered, That Mr. Fisher, Col. Bowers, Col. Gerrish, Mr. Bayley and Mr. Slead, be a committee to consider the two returns of members from Eastham.

The returns of three members from Hardwick, who are to attend this Congress severally, each two months, was approved of.

The committee appointed to consider Gen. Thomas's letter, reported verbally ; the report was accepted, and ordered to be committed to

---

(1) A remonstrance was presented against the return of Mr. Amos Knowles, Jr., one of the members returned from Eastham, with testimony tending to prove, that he had used expressions reflecting on the wisdom and fidelity of Congress, and that he entertained sentiments unfavorable to its policy and measures. These charges were denied, and the origin attributed to personal or party hostility by the respondent. The election of the members from Eastham and Williamsburg was contested, on the ground that the town meetings were not properly notified.

(2) The sermon of Doct. Langdon was from ISAIAH i. 26. *"And I will restore thy judges as at the first, and thy counsellors as at the beginning ; afterwards thou shalt be called the city of righteousness, the faithful city."* The discourse was printed at Cambridge.

writing, and one copy sent to the camp at Cambridge, and another to the camp at Roxbury.

Ordered, That Col. Palmer, Mr. Williams and Deacon Cheever, be a committee to introduce to this Congress a committee from the reverend gentlemen of the clergy, in convention at Watertown, now at the door.

The committee were accordingly introduced, and informed the Congress that the said convention would be glad of the use of the meeting-house to-morrow morning, at eight o'clock. Then the said committee withdrew.

Ordered, That Col. Palmer, Mr. Williams and Deacon Cheever, be a committee to inform the reverend gentlemen of the convention, that this Congress comply with their request, and that the committee lay before the said convention, a copy of the resolve of the last Congress, respecting chaplains.

Resolved, That Mr. Hastings, who attended the last Congress as door-keeper, be desired to attend this Congress till further orders.

Ordered, That the papers relative to the fortresses at Ticonderoga, &c., be laid before the Congress.

The papers being read, *Resolved*, that Mr. Phelps, who was the bearer of some of them, be introduced to the Congress.

After information from Mr. Phelps, *Ordered*, that the president, Mr. Glover, Col. Nicholson, Doct. Taylor, Mr. Edwards, Col. Dwight, Doct. Wheeler, Mr. Hale and Doct. Whiting, be a committee to take said papers into consideration, to sit forthwith, and report as soon as may be.

Ordered, That the Hon. Mr. Spooner, Mr. Hopkins, Mr. Greenleaf, Capt. Batchelder and Col. Otis, be a committee to consider a letter from the committee of correspondence of the colony of New Hampshire, to the committee of correspondence of Newburyport.[1]

The Congress then adjourned to ten o'clock to-morrow morning.

(1) The following letter, from the committee of correspondence of New Hampshire, was received in Newburyport May 30th, and immediately forwarded to Congress:

PORTSMOUTH, 29th May, 1775.

" GENTLEMEN :—We had two provision vessels seized at the mouth of our harbor the last night, by the Scarborough: and upon application to Capt. Barclay for their release, find he has positive orders from the admiral to take possession of all vessels laden with provisions, salt, or molasses, and send them to Boston ; and he says further, those orders are circular through the continent. We give this earliest intelligence for your government, and also inform you, that the Canceaux, a small ship of six or eight guns, sails, the first fair wind, to convoy the two vessels already seized, to Boston, and are sorry to find ourselves unable to prevent it, as we have our harbor blocked up, by a twenty gun ship, and have no vessel of force able to retake them. One reason of our mentioning this cir-

THURSDAY, June 1, 1775.

The committee appointed to consider Gen. Thomas's letter, brought in the following report, which was accepted, and a copy of it ordered to be sent to the muster master at Cambridge, and another to the muster master at Roxbury, viz. :

The committee appointed to consider a letter from Gen. Thomas, relative to immediately paying the army the advance pay, have attended that service, and beg leave to report, that they have waited on the receiver general, to know of him how soon he can furnish the muster masters with the notes proposed for the army; and were informed by the receiver general, he now had several hundred notes ready to deliver; and that he had provided all necessary helps, and would make the greatest despatch possible; and that he should be able, at least, to pay off one regiment every day, and perhaps more; and that he would, from day to day, deliver one half of said notes to the muster master at Cambridge, and the other half to the muster master at Roxbury.

Ordered, That a copy of the above be sent to the muster masters.

Ordered, That Col. Jones and Mr. Orne, be added to the committee who were appointed to consider the returns of members from Eastham.

Resolved, That the following members be, and hereby are appointed, monitors in this Congress, viz. : 1st. Col. Gerrish: 2d. Mr. Durfee: 3d. Col. Farley: 4th. Doct. Taylor: And that the division of the house be as follows, viz. :

First Division: the pews at the right hand of the pulpit, and all the pews on the west and south part of the meeting-house, from the aisle that bounds the seats and the body pews :

Second Division : the pews on the left hand of the pulpit, and all the pews on the north and east part of the house, from the aisle that bounds the seats and the body pews:

Third Division: all the body pews and seats on the left hand of the broad aisle :

Fourth Division : all the body pews and seats on the right hand of the broad aisle.

Resolved, That this Congress will adopt and observe the rules and orders established by the last Congress.

cumstance, and sending an express this night with it, is, because we have just heard that you have an armed vessel in your port."

" We have ordered two small vessels to cruize off and on, and, if possible, give this intelligence to all vessels bound to this or any other port, and trust you will do the same.

By order of the Committee.

Your most humble servant,

H. WENTWORTH, *Chairman*."

To the Committee of Correspondence, Newbury.

Ordered, That Col. Prescott, Mr. Slead, Col. Barrett, Mr. Thatcher, and Mr. Partridge, be a committee to consider what number of the poor of the town of Boston should be sent to the town of Ashby, or other towns, not mentioned in the schedule annexed to a resolve passed in the last Congress.

[The committee presented the following report, which was read and accepted:]

Whereas, the poor of the town of Boston, by a resolve of Congress passed the first day of May last, are confined to a certain number of towns and districts in this colony, as appears by a schedule annexed to said resolve, and some of said poor having relations and connections in other towns and districts than are mentioned in said schedule, and being desirous to go and reside in such places, it is, therefore, *Resolved*, that the poor of Boston may be removed into any other town or district in this colony, where the selectmen of such town or district shall see fit to receive them, all such towns and districts observing the rules, regulations and directions given in the resolve aforesaid, and shall be entitled to the same rewards and privileges as mentioned in said resolve.

Ordered, That Deacon Fisher, Mr. Spaulding, Mr. Stickney, Mr. Partridge and Major Perley, be a committee to consider the proposal of the reverend gentlemen of the clergy, now in convention at Watertown, [which is as follows:]

To the Hon. Joseph Warren, Esq., President of the Provincial Congress of the Colony of the Massachusetts Bay, &c.:

SIR:—We, the pastors of the congregational churches of the colony of the Massachusetts Bay, in our present annual convention, gratefully beg leave to express the sense we have of the regard shewn by the honorable Provincial Congress to us, and the encouragement they have been pleased to afford to our assembling as a body this day. Deeply impressed with sympathy for the distresses of our much injured and oppressed country, we are not a little relieved, in beholding the representatives of this people, chosen by their free and unbiassed suffrages, now met to concert measures for their relief and defence, in whose wisdom and integrity, under the smiles of Divine Providence, we cannot but express our entire confidence.

As it has been found necessary to raise an army for the common safety, and our brave countrymen have so willingly offered themselves to this hazardous service, we are not insensible of the vast burden that their necessary maintenance must [devolve] upon the people. We, therefore, cannot forbear, upon this occasion, to offer our services to the public, and to signify our readiness, with the consent of our several congregations, to officiate, by rotation, as chaplains to the army.

We devoutly commend the Congress, and our brethren in arms, to the guidance and protection of that Providence, which, from the first settlement of this country, has so remarkably appeared for the preservation of its civil and religious rights.

SAMUEL LANGDON, Moderator.

At the Convention of the Ministers of the Massachusetts Bay, June 1, 1775:

" The convention, taking into consideration the method of furnishing the army with chaplains, agreeably to the offer they have made to the honorable Congress, think it most expedient, that a sufficient number of persons should be chosen out of their number, by the officers of the army, to officiate statedly, rather than by quick rotation, in that character; and the convention depend, that the parochial duties of those ministers who shall serve in the army, will be performed by their brethren in the vicinity.

A true copy.   Test: AMOS ADAMS, Scribe."

Ordered, That Major Fuller, Col. Cushing and Major Whittemore, be a committee to inquire how many armourers are already appointed in the Massachusetts army, and how many more are necessary.

Ordered, That Major Brooks, Capt. Stone and Mr. Crane, be a committee to consider the letter from the selectmen of the town of Hopkinton, and that they sit forthwith.[1]

The committee appointed to consider the letter from the committee of correspondence for the colony of New Hampshire, reported, verbally, that it was their opinion, that it would be expedient to forward, forthwith, a copy of said letter to the committee of correspondence for the colony of Rhode Island, and another to the colony of Connecticut, and that the several members of the sea port towns, or of the towns adjacent, should write to the committee of such sea port towns, informing them of the subject of said letter.

---

(1) This letter states, that a false alarm having been spread in the town of Hopkinton and the country adjoining, the people were called from their labors, and much and useless loss of time and expense incurred; to prevent a repetition of such alarms, a meeting of the inhabitants was held, and a committee of safety, consisting of Gilbert Dench, Samuel Park, Ebenezer Claflin, Samuel Hayden and Jonathan Hale, appointed, to determine when it should be necessary for the people of the town to march on any alarm; and desired the Congress to establish some signal, by which authentic intelligence might be distinguished from false reports.

Ordered, That Col. Thompson, Col. Freeman and Mr. Jewett, be a committee to consider a letter from the committee of safety for the town of Salem, and report.[1]

The committee on the Eastham returns, reported, that in their opinion neither of the members were legally chosen ; the report, after debate, was not accepted.

Resolved, That this last vote be reconsidered, and that a recommendation be sent to the town of Eastham, to choose one or more members, as to them shall seem meet, to represent them in this Congress.

Afternoon.

The committee appointed to consider the letter from the committee of safety of the town of Salem, reported; which report was accepted, and is as follows, viz. :

The committee appointed by the honorable Provincial Congress, to take into consideration the letter from the committee of safety, and town clerk, for the town of Salem, respecting the answers of Mr. Stephen Higginson to questions asked him before the House of Commons of Great Britain, &c., beg leave to report: that they have critically examined that matter, and are of opinion that the intentions of said Higginson, in those answers, were friendly to the inhabitants of Salem and Marblehead, and to the colonies in general, and that he ought to be honorably acquitted by this Congress, and recommended to the favor of the public.

(1) A petition against the fishery bill, having been presented in the House of Commons of Great Britain, in the spring of 1775, setting forth that a great number of innocent persons, particularly in the island of Nantucket, would be reduced by it to extreme distress, " Mr. Stephen Higginson, a native of Salem, in New England," says a London paper, " was called to the bar, to prove the allegations in the petition. He stated that the colonies of Massachusetts Bay and New Hampshire, Connecticut and Rhode Island, did not collectively produce sufficient for the subsistence of their inhabitants, and that they received considerable from the Carolinas, Virginia, Maryland, Pennsylvania and New York ; that there were then employed in the cod fisheries about 700 vessels, from 15 to 70 tons, which carried about 4200 men, and that about one half of that number were employed on shore in curing the fish ; that about 350 vessels from 50 to 180 tons, were employed in conveying the fish to market, which carried about 3000 men ; that if the cod fisheries should be prohibited, about 10,000 men must be under the necessity of seeking employment ; and that as the major part of them would not settle at Halifax, on account of its being a military government, they must either stay at home and want bread, emigrate to the southward, or go to the French at Miquelon and St. Pierre ; and as many of the inhabitants at and near Marblehead were Portuguese, Dutch, and other foreigners, it was not unlikely but they might easily be induced thereto." The above statements of Mr. Higginson were printed in the *Essex Gazette,* vol. vii, number 353, and gave offence to many of the inhabitants of Salem and Marblehead, as being designed to injure the province. Upon the return of Mr. Higginson from London, he immediately presented himself before the committee of safety of Salem, who, after an examination, were entirely satisfied of his innocence and good intention in the matters complained of, and recommended that he wait on the Provincial Congress, and obtain the decision of that body to quiet the minds of the people. The communications of Richard Derby, Esq., chairman of the committee of safety, and of Timothy Pickering, Jr., Esq., clerk of the town of Salem, presented these facts for the consideration of Congress.

Ordered, That the Hon. Mr. Dexter, be directed to inquire of the receiver general, if he has received the money from the Hon. Mr. Russell, agreeably to the resolve of the last Congress.

Ordered, That Deacon Bayley, Capt. Holmes and Col. Thompson, be a committee to draw up a resolve, recommending to the town of Eastham to choose a new member or members to represent them in this Congress.

Ordered, That three hundred passes, of the following form, be printed, viz. : .

To the Guards of the Colony Army:

Pursuant to a resolve of the Provincial Congress, you are hereby ordered to permit —— ——, a member of said Congress, to pass and repass, with such as may accompany him, at all times.

—— ——, *President.*

June 1775.

Hon. Mr. Dexter reported to the Congress, that he had made inquiry of Mr. Gardner, the receiver general, as directed, and that the receiver general informed him he had not seen Mr. Russell since the order of Congress, respecting his paying the public moneys he has in his hands to Mr. Gardner.

The committee appointed to consider the letter from the selectmen of Hopkinton, reported : the report was recommitted, and Mr. Phillips, Mr. Partridge, Col. Richmond and Mr. Sawyer added to the committee.

Ordered, That Doct. Taylor, Hon. Mr. Dexter and the Hon. Col. Bowers, be a committee to consider the application made to this Congress by Col. Barrett, in behalf of the Rev. Mr. Emerson, for the use of one of the horses taken from the regulars, during the absence of the Hon. Thomas Cushing, Esq., who has Mr. Emerson's horse now in the public service.

The committee appointed to consider the request of Mr. Emerson, reported. The report was accepted, and is as follows, viz. :

The committee appointed to consider the request of the Rev. William Emerson of Concord, respecting the use of a horse taken upon the 19th of April last, from one of the regulars, by Mr. Isaac Kittridge of Tewksbury, Capt. Nathan Barrett, and Henry Flint of Concord, beg leave to report, by way of resolve, that said horse be delivered to said Emerson, by the person or persons in whosesoever possession he may be found, he, the said Emerson, paying a reasonable price for keeping said horse, and Mr. Emerson is hereby permitted to keep and use said horse, till the further order of this Congress.

The committee appointed to consider the papers relating to Ticonderoga, &c., reported a letter to Col. Arnold, another to the Hon. William Williams, Esq., speaker of the assembly of the colony of Connecticut, and another to the Provincial Congress of New Hampshire, which were read and accepted, and ordered to be authenticated, and sent forward, and are as follow, viz. :

Letter to Col. Benedict Arnold :

Sir :—This Congress have received yours of the 19th and 23d of May ult., per Capt. Brown and Capt. Phillips, a copy of which has been sent to New Hampshire ;[1] they highly approve of, and take great satisfaction in the acquisitions you have made at Ticonderoga, Crown Point, on the lake, &c. As to the state you are in respecting men, provision, &c., we have advices from Connecticut and New York, that ample preparation is making, with the greatest despatch, in those two colonies, from whence you may depend on being seasonably supplied. They are sorry to meet with repeated requests from you, that some gentleman be sent to succeed you in command; they assure you, that they place the greatest confidence in your fidelity, knowledge, courage, and good conduct ; and they desire that you, at present, dismiss the thoughts of quitting your important command at Ticonderoga, Crown Point, Lake Champlain, &c., and you are hereby requested to continue your command over the forces raised by this colony, posted at those several places, at least until the colony of New York or Connecticut shall take on them the maintaining and commanding the same agreeably to an order of the Continental Congress.

   To Col. Benedict Arnold,
          Ticonderoga.

P. S.—We have just received intelligence, by a letter from Gov. Trumbull, that the general assembly have ordered a thousand men to march immediately to reenforce the army now at Crown Point, Ticonderoga, &c., also [to send] 500 lbs. powder, and also that each soldier is furnished with one pound of powder, &c. The Congress further advise, that in case your present necessity requires it, you make use of the £160 you found on board the sloop, for the service of this colony, you accounting for the same to this or some other congress, or house of

---

(1) These, with other letters of Col. Arnold, and documents relating to the capture of Ticonderoga, too voluminous to be annexed to the text as notes, are inserted in the Appendix.

representatives of this colony; and they hereby assure you, that this colony will repay it, whenever it shall be ordered by the Continental Congress; and that you also complete the raising the number of four hundred men in the pay of this colony, if you judge it necessary.

[*To the House of Assembly of Connecticut :*]

GENTLEMEN :—We gratefully acknowledge the receipt of your favor of the 27th ult. We fully concur in opinion with you, that maintaining a post at Ticonderoga or Crown Point, is of the utmost importance : therefore, take particular satisfaction, that you have, on this subject, so early, and repeatedly expressed your minds to the Continental Congress.

By private intelligence of the 29th ult., sent to Capt. Joseph Trumbull, we are informed, that the Provincial Congress of New York, do not understand the resolve of the Continental Congress, concerning said fortresses, to extend so far as wholly to dismantle them; but so far, only, as to supply any fortifications that may be built at the south end of Lake George; which resolve, in this sense of it, they are, with despatch, executing : therefore, in our present distressing situation, we have postponed sending further assistance to ||ᵃCol.|| Arnold, especially since New York have not requested it.

To the Hon. William Williams,
Speaker of the House of Assembly of the Colony of Connecticut.

[*To the Provincial Congress of New Hampshire :*]

GENTLEMEN :—We send you enclosed, a copy of a letter from Col. Arnold, commander of the troops at Ticonderoga and Crown Point, together with a copy of a letter from the speaker of the house of representatives for the colony of Connecticut, by which you will be acquainted with the present situation of those fortresses, and the measures necessary to be taken for securing and defending so valuable acquisitions.

You will, doubtless, agree with us in sentiment, that it is a matter of the greatest importance, that those places remain in our possession, in order to secure our frontiers from the depredations of our enemies, if they should attempt to attack us from that quarter, of which there appears to be great danger.

It was the agreement of this colony, that four hundred men, and £100 in money, should be raised for the reduction of the place; and

a ||Captain.||

it is our determination to contribute our full proportion toward securing the acquisition. By the letter from the speaker of the house of representatives for Connecticut, you will find, that that colony have voted to send immediately to their assistance, four companies, and 500 pounds weight of powder; and we suppose the troops are on the march there : and we most earnestly request, that you would contribute your endeavors, likewise, for the speedy and effectual security of the aforementioned places, which, considering the importance of the affair, and the ready disposition which you have discovered for the defence of the common cause, leaves us no room to doubt of your compliance therewith.

To the Provincial Congress of New Hampshire.

Resolved, That the secretary be, and hereby is empowered, to appoint some person to assist him in his office.

Adjourned till to-morrow morning, eight o'clock.

FRIDAY, June 2, 1775.

The committee appointed to bring in a resolve recommending to the town of Eastham to choose one or more members to represent them in this Congress, reported; the report was accepted, and is as follows, viz. :

Whereas, this Congress, upon examination, judge that the persons returned as delegates for Eastham, in the county of Barnstable, were not legally chosen, and that the allowing either of them a seat in this house would be attended with many inconveniences; therefore, *Resolved,* that it be, and it hereby is recommended, to the said town of Eastham, that they forthwith elect or depute one or more persons, to serve for, and represent said town, in the Provincial Congress, now held at the meeting-house in Watertown, to be chosen by such only as are qualified to vote for representatives in the general assembly, and to be continued by adjournment, as they shall see cause, until the expiration of six months from the first sitting of this Congress, and no longer, and to consult, and deliberate, and resolve, upon such further measures, as, under God, shall be effectual, to save this people from impending ruin, and to secure those inestimable liberties, derived to us from our ancestors, and which it is our duty to preserve for posterity.

Resolved, That ten o'clock, this forenoon, be assigned for the choice of a chaplain for this Congress.

37

Ordered, That Mr. Fisher, Col. Barrett, Capt. Holmes, Col. Bowers and Col. Sawyer, be a committee to bring in a resolve for making further provision for distributing the poor of Boston to such towns in the colony as the committee may think convenient.

Ordered, That Col. Gerrish, Mr. Spooner, Mr. Sever, Col. Bowers, and Mr. Fisher, be a committee to take into consideration the petition and memorial of the several committees of correspondence for the county of Worcester, and report.[1]

The committee appointed to consider the resolve and proposals of the reverend gentlemen of the clergy, reported; the report was accepted, and is as follows, viz.:

Whereas, it is of the greatest importance that our colony army be furnished with gentlemen to act as chaplains, on whose virtue, firmness and patriotism they can safely rely; and whereas, the reverend convention of the clergy of this colony have, most nobly and without reward, tendered their services in their country's cause:

Therefore, *Resolved*, That the general and field officers be, and they hereby are empowered and directed, to choose nine gentlemen of the clergy of this colony, to act as chaplains to said army: provided that not more than two of them belong to any one county; and the general officers of said army are hereby empowered to determine the regiments to which each chaplain shall be desired to officiate; and also, the committee of supplies are hereby directed to make suitable provision for said chaplains during their continuance in camp.

Ordered, That Mr. Spooner, Col. Richmond and Col. Dwight, be a committee to take into consideration the expense Capt. Phelps has been at, in supplying the Massachusetts forces at Ticonderoga, and report.

Ordered, That Doct. Whiting and Doct. Bailies, be added to the committee which was appointed by the last Congress, to examine those persons who might be nominated for surgeons of the Massachusetts army.

Ordered, That Deacon Bayley, Hon. Joseph Gerrish, Esq., Josiah Johnson, Esq., Mr. John Hale, Hon. William Sever, Esq., Col. Joseph Otis, Hon. Jerathmiel Bowers, Col. Cutt, Capt. Stephen Maynard, Col. Thompson, Mr. Joseph North and Timothy Edwards, Esq., be a committee to take into consideration the situation and circumstances of

---

(1) The purport of this memorial may be inferred from a resolution of the convention of committees of correspondence of the county of Worcester, May 31, 1775: "*Voted*, That a committee be chosen to draw up a remonstrance to the Provincial Congress, that no man be allowed to have a seat therein, who does not vote away his own money for public purposes, in common with the other members and his constituents."

the sea port towns and islands in this colony, which are exposed to the excursions and ravages of the enemy, and in particular to consider the letter of Mr. Stephen Nye to Col. Freeman ; the petition from the town of Kittery ; the resolve of the last Congress relative to the invasion of the enemy on our sea coasts, &c. ; and a petition from some of the inhabitants of Deer Island, and sit forthwith, and report as soon as may be.[1]

Order of the day moved for.

Ordered, That Mr. Jones, Mr. Bliss and Mr. Toby, be a committee to receive, sort and count the votes for a chaplain. The committee having attended that service, reported, that the Rev. Mr. [William] Gordon was chosen.

Ordered, That Col. Davis, Mr. Wheeler and Major Bliss, be a committee to wait upon the Rev. Mr. Gordon, informing him that this Congress have made choice of him to officiate as their chaplain during its session in this place.

The committee appointed to inquire how many armourers were appointed, &c., reported, that the committee of safety informed them that there were thirteen appointed, and several others nominated, and that the general officers had agreed that thirteen was a sufficient number, but that they were in want of tools and stock.

                                        Afternoon.

Ordered, That commissions be given to the officers of Col. Scammell's regiment, except such captains as have already received their commissions, agreeably to the list by him exhibited.

Ordered, That Col. Prescott, Col. Freeman, Hon. Mr. Spooner, Mr. Partridge, Col. Cushing, Col. Spaulding and Col. Sayer, be a committee to consider the petition of Capt. Jacob Gerrish, and seven other captains in the Massachusetts army.

Ordered, That Col. Richmond be, and hereby is appointed, to countersign the notes, which were ordered to be prepared for the soldiers' advance pay, in the room of Major Fuller, who declines serving further in that business.

Ordered, That Deacon Baker, Major Brooks, Mr. Nichols and Col. Grout, be added to the committee who were appointed by the last Congress, to draw up some easy and concise method of making salt petre.

(1) All the petitions from the sea port towns, represent, in substance, that the harbors lie open to the enemy, that the lives and property of the inhabitants of the Atlantic coast are exposed to danger from the incursions of the British troops ; that the want of arms and ammunition prevents prudent preparations for defence ; and some papers contain moving descriptions of alarm and peril from the approach of the king's war ships, and of suffering and distress from the scanty supply of food. Such was the general tenor of the memorials mentioned in the text.

Ordered, That the officers of Col. Gardner's regiment be commissioned agreeably to the list by him exhibited.

Ordered, That Capt. Parker, Capt. Thatcher, Mr. Jewett, Col. Porter and Mr. Singletary, be a committee to consider what is best to be done with the horses lately taken from Noddle's Island.

The committee appointed to take into consideration the petition of Capt. Jacob Gerrish and others, reported, verbally, that they think it expedient that Col. Gerrish be notified to attend said committee, to-morrow morning, at eight o'clock, at the house of Mr. Learned, in Watertown, if he sees cause: thereupon,

Ordered, That the same committee be directed to bring in a short resolve for this purpose.

The committee appointed to consider what is best to be done with the horses taken from Noddle's Island, reported. The report was accepted, and is as follows, viz. :

The committee appointed to consider what shall be done with the horses taken by our forces from Noddle's Island, which belong to our enemies, beg leave to report : that the same horses be delivered to the committee of supplies, to be by them used and improved for the benefit of the colony, as they shall think fit, until further order from this or some future congress, or house of representatives.

Ordered, That Col. Farley, Deacon Baker and Mr. Batchelder, be a committee to inquire of the committee of safety, what progress has been made in the raising a regiment for the train.

The committee appointed to bring in a resolve, whereby to notify Col. Gerrish to appear before said committee to-morrow morning, reported the following, which was read and accepted, and Capt. Thatcher was desired to carry it to Col. Gerrish this evening. It is as follows, viz. :

To Col. Samuel Gerrish:

A number of gentlemen have presented a petition to this Congress, in behalf of themselves and the men they have enlisted, praying that Capt. Moses Little and Mr. Isaac Smith may be appointed and commissioned as two of the field officers over them. Six of the said petitioners are returned by you as your captains, as appears by your return, and the petition has been committed to a committee, to hear the petitioners and report to the Congress; and it is, therefore, *Ordered*, that the said Col. Samuel Gerrish be notified, and he is hereby notified, to attend the said committee, at the house of Mr. Learned, in Watertown, the 3d day of June instant, at eight o'clock in the forenoon.

Read and accepted, and Capt. Thatcher was desired to carry this resolve to Col. Gerrish this evening.

The committee appointed to consider the subject of the letter from the selectmen of Hopkinton, again reported. The consideration of the report was ordered to be put off till to-morrow morning, eleven o'clock.

The committee appointed to wait on the Rev. Mr. Gordon, reported, that they had informed Mr. Gordon that this Congress had appointed him their chaplain, and that Mr. Gordon told them he would attend this Congress to-morrow morning.

The committee appointed to consider the expense Mr. Phelps had been at, in supplying the Massachusetts forces at Ticonderoga, exhibited an account, which they looked upon was not supported by any vouchers, and therefore submitted the matter to Congress. *Ordered*, that the consideration of the same be put off to to-morrow morning.

The Congress then adjourned to nine o'clock to-morrow morning.

SATURDAY, June 3, 1775.

Ordered, That Col. Palmer, Col. Davis, Mr. Glover, Deacon Gould and Mr. Webster, be a committee to consider a resolve of the committee of safety, respecting a person in Brookline, who is broke out with the small pox, and that they sit forthwith.

The committee appointed to consider the situation and circumstances of the islands and sea coasts, reported :

1st. That the petition of Col. Lithgow be committed to the committee of supplies :

2d. A resolve on the subject of Mr. Nye's letter, [which is as follows :]

[Whereas, the forces under the command of general Gage, are frequently plundering and making depredations on the islands and sea coasts of this province, particularly on the island of Nashawn, and others adjacent ; whereby, not only individuals, but the public, are much injured, and our enemies strengthened. *Resolved*, therefore, that it be recommended to all those persons occupying the islands or sea coasts aforesaid, which are exposed to be ravaged or plundered, and cannot be defended by the inhabitants ; to remove all their hay, cattle, horses, sheep, &c., so far into the country, or otherwise dispose of them, that they may be out of the way of our implacable enemies ; also, that it be recommended to the committee of correspondence, in each town and district, or selectmen, where no such committee is chosen, to take effectual care that this resolve be immediately, strictly and fully executed, and that all persons who refuse to comply herewith, be viewed as disposed to furnish our enemies with such unremoved hay and stock, and shall therefore be held as inimical to the liberty and rights of this country.]

The committee appointed to consider a resolve of the committee of safety, reported the following resolve, which was accepted, viz. :

Whereas, a person is now broke out with the small pox, at Brookline, on the road between Cambridge and Roxbury, whereby the public in general, and the camps in particular, will be greatly endangered, if said person is suffered to remain in said house :

Therefore, *Resolved*, That said person be immediately removed to the house of Ebenezer Smith in Little Cambridge, wherein the small pox has lately been; and that the selectmen of Brookline are hereby directed to remove said person to said house, in the most careful manner, at the expense of said town of Brookline; and the selectmen of Cambridge are hereby directed to receive said person into said Smith's house.

Ordered, That Mr. Gerry, Hon. Mr. Spooner, Major Bliss, Hon. Mr. Sever, Col. Freeman, Col. Farley and Col. Richmond, be a committee to consider a resolve of the committee of safety, relative to a reenforcement of the Massachusetts army, for the protection of the sea coasts, &c. ; and that this committee be directed to confer with the committee of safety on the subject of it; and that those gentlemen, who have been appointed and commissioned as general officers, be invited to the conference.

Also, *Resolved*, That eight o'clock, on Monday morning next, be assigned for such conference, to be held at Cambridge, and that the committee of safety, and the said general officers, be served with a copy of this resolve.

A number of papers from the committee of safety, respecting Col. Jonathan Brewer, were read.[1]

Resolved, That the further consideration of the papers relative to Col. Jonathan Brewer, be referred to the afternoon, three o'clock.

, Afternoon.

Ordered, That a commission be prepared, and delivered to Col. John Nixon.

Ordered, That Mr. Greenleaf, Capt. Bragdon and Mr. Sawyer, be a

(1) The committee of safety charged Col. Brewer with having obtained the men enlisted into the regiment he had formed, from others corps, by wrong representations ; and with converting private property to his own use without proper authority.

committee to consider the petition of a number of persons of the town of Dartmouth.[1]

The committee on the petition of Jacob Gerrish and others, reported verbally: agreeably to which report,

Resolved, That the petition be so far granted, as that the petitioners be directed to apply to the committee of safety, for a recommendation to this Congress, to commission Capt. Moses Little as colonel of a regiment in the Massachusetts army.

Ordered, That Col. Dwight, Hon. Mr. Sever, Col. Farley, Major Bliss and Mr. Edwards, be a committee to take into consideration a letter from Col. James Easton, and report.

[The] order of the day [was] moved for.

The papers respecting Col. Brewer were read.   After debate,

Moved, That the matter subside; the question being put, it passed in the negative.   *Moved*, that the petitioner be admitted on the floor; the question was put, and it passed in the negative.

Resolved, That Tuesday next, at eight o'clock, A. M., be assigned for hearing Col. Jonathan Brewer, on the subject of certain papers laid before this Congress by order of the committee of safety, and that the committee of safety, as also Col. Brewer, be served with a copy of this resolve, and that Col. Brewer be directed to bring with him a return of the number of men enlisted in his regiment, distinguishing how many are present at head quarters, and how many are absent.

Agreeably to an order of Congress, a colonel's commission was delivered to Col. John Nixon.

The committee on the petition from Dartmouth, reported.   The report being amended, was accepted, and is as follows, viz. :

On the petition of David Shepherd and others, from Dartmouth, representing that uneasiness has arisen on account of said petitioners fitting out sundry vessels for whaling voyages, and for the West Indies, *Resolved*, that the petitioners be informed, that this Congress know of no objection to their pursuing the above voyage, or any other where they are willing to risk their interest, provided that the owners and

---

(1) The petition of David Shepherd and eighteen others, dated Dartmouth, June 1, 1775, shows, "that the subscribers have, at great expense, fitted out some of our vessels for whaling voyages, and one or two with lumber, &c. for the West Indies, some of which are now ready for sea, being advised thereto by the committee of correspondence of the town, and not being restricted therefrom by the Continental or Provincial Congress, the advice and directions of whom we are determined to abide by in this affair; notwithstanding which, some people manifest uneasiness that we should send our vessels to sea, and will not be satisfied unless we have the advice of the honorable the Provincial Congress, now sitting, thereon, which will quiet the minds of the people, and give them and us satisfaction relative to the matter. Therefore, the petitioners pray advice and direction."

masters of such vessels strictly adhere to the resolutions of the Continental Congress.

Ordered, That a messenger be forthwith sent to the receiver general with the following letter, viz. :

SIR :—The absolute necessity of paying the colony forces immediately, having been duly considered by this Congress, and not being able to make necessary payments, to prevent the troops from returning home, without your being present: you are therefore directed, upon the receipt of this order, immediately to repair to this place, and make the utmost despatch in completing the signing of the bills wanted for the above purposes.

P. S.—The Congress is just informed, that a gentleman at Salem has £500, which he is willing to lend the province; which would be of the greatest importance to pay immediately to the soldiers, and might prevent the greatest mischiefs.

Resolved, That Mr. Phillips be desired to repair to Salem to Mr. Becket, desiring him to bring, or send, the money he has offered to lend the province, to this place, to-morrow morning, and take a note therefor from the receiver general.

Ordered, That Capt. Stone be directed to apply to Mr. Revere, desiring him to attend the business of stamping the notes for the soldiers, all the ensuing night, if he can, and to finish them with the greatest despatch possible; and also to despatch a messenger to Major Fuller, desiring him to attend to countersign them.

Adjourned to eight o'clock to-morrow morning.

SUNDAY, June 4, 1775.

Resolved, That Col. Henshaw be admitted to give an account of his proceedings at Connecticut, where he was sent by the last Congress on the affair of Ticonderoga.

Resolved, That Col. Asa Whitcomb be directed to pay the advance pay to those companies of Col. Patterson's regiment, who came from the county of Berkshire, out of the first money he may receive from the receiver general.

Resolved, That Col. Lemuel Robinson be directed to pay the advance pay to the three companies of Col. [Fellow's] regiment, which came from the county of Berkshire, out of the first money he may receive from the receiver general.

Ordered, That the papers exhibited by Col. Henshaw be put into the hands of the committee of safety, and the committee of this Congress, who are appointed to confer with them to-morrow morning.

Ordered, That Mr. Sullivan, Hon. Mr. Spooner and Col. Prescott, be a committee to inquire what number of colony notes are struck off, how many are signed, whether the press is now going, and to make a thorough inquiry in this respect, and report at the adjournment.

Ordered, That Doct. Whiting be appointed to employ a messenger, to be sent to Major Fuller, directing his attendance to the service of countersigning the notes, immediately.[1]

Ordered, That Capt. Bragdon and Col. Thompson, be appointed to attend Mr. Revere whilst he is striking off the notes for advance pay to the soldiers, night and day, [aalternately,] till they are all struck off.

The committee on Col. Easton's letter, reported, that it was their opinion it would be best to commit it to the committee who were appointed to confer with the committee of safety, to-morrow morning: it was accordingly given to the Hon. Mr. Spooner.

Ordered, That the key and billet delivered to this Congress, from Major Fuller, by Capt. Stone, be put into the hands of the committee who were appointed to make inquiry respecting the colony notes.

Adjourned to twelve o'clock.

[Noon.]

Met at twelve o'clock.

Ordered, That Col. Richmond be excused from serving on the committee who were appointed to confer with the committee of safety, being engaged in countersigning the notes, and that Col. Gerrish attend that service in his stead.

Adjourned to four o'clock, afternoon.

[Afternoon.]

Met at four o'clock, and adjourned to Monday morning, eight o'clock.

MONDAY, June 5, 1775.

A petition from Truro for powder was read.

Resolved, That the petitioners have leave to withdraw their petition.

Ordered, That Col. Foster be, and hereby is appointed, to countersign the $20, $14, and $6 notes.

Ordered, That Mr. Pickering, Mr. Phillips and Mr. [bGoodwin,] be appointed to number the notes which are preparing for advance pay for the soldiers. Mr. Pickering, to number the sheets struck off on the first plate; Mr. Phillips, those of the second; and Mr. [bGoodwin,] those of the third.

a [alternatively.]   b [Gooding.]

(1) Major Fuller was detained, by sickness, from attendance on the committee.

Ordered, That the letter from Gov. Trumbull, just received and read, be committed to the committee of safety, and the committee appointed to confer with them.

Ordered, That Col. Foster bring in a resolve, appointing some persons to examine and inspect the mineral earth, brought by him to this place.

Col. Foster brought in a resolve accordingly, which was accepted, and is as follows :

Resolved, That Doct. Whiting, Deacon Baker and Col. Grout, be a committee to inquire into the nature and quality of the said mineral earth, and in such inquiry to consult the Hon. Joseph Warren, Esq. and Mr. Professor Sewall, and such other persons as they may think proper, and report to this Congress as soon as may be.

Ordered, That Mr. Sullivan, Mr. Greenleaf, Mr. Partridge, Col. Cushing and Mr. Edwards, be a committee to hold a conference with the general officers of the American army, and to inquire of them whether there is any thing this Congress can do to preserve the health of said army.

A petition, signed by Phillip Hubbard and others, was read, and ordered to lie on the table.

Ordered, That Mr. Sullivan, Col. Cushing, Capt. Holmes, Mr. Partridge and Mr. Currier, be a committee to consider what order it would be proper for this Congress to take relative to any letters which have been or may be intercepted.

Ordered, That Mr. Edwards, and Mr. Stone of Lexington, be appointed to inquire what is become of a letter said to be sent by the Stockbridge Indians to this Congress.

The committee appointed to bring in a resolve respecting intercepted letters, reported ; the report was read and accepted, and is as follows, viz. :

Whereas, it has been represented to this Congress, that several letters, and packets of letters, of public concernment, wrote to and by the avowed enemies of this country, have fallen into the hands of sundry persons in this colony ; and, whereas, it appears absolutely necessary that all such letters should be immediately laid before this Congress, for their consideration ; therefore, *Resolved,* that all persons who now are, or shall hereafter be possessed of such letters, shall lay them, as soon as may be, before this, or some future Congress, for their advisement thereon.

Afternoon.

Resolved, That the resolve which passed this Congress, relative to accommodating the Rev. Mr. Emerson with one of the horses taken from the regulars, be so far reconsidered, as that it be recommitted, for a plainer description of the horse intended to be delivered to him; and that Col. Batchelder and Col. Dwight be added to the committee, in the room of Doct. Taylor and Col. Bowers, who are absent.

Ordered, That commissions be delivered to the officers of Col. Nixon's regiment, agreeably to the list by him exhibited.

Ordered, That Mr. Fisher, Col. Barrett, Capt. Holmes, Col. Bowers and Col. Sawyer, be a committee to consider the proposal of Capt. Foster, relative to removing the poor, and the goods of the poor, of the town of Boston, into the country.

Resolved, That the committee of supplies be directed to lay before this Congress, in writing, an account of their proceedings, with respect to the memorandum of Gen. Ward for sundry military stores, committed to them by the last Congress.

Ordered, That Capt. Stone, Capt. Smith and Col. Goodrich, be a committee to inquire of the committee of supplies, if they have sent to New York for any of the powder, which, it is said, is lately arrived there.

Ordered, That Mr. Fisher, Capt. Holmes, Mr. Sawyer, Col. Grout and Mr. Webster, be a committee to bring in a resolve in addition to the resolve of the last Congress, respecting the poor of the town of Boston, passed the first ultimo, which shall extend to such of the poor of said town, sufferers by the Boston port bill, as were removed out of that town before the date of said resolve.

The committee appointed to inquire into the nature and qualities of the mineral earth, brought by Col. Foster from Brookfield, reported, that it was their opinion, and the opinion of those whom they conversed with thereon, that it contains a matter useful for the production of nitre, but that there was too small a quantity for an experiment:

Whereupon, *Ordered*, That this committee be directed to appoint some suitable person, to repair to Brookfield, to make some experiment with the mineral earth, which is said to be there in large quantities.

Ordered, That the Hon. Mr. Dexter, Col. Otis, Col. Porter, Capt. Stone of Oakham, and Capt. Stone of Framingham, be a committee to bring in a resolve for the purpose of giving a currency to the bills of credit of all the governments on the continent.

The committee appointed to bring in a resolve descriptive of the horse designed for Mr. Emerson, reported; the report was read and accepted, and is as follows:

Whereas, in a resolve of this Congress, passed the 1st instant, the horse appointed for the use of the Rev. Mr. Emerson of Concord, was not so fully described as that Thomas Read of Woburn, the keeper of said horse, could, with safety, deliver him to said Emerson ; therefore, *Resolved*, that said Read be, and hereby is directed, to deliver a certain sorrel horse, that was taken by the guards, at Roxbury, from an officer of general Gage's troops, on the 20th of April last, to said Emerson, he paying a reasonable sum for the keeping said horse, and said Mr. Emerson is hereby permitted to keep and use said horse, until the further order of this Congress.

Ordered, That Col. Porter, Capt. Stone of Oakham, Capt. Partridge, Col. Otis and Deacon Baker, be a committee to consider the letter from Mr. Gridley to the committee of safety, and to confer with them thereon, and also on the state of the artillery in general.

Resolved, That the four prisoners brought to this Congress by sergeant John Parker, be committed to the custody of the guard, which is appointed to guard the public stores in Watertown, till further orders of this Congress ; and that the commissary be directed to provide what provisions they may stand in need of, till to-morrow morning.

Ordered, That Mr. Sullivan bring in a resolve, for the purpose of discouraging and preventing persons from taking any notes or bills of credit, of this, or the other colonies, under the value specified therein.

The committee appointed to bring in a resolve for giving currency to the notes of the other governments, reported : the report was ordered to lie on the table, till Mr. Sullivan had brought in the resolve for which he was just now appointed.

Ordered, That Col. Cutt, Capt. Parker, Mr. Page, Capt. Morton and Capt. Stone, of Oakham, be a committee to make some establishment for an allowance of provisions for the soldiers of the Massachusetts army.

Resolved, That Friday next, at three o'clock, P. M., be assigned for the consideration of the report of Col. Thompson, relative to his proceedings at Kennebeck.

Adjourned to eight o'clock to-morrow morning.

TUESDAY, June 6, 1775.

Ordered, That Mr. Sullivan, Col. Cushing, Mr. Partridge, Mr. Greenleaf and Col. Glover, be a committee, to devise some means whereby the army may be more regularly supplied with the necessaries procured for it by the colony.

[The] order of the day [was] moved for.

Resolved, That those members who are out upon committees be directed to attend.

Resolved, That three o'clock, P. M., be assigned for the choice of a vice president.

Ordered, That Col. Thompson, Major Brooks and Col. Cutt, be a committee to inquire into the circumstances of bringing the four prisoners to this place yesterday.

Moved, That the Congress take some order at this time relative to the prisoners : the question being put, it passed in the negative.

The papers respecting Col. Brewer were read, and Col. Brewer was then admitted, and, on his request, *Resolved*, that Capt. Edwards, Capt. Butler, Lieut. Tuckerman, Col. Buckminster, Mr. Cudworth, Thomas Withington and Capt. Gray, be admitted on the floor of this house, as [*witnesses] in the cause.

The complaint of the committee of safety being read, and Col. Brewer having had leave of making his defence, he was fully heard therein, as were also the witnesses by him produced, the galleries being first opened for any who were inclined to hear the cause.

Col. Brewer, having offered what he saw fit, withdrew with his witnesses, and the galleries being cleared, *Resolved*, that the further consideration of this matter be referred to the afternoon.

The committee appointed to bring in a resolve for giving currency to the bills of credit of the other governments, reported : the report was ordered to lie upon the table till the afternoon.

[Afternoon.]

Voted, That the resolve, which passed in the forenoon, for choosing a vice president, be reconsidered.

The Congress [ᵇresumed] the consideration of the case of Mr. Brewer; and, after a long and full debate, it was *Moved*, that the question be put whether the president should be directed to deliver a commission to Mr. Brewer, as colonel of a regiment in the Massachusetts army, and it passed in the negative : the number of members present being 150, and but 70 for the question.

Mr. Cushing informed the Congress, that Mr. Benjamin Edwards, on hearing, at the door of this house, of the determination of the Congress respecting Mr. Brewer, made use of the following expression, viz.: "By God, if this province is to be governed in this manner, it is time for us to look out, and 'tis all owing to the committee of safety, a pack of sappy-head-fellows. I know three of them myself." Whereupon, *Resolved*, that Mr. Edwards be directed to attend this house to make answer to the above charge. Mr. Edwards being called in, and

a [evidence.]   b [reassumed.]

having heard the charge alleged against him, it was *Resolved*, that Mr. Edwards have leave to withdraw, and that he be directed to attend this Congress to-morrow morning, at ten o'clock.

The petition of Major Baldwin,[1] being read and considered, it is thereupon *Ordered*, that the Rev. president Langdon be requested to furnish Major Baldwin, out of the college apparatus, with [such] instruments as he stands in need of, to perform the public services therein mentioned, he giving his receipt therefor, to return the same in good order, as soon as the said services shall be performed.

A resolve of the committee of safety, relative to the [*admission] of slaves into the army was read, and ordered to lie on the table for further consideration.

The committee appointed to bring in an additional resolve, relative to making provision for the poor of Boston, reported: the report was read, amended and accepted, and ordered to be printed in the Cambridge, Watertown and Worcester papers; and is as follows:

Whereas, the provision already made for the removal of the poor of Boston, suffering by the cruel hand of arbitrary power, has not answered the salutary purposes intended, and it becomes necessary that further provision be made, therefore, *Resolved*, that such suffering poor shall be allowed to remove into any town or district in the colony, other than such towns or districts as are already ordered to provide for and receive the number of said poor to them assigned; and every town and district in the colony, that shall receive and provide necessary support for such suffering poor, shall be indemnified, in every respect, as fully as any other town or district in the colony, provided they observe and comply with directions already given relative to said poor. And, whereas, in the present distressed circumstances and confusion of the town of Boston, some of said poor have or may remove out of said town without proper certificates from the committee of donations, and the town to which such persons remove, may refuse to receive them for want of the same; *Resolved*, that it be recommended to the selectmen of the several towns and districts in this colony to which such persons may remove, that such provision be made, as is necessary to prevent their suffering, until such certificate can be procured; and such town or district shall be indemnified, as before provided, they observing the directions given in the resolve passed by the last Con-

a [inadmission.]

(1) The petition of Loammi Baldwin represented, that Gen. Ward had approved of a proposal for taking surveys of the ground between the camp of the Massachusetts army and the posts of the British troops, and requested the loan of mathematical instruments from the apparatus of Harvard College, to be used in the execution of this service.

gress relative to said poor; and such persons shall be considered as part of their assignment. And, whereas, it is found extremely difficult for the committees at Charlestown and Roxbury to remove said poor to the several towns and districts to which they are destined, for want of teams to go such a distance as is necessary in many cases, it is further recommended to the selectmen of each town and district in this colony, that they assist in removing said poor, upon every necessary occasion, when it is in their power, to the several places of their assignment, keeping a particular account of their trouble and expense, and the names of the persons they assisted, and they shall be paid in manner as before provided. And the committees at Charlestown and Roxbury, who were appointed by this Congress to make provision for such poor as might come out of the town of Boston, are desired to procure a list of said poor from the committee of donations for future use: and also, to take the advantage of the teams that may come from the westward, for the removal of said poor by every opportunity in their power.

Ordered, That the committee appointed to inquire into the circumstances of bringing four prisoners from Cambridge, be directed to make such provision for them as is necessary, till further orders from this Congress, and that Mr. Robinson be added to the committee, and that said committee report what they think would be best to be done with them.

Adjourned to Wednesday morning, eight o'clock.

WEDNESDAY, June 7, 1775.

Ordered, That Mr. Sullivan, Col. Parker, Mr. Webster, Major Fuller and Col. Prescott, be a committee to wait on General Ward, requesting him to exhibit to this Congress a return of the number of men in the Massachusetts army, and that Mr. Sullivan, Doct. Holten and Mr. Cushing be a committee, to bring in a resolve for this purpose.

The committee appointed to consider what is best to be done with the four prisoners brought from Dartmouth, via Cambridge, reported : the report was recommitted.

A petition from the inhabitants of Machias was read and committed to Mr. Batchelder, Col. Otis, Mr. Nichols, Mr Lothrop and Mr. Webster, to consider thereon and report.[1]

---

(1) The following is the petition mentioned in the text. It was subscribed by Jonas Longfellow and thirty-seven other citizens.

To the Honorable Congress of the Massachusetts Bay :

"GENTLEMEN:—With the highest satisfaction, we now consider you as the guardians of this

The committee appointed to inquire what is become of the original letter from the Stockbridge Indians, reported, that they think it probable, from what they have on inquiry heard, that it is in the hands of the Hon. Mr. Hancock.

The committee appointed to consider of Col. Gridley's letter to the committee of safety, beg leave to report in part, that an ordnance storekeeper be immediately appointed, and recommend that Major Nathaniel Barber be appointed to that employment, and beg leave to sit again, to report a proper establishment, as also to report what further [ªsteps] are necessary to be taken as requested in Col. Gridley's letter.

Ordered, That commissions be delivered to the lieutenants and ensigns of Col. Mansfield's regiment, agreeably to the list by him exhibited.

Ordered, That Mr. Edwards, Col. Porter, Doct. Whiting, Mr. Wheeler and Mr. Goodridge, be a committee to consider the letters from the Stockbridge Indians, and report.

extensive and wealthy province, and relying on your wisdom, the wisdom of the Continental Congress, the justice of our cause, and the tender mercy of our fathers' God, we promise ourselves, in due time, a happy deliverance from the iron chains of tyranny, which were forming for us, and from servitude equal to Egyptian bondage."

"As a part, therefore, of your charge, we, the distressed inhabitants of Machias, beg leave to approach your presence, and to spread our grievances at your feet. We dare not say we are the foremost in supporting the glorious cause of American liberty; but this we can truly affirm, that we have done our utmost to encourage and strengthen the hands of all the advocates for America with whom we have been connected; that we have not even purchased any goods of those persons, whom we suspected to be inimical to our country, except when constrained by necessity; and that none on the continent can more cheerfully risque all that is dear to them on earth, when called, in support of those precious privileges which God [gave,] and our venerable ancestors, as a most invaluable legacy, have handed down to us."

"We must now inform your honors, that the inhabitants of this place exceed one hundred families, some of which are very numerous, and that divine Providence has cut off all our usual resources, A very severe drought last fall prevented our laying in sufficient stores; and had no vessels visited us in the winter, we must have suffered; nor have we this spring been able to procure provisions sufficient for carrying on our business. Our laborers are dismissed; some of our mills stand still; almost all our vessels have forsaken us; our lumber lies by us in heaps; and, to complete our misfortunes, all our ports are to be shut up on the first of July next; we must add, we have no country behind us to lean upon, nor can we make an escape by flight; the wilderness is impervious, and vessels we have none."

"To you, therefore, honored gentlemen, we humbly apply for relief. You are our last, our only resource, and, permit us again to say, you are our guardians, and we rejoice and glory in being subject [to you]. Pardon our importunity. We cannot take a denial, for, under God, you are all our dependance, and if you neglect us, we are ruined. Save, dear sirs, one of your most flourishing settlements from famine, and all its horrors. We ask not for charity; we ask for a supply, to be put into the hands of Messrs. Smith and Stillman, or any other person or persons your wisdom may point out, who shall obligate themselves to pay the whole amount on demand in lumber, the only staple of our country."

"That God may long preserve you, and make you happily instrumental in his hand, in bestowing all the sweets of peace and liberty to this much injured country, and even to Great Britain herself, is the constant and fervent prayer of, gentlemen, your most humble petitioners."

"*Machias, May* 25, 1775."

a [stores.]

A petition from Col. Brewer, and another from several nominal captains under him, were read and ordered to lie on the table.

Two resolves from the Continental Congress were read, and ordered to be printed in hand bills, and dispersed throughout the colony.

Col. Porter, Col. Tyng and Mr. Jewett, were appointed a committee to prepare a resolve for the purpose of carrying into execution the said resolves.

Resolved, That Mr. Edwards be called in, and admonished by the president: which was done accordingly.

Ordered, That commissions be delivered to Col. Fellowes and the officers of his regiment, agreeably to the list exhibited by his lieutenant colonel.

The committee appointed to bring in a resolve, expressive of the duty of the committee who were appointed this day to wait on General Ward, reported. The report was read and accepted, and is as follows, viz.:

Ordered, That Mr. Sullivan, Col. Parks, Mr. Webster, Major Fuller and Col. Prescott, be a committee to wait on the hon. general Ward, and hold a conference with him on the state of the army, and to desire him to make a return, as soon as may be, to this Congress, of the number and equipments of the troops raised by this colony, and now in the camps at Cambridge and Roxbury, and stationed elsewhere, that due advisement be had thereon.

The Hon. Mr. Spooner, Hon. Mr. Sever, Hon. Col. Bowers, appointed to consider a memorial from the convention of Worcester, being absent, *Ordered*, that the Hon. Mr. Dexter, Col. Dwight, and Capt. Stone, be appointed in their stead.

A memorial from the selectmen of the town of Salem was read, and committed to Col. Glover, Doct. Taylor and Mr. Wheeler.

The report of the committee appointed to bring in a resolve for giving currency to the bills of credit of the other governments, was read and recommitted.

Ordered, That Mr. Orne, Col. Porter and Mr. Whittemore, be a committee to consider the petition of Benjamin Ames, and seven other companies of Col. Fry's regiment, and report.

The committee on the petition of the inhabitants of Machias reported. The report was ordered to lie upon the table for further consideration.

[Afternoon.]

Ordered, That Col. Warren, Hon. Mr. Dexter, Col. Gerrish, Col. Otis and Col. Farley, be a committee to confer with the two gentlemen,

39

members of the Congress of New Hampshire, who have brought a letter from that Congress to this.

Resolved, That to-morrow, four o'clock, P. M., be assigned for the choice of two gentlemen to act as major generals in the Massachusetts army.

The report of the committee on the letter from Hopkinton was read: the consideration of it was put off to five o'clock this afternoon.

On the representation of the town clerk of Lunenburg, in his letter to Doct. Taylor, respecting their town's stock of powder, &c., *Resolved*, that that town be excused from delivering out of their stock any more than one half barrel; the resolve of the former Congress, directing the selectmen of said town to deliver two [barrels], to the order of the committee of supplies, notwithstanding.

Ordered, That Mr. Orne and Mr. Vose, be of the committee appointed to collect the letters of the late Governor Hutchinson, in the room of Doct. Perkins and Mr. Ellis, who are absent.

The committee appointed to inquire into the circumstances of the four prisoners, reported. The report was amended and accepted, and is as follows:

[The committee appointed to take into consideration the circumstances of four prisoners brought to this Congress on the second day of June instant, said to be taken at Dartmouth, since the nineteenth of April last, beg leave to report: that it is the opinion of this committee, that the said four prisoners, viz.: Richard Luckus, mate of the ship Falcon, John Dunkinson, surgeon's mate, Jonathan Lee and Robert Caddy, be sent to Concord, to the care of the selectmen of said town, to be by them secured and provided for, agreeably to their rank, at the expense of this colony, until they receive some further order, from this or some other Congress or house of representatives of this colony.]

The committee appointed to confer with the gentlemen from the New Hampshire Congress, reported, verbally; whereupon, *Ordered*, that said committee be directed to reduce their report to writing.

The report of the committee on the petition from the inhabitants of Machias, being again read, was accepted, and is as follows, viz.:

The committee appointed to consider the petition of the inhabitants of Machias, beg leave to report, that it be recommended by this Congress to the committee of correspondence of the town of Salem, or to the like committees of any other towns within this province, to supply Messrs. Gardner & Smith, of said Machias, for the present relief of the said inhabitants, with the following articles, viz.: one hundred bushels of indian corn; ten barrels of pork and beef; one cask of molasses; and one cask of rice; and take, in return for the same, wood, or such other payment as the said Gardner and Smith may be able to make: and in case they, or their constituents, the above said inhabitants, should not make satisfaction for the same in a reasonable time, it shall be allowed and paid out of the public treasury of this province, and the said inhabitants shall refund the same as soon as may be. Your committee further report, that a recommendation go from this Congress to the governor and company of the colony of Connecticut, to suffer the inhabitants of the eastern parts of this colony, to purchase and carry out of said colony of Connecticut, such provisions as their necessitous circumstances may require.

The committee appointed to confer with the gentlemen from New Hampshire, having reduced their report to writing, the same was read and accepted, and is as follows, viz.:

Resolved, That an application be made by this Congress to the Continental Congress, desiring them to take such measures as to them shall appear proper, to quiet and conciliate the minds of the inhabitants of Canada, and the several tribes of Indians adjacent to these colonies, and prevent any unfavorable apprehensions, from the military preparations of the several colonies in America, and that the other three New England colonies, with the colony of New York, be desired to join in such an application.

Resolved, That letters be immediately written to the colonies of Connecticut, Rhode Island and New Hampshire, desiring them, severally, to appoint committees, to meet a committee appointed by this Congress, at the town of Worcester, in this colony, on Wednesday, the 28th day of June current, in order to settle and determine the number of men to be raised on the present emergency, by each of the New England colonies; and likewise to determine where they shall be stationed and employed.[1]

(1) The resolutions were founded on propositions of the Provincial Congress of New Hampshire, communicated by delegates attending on the assembly of Massachusetts, and expressed in the following letter:

In Provincial Congress, at Exeter, June 3, 1775.

"GENTLEMEN:—Having undoubted evidence of the attempts of the British ministry to engage the Canadians and savages in their interest, in the present controversy with America, and of actual movements in Canada in consequence thereof, we have thought it necessary that measures should be immediately taken, to defend, and quiet the minds of the people more especially exposed in the frontiers; and accordingly have resolved to send a number of troops as soon as may be; three companies, for the present, to be employed where and in such manner as may best answer that important end.

"We thought it expedient to give you the earliest intelligence of what we have done in this way, earnestly praying, and nothing doubting, but that you will concur in such measures, as, in your wisdom, you shall judge reasonable and necessary for the defence and safety of the back settlements, for whom both you and we must very sensibly feel.

Whereupon, *Ordered*, that the president, Hon. Mr. Sever, and the Hon. Mr. Dexter, be a committee, to prepare an application to the Continental Congress, and a letter to each of the colonies of Connecticut, Rhode Island and New Hampshire, and a letter to New York, agreeably to the foregoing resolve.

Resolved, That to-morrow, 5 o'clock, P. M., be assigned for the choice of three members of this Congress, as a committee, to meet committees from the colonies of Connecticut, Rhode Island and New Hampshire, agreeably to the foregoing resolve.

The committee appointed to confer with the committee of safety, on the subject of their resolve relative to a reinforcement of the army, reported, [as follows:]

[The committee appointed to consider a resolve of the committee of safety, of the 2d instant, relative to a reinforcement of the Massachusetts army, have attended that service, and having, agreeably to the order of Congress, conferred with the committee of safety and general officers upon the subject matter of the resolves, beg leave, upon mature deliberation, to report, that it appears to the committee inexpedient and unnecessary for this colony to augment, at present, the forces already voted by it to be established for the defence of this and the other American colonies.   ELBRIDGE GERRY, *Chairman*.]

Whereupon, *Resolved*, That to-morrow, nine o'clock, be assigned for the consideration of the said report, and that the committee of safety, the committee of supplies, and the several committees for this Congress, be notified of this assignment, and be desired to attend at that time, if they can with conveniency.

Ordered, That the Hon. Col. Warren, Mr. Pitts, Mr. Gerry, the president, Col. Freeman, Mr. Pickering, Mr. Batchelder, Hon. Mr. Dexter and Mr. Greenleaf, be a committee, to consider the expediency of establishing a number of small armed vessels, to cruise on our sea

"We furthermore think it suitable, just to suggest, that we have some apprehensions, lest our military manœuvres in the frontiers, should raise a jealousy in the minds of the Canadians, and awaken their fears of direct intentions of hostilities against them. We should give them the most positive assurances upon this head, that we desire nothing more than our own security; and that it is our most hearty wish to remain in steady terms of friendship with them. And in order to the more regular, harmonious, and effectual prosecution of the important object aforesaid, as also other valuable purposes, that we conceive it may answer, we would humbly move for a conference by a committee, with a committee from you, at such time and place as you shall please to appoint, and to consider of an address to be forwarded to the Canadians: and put it in the power of this Congress to join with you, and, if it might be, with the other New England colonies, and New York, that this negotiation might answer the most effectual purpose. By order of Congress.

I am your most obedient, humble servant,

MATTHEW THORNTON, *President*."

To the Hon. Provincial Congress of the Massachusetts Bay.

coasts, for the protection of our trade, and the annoyance of our enemies: and that the members be enjoined, by order of Congress, to observe secrecy in this matter.

Ordered, That Mr. Sullivan, Col. Porter, Hon. Mr. Sever, Mr. Greenleaf and Mr. Partridge, be a committee to consider at large on some measure for [*commissioning] the officers of the army.

Ordered, That the secretary be directed to serve General Ward with a list of the officers of the army, commissioned by this Congress.

Adjourned to nine o'clock to-morrow morning.

THURSDAY, June 8, 1775.

An account of the taking a sloop which sailed from Boston for Annapolis for hay and other stores for the use of the army at Boston, from the committee of the town of Arundel,[1] was read, as also several letters which were found on board said sloop. Whereupon,

Resolved, That the thanks of this Congress be given to said committee for their care and judicious conduct in this affair.

The order of the day [was] moved for.

Resolved, That this Congress will resolve itself into a committee of the whole house, which was done accordingly.

The committee of the whole house, by Col. Warren, their chairman, reported, that the committee have not sufficient time to deliberate on a matter of such importance, and therefore desire leave to sit again; which report was accepted by the Congress.

Afternoon.

The committee of the house reported, that it was the opinion of said committee, that the report of the committee, who were appointed to confer with the committee of safety, on the augmentation of the army, be accepted; which report was accordingly accepted by this Congress.

Ordered, That a commission be delivered to Thomas Poor, Esq., as major of a regiment under the command of Col. Fry.

' a [commissionating.]

(1) The committee of Arundel state, that the sloop Polly, belonging to that town, with Ephraim Perkins, master, while returning from a coasting voyage to Plymouth, was seized by a British armed vessel, carried into Boston harbor, and there detained. The cargo was taken into the custody of General Gage, and the owner obtained payment of the original cost of the articles. A proposition was made to Mr. Perkins, to enter into the king's service, and accepted, as affording means of escape. The sloop was chartered for Windsor, in Nova Scotia, to receive hay and grain for the supply of the troops, and went out with Josiah Jones supercargo, and Jonathan Hicks passenger. The master sailed directly for Arundel, where he arrived on the 2d of June, and surrendered his companions as prisoners. The papers transmitted to Congress, were the charter party, orders, instructions, and letters subscribed by Major William Shirreff, deputy quarter master general, relating to the objects and business of the voyage.

Resolved, That the choice of two major generals be deferred to four o'clock, to-morrow afternoon.

Ordered, That the committee appointed to consider the expediency of establishing several small armed vessels, sit forthwith.

The committee appointed to consider on some measures for commissioning the officers of the army, reported the following resolve, which was read and accepted, and an hundred of them ordered to be printed, and dispersed among the army. It is as follows, viz.:

Whereas, it is necessary to have, as soon as may be, a return of the number and equipments of the forces raised by this colony; and whereas, it is of the utmost importance that such returns should be consistent with the strictest truth: it is therefore *Resolved*, that if any officer now commissioned in the forces aforesaid, or that shall hereafter be commissioned therein, shall, wittingly and willingly, after his being so commissioned, make any false return of the numbers or equipments of the men under his command, and shall be thereof convicted before this, or any future Congress of this colony, or before a general court martial of the army raised by this colony, such officer shall be immediately cashiered. And every person now under nomination, or that shall hereafter be nominated to any office in said forces, that shall, wittingly and willingly, make such false return, shall be deemed incapable of holding any commission or command in the forces aforesaid, until the last day of December next.

The petition of Col. Henshaw was read, and committed to the committee who were appointed to consider on some measure for commissioning the officers of the army.

Resolved, That the choice of three delegates to meet delegates from the other colonies in New England, at Worcester, be put off to ten o'clock, to-morrow morning.

Ordered, That Mr. Cushing of Hanover, Capt. Stone of Oakham, and Dummer Jewett, Esq., be a committee to take into consideration a petition from the committees of correspondence for the county of Cumberland, and that they sit forthwith.

Ordered, That Major Bliss, Major Brooks and Mr. Sayer, be a committee to consider the account of Capt. Phelps, and to consider what sum is necessary to supply Capt. Phelps with, for transporting to Ticonderoga the pork he has purchased for our forces there, and bringing the cannon from thence.

Ordered, That Mr. Wheeler be appointed to number the small colony notes, in the room of Mr. Goodwin, who has leave to go home.

The committee appointed to consider the letter from the Stockbridge

Indians, reported the following, which was accepted, and ordered to be authenticated by the secretary, if the president is not in Watertown, and sent forward.[1]

To the Moheakounuck tribe of Indians, living in and about Stockbridge:

BROTHERS: We, this day, by the delegate from Stockbridge, first heard your friendly answer to our speech to you, by Capt. William Goodrich; which answer, we are told, you made to us immediately, by a letter, which we have not yet received. We now reply.

BROTHERS: You say that you were once great, but that you are now little; and that we were once little, but are now great. The Supreme Spirit orders these things. Whether we are little or great, let us keep the path of friendship clear, which our fathers made, and in which we have both travelled to this time.

The friends of the wicked counsellors of our king fell upon us, and

---

(1) The *talk* of the *Moheakounuck* or *Muhhekaneok* indians was delivered by Solomon Uhhaunnauwaumut, their chief sachem, at Stockbridge, the seat of the tribe, April 11, 1775, after a council of two days. The letter of the interpreter, containing the speech, was delayed in transmission or communication to a late period: it is copied below.

"Brothers! We have heard you speak by your letter—we thank you for it—we now make answer."

"Brothers! You remember when you first came over the great waters, I was great, and you was little, very small. I then took you in for a friend, and kept you under my arms, so that no one might injure you: since that time we have ever been true friends; there has never been any quarrel between us. But now our conditions are changed. You have become great and tall. You reach to the clouds.—You are seen all round the world, and I am become small, very little. I am not so high as your heel. Now you take care of me, and I look to you for protection."

"Brothers! I am sorry to hear of this great quarrel between you and Old England. It appears that blood must soon be shed to end this quarrel. We never till this day understood the foundation of this quarrel between you and the country you came from."

"Brothers! Whenever I see your blood running, you will soon find me about you to revenge my brother's blood. Although I am low and very small, I will gripe hold of your enemy's heel, that he cannot run so fast, and so light, as if he had nothing at his heels."

"Brothers! You know I am not so wise as you are, therefore I ask your advice in what I am now going to say. I have been thinking before you come to action to take a run to the westward, and feel the mind of my Indian brethren, the Six Nations, and know how they stand, whether they are on your side, or for your enemies. If I find they are against you, I will try to turn their minds. I think they will listen to me, for they have always looked this way for advice concerning all important news that comes from the rising of the sun. If they hearken to me, you will not be afraid of any danger from behind you. However their minds are affected, you shall soon know by me. Now I think I can do you more service in this way, than by marching off immediately to Boston, and staying there: it may be a great while before blood runs. Now, as I said, you are wiser than I, I leave this for your consideration, whether I come down immediately, or wait till I hear some blood is spilled."

"Brothers! I would not have you think by this that we are falling back from our engagements. We are ready to do any thing for your relief, and shall be guided by your counsel."

"Brothers! One thing I ask of you, if you send for me to fight, that you will let me fight in my own Indian way. I am not used to fight English fashion, therefore you must not expect I can train like your men. Only point out to me where your enemies keep, and that is all I shall want to know."

shed some blood, soon after we spake to you last, by our letter. But we, with a small twig, killed so many, and frightened them so much, that they have shut themselves up in our great town, called Boston, which they have made strong.

We have now made our hatchets and all our instruments of war sharp and bright. All the chief counsellors who live on this side the great water, are sitting in the grand council house in Philadelphia. When *they* give the word, we shall all, as one man, fall on, and drive our enemies out of their strong fort, and follow them till they shall take their hands out of our pouches, and let us sit in our council house, as we used to do, and as our fathers did in old times.

BROTHERS : Though you are small, yet you are wise: use your wisdom to help us. If you think it best, go and smoke your pipe with your indian brothers, towards the setting of the sun, and tell them all you hear, and all you see, and let us know what their wise men say. If some of your young men should have a mind to see what we are doing here, let them come down, and tarry among our warriors. We will provide for them while they are here.

BROTHERS : When you have any trouble, come and tell it to us, and we will help you.

To Capt. Solomon Uhhaunnauwaunmut, Chief Sachem of the Moheakounuck tribe of Indians, at Stockbridge.

[Whereas, it appears to this Congress, that great benefit may arise to the American cause, should our friends of the Stockbridge, or Moheakounuck tribe of Indians, send belts and messengers to the several tribes connected with them; and as the same may be attended with expense; therefore, *Resolved*, that the selectmen of the town of Stockbridge, for the time being, be a committee to promote the forwarding such messengers and belts, and that the committee aforesaid be allowed to draw out of the public moneys, in the hands of Stephen Nash, late collector for the town of Stockbridge aforesaid, any sum or sums, not exceeding fifteen pounds, for which said committee shall account to this, or some future Congress, or house of representatives, and be allowed all reasonable charges that have or may arise for promoting and forwarding the premises.]

The committee appointed to establish an allowance of provisions for the soldiers, reported. The further consideration of the report was put off to nine o'clock to-morrow morning.

A colonel's commission was delivered to Col. John Fellowes.

Adjourned to eight o'clock to-morrow morning.

A petition from the selectmen and others of the town of Manchester[1] was read, and committed to the committee who were appointed to consider the circumstances of the sea port towns.

Col. Bowers and Mr. Fisher, who were of the committee appointed to consider the petition of the convention of committees of the county of Worcester,[2] being absent, *Ordered*, that Major Bliss and Doct. Taylor be appointed in their room.

Col. Bowers, who was on the committee appointed to consider the situation and circumstances of the sea coasts, being absent, *Ordered*, that the Hon. Mr. Spooner be appointed in his room.

Ordered, That Capt. Stone of Oakham, Deacon Hovey, Col. Prescott, Col. Farley and Col. Grout, be a committee to consider what is proper to be done with the prisoners brought to this place from Arundel.

Ordered, That Capt. Goodrich, Mr. Mitchel and Mr. Johnson, be a committee to consider a petition from Abiathar Angel, and report.

A petition from the town of Berwick was read, and committed to the committee appointed to consider the situation and circumstances of the sea coasts.

The committee appointed to bring in a resolve for the purpose of enforcing two resolves of the Continental Congress, reported : the report was accepted, and with the said resolves of Congress here follow, viz. :

IN CONGRESS, May 17, 1775, *at Philadelphia.*

Resolved, That all exportations to Quebec, Nova Scotia, the Island of St. Johns, Newfoundland, Georgia, except the parish of St. Johns, and to East and West Florida, immediately cease; and that no provisions of any kind, or other necessaries, be furnished to the British fisheries on the American coasts, until it be otherwise determined by the Congress.

May 29.

Resolved, That no provisions or necessaries of any kind be exported to the island of Nantucket, except from the colony of the Massachu-

(1) The people of Manchester, suffering under the pressure of military duty, which interrupted the cultivation of the fields and the prosecution of the fishery, requested liberty to raise and employ a company of men for the defence of the town, to be placed on the provincial establishment, and attached to the regiment of the army stationed nearest to the petitioners.

(2) The convention of the committees of Worcester county, in addition to a former memorial, voted to remonstrate against the right of the delegates returned from the districts of Charlton and Paxton to hold their seats in Congress. The objections against the validity of the elections are not stated in the records.

setts Bay, the convention of which colony is desired to take measures for effectually providing the said island, upon their application to purchase the same, with as much provision as shall be necessary for its internal use, and no more. The Congress deeming it of great importance to North America, that the British fishery should not be furnished with provisions from this continent through Nantucket, earnestly recommend a vigilant execution of this resolve to all committees.

A true copy from the minutes.

CHARLES THOMPSON, *Sec'ry*.

The foregoing resolves of the Continental Congress, being read and considered, *Resolved*, that the same be forthwith printed in hand bills, together with this resolve, and dispersed in the several sea port towns in this colony, that due obedience may be paid to the same. Further, *Resolved*, that the inhabitants of the island of Nantucket have liberty to purchase such provisions as are necessary for the internal use of said island, in any of the New England governments; provided, nevertheless, that no provisions or necessaries of any kind be exported to the said island of Nantucket, without a permit in writing from the committee of safety of this colony, or such person or persons as they shall appoint to give such permit, expressing the quantity so to be transported, be first had and obtained; and that the same be exported from such port only, in this colony, as shall be expressed in the same permit.

The order of the day was moved for.

The report of the committee on the establishment of an allowance of provisions for the soldiers, was read and considered, and after debate thereon, was recommitted.

The committee on the petition from the county of Worcester reported, that it is the opinion of the committee, that the delegates chosen by the districts of Paxton and Charlton, as mentioned in said petition, have not a right to seats in this house.

Moved, That a commission be delivered to Col. John Glover, as colonel of a regiment in the Massachusetts army.

[Afternoon.]

The report of the committee on the petition from the county of Worcester was considered, and, after much debate, the question was put, whether said report be accepted, and it passed in the negative.

Ordered, That the guard who has in custody the prisoners from Arundel, be relieved by a guard from the town of Watertown.

Ordered, That Mr. Sayer be added to the committee, who were appointed to consider some measures for commissioning the officers of the army, in the room of Col. Porter, who has leave of absence.

Leave of absence was granted to the Rev. Mr. Thayer, and the Rev. Mr. Curtis, and it being moved that they be directed to return as soon as may be, the question was put, and it passed in the negative.

Col. Porter, who was of the committee to consider the letter of Mr. Gridley to the committee of safety, relative to the train, being absent, Mr. Partridge was appointed in his room.

Resolved, That the committee of safety be required, as soon as may be, to certify to this Congress, the names of such gentlemen as are candidates for the command of a regiment, with the number of privates that have been enlisted under them, and any other claims or pretensions that any gentleman may have to a commission in the service.

Ordered, That the papers exhibited to this Congress by Capt. Phelps be returned to him by Major Bliss.

Adjourned to nine o'clock to-morrow morning.

SATURDAY, June 10, 1775.

Ordered, That the committee of safety be directed to make return, in writing, to this Congress, as soon as may be, of the names of all those persons who claim, or offer themselves to be commissioned as colonels of regiments in the colony army, and are not commissioned, with any agreement that may have been made with any such persons by the committee of safety; as also, a state of those regiments, which such persons claim the command of, as to their numbers, equipments, and the time they have been engaged in service.

The committee appointed to consider what is proper to be done with the prisoners brought from Arundel, reported as follows, viz.:

The committee appointed to examine the persons and papers sent to this Congress, by the committee of the town of Arundel, have attended that service; and, after due perusal of said papers, Josiah Jones and Jonathan Hicks, therein referred to, were brought before them. Said Jones in his defence says, he had no concern with the sloop Polly, otherwise than as a passenger in her to Nova Scotia; notwithstanding which, it appears clearly to this committee, by said papers, as also by the evidence of Capt. Smith, master, herewith transmitted, that said Jones went on board said sloop as supercargo, in the service of general Gage, to bring hay and other articles to Boston, to supply our enemies. We find by said Jones' account of himself, that he went to Boston soon after the memorable Lexington battle, of the 19th of April last, in company with John Ruggles, of Hardwick, who was ordered by a committee to the said town of Hardwick; and that said Jones was know-ing to the proceedings of said committee against said Ruggles, before they set out together from Weston to take refuge in Boston; and that they left the common road, and went in the woods and difficult places, to pass the town of Roxbury. The committee, upon the whole, have not the least reason to doubt, of said Jones' being a notorious enemy to his country, and of his having been in the actual employment of our enemies against the just liberties of the people. [They] therefore beg leave to report the following order, viz. :

In Provincial Congress, June 10, 1775.

Ordered, That Josiah Jones, taken from the sloop Polly, be sent, with a sufficient guard, to the town of Concord, in the county of Mid-dlesex, and committed to the common jail, there to remain until the fur-ther orders of the Congress, or house of representatives of this colony.

Said Jonathan Hicks in his defence says, that since the public dis-putes respecting the liberties of the country, he has not liked the part that has been acted, in many respects, on either side, therefore could not see his way clear to join with any. Upon examination, the com-mittee find by evidence, that at Gardinerston, while he lived there, he expressed himself highly against committees of correspondence, &c., calling them rebels, and using other opprobrious language against the people who appeared for liberty, and endeavored to hinder their unity. That, also, while he the said Hicks lived at Plymouth, he was esteem-ed by the good people there, inimical to the liberties of his country by his general conduct, and that at certain times he appeared very high, and once drew his sword or spear upon certain persons. Said Hicks, upon the whole, owns his general conduct has been such, as the people for liberty call tory, but still says he is against the oppressive acts.

Said Hicks confesses, that the evening after the battle of Lexington aforesaid, he left Plymouth, and took shelter with the troops at Marsh-field, not thinking himself safe in the country; that he went with them to Boston, and there remained until he went on board the sloop Polly, with Jones, and says he designed for Halifax, there to tarry, if he could find business, in order to be out of the noise.

Capt. Smith, master of said sloop, can give no account of Hicks' business on board; all he can say is, he in general appeared inimical, calling the liberty people rebels, &c. The committee, therefore, beg leave to report the following order :

In Provincial Congress, *Watertown,* June 10, 1775.

Ordered, That Jonathan Hicks, taken from the sloop Polly, be sent, with a sufficient guard, to the town of Concord, in the county of Middlesex, and committed to the common jail, there to remain until the further orders of the Congress, or house of representatives of this colony.

Resolved, That the keeper of the jail in the county of Middlesex be directed to receive Messrs. Jones and Hicks, who were taken prisoners from the sloop Polly, at Arundel, and keep them in safe custody till further order, and provide them necessaries for their subsistence whilst in jail, and that the committee of correspondence for the town of Watertown, be directed to see that the resolves of Congress, respecting the said Jones and Hicks be forthwith carried into execution, and to take such guards as they think necessary for that purpose.

Ordered, That the Hon. Mr. Sever, Col. Otis and Mr. Davis, be added to the committee, who were appointed to consider the expediency of establishing a number of armed vessels for the protection of the sea coasts.

Ordered, That Major Hawley, Capt. Stone, of Framingham, Col. Parks, Hon. Mr. Sever, Mr. Johnson, Hon. Mr. Spooner and Deacon Plympton, be a committee to take into consideration the artificers which may be necessary for the army in the pay of this colony, and that they report, as soon as may be, in what way such artificers shall be established, the numbers wanted for the army at Cambridge and Roxbury of each kind, and the sum that is proper to be allowed them per month.

Ordered, That Mr. Whittemore, Capt. Dwight and Mr. Kollock, be a committee to bring in a resolve for the appointment of a number of armorers for the Massachusetts army, and for the establishment of their pay.

The resolve for establishing an allowance of provisions for the soldiers was again read, and accepted: and ordered to be printed in hand bills, and is as follows, viz.:

The committee appointed to make an establishment for the allowance for provisions for the soldiers of the Massachusetts army, beg leave to report the following resolve, viz.:

Resolved, That each soldier in the Massachusetts army shall have the following allowance per day, viz.:

1st. One pound of bread: 2d. Half a pound of beef and half a pound of pork; and if pork cannot be had, one pound and a quarter of beef; and one day in seven they shall have one pound and one quarter of salt fish, instead of one day's allowance of meat: 3d. One pint of milk, or, if milk cannot be had, one gill of rice: 4th. One quart of good spruce or malt beer: 5th. One gill of peas or beans, or other sauce equivalent: 6th. Six ounces of good butter per week: 7th. One pound of good common soap for six men per week: 8th. Half a pint of vinegar per week per man, if it can be had.

The committee appointed to inquire into the state of the army, reported, that, in order to execute their commission, it is necessary that they should be furnished with a copy of all recommendations for commissions, sent to this Congress by the committee of safety, and a list of all officers commissioned by the Congress, and asked leave to sit again. The report was accepted.

Ordered, That Mr. Sayer, Mr. Edwards and Major Fuller, be a committee to consider the proposal of the Hon. General Ward, respecting furloughs for the soldiers, and report.

Afternoon.

The petition of a number of the freeholders of Williamsburg[1] [was] read, and committed to Mr. Hale, Mr. Lyman and Col. Danielson.

The petition of Davis & Coverly[2] [was] read, and committed to Mr. Fairbanks, Mr. Webster and Col. Sawyer.

Monday next, three o'clock, P. M., was assigned to make choice of three delegates to meet those that may be sent from the other New England colonies.

The choice of two major generals [was] referred to Monday, five o'clock, P. M.

Hon. Col. Warren, Hon. Mr. Spooner, Doct. Taylor, Capt. Stone, Mr. Edwards, Col. Cobb, Col. Thompson, were appointed a committee to consider the expediency of establishing a number of armed vessels.

SUNDAY, June 11, 1775.

[The Congress] met at eight o'clock, and adjourned to half past three, P. M.

Resolved, That the Hon. Major Hawley, Hon. Mr. Spooner, Hon. Col. Warren and Hon. Col. Foster, have leave to offer, for the consideration of this Congress, an address which they have prepared for the Continental Congress. The same being read and amended, was accepted, and ordered to be transcribed, and signed by the Hon. Major Hawley as vice president, and sent immediately, by express, to Philadelphia; and that the committee of supplies be desired to procure some person to carry it. It is as follows, viz. :

(1) Letters from the town clerk and other inhabitants of Williamsburg declare that the meeting held for election of a member of the Congress was illegal, but assign no specific informalities.

(2) The petitioners asked leave to exchange a quantity of goods owned by them in Boston, for similar merchandise in Marlborough, the property of a merchant residing in the former town.

May it please your honors:

The situation of any colony, or people, perhaps was never before such as made it more necessary for fully exercising the powers of civil government, than the present state and situation of the colony of the Massachusetts Bay. The embarrassments, delays, disappointments and obstructions, in executing every undertaking necessary for the preservation of our lives, and much more of our property, are so great and many, as that they cannot be represented, or enumerated: and that is chiefly to be attributed to our want of a settled civil polity or government: besides, every thing necessary for the abovesaid most important purposes, which is in some degree effected, is done in the most expensive manner: in short, although the times we are fallen into, and the prospects before us, are such as require the utmost economy, yet, nothing of the kind can be preserved in our present state.

There are, in many parts of this colony, alarming symptoms of the abatement of the sense, in the minds of some people, of the sacredness of private property, which is plainly assignable to the want of civil government; and your honors must be fully sensible, that a community of goods and estate, will soon be followed with the utter waste and destruction of the goods themselves; besides, the necessity of civil government appears more and more apparent from the extreme difficulty of maintaining the public peace without it; although we can truly say, much fewer enormities and breaches of the peace have happened among us, than it was natural to expect, from the contemplation of such a state as we have been cast into.

May it please your honors: The pressing weight of our distresses has necessitated the sending a special post to obtain your immediate advice upon this subject; and we do most earnestly entreat, that you would, as soon as possible, despatch the messenger with such advice.

Our former application to you, of the 16th of May last, has rendered it unnecessary that we should further enlarge upon this subject; and, to prevent repetition, we beg leave to refer you to our letter of that date.

The army under the command of general Gage, we estimate to amount, at least, to 5000 men, well appointed, under the command of generals of character and experience, and prepared with every thing necessary for action, exclusive of the additional strength derived from negroes, which the general has taken into his service, and disaffected Americans. We have great reason to apprehend, that a reenforcement of at least eight regiments of foot and one of horse may be hourly expected. We enclose a copy of an intercepted letter from Major Sherriff, which exhibits to you one ground of this apprehension.[1] We have had under our consideration, the propriety and necessity of augmenting our army, notwithstanding our great embarrassment, and though we have not yet adopted it, nothing, perhaps, but the more ample provision of the neighboring colonies, will relieve that necessity.

The depredations and piracies frequently committed on our sea coasts, and the little trade which remains to us, whereby, among other capital articles, the importation of ammunition and provisions is almost totally obstructed, and threatens our ruin; have also occasioned our contemplating steps to prevent those inconveniences, by [*fitting] out a number of armed vessels, with sufficient strength to encounter their small though numerous cutters.

We shall only add, that, as the seat of war, with all its attendant distresses, have, for the present, taken their principal residence here, we should consider it as a happy event, if you should think proper to adjourn to some part of the continent not so far distant, that the advice and aid of the [bContinental Congress] may be more expeditiously afforded upon any emergency.

Adjourned to Monday morning, eight o'clock.

MONDAY, June 12, 1775.

Ordered, That Mr. Wheeler, Deacon Baker and Mr. Webster, be a committee to consider some measures for preventing the violation of the sabbath, and to bring in a resolve for this purpose.

Resolved, That five o'clock in the afternoon, be assigned for the consideration of the report of the committee, who were appointed to bring in a resolve for giving a free currency to the bills of credit of this and the other colonies.

Ordered, That the Hon. Mr. Spooner, Hon. Col. Gerrish and Doct. Whiting, be a committee to consider the petition from the committee at Charlestown, and report.

Resolved, That the secretary have liberty to procure such assistance, from time to time, as he shall think necessary.

a [fixing.]   b [continent.]

(1) The letter of Major William Sherriff, deputy quarter master general, was dated at Boston, May 29, 1775, and addressed to Thomas Williams, Esq., keeper of the king's ordnance at Annapolis, in Nova Scotia. The writer speaks of the profits and rewards the people of the eastern province might receive, if they would collect forage and provisions for the royal army in Massachusetts. "On the other hand," he says, " if they give themselves airs, and follow the example of these mad men, they will consider how easily government can chastise them, and they may rely upon it they will, and that immediately too: but I hope they will consider their interest better, and make all the money they can" .... " We are in the same situation, as when I wrote you last, except the addition of twelve hundred troops lately arrived from England. The regiment of horse, and eight other regiments are hourly expected, when I hope you will hear better accounts from us."

Resolved, That two persons be appointed to repair to the fortress of Ticonderoga, to examine into the state of that fortress, and of affairs there, and to act in such a manner as they shall be directed by this Congress, and that four o'clock in the afternoon be assigned for the choice of such persons, by ballot, and that the Hon. Major Hawley, Hon. Col. Warren and Mr. Sullivan, be a committee to prepare instructions for such delegates.

The committee who were appointed to consider the expediency of establishing a number of armed vessels, reported : the consideration of the report was put off to ten o'clock to-morrow morning.

Hon. Mr. Dexter, one of the committee who were appointed to prepare letters to the Continental Congress, New York and the New England governments, being absent, *Ordered*, that the Hon. Mr. Spooner be appointed in his room.

Ordered, That Mr. Sayer be directed forthwith to fill up and deliver commissions to the officers of Col. Whitcomb's regiment.

Ordered, [That] Mr. [*Holten], Mr. Mitchell and Mr. Colvill, be a committee to consider the petition of Mr. Ebenezer Prout.

Ordered, That Doct. Whiting, Doct. Taylor and Mr. Parks, be a committee to consider some method of supplying the several surgeons of the army with medicines.

The committee appointed to prepare a letter to the Continental Congress, &c., reported the following, which was accepted, viz. :

May it please your honors:

The views of administration having been made evident, by their conduct for some years past, and the late regulations of civil and ecclesiastical polity of Quebec having clearly discovered an intention to make use of the Canadians as engines to reduce this continent to slavery, it has been found absolutely necessary for the preservation of the liberties of America, to take possession of the important pass of Ticonderoga, and to send forward a sufficient force to hold the same against any attempt which may be made to retake it, and to prevent general Carlton from sending forces by the way of the lakes to annoy and distress the frontiers; but, as we apprehend, there never has been any intention to give the least disturbance to our brethren of Canada, to whom we most sincerely wish the full and free enjoyment of their civil and religious rights. We humbly request, that your honors would take such steps, to prevent any false impressions, which our enemies may attempt to make on their minds concerning our designs, or to remove any such

a [Folten.]

41

as have already been made, as you, in your wisdom, shall think most expedient : as we look upon it to be of the utmost importance that there should no jealousies subsist between them and the other colonies. We also have had the most disagreeable accounts of methods taken to fill the minds of the Indian tribes adjacent to these colonies with sentiments very injurious to us ; particularly we have been informed that Col. Guy Johnson has taken great pains with the Six Nations, in order to bring them into a belief, that it is designed by the colonies to fall upon them and cut them off. We therefore pray you would, with all the speed convenient, use your very great influence in guarding against the evil intended by this malevolent misrepresentation. And we have wrote to our sister colonies in New England, and to New York, requesting they would make a similar application to you respecting these matters.

We are your most obedient, humble servants.

Resolved, That the vote for choosing two persons to repair to the fortress of Ticonderoga be so far reconsidered, as that there be three persons chosen, instead of two, for that service.

[Afternoon.]

Ordered, That Col. Farley, Major Brooks and Mr. Cross, be a committee to consider and report what is proper to be done with the grass growing on the estates of the refugees at Cambridge, Charlestown, Roxbury and Milton, [who reported as follows :]

The committee appointed to take into consideration the resolve of the committee of safety relative to certain quantities of grass growing on the lands of the refugees in and about Cambridge, have attended that service, and beg leave to report by way of resolve.

Resolved, That it be recommended to the committee of safety, that they appoint some person or persons in the towns hereafter mentioned, viz. : Cambridge, Charlestown, Roxbury and Milton, to cut the grass and secure the hay growing on the estates of the refugees, in the above mentioned towns, in some convenient place, for the benefit of the colony, as to them shall seem meet.

Ordered, That Mr. Sullivan, Hon. Col. Warren and Col. Gerrish, be a committee to consider what is best to be done with respect to a vessel said to be going from Salem to New Providence for fruit and turtle for the army at Boston.

Resolved, That Mr. Gerry have leave to bring in a resolve for preventing the exportation of fish and other provisions.

The resolve was accordingly read and accepted, and ordered to be printed in hand bills, and sent to the several maritime towns in this colony, and is as follows, viz. :

Whereas, the enemies of America are multiplying their cruelties towards the inhabitants of the New England colonies, by seizing provision vessels, either the property of, or intended to supply them, and also by plundering the stock of cattle, sheep, &c., on their sea coasts; [therefore] *Resolved*, that it be, and it is hereby, recommended to the inhabitants of the towns and districts in this colony that they forthwith exert themselves to prevent the exportation of fish and all other kinds of provision, excepting such only, as shall be intended to supply the inhabitants of the colonies aforesaid, and as, in the opinion of the selectmen, and committee of correspondence, and committees of safety of the towns where the same shall be stored, may, with prudence, be shipped for conveyance by water for the purpose aforesaid. And it is strongly recommended to the selectmen, committees of correspondence, and committees of safety, thoughout the colony, that they cause this resolve to be strictly executed.

The committee appointed to consider some method for supplying the surgeons in the army with medicine, reported : the report was read and accepted, and is as follows, viz. :

The committee appointed to take into consideration a complaint that the surgeons in the army are not properly furnished with medicines, have attended that service, and beg leave to report : that whereas, it appears that there is not, as yet, a sufficient number of medicine chests provided, to furnish each regiment with a distinct chest; and whereas, the committee of supplies are making provision for the supplying of each regiment with such medicine chests as soon as possible : therefore, *Resolved*, that the committee of supplies be, and hereby are directed, immediately to furnish the surgeon of the first regiment at Cambridge, and also the surgeon of the first regiment at Roxbury, each of them, with a medicine chest, for the present; and that all the other surgeons in the army at Cambridge and Roxbury, have free recourse to the said chests, and be supplied from them, from time to time, as they shall find occasion, until more ample provision shall be made for them : all which is humbly submitted, and the committee beg leave to sit again.   WILLIAM WHITING, *per order.*

Ordered, That the same committee be appointed to examine into the medical stores, and make a list of what is necessary for the supplying each regiment, that the same may be laid before the committee : and that the same committee consider what medicines are necessary, and bring in a list of what medicines are in the medicinal store : and that they be directed to report what instruments are necessary for the surgeons of the army.

The committee appointed to consider what is best to be done relative to a vessel going from Salem to New Providence, reported : the report was read and accepted, and is as follows :

Whereas, this Congress has been informed, that a schooner belonging to the Ervings, in Boston, is fitted out, under color of being chartered by one Thompson, who has lately fled from Medford to Boston ; but is really destined to Salem, and from there to New Providence, to get fruit, turtle, and provisions of other kinds, for the sustenance and feasting of those troops, who are, as pirates and robbers, committing daily hostilities and depredations on the good people of this colony, and all America ; it is, therefore, *Resolved*, that Capt. Samuel McCobb, a member of this Congress, be immediately despatched to Salem and Marblehead, to secure said Thompson, and prevent said vessel from going said voyage, and cause the said Thompson to be brought to this Congress : and the committees of correspondence, safety and inspection of said towns, and all the good people of this colony, are directed to give the said Capt. McCobb all needed assistance therein.

Ordered, That Mr. Sullivan, Capt. Stone and Major Bliss, be a committee to count and sort the votes for three gentlemen as a committee to meet committees from the other governments of New England, at Worcester, on the 28th of June current.

The committee, having attended that service, reported, that the Hon. Mr. Dexter, the Hon. Major Hawley and the Hon. Mr. Sever, were chosen. The Hon. Major Hawley and the Hon. Mr. Sever, having desired to be excused, and having offered their reasons therefor, they were excused accordingly ; whereupon,

Resolved, That ten o'clock to-morrow morning, be assigned for the choice of two persons, in the room of Major Hawley and Mr. Sever, to attend the said convention at Worcester, on the 28th of June current.

Ordered, That Mr. Sullivan, Capt. Stone and Major Bliss, be a committee to count and sort the votes for three gentlemen to go to Ticonderoga.

The committee having attended that service reported, that the Hon. Mr. Spooner, Hon. Col. Foster and Mr. Sullivan, were chosen.

Resolved, That the choice of two major generals, be referred to to-morrow morning, eleven o'clock.

Ordered, That the petition from the county of Cumberland, laid on the table by the committee who were appointed to consider of it, be committed to the committee who were appointed to consider the circumstances of the sea coasts.

The report of the committee of safety, relative to the claims of those who stand as candidates for commissions in the army, &c., was read, and, with the papers accompanying it, was committed to the Hon. Major Hawley, Col. Farley, Capt. Greenleaf, Doct. Taylor, Capt. Stone, Mr. Partridge and Col. Sayer.

The committee on Mr. Prout's petition reported, that he have leave to withdraw it. The report was accepted.

It was moved and seconded, that the resolve for choosing committees to meet committees from the other governments in New England, at Worcester, the 28th current, be reconsidered: and it was thereupon *Resolved*, that the further consideration of this motion be referred to ten o'clock to-morrow morning.

The petitions of Col. Brewer and his officers, being read, were committed to the committee to whom were this day committed the report of the committee of safety, and the papers accompanying it.

The committee on the petition of Davis & Coverly, reported: the report was read and accepted, and is as follows:

Whereas, application has been made to this Congress by Messrs. Davis & Coverly, merchants of Boston, representing that they have a quantity of English goods now in Boston, and that Henry Barns, of Marlborough, has a quantity of English goods, nearly of the same quality, in said Marlborough, and therefore pray that they may have leave to make an exchange: *Resolved*, that the prayer of said petition be granted, and that the petitioners have leave to make the exchange asked for.

The committee appointed to bring in a resolve for appointing a number of armorers, reported.[1] The report being read and amended, was [ªaccepted.]

TUESDAY, June 13, 1775.

A letter from Governor Trumbull was read, enclosing a letter from Col. Arnold, and three resolves of the Continental Congress: all which were committed to the committee who were appointed to prepare instructions to the committees that are to repair to Ticonderoga.

Resolved, That there be twenty-three regiments commissioned, exclusive of the regiment of matrosses.

Ordered, That Mr. Webster, Col. Richmond and Major Wood, be

a [accepted and is as follows.]

(1) The report has not been entered on the journal, nor is it preserved on the files.

a committee to consider the petition of Abner Graves and others, and that they hear the petitioners, and notify Capt. Dexter of time and place.[1]

[The] order of the day [was] moved for.

Absent members [were] directed to attend.

Resolved, That the further consideration of the report relative to the establishment of armed vessels, be put off to three o'clock, in the afternoon, and that the committee of safety and committee of supplies be notified of this resolve.

Ordered, That Col. Otis and Col. Grout be added to the committee who were appointed to deliver out commissions.

Resolved, That the resolve for the appointment of a convention of committees from the several governments at Worcester, be reconsidered, as well as the vote whereby a committee was appointed by this Congress, and the vote assigning a time for the choice of two members in the room of two members of that committee who were excused.

Ordered, That Mr. Partridge, Mr. Sayer, and Major Brooks, be a committee to receive and count the votes for the major generals.

Ordered, That only one major general be chosen at a time, and that the gentleman first chosen be the first major general.

Resolved, That the committees who may at any time be appointed to receive and count votes for the choice of any person to any office or appointment, be strictly enjoined to allow no member to shift or change a vote after it is put into the hat.

The committee appointed to receive the votes for the first major general, reported, that Col. John Whitcomb was chosen.

Resolved, That the choice of the second major general be referred to five o'clock in the afternoon.

An account of Mr. Charles Cotton was read, and committed to Mr. Pickering, Mr. Batchelder, and Mr. Dwight.

An account from Mr. Taylor, was likewise exhibited, and committed to Col. Richmond, Mr. Singletary, and Mr. Hale, to examine, consider of, and report upon.

Two accounts of Mr. John Brown were also read, and committed to Mr. Hale, Mr. Edwards, Mr. Vose, Col. Thompson, and Major Bliss.

Ordered, That Mr. Lothrop, Mr. Fox, and Mr. Fessenden, be a committee to consider the expediency of appointing Ensign Foley to be an armorer in the Massachusetts army, in addition to the number

(1) The petition related to military rank and organization.

which this Congress have ordered to be appointed, and to consider what his pay shall be, if they think it proper he should be appointed.

The committee on Charles Colten's account, reported; whereupon, *Resolved*, that the receiver general be, and hereby is directed, to pay to Mr. Charles Colten out of the public treasury, the sum of £13 18s. 8d. in full for his account this day exhibited to, and allowed by, this Congress.

The committee appointed yesterday to consider the report of the committee of safety, reported the following resolve, which was accepted; and Capt. Stone, Capt. Dwight, and Mr. Kollock, were ordered to give due information thereof to the colonels therein mentioned, viz :

Resolved, That Colonels Glover, Heath, David Brewer, Robinson, Woodbridge, Henshaw, Little, Jonathan Brewer, be directed, by next Thursday morning, at 8 o'clock, to make a true return to the committee on the claims and pretensions of the several gentlemen claiming to be commissioned as colonels; of the number of captains, who, with their respective companies, do choose to serve under the above named gentlemen respectively as colonels; and of the number of men; and of the number of effective fire-arms in each company; and of the place or places where said companies are : on pain of forfeiting all pretensions to a commission of a colonel, in case of making a false return.

Afternoon.

An account of Mrs. Dorothy Coolidge was read, and committed to Doct. Taylor, Col. Thompson, and Mr. Bent.

[The] order of the day [was] moved for.

The report of the committee on the expediency of establishing a number of armed vessels was considered, and after a very long debate, the further consideration of it was referred to Friday next, at eleven o'clock, A. M.

The committee who were appointed to prepare instructions to the gentlemen chosen by this Congress to repair to Ticonderoga, reported : the report was read, and accepted, and is as follows, viz.:

To Walter Spooner, Jedediah Foster, and James Sullivan, Esquires :

You are directed to proceed, as soon as may be, to the posts of Ticonderoga and Crown Point, by the road through the new settlements, called the New Hampshire Grants; that you carefully observe the quality of the said road, and judge of the feasibleness of transporting provisions by the said road to the waters of Lake Champlain; that you take with you copies of the commission and instructions of the committee of safety to Col. Benedict Arnold, and inform yourselves as fully as you shall be able, in what manner the said Col. Arnold has executed his said commission and instructions.

That you make and give to the said Arnold, and any men whom he shall, by virtue of the said commission and instructions retain in the service of this colony, such orders as to you shall seem meet : provided always, that you do not authorize the said Arnold to engage and retain in the pay of this Colony, as soldiers, a greater number than that specified in his said commission and instructions, and provided that the said Arnold and his men whom he has retained are free and willing to continue at one or both of the said posts, under the command of such chief officer as is, or shall be appointed by the government of Connecticut; and in case you shall order such number of men to be continued at or near the said posts in the pay of this colony, as you shall judge it necessary there should be, that you appoint a committee of one or more persons, in the pay of this colony, to provide supplies for such men, and a commissary to deal out such supplies to them : which committee and commissary you are to appoint in writing under your hands.

And you are to determine and order, respecting the said Arnold's continuing in the commission and pay of this colony, as to you shall appear most for the general service and safety, after having made yourselves fully acquainted with the spirit, capacity, and conduct of the said Arnold. And in case you shall judge it proper to discharge the said Arnold, that you direct him to return to this colony, and render his account of the disposition of the money, ammunition, and other things which he received at his setting out upon his expedition, and also of the charges he has incurred, and the debts which he has contracted in behalf of this colony, by virtue of the commission and instructions aforesaid.

And in case you shall find any men at the said posts properly retained, and engaged there in the service of this colony, that you cause them and their arms to be mustered, and that to such as shall pass muster, you pay out of the money which you shall receive from our receiver general for that purpose, the same advance pay as is by order of Congress paid to such men as are retained and mustered to serve within the colony ; and in case you shall not find any men at the said posts, properly engaged and retained in the service of this colony, or that the number which you shall find so retained, shall be much short of the number which said Arnold was empowered to enlist, that then you, if you shall judge that the effectual security of the said posts shall require it, and if you shall also find a proper person in those parts, fit and suitable for the command of four hundred men, or such less number, as together with such as you shall find ordered and posted there by any other colony or colonies, and shall also find that soldiers can be raised in those parts so seasonably, as that thereby the effectual maintenance of the said posts may be served or promoted ; you are to appoint meet persons to be officers and commanders for such a number of men as you shall order to be enlisted, and give the necessary orders for raising, enlisting, and maintaining them, for such term as you shall judge necessary for defence of said posts, and also appoint some sufficient and faithful man as muster master and pay master of such men, and leave sufficient money in his hands for that purpose, taking proper receipts and his security that the money so left shall be applied to that use. And you are to take a careful survey of the ordnance stores, and ordnance at those posts, together with all other articles necessary for the maintenance thereof, and report the state thereof to this Congress. And if you shall find it necessary to purchase powder for the men who shall be retained there on the part of this colony, that you procure the same, and so much as you shall judge needful, in the best and most expeditious way you can, on the credit of this colony.   And in general, you are hereby fully empowered to do every thing, in behalf of this colony, for the effectual securing and maintaining those posts which you shall judge necessary, equal to the importance of the same.

You are further directed, when you shall have transacted what you are by the foregoing instructions authorized to do and transact, at the posts abovesaid, by the very first opportunity, to advise the General American Congress thereof, as also of your opinion of the necessity and importance of maintaining the said posts for the general defence of these colonies : and when you shall have made yourselves fully acquainted with the state and condition of the said posts, and the dispositions and establishments which you shall find are made for maintaining of them, if you shall judge that any further provisions are necessary for securing and maintaining them, you are directed, fully and respectfully, to signify your thoughts thereon to the General Congress. You are also directed to advise the general convention of the colony of New York, and the governor of the colony of Connecticut, respectively, of what you shall order and transact, by virtue of the said instructions.

The committee appointed to consider the expediency of appointing Ensign Falley, of Col. Danielson's regiment, an armorer in the Massa-

42

chusetts army, in addition to the number already ordered, and to consider what his pay shall be, if it is thought proper by this Congress, he should be appointed, have attended that service, and beg leave to report as follows, viz :

That, whereas, it has been represented to your committee, that the armorers, or many of them, who are already established, are very imperfect in the business they profess, and that the above said Falley is a complete master of the same ; in consideration of which, your committee think it of the highest importance, that he (the said Falley) should be employed in said department, and be allowed and paid forty shillings per month, in addition to his pay as an ensign, and be under the same rules and regulations as the other armorers already appointed, or to be appointed ; all which is humbly submitted.

ISAAC LOTHROP, *per order.*

Ordered, That the president, Col. Warren, Col. Palmer, Mr. Sever and Doct. Taylor, be a committee to consider the subject matter of a late extraordinary proclamation of general Gage.[1]

---

(1) The celebrated proclamation of general Gage was promulgated June 12, 1775.

By his excellency, the honorable Thomas Gage, Esq., governor and commander in chief, in and over his majesty's province of Massachusetts Bay, and vice admiral of the same :

A PROCLAMATION.

" Whereas, the infatuated multitudes, who have long suffered themselves to be conducted by certain well known incendiaries and traitors, in a fatal progression of crimes against the constitutional authority of the state, have, at length, proceeded to avowed rebellion ; and the good effects which were expected to arise from the patience and lenity of the king's government, have been often frustrated, and are now rendered hopeless, by the influence of the same evil counsels ; it only remains for those who are entrusted with supreme rule as well for the punishment of the guilty as the protection of the well affected, to prove they do not bear the sword in vain."

" The infringements which have been committed upon the most sacred rights of the crown and the people of Great Britain, are too many to enumerate on one side, and are all too atrocious to be palliated on the other. All unprejudiced people who have been witnesses of the late transactions in this and the neighboring provinces, will find, upon a transient review, marks of premeditation and conspiracy that would justify the fulness of chastisement : and even those who are least acquainted with facts, cannot fail to receive a just impression of their enormity, in proportion as they discover the arts and assiduity by which they have been falsified or concealed. The authors of the present unnatural revolt, never daring to trust their cause or their actions to the judgment of an impartial public, or even to the dispassionate reflection of their followers, have uniformly placed their chief confidence in the suppression of truth : and while indefatigable and shameless pains have been taken to obstruct every appeal to the real interest of the people of America, the grossest forgeries, calumnies, and absurdities that ever insulted human understanding, have been imposed upon their credulity. The press, that distinguished appendage of public liberty, and when fairly and impartially employed, its best support, has been invariably prostituted to the most contrary purposes : the animated language of ancient and virtuous times, calculated to vindicate and promote the just rights and interest of mankind, has been applied to countenance the most abandoned violation of those sacred blessings ; and not only from the flagitious prints, but from the popular harangues of the times, men have been taught to depend upon activity in treason, for the security of their persons and properties : till, to complete the horrid profanation of terms and of ideas, the name of GOD has been introduced in the pulpits, to excite and justify devastation and massacre."

" The minds of men having been thus gradually prepared for the worst extremities, a number of

Resolved, That Mr. Sullivan have liberty to use the horse in Mr. Fowle's pasture in this town, which was taken lately from Noddle's island, for his journey to Ticonderoga.

Adjourned till to-morrow morning, eight o'clock.

armed persons, to the amount of many thousands, assembled, on the 19th of April last, and, from behind walls and lurking holes, attacked a detachment of the king's troops, who, not expecting so consummate an act of phrenzy, unprepared for vengeance, and willing to decline it, made use of their arms only in their own defence. "

"Since that period, the rebels, deriving confidence from impunity, have added insult to outrage ; have repeatedly fired upon the king's ships and subjects, with cannon and small arms; have possessed the roads, and other communications by which the town of Boston was supplied with provisions ; and with a preposterous parade of military arrangement, they affect to hold the army besieged ; while part of their body make daily and indiscriminate invasions upon private property, and with a wantonness of cruelty over incident to lawless tumult, carry depredation and distress wherever they turn their steps. The actions of the 19th of April are of such notoriety, as must baffle all attempts to contradict them ; and the flames of buildings and other property from the islands and adjacent country, for some weeks past, spread a melancholy confirmation of the subsequent assertion."

"In this exigency of complicated calamities, I avail myself of the last effort within the bounds of my duty to spare the effusion of blood, to offer, and I do hereby, in his majesty's name, offer and promise his most gracious pardon to all persons who shall forthwith lay down their arms, and return to the duties of peaceable subjects: excepting only from the benefit of such pardon, SAMUEL ADAMS and JOHN HANCOCK, whose offences are of too flagitious a nature to admit of any other consideration than that of condign punishment."

"And, to the end, that no person within the limits of this proffered mercy, may plead ignorance of the consequence of refusing it, I, by these presents, proclaim, not only the persons above named and excepted, but also all their adherents, associates and abettors ; meaning to comprehend in these terms, all and every person, and persons, of what class, denomination, or description soever, who have appeared in arms against the king's government, and shall not lay down the same as before mentioned ; and likewise all such as shall so take arms after the date hereof, or shall, in any wise, protect or conceal such offenders, or assist them with money, provision, cattle, arms, ammunition, carriages, or any other necessary for subsistence, or offence ; or shall hold secret correspondence with them, by letter, message, signal, or otherwise ; to be rebels and traitors, and as such to be treated."

"And whereas, during the continuance of the present unnatural rebellion, justice cannot be administered by the common law of the land, the course whereof has, for a long time past, been violently impeded, and wholly interrupted, from whence results a necessity for using and exercising the law martial ; I have, therefore, thought fit, by the authority vested in me by the royal charter to this province, to publish, and I do hereby publish, proclaim and order, the use and exercise of the law martial, within and throughout this province, for so long a time as the present unhappy occasion shall necessarily require ; whereof all persons are hereby required to take notice, and govern themselves, as well to maintain order and regularity among the peaceable inhabitants of the province, as to resist, encounter, and subdue the rebels and traitors above described by such as shall be called upon for those purposes."

"To these inevitable, but I trust salutary measures, it is a far more pleasing part of my duty to add the assurance of protection and support, to all, who, in so trying a crisis, shall manifest their allegiance to the king, and affection to the parent state: so that such persons as may have been intimidated to quit their habitations in the course of this alarm, may return to their respective callings and professions ; and stand distinct and separate from the parricides of the constitution, till GOD in his mercy shall restore to his creatures in this distracted land, that system of happiness from which they have been seduced, the religion of peace, and liberty founded upon law."

"Given at Boston, this twelfth day of June, in the fifteenth year of the reign of his majesty George the third, by the grace of God, of Great Britain, France and Ireland, king, defender of the faith, &c. Anno domini, 1775.   THOMAS GAGE."

"By his excellency's command,   THOMAS FLUCKER, *Secretary.*"

"*God save the King.*"

WEDNESDAY, June 14, 1775.

Resolved, That the receiver general be and hereby is directed to pay the sum of four hundred pounds to the committee who have been appointed by this Congress to repair to Ticonderoga, to be by said committee appropriated as advance pay to the men enlisted under Col. Benedict Arnold : said committee to be accountable therefor.

Resolved, That the receiver general be, and hereby is directed, to advance the sum of twenty pounds to the committee, who have been appointed by this Congress to go to Ticonderoga, in cash, or bills of credit, at the option of said committee, for their expenses, they to be accountable therefor.

The committee appointed to consider the petition of Abner Graves and others, reported, that the petitioners have leave to withdraw their petition. The report was accepted.

Ordered, That Capt. Stone, Col. Warren, Col. Grout, Mr. North and Col. Otis, be a committee to consider the report of Col. Thompson and the petition of Mr. Parry, and report.

Resolved, That the first Thursday in July next, be appointed to be observed as a day of fasting and prayer throughout this colony, and that the Hon. Col. Palmer, Hon. Mr. Sever and Mr. Hopkins, be a committee to bring in a resolve for this purpose.

Ordered, That Col. Robinson, Mr. Webster, Major Fuller, Capt. Holmes and Mr. Edwards, be a committee to consider some way and means of furnishing those who are destitute of arms in the Massachusetts army.

Ordered, That the committee who were chosen to repair to Ticonderoga, be directed to revise the papers that respect the fortress there, and take such as they may think they shall want, and that this Congress will not have occasion for.

Ordered, That Mr. Phillips, Mr. Jewett and Mr. Hopkins, be a committee to devise some means for securing the library and apparatus of Harvard College.

Ordered, That Col. Gerrish, Mr. Parker and Mr. Caldwell, be a committee to consider the request of Joseph Palmer (quarter master general) for providing tents or barracks for the army at Cambridge.

Ordered, That three o'clock this afternoon be assigned for the choice of a second major general, and the committees who are now out be notified of the same.

Ordered, That the consideration of a report for giving a currency to the bills of credit of the other governments, be referred to four o'clock this afternoon.

Ordered, That Mr. Chadwick, Mr. Lothrop, Col. Smith, Mr. Stearns and Capt. Ellis, be a committee to consider the propriety of supplying the generals of the Massachusetts army at Cambridge and Roxbury, with some necessary household furniture.

Ordered, That Col. Coffin, Doct. Taylor and Mr. Pickering, be a committee to disperse the resolves of Congress relative to the embargo laid upon the exportation of fish, &c.

[Afternoon.]

Upon a motion made, Col. Prescott was chosen to countersign the notes, instead of Col. Foster, absent, who was appointed for that purpose.

The order of the day [was] moved for.

Mr. Lothrop, Capt. Cushing and Capt. Dwight, were chosen a committee to count and sort the votes for a second major general, who reported that Doct. Joseph Warren was chosen.

Resolved, That Col. Grout, Col. Berry and Col. Otis, be a committee to wait on the Hon. John Whitcomb, Esq., and inform him this Congress have made choice of him for first major general of the Massachusetts army, and desire his answer to this Congress of his acceptance of said trust; also, to wait on the Hon. Joseph Warren, Esq., and inform him this Congress have made choice of him for second major general of the Massachusetts army, and desire his answer to this Congress of his acceptance of said trust.

The committee appointed to consider some measures for preventing the violation of the sabbath, reported : the report was recommitted.

The committee appointed to devise some measures for securing the library and apparatus of Harvard College, reported : the report was recommitted for amendment.

Mr. Smith, Mr. Lothrop and Major Brooks, were chosen on the committee appointed to take into consideration the artificers, which may be necessary for the army in pay of this colony, instead of Major Hawley, Capt. Stone of Framingham, and Hon. Mr. Spooner, absent.

Major Davis [was] chosen instead of Hon. Mr. Spooner, absent, on the committee appointed to consider a petition from Charlestown.

The committee appointed to bring in a resolve for a day of fasting and prayer, reported : the report was recommitted for amendment, viz : that the following things might be mentioned : blessing on the Continental Congress; unity of the colonies; health; fruitful seasons; &c., &c.

Col. Richmond, per order, reported the following resolve :

Whereas, it appears to this Congress, that it is absolutely necessary that proper officers be put in commission to command the train of artillery, and that it be done without delay: *Resolved*, that the committee of supplies be directed forthwith to recommend such officers to this Congress, as they shall think proper for the purposes aforesaid.

The consideration of the currency of the notes for the payment of soldiers, [was] assigned to to-morrow morning, nine o'clock.

Mr. Samuel Thatcher was appointed to number the notes, instead of Mr. Samuel Phillips, who is otherwise engaged.

Resolved, That the receiver general be, and hereby is directed, to supply Col. Robinson to-morrow, with such money for advance pay for the soldiers, as he was to have received this day.

THURSDAY, June 15, 1775.

Ordered, That Mr. Gridley's letter respecting officers of the train, and artificers, be committed to the committee who were appointed the 10th instant, to consider how many artificers were necessary, &c.

Ordered, That Col. Barrett, Capt. Dwight and Capt. Page, be a committee to consider what measures it would be proper to take, that the army may be supplied with no provisions but what are good in kind.

The resolve relative to securing the library and apparatus of Harvard College, was read and accepted, and is as follows, viz. :

Whereas, it is expedient that those apartments in Harvard Hall, under the immediate charge of the professor of philosophy and librarian of Harvard College, be evacuated, *Resolved*, that the library, apparatus, and other valuables of Harvard College, be removed, as soon as may be, to the town of Andover; [and] that Mr. Samuel Phillips, Mr. Daniel Hopkins, and Dummer Jewett, Esq., be a committee to consult with the reverend, the president, the Hon. Mr. Winthrop and the librarian, or such of them as may be conveniently obtained, and with them to engage some suitable person or persons in said town, to transport, receive, and take the charge of the above mentioned effects; that said committee join with those gentlemen, in employing proper persons for packing said library, apparatus, and such other articles as they shall judge expedient, and take all due care that it be done with the greatest safety and despatch: and as the packages shall be completed, that they give notice to those engaged to receive them: the charges to be laid before this, or some future Congress, or house of assembly of this province.

Ordered, That the letters prepared for the Continental Congress,

New York, and the several governments in New England, be authenticated and sent forward as soon as may be. They are as follow, viz. :

Considering the exposed state of the frontiers of some of the colonies, the danger that the inhabitants of Canada may possibly have disagreeable apprehensions from the military preparations making in several of the other colonies, and the rumors that there are some appearances of their getting themselves in readiness to act in a hostile way, this Congress have made application to the Hon. Continental Congress, desiring them to take such measures as to them shall appear proper, to quiet and conciliate the minds of the Canadians, and to prevent such alarming apprehensions. We have also had the most disagreeable accounts of methods taken to fill the minds of the Indian tribes adjacent to these colonies, with sentiments very injurious to us: particularly we have been informed, that Col. Guy Johnson has taken great pains with the Six Nations, in order to bring them into a belief, that it is designed by the colonies to fall upon them, and cut them off.

We have therefore desired the Hon. Continental Congress, that they would, with all convenient speed, use their influence in guarding against the evil intended by this malevolent misrepresentation. And we desire you to join with us in such application.

To the Continental Congress, New York, and the several governments in New England.

Voted, To accept the report for directing the committee of safety to take immediate care to provide houses for the soldiers near the camp in Cambridge, if tents cannot be had, at the expense of the colony. It is as follows, viz : The committee appointed to take under consideration the petition of the quarter master general, and committee of safety, have attended that service, and report, that the committee of safety be directed to take immediate care to provide houses for the soldiers near the camp in Cambridge, if tents cannot be had, at the expense of the colony.

Ordered, That to-morrow, at three o'clock in the afternoon, be assigned for the choice of four brigadier generals, two adjutant generals, and two quarter master generals.

Ordered, That the petition of Ephraim Perry, and four others, inhabitants of Fox Island, be committed to the committee appointed to consider the circumstances of the sea coasts.

Voted, To accept the report for advising a number of towns and districts, as per schedule annexed to the report, who have fire-arms, to deposit the same with their respective town or district treasurers, for the use of the army. It is as follows, viz :

Whereas, some of the inhabitants of the plantations in this colony not incorporated, and some of the inhabitants of the neighboring colonies, together with a number of the late inhabitants of the town of Boston, have enlisted into the army now raising in this colony; therefore, [are] not provided with arms by a resolve of Congress, dated May 9th, 1775, empowering the selectmen to supply the inhabitants of their respective towns, with arms, &c. : therefore, *Resolved*, that the inhabitants of the several towns and districts in the counties of Worcester, Hampshire, and other counties specified in a list hereunto annexed, who may have good and sufficient fire-arms and bayonets, be advised hereby, immediately to deposit the same with the respective town or district treasurers, to the number at least of so many in each town or district, as is specified in said list, for which arms and bayonets, or arms alone, where bayonets are not to be had, each owner shall receive so much as his arms and bayonets shall be valued [at], by the selectmen of the town or district in which he dwells, of the treasurer of said town or district, in bills of credit of this colony, within thirty days after the arms are delivered, for which bills are to be taken, in the name of this colony, attested by the selectmen aforesaid.   And the amount of such bills, with an order from such treasurer, the committee of supplies of this colony are hereby ordered to pay, together with the expense of transporting said arms to the store of said committee in Watertown. And further, the selectmen and committees of correspondence, together with the treasurers of the towns and districts aforesaid, are hereby directed to give their aid in collecting and transporting said arms with the greatest despatch.

County of Worcester.—Worcester, 30; Lancaster, 32; Mendon, 24; Brookfield, 31; Oxford 11; Charlton, 11; Sutton, 31; Leicester, 12; Spencer, 10; Paxton, 6; Rutland, 15; Oakham, 6; Hubbardston, 2; New Braintree, 10; Southborough, 12; Westborough, 12; Northborough, 8; Shrewsbury, 22; Lunenburg, 16; Fitchburg, 6; Uxbridge, 16; Harvard, 16; Dudley, 10; Hutchinson, 13; Bolton, 15; Upton, 6; Sturbridge, 12; Leominster, 12; Hardwick, 17; Western, 11; Holden, 8; Douglas, 7; Grafton, 12; Petersham, 12; Royalston, 2; Westminster, 10; Athol, 6; Templeton, 8; Princeton, 8; Ashburnham, 3; Winchendon, 3;   514

Hampshire.—Springfield, 22; West Springfield, 23; Wilbraham, 10; Northampton, 22; Southampton, 8; Hadley, 9; South Hadley, 7; Amherst, 10; Granby, 5; Hatfield, 11; Whateley,

4; Williamsburg, 3; Westfield, 16; Deerfield, 12; Greenfield, 8; Shelburne, 4; Conway, 5; Sunderland, 7; Montague, 6; Northfield, 8; Brimfield, 13; South Brimfield, 8; Monson, 6; Pelham, 12; Greenwich, 8; Blanford, 5; Palmer, 8; Granville, 14; New Salem, 6; Belchertown, 8; Colraine, 5; Ware, 4; Warwick, 3; Bernardston, 4; Murrayfield, 5; Charlemont, 3; Ashfield, 4; Worthington, 2; Shutesbury, 4; Chesterfield, 6; Southwick, 6; . . , . . . 334

Suffolk.—Wrentham, 25; Medway, 10; Bellingham, 6; Walpole, 8; 49

Middlesex.—Marlborough, 20; Littleton, 10; Hopkinton, 10; Westford, 10; Stow, 7; Groton, 8; Shirley, 4; Pepperel, 6; Townshend, 5; Dracut, 7; Holliston, 6; Acton, 5; Dunstable, 4; 102

Plymouth.—Bridgewater, 25; Middleborough, 16; . . 41

Bristol.—Attleborough, 10; Rehoboth, 15; . . . 25

Worcester, 514; Hampshire, 334; Suffolk, 49; Middlesex, 102; Plymouth, 41; Bristol, 25: in all, ... 1065

Voted, To accept the report for providing a magazine of fire-arms for this colony: also, that said report be printed in the several newspapers, viz:

Whereas, it is necessary that this colony be provided with a magazine of arms which are good and sufficient; therefore, *Resolved,* that any person or persons, who may have such to sell, shall receive so much for them, as the selectmen of the town or district in which he or they may dwell, shall appraise said arms at, upon the delivery of the same to the committee of supplies at Watertown, and exhibiting a certificate of said appraisement, attested by said selectmen, to the committee aforesaid; provided said delivery be made within one month from the date hereof.

Afternoon.

Ordered, That Mr. Parker, Col. Thompson, and Mr. Aiken, be a committee to apply to the committee of supplies, and the generals of the army, and inquire whether the army is sufficiently supplied with ammunition.

Ordered, That Daniel Davis, Esq., be on the committee appointed to take care of the estates of the refugees, in the room of Mr. Partridge, who is absent.

The committee appointed to examine and consider two accounts exhibited to this Congress by Mr. John Brown, reported: The report on each of them, was accepted, and is as follows, viz: The committee appointed to examine the within account, beg leave to report, that the same be laid on the table till Mr. Brown exhibits an account of particulars with his journal.				JOHN HALE, *per order.*

The committee appointed to examine the within account, beg leave to report, that it does not appear to them that the within mentioned services were rendered in consequence of an application by any person employed by this colony.				JOHN HALE, *per order.*

Ordered, That Col. Warren, Mr. Sever, and Col. Otis, be a committee to consider the application of the Reverend Dr. Langdon, president of Harvard College, and report thereon.

The committee appointed to consider the claims and pretensions of several colonels in the army, reported: which report was accepted: whereupon, *Ordered*, that Col's. Glover, David Brewer, Woodbridge, Little, and Jonathan Brewer, be commissioned as colonels in the Massachusetts army, and that [Joseph] Haven, Esq., administer the oath prescribed by Congress. The report is as follows, viz:

The committee appointed to consider the claims and pretensions of the several gentlemen hereafter named, who suppose that they have just grounds to expect of this honorable Congress, that they should receive commissions appointing them severally to be chief colonels in the Massachusetts army, now raising for the defence of the rights of this and the neighboring colonies, namely: Col. Glover, Gen. Heath, Col. David Brewer, Col. Robinson, Col. Woodbridge, Col. Little, Col. Henshaw, and Col. Jonathan Brewer, beg leave to report the following state of facts to this Congress, viz: That the colonels Glover, David Brewer, Woodbridge, Little, Henshaw, and Jonathan Brewer, have exhibited their claims to your committee, and according to the returns which the said gentlemen have respectively made to us, the said Col. Glover has levied ten companies, making in the whole 505 men, inclusive of officers; and about three quarters of the said number armed with effective firelocks; who are willing and choose to serve in the said army, under him the said Glover; all now at Marblehead:

That the said David Brewer has levied nine companies, amounting, inclusive of officers, to the number of 465 men, who choose to serve under him as their colonel; and that 307 of the said men are armed with effective fire-arms; and that said companies, excepting 34 men who are on their way to head quarters, are posted at Roxbury, Dorchester, and Watertown:

That the said Woodbridge has levied eight companies, amounting, inclusive of officers, to the number of 354 men, who choose to serve under him as their chief colonel, and that 273 of the said men, are armed with good effective firelocks, and that all the said men, excepting seven, are now in the camp at Cambridge; the said seven men are on the road hither:

And that the said Little has raised eight companies, according to General Ward's return, amounting, inclusive of officers, to the number of 509 men, who choose to serve under him as their chief colonel; and all the said men are armed with good effective firelocks, and 382 of them with good bayonets, fitted to their firelocks; and that seven of the said companies are at the camp in Cambridge, and one company at Cape Ann, by order of the committee of safety:

And that the said Jonathan Brewer has levied eight companies, amounting, inclusive of officers, to the number of 397 men, who choose to serve under him, the said Jonathan, as their chief colonel; and that 302 of the said men are armed with good firelocks; and that all the said men, excepting 27 who are on the road hither, are posted at Cambridge and Brookline; and the said Brewer supposes, from accounts he has received, that one Capt. Murray is on the road from Hatfield hither with a full company:

And that the said Col. Henshaw has returned to us, that he has a prospect of several companies arriving shortly here, who, he supposes, would be inclined to serve under him as their chief colonel:

And that general Heath, and Col. Robinson, have made no returns to us, your committee, of their levies, or whether they are willing to serve in the said army as colonels:

And upon these facts, your committee are clearly of opinion, that the safety of the country, and the promoting the public service, make it highly necessary and expedient, that the said colonels Glover, David Brewer, Woodbridge, Little, and Jonathan Brewer, be, without any delay, commissioned as chief colonels in the army aforesaid: and that their field officers, captains, and subalterns, be also commissioned, as soon as a list of them can be settled, inasmuch as your committee are fully satisfied from good documents, that all the men contained in the 19 regiments already organized, together with all the men levied by the said Colonels Glover, D. Brewer, Woodbridge, Little, and Jonathan Brewer, together with an allowance of 450 men, which may have been enlisted by general Heath, and the like number by Col. Robinson, will fall considerably short of amounting to 13,600 men; and also, because your committee apprehend that this Congress may, without any injustice to the field officers already commissioned, or any other, make such orders, that the amount of the pay of the whole army may not be unreasonably enhanced by a greater number of regiments, than, by the last establishment it was intended the army should consist of; all which is most humbly submitted by your committee.

JOSEPH HAWLEY, *per order.*

Adjourned to Friday morning, 8 o'clock.

FRIDAY, June 16, 1775.

Resolved, That this Congress will take into consideration a resolve offered to the Congress by the committee of supplies, through the hands of Major Fuller, relative to supplying the soldiers with rum.

The resolve was accordingly considered and accepted, and is as follows, viz :

Whereas, by a resolve of Congress, relative to the allowance of soldiers, no provision is made for the delivery of rum, or spirituous liquors, upon extraordinary occasions : *Resolved,* That the commanding officer of the army, the lieutenant general, the major generals, and the brigadier generals, be, and hereby are respectively empowered, to draw on the commissary for spirituous liquors, for such soldiers, as from time to time, they may think necessary to supply therewith ; provided always, that the said general officers shall not allow any soldiers spirituous liquors as aforesaid, unless upon extraordinary duty, or otherwise particularly circumstanced.

Ordered, That the Hon. Major Hawley, Hon. Col. Gerrish, Hon. Col. Warren, Col. Prescott, Col. Farley, Mr. Aiken, and Doct. Hall, be a committee to consider a resolve of the committee relative to an augmentation of the army, a supply of arms to the soldiery, &c., and report thereon.

[The] order of the day [was] moved for, for further considering the report of the committee, respecting the expediency of fitting out some armed vessels : *Voted,* that there be a further assignment thereof, viz : to three o'clock, P. M.

Ordered, That John Row, captain ; Mark Pool, lieutenant ; Ebenezer Cleveland, ensign ; be commissioned in Col. Bridge's regiment.

Ordered, That Col. Richmond, Doct. Taylor, and Mr. Partridge, be a committee to draw a complaisant letter to Gen. Whitcomb, to desire a more explicit answer respecting his acceptance of the post of first major general, [who reported the following :]

WATERTOWN, June 16, 1775.

SIR :—Your letter wherein you express yourself willing to continue in the service of this colony, until the army is regulated and properly encamped, and then rely on a discharge, was read with much concern by this Congress, who earnestly hope you will continue in office till the conclusion of the campaign, and must beg your further and more explicit answer.

Col. Jonathan Brewer [was] sworn and commissioned.

Col. David Brewer [was] sworn and commissioned.

Col. Glover [was] sworn and commissioned.

The committee on Col. Henshaw's petition for an allowance for his journey to Connecticut, reported : [which report was] amended and accepted, and is as follows, viz :

The committee appointed to consider the within account, beg leave to report that they think it reasonable to allow Col. Joseph Henshaw, for his expenses, £4 7s.; horse travel for him and servant, £1 5s.; time, £2 16s.—£8 8s.; deduct 2s. per day from the sum charged for the time of Col. Henshaw and his servant, 14s.—£7 14s. Receiver general directed to pay it.   SAMUEL HARDING, *Chairman*.

Doct. Hall and Doct. Jones were added to the committee to examine surgeons for the army. *Resolved*, that any three of said committee shall be a quorum.

Ordered, That commissions be delivered to two companies in Col. Nixon's regiment, agreeably to his list exhibited.

[Afternoon.]

Ordered, That Col. Otis and Mr. Johnson be added to the committee who were appointed to consider the late extraordinary proclamation of general Gage.

Ordered, That Mr. Benjamin Ely, be appointed to obtain of the committee of safety, as soon as possible, a list of such gentlemen as they can recommend to be commissioned as officers of the train.

Resolved, That the receiver general be, and hereby is directed to pay to Col. Joseph Henshaw, the sum of seven pounds, fourteen shillings, in full for his account reported and accepted by the Congress.

Ordered, That commissions be delivered to the following officers of Col. Nixon's regiment, viz : Capt. Ebenezer Winship, Lieut. William Warren, Ensign Richard Buckminster.

Ordered, That Mr. Orne, Mr. Glover, and Major Brooks, be a committee to consider what may be done with respect to such vessels as are now ready to sail, with fish on board, there being a resolve of this Congress against the exportation of fish, &c.; and in particular the cases of Mr. Ellis Gray and Richard Hinckley which has been laid before this Congress.

The committee on the violation of the Sabbath reported ; [which report was] accepted, and is as follows, viz :

As it has pleased Almighty God in his providence, to suffer the calamities of an unnatural war to take place among us, in consequence of our sinful declensions from him, and our great abuse of those invaluable blessings bestowed upon us : and as we have reason to fear, that unless we become a penitent and reformed people, we shall feel still severer tokens of the divine displeasure : and as the most effectual way to escape those desolating judgments which so evidently hang over us, and if it may be, obtain the restoration of our former tranquillity, will be, that we repent and return, every one from his iniquities, unto Him that correcteth us ; which, if we do in sincerity and truth, we have no reason to doubt but he will remove his judgments, cause our enemies to be at peace with us, and prosper the work of our hands : and as, among the prevailing sins of this day, which threaten the destruction of this land, we have reason to lament the frequent profanations of the Lord's day or the Christian Sabbath ; many spending their time in idleness or sloth, others in diversions, and others in journeying, or business, which is not necessary on said day : and as we earnestly desire that a stop might be put to this great and prevailing evil, it is therefore *Resolved*, that it be recommended by this Congress to the people of all ranks and denominations throughout this colony, that they not only pay a religious regard to that day, and to the public worship of God thereon, but that they also use their influence to discountenance and suppress any profanation thereof in others : and it is further *Resolved*, that it be recommended to the ministers of the gospel, to read this resolve to their several congregations, accompanied with such exhortations as they shall think proper : and whereas, there is great danger that the profanation of the Lord's day will prevail in the camp, we earnestly recommend to all the officers, not only to set good examples, but that they strictly require of their soldiers to keep up a religious regard to that day, and attend upon the public worship of God thereon, so far as may be consistent with other duties.

Ordered, That the foregoing resolve be printed in hand bills, and sent to the several ministers in each town and district in the colony.

General Heath and Col. Robinson returned a list of their companies, and whereas there are several of the same companies returned in each, *Ordered*, that Mr. Batchelder, Mr. Durfee, Major Perley, Major Fuller of Middleton, Major Bliss, be a committee to consider of the same, and report.

A further time was assigned to make choice of brigadier generals, quarter masters general, and adjutants general, viz. : to-morrow morning, eleven o'clock.

Col. Coffin, Mr. Stephen Hall and Col. Davis, were chosen a committee to consider the petition of James Kirkwood.

The committee on the petition of Ellis Gray and Richard Hinckley, &c., reported : the two reports were accepted, and are as follow :

The committee appointed to take under consideration the petition of Messrs. Ellis Gray and Richard Hinckley, relative to eighty hogsheads of Jamaica cod fish, laden on two vessels bound to the West Indies; the one of which would have sailed before the resolve of this honorable Congress forbidding the exportation of fish was published, had she not been detained by the elopement of her hands, beg leave to report : that being fully convinced, from the accounts given us by Mr. Gray and Mr. Hinckley, that the fish those gentlemen were about to export, is of such a kind, being old Jamaica fish, as, if detained, cannot possibly be of any advantage to this colony, but must perish, the colony being plentifully supplied with new fish, that permission be given by this Congress, to the owners of said vessels, for their proceeding on their voyages ; provided, there is no other kind of provision on board, except what is for the ship's use; and further, that toleration be given to all other owners of vessels, for their departure, who shall convince this Congress, or a committee thereof, that their vessels and cargoes are in the same predicament, as no possible advantage can accrue from their detention.   J. ORNE, *per order*.

The committee appointed to examine the bearer of a certificate from Newburyport, setting forth, that Jonathan Titcomb and Stephen Hooper, Esq., of Newburyport, have shipped on board two vessels, 130 hogsheads of Jamaica fish, which is said to be old fish, beg leave to report : that they are fully convinced, the fish above mentioned is of such a kind as is expressed in the certificate, and that the vessels who have laden it, have no other provisions but a supply for the ship's use ; and, as such, are of opinion that the owners of said vessels be tolerated to despatch them on their voyages, agreeably to a resolve of this Congress just now past, granting indulgence to the owners of vessels in such predicament for so doing.   J. ORNE, *per order*.

The committee appointed to consider a late extraordinary proclamation, signed, Thomas Gage, reported [as follows :]

[IN PROVINCIAL CONGRESS, *Watertown*, June 16, 1775.]

[*Resolved*, That the following proclamation be signed by the president, printed and published throughout this colony.]

[By the Provincial Congress.]

[The confidence which our countrymen have reposed in us, lays us under the strongest obligation to watch and guard against all the malignant designs of their inveterate enemies.]

[That the British administration have formed, and have been for several years executing, a plan to enslave this and the other American colonies, is a proposition so evident, that it would be an affront to the understanding of mankind to adduce proofs in support of it. We shall therefore only advert to those unhappy circumstances, which have been the immediate causes of plunging this people into the horrors of war and desolation. When a fleet and army were sent forth to deprive us of every thing that man holds dear : when the capital of this colony became a garrison, and fortifications were erected upon the only land entrance into the metropolis : when the commander of the army so far manifested his designs against us, as to send out his soldiers in the night, to remove the public magazines of the colony from their safe lodgment in the country, and place them under the command of a foreign army : when he evidenced his enmity to the liberties of this country, by sending a detachment from that army against the peaceable inhabitants of one of our principal towns, only because they were assembled, quietly to concert measures to save themselves from ruin : when we were totally deprived of the benefit of a legislative body : when the whole system of distributive justice was so mutilated, that there could be no reason to hope for any advantages from it : when an act of parliament was passed, which the general of the army resolved to execute, by which our countrymen were given up as a prey to a lawless soldiery, who were screened from punishment here, for the murders they might commit : in fine, when the army and navy breathed nothing but blood and slaughter, and all our accounts from England but too strongly proved the inhuman intentions of those in power ; it became us as men, as freemen and as christians, to take some steps to preserve our own lives and properties, as well as to secure the inheritance, purchased at no less a price than the blood of many thousand of our brave ancestors, entire and undiminished for succeeding generations. The Congress, whom this people then chose, recommended it to them, to provide themselves with such articles for their defence as the law of the land required, and further recommended it to them, to appropriate some part of their property for the purchasing such stores, to be laid up in public magazines, as might be useful for the general defence, in case an attack should be made upon us by the army. The recommendation was cheerfully complied with, and stores were procured, in the most peaceable and quiet manner, and deposited in magazines, where they were to have continued without the least injury or disturbance to any one, unless drawn out by necessity, to save the country from destruction.   But the possibility of our making resistance to the bloody schemes of our adversaries was the source of continual terror to the traitors, whose aim was to enslave this country, and general Gage, after many little pilferings, and several humiliating disappointments in his attempts to rob the people, at length determined to destroy the magazines at Concord; he sent the grenadiers and detachments of light infantry of every regiment, about one thousand in number, secretly, by night, over Charles river.   On their way, some of the officers captured, and otherwise infamously abused several of the inhabitants, and, when the body arrived at Lexington meetinghouse, which was very early in the morning of the ever memorable nineteenth of April, they, in a most barbarous and infamous manner, fired upon a small number of the inhabitants, and cruelly murdered eight men.   The fire was returned by some of the survivors, but their number was too inconsiderable to annoy the regular troops, who proceeded on their errand, and, upon coming up to Concord, began to destroy, by fire and water, the stores and magazines, until a party of them again fired upon and killed two more of the inhabitants. The native bravery of our countrymen could now no longer be restrained; a small party, consisting of about two or three hundred men, attacked them with such spirit and resolution as compelled them soon to retreat.   At Lexington, they met a reenforcement of regular troops, consisting of about eight hundred, with two field pieces, commanded by Lord Percy; this, however, did not encourage them to keep their ground : but they continued their route towards Charlestown, marking their way with every species of desolation and cruelty which their haste would permit.   The burning and robbing of houses, the abuses and barbarities offered to defenceless women and children, the wanton slaughter of the aged and helpless, will be perpetual memorials of the base spirit which actuated the perpetrators.   Upon their arrival at Charlestown, our countrymen quitted the pursuit, and the next day suffered them, without annoyance, to cross the river, and return to Boston.   This action of the troops destroyed every hope of coming to any accommodation with them; we, therefore, were compelled to raise an army to prevent such bloody excursions in future ; an army is, therefore, raised and appointed for that purpose, and we are, with the greatest reluctance, obliged to declare, that we have now nothing to depend upon, under God, to preserve America from slavery and destruction, but our

44

own arms. To these we have been forced to make our appeal, and by these we are determined to maintain our rights: and we are obliged to declare, and do now publicly declare, all persons, who shall afford any aid, assistance, or relief, or hold any manner of communication of any kind whatsoever, with general Gage, admiral Graves, or the army, or navy, or any one of those now under their command, who are stationed in our metropolis and the harbor of Boston, or elsewhere, or any persons who are known, or shall hereafter be known, to have afforded such aid, or to have had such communication with them, or either of them, to be enemies and traitors to their country, and they shall be proceeded against and treated as such; excepting only, such of the unhappy inhabitants of Boston, as have, by a treacherous and most infamous breach of faith in general Gage, been prevented from removing out of the town of Boston, whose peculiar circumstances this Congress will, at all times, make due allowance for, so long as they shall avoid doing any thing to obstruct or counteract such steps as this Congress shall think fit to take ; but the said inhabitants are strictly forbidden, whatever may be the consequence of their refusal, to be in any, the least degree, instrumental in assisting the enemy, or opposing the country, as they would avoid the penalties due to the enemies thereof. From a real tenderness to our fellow men, we most sincerely regret the unhappy situation of the soldiery and sailors in the army and navy now stationed in the town and harbor of Boston, and assure them, upon that faith, which never has been, and we trust never will be violated, that, upon their quitting the infamous service in which they are, as we must in charity suppose, contrary to their own inclinations and principles engaged; we will receive them as brethren and fellow subjects, and protect them against every attempt that may be made by our enemies to force them again into the disgraceful and inhuman service, in which they are now employed.]

[And, that our earnest desire to discover our tender regard to our few misguided fellow countrymen, and our readiness to forgive even those who have knowingly offended, we do promise and engage a full and free pardon to all persons who have fled to the town of Boston for refuge, and to other public offenders against the rights and liberties of this country, of what kind or denomination soever ; excepting only from the benefit of such pardon, Thomas Gage, Samuel Graves; those counsellors who were appointed by mandamus and have not signified their resignation, viz., Jonathan Sewall, Charles Paxton, Benjamin Hallowell; and all the natives of America, not belonging to the navy or army, who went out with the regular troops on the nineteenth of April last, and were countenancing, aiding, and assisting them in the robberies and murders then committed; whose offences are of too flagitious a nature to admit of any other consideration than that of condign punishment: provided, they take the benefit hereof, by making a surrender of themselves to any general officer belonging to the Massachusetts army, and subscribe a declaration of their readiness to comply with, support, and abide by, all the resolutions and determinations which are already made by this or any former Congress, or that shall hereafter be made by this or any future Congress, or house of representatives of this colony, within thirty days from the date hereof. And it is earnestly enjoined upon the selectmen, committees of correspondence, committees of safety, and all other officers, of every town in this colony, that they use their utmost diligence to discover and make known to this Congress, any person or persons, who shall, in any respect, attempt to do any thing tending to render ineffectual their designs and doings; and we trust, that the God of armies, on whom we rely for a blessing upon our arms, which we have taken up in support of the great and fundamental principles of natural justice and the common and indefeasible rights of mankind, will guide and direct us in our designs; and at last, in infinite goodness to this his injured people, restore peace and freedom to the American world.]

Voted, That Tuesday next, ten o'clock before noon, be assigned for the further consideration thereof.

Ordered, That Mr. Lothrop, Col. Grout and Mr. Crane, be a committee to fill commissions for the field officers of the regiment of artillery, as recommended by the committee of safety.

Resolved, That a commission be made out for Mr. Heath, as colonel of a regiment of the Massachusetts army.

Resolved, That Deacon Plympton be appointed to countersign the small notes, instead of Col. Richmond.

The committee appointed to consider the application of president Langdon, reported; which report was accepted, and is as follows, viz.:

Resolved, That it be and hereby is recommended to as many of the overseers of Harvard College as can be called together, under the present circumstances of the college and the country, to meet and join with the corporation of said college, in conferring academical degrees at the approaching season of the annual commencement, on such candidates as may offer themselves and be judged qualified for the same; and to transact any other important matters relative to that society, in the

same manner, and to all intents and purposes, as the whole body of
the overseers might do, if present.

Voted, That the receiver general, Henry Gardner, Esq., as also
Deacon Plympton, have leave of absence from to-morrow afternoon until Monday morning.

Adjourned till eight o'clock to-morrow morning.

SATURDAY, June 17, 1775.

The committee on account of Mrs. Coolidge, reported : the report
was ordered to lie on the table, till the president came into Congress.

The Congress granted leave of absence to Mr. J. Orne, being bound
on a journey to Philadelphia.

The committee appointed to take into consideration the property of
some persons, who have left their habitations in sundry towns in this
colony, and also have discovered themselves to be enemies to the rights
of this colony and the continent, &c., reported.

Ordered, That Mr. Edwards, Col. Thompson and Col. Glover, be a
committee to consider upon the expediency and means of procuring
fire arms and powder from Philadelphia, and elsewhere ; which committee reported : the report was read and accepted, and is as follows,
viz. :

The committee appointed to consider upon the expediency and
means of procuring fire arms and powder from Philadelphia and elsewhere, and to report in the form of a resolve, report accordingly :

Resolved, That the committee of supplies be directed to employ Mr.
Joshua Orne, a member of this Congress, for this end, and that they,
by letter, desire that the honorable Continental Congress would be
pleased to grant to Mr. Orne their aid in the premises.

The committee appointed to take into consideration the resolve of
the committee of safety, respecting the augmentation of the army, and
supplying the army with arms, &c., reported in part ; the report was
considered and accepted, and is as follows, viz. :

Whereas, the hostile incursions this country is exposed to, and the
frequent alarms we may expect from the military operations of our enemies, make it necessary that the good people of this colony be on
their guard, and prepared at all times to resist their attacks, and to aid
and assist their brethren : therefore, *Resolved*, that it be, and hereby is
recommended to the militia, in all parts of this colony, to hold themselves in readiness to march at a minute's warning, to the relief of any
place that may be attacked, or to the support of our army, with at least
twenty cartridges, or rounds of powder and ball ; and, to prevent all

confusion or delay, it is further recommended to the inhabitants of this colony living on the sea coasts, or within twenty miles of them, that they carry their arms and ammunition with them to meeting on the sabbath, and other days when they meet for public worship.

Resolved, That all vacancies occasioned by the officers going into the army, or otherwise, in the several regiments of militia, be immediately filled up: and it is recommended to the regiments, where such vacancies are, to supply them, in manner and form as prescribed by the resolutions of Congress.

· *Ordered*, That the resolve before mentioned, brought in by said committee last mentioned, be immediately printed in handbills, and that the number be three hundred.

Voted, That Capt. Goodman, Mr. Brown, and Major Bliss, be and hereby are appointed a committee, to get said three hundred handbills printed, and distribute the same to the several towns and districts in this colony.

Resolved, That Doct. Moses Gunn, be and hereby is appointed to countersign the large notes, instead of the Hon. Joseph Warren, Esq.

Col. Jonathan Brewer's list of officers in his regiment, was presented: *Ordered*, that a commission be delivered to each of the said officers, except to Joseph Stebbins, who has but 21 men in his company.

Col. David Brewer's list of officers in his regiment, was presented: *Ordered*, that a commission be delivered to each of said officers.

Resolved, That Capt. Holmes, Major Brooks, and Capt. Smith, be a committee to confer with the printers, Edes, Hall, and Thomas, and know of them respectively, upon what terms they will print handbills, and also such pieces as may be desired by this Congress to be put in the weekly papers, and make report to this Congress in writing, with all convenient speed.

The petition of sundry persons from Egamagon Reach was read, and committed to the committee on the state of the sea coasts, [who reported as follows:]

On the petition of a number of the inhabitants of Egamagon Reach, No. 4., so called, praying for a small supply of provisions:

Resolved, That it be recommended by this Congress to the committee of safety of the town of Salem, or to the like committee or committees of correspondence of any other towns within this province, to supply Messrs. Robert Byard and Alexander Greenlaw, of said Egamagon Reach, No. 4., for the present relief of the said inhabitants, with the following articles, viz.: forty bushels of Indian corn, and five barrels of pork; and take in return for the same, cord wood, or such other payment as the said Robert Byard, and Alexander Greenlaw, may be able to make; and in case they, the said Bayard and Greenlaw, should not make satisfaction for the same, in a reasonable time, it shall be allowed and paid out of the public treasury of this province, and the said Byard and Greenlaw shall refund the same as soon as may be.

Several of the committee who were appointed to consider the state and circumstances of the sea-coasts, viz.: Hon. Mr. Sever, Hon. Mr. Spooner, Col. Cutt, and Capt. Maynard, being absent, *Ordered*, that Major Hall, Mr. Aiken, Capt. Morton, and Capt. King, be appointed in their stead.

Resolved, That the vote for choosing brigadier generals from the colonels who have been commissioned by this Congress, be so far reconsidered, as that Col. Heath, though he has not yet received his commission, may be eligible to that office.

The committee appointed to consider the resolutions of the committee of safety, reported the following resolve and schedule, which were accepted.

Whereas, some of the inhabitants of the new plantations in this colony, not incorporated, and some of the inhabitants of the neighboring colonies, together with a number of the late inhabitants of the town of Boston, have enlisted into the army now raising in this colony, to whom the resolve of Congress, dated May 9, 1775, empowering the selectmen to supply the inhabitants of their respective towns with arms, &c., did not extend; and, by that means, many of such men are not provided with sufficient arms: therefore, *Resolved*, that the inhabitants of the several towns and districts in the counties specified in a list hereunto annexed, who may have good and sufficient firelocks, be and hereby are most earnestly advised, as soon as possible, to provide and deliver to such person or persons as are to be now appointed by this Congress to receive the same, the full number of good, effective firelocks, specified in the said list for each town and district to supply, for which firelocks every owner thereof shall receive such sum, in the bills of credit of this colony, as the person or persons now to be appointed by this Congress to receive such firelock, and the owner thereof, shall agree to be the value of the same, within forty days after the delivery of such firelock. For all which firelocks delivered as aforesaid, the person to be appointed by this Congress to receive the same, shall give his receipt therefor in the form following:

The   day of   1775.

Received of A. B.   firelock , to the use of the colony of the Massachusetts Bay, of the value of   ; which sum the receiver general of the said colony is directed, in forty days after the date hereof, to pay to the said A. B. or order, in bills of credit of this colony.

And the said receiver general, upon such receipt being produced to him, is empowered and required to pay, out of the treasury of this colony, the sum specified in such receipt, in the bills of credit aforesaid, to the person named therein, or his order ; and, furthermore, the selectmen and committees of correspondence of the several towns and districts aforesaid, are hereby most earnestly requested to afford all possible aid and assistance to the persons to be appointed by this Congress, to procure the said firelocks ; that so the said arms may be supplied to our army with the greatest expedition.   And the persons to be appointed to procure said firelocks, are hereby severally empowered and directed to employ such wagoners and teamsters as shall be necessary, with great despatch, to convey the same to the army, and to order the receiver general of this colony to pay, out of the treasury of the same, in bills of credit as aforesaid, such sums as they shall agree on and draw for ; and the said receiver general is hereby authorized and directed to pay the orders so drawn.

Worcester County.—Worcester, 30 ; Lancaster, 32 ; Mendon, 24 ; Brookfield, 31 ; Oxford, 11 ; Charlton, 11 ; Sutton, 31 ; Leicester, 12 ; Spencer, 10 ; Paxton, 6 ; Rutland, 15 ; Oakham, 6 ; Hubbardston, 2 ; New Braintree, 10 ; Southborough, 12 ; Westborough, 12 ; Northborough, 8 ; Lunenburg, 16 ; Fitchburg, 6 ; Uxbridge, 11 ; Northbridge, 5 ; Harvard, 16 ; Dudley, 10 ; Hutchinson, 13 ; Bolton, 15 ; Upton, 6 ; Shrewsbury, 22 ; Sturbridge, 12 ; Leominster, 12 ; Hardwick, 17 ; Western, 11 ; Holden, 8 ; Douglass, 7 ; Grafton, 12 ; Petersham, 12 ; Royalston, 2 ; Westminster, 10 ; Athol, 6 ; Templeton, 8 ; Princeton, 8 ; Ashburnham, 3 ; Winchendon, 3 ;   .   .   .   514

Hampshire.—Springfield, 26 ; West Springfield, 25 ; Wilbraham, 11 ; Northampton, 25 ; Southampton, 10 ; Hadley, 11 ; South Hadley, 9 ; Amherst, 12 ; Granby, 7 ; Hatfield, 14 ; Westfield, 19 ; Deerfield, 15 ; Greenfield, 10 ; Sunderland, 9 ; Montague, 8 ; Northfield, 10 ; Brimfield, 15 ; South Brimfield, 10 ; Monson, 8 ; Pelham, 14 ; Blandford, 9 ; Palmer, 11 ; Granville, 16 ; New Salem, 9 ; Warwick, 5 ; Ashfield, 8 ; Southwick, 8 ;   334

Suffolk.—Wrentham, 25; Medway, 10; Bellingham, 6; Walpole, 4; Medfield, 4;   49

Middlesex.—Marlborough, 20; Littleton, 6; Hopkinton, 9; Westford, 6; Groton, 7; Shirley, 2; Pepperell, 4; Townsend, 4; Dracut, 5; Acton, 5; Dunstable, 5; Tewksbury, 4; Chelmsford, 7; Billerica, 7; Stow, 4; Framingham, 3; Wilmington, 4;   102

Plymouth.—Bridgewater, 25; Middleborough, 16; .   41

Bristol.—Attleborough, 10; Rehoboth, 15; . .   25

Worcester, 514; Hampshire, 334; Suffolk, 49; Middlesex, 102; Plymouth, 41; Bristol, 25; total, . . .   1065

Resolved, That four o'clock, P. M. be assigned for choosing committees to receive and purchase fire arms agreeably to the foregoing resolve.

Afternoon.

A letter from the president of the Continental Congress, and a resolve containing several recommendations to this and the other colonies, and two letters, one to the Lieut. Gov. of Rhode Island, and one to the Provincial Congress of New Hampshire, brought express by Mr. Fessenden, were read; whereupon, *Ordered*, that Capt. Morton take charge of the letter to New Hampshire, and Mr. Slead that to Rhode Island, to deliver them immediately, and return to the Congress as soon as may be.

Resolved, That the Hon. Col. Warren, Hon. Major Hawley, Hon. Col. Gerrish, Mr. Gerry, Col. Prescott, Deacon Cheever, Capt. Brown, and Capt. Robinson, and the secretary of the Congress, be a committee to notify and call together the members of this Congress in any extraordinary emergency, at any other time, or to any other place, than [that] to which it may stand adjourned.

The order of the day [was] moved for:

Whereupon, committees were chosen to purchase arms agreeably to the resolve passed in the forenoon: the names of the committees chosen are expressed in the following resolve, viz.:

For the county of Worcester: Capt. William Page of Hardwick, Capt. Abiel Saddler of Upton, Mr. Hemmenway of Shrewsbury :—*For the county of Hampshire:* Major Benjamin S. Ely of West Springfield, Major John Bliss of Hadley :—*For the county of Suffolk :* Capt. Lemuel Kollock of Wrentham :—*For the county of Middlesex :* Col. Simeon Spaulding of Chelmsford, Capt. Josiah Stone of Framingham : —*For the county of Plymouth :* Major Ebenezer White of Rochester : —*For the county of Bristol :* Col. George Williams of Taunton.

Adjourned to Sunday morning, eight o'clock.

Sunday, June 18, 1775.

Resolved, That the records and papers of the Provincial Congress be secured and taken care of, at the discretion of the secretary ; and that the committee of supplies be, and hereby are directed, to procure a horse for the secretary, that he may have one ready for that purpose on any emergency.

A petition from the committee of Waldoborough for powder, was read ; whereupon, *Resolved,* that the petitioners have leave to withdraw their petition.

Ordered, That Mr. Lothrop appoint some messenger to go to Doct. Church, for the letters it is said he has brought from Philadelphia.

Ordered, That Major Hawley, Col. Warren, Mr. Kollock, Mr. Edwards, Col. Gerrish, Doct. Church and Col. Otis, be a committee to prepare a letter to the Continental Congress on the late attack of the king's troops at Bunker's hill, &c., and such other matters as they may think proper, and report to this Congress : and also that they take into consideration a letter from the president of the Continental Congress, and several recommendations of the said Continental Congress therein enclosed, received by Mr. Fessenden, and another letter from the said president, with a resolve enclosed relative to a mode of government for this colony ; and also to inquire of the committee of supplies, what steps they have taken to procure powder from the other governments of New England.[1]

(1) The letters of the Hon. John Hancock, president of the Continental Congress, with the resolutions enclosed, except that inserted in the journal, are copied below. The despatches for the governments of Rhode Island and New Hampshire, covered transcripts of the same documents.

" PHILADELPHIA, June 10th, 1775

" GENTLEMEN :—In consequence of your application to this Congress for advice respecting a form of government to be adopted in the Massachusetts Bay, under your present circumstances, I am directed by the Congress to transmit you their resolution thereon, which is here enclosed. I am also to inform you that the Congress have been so pressed with business, that they have been prevented determining upon the other matters mentioned in your letters to them : but they will very soon come under their consideration, and their resolutions thereon shall be forwarded to you."

" I also enclose you a resolve of Congress, for furnishing our army with flour ; this you will keep secret, at least as far as the nature of it will admit, as the publication may give an alarm, which may prevent the good effects of it."

" Last evening, Mr. Fessenden, your express, arrived, with your despatches of June 4th, which I

Ordered, That the committee of supplies be directed to write to Rhode Island and New Hampshire, touching the article of powder; also to send to each of said governments a copy of the recommendations of the Provincial Congress.

shall this morning lay before the Congress, and, when considered by Congress, their determination shall be immediately transmitted you."

"I am, with much esteem, gentlemen, your most obedient, humble servant,

JOHN HANCOCK, *President.*"

"*To the gentlemen of the Provincial Congress, Massachusetts Bay.*"

"In Congress, June 9th, 1775.

"*Resolved,* That the Provincial Convention of New York be requested to convey, as soon as possible, to Providence, in Rhode Island, or to any port in the government of Massachusetts Bay, five thousand barrels of flour, for the use of the continental army."

"That the committee of correspondence at Providence, or in the government of Massachusetts Bay, where the said flour may be carried, be desired to receive the same, and to forward it to the camp before Boston, as soon as may be, and to lodge such parts thereof as cannot immediately be sent thither, in places of security."

"That this Congress will make provision for defraying the expenses incurred for this service."

"Secret as the nature of it will admit, for fear of an alarm being given, and a stop.   J. H."

"PHILADELPHIA, June 10th, 1775.

"GENTLEMEN:—By order of the Congress, I transmit you the inclosed resolutions, passed by the Congress this morning. The necessity of the present emergency requires a speedy compliance with the first, and I need not inform you that the nature of the service requires it to be done with as much secrecy as possible."

"I am also directed by the Congress to request you will please to transmit to them, as soon as may be, an estimate of the powder, arms, and ammunition in your colony, including private as well as public stocks."

"By Doctor Church, this morning, I forwarded you the resolution of Congress respecting the mode of government."

"I am your most obedient servant,

JOHN HANCOCK, *President.*"

"The inclosed letters for the lieutenant governor of Rhode Island, and the gentlemen of New Hampshire, please immediately, on receipt, to send off by express; pray don't fail."

"*To the members of the Provincial Congress, Massachusetts Bay.*"

"In Congress, June 10, 1775.

"The Congress earnestly recommend to the several colonies of New Hampshire, Rhode Island, Connecticut, and the internal towns of the Massachusetts Bay, that they immediately furnish the American army before Boston, with as much powder, out of their town and other public stocks, as they can possibly spare, keeping an exact account of the quantity supplied, that it may be again replaced or paid for by the continent: this to be effected with the utmost secrecy and despatch."

"*Resolved,* That it be recommended to the committees of the several towns and districts of Massachusetts Bay, New Hampshire, Rhode Island, Connecticut, New York, and the eastern division of New Jersey, to collect all the saltpetre and brimstone in their several towns and districts, and transmit the same, with all possible despatch, to the Provincial Congress of New York."

"That it be recommended to the Provincial Congress of New York, to have the powder mills in that colony put into such a condition, as immediately to manufacture into powder, for the use of the continent, whatever materials may be procured in the manner above directed."

"*Resolved,* That it be recommended to the several inhabitants of the colonies, who are possessed of saltpetre and sulphur for their own use, to dispose of them, for the purpose of manufacturing gunpowder."

"*Resolved,* That the saltpetre and sulphur, to be collected in consequence of the resolves of Congress for that purpose, be paid for out of the continental fund."

"A true copy from the minutes.   CHA'S THOMPSON, *Sec'y.*"

[Afternoon.]

Ordered, That Col. Thurston, Col. Parks and Doct. Corbett, be a committee to consider a petition from Egamagon Reach; and also a petition from Deer Island, [for supplies of provisions.]

Adjourned to Monday morning, eight o'clock.

MONDAY, June 19, 1775.

Ordered, That Mr. Bonney, Mr. Foster and Col. Thompson, be and hereby are appointed a committee to repair immediately to Cambridge, and inquire what methods are taking to supply the army at the intrenchments with victuals and drink, and take effectual care that they be well supplied without delay.

Ordered, That Col. Parks, Deacon Fairbanks and Doct. Whiting, be, and hereby are appointed a committee to take into consideration a letter from General Ward, respecting the supplying the soldiers with blankets and other articles lost in battle, also for providing spears for defence.[1]

Doct. Hall, Doct. Jones and Mr. Bigelow, were appointed a committee to consider the expediency of establishing another hospital for the sick and wounded of the army, and ordered to sit forthwith.

Deacon Bailey, Capt. Goodman and Mr. Fisher, were appointed a committee, to inquire of the committee of supplies, how far they have proceeded to supply the soldiery with blankets, &c., and make report.

Capt. Goodrich, Mr. Aikin and Capt. Dwight, were appointed to consider a letter from the Hon. Jedediah Preble and Hon. Enoch Freeman, respecting Col. Phiney's regiment being commissioned for the defence of the sea coasts.[2]

(1) Two letters were received from Gen. Ward, on the 19th of June, addressed to the president of Congress.

"CAMBRIDGE, June 19, 1775.

"SIR :—The honorable Congress are hereby informed, that, in the late action, many of the soldiers lost their blankets and clothes ; they are now in a very suffering condition on that account, and must, in order to fit them for duty, be immediately supplied, especially with blankets ; and many that were not in the action are destitute of blankets."

"It is requested, that the troops may be supplied also with a large number of spears or lances, for defending the breastworks. In the late action, spears might have saved the intrenchment.

By order of the general.   JOSEPH WARD, Sec'ry."

"HEAD QUARTERS, June 19, 1775.

"SIR :—I must earnestly entreat the Congress to furnish the train of artillery, with a company of artificers immediately, as the army suffers greatly for want of them. This ought to have been one of the first establishments, and I hope the Congress will not delay the matter a day longer.

I am, sir, your most obedient, humble servant,

ARTEMAS WARD."

(2) The letter from the Hon. Jedediah Preble and Hon. Enoch Freeman follows :

"FALMOUTH, June 14, 1775.

"HONORED SIR :—These wait on you by Colonel Phiney, who informs us, he has ordered the

The committee appointed to consider the expediency of establishing certain officers for taking care of the ordnance stores, viz., storekeeper, conductors, and clerk; also, the establishment of a company of artificers, &c., reported: the report was amended and accepted, and is as follows, viz. :

The committee appointed to consider the expediency of establishing certain officers for taking care of the ordnance stores; also what artificers, and the number, that may be necessary for the army, and in what way they shall be established, have attended that service, and beg leave to report as follows: That, in addition to the storekeeper already appointed by this Congress, there be established four conductors of stores, and two clerks for the ordnance department; and a company of artificers, to consist of a master carpenter or overseer, with 49 privates; and the committee of safety be desired to recommend to this Congress, fit persons for the offices abovenamed; and if any such privates, who are now engaged in either of the regiments of the Massachusetts army, are inclined to join the abovesaid company, they may have leave so to do, they relinquishing their pay as soldiers, from the time they engage as artificers, and be equipt with fire arms, and accoutrements; and the overseer, when appointed, be ordered to consult the chief engineer with respect to the number of each kind of artificers that may be necessary, and that he complete his company, and make return thereof to this Congress, with all possible despatch. Your committee, furthermore, beg leave to report an establishment for the officers and privates above mentioned, viz, :

The storekeeper, $80 per month: four conductors, each $48 do. : one master carpenter, or overseer, $80 do. : two clerks, each $48 do. : 49 privates, they to find their own tools, $50 do. each. All which is humbly submitted.   ELISHA PARKS, *per order*.

Resolved, That three o'clock, P. M., be assigned for the choice of a president of this Congress, in the room of the Hon. Joseph Warren, Esq., supposed to be killed in the late battle of Bunker Hill.

The committee appointed to take into consideration the resolve of

men lately enlisted in this county, to guard the sea coasts and islands within said county, to secure the cattle and sheep from the ravages of cruisers from the navy : but, as no provision is made for their subsistence, it cannot be expected they can continue to do duty without. We refer you to Colonel Phiney for particulars. Four Indian chiefs arrived here this day, with Captain Lana, from the Penobscot tribe. We hope their expectations will be answered, which will lay a foundation for the securing to our interest the whole tribe."

         "We are, honored sir, your most obedient, humble servants,

                                        JEDEDIAH PREBLE,
                                        ENOCH FREEMAN."

Hon. Joseph Warren, Esq., to be communicated.

the honorable Continental Congress, respecting the method of establishing civil government in this colony, reported: [The report was] read and debated, and *Resolved*, that the further consideration of said report be put off until Doct. Church, who was at Philadelphia at the time said resolve of the Continental Congress passed, shall be present.

The committee appointed to take into consideration a letter from General Ward, respecting supplying the soldiers with blankets, &c., lost in battle, and providing spears &c., reported: The report was recommitted.

Col. Prescott and Mr. Wheeler, were added to the committee chosen to fill up commissions for the officers of the army.

Afternoon.

[The] order of the day [was] moved for.

Ordered, That Col. Prescott, Doct. Hall, and Col. Otis, be a committee to receive, sort, and count, the votes for a President.

The committee having attended that service, reported, that the Hon. James Warren, was chosen.

Resolved, That nine o'clock to-morrow morning, be assigned for the consideration of the report of the committee on the establishing armed vessels.

The committee appointed to inquire of the committee of supplies, what they had done relative to providing blankets and coats, reported, verbally; that they had conformed to the resolve of Congress relative thereto, and looked upon it to be their duty, to pay such orders as the selectmen might draw on them for the blankets they should purchase, but that they had only paid one town as yet.

Resolved, That the same committee report to this Congress, the price proper to be given for blankets throughout the whole colony, and that the committee of supplies be directed to suspend the payments for blankets till some further day, and that the said committee bring in a resolve expressive of the reason thereof.

The committee appointed to consider the expediency of establishing another hospital for the army, reported, that a house belonging to Doct. Spring, of this place, may be had for that purpose, whereupon,

Resolved, That said committee be directed to inquire at what rate, per month, Doct. Spring will let the same.

Resolved, That the secretary be directed to subscribe the name of the late president, to all commissions that are to be delivered out to the officers of the army, bearing date the 19th of May.

The report of the committee appointed to consider General Ward's letter relative to spears, was again read and accepted, and it is as follows, viz.:

The committee appointed to take into consideration a letter from the general, informing that a number of the soldiers in the late action, lost their clothes and blankets, and also proposing that the soldiers in the intrenchments be furnished with lances and spears, have attended that service, and beg leave to report by way of resolve.

[*Resolved*,] That the committee of supplies be, and they are hereby directed, to furnish those destitute soldiers with clothes and blankets, as soon as may be, who shall produce from the colonel of the regiment they belong to, certificates of their having lost such clothes and blankets in the late engagement: and that a committee be chosen, immediately to procure, from such as can most speedily and conveniently supply them, a sufficient number of good spears, not exceeding 1500, either by purchase or hire; and that the same be transmitted to the army at Cambridge as soon as possible; all which is humbly submittted.   ELISHA PARKS, *per order.*

Adjourned to eight o'clock, to-morrow morning.

                              TUESDAY, June 20, 1775.

The committee appointed to consider the request of Col. Phiney, reported.

The report was ordered to lie on the table till the matter respecting armed vessels is considered.

Ordered, That Major Brooks, Col. Mitchell, Mr. Ellis, Mr. Kollock, Deacon Fairbanks, Mr. Perry, and Major Fuller, be a committee to purchase spears, agreeably to a resolve which passed the .Congress yesterday; said committee to proceed on the business forthwith; to consult with and receive directions from the general, respecting the form, &c., of the spears; and to engage payment for the same, in bills of credit of this colony.

The committee on the resolve of the Continental Congress respecting government, reported a letter to the several towns in the colony, which was read and accepted, and ordered to be printed in hand bills with the resolve of the Continental Congress at large: and Mr. Whitney, Col. Freeman, Capt. Stone, Doct. Church, and Deacon Cheever, were appointed a committee to ascertain the number to be printed; to get them printed, and to disperse the same to the several towns and districts in this colony: and also to consider in what manner the late inhabitants of the towns of Boston and Charlestown, should choose members to represent them.   The resolve of the Continental Congress and the letter to the towns, follow, viz. :

IN CONGRESS, FRIDAY, June 9, 1775.

Resolved, That no obedience being due to the act of parliament for altering the charter of the colony of Massachusetts Bay, nor to a governor and lieutenant governor, who will not observe the directions of, but endeavor to subvert that charter; the governor and lieutenant governor are to be considered as absent, and their offices vacant.   And as there is no council there, and the inconveniences arising from the suspension of the powers of government are intolerable, especially at a time when general Gage hath actually levied war, and is carrying on hostilities against his majesty's peaceful and loyal subjects of that colony; that in order to conform, as near as may be, to the spirit and substance of the charter, it be recommended to the Provincial Congress, to write letters to the inhabitants of the several places, which are entitled to representation in assembly, requesting them to choose such representatives; and that the assembly, when chosen, should elect counsellors; which assembly and council should exercise the powers of government, until a governor of his majesty's appointment will consent to govern the colony according to its charter.

A true copy from the minutes.

CHARLES THOMPSON, *Secretary.*

By order of the Congress.   JOHN HANCOCK, *President.*

COLONY OF THE MASSACHUSETTS BAY.

In observance of the foregoing resolve of the Hon. Continental Congress, now sitting at Philadelphia, these are to request you, forthwith, to cause the freeholders and other inhabitants of your town, that have an estate of freehold in land, within this province or territory, of forty shillings per annum, at the least, or other estate to the value of forty pounds sterling, to assemble, at such time and place as you shall appoint, then and there to elect and depute one or more freeholders, resident in the same town, according to the numbers set and limited by an act of the general assembly, entitled an act for ascertaining the number and regulating the house of representatives, to serve for, and represent them in a great and general court or assembly, to be convened, held, and kept, for the service of the said colony, until the end of the day next preceding the last Wednesday of May next, if necessary, and no longer, at the meeting-house in Watertown, upon Wednesday, the 19th day of July next ensuing the date hereof, and to warn the person or persons so elected by the major part of the electors present at such election, to be timely notified, by one or more of the constables of your town, to attend the service of this colony in the said general court or assembly, on the day above prefixed, by nine o'clock, in the forenoon, and so from day to day, during their session and sessions. Hereof we desire you not to fail, and make return of this letter, with the name or names of the person or persons so elected or deputed, and of their being notified, unto the said general assembly, at the time and place abovementioned for its meeting.

Given under my hand, this nineteenth day of June, anno domini, 1775.   By order of Congress.

                                                        President.

To the selectmen of the town of
    Attest,   *Secretary.*

Resolved, That 3 o'clock, P. M. be assigned for the choice of a major general in the room of the late Doct. Warren, and also for the choice of one brigadier general.

Several letters from Penobscot, viz.; from Mr. John Lane, and others, were read and committed to Capt. Webster, Col. Farley, Capt. Holmes, Doct. Taylor, and Major Perley.[1]

Doct. Gunn was appointed to report a resolve on the proposal made by the committee of safety, relative to the killed and wounded in the late battle.

A petition from the district of Woolwich[2] was presented and read: and thereupon, *Resolved,* that the petitioners have leave to withdraw their petition.

Upon a motion made, *Resolved,* that the house of Mr. Hunt, at Cambridge, be hired for a hospital, and that the committee appointed to treat with Doct. Spring, be a committee to hire the same.

(1) The substance of the communications from Penobscot, is contained in a letter from Gen. Preble.

                                        " FALMOUTH, June 15, 1775.

"HONORED SIR:—Mr. Lane is returned here, with four of the Penobscot tribe ; we have furnished them with carriages to convey them to you, and Mr. Lane with money to pay their expenses. Orono, the chief man, seems to be sensible, and hearty in our cause : he reserves what he has chiefly to say, till he comes to the Congress. We gave them assurances that they might depend upon being provided for, while there, as well as on their return back again, wished them a pleasant journey, and that the event might be happy to them and us. We suppose Mr. Lane will give account of the expense, therefore we have sent none."

"Wishing success to our righteous cause, we are, your honors, most obedient humble servants, the committee of correspondence,   JEDEDIAH PREBLE, *Chairman.*"

" *Hon. Joseph Warren, President.*"

(2) This petition was for a supply of powder.

Ordered, That Doct. Church, Doct. Taylor, and Doct. Whiting, be a committee to consider what method is proper to be taken to supply the hospitals with surgeons : and that the same gentlemen be a committee to provide medicines, and all other necessaries for the hospitals.

The report of the committee on the expediency of establishing armed vessels, was considered, and after debate, the matter was ordered to subside.[1]

The committee appointed to confer with Doct. Spring, relative to the use of his house for another hospital, reported : the report was read and accepted, and is as follows, viz. :

The committee appointed to consider of the expediency of establishing another hospital for the sick and wounded of the army, having attended that service, beg leave to report, that they judge it is really expedient to have another established, and they judge that the house of Doct. Spring, in Watertown, is convenient for that purpose ; and that he is willing said house should be improved by the province for that use, but that he cannot at present ascertain the damage it may be to him, but is willing to submit that matter to the judgment of a committee to be hereafter appointed by this honorable Congress or the house of assembly.   By order,   J. HALL.

Ordered, That Doct. Church, Doct. Taylor, and Mr. Pickering, be a committee to consider the petition of Mr. Pigeon, commissary general.

Ordered, That Mr. Wheeler, Doct. Whiting, and Capt. Pilsbury, be a committee to consider a petition of Col. John Patterson, [who reported as follows :]

The committee appointed to take into consideration the petition of Col. Patterson, have attended that service, and beg leave to report by way of resolve.

[*Resolved*,] That the committee of supplies be directed to give immediate orders for the supplying said destitute soldiers with blankets, agreeably to the said petition.

The committee on the petition of Mr. Pigeon, reported. The report was accepted, and is as follows, viz. :

Resolved, That Mr. John Pigeon, commissary general, requesting a dismission from his said office, being under a mistake, have liberty to withdraw his petition ; that the conduct of said commissary general in his office, has been such as to merit the approbation of this Congress,

(1) The resolve reported by the committee, provided for fitting out a number of armed vessels not less than six, to mount from eight to fourteen carriage guns, to cruise under the orders of the committee of safety, for the protection of the commerce and property of the towns of the sea-coast against the depredations of the enemies of the province, and for the capture and destruction of its foes.

and of the public in general ; and that said John Pigeon be desired to attend his business as commissary general in the service of this province.

At the request of Mr. Pigeon, the commissary general, *Ordered*, that Doct. Holten, Mr. Devens, and Col. Palmer, be a committee to consult, and with their advice, assist Mr. Pigeon in such matters as appertain to his office.

Resolved, That there be one deputy commissary appointed to each regiment, and that Mr. Pigeon, the commissary general, be desired to lay before the Congress a list of persons proper to be appointed for this business, and to propose an establishment for their pay.

Ordered, That Mr. Edwards, Mr. Hopkins, Doct. Taylor, Mr. Batchelder, and Doct. Church, be a committee to confer with four Indians, this day arrived from Penobscot, under the conduct of Mr. John Lane, and to provide proper entertainment for them while in this place, and for their return home.

Ordered, That Mr. Pickering, Mr. Langdon, and Col. Sawyer, be a committee to consider the desire of Capt. George Dodge for liberty to export a quantity of old Jamaica fish.

On a motion made in behalf of Capt. Thomas Mason and Capt. George Dodge, that they might have liberty from this Congress to ship off for the West Indies, one hundred and thirty hogsheads of last year Jamaica cod fish, or a quantity not exceeding the same :

Resolved, That it appears to this Congress, that the detention of said fish can be of little or no service to this colony, and that they be allowed to export the same : and the committee of safety for the town of Salem is directed to see that this resolve be effectually carried into execution, and that no other provisions, except for the vessel's use, be shipped off in the same.

Resolved, That five o'clock, P. M., be assigned for the choice of some person to preach an election sermon on the 9th of July next.

[Afternoon.]

The committee appointed to consider a petition from the committee chosen to take care of the poor at Charlestown, reported; the report was accepted, and is as follows, viz. :

The committee chosen to take the within petition into consideration report, that it is their opinion, that the poor of the town of Charlestown be provided for by the selectmen of the several towns to which they remove, until the further order of this or some future Congress, or house of representatives.

Ordered, That Col. Cushing, Major Perley, Col. Prescott, Col. Barrett, and Deacon Fisher, be a committee to inquire into the grounds of a report which has prevailed in the army, that there has been treachery in some of the officers; and that, if they find that such report is without foundation, they bring in a resolve for quieting the minds of the people, in respect thereof.

Ordered, That the committee appointed to consider the request of Capt. George Dodge, should likewise consider a request made by Deacon Cheever, in behalf of Mr. Russell, for a similar purpose.

On a motion made in behalf of Mr. Thomas Russell, merchant, that he might be allowed to ship off from this colony, one hundred hogsheads of last year's Jamaica fish, for the West Indies:

Resolved, That it appears to this Congress, that the detention of said fish can be of little or no service to this colony, and that he be allowed to export the same; and as part of said fish is now at Salem, and part at Newburyport, it is further *Resolved*, that the said Russell be allowed to send or transport the fish which is at Salem to Newburyport, in order to be shipped off as aforesaid: and the respective committees of safety of both said towns, are directed to take care, in their own departments, that this resolve be effectually carried into execution, and that no other provisions, except for the vessel's use, be shipped off in the same.

The order of the day [was] moved for.

Ordered, That Capt. Webster, Mr. Wheeler, and Mr. Fox, be a committee to receive and count the votes for a major general.

The committee having attended that service, reported that Col. Heath was chosen.

Resolved, That eleven o'clock, to-morrow morning, be assigned for the choice of four brigadier generals.

A return of a member, (viz. : Mr. Beriah Norton,) from Edgartown, was read, and considered; and the question being put, whether Mr. Norton be regularly returned a member for said town, it passed in the negative.

Ordered, That the secretary transmit to General Heath a certificate of his being chosen by this Congress a major general in the Massachusetts army, and to desire his acceptance, and that he would attend this Congress, as soon as may be, to receive his commission.

Ordered, That Mr. Wheeler, Mr. Lothrop, and Mr. Sayer, be a committee to make out a commission for Major General Heath.

Ordered, That Col. Freeman, Mr. Webster, and Doct. Taylor, be a committee to prepare the form of a return, to be printed on the back of the letter to be sent to the several towns and districts for choosing representatives.

Ordered, That Deacon Fisher, Capt. Stone, and Capt. Thatcher, be a committee to consider a letter from the committee of safety relative to their recommendation of Mr. John Wiley as captain of a company of the train of artillery, and that they notify the said Wiley to be heard thereon.

Ordered, That Capt. Batchelder, Mr. Hopkins, and Major Fuller, be a committee to consider a petition from Robert Haskell.[1]

Ordered, That Capt. Brown be of the committee, in the room of Major Hall, to agree with Mr. Hunt for his house in Watertown, to be used as a hospital.

Ordered, That Deacon Nichols, Deacon Fisher, and Mr. Hinsdale, be a committee to distribute Doct. Langdon's sermons, one to each minister in the colony, and one to each member of the Congress.

The committee appointed to prepare the form of a return to be printed on the back of the letters to the selectmen of the several towns and districts, &c., reported. The report was read, and accepted, and is as follows, viz.:

Pursuant to the letters within written, the freeholders and other inhabitants of the town of   , qualified as is therein directed, upon due warning given, assembled and met together, the   day of   , 1775, and did then elect and depute   to serve for and represent them, in the session and sessions of the great and general court, or assembly, appointed to be convened, held, and kept, at the meeting-house in Watertown, upon Wednesday, the nineteenth day of July, 1775; the said person being chosen by the major part of the electors present at said meeting. Dated at aforesaid, the   day of   , Anno Domini, 1775.

} *Selectmen of*

The person chosen as aforesaid notified thereof, and summoned to attend accordingly, by me,

Constable of

(1) Robert Haskell represented, that he was a native of Beverly, where he resided until 1762, when he removed to Yarmouth in Nova Scotia, and cultivated a small farm. Returning to Beverly in 1773, he engaged in the coasting trade; but the wreck of his vessel, and the loss of her cargo, had deprived him of the means of support, and rendered him desirous of returning to his lands. Having contracted for his passage in an old ship, the committee of safety of Beverly had refused their permission for his departure on the contemplated voyage. He prayed that Congress would give him liberty, under the unfortunate circumstances of his condition, to revisit his home and family.

The committee appointed to prepare a letter to the Continental Congress, reported. The report was read, paragraph by paragraph, and accepted, and ordered to be transcribed, authenticated, and sent forward, [and is as follows, viz :]

To the Honorable, the Continental Congress, now sitting at Philadelphia :

May it please your honors :

Having been favored with your resolve respecting the assumption of government in this colony, we seize the earliest opportunity to express our grateful [*sentiments] for that compassion, seasonable exertion, and abundant wisdom, evidenced in your recommendation to this people on that head, and for the generous provision you have made for our support, in our efforts for the defence of the common liberty and essential rights of the whole continent. As we are plunged into the accumulated distresses of a domestic war, our constant attention to the calls of our brethren in the field, will leave us but little time to contemplate the acts of ordinary legislation ; but, as we are impressed with the indispensable necessity of rescuing this people from the danger they are in, of falling into a state of anarchy, and that our public resolutions may be taken and executed with greater despatch, we shall apply ourselves, with all diligence, to fulfil your benevolent intentions, and establish the form of government recommended by your honors ; that so, order and government may be restored to this disturbed community.

We think it our indispensable duty to inform you, that reenforcements from Ireland, both of horse and foot, being arrived, the number unknown, and having good intelligence that general Gage was about to take possession of the advantageous posts in Charlestown, and on Dorchester point, the committee of safety advised, that our troops should prepossess them, if possible ; accordingly, on Friday evening, the 16th instant, this was effected by about twelve hundred men. About daylight, on Saturday moning, their line of circumvallation, on a small hill south of Bunker's hill, in Charlestown, was closed. At this time, the Lively, man of war, began to fire upon them. A number of our enemies' ships, tenders, cutters, and scows, or floating batteries, soon came up : from all which the fire was general by twelve o'clock. About two, the enemy began to land at a point which leads out towards Noddle's island, and immediately marched up to our intrenchments, from which they were twice repulsed ; but, in the third attack, forced them. Our

a [resentments.]

forces, which were in the lines, as well as those sent for their support, were greatly annoyed on every side, by balls, and bombs, from Copp's hill, the ships, scows, &c.   At this time, the buildings in Charlestown appeared in flames, in almost every quarter, kindled by hot balls, and are since laid in ashes.   Though this scene was most horrible, and altogether new to most of our men, yet many stood and received wounds by swords and bayonets, before they quitted their lines.   At five o'clock, the enemy were in full possession of all the posts within the [isthmus.] In the evening and night following, General Ward extended his intrenchments, before made at the stone house, over Winter hill.   About six o'clock, P. M., of the same day, the enemy began to cannonade Roxbury, from Boston neck and elsewhere, which they continued twenty four hours, with little spirit and less effect.

The number of killed and missing on our side is not known; but supposed by some to be about sixty or seventy, and by some, considerably above that number.   Our most worthy friend and president, Doct. Warren, lately elected a major general, is among them.   This loss we feel most sensibly.   Lieut. Col. Parker, and Major Moore, of this colony, and Major McClary, from New Hampshire, are also dead.   Three colonels, and perhaps one hundred men are wounded.   The loss of the enemy is doubtless great.   By an anonymous letter from Boston, we are told, that they exult much in having gained the ground, though their killed and wounded amount to about one thousand; but this account exceeds every other estimation.   The number they had engaged is supposed to be between three and four thousand.   If any error has been made on our side, it was in taking a post so much exposed.

As soon as an estimate can be made of public and private stocks of gunpowder in this colony, it shall be transmitted without delay; which, we are well assured, will be very small, and by no means adequate to the exigencies of our case.

We apprehend, that the scantiness of our stock of that article cannot fail to induce your honors still to give your utmost attention to ways and means of procuring full supplies of it.   We feel ourselves infinitely obliged to you for your past care in this respect.

We beg leave humbly to suggest, that, if a commander in chief over the army of the United Colonies should be appointed, it must be plain to your honors, that no part of this continent can so much require his immediate presence and exertions, as this colony.

Ordered, That the Hon. Major Hawley, and Mr. Phillips, be a committee to draw up a resolve, to be sent to General Ward, suggesting to him the expediency of drawing part of the forces stationed at Roxbury, to the camp at Cambridge.

The said committee reported the following letter, which was accepted, and ordered to be sent, by Mr. Thaxter, to the camp at Cambridge, immediately:

SIR:—This Congress, considering the present situation of the enemy, and that of the division of our army at Cambridge, think proper to suggest to your serious consideration, whether it is not proper and expedient, that there should be an immediate draft of a regiment or more from the Roxbury camp to that at Cambridge. Your good sense will undoubtedly incline you to consult General Thomas, before you determine absolutely on this measure; but we conceive the consideration of this matter ought not to be delayed a moment.

To the Hon. General Ward.

Adjourned to Wednesday morning, eight o'clock.

WEDNESDAY, June 21, 1775.

Resolved, That the vote of this Congress for ranking the major generals agreeably to the order of their choice, be reconsidered.

The commission prepared for General Heath, was presented to Congress, read, and accepted, and is as follows:

The Congress of the Colony of Massachusetts Bay, to the Hon. William Heath, Esq.   Greeting.

We, reposing especial trust and confidence in your courage, and good conduct, do, by these presents, constitute and appoint you, the said William Heath, to be a major general of all the forces raised by the Congress aforesaid, for the defence of this and the other American colonies.

You are, therefore, carefully and diligently to discharge the duty of a major general, in leading, ordering, and exercising the said forces in arms, both inferior officers and soldiers, and to keep them in good order and discipline: And they are hereby commanded to obey you as their major general: And you are, yourself, to observe and follow such orders and instructions, as you shall, from time to time, receive from the general and commander in chief of said forces, or any other your superior officers; and to demean yourself according to military rules and discipline established by said Congress, in pursuance of the trust reposed in you. Dated at Watertown, the 21st of June, 1775.

By order of Congress.

President.

Ordered, That Col. Gerrish, Major Hawley, Doct. Taylor, Mr. Durfee, and Mr. Jewett, be a committee to consider the expediency of directing General Ward, to call Col. Glover's regiment, now stationed at Marblehead, to the camp at Cambridge, and report.

The committee on the petition of Robert Haskell, reported: The report was accepted, and is as follows, viz.:

The committee appointed to take into consideration the petition of Robert Haskell, beg to report by way of resolve,

Resolved, That the petitioner, Robert Haskell, be, and he hereby is permitted to proceed from Beverly to Nova Scotia, in a fishing vessel about 17 years old, that he hath procured for that purpose; also to carry three or four persons with him, and the following provisions, viz.: one barrel of pork; two of bread; sixteen gallons of molasses; sixteen gallons of rum; a half bushel of beans or peas; and two bushels of salt; but no more provisions of any kind whatever: and that such proceeding will not be contrary to the resolve passed by the Grand American Congress, the 17th of May last, or any other resolve that honorable Congress have yet published.

Resolved, That Col. Phiney, be admitted into this house, to inform the Congress of the state of the regiment enlisted in the county of Cumberland.

The committee appointed to consider the expediency of directing General Ward, to call to the camp at Cambridge, the regiment at Marblehead, reported. The report was [ªaccepted][1].

Ordered, That Col. Sayer wait on General Ward with it.

Ordered, That Mr. Sayer, draw, in the form of a resolve, the report of the committee relative to the estates of the refugees.

Ordered, That the president sign the resolve relative to the violation of the sabbath, which passed the 16th instant.

Ordered, That Doct. Jones, Capt. Stone, and Capt. Bragdon, be a committee to consider the petition of Thomas Twining.

Mr. Sayer reported a resolve relative to the estates of the refugees, which was accepted, and ordered to be printed in the Cambridge, Watertown, and Worcester papers, and is as follows, viz.:

Whereas, the property of some persons who have left their habitations in sundry towns in this colony, and have discovered themselves to be enemies to the rights of this colony, and the continent of Ameri-

a [accepted and is as follows.]

(1) The resolution, unfortunately lost from the journal and files, appears to have directed the removal of the regiment from the coast to the camp, as soon as the troops could abandon their post with safety to the inhabitants.

ca, in general, and have taken refuge in Boston, and other places, under the protection of the enemies to said colony and continent : therefore, *Resolved*, that it be recommended to the selectmen and committees of correspondence of the several towns and districts of this colony, where any property is to be found belonging to any of the aforesaid persons, that they take the same into their care, and make the best improvement thereof in their power ; and also, that it be recommended to the said committees or selectmen, to use their endeavor, that no strip or waste be made on such property, and to keep an account of all the rents and profits arising from the same, and to be accountable for the same, to this, or some other Congress or assembly of this colony, when thereto required ; they having a reasonable allowance made for their trouble.

Afternoon.

Ordered, That Major Hawley, Mr. Gerry and Major Fuller, be a committee to bring in a resolve, for the purpose of calling the general assembly at another time than that at which it is to be held, if the exigencies of the times should make it necessary.

Resolved, That another major general be chosen by this Congress, in addition to the two already chosen, and that six o'clock, this afternoon, be assigned for such choice.

Ordered, That Major Fuller, Col. Farley and Mr. Wheeler, be a committee to inquire how and where materials for making good paper, proper for bills of credit, may be had, if any such bills should be emitted.

Ordered, That Capt. Bragdon and Col. Davis, be a committee to apply to Mr. Paul Revere, desiring him to take care, that he does not leave his engraving press exposed, when he is absent from it ; and said committee are directed to take the plates into their hands, and deliver them to this Congress, when the notes are all struck off.

The committee who were appointed to confer with the Indians, reported as follows, viz. :

The committee appointed by the honorable colony Congress, now sitting, to treat with the chiefs from the Penobscot tribe, after an introduction on their part, received from the [chief of the] Indians the following address, viz. :

The representation he now makes, and the engagements he enters into, are in behalf of the whole tribe he represents.

His heart is good, honest, and upright, in all he says.

The English are a people old and strong ; but they are children and weak. They have a large tract of land, which they have a right to

47

call their own, and have possessed, accordingly, for many years. These lands have been encroached upon by the English, who have, for miles on end, cut much of their good timber. They ask that the English would interpose and prevent such encroachments for the future; and they will assist us, with all their power, in the common defence of our country; and they hope, if the Almighty be on our side, the enemy will not be able to deprive us of our lands.

They request that Capt. Lane be an agent for them, to settle all matters relative to the above difficulties respecting their lands.

They desire a commissary may be sent among them, of whom they may purchase goods. They desire provisions, powder, &c., may be sent them, which they will buy at a reasonable rate.

They say, they have been much imposed upon by our traders, and desire such evils may be, by us, prevented.

Ordered, That the request of the Indians, as mentioned in said report, be considered by the committee aforesaid.

Ordered, That Mr. Haven administer the oaths to General Heath, as colonel, and as major general of the Massachusetts army.

The president then delivered General Heath a commission as colonel, and another as a major general of the Massachusetts army.

Ordered, That Mr. Pickering, Mr. Lothrop and Mr. Pitts, be a committee to deliver commissions to the following officers in General Heath's regiment, viz.: Jotham Loring 2d, major: Charles Cushing, captain: Elias Whitton, lieutenant: Benjamin Beal, ensign.

Ordered, That the president, Major Hawley, Mr. Gerry, Col. Thompson, Capt. Goodman, Col. Lincoln and Col. Freeman, be a committee to inquire into the reason of the present want of discipline in the Massachusetts army, and to report to this Congress what is the most proper way to put said army into a proper regulation.

A commission was delivered to Col. Benjamin Ruggles Woodbridge, as colonel of a regiment in the colony army.

Ordered, That commissions be delivered to the officers of Col. Woodbridge's regiment, agreeably to a list by him exhibited to the committee of safety.

The order of the day [was] moved for.

Ordered, That Col. Lincoln, Mr. Pitts and Mr. Lothrop, be a committee to receive, sort, and count the votes for another major general: which committee reported, that they had attended that service, and that Joseph Fry, Esq., was chosen.

Ordered, That Mr. Phillips be appointed, forthwith to wait on Col.

Fry, to inform him of such choice, and to know if he will accept that trust.

The committee appointed to consider the request of the Indians, now in Watertown, reported: the report was accepted, and is as follows, viz. :

We, the delegates of the people of this province, assembled in Congress, being appointed to transact the public business, have no doubt that any engagement we shall make, for and in behalf of our constituents, will, on their part, be faithfully ratified and adhered to. We do not doubt of the integrity and honest intentions of our brethren of the Penobscot tribe, and hope, on their part, that they entertain no jealousy of the uprightness and fidelity of us, their brethren. The inhabitants of this colony disdain to make use of unjustifiable force or artifice, to rob their unsuspecting brethren of their rights; and are heartily disposed to prevent any injuries and encroachments upon their neighbors, and to restrain and chastise such invaders as have evidenced any such unjustifiable dispositions. And we hereby strictly forbid any person or persons whatsoever, from trespassing or making waste, upon any of the lands and territories, or possessions, beginning at the head of the tide on Penobscot river, extending six miles on each side of said river, now claimed by our brethren, the Indians of the Penobscot tribe, as they would avoid the highest displeasure of this Congress.

We thank our brethren of the Penobscot tribe, for their generous offers of friendship and assistance in our present war with our brethren in Great Britain, who are endeavoring, by murder and violence, to rob us of our lands and property, and hereby engage to [support] their just claims against every invader. As soon as we can take breath, from our present fight, we will take care that our brethren, the Penobscot tribe, shall be furnished with a proper commissary, who shall be directed to furnish them with provisions, ammunition, and goods, at a reasonable rate; and proper and effectual measures shall then be taken, to prevent any dishonest persons from carrying on a fraudulent traffic with them.

We accept of Capt. Lane, as an agent, appointed by our brethren of the Penobscot tribe, who is hereby authorized and empowered to take cognizance, and make report to this Congress, or any future assembly of this colony, of any molestation or depredations, which the Indians of the Penobscot tribe may hereafter sustain, from any person whatsoever; so that seasonable and effectual measures may be taken to afford those, our brethren, such redress as their circumstances may require. To the Fountain of all Justice we dare appeal, that our intentions are equitable towards all our neighbors, and on that Almighty Being we rely, that, while we are struggling against rapine and tyranny, we shall be supported in the conflict, and our just endeavors be finally crowned with success.

The committee likewise reported, verbally, that it is their opinion, the said Indians should have, each of them, two yards of blue broad-cloth, and one piece of ribbon, and have their expenses paid, out and home : which report was accepted, and the committee of supplies directed to furnish said Indians with the said ribbon and cloth.

A copy of a letter from the president of the New York Congress to Major General Wooster, at Greenwich, forwarded to head quarters at Cambridge, was read, and committed to the committee just now appointed to consider some methods for regulating the army immediately.[1]

(1) The letter of the New York Congress was forwarded by Gov. Trumbull, with the communications which follow :

"LEBANON, June 19, 1775, A. M., 7 o'clock.

"SIR :—Inclosed are copies of notes taken by the Provincial Congress at New York, of the intelligence brought by Capt. Thompson, of the embarkation of four regiments from Ireland for New York, in consequence whereof Major General Wooster is requested by that Congress to march immediately within five miles of the city ; and the latter informs me, that Capt. Sears informed him, that the people of New York intend to quarter our troops in the city. The military stores, which were at Turtle Bay, have fallen into the hands of General Wooster, consisting of too many articles to be enumerated ; among which are, about five hundred good horse harnesses, a very considerable number of 13 and 10 inch carcasses, [shells and pots,] all well charged, a very great plenty of grape shot, cannon balls from 24 pounders down to 3, &c., &c."

"The Provincial Congress of New York forwarded, for the use of your camp at Cambridge, 655 lbs. of powder, which came as far as Stanford. They desired the same quantity might be forwarded from our eastern magazines. The governor, with his council here, agreed, on Saturday last, to send forward ten barrels of powder, containing 1100 lbs., from Norwich. Immediately after receiving the letter of Mr. Gerry, of 17th June, at 7 and 8 o'clock, P. M., I sent to Norwich directions to forward the same, night and day. The remainder of Col. Parson's regiment were ordered to march, forthwith, to join the rest at camp, with one pound powder, three do. ball, and six flints each. I have sent to hasten them on. I have, this moment, received advice from Col. Arnold at Crown Point, of 13th instant, that the Indians of the Cagnawaga tribe are determined not to assist the king's troops, and have passed a law, that the first of their tribe, who takes up arms against us, shall be put to death ; which he says, is confirmed by five chiefs of that tribe there with their families, and they press hard for our army to march into Canada, as they are much disgusted with the regular troops. Three Indians, sent by him to Canada, it seems, have been much abused by the regulars, and are returned, and confirm that account : it is also confirmed, he says, by a gentleman of probity at Montreal ; and that numbers of the Canadians have expected our army there, and are impatient of our delay, being determined to join us as soon as sufficient force appears to support them : that Gov. Carlton, by every art, can raise no more than twenty Canadians of the noblesse : that he threatens to burn Montreal, if the merchants won't defend the city, in case of an attack : that he has only 550 effective men, and thinks it would be very easy to possess ourselves of the whole country."

"Col. Hinman writes, that he is in quiet possession of Ticonderoga, and does not find that there are any enemies about him."

"I am, with great truth and regard, gentlemen, your obedient, humble servant,

JONA. TRUMBULL."

"*Joseph Warren, Esq., President of the Massachusetts Congress, and Elbridge Gerry, Esq., chairman of the committee of supplies at Massachusetts.*"

Ordered, That commissions for the several officers of the train of artillery hereafter mentioned, be prepared and delivered, viz. : To Col. Richard Gridley, colonel : Mr. William Burbeck, lieutenant colonel . Mr. David Mason, 1st major : Mr. Scarborough Gridley, 2d major.

Resolved, That commissions be delivered to the several officers of the train of artillery, agreeably to the list exhibited by the committee of safety, except to Mr. John Wiley's company: and that the said committee be desired to recommend some persons for that company anew.

Ordered, That Mr. Lothrop, Mr. Pickering and Col. Sawyer, be a committee to prepare commissions for the several officers of the train, agreeably to the foregoing resolve of Congress.

Notes of the Intelligence brought by Capt. Thompson.

" Capt. Thompson arrived at New York, Tuesday, 13th June, 1775 ; left Cork, in Ireland, on the 6th of May last, and informs, that six regiments had sailed, in 24 transports, for Boston, one regiment of horse included, which sailed 30th April. Three regiments were embarked, and the fourth embarking, to sail for New York, with the first fair wind. The regiments were all full, 700 men each, filled by drafts from the regiments that remain. Their places were to be filled by new recruits. The general report was, that these four regiments were coming to New York, and some captains, and other officers belonging to the troops, told Capt. Thompson in person, that they were coming to New York. One regiment arrived at Cork, from Kilkenny, the day Capt. Thompson sailed, which was the last regiment to embark for New York. He saw 12 large transports destined for New York : he heard that 16 were to sail : one general officer was to come to New York."

" The troops coming to New York are to protect the people's property, and assist against mobs : the report in Ireland was, that those troops had been wrote for by persons here. The troops, in general, disliked the service : some officers had sold out: no ships of war were coming with the transports : a report prevailed in Ireland, that nine new regiments were to be raised. He heard that 30,000 Russians were ready at a moment's warning. The people of Ireland, in general, are well affected to the Americans, and are averse to the Americans' being taxed by the parliament of Great Britain. Capt. McIlvaine sailed (before Capt. Thompson) for Philadelphia, and has the numbers of the regiments coming to America."

" PROVINCIAL CONGRESS, *New York*, 17th June, 1775."

" SIR :—Being well informed that four regiments, containing near three thousand effective men, have sailed, in transports, for this city, we took the liberty to request the assistance of those brave sons of freedom who are under your command. We are, this instant, further informed, that the Mercury, ship of war, was cruising upon our coast, and is now at Sandy Hook, to order those transports to Boston immediately, and did, on Tuesday last, thirty leagues to the southeast of the Hook, deliver her orders to the old Spy, man of war, now a transport, with part of the forty fourth regiment on board, which immediately altered her course. From hence, we conclude, that a very capital stroke is meditated against our brethren of the Massachusetts Bay. You best can determine, sir, whether it is proper, on this occasion, for the forces under your command to march westward ; but we are led to believe, that it is of more important consequence to secure the several passes with which nature hath bounteously fortified the eastern country, that, if some unexpected chance of war should prove fatal to us, in the first contest, the enemy may, by such means, receive a check in his career of vengeance. We beg you to transmit this intelligence to the provincial camp with the utmost despatch.   We are, sir, your most humble servants.

By order of the Congress.   PETER V. B. LIVINGSTON, *President.*"

" *To Major Genrral Wooster, at Greenwich.*"

" The above is a true copy of a letter just received from the Provincial Congress of New York, and now forwarded by express.

By order of General Wooster.   JAMES LOCKWOOD, *Sec'ry.*"

Ordered, That Major Whittemore wait upon Col. Gridley, to desire him to attend this Congress, to-morrow, to receive his commission.

Ordered, That Deacon Nichols, Mr. Bent and Deacon Fisher, be a committee to consider the petition of Capt. Briant Morton.

Ordered, That Col. Gridley's list of staff officers be committed to the committee just now appointed to prepare commissions for the officers of the train.

Adjourned to Thursday morning, nine o'clock.

THURSDAY, June 22, 1775.

Ordered, That the secretary, Col. Cushing and Mr. Wheeler, be a committee to make a list of such officers of the army, as have been commissioned, and also to inquire who have not yet received their commissions.

Ordered, That an ensign's commission be delivered to Mr. Stephen Frost, of Capt. Locke's company, in Col. Gardner's regiment.

Ordered, That the selectmen of the town of Ashby, be directed to deliver the selectmen of the town of Townshend one half barrel of powder, provided they have two half barrels, the selectmen of Townsend giving a receipt for the same.

Ordered, That the petition of Col. Paul Dudley Sergent be committed to Col. Parks, Major Fuller of Middleton, and Mr. Nye.

Ordered, That the petition from Penobscot [for ammunition and provisions] be recommitted.

Ordered, That Doct. Francis Kittridge be desired to attend the hospital, as a surgeon, till the further order of Congress, and that Mr. Kendall be desired to inform Doct. Kittridge of his appointment.

Ordered, That the colonels of the several regiments in the Massachusetts army, be directed to recommend, immediately, suitable persons for surgeons and surgeons' mates.

Ordered, That a recommendation from the committee of safety, respecting aids de camp, be committed to Col. Glover, Major Goodwin and Dr. Whiting.

Ordered, That Major Whittemore, Mr. Davis and Deacon ['Gould,] be a committee to distribute the handbills respecting the due observance of the Lord's day.

Ordered, That Mr. Pickering be appointed, in the room of Col. Coffin, to consider the petition of Mr. Kirkwood, keeper of the lighthouse on Thatcher's island.[1]

a [Gool.]

(1) James Kirkwood represented, that he had been deprived of his salary for two years, and had not been remunerated for his disbursements in maintaining the lights on Thatcher's island, and

Ordered, That Mr. Hinsdale, Col. Farley and Capt. Batchelder, be a committee to take into consideration a petition from George Vincent of Salem.

Ordered, That Doct. Whiting be appointed to draft a resolve, that application be made to the committee of safety by every person that is to be appointed a military officer.

Ordered, That the proclamation for a fast be recommitted for amendment, and that Mr. Webster and Deacon Fisher be added to the committee.

Ordered, That a hospital be provided for the camp at Roxbury, and that Col. Davis, Doct. Taylor and Doct. Whiting, be a committee to provide one accordingly, and to supply the same.

Ordered, That Major Fuller of Newton, be appointed to take care of the plates, until the further order of this Congress, or some future house of representatives of this colony.

Ordered, That Major Hawley, Mr. Webster and Col. Gerrish, be a committee to take into consideration Col. Phiney's regiment.

Ordered, That Mr. Goodman be appointed, in the room of Col. Grout, on the petition of Mr. Parry.

Afternoon.

Ordered, That Mr. Paul Revere's account[1] be committed to Col. Farley, Mr. Hall and Mr. Bailey.

Ordered, That Capt. Batchelder, Major Goodwin and Mr. Hobart, be a committee to consider the propriety of commissioning the officers in Col. Gerrish's regiment.

Ordered, That Mr. Pickering be appointed, to fill up commissions for Samuel Patch, as captain, and Zachariah Walker and Joshua Brown, as lieutenants, in Col. William Prescott's regiment.

Ordered, That a letter be sent to General Ward, in answer to his letter, and that Col. Lincoln be appointed for that service.

Voted, That a particular number of men shall be settled, to entitle Col. Phiney to the command of a regiment.

Voted, That Col. Phiney be directed to bring up to the camp four hundred men with effective fire arms, and that a time be limited to bring up one hundred more, at least, with effective fire arms, and in that case [he] to be entitled to a colonel's commission, and not otherwise.

prayed relief from the pecuniary difficulties he experienced by reason of the postponement of the payments due for his services and expenses.

(1) Col. Paul Revere charged for engraving four copper plates of the colony notes, at 6*l*. each, 24*l*. : and for printing 14,500 impressions, at 3*l*. 6*s*. 8*d*. the thousand, 48*l*. 6*s*. 8*d*.

Ordered, That Mr. Pickering be appointed, to make out commissions to the officers in Col. Gerrish's regiment.

Ordered, That the committee of safety be directed, as soon as possible, to prepare and transmit to this Congress, perfect lists of the names of such gentlemen as they judge fit and worthy to be commissioned in the several regiments granted by this Congress, and for which the said committee have not already transmitted lists, that so our army may be organized as soon as possible.

On the petition of the selectmen of the town of Townshend, *Resolved,* that it be recommended to the selectmen of the town of Ashby, to deliver to the selectmen of the town of Townshend, one half barrel of gunpowder for the use of the inhabitants of said Townshend; which shall be replaced in the town of Ashby by this Congress, or a house of representatives, so soon as the state of our magazines will admit; or otherwise, said town of Ashby shall be fully paid for said powder, out of the public treasury : provided the said town of Ashby have two half barrels, as has been represented to this Congress.

The committee appointed to consider by what means the army before Boston, may be effectually and most expeditiously strengthened, beg leave to report in part, that they judge it absolutely necessary that the eight companies stationed in the county of Plymouth, belonging partly to General Thomas's regiment, and partly to Col. Cotton's regiment, be immediately ordered to join the army as soon as possible, and that directions be immediately given to General Ward for that purpose.

JOSEPH HAWLEY, *per order.*[1]

[The committee reported the following letter to general Ward, which was accepted :]

SIR :—As it appears to this Congress highly probable, that the army of our enemies will speedily make the utmost efforts to force your lines and penetrate into the country, they have judged it absolutely necessary for the strengthening of the army before Boston, that the eight companies now posted in the county of Plymouth, belonging partly to General Thomas's regiment, and partly to Col. Cotton's regiment, should immediately join the said army. You are therefore directed, without delay, to give the orders necessary for the marching the said eight companies to the said army as soon as may be.

---

(1) In the original journal, the resolve in relation to the removal of the troops from Plymouth, is repeated, under the date of June 23.

Resolved, That [ᵃ the colonels] in the Massachusetts army, be and they are hereby directed, immediately to inform the committee appointed by Congress to examine the surgeons for said army, whom they recommend for the surgeons and surgeon's mates of their respective regiments, and send them to said committee for examination, without delay; except such as have been examined.

Resolved, That George Vincent be, and he hereby is permitted to export from Salem to the West Indies, about forty one barrels of alewives, and said Vincent is also permitted to take on board his vessel, provisions sufficient for his voyage to the said West Indies, and no more, and the committee of safety of the town of Salem, are hereby directed to see this resolve strictly complied with.

On a petition of a number of the inhabitants settled on Penobscot river, the inhabitants of Belfast, Majabigwaduce, and Benjamin's river, representing the difficulties and distress said inhabitants are under, in respect to the scarcity of corn and ammunition, and praying for some relief, *Resolved*, that it be recommended by this Congress, to the committee of safety of the town of Gloucester, or Newburyport, or to the like committees of safety, or correspondence, of any other towns within this colony, to supply Capt. Jonathan Buck, one of the petitioners, for the use of said inhabitants, for their present relief, with two hundred bushels of indian corn, or to that amount in corn and rye, and take, in return for the same, cord wood, or such other payment as the said Buck may be able to make, on his security therefor; and in case the said Buck shall not make satisfaction for the same, in a reasonable time, it shall be allowed and paid, out of the public treasury of this colony, and the said Buck shall refund the same as soon as may be: and that Col. Goldthwait deliver up all the public arms and ammunition in his possession, to the petitioners, or a committee appointed by them for that purpose: and, as to powder, they shall be reasonably supplied therewith, as soon as the state of our magazine will admit thereof.

FRIDAY, June 23, 1775.

Ordered, That Col. Cushing, Mr. Lothrop, Mr. Pickering, Mr. Wheeler, and Mr. Langdon, be a committee to fill up commissions, and that no one of said gentlemen quit the house without leave.

Ordered, That the officers in Col. Glover's regiment, be commissioned, except Capt. Lee and his subalterns.

Ordered, That the pay of the ensigns be augmented to three pounds

ᵃ [each colonel.]

ten shillings, and those that are returned as ensigns, be commissioned as second lieutenants.

Ordered, That the petition of Bridget Philips, be dismissed; that directions be given to General Ward, not to permit Bridget Philips, wife to an officer in Boston, to go into Boston, nor any other person whatever, and that Major Goodwin, be directed to bring in a resolve for that purpose.

Ordered, That a commission be given to Col. Gridley, as chief engineer and colonel, with the rank of major general, and that the lieutenant colonel of the train have the rank of colonel, and that the majors have the rank of lieutenant colonels; and that the captains [have] the rank of majors, captain lieutenants and first lieutenants the rank of captains; and that the rank of the other officers be suspended for the present.

Ordered, That the report respecting Col. Phiney's regiment be recommitted, in order to bring in a resolve directing Col. Phiney, to bring to the camp, 400 men with effective fire arms, and in that case [he] to be commissioned as first colonel, with a major under him; and in case he brings up 500 men, all the officers to be appointed; and in case he brings up but 300 men, [he] to receive a commission as lieutenant colonel; also, that his men be brought up to camp at the expense of the government.

Ordered, That the committee appointed to disperse the handbills respecting the due observance of the Lord's day, be directed to make a computation what number are wanted, and order them to be printed, and that one be struck off for each parish.

Ordered, That General Fry be commissioned as a major general, and that the president be directed to administer the oath to him.

Ordered, That the oath for general officers be altered, and that the words, "or house of representatives, or legislative body of said colony," be added.

Ordered, That Mr. Lane's account for bringing up the Indians, be committed to Mr. Langdon, Capt. Goodman, Capt. Holmes, Capt. Parker, and Capt. Carpenter, to take the same into consideration, and report thereon.

The committee appointed to provide a hospital for the camp in Roxbury, reported as follows: That they have appointed the house belonging to Joshua Loring, in said Roxbury, for a hospital, and for the use of said camp. The report was accepted.

Ordered, That the account of Capt. Kirkwood, be recommitted to the committee appointed to take that matter into consideration, and that Major Whittemore, and Mr. Glover, be added to the committee.

Ordered, That the consideration of the appointment of quarter master generals, and adjutant generals, be deferred to four o'clock, P. M., and that Mr. Hobart, be appointed to wait on General Ward, to [request him to] nominate an adjutant general.

Ordered, That to-morrow, eleven o'clock, A. M., be assigned to come to the choice of four brigadier generals.

Ordered, That a committee be appointed to draw up the form of warrants for staff officers, and that the committees appointed to deliver out commissions be appointed for that purpose.

The committee appointed to take into consideration Col. Phiney's regiment, reported.   The report was accepted, and is as follows, viz. :

Resolved, That Col. Edmund Phiney, heretofore authorized by the committee of safety to raise a regiment for the service of this colony, but [who] has not yet effected it, be directed to proceed, with the greatest diligence and despatch in that business, and in case he shall, on or before the fifteenth day of July next, join the army of this colony, now before Boston, with four hundred effective men, each armed with a good effective firelock, the said Phiney, shall be entitled to be commissioned as a colonel, on the pay established by this Congress for a chief colonel; and that there shall be also allowed to the said body, one major, and no other field officers; and in case the said Phiney, shall procure an addition of one hundred effective men, or upwards, and each armed with an effective firelock, by the last day of July next, that, in such case, the said one hundred men shall be joined to the aforesaid four hundred men, and both the said numbers shall constitute one regiment, and then the choice of field officers shall be completed, and a proper number of subordinate officers, commissioned : but in case the said Phiney shall fail of procuring four hundred effective men, armed as aforesaid, but shall [ªprocure] to be enlisted, and brought to the said army, by the said fifteenth day of July next, a number of effective men, all armed as aforesaid, less than four hundred, and not less than three hundred, he shall be entitled to be commissioned as a lieutenant colonel, and that allowance shall hereafter be made of all reasonable expenses in marching said men to the said army.   And that the said Phiney, be specially instructed not to march any man to the said camp, who is not furnished with a good effective firelock, and that no man without a firelock, shall be accounted, or reckoned, as going to constitute the numbers above mentioned, which shall entitle him to either of the aforesaid commissions proposed for him.

Ordered, That the secretary be directed to make out a copy of the resolve respecting Col. Phiney's regiment.

Afternoon.

The committee appointed to take into consideration the price of blankets, to be given the soldiers, reported as follows; which [report] was accepted, viz. :

Resolved, That the sum of twelve shillings, lawful money, be the stated price for each blanket allowed to the soldiers in the Massachusetts army; and such soldiers as have, or shall be supplied with blankets of less value, as may appear by the appraisement of the selectmen, shall have the overplus made up to them by those who supplied said soldiers, and the aforesaid twelve shillings shall be allowed, out of the. public treasury, for each blanket.

Ordered, That nine o'clock, to-morrow morning, be assigned to take into consideration an establishment for the brigadier generals, and quarter master generals, and adjutant generals.

Ordered, That the time assigned for the choice of quarter master generals, and adjutant generals, be deferred to to-morrow morning, at ten o'clock, A. M.

Ordered, That a letter from Mr. Hooper of Newburyport,[1] be referred to the committee of supplies, they to make report.

Ordered, That Daniel Noyes, of Ipswich, be appointed a postmaster, in the room of Mr. James Foster, who has resigned that office.

Ordered, That Major Fuller of Middleton, be directed to wait on General Whitcomb, and desire him to attend this Congress, and receive his commission.

Ordered, That Doct. Taylor, Major Fuller of Middleton, and Col. Thompson, be a committee to take into consideration the regiment that was moved from Marblehead to Cambridge, immediately, and that the committee be directed to go to Cambridge, and inquire into it, and make report.

Ordered, That the committee appointed to fill up commissions, be directed to fill up a commission for General Whitcomb.

Ordered, That Mr. Nye, be appointed to number the notes signed by Deacon Plympton.

(1) Stephen Hooper, Esq. states, that the committee of Portsmouth had received from Baltimore, fifty barrels of flour, intended as a donation for the inhabitants of Boston: but, as the New Hampshire troops needed supplies, they desired to purchase and retain the flour.

Ordered, That Capt. Sprague, Capt. White and Doct. Whiting, be a committee to take into consideration a petition from the town of Malden.

Ordered, That Mr. Hopkins, Capt. Bragdon and Mr. Phillips, be a committee to take into consideration the circumstances of the Reverend Doct. Langdon, president of the college, and report thereon.

Ordered, That a committee be appointed to consider of proper expedients to augment the army, and, in particular, to write to the other New England governments on the subject, and that they be directed to attend the service immediately.

Ordered, That Mr. Nye be excused from attending the service, in numbering the notes signed by Deacon Plympton, and that Mr. Holmes be appointed in his room, and be directed to attend that service immediately.

Ordered, That the report of the committee, who were ordered to inquire into the misconduct in the late engagement, lie on the table till they are ready to report in full.

Ordered, That the committee of safety be directed to make out a new list for officers of the train of artillery, and that no person unworthy of the office be appointed.

The committee appointed to take into consideration Capt. Lane's account for bringing up the Indians from Penobscot, reported, that his account be allowed, and that the receiver general be directed to pay said account to Capt. Lane, or order ; and likewise, that the sum of nineteen pounds, ten shillings, eight pence, lawful money, be paid by the receiver general to Capt. Lane, to defray his expenses in carrying the Indians back to Penobscot, and that Mr. Langdon be appointed to draft a resolve for that purpose.

The committee appointed to take into consideration a letter from Mr. Stephen Hooper of Newburyport, reported as follows, viz. :

Resolved, That those of the committee of donations of the town of Boston, who have left said town, viz., Messrs. Benjamin Austin, Nathaniel Barber and —— Proctor, be advised to sell the fifty barrels of flour sent from Baltimore for the use of the poor of Boston, now in the hands of the committee of correspondence of Portsmouth, to the same committee, for the use of the New Hampshire troops.[1]

The committee appointed to take into consideration the request from the town of Malden, reported as follows, which was accepted, viz. : the

(1) The report of the committee to consider what measures should be adopted to strengthen the army before Boston, in relation to the removal of the troops from Plymouth county, inserted in the journal of the proceedings of the twenty-second of June, and repeated in the original, has been omitted.

committee beg leave to report, that the inhabitants of the town of Malden be [directed] to make the best use of their artillery they can, for their defence, in case they shall be attacked by the enemy, and that they make their application for assistance to the general of the army, who, doubtless, will furnish them with such detachments from the army, as they shall judge necessary and expedient.

The committee appointed to draft a resolve for the receiver general to pay to Capt. Lane £19 10s. 8d., for defraying the expense of carrying the Indians back to Penobscot, reported as follows, viz.:

Resolved, That there be paid, out of the public treasury of this colony, to Mr. John Lane, or order, the sum of £19 10s. 8d., to pay the expenses of himself, four Indian chiefs, and an interpreter, from Watertown to Penobscot, and the receiver general is hereby directed to pay the same accordingly.

Voted, That the former vote respecting the removal of the library, apparatus, and other valuable effects of Harvard College, be reconsidered, and that the following resolve be accepted, viz.:   Whereas, it is expedient that those apartments in Harvard Hall, under the immediate charge of the professor of philosophy and librarian of Harvard College, be evacuated: *Resolved,* that the library, apparatus, and other valuables of Harvard College, be removed, as soon as may be; that Mr. Samuel Phillips, Mr. Daniel Hopkins and Dummer Jewett, Esq., be a committee to consult with the reverend, the president, the Hon. Mr. Winthrop and the librarian, or such of them as may be conveniently obtained, and, with them, to engage some suitable person or persons in the town of Andover, and such other places as they may think best, to receive and take the charge of the above mentioned effects; that said committee join with those gentlemen, in employing proper persons for packing said library, apparatus, and such other articles as they shall judge expedient, and take all due care, that it be done with the greatest safety and despatch; and, as the packages shall be completed, that they take due care for their transportation: the charges to be laid before this, or some future Congress, or house of assembly of this province.

Ordered, That Mr. Hale, Capt. Parker and Capt. Bragdon, be a committee to take Capt. Lane's account of his time into consideration, and report thereon.

Resolved, That Winthrop Sergeant of Gloucester, merchant, be allowed to ship off for the West Indies, a quantity of old Jamaica fish, not exceeding forty hogsheads, it appearing to this Congress, that the said fish, if stopped, will be of little or no service to this colony; and the committee of safety for Gloucester are directed to cause this resolve to be so carried into execution, as that no other provisions, except for the vessels' use, be shipped off in the same.

Voted, That the receiver general be directed to pay to the Reverend Doct. Langdon, president of the college, £100, lawful money, in bills of credit of this colony.

Ordered, That the committee appointed to consider by what means the army before Boston, may be effectually and most expeditiously strengthened, be directed to write a letter to General Ward; who reported a letter to General Ward, directing him to call on the eight companies stationed in the county of Plymouth.[1]

The committee appointed to take into consideration the petition of Robert Haskell, beg leave to report by way of resolve : *Resolved*, that the petitioner, Robert Haskell, be permitted to proceed from Beverly to Nova Scotia in a fishing vessel, about seventeen years old, that he hath procured for that purpose, also to carry three or four persons with him, and the following provisions, viz. : one barrel of pork, two hundred [pounds] of bread, sixteen gallons of rum, sixteen gallons of molasses, half a bushel of beans or peas, and two bushels of salt ; but no more provisions of any kind whatever : and that such proceeding will not be contrary to the resolve passed by the grand American Congress, the 17th of May last, or any other resolve that honorable Congress have yet published.

Resolved, That the committee of safety be directed to make out a new list for officers of the train of artillery, that no person unworthy of office be appointed.

SATURDAY, June 24, 1775.

Ordered, That Doct. Taylor, Col. Sawyer and Capt. Batchelder, be a committee to consider some method for regulating trade with the Indians.

Major Fuller, Doct. Bailey and Capt. Goodman, [were] appointed a committee to consider the expediency of part of Col. Phiney's regiment being stationed in the counties of Cumberland and Lincoln.

Ordered, That Mr. Langdon, Col. Sawyer and Capt. Goodman, be a committee to consider what is further necessary to be done respecting the bills of credit of this colony.

Voted, That there shall be two surgeons and two mates appointed for each hospital, and commissioned accordingly.

Ordered, That the committee appointed to examine the surgeons, be desired to report an establishment for surgeons of hospitals.

---

(1) This paragraph seems, in making up the journal, to have been inadvertently inserted, the subject having been disposed of on the preceding day.

The committee appointed to consider an establishment for the surgeons of hospitals, reported : the report was accepted, and is as follows, viz. : that it is their opinion, that the establishment of the chief surgeons should be at the rate of eight pounds per month, and each mate, four pounds, ten shillings, per month.

Ordered, That Col. Freeman, Col. Farley and Capt. Stone, be a committee to get the resolve for a fast printed, and one sent to each religious society in this colony : [which is as follows, viz. :]

[Whereas, it hath pleased Almighty God, the wise and good Governor of the Universe, in his righteous providence, for our many sins, to suffer the sword of the British troops to be unsheathed against the inhabitants of this colony, in such a cruel and unnatural manner as must give the world the most indisputable proofs of the wicked designs to destroy or enslave this whole continent : as in the unprovoked and unnatural instances of hostilities, cruelty and barbarity, of the ever memorable 19th of April last, whereby so many of the brave and inoffensive inhabitants of this colony were murdered : and the several attacks which have since been made by the said troops on us between that day and the 17th instant, when our country resounded with the roar of cannon from the once peaceful shores and harbor near the capital, when there was scarce aught but smoke, fire, and blood, to be seen there, whereby the lives of many of our countrymen, bravely fighting in defence of the rights of America, were lost; together with their laying the opulent town of Charlestown, in a most savage manner, in ashes :]

[And whereas, some more late oppressive acts of the British parliament are designed by them soon to be enforced upon the Americans; and as large reenforcements are arrived and arriving to join our enemies in Boston, which will probably induce them to make another trial of military prowess, to penetrate into the country; and we, being taught, not only by these sore trials, but also by the great mercies of our God, who has hitherto so remarkably covered the heads of our people in the day of battle, to be deeply impressed with a sense of our absolute dependance upon the Lord of Hosts, and God of Armies, for success in this important war, into which we are driven by our enemies, do renounce all confidence in our own strength; but, being fully assured our cause is just, and relying on the mercy of God for his divine protection and assistance therein : therefore, *Resolved,* that Thursday, the 13th day of July next, be observed as a day of public fasting and prayer, throughout this colony, that we may all, at one time, sincerely humble ourselves before the searcher of hearts for all our many sins, as a people, and as individuals, and humbly and earnestly beseech his forgiveness, and his blessing on us : that he would graciously afford his divine direction and assistance in our military operations, and speedily cause our enemies to be at peace with us upon a just and permanent foundation, that not only a stop may be put to the wanton effusion of human blood, but that Great Britain and these colonies may again rejoice in the free and undisturbed exercise of all those rights, liberties and privileges, civil and religious, for the enjoyment of which our pious ancestors braved every danger, by which they have rendered their memory dear to us, their posterity, and set an example worthy the imitation of all succeeding generations : that he would grant us health in our army and in all our habitations, succeed us in all our lawful employments, give us rain from heaven to water the dry and thirsty earth, and fruitful seasons, and fill our hearts with food and gladness : that he would bestow his blessing upon the various means used for the recovery and preservation of our just rights, particularly on the congresses and houses of assembly of this and the sister colonies, and especially on the American Congress, that they may all be inspired with that wisdom that is necessary in this day of difficulty and distress : that he would smile on the measures taken for the exercise of civil government in this colony: above all, that he would sanctify to us the various dispensations of his righteous providence, that we may be prepared for whatever he may call us to do or suffer, be a peculiar people to himself, and our persons and services accepted of him through Christ our Redeemer. And it is hereby earnestly recommended to each and every religious society, of whatever denomination, in this colony, strictly to abstain from all servile labor and recreation on said day, to mix their fasting with humble thankfulness for the many signal and undeserved mercies we enjoy, and observe said day in a religious manner, by turning every one from his evil ways to God, that so he may turn unto us and not forsake his heritage.]

The committee appointed to take into consideration the wages of Capt. John Lane and Mr. Gilmore, for their attendance in bringing up four Indians from Penobscot, reported. [The report is as follows, viz. :] The committee for examining the account of Mr. John Lane, have attended that service, [and] found the said Lane's account well supported, excepting a few inaccuracies in casting; they therefore beg leave to report by way of resolve, viz. :

Resolved, That there be paid, out of the public treasury of this colony, to Mr. John Lane, the sum of forty-seven pounds, eighteen shillings, and eleven pence half penny, for his expenses in bringing up to the Congress four of the chiefs of the Penobscot tribe of Indians, with

49

an interpreter; and the receiver general of this colony, is hereby directed to pay the said John Lane, or order, the aforesaid sum of forty-seven pounds, eighteen shillings, eleven pence half penny.

Mr. Freeman, and Capt. Bragdon, were added to the committee appointed to consider the expediency of stationing part of Col. Phiney's regiment in the county of Cumberland.

Ordered, That Capt. Lane be admitted on the floor of the house, in order to answer such questions as the Congress shall propose to him.

Ordered, That the committee of supplies be directed to supply the four Indians brought up by Capt. Lane, with a pair of shoes each.

Ordered, That Mr. Mighill, Mr. Hobart, Capt. Webster and Mr. Lothrop, be added to the committee to consider the petition of Edward Parry.

The committee appointed to take into consideration the circumstances of the Rev. Doct. Langdon, president of the college, reported as follows, viz.: *Resolved,* that there be allowed and paid out of the public treasury of this colony, the sum of £100, lawful money, in bills of credit of this colony, to the Rev. Doct. Langdon, president of Harvard College, in part for his services in that station, since his appointment thereto: and the treasurer and receiver general is hereby directed to pay the said sum in bills of credit, accordingly.[1]

Ordered, That the report of the committee to consider Capt. Lane's services be recommitted.

Ordered, That Col. Gerrish, Mr. Wheeler and Col. Farley, be a committee to consider and report what is to be done with the overplus bills.

Ordered, That Deacon Fisher be appointed in the place of Capt. Bragdon, to consider the services of Capt. Lane, in bringing up four Indian chiefs.

The committee appointed to take into consideration the petition of James Kirkwood, keeper of the lights on Thatcher's island, reported: the report was accepted, and is as follows, viz.:

Resolved, That there be allowed and paid, out of the public treasury, to Capt. James Kirkwood, sixty pounds, for one year's salary as keeper of the light-houses on Thatcher's island, and also eighteen pounds, eighteen shillings more, being for his disbursements, in repairing buildings, and other work done there, box of medicines, and several other necessaries, as per his account, herewith exhibited: and the receiver general is, accordingly, hereby directed to pay the said Capt.

(1) The appropriation for the salary of Doct. Langdon had been made on the preceding day: the grant is set out more formally in this resolution, than in that of June 23.

Kirkwood, the aforesaid sums, amounting to seventy-eight pounds, thirteen shillings, the same to be paid in bills of credit of this colony.

Ordered, That three o'clock, P. M., be assigned to come to the choice of a gentleman to preach the election sermon.

The committee appointed to draft a resolve respecting Bridget Phillips, wife of an officer in General Gage's army, reported : the report was read and accepted, and is as follows, viz. : *Resolved,* that General Ward do not suffer or permit Bridget Phillips, wife to an officer under General Gage, to go into Boston, nor any other person whatever, without leave first obtained of this Congress, or some future house of representatives; and that an express be forthwith sent to the committee of safety for the town of Newburyport, to order them to take the most effectual measures to prevent the said Bridget from going out of this province, or to Boston.

The committee appointed to take into consideration, and report the form of a commission for brigadier generals, quarter master generals, and adjutant generals, adjutants, quarter masters, and surgeons, reported a form, which was accepted.

Ordered, That the form of a commission lie on the table.

The committee appointed to hire a house of John Hunt, Esq., for a hospital, reported the following proposal, which was accepted, viz. :

GENTLEMEN :—With respect to the hire of the house belonging to John Hunt, Esq., for a hospital, the proprietor only expects such a consideration from the colony, as will be a satisfaction for the necessary damage to the house, expecting proper care will be taken that the out-houses, &c., be kept in good order.

W. HUNT, in behalf of the proprietor.

Ordered, That the committee appointed to procure spears for the army, be directed to use their discretion in procuring poles for the handles of the spears.

Afternoon.

The committee appointed to prepare a letter to the lieutenant governor and company of Rhode Island, reported : the report was accepted, and similar letters, so far as circumstances will admit, ordered to be sent to Connecticut and New Hampshire. [The letter to the governor of Connecticut is as follows :]

GOVERNOR TRUMBULL.

May it please your honor :—From advices received divers ways, we have the greatest reason to determine, that all the British troops already destined, or that may be yet ordered to America this season, will come to Boston, it being evidently their design, if possible, to rout our army before that place, destroy all our magazines, and thereby to strike terror and faintness into the hearts of all the friends to right and liberty throughout the continent, to revive and animate the scattered friends, and break the union of the colonies, and in that way insure final success to their tyranny. This being undoubtedly the plan of our enemies, it is of inexpressible consequence, that the ground which we have taken should at all events be maintained. Your honor is, no doubt, fully sensible that our army, for the present, is unavoidably checked, with regard to offensive operations, for a reason of which you are not unapprized : but, however, we have the means of acting on the defensive.

As Boston is impregnable against every thing but great artillery, very few troops are sufficient to keep it ; and as there are two passes at least, very distant from each other, by which the enemy will probably attempt to advance into the country, it is thereby rendered necessary that we should throw our army into at least two grand divisions, each of which ought to be able to withstand almost the whole strength of the enemy. Your honor is acquainted, that it was, at first, supposed to be necessary, that 30,000 men should be raised, and stationed to act for this season in the environs of Boston. Thirteen thousand, six hundred, was the number supposed by our Congress, to be the colony's proportion of such an army : and that number we have, to our utmost, been endeavoring fully to complete; but, because there are deficiencies in our regiments, as your honor well knows there always will be in such cases, in order to make that quota good, we have been obliged to increase the number of the regiments ; but still, there is a deficiency, and, because of the inexpressible importance of having our army effectually strong, we are, with unremitted efforts, and by every device, at vast expense, laboring to make that number fully complete, or rather to exceed it.

May it please your honor :—Because we are so vastly apprehensive of the fatal consequences of a general defeat of this army to the whole American cause, and are so unutterably solicitous to have it effectually strengthened, we have called in every individual of our levies from all our outposts, to join the army; although, by that measure, we expose all our towns on the sea coasts to the rage and depredations of the enemy, and run the dreadful risk of the best of our towns being reduced to ashes, and taking the miserable fate of Charlestown.

We beg leave to acquaint your honor, that it is most clearly our opinion, and that we have the best grounds to suppose, that, as soon as the enemy have recovered a little breath from their amazing fatigues of the seventeenth of June, and the surprising losses which they then undoubtedly sustained, shall be made up by arrivals of new troops, which is almost daily taking place, they will direct all their force to some one point, and make the utmost efforts to force our lines, destroy our magazines, and thereby strike general terror and amazement into the hearts of the inhabitants of the whole continent.

From this view of the case, we cannot, a moment longer, forbear addressing your honor, and most earnestly suggesting to the immediate consideration of your general assembly, not only the expediency, but indispensable necessity, of an immediate augmentation of the troops from your colony, for the more effectual strengthening of the army. What the number of the augmentation ought to be, we most cheerfully submit to the good judgment of your assembly, not in the least doubting, but their wisdom and justice will direct and dispose them to do all that is proper, in so important a crisis as we really consider the present.

We need not express to your honor, the indispensable necessity of despatch in making reenforcements, nor the propriety and advantage of marching any new levies, which your assembly may order, with all possible speed, without the first raised companies waiting for the completing of others; inasmuch as your colony has here, on the spot, all the proper officers to make the necessary disposition for their reception, and as the season of their being of any advantage for the support of our army, may be irrevocably lapsed before their arrival, if the least unnecessary delay should be indulged.

We have made a representation to the lieutenant governor of Rhode Island, similar to the foregoing, and are about to make a like representation to the congress of New Hampshire, and to send the same by special express.

We suppose the whole number of our enemy's land forces, when joined with the four regiments which were ordered to New York, will amount to upwards of ten thousand, exclusive of negroes and tories, who are every way provided and furnished, in the best manner, for action.

We have the fullest confidence, that your honor's zeal and ardor for the salvation of our country, and the preservation of our inestimable rights, will render any importunity unnecessary, to induce you to take all the requisite steps to effect the proposed augmentation, for which we are most solicitous.

Ordered, That Major Hawley, Col. Gerrish and the president, be a committee to take into consideration, and report thereon, a letter from General Ward, informing of the desertion of Lieut. Cox of Salem, and a number of men.

Ordered, That Major Hawley and the president be excused, and that Col. Porter and Doct. Church be appointed in their room.

The committee appointed to consider the expediency of stationing part of Col. Phiney's regiment in the counties of Cumberland and Lincoln, reported: the report was accepted, and is as follows, viz.: Whereas, it appears to this Congress to be necessary, that some provision should be made for the defence and protection of the sea coasts in the counties of Cumberland and Lincoln; therefore, *Resolved*, that the resolve which passed yesterday, relative to Col. Phiney's regiment, be so far reconsidered, as that the remainder of said regiment, after 400 thereof have marched to the camp at Cambridge, be immediately raised and stationed in such places in the said counties, as shall be thought best by General Preble, Col. Enoch Freeman and Major Wheaton of St. Georges, until they receive further orders from the Congress, or a general assembly of this colony: and that, after they are at first stationed, they shall be under the direction of Col. Enoch Freeman, who is hereby empowered to order and dispose of them, as, in his opinion, will most conduce to the general interest. And the committee of supplies are hereby directed to supply said troops with provisions, agreeably to the allowance as established by this Congress.

And it is recommended to the selectmen of the several towns in the counties aforesaid, to supply the said troops with ammunition, which shall be replaced as soon as the colony magazine can be supplied, or paid for out of the public treasury; and that Col. Freeman be, and hereby is appointed, to muster the said men, and to see that they are all well prepared with fire arms and other accoutrements.

Mr. Hubbard was appointed in the room of Col. Farley on Mr. Revere's account.

Ordered, That the proclamation for a fast be suspended.

The committee appointed to consider the letter from General Ward, reported: the report was accepted, and is as follows, viz.:

Resolved, That it be recommended to General Ward, immediately to take effectual measures to apprehend Lieut. Cox, and such privates as have been induced by the said Lieut. Cox to desert their duty, and forthwith to bring [said] Cox, and such other deserters as may be apprehended, to their trial, that the said Lieut. Cox and his accomplices may [receive] such condign punishment for their aggravated offences, as, in the rules and orders of war, is provided for; and it is further recommended to the committees of all denominations, and the select-men of any town where said deserters may be, to afford all possible aid and assistance to the general in apprehending them.

Ordered, That the president, Mr. Gerry, Major Hawley, Deacon Cheever, Col. Gerrish, Col. Lincoln and Col. Porter, be a committee to consider what steps are proper to be taken for receiving General Washington with proper respect, and to provide a house for him accordingly.

The committee appointed to consider what allowance is adequate to the services of Capt. John Lane, &c., in bringing up four Indians from Penobscot, reported: the report was accepted, and is as follows, viz.:

The committee appointed to consider what allowance is adequate to the services of Capt. John Lane and Mr. Gilman, for their attendance in bringing up to this town, four Indians of the Penobscot tribe, beg leave to report: that the said Mr. Lane proceed to raise a company of fifty-six effective men, including sergeants, to join the army at Cambridge, agreeably to the order of the committee of safety; and upon his raising said men, that he be entitled not only to a captain's commission, but to the pay established for captains, to commence at the time he received his orders from the committee of safety: that Mr. Gilman be allowed for forty days' attendance as an interpreter to Mr. Lane, at three shillings per day, six pounds; and that the said Mr. Gilman be presented with an honorary commission, with the rank of lieutenant, and be desired to use his influence to cultivate a peaceable disposition in the Indians at St. Francois, and other parts adjoining, and give intelligence of their temper and disposition, from time to time, as he shall have opportunity, and as the importance of affairs may require; and all necessary charge and trouble for any important intelligence so [communicated,] shall be suitably rewarded.[1]

The committee for giving out commissions, were directed to make out an honorary commission for Mr. Gilman, agreeably to the foregoing report.

Mr. Pickering [was] appointed to draw a resolve, directing the treasurer to pay Mr. John Lane and Andrew Gilman, agreeably to said report.

Col. Porter was appointed to procure a scythe, and carry it to a blacksmith, to be fixed for a spear, in such a manner as he thinks fit, and bring it before this Congress, when fixed.

(1) This resolve is repeated in the journal of the next day.

Mr. Pickering brought in a resolve as directed, which was accepted, and is as follows, viz. :

Resolved, That there be allowed and paid out of the public treasury of this colony, to Mr. Andrew Gilman, the sum of six pounds, in bills of credit of this colony, for forty days' attendance as an interpreter to four Indians of the Penobscot tribe, in their late attendance at an embassy to this Congress ; and the receiver general is hereby directed to pay the same sum of six pounds to Mr. Andrew Gilman, in bills of credit, accordingly.

Ordered, That any one of the committee appointed to procure spears, be empowered to order the blacksmith to work on the sabbath, to complete the same as soon as possible.

Resolved, That it be recommended to our good brothers, the Indians of the Penobscot tribe, to immediately apply to General Preble and Col. Freeman of Falmouth, for a supply of provisions and all other necessary goods, and would recommend said gentlemen, as the most suitable persons to supply the Indians, who will undoubtedly do them justice ; and it is hereby recommended to General Preble and Col. Freeman, to supply said Indians with provisions, and all other necessary articles, upon the most equitable terms, and to receive their fur, and other skins, in payment ; and the said General Preble and Col. Freeman, are hereby desired to supply said Indians at the truck-house at Penobscot.

Ordered, That Capt. Stone, Col. Thompson and Capt. Bragdon, be a committee to consider the request of Col. Freeman, to have the minute company of the town of Sandwich stationed at Naushan island.

Monday morning, nine o'clock, was assigned, agreeably to a resolve of the committee of safety, to choose a proper person to superintend the armorers in the camp, and to see that they do their duty.

A letter from George Stillman to Col. Otis was read, and committed to Mr. Goodwin, Mr. Langdon and Doct. Whiting.[1]

Mr. Lothrop, Mr. Dickerson and Mr. White, were appointed a committee to get the proclamation of the Continental Congress for a fast, reprinted, and dispersed one to each religious assembly in the colony.[2]

(1) This letter related to the capture of a tender ; which is fully described in the memorial of the inhabitants of Machias.

(2) The fast appointed by the Continental Congress superseded that directed by the provincial assembly. The proclamation which follows was distributed and read from the desk of every church of Massachusetts, instead of that adopted, and entered in the journal, page 384.

IN CONTINENTAL CONGRESS, June 12, 1775.

As the great Governor of the world, by his supreme and universal providence, nor only conducts the course of nature with unerring wisdom and rectitude, but frequently influences the minds of men to serve the wise and gracious purposes of his providential government ; and it being, at all

Mr. Lothrop, Deacon Fisher and Mr. Parker, were appointed a committee to count and sort the votes for some person to preach an election sermon on the 19th of July next.

The committee reported, that Mr. Gordon was unanimously chosen, and the president was appointed to inform him of this choice.

Adjourned to eight o'clock to-morrow morning.

SABBATH DAY, June 25, 1775.

Ordered, That Capt. Brown, Major Fuller, Mr. Bigelow, Major Brooks, Col. Smith and Deacon Stone, be a committee to procure four hundred spades and shovels for the use of the army, immediately. And the said committee is directed to make a list of such persons, of whom they may procure said spades and shovels, with the number received of each person, and the value thereof, and, when procured, that they immediately forward them to the army at Cambridge.

The committee appointed to prepare an honorary commission for Mr. Gilman, reported a form, which, being duly amended, was accepted, and is as follows, viz. :

The Congress of the Colony of the Massachusetts Bay, to Andrew Gilman, gentleman, Greeting.

We, entertaining a good opinion of your prudence, courage, and good conduct, do appoint, and you the said Andrew Gilman are hereby

times, our indispensable duty devoutly to acknowledge his superintending providence, especially in times of impending danger and public calamity, to reverence and adore his immutable justice as well as to implore his merciful interposition for our deliverance.

This Congress, therefore, considering the present critical, alarming, and calamitous state of these colonies, do earnestly recommend, that Thursday, the 20th day of July next, be observed, by the inhabitants of all the English colonies on this continent, as a day of public humiliation, fasting, and prayer: that we may, with united hearts and voices, unfeignedly confess and deplore our many sins ; and offer up our joint supplications to the all-wise, omnipotent, and merciful Disposer of all events ; humbly beseeching him to forgive our iniquities, to remove our present calamities, to avert those desolating judgments, with which we are threatened, and to bless our rightful sovereign, king George the third, and to inspire him with wisdom to discern and pursue the true interests of his subjects, that a speedy end may be put to the civil discord between Great Britain and the American colonies, without farther effusion of blood : and that the British nation may be influenced to regard the things that belong to her peace, before they are hid from her eyes: that these colonies may ever be under the care and protection of a kind Providence, and be prospered in all their interests : that the divine blessing may descend and rest upon our civil rulers, and upon the representatives of the people, in their several assemblies and conventions, that they may be directed to wise and effectual measures for preserving the union, and securing the just rights and privileges of the colonies ; that virtue and true religion may revive and flourish throughout our land ; and that all America may soon behold a gracious interposition of Heaven for the redress of her many grievances, the restoration of her invaded rights, a reconciliation with the parent state, on terms constitutional, and honorable to both ; and that her civil and religious privileges may be secured to the latest posterity.

And it is recommended to Christians, of all denominations, to assemble for public worship, and to abstain from servile labor, and recreation on said day.

50.

appointed, to the honorary title of lieutenant; and you are to be considered of that rank, not only among the good people of this province, but also among all our friends and brethren through the continent; and we confide in your readiness to promote the common cause of America, among our good brothers, the Indians of the several tribes which you may have opportunity to be acquainted with, as well as with the inhabitants of the province of Quebec.

By order of the Congress.

——— ——— *President.*

The petition of John Lane was read, the prayer whereof was granted, and Col. Lincoln appointed to draw up a resolve thereon.

Col. Lincoln drew up a resolve accordingly, which was accepted, and is as follows, viz.: *Resolved,* that Henry Gardner, Esq., receiver general, be, and he is hereby directed, to pay unto Capt. John Lane, or his order, the sum of twelve pounds, lawful money, being two months pay for a captain in the colony service, he the said Lane to be accountable for that sum, to this, or some future Congress, or constitutional assembly of this colony.

Resolved, That Capt. John Lane proceed to raise a company of fifty six effective men, including sergeants, to join the army at Cambridge, agreeably to the order of the committee of safety: and, upon his raising said men, that he be entitled not only to a captain's commission, but to the pay established for captains, to commence at the time he received his orders from the said committee of safety.[1]

Ordered, That Deacon Fisher draw, in form of a resolve, the report of the committee relative to Andrew Gilman.

Ordered, That Col. Lincoln draw up a resolve, empowering Mr. Grannis to employ thirty men to protect the Elizabeth islands.

Mr. Fisher, agreeably to order, presented the following resolve, which was accepted, and is as follows, viz.:

Resolved, That Lieut. Andrew Gilman be, and hereby is, ordered and instructed to use his utmost influence to cultivate a friendly and peaceable disposition in the Indians at St. Francois, and all other parts adjoining, and to give intelligence of their temper and disposition, from time to time, as he shall have opportunity, and as the importance of affairs may require, and also of the Canadians at Quebec, and other adjacent parts of Canada, so often as it may be in his power, for which service he shall receive a proper reward.

Col. Lincoln, agreeably to order, presented the following resolve,

(1) The substance of this resolve is inserted in the Journal of June 24.

which was accepted : *Resolved*, that Capt. John Grannis be, and he hereby is empowered, immediately, to engage thirty good, able bodied, effective men, to be paid by this colony, well provided with arms and ammunition, and to cause them to be provided with suitable provisions, to repair, without delay, to the Elizabeth islands, so called, in [*Dukes county,] there to protect the stock, and to impress such a number of boats, &c., [as] he shall want to transport the men to and from said islands, as occasion may require, from time to time, until the further order of this, or some future Congress, or constitutional assembly of this colony.

Ordered, That commissions for the officers of the train be immediately sent to the committee of safety, and that they be directed to deliver them to such officers, to whom there is no exception, and that Col. Porter be appointed to carry said commissions to the committee of safety, with this order, immediately.

Ordered, That commissions be delivered to certain officers of Col. Prescott's regiment, agreeably to the recommendation of the committee of safety.

Afternoon.

A draft of a letter to Governor Trumbull, was presented by the committee appointed to prepare one, and was read and accepted, and the committee of supplies directed to forward it by express.[b][1]

The committee appointed to consider what steps are proper to be taken for the reception of General Washington, reported ; the report was ordered to lie on the table.

A letter from the committee of Machias was read, respecting the capture of a king's cutter, and committed to the committee which was yesterday appointed to consider a letter on the same subject to Col. Otis.[2]

a [the county of Duke's county.]   b [and is as follows.]

(1) The letter to Governor Trumbull is the same which has already been inserted in the Journal of June 2, page 311.

(2) The letter of the committee of Machias contains the relation of a bold exploit. It was dated June 14, 1775.

" *To the Honorable Congress of the Massachusetts Bay.*"

"GENTLEMEN :—We, the faithful and distressed inhabitants of Machias, beg leave, once more, in the most respectful manner, to approach your presence, and spread before you a just and full representation of our very critical situation."

" On the 2d instant, Capt. Ichabod Jones arrived in this river with two sloops, accompanied with one of the king's tenders. On the third instant, a paper was handed about for the people to sign, as a prerequisite to their obtaining any provisions, of which we were in great want. The contents of this paper, required the signers to indulge Capt. Jones in carrying lumber to Boston, and to protect him and his property, at all events : but, unhappily for him, if not for us, it soon expired, after producing effects directly contrary in their nature to those intended. The next effort, in order to carry those favorite points, was to call a meeting, which was accordingly done. On the 6th, the people generally assembled at the place appointed, and seemed so averse to the measures proposed, that Capt. Jones privately went to the tender, and caused her to move up so near the town that her guns

Mr. Holmes was appointed in the room of Col. Sawyer, on the committee appointed to bring in a resolve for making the notes of this colony, a currency and tender for payment in all cases.

would reach the houses, and put springs upon her cables. The people, however, not knowing what was done, and considering themselves nearly as prisoners of war, in the hands of the common enemy, which is our only plea for suffering Capt. Jones to carry any lumber to Boston, since your honors conceived it improper, passed a vote, that Capt. Jones might proceed in his business as usual without molestation, that they would purchase the provision he brought into the place, and pay him according to contract. After obtaining this vote, Capt. Jones immediately ordered his vessels to the wharf, and distributed his provisions among those only, who voted in favor of his carrying lumber to Boston. This gave such offence to the aggrieved party, that they determined to take Capt. Jones, if possible, and put a final stop to his supplying the king's troops with any thing. Accordingly, they secretly invited the people of Mispecka and Pleasant river to join them; accordingly, a number of them came, and, having joined our people, in the woods near the settlement, on the 11th, they all agreed to take Capt. Jones and Stephen Jones, Esq., in the place of worship, which they attempted, but Capt. Jones made his escape into the woods, and does not yet appear; Stephen Jones, Esq., only was taken, and remains, as yet, under guard. The captain and lieutenant of the tender, were also in the meeting-house, and fled to their vessel, hoisted their flag, and sent a message on shore to this effect: " that he had express orders to protect Capt. Jones; that he was determined to do his duty whilst he had life; and that, if the people presumed to stop Capt. Jones's vessels, he would burn the town." Upon this, a party of our men went directly to stripping the sloop that lay at the wharf, and another party went off to take possession of the other sloop, which lay below, and brought her up nigh a wharf, and anchored her in the stream. The tender did not fire, but weighed her anchors as privately as possible, and, in the dusk of the evening, fell down and came to, within musket shot of the sloop, which obliged our people to slip their cable, and run the sloop aground. In the mean time, a considerable number of our people went down in boats and canoes, lined the shore directly opposite to the tender, and, having demanded her to surrender to America, received for answer, " fire and be damned ;" they immediately fired in upon her, which she returned, and a smart engagement ensued. The tender, at last, slipped her cable, and fell down to a small sloop, commanded by Capt. Toby, and lashed herself to her for the remainder of the night. In the morning of the 12th, they took Capt. Toby out of his vessel, for a pilot, and made all the sail they could to get off, as the wind and tide favored; but, having carried away her main boom, and meeting with a sloop from the Bay of Fundy, they came to, robbed the sloop of her boom and gaff, took almost all her provision, together with Mr. Robert Avery of Norwich, in Connecticut, and proceeded on her voyage. Our people, seeing her go off in the morning, determined to follow her. About forty men, armed with guns, swords, axes, and pitch forks, went in Capt. Jones's sloop, under the command of Capt. Jeremiah O'Brian: about twenty, armed in the same manner, and under the command of Capt. Benjamin Foster, went in a small schooner. During the chase, our people built them breastworks of pine boards, and any thing they could find in the vessels, that would screen them from the enemy's fire. The tender, upon the first appearance of our people, cut her boats from the stern, and made all the sail she could; but, being a very dull sailor, they soon came up with her, and a most obstinate engagement ensued, both sides being determined to conquer or die: but the tender was obliged to yield; her captain was wounded in the breast with two balls, of which wounds he died next morning; poor Mr. Avery was killed, and one of the marines, and five wounded. Only one of our men was killed, and six were wounded, one of whom is since dead of his wounds, The battle was fought at the entrance of our harbor, and lasted for near the space of one hour. We have in our possession, four double fortified three pounders, and fourteen swivels, and a number of small arms, which we took with the tender, besides a very small quantity of ammunition, &c. Thus we have given your honors as particular an account of this affair as possible. We now apply to you for advice, and for a supply of ammunition and provisions, the latter of which we have petitioned your honors for already, which, if we could be fully supplied with, we doubt not but, with the blessing of heaven, we should be prepared to defend ourselves. We purpose to convey the prisoners to Pownalborough jail, as soon as possible, there to await your orders."

"We are, with deference, your honors' most obedient, humble servants."

"By order of the committee,   JAMES LYON, *Chairman.*
                                                     GEORGE STILLMAN, *Clerk.*"

"*Machias, June 14th, 1775.*"

Mr. Davis was appointed, in the room of Capt. Stone, on the committee who were appointed to consider the petition from Edward Parry.

Adjourned to Monday morning, eight o'clock.

MONDAY, June 26, 1775.

Ordered, That the committee appointed to consider the petition of Mr. Edward Parry, and the report of Col. Thompson relative to his conduct at Kennebec, be directed to consider his the said Thompson's conduct at Falmouth, with respect to Capt. Mowat and Capt. Coulson, and his laying Mr. Bernard under bonds.

Ordered, That the committee appointed to deliver out commissions, be directed to draw a fair list of all those officers in the army, who have been commissioned, which list shall be attested by the secretary, and transmitted to General Ward.

A letter from the committee of safety, proposing that the Congress should appoint two persons to superintend the supply of the army, was read, and committed to the committee who have under consideration the regulation of the army.

Ordered, That Mr. Pickering, Mr. Nye and Mr. Fisher, be a committee to inquire into the state of the towns' stocks of ammunition, in the counties of Worcester and Hampshire, and that said committee sit forthwith.

Ordered, That all the commissions for the officers of the train, be forthwith signed by the secretary, except John Wiley's, Samuel Gridley's and John Callender's, and sent to the committee of safety.

Ordered, That no handles be made to spears, or other weapons of war, or any tools for the use of the army, of chesnut, or any other brittle wood.

Ordered, That the committee appointed to inquire into the grounds of a report which has prevailed, that there has been treachery in some of the officers of the army, be directed to proceed in their inquiries.

Ordered, That Col. Porter, Col. Gerrish and Capt. Thatcher, be a committee to consider and report, to whom the arms obtained by a committee of Congress, shall be delivered, and, when distributed, how the persons receiving them shall be made accountable.

Resolved, That every person who has in possession any of the precepts lately issued by this Congress for calling a general assembly, be desired *to dele* the word "*warn*," and in its stead insert the word "*cause*," and that Mr. Edes be desired, in his next paper, to give notice of the mistake made by printing the said word "*warn*" instead of the word "*cause*."

Resolved, That Major Fuller be desired, immediately, to go home, to get the returns of the towns' stocks of ammunition.

The report of the committee appointed to consider what steps are proper to be taken for the reception of General Washington, was again considered, amended, and accepted, and is as follows, viz. :

Resolved, That Doct. Benjamin Church and Mr. Moses Gill,[1] be a committee to repair to Springfield, there to receive Generals Washington and Lee, with every mark of respect due to their exalted characters and stations ; to provide proper escorts for them, from thence, to the army before Boston, and the house provided for their reception at Cambridge ; and to make suitable provision for them, in manner following, viz. : by a number of gentlemen of this colony from Springfield to Brookfield ; and by another company raised in that neighborhood, from there to Worcester ; and by another company, there provided, from thence to Marlborough ; and from thence, by the troop of horse in that place, to the army aforesaid : And [to make suitable provision for] their company at the several stages on the road, and to receive the bills of expenses at the several inns, where it may be convenient for them to stop for refreshment, to examine them, and make report of the several sums expended at each of them, for that purpose, that orders may be taken by the Congress for the payment of them : and all innkeepers are hereby directed to make provision agreeably to the requests made by the said committee : and that General Ward be notified of the appointment of General Washington, as commander in chief of the American forces, and of the expectation we have, of his speedy arrival with Major General Lee, that he, with the generals of the forces of the other colonies, may give such orders for their honorable reception, as may accord with the rules and circumstances of the army, and the respect due to their rank, without, however, any expense of powder, and without taking the troops off from the necessary attention to their duty, at this crisis of our affairs.

Resolved, That three o'clock in the afternoon, be assigned for the purpose of choosing three persons as a committee to repair to Springfield, to receive Generals Washington and Lee, agreeably to the foregoing resolution.

Resolved, That the president's house in Cambridge, excepting one room reserved by the president for his own use, be taken, cleared, prepared, and furnished, for the reception of General Washington and

---

(1) In making up the journal of the proceedings of the day, the names of the gentlemen elected to receive the generals of the army at Springfield were inserted in the report of the committee, although they were not elected to discharge that duty until after the report had been accepted.

General Lee, and that a committee be chosen immediately to carry the same into execution.

The committee appointed to consider what preparations are proper to be made for the reception of General Washington, reported the [*foregoing] resolve, which was accepted, and Capt. Partridge, Capt. Thatcher, and Mr. Philips, Major Goodwin, and Mr. Caldwell, appointed a committee for the purpose therein mentioned.

Mr. Crane was appointed, in the room of Mr. Hall, on the committee chosen to consider Mr. Revere's account.

Resolved, That the committee appointed to prepare letters to the several governments in New England for a reenforcement of men, omit preparing one for the colony of New Hampshire.

Ordered, That Doct. Taylor, Capt. Goodman, and Mr. Philips, be a committee, to bring in a resolve for the purpose of preventing all imposition on the committee who have been heretofore directed to examine those persons who may be suspected as inimical to their country, by any person whatever.

The committee to consider the letter from Machias reported: the report was accepted, and is as follows, viz:

Resolved, That the thanks of this Congress be, and they are hereby given to Capt. Jeremiah Obrian, and Capt. Benjamin Foster, and the other brave men under their command, for their courage and good conduct in taking one of the tenders belonging to our enemies, and two sloops belonging to Ichabod Jones, and for preventing the ministerial troops being supplied with lumber; and that the said tender, sloops, their appurtenances and cargoes, remain in the hands of the said Captains Obrian and Foster, and the men under their command, for them to use and improve, as they shall think most for their and the public advantage, until the further order of this, or some future Congress, or house of representatives: and that the committee of safety for the western parish in Pownalborough, be ordered to convey the prisoners taken by the said Obrian and Foster, from Pownalborough jail to the committee of safety or correspondence, for the town of Brunswick; and the committee for Brunswick, to convey them to some committee in the county of York, and so to be conveyed from county to county, till they arrive at this Congress.

Afternoon.

Ordered, That commissions be delivered to Ezra Badlam, captain of the train of artillery, in the room of John Wiley; John Sibley, lieutenant; Samuel Dagget, second lieutenant; and John Blanchard,

a [following.]

second lieutenant; agreeably to the recommendation of the committee of safety.

Ordered, That Col. Porter, Mr. Fisher, and Capt. Goodridge, be a committee to consider a letter from General Ward, this day received.

Ordered, That Mr. Fisher, Doct. Whiting, and Major Brooks, be a committee to receive, sort and count the votes for three gentlemen to go to Springfield to meet Generals Washington and Lee.

The committee having attended that service, reported, that Doct. Church, Mr. Gill, and the Hon. Major Hawley, were chosen.

The Hon. Major Hawley moved, that he might be excused from that service, and, having offered his reasons, the question was put, and he was excused accordingly.

Resolved, That the vote for choosing three persons to go to Springfield to meet Generals Washington and Lee, be reconsidered, so far as that only two persons should be appointed to repair thither on that service.

Resolved, That Capt. Mc Kinster, and Capt. Porter, who have each of them raised a company at New York and Connecticut, be permitted to join Col. Patterson's regiment, provided their companies are complete and equipt: and that Major Goodwin bring in a resolve for this purpose.

Resolved, That General Whitcomb's commission be dated the 21st day of June.

Resolved, That the president be desired to administer to General Whitcomb the oath appointed to be administered to the general officers of the army.

The president delivered to General Whitcomb a commission, as a major general of the Massachusetts army.

A petition from the committee of correspondence for the town of Plymouth was read,[1] whereupon, *Resolved*, that the prayer thereof

(1) The committee of Plymouth earnestly remonstrated against the removal of the detachments of troops stationed along the coast to afford protection to the inhabitants. The petition follows:

To the Honorable the Provincial Congress, now sitting at Watertown:

The petition of the committee of correspondence for the town of Plymouth humbly sheweth, that your petitioners have this day received intelligence that a vote passed your house the instant, determining to remove to head quarters, that part of Col. Cotton's regiment, which has been, by order of your most respectable body, stationed in this place, for the security and protection of the lives and property of this greatly exposed and much threatened town; we, your petitioners, have lately received undoubted intelligence by one of our townsmen, who has been taken by a tender, and carried into Boston, that Admiral Graves made particular inquiry into the circumstances of this town, and said that we were a rebellious people, and that, in consequence of our building a fort in opposition to the king's troops, it should not be long before he would blow the town about our ears. Your petitioners are very sensible, that, should the troops be called away from be granted, and that General Ward be directed to countermand his orders for drawing off the forces stationed at Plymouth.

On a motion made, *Voted*, that this last resolve be reconsidered, and *Ordered* that the petition from Plymouth be committed to Capt. Parker, Col. Lincoln, Col. Davis, Mr. Phillips, and Mr. Webster.

Ordered, That commissions be delivered to the officers of Col. Little's regiment, agreeably to a list recommended by the committee of safety.

A list of the officers and soldiers of Capt. Samuel Sprague's company, was presented to the Congress: whereupon, *Ordered*, that commissions be delivered to the said officers, viz: Samuel Sprague, captain; Joseph Cheever, lieutenant; William Oliver, [ensign]; and that the company be joined to Col. Gerrish's regiment.

Mr. Goodwin, agreeably to order, reported the following resolve, which was accepted, viz: Whereas, Capt. Mackinster of Spencer, and Capt. Porter of Becket, have enlisted, each, a company of men, on the establishment of this colony, and not joined as yet to any regiment, *Resolved*, that the said companies be joined to Col. John Patterson's regiment, now stationed at Cambridge, immediately; provided said companies are full, or near full, and that each man is equipt with a good and sufficient firelock, and [that they] join their regiment as soon as may be.

Ordered, That commissions be delivered to Capt. Reuben Dow, and Lieut. John Goss, as officers, agreeably to the respective titles affixed to their names in Col. Prescott's regiment.

The committee appointed to consider and report to whom the arms procured by a committee of this Congress should be delivered, &c., reported the following resolve, which was read and accepted, viz:

this station, the town of Plymouth, as well as the adjacent villages, will lie open to the ravages of our enemies, and that it will be no difficult matter for them to plunder and destroy us. The poor of this town are already much distressed, by reason of the stop put to the fishery, and can scarcely subsist upon what they get out of the clam banks, and by fishing in boats, and should they be driven from their huts into the barren country that surrounds us, they must, (for aught we see,) perish with hunger, and for want of habitations, there not being houses within twenty miles sufficient to receive them. These poor people consist principally of women and children, their husbands and parents having enlisted themselves into the service of the colony. Your petitioners are very far from desiring to create any unnecessary expense to the colony, but, at the same time, think it necessary that said troops remain with us, and are of opinion, that, should they be withdrawn, the town will be immediately evacuated, and, for the above reasons, your petitioners as in duty bound, &c. For and by order of the committee of correspondence for the town of Plymouth.

ANDREW CROSWELL, *Clerk*,
GAMALIEL BRADFORD, Jr.,
JOHN GRAY, *by order*."

"The committee of correspondence for the town of Duxbury and Kingston which lie on Plymouth Bay, join in the general prayer of the above petition."

Whereas, this Congress has ordered a number of fire arms to be furnished from several towns and districts in this colony, to be forwarded to the army, to supply those who are destitute of arms; but no provision is made for delivering them out, and taking proper receipts for the same, therefore, *Resolved*, that all the small arms that are, or may be procured by the above order, be delivered to Major Nathaniel Barber, military storekeeper at Cambridge; he to give his receipt for the same, to the person from whom he receives them; that the same be delivered out to such officers as shall produce orders therefor from the Hon. General Ward, they giving receipts for the same to the said Major Barber, to be returned in good order, unless lost in the service of the colony. And every soldier who shall receive any such fire arms, shall give his receipt for the same to the officer from whom he shall receive it, to be returned as aforesaid; and in case the same shall not be returned, at the close of the campaign, or sooner, the value of the said fire arm shall be deducted out of the wages of the person receiving the same; and also that the sum of six shillings shall be deducted out of the wages of each soldier, who shall receive such fire arm, for the use of the same, in case he return it again in good order.

The committee on the petition of Edward Parry, &c., reported. The report was read, amended, and [ªaccepted].[1]

The committee on the petition from Plymouth reported: the report was read but not accepted.

Ordered, That the Hon. Col. Gerrish, Capt. Bragdon, Col. Thompson, Col. Freeman, and Mr. Lothrop, be a committee to consider what measures are proper to be taken for the defence and protection of the sea coasts.

Ordered, That the committee last chosen, consider several petitions which were committed to the committee sometime since appointed to consider the state of the sea coasts, and that said committee first consider the case of the town of Plymouth, as represented in the petition from that town.

The committee appointed to consider the conduct of Col. Thompson, at Falmouth, with respect to Capt. Mowat, reported. The report was ordered to subside. [It was as follows:]

[The committee appointed to consider the conduct of Colonel Thompson at Falmouth with respect to Capt. Mowatt, &c., and his laying Mr. Bernard under bonds, are of opinion, that said Thompson's

a [accepted and is as follows.]

(1) The report referred to in the text is neither entered on the journal, nor preserved on the files of Congress.

conduct was friendly to his country, and the cause of liberty : and that said Barnard's conduct appears to have been inimical to both.]

Adjourned to Tuesday morning 8 o'clock.

TUESDAY, JUNE 27, 1775.

A letter from the committee of Albany was read, whereupon *Ordered*, that Doct. Whiting, Mr. Greenleaf, and Mr. Hopkins, be a committee to consider the same and prepare an answer thereto.[1]

Resolved, That four persons be added to the committee of supplies, and that 11 o'clock this forenoon, be assigned for the choice of them.

The committee appointed yesterday to consider General Ward's letter, reported a resolve,[2] which was accepted, and ordered to be printed in hand bills, and dispersed throughout the colony, and thereupon *Ordered*, that Capt. Goodridge, Mr. Partridge, and Mr. Caldwell, be a committee for that purpose.

A letter from Isaac Stone relative to Francis More, a baker, was read and ordered to be transmitted to the committee of supplies.[3]

Ordered, that the resolve just now past, in consequence of General Ward's letter be reconsidered, and that it be recommitted, together with the resolve passed relative to absconding soldiers, to Mr Partridge, Mr. Hopkins and Capt. Goodrich.

Ordered, That Mr. Thatcher be appointed to apply to the brother

---

(1) The letter from the committee of Albany follows :

" ALBANY, COMMITTEE CHAMBER, 23o JUNE, 1775.

" BRETHREN,—

We have received a vague and uncertain account from your colony, of an engagement, which your troops have had with the enemies of our country, at or near Charlestown. As we feel ourselves deeply interested in every event affecting the general weal of America, it gives us great pleasure, that, though with the loss of many brave men, you have been able, if our information be true, to drive, with considerable loss, the tools of tyranny and oppression back to their asylum. Strongly impressed with the warmest disposition to cultivate harmony with you, and, if necessary, to afford you all the assistance in our power, we have, therefore, sent you this by Mr. Price, in order to receive from you a circumstantial detail of the late engagement and its consequences. May that God, who has so often signally espoused our cause in the arduous struggle for liberty and humanity, still continue to you his gracious guidance and protection."

" We expect daily an attack upon Ticonderoga from Canada."

" We are at a loss to know what must be done with the donations collected in this city for the poor of Boston, and beg to be informed by you, as the chief of the contributions are in grain, whether we shall dispose of it here, and convert it into cash, or otherwise wait your directions. We are, brethren, your very humble servants.

By order of the committee, SAMUEL STRINGER, *Chairman*."

To the Provincial Congress of the Colony of Massachusetts Bay, if sitting ;
otherwise to the Committee of War at Cambridge or elsewhere.

(2) The resolve relating to absconding soldiers is inserted in the Journal of June 28 following.

(3) The letter of Isaac Stone charges one of the bakers of the army with using the flour furnished from the stores of the province for the supply of his own customers.

of our late president for such papers belonging to this Congress, as he may have in his possession.

Ordered, That Doct. Taylor, Col. Coffin, and Capt. Webster, be a committee to consider a letter from General Thomas respecting a petition for liberty to permit provisions to be carried to those who were taken prisoners by Gage's troops, on the 17th instant, now in Boston.

A number of letters were presented to the Congress by Mr. Palfrey, lately arrived from England, some of which were read, and then the whole were committed to Doct. Taylor, Mr. Partridge and Capt. Brown.[1]

Ordered, That Mr. Bigelow be appointed to go to Cambridge, to inquire if there are any blank commissions at the committee of safety's room.

Ordered, That Mr. Webster, Mr. Partridge, and Capt. Goodman, be a committee to receive and sort the votes for four gentlemen to be added to the committee of supplies.

The committee having attended that service, reported, that Col. James Prescott, Col. Elisha Porter, Major Brooks, and Capt. Vose, were chosen.

Major Brooks, having requested that he might be excused, was excused, and Col. Barrett was chosen in his room.

Ordered, That the secretary make out a proper certificate of the choice of the abovenamed four gentlemen on the committee of supplies.

The committee on the account of Mr. Paul Revere reported: the report was recommitted.

A letter from General Ward was read, nominating Col. William Henshaw, to be an adjutant general in the Massachusetts army, whereupon, *Ordered,* that a commission be made out for him accordingly.

Ordered, That the Hon Major Hawley, Mr. Pickering, and Col. Porter, be a committee, to prepare letters to the Continental Congress, requesting their aid in furnishing us with gunpowder: and also to prepare another letter to Governor Trumbull, requesting him to take some steps for collecting powder from the several towns in the colony of Connecticut, to be sent to head quarters at Cambridge, as this colony is now doing.

A letter from General Thomas was read, nominating Mr. Samuel Brewer, to be an adjutant general in the Massachusetts army: whereupon *Ordered,* that a commission be made out for him accordingly.

(1) The letters from England, so far as the contents of all can be inferred from the few preserved, gave information of the embarkation of regiments of troops, and the preparations of the administration to reduce the colonies to subjection.

Resolved, That Mr. Ezekiel Chever be appointed store keeper of the ordnance in the room of Major Barber, who has declined acceptance of that trust, and that 5 o'clock P. M. be assigned for considering the expediency of augmenting the pay of the store keeper of the ordnance.

Ordered, That Capt. Holmes, Capt. Brown, and Capt. Batchelder be a committee to examine Ensign Robert Campbell, lately arrived from England, and now a prisoner in this town, and to report what is proper to be done with him.

Afternoon.

Ordered, That Capt. Farley, Capt. Dwight, and Mr. Webster, be a committee to prepare an address to the several towns in the colony, who may be applied to, to furnish the army with powder.

Resolved, That Mr. Edes be desired to print 300 blank commissions, in the form lately made use of for the officers of the army.

A petition from Jonathan Hicks, and Josiah Jones, prisoners in Concord jail, was read, and ordered to lie on the table.[1]

A letter from S. L. was read, and ordered to lie on the table.[2]

A petition from the committees of the several townships of Goldsborough, Narragaugus and Number Four, was read, and committed to Capt. Parker, Col. Smith and Capt. Ellis, who are directed to consider the propriety of supplying the inhabitants of Machias with some three pounders, and some swivel balls.[3]

(1) These gentlemen, captured in a sloop bound to Nova Scotia and ordered to be put in confinement, by a resolve of Congress, June 10, (page 315,) in their memorial, admit, that they had entertained opinions at variance with those of their countrymen : while they refused to assent to the justice of every ministerial claim, they had deemed it inexpedient and unsafe to bear arms against the power of Great Britain. " We declare" they say " before God and man, with perfect sincerity, that we do, most affectionately wish prosperity to our native land, and to the inhabitants in general of these American colonies ; and we are ready, at any time, and at all times, so far as our abilities extend, to do any thing within the limits of justice, that appears to us subservient to this important end." Protesting that it was with the view to avoid danger, and not from want of regard to the cause of the country, that they had taken up their residence in Boston, they earnestly entreat that they may be liberated from imprisonment, on giving obligations to observe a patriotic course of conduct.

(2) A letter, subscribed with the initials S. L., strongly urges the expediency of fitting out armed vessels without delay. The writer apprehended, that the squadron under Admiral Graves, with the small ships of war and tenders, might interrupt the vessels bringing provisions to Massachusetts, and reduce the army and inhabitants to a state of famine. He suggests that a ship, then ready to launch at Danvers, of about 300 tons burden, might be commissioned, and many ships, lying idle at the wharves of the sea coast, might be usefully employed in bringing grain from the southern colonies, transporting powder, cannon, and arms, from Spain or France, and collecting saltpetre from ports where that article could be purchased.

(3) All the eastern towns suffered severely from scarcity of food and deficiency of arms and ammunition. Among the constant applications for relief was that mentioned in the text. In a letter from Col. Enoch Freeman dated at Falmouth, he states : " A man from Deer Island, near

Ordered, That Capt. Shillaber be directed to bring in a resolve for the purpose of assuring the officers and soldiers, that, notwithstanding the date of the officers' commissions, the pay of both officers and soldiers shall commence at the time of their enlistment.

Ordered, That commissions be made out to the subaltern officers of Capt. Edward Crafts' company in the train, agreeably to the recommendation of the committee of safety.

A letter from Elisha Phelps was read, and ordered to lie on the table.[1]

The letter from Mr. Isaac Stone which was this day transmitted to the committee of supplies, was, by that committee, returned, and again read, and thereupon *Ordered,* that Major Fuller be directed to notify the commissary general to attend this Congress on the subject thereof.

The committee appointed to consider in what way the sea coasts should be protected, reported, whereupon *Ordered,* that the committee of supplies, and all committees of the house now out, be directed immediately to give attendance.

Ordered, That the committee appointed to provide hospitals for the army, be directed to provide another hospital, to be appropriated solely for such of the army as may be taken with the small pox, and to consider what measures can be taken to prevent the spreading of that distemper, and that Doct. Rand, and Doct. Foster, be added to the committee.

Resolved, That the resolve passed yesterday, directing how the fire arms should be distributed, be reconsidered. The same being amended, was again accepted and is as follows, viz: Whereas, this Congress has ordered a number of fire arms to be furnished from several towns and districts in this colony, to be forwarded to the army, to supply those who are destitute of arms, but no provision is made for delivering them out, and taking proper receipts for the same, therefore, *Resolved,* that all the small arms that are, or may be procured by the above order, be delivered to the committee of safety at Cambridge; they to give their receipt for the same, to the person from whom they receive them: that the same be delivered out to such officers, as shall

---

Penobscot, was here this afternoon, and gives a melancholy account of the distress the people are in, that way, for want of bread, owing to the stoppage of trade. He heard that several children had died of hunger. What will become of them, God only knows. We are not able to help them or ourselves. I don't know what can be done for them or us, without some vessels of superior force to the tenders should be provided to bring bread."

(1) Capt. Phelps was sent to Connecticut for the purpose of procuring aid in transporting cannon from Tyconderoga to the camp near Boston. He stated that Gov. Trumbull declined authorizing the removal of the guns from the northern fortress, without the direction of the Continental Congress.

produce orders therefor, from the Honorable General Ward, they giving receipts for the same, to the said committee of safety, to be returned in good order, unless lost in the service of the colony. And every soldier who shall receive any such fire arm, shall give his receipt for the same, to the officer from whom he shall receive it, to be returned as aforesaid; and the officer shall return the said receipts to the committee of safety; and in case the same shall not be returned, at the close of the campaign, or sooner, the value of the said fire arm, shall be deducted out of the wages of the person receiving the same; and that the committee of safety shall appraise all such arms, as have not already been appraised, and take an account of the whole.

Ordered, That Col. William Henshaw, an adjutant general, take the oath appointed to be taken by the officers and soldiers of the Massachusetts army, and that a commission as adjutant general be delivered to him.

The committee appointed to examine Ensign Robert Campbell, reported the following resolve, which was accepted. The committee appointed to take into consideration the case of a prisoner, bound to Boston to join the army under the command of General Gage, have examined said prisoner, and his account of himself is, that his name is Robert Campbell, about seventeen years old, son of Lieut. Col. Alexander Campbell, who is now lieutenant governor of Fort George, in Inverness, and is of one of the first families in Scotland. Said Robert Campbell further says, he was born in the army, and now has a recommendation for an ensign's commission in the 35th regiment.

Resolved, That Robert Campbell be sent immediately to the care of the selectmen of Concord, to be by them put under keepers, or into prison, and provided for, as their prudence shall direct, until the further order of this Congress, or some future house of representatives, and that he be delivered to Col. Barrett, to be conveyed to said selectmen of Concord.

An account of Simeon Fish, and John Toby, of the expenses of bringing Ensign Robert Campbell from Falmouth to this Congress, was read, and committed to the committee, who were appointed to examine said Campbell.

The committee appointed to inquire into the state of the several towns stocks in the counties of Hampshire and Worcester, reported a schedule, containing an account of the stocks of several towns in said counties, which was committed to Mr. Singletary, Mr. Nye, and Mr Cut, who were directed to consider what quantity should be drawn from each town, for the use of the army.

The committee appointed to consider the letter of General Thomas, relative to the request of a number of our wounded friends, in captivity in Boston, reported : the report was accepted, and a copy of it ordered to be sent to General Thomas, and is as follows, viz : the committee appointed to consider the request of a number of our wounded friends, now in captivity in Boston, beg leave to report, that General Thomas be requested moderately to supply said prisoners with fresh meat, in case he can convey it to them, and them only.

The report of the committee appointed to consider some means for protecting the sea coasts, was again read and considered, and after debate, the further consideration of it was put off till to-morrow morning.

Adjourned to to-morrow morning 8 o'clock.

WEDNESDAY, June 28, 1775.

The committee appointed to prepare an answer to the letter from Albany, reported.

Ordered, That Col. Lincoln bring in a resolve, making five of the committee of supplies to be a quorum, or in defect of five, that any three may be a quorum, provided the chairman be one of the three.

[Col. Lincoln reported a resolve, which was read, accepted, and is as follows, viz :]

Whereas, The public interest often makes it necessary, that a very considerable number of the committee of supplies should be absent on business of the colony, and as no orders can be paid by the receiver general, but such as are signed by the said committee, or the major part of them; by reason whereof, the public service may be obstructed, and greatly delayed; for prevention of which, it is *Resolved,* That three of said committee of supplies, the chairman, David Cheever, Esq. being always one of the three, shall, when there are less than five present, be considered as a quorum; and all orders, bargains, and contracts, by them made, shall be held good, to all intents and purposes, as fully as though the whole of said committee were present, and assenting to such orders, bargains, and contracts. And the receiver general of this colony be, and is hereby directed to govern himself accordingly.

The letter prepared to be sent to the committee of Albany, was accepted, and is as follows :

Gentlemen; This Congress have received your very obliging letter, by Mr. Price, of the 23d ultimo, and they cheerfully embrace the opportunity to forward to you by the same hand, as particular an account of the late engagement with the enemies of America, as we, in the present hurry of our public affairs, are able to do. On the night of the 16th of June instant, a body of our troops took possession of a hill in Charlestown, where they began some entrenchments; but as soon as the morning light appeared, they were fired upon by some of the ships in Boston harbor, and also from a battery on Copp's hill, which is on Boston side. Soon after, several ships and floating batteries drew up, as near as possible on each side [of] Charlestown neck, in order, with their cannon, to annoy our people, and prevent any recruits going from our main body to their relief. About two o'clock, P. M., a large body of regular troops, consisting of several thousands, commanded by Lord Howe, suddenly crossed Charles river, and landed near the hill on which our people were posted. They immediately marched up, in order to force our infant entrenchments: but our people gave them so warm a reception, that they thought best to retreat; but soon renewed their attempts; but were repulsed the second time with great slaughter; but, on their third attempt, our people, being almost destitute of ammunition, as the enemies' constant fire from their ships and floating batteries had prevented any supplies from our main army, were obliged to retreat, with the loss of about 50 men killed, and 200 wounded, as near as has yet been ascertained, and about 30 taken prisoners, many of whom were wounded, and some are since dead of their wounds. The loss on the part of our enemies is much greater; some persons who were on the field of battle soon after the fight, affirm they saw 800 men dead on the ground, and that there were as many more wounded; the lowest account we have had, is, 1000 killed and wounded, among whom are 84 commissioned officers. On the same day, the town of Charlestown, consisting of near 500 houses and other buildings, was, by those bloody incendiaries, set on fire and consumed to ashes. We cannot, however, but assure you, gentlemen, that, notwithstanding our present distressed situation, we feel a peculiar satisfaction in finding our patriotic brethren of the city and county of Albany, so cordially interesting themselves in our particular welfare, and so kindly offering us their assistance, as well as manifesting their zeal for the rights and liberties of America in general. It is our ardent desire to cultivate harmony and friendship with all our neighboring brethren, and, we hope, you will not fail to continue your favors, and we assure you, that we shall always take pleasure in conveying to you any intelligence that shall afford satisfaction. As to the benevolent donations you mention, which are collected for our distressed brethren, as the transporting the article you make mention of, is almost impracticable, [we] think it had better be exchanged for cash, or some necessary specie, which may be more easily transported. We are sorry to hear there is any prospect of an attack upon Ticonderoga, &c., but, we trust, those important fortresses are sufficiently garrisoned, and doubt not, but our brave countrymen stationed there, will be able to repulse any force which can be sent against them from Canada. Finally, brethren, we ardently wish, that the great Supreme Being, who governs all things, may so direct all our military operations, that they may speedily issue in the full restoration and peaceable possession of the natural and constitutional rights and liberties of every American.

P. S. Some make the number of our killed and missing to be near a hundred.

The committee on the account of Messrs. Fish and Toby, reported : the report was accepted, and is as follows, viz. : *Resolved*, that Simeon Fish and John Toby be allowed and paid, out of the public treasury of this colony, six pounds, seven shillings, for their time and expenses in bringing Robert Campbell, a prisoner, from Falmouth to this Congress, and also for their time and expenses back to Falmouth again ; and the receiver general is hereby directed to pay the said sum of six pounds, seven shillings, to the said Fish and Toby, in full discharge of their expenses as aforesaid.

The committee who were appointed to consider the resolves of this Congress relative to absconding soldiers, reported : the report was recommitted.

Mr. Pigeon was introduced on the subject of Capt. Stone's letter respecting Mr. More.

Ordered, That Deacon Fisher, Capt. Batchelder and Capt. Stone of Framingham, be a committee, to join with Mr. Pigeon in an inquiry into the conduct of said More, and report to this Congress.

Ordered, That Capt. Batchelder, Col. Coffin and Capt. Goodman, be a committee to bring in a resolve for the purpose of saving provisions in the army.

A list of persons recommended as deputy commissaries was read, and committed to Mr. Greenleaf, Capt. Carpenter and Mr. Johnson.

The committee appointed to bring in a resolve for giving a currency to the notes or bills of credit of this colony, reported : the report was recommitted for the purpose of introducing the large notes issued by this colony.

Ordered, That commissions be delivered to such officers of Col. Gerrish's regiment as are not yet commissioned.

A petition of John Obrian was read, and committed to Major Perly, Major Fuller of Middleton, and Mr. Cutt.[1]

The report of the committee appointed to consider some measures for defending the sea coasts was again taken into consideration, amended and accepted, and Col. Freeman, Col. Gerrish and Capt. Carpenter, were appointed to fix the pay of the officers in proportion to that of the soldiers agreeably to said report.

The report of the committee respecting absconding soldiers, was put off to three o'clock, P. M.

The committee appointed to consider some method of saving provisions in the army, reported : the report was accepted, and is as follows : The committee appointed to consider of the most effectual means to prevent any waste of provision in the army, beg leave to report by way of resolve.

Resolved, That the commissary general be, and he hereby is directed, to purchase all the provisions that any of the soldiers may have to spare of their allowance, for the use of our army, and pay a reasonable price for such provision.

Afternoon.

The following gentlemen were appointed a committee to station the troops in the county of Essex, agreeably to the resolve of Congress, which passed in the forenoon, viz. :

Lynn—Mr. Edward Johnson. *Manchester*—Mr. Andrew Woodbury. *Gloucester*—Col. Coffin. *Salem*—Mr. Pickering. *Ipswich*—Col. Farley. *Newburyport*—Capt. Greenleaf. *Marblehead*—Elbridge Gerry, Esq. *Beverly*—Capt. Batchelder. *Newbury*—Col. Gerrish. *Salisbury*—Capt. Nathaniel Currier.

And the following gentlemen for the county of York, viz. :

York—Capt. Bragdon. *Berwick*—Major Goodwin. *Arundel*—Deacon Hovey. *Kittery*—Edward Cutt, Esq. *Wells*—Col. Sawyer. *Biddeford*—James Sullivan, Esq.

The following gentlemen were likewise appointed, agreeably to said resolve, to give out enlisting orders, viz. :

For the County of Essex—Mr. Hopkins, Mr. Greenleaf, and Col. Farley. *For the County of Plymouth*—Hon. Col. Warren, Mr. Lothrop, Capt. Partridge. *For the County of Barnstable*—Col. Freeman, Col. Otis, Daniel Davis, Esq. *For the County of Dukes*—

---

(1) The petitioner represented that the inhabitants of Machias were one thousand souls, who had not provisions, nor any method to procure supplies, in the bad condition of the times. The provision made for their support by Congress, filled them with gratitude : but the quantity furnished was so small, that without further aid they could not subsist, and must be obliged to abandon their habitations.

Mr. Nye. *For the County of Bristol*—Mr. Durfee, Hon. Mr. Spooner, Capt. Holmes. *For the County of York*—Col. Sawyer, Edward Cutt, Esq., Capt. Bragdon. *For the County of Cumberland* —Hon. Col. Freeman, Col. Thompson, Mr. Mitchell. *For the County of Lincoln*—Mr. D. Sewall, Mr. Langdon, Mr. E. Witcher.

Ordered, That Col. Freeman, Mr. Langdon and Mr. Greenleaf, be a committee to get two hundred of the resolves for stationing companies on the sea coast, printed.

The resolves being completed, are as follow, viz. : The committee appointed to take into consideration and report some way of defending and supporting the towns upon the sea coast in this colony, having considered of the same, report the following resolves, viz. :

Resolved, That there be immediately raised in the county of Essex, ten companies, to consist of fifty men each, officers included, to be stationed upon the sea coast in that county, in such manner and proportion as shall be agreed upon by a joint committee, consisting of one member to be appointed by this Congress from each of the towns of Lynn, Manchester, Gloucester, Marblehead, Salem, Beverly, Ipswich, Newbury, Newburyport, and Salisbury, in said county, and to be under the direction of the committees of correspondence of each town where they may be stationed. Also, that there be raised in the counties of Plymouth and Barnstable, nine companies, each to consist of the number of fifty men, four of which companies to be stationed in the county of Plymouth, according to the direction of the field officers of the first regiment of the county of Plymouth, under whose direction they shall be considered; the other five companies to be stationed in the county of Barnstable, in such manner as the field officers of the two regiments there shall agree, and to be under their directions; and that the county of Barnstable shall have the liberty of raising eight of those companies; likewise, that there be raised in the county of Bristol, including the towns of Wareham and Rochester, two companies, consisting of fifty men each, to be stationed, one company in Dartmouth, and the other company in Wareham and Rochester equally, and to be under the direction of the committees of correspondence of the respective towns. Also, that there be raised in the county of York, four companies, consisting of fifty men each, to be stationed in that county, according to the agreement of a joint committee consisting of one member from each of the towns upon the sea coast in that county, to be chosen for that purpose; when stationed, to be under the direction of the field officers in that county. Also, that there be raised in the county of Cumberland, five companies, consisting of fifty men each, to be stationed as shall be agreed upon by a joint committee appointed by each town upon the sea coast, viz.: two members to be chosen by the town of Falmouth and Cape Elizabeth, one by Scarborough, one by North Yarmouth, one by Brunswick, and one by Harpswell, and after the division and station is ordered, to be under the direction of the committees of the respective towns where they shall be stationed. And also, that there be raised in the county of Lincoln, three companies, consisting of fifty men each, to be stationed by a committee consisting of members to be chosen, one by each town upon the sea coast in said county, as they shall agree, and then to be under the direction of the committees of correspondence of the respective towns and plantations where they shall be stationed, and of the assessors where no such committees are appointed. Also, *Resolved*, that a committee of three persons be appointed in each county, to give out enlisting orders in their respective counties, where such men are to be raised, and to muster them; and also, that Col. Phinney be directed to march the whole of his regiment, who are equipt with arms, to the camp at Cambridge, and those who are not equipt, to dismiss. Likewise, further *Resolved*, that the thirty men ordered to be raised from the town of Falmouth, and stationed on the Elizabeth Islands, be augmented to fifty, officers included, and under the same wages and subsistence, as is hereafter provided, and to remain there for protection of the stocks on those islands; and that each private soldier of the several companies herein mentioned, shall be entitled to the sum of $36 per month, and subsistence as the other companies raised for the colony service, till the further order of this, or some future Congress or House of Representatives; and that the pay of the officers be reduced in the same proportion as the pay of the soldiers, viz.: captains' pay, £5 8s.; 1st lieutenant, £3 12s.; 2d lieutenant, £3 3s.; sergeants, £2 4s.; corporals, fifers, and drummers, £2.

Resolved, That each soldier who shall enlist, shall furnish himself with a good and sufficient firelock, and that no man shall be mustered as a soldier who is not so furnished, accordingly.

Also, *Resolved*, That each town where soldiers shall be stationed as above, shall furnish them with ammunition, out of their stocks, for which they shall be paid out of the public treasury of this colony.

A petition of Robert Shillaber [for leave to export fish,] was read, and committed to Capt. Batchelder, Capt Goodman, and Major Fuller, of Middleborough.

Ordered, That Deacon Bayley, Major Goodwin, Mr. Batchelder, Col. Coffin, and Col. Gerrish, be a committee to consider what method would be most expedient, by which to supply the soldiers to be raised for the defence of the sea coast, with provisions.

Ordered, That Doct. Taylor, Capt. Stearns, and Mr. Starkweather, be a committee to consider the petition of several officers in Col. Prescott's, Col. Fry's, and Col. Bridge's regiments.[1]

The report of the committee relative to absconding soldiers, was again considered, and accepted, and is as follows, viz. :

Whereas, in consequence of [ᵃan] application made to the Provincial Congress, sitting in this town in May last, by the officers of the army, that some effectual method should be taken for the speedy return of absconding soldiers, or such as should tarry beyond the time limited by furlough, it was then *Resolved*, that it should be, and accordingly was recommended to the committees of correspondence in the several towns and districts in this colony, or to the selectmen, where no such committees were appointed, that they should take effectual care, that such absconding or delinquent soldiers should be sent back immediately to their respective regiments ; yet it appears to this Congress, that the above resolution has not, in every instance, had the desired effect ; therefore, *Resolved*, that it be further recommended to the several committees of correspondence in each town and district in this colony, or to the selectmen, where no such committees are appointed, that they take the most speedy and effectual care, that said resolve be strictly adhered to and punctually executed ; and it is also recommended to the good people in the several towns and districts aforesaid, to give their utmost aid and assistance to said selectmen or committees in executing said resolve, as the existence of the army very much depends thereon.

And it is further *Resolved*, that all necessary expenses, which may accrue by returning said absconding or delinquent soldiers to their respective regiments, be paid, and deducted out of the wages of said soldiers.

Ordered, [That the foregoing resolves] be printed in the Cambridge, Watertown, and Worcester papers.

The committee appointed to consider what preparations are necessary to be made relative to making paper bills of credit, reported. The report was ordered to lie till there is a fuller house.

Ordered, That Col. Lincoln, Major Fuller, of Newton, Mr. Singletary, Mr. Durfee, and Mr. Dexter, be a committee to consider what

a [our]

(1) These petitions related to the organization of the regiments and the rank of the officers.

method is best to be taken for providing each of the soldiers with a coat.

The form of a warrant for the surgeons was read and accepted, and is as follows, viz. :

The Congress of the Massachusetts Bay, to A. B.   Greeting.

Being informed of your skill in surgery, and reposing especial trust and confidence in your ability and good conduct, we do, by these presents, constitute and appoint you the said A. B., to be surgeon of the regiment of foot, whereof —— —— is colonel, raised by the Congress aforesaid, for the defence of said colony.   You are, therefore, carefully and diligently to discharge the duty of a surgeon to the said regiment, in all things appertaining thereunto, observing such orders and instructions as you shall, from time to time, receive from the colonel of said regiment, according to military rules and discipline established by said Congress, or any your superior officers, for which this shall be your sufficient warrant.

By order of the Congress,

—— —— *President.*

Dated at Watertown.

Ordered, That the committee appointed to make out commissions for the officers of the army, be directed to make out warrants for the surgeons agreeably to the above form, as soon as they have been examined and appointed.

Ordered, That Deacon Fisher, Col. Thompson, and Mr. Wiswall, be a committee to bring in a resolve for the purpose of preventing the unnecessary [ªexpenditure] of gunpowder.

The committee appointed to consider the petition of Mr. Obrian, reported verbally ; that the petitioner be served with a copy of the report of this Congress on the petition of a number of the inhabitants of Machias.   The report was accepted, and the petitioner had leave to withdraw his petition.

The report of the committee relative to making the notes and bills of credit of this and the other colonies, a tender, being amended, was accepted, and ordered to be authenticated and printed in the Cambridge, Watertown, and Worcester papers, and is as follows :   Whereas, a former Congress of this colony, ordered their receiver general to issue notes and bills upon the credit of this colony, for the payment

ª [expense]

and supply of their army, and other necessary expenses of this colony; and whereas, divers others of the sister colonies have issued notes or bills, for the payment of their respective forces; and it is necessary, that the notes and bills of this and the sister colonies should have free currency; therefore, *Resolved*, that the notes and bills of the colony of Rhode Island, at and after the rate of six shillings and nine pence an ounce for silver, and the bills and notes of this and all the other colonies, excepting Nova Scotia and Canada, at and after the rate of six shillings and eight pence an ounce for silver, shall be taken and received, and accounted a good and sufficient tender for the payment of all debts, and the damages that may arise upon the non-performance of any promises, and also be received into the public treasury of this colony, without any discount or allowance whatever. And if any person whatever, shall refuse to take any of the notes or bills of the colonies aforementioned, at the rates before expressed, for any debt, or in satisfaction for the damages sustained by reason of the non-performance of any promise, or shall ask, demand, or receive, any discount, gratuity, or premium, for receiving any of the bills or notes aforementioned, he or she so offending, shall be deemed an enemy to the country. And the several committees of correspondence, inspection, and safety in their respective towns, are required to return the names of all persons who shall contravene this resolve, to this or some future Congress, or House of Representatives, that they may take order thereon as to them shall seem meet.

The resolve relative to the commencement of the pay of the officers and soldiers, was considered, and recommitted, and Mr. Batchelder and Major Fuller added to the committee.

Ordered, That Mr. Webster, Major Perley, and Mr. Mighill, be a committee to bring in a resolve for the purpose of recommending to the governor and company of the colony of Connecticut, to suffer the inhabitants of the eastern parts of this colony, to purchase and carry out of said colony such provisions as their necessitous circumstances may require.

Resolved, That the committee appointed to prepare a letter to the Continental Congress, be empowered and directed to communicate it to the committee of supplies, and then to forward the same to the delegates of this colony at said Congress, without reporting it to this Congress, said delegates to communicate it to the Continental Congress, if they think proper.

Ordered, That Mr. Starkweather, Capt. Partridge, and Col. Dexter, Mr. Singletary, and Col. Coffin, be a committee to examine into the conduct and books of Mr. John Pigeon, commissary general, Mr. Pigeon having desired that a committee might be appointed for that purpose, and that said committee consider the expediency of furnishing Mr. Miller, a deputy commissary, with a horse.

Resolved, That tomorrow morning, ten o'clock, be assigned for the purpose of considering the proposal of the commissary general, for an allowance of molasses to the soldiers.

The committee appointed to bring in a resolve relative to the commencement of the pay of the officers and soldiers, reported the following, which was accepted, and ordered to be published in the papers, and is as follows, viz. :

Resolved, That each commissioned officer in the colony army shall draw pay, according to the present establishment, from the time of his first engaging in the public service or receiving beating orders, and that each non-commissioned officer and private draw pay from the time of his enlisting in said service; also, that such of the minute men and militia, as marched into the field on the 19th April, and soon after, and have remained there, and since engaged in said army for the defence of the colony, shall be paid for their service, agreeably to the present establishment, from the time of their first marching into the field.

Ordered, That Doct. Taylor, Mr. Hall, Major Brooks, Mr. Partridge, and Deacon Fisher, be a committee to consider the written proposal of Doct. Whiting, relative to saltpetre.[1]

Adjourned to eight o'clock, tomorrow morning.

THURSDAY, JUNE 29, 1775.

A petition from Mr. John Calef[2] was read, and committed to Major Fuller, Col. Coffin, Mr. Hopkins, Capt. Parker, and Mr. Mighill.

The committee appointed to bring in a resolve for the purpose of recommending to the governor and company of Connecticut, to supply the eastern country with provisions, reported : the report was accepted.[a][3]

A letter from the committee of safety, enclosing a letter from Mr. Samuel Smith, chairman of the committee of Northfield, was read, and ordered to be sent to the committee of supplies.[4]

a [and is as follows.]

(1) Doct. Whiting recommended, that information in relation to the manufacture of saltpetre should be obtained from skilful persons in New York.

(2) This petition was for leave to send a ship fitted out in Salem, upon a foreign voyage.

(3) The substance of the resolve is stated in the text : the original has not been preserved.

(4) The committee of Northfield informed Congress, that two small cannon belonging to Massa-

The committee appointed to consider the petition from Narraguagus and other towns at the eastward, reported. The report was ordered to subside, and the petitioners had leave to withdraw their petition.[1]

Ordered, That the President, Major Hawley, Doct. Whiting, Mr.
Hopkins, and Mr. Greenleaf, be a committee to prepare an address to
Generals Washington and Lee, to be presented to them on their arri-
val here.

The committee appointed to consider the petition of officers belonging to Col. Prescott's, Col. Fry's and Bridge's regiments, reported:
which report was accepted.[a] [2]

Ordered, That the resolve passed the 19th instant, relative to spears,
&c., be recommitted to Major Goodwin for amendment.

The committee appointed to consider a proposal made by Doct.
Whiting, for sending some person to New York, to advise with Doct.
Graham and others, and procure from them directions for the manufacture of saltpetre, reported; which report was ordered to lay on the
table, and Mr. Phillips and Doct. Whiting were appointed to confer
with Mr. Professor Sewall, on the subject matter contained therein.

The committee appointed to consider some methods for supplying
the soldiers, stationed on the sea coasts, with provisions, reported.
The report was amended and accepted, and is as follows, viz.: *Resolved,* that the selectmen of the several towns or plantations on the
sea coast, or, where there are no selectmen, the assessors of such
place where any such soldiers shall be stationed for their defence, be,
and they hereby are directed, to supply the officers and soldiers with
suitable provisions for their support, so long as said men continue in
the colony service, and do their duty of soldiers in their several stations, for which provisions, the said selectmen or assessors shall be
paid, out of the public treasury, the sum of five shillings for each man,
per week, who shall be so supplied. And it is recommended to the
owners of the Elizabeth Islands, to supply the soldiers that may be
stationed on said islands, for which they shall be allowed, out of the
treasury aforesaid, the same sum per week, which is allowed for the

---

a [and is as follows.]

chusetts, and a double fortified gun of New Hampshire, were left at Fort Dummer when that fortress was dismantled, and a cannon at Fort Hinsdale, above Northfield; all four pounders, which
might be conveyed to the army.

(1) The scarcity of provisions and the deficiency of arms were assigned as the reasons for de-
clining to make the appropriations requested by the petitioners.

(2) The report appears to have pointed out a mode of adjusting difficulties which had arisen in
relation to the rank of some of the officers of the regiments.

supply of the soldiers to be stationed in the other parts of the sea coast.

Ordered, That Mr. Hobart, Col. Farley and Mr. Webster, be a committee to inquire of the committee of supplies, in what manner the military stores in Watertown are guarded, and that they take effectual care that they be properly guarded, and that there be not so large a quantity kept together, as there now is in one place.

A letter from the committee of safety, respecting Gen. Ward's ordering them to deliver out small arms to such officers as may apply, was read; the consideration whereof was referred to 9 o'clock, to-morrow morning.

The committee on the petition of Mr. John Calef, reported. The report was accepted, and is as follows, viz. : It appearing to this Congress inconsistent with the best interest of this colony, that the within mentioned ship should proceed on her voyage as requested by the within memorialist, therefore, *Resolved,* that the said ship do not accordingly proceed on said voyage, till further order from this Congress, or some future house of representatives.

Afternoon.

Ordered, That Col. Freeman, Doct. Taylor and Mr. Lothrop, be a committee to consider in what manner enlisting orders and commissions shall be given to the officers of the several companies to be stationed on the sea coasts.

Mr. Palfrey was introduced to this Congress, who brought with him a number of letters, which were brought from England by Capt. Jenkins.[1]

Resolved, That Ensign Campbell, now a prisoner at Concord, be sent for to this Congress, and that Doct. Taylor and Capt. Stone be directed to search his packages, and see that he is brought to this Congress, and that Mr. Partridge be directed to bring in a resolve empowering said gentlemen to [perform] this service.

Ordered, That the letters directed to gentlemen in Rhode Island, be sent to the officers of the Rhode Island forces; those to Connecticut to the officers of the Connecticut forces; and those directed to New Hampshire, to the officers of the New Hampshire forces.

Ordered, That Doct. Whiting, Mr. Webster and Col. Freeman, be a committee to take under consideration a resolve of Congress, empowering the committee for procuring guns, to draw on the treasurer,

(1) Some of these letters contained the expression of friendly sentiments, others information of the preparations for reducing the colonies to obedience ; and among them were many addressed to individuals on affairs of business and trade.

for the value of what they purchase, and to report what alterations are necessary to be made therein.

Ordered, That Mr. Hopkins, Mr. Phillips and Col. Farley, be a committee to supervise the letters brought to this Congress by Mr. Palfrey.

Resolved, That the committee of supplies be directed to furnish the committee appointed to go to Concord, with horses.

Mr. Partridge, agreeably to order, reported the following resolve, which was accepted.

Resolved, That Doct. Taylor, and Capt. Stone of Framingham, be a committee, whose duty it shall be to repair to the town of Concord, and make search, or cause strict search to be made, into the pockets and packages of Ensign Campbell, now a prisoner at Concord, and is suspected of having letters of public concernment concealed in his possession ; and that they cause said Campbell to be brought immediately to the door of this Congress, in order for examination, if they judge it necessary.

The committee appointed to prepare an address to the several towns in the counties of Hampshire and Worcester, recommending them to supply the army with powder, reported. The report was accepted, and is as follows, viz. :

To the several Towns in the Counties of Hampshire and Worcester :

This Congress, taking into their most serious consideration, the great want of powder in our public magazines, and considering how much depends on that important and most necessary article, which, under God, if provided, may prove the salvation of America ; and as your towns lay the least exposed to the ravages of our enemies, therefore, it is most earnestly recommended by this Congress, to the selectmen of each town and district in the county of Worcester, that they deliver the whole of the towns' stocks, in said county of Worcester, to Mr. John Caldwell, Mr. Amos Singletary and Deacon Israel Nichols, a committee appointed by this Congress to receive the same ; and it is likewise recommended to the selectmen of each town and district in the county of Hampshire, to deliver their respective towns' stocks of powder, to Capt. Noah Goodman, who is appointed by this [Congress] to receive the same from said county of Hampshire ; except so much as is allowed to be kept in each town, which will appear by the schedule hereunto annexed, and that it be replaced, as soon as the state of the colony magazines will admit thereof, or otherwise will be paid for in money.[1]

Ordered, That Mr. Caldwell, Mr. Singletary and Deacon Nichols, be a committee to procure powder from the several towns in the county of Worcester, agreeably to said schedule, and Capt. Goodman, from the county of Hampshire.

Ordered, That Capt. Brown, Col. Davis and Mr. Fairbanks, be a committee to inquire where safe and convenient stores may be had, for storing what gunpowder is or may be procured for the use of this colony, and that they sit forthwith.

An account exhibited by Mr. Ichabod Goodwin, was read, and committed to Deacon Stickney, Capt. King and Mr. Thompson.

The report of the committee on the motion of Doct. Whiting, was again read, amended and accepted, and is as follows, viz.: The committee appointed to take into consideration a motion made for sending some proper person to New York, in order to advise with Doct. Graham and others, and procure from them directions for the manufacturing of saltpetre, have attended that service, and beg leave to report, by way of resolve, that Doct. William Whiting be a committee to repair to New York, and confer with Doct. Graham, or any other gentlemen that have had experience in the manufacturing of saltpetre, and that he be directed to procure from him or them, the most minute, particular, and intelligible account, relative to the manufacturing of this article, possible, and that, if to be found, he procure and engage some ingenious person, who has been used to work in the business of making saltpetre, to come immediately to this place, who shall be employed in said business, and that the expenses of said journey to New York, and the travel of said workman to this place, be paid out of the public treasury of this colony.

The report of the committee on the account of Mr. Paul Revere, was read, whereupon, *Ordered,* that tomorrow morning, ten o'clock, be assigned for the consideration thereof.

The committee on the petition of Robert Shillaber, reported. The report was accepted, and is as follows, viz.: *Resolved,* that Mr. Robert Shillaber be, and he hereby is permitted, to export to the West Indies, eighty hogsheads of Jamaica fish : provided, that no other provision be shipped with the said fish, except so much as will be sufficient for such a voyage ; and the committee of safety in Salem, are directed to see this resolve strictly complied with.

(1) The vote accepting this report was reconsidered. The revised schedule is inserted in the journal of June 30.

Ordered, That Major Goodwin, Col. Dwight, and Capt. Bragdon, be a committee to prepare instructions to the committee who were appointed to procure powder from the counties of Hampshire and Worcester, and that they sit forthwith.

The committee on the account of Major Goodwin, reported. The report was accepted, and is as follows, viz. : *Resolved*, that the receiver general be, and he hereby is ordered, to pay to Major Ichabod Goodwin, £2 17s 8d, for his time, horse, and expenses, in going express to Falmouth, by order of the committee of safety.

Adjourned to Friday morning, eight o'clo ck.

FRIDAY, JUNE 30, 1775.

Ordered, That Mr. Wheeler, Major Fuller, and Mr. Greenleaf, be a committee to bring in a resolve for the purpose of appointing some person to convey one Green, a captive, to Worcester gaol, there to be confined till further order of this Congress.

The committee appointed to consider what was best to be done with the supernumerary sheets of colony notes, reported. The report was accepted, and is as follows, viz. : The committee appointed to consider what shall be done with the supernumerary sheets, struck off from the plate containing the twenty, fourteen, and six shilling bills, have attended to that service, and find, upon examination, that there are one hundred and twenty-seven sheets above the number proposed, which make the sum of two hundred and fifty-four pounds; and beg leave to report, that it is their opinion, that an order of Congress be taken, for committing said sheets to the care of the receiver general, until the further order of the Congress or House of Representatives.

Ordered, That Major Hawley bring in a resolve, directing the committee of safety to consider the expediency of granting a further emission of bills of credit.

A letter from the committee of safety, enclosing one from the committee of safety of Portsmouth, to Doct. Langdon, and an anonymous letter wrote from Boston to Portsmouth, which was intercepted by the said committee at Portsmouth, was read, and *Ordered*, that a copy of the letter from the committee of safety of Portsmouth, be transmitted to the committee of supplies, and that the anonymous letter lie on the table.[1]

---

(1) The intercepted letter was addressed to Hugh Henderson, and is without signature. The copy follows :

" BOSTON, 22 JUNE, 1775."

"DEAR HUGH :—I take this opportunity of letting you know our welfare. We have had a great deal of confusion last Saturday ; but we have great reason of thankfulness that the troops got the

Ordered, That such of the committee who were appointed to deliver out commissions, as are now present, be directed to attest the list of officers commissioned.

Ordered, That Mr. Wheeler, be directed to deliver the supernumerary bills to the receiver, and take his receipt for the same.

A petition of Doct. William Whiting was read,[1] whereupon, *Resolved*, that the receiver general be, and he is hereby directed, to pay to Doct. Whiting, the sum of eight pounds, in colony notes, towards defraying the expenses of the said Doct. Whiting, which may accrue in his journey to New York, said Whiting to be accountable for the same to this Congress or some future House of Assembly of this colony.

The committee appointed to consider some measures to prevent the spreading of the small pox, were directed to sit forthwith.

Ordered, That Deacon Fisher, Mr. Lothrop, and Col. Richmond, be a committee to consider a resolve of the committee of safety, relative to artificer's accounts, and that said committee be directed to consider such accounts as may be transmitted to this Congress, by the committee of safety, and to report thereon.

Resolved, That the resolve of this Congress relative to procuring powder from the counties of Hampshire and Worcester, be reconsidered, and that the same, together with the report of the committee appointed to prepare instructions to the committee appointed to procure powder from said counties, be recommitted.

Ordered, That Capt. Stone, Mr. Plympton, and Mr. Johnson, be a committee to bring in a resolve for the purpose of making provision for the poor of the town of Charlestown.

Ordered, That Col. Coffin, Mr Lothrop, Capt. Nye, Capt. Bragdon, and Col. Mitchell, be a committee to inquire into the state of the two light houses at Cape Ann, and the light house at the entrance of Boston harbor, and also, that at Plymouth, and consider whether it is expedient to continue the lights therein.

better of the people. It was one of the boldest attacks almost of the age, as they had [Bunker Hill] very strong; but they did not keep it fifteen minutes after the attack begun, and such firing I never heard, so constant, I saw it all the time. There are a great many country people killed and among them is Doctor Warren: About thirty are taken prisoners and are in town. One vessel of the second fleet came in last night; so, I am in hopes the troops will be soon enabled to bring them to a sense of duty."

" If you have any apprehension of danger, I think you had best come to town."

" Yours, &c."

The committee of Portsmouth informed Congress, that a ship had been sent from Boston, to procure provisions from the islands.

(1) Doctor Whiting stated, that he had not received pay for attendance on the sessions of Congress from the town he represented ; and requested, that funds might be advanced from the public treasury to defray the expenses of his mission to New York.

Major Hawley, agreeably to order, brought in the following resolve, which was accepted.

Resolved, That the committee of safety be a committee, forthwith to consider, whether the exigencies of this colony do require, that there should be, as soon as possible, a grant made by this Congress of a further emission of notes or bills of credit, and that they consider of what sum it is proper that grant should consist, and of what denominations such bills should be, and whether they should bear any interest, and if any, what the rate of such interest should be, and at what time such notes or bills should be payable or redeemed, and whatever other regulations the said committee shall judge it expedient such notes or bills should be issued upon, and that the said committee report as soon as may be.

Ordered, That Deacon Fisher bring in a resolve, directing the receiver general to pay the sum of three pounds ten shillings, to the committee appointed to procure powder from the county of Worcester, and two pounds ten shillings, to Capt. Goodman, who is appointed to procure powder from the county of Hampshire.

Afternoon.

The form of a warrant for surgeons of the hospital, was read and accepted, and is as follows, viz. :

The Congress of the Colony of the Massachusetts Bay, to ———
——— Greeting.

Being informed of your skill in surgery, and reposing special trust and confidence in your ability and good conduct, [we] do by these presents, constitute and appoint you, the said ——— ——— to be a surgeon of the hospital, established by order of the Congress, in ——, for the sick and wounded of the colony army. You are, therefore, carefully and diligently to discharge the duty of a surgeon of said hospital, in all things appertaining thereto, observing such orders and instructions as you shall, from time to time, receive from any, your superior officers, according to the rules and discipline established by said Congress, for which, this shall be your sufficient warrant.

By order of Congress,
Dated the —— day of —— A. D. 1775.

Ordered, That warrants be made out to the following officers, viz. : Doct. Lemuel Cushing, surgeon ; Doct. Gad Hitchcock, surgeon's mate ; Adam Bayley, quarter master ; Luther Bayley, adjutant ; in

General Thomas's regiment: Doct. Lemuel Howard, surgeon to the Roxbury Hospital.

Mr. Jabez Matthews was admitted to give an account of his embassy to Quebec.

Ordered, That commissions be delivered to sundry officers in Col. Whitcomb's regiment, agreeably to a list of this date, by him exhibited.

Deacon Fisher, agreeably to order, reported the following resolves, which were accepted:

Resolved, That the sum of three pounds and ten shillings, be paid out of the public treasury, by the receiver general, who is directed to pay the same, to John [ᵃCaldwell,] Esq., for the use of the committee that was chosen to collect gunpowder within the county of Worcester, for the use of the army, and that they be accountable to this Congress or some future House of Representatives.

Resolved, That the sum of two pounds and ten shillings, be paid out of the public treasury, by the receiver general, who is hereby directed to pay the same, unto Mr. Noah Goodman, to bear his expenses in collecting gunpowder within the county of Hampshire, for the use of the army, he to be accountable for the same to this Congress or some future House of Representatives.

The committee appointed to prepare a form of a commission, &c., for the officers of those companies, who are to be stationed on the sea coasts, reported. The report was accepted, and is as follows:

The committee appointed to take into consideration in what manner and form commissions, beating and enlisting orders, be made out to the officers to be appointed and raised for defence of the sea coast, having taken the premises into consideration, would humbly report the following draught of a blank for commissions, viz.:

The Congress of the Colony of the Massachusetts Bay, to ——— ———, Gentleman,   Greeting.

We, reposing especial trust and confidence in your courage and good conduct, do, by these presents, constitute and appoint you, the said ——— ——— to be a ———, of a company of foot, appointed by said Congress, to be raised for the protection and defence of the sea coast in this colony. You are, therefore, carefully and diligently to discharge the duty of a ———, in leading, ordering, and exercising the said company in arms, both inferior officers and soldiers, and to

a [Colvill.]

keep them in good order and discipline; and they are hereby commanded to obey you as their ———, and you are yourself to observe and follow such orders and instructions as you shall, from time to time, receive from your superior officers, or from those who are or may be appointed to have the direction of the said company or companies, in the several towns or counties where you may be stationed, according to military rules and discipline in war, in pursuance of the trust reposed in you.   By order of Congress.

——— ———, *President.*

——— the ——— day of ———, A. D. 1775.
Attest,   ——— ———, *Secretary.*

Also, your committee beg leave to report the following blank or form for beating orders, viz. :

To ——— ———.

Sir :—You are hereby empowered, immediately, to enlist a company, to consist of forty-seven able-bodied, effective men, including sergeants, corporals, drummers, &c., as soldiers in the Massachusetts service, for the defence of the sea coast in this colony, and cause them to pass muster as soon as may be.

By order of Congress,

——— ———, *President.*

——— day of ———, A. D. 1775.
Attest,   ——— ———, *Secretary.*

Your committee likewise report the following form of an enlistment, viz. :

We, the subscribers, do hereby solemnly engage and enlist ourselves, as soldiers in the service of the Massachusetts colony, for the defence and protection of the sea coasts in said colony, from the day of our enlistment to the last day of December next, unless the said service should admit of a discharge of a part, or the whole, sooner, which is to be determined by the Congress or General Court, or Assembly of said colony. And we do hereby promise to submit ourselves to all the orders and regulations of the army, and faithfully to observe and obey all such orders as we shall, from time to time, receive from our superior officers.

Your committee also beg leave to report, that the committees in the several counties, appointed by this Congress, to give out beating and enlisting orders, be directed to fill up said commissions and orders, and to deliver the commissions to the officers as soon as their companies are full ; also, that a person be appointed in each of those counties upon the sea coast, to administer the oath to officers and soldiers.

NATHANIEL FREEMAN, *Chairman*.

Resolved, That there be one hundred and twenty blank commissions printed, sixty beating orders and one hundred and twenty enlisting orders.

Ordered, That Col. Freeman, Doct. Taylor, and Col. Farley, be a committee to consider in what manner crimes shall be punished, which may be committed by any of the officers or soldiers of the forces stationed on the sea coasts.

Resolved, That all warrants for staff officers, which may in future be delivered, be dated the day they are delivered.

Resolved, That all commissions to fill up vacancies, be dated the day they are delivered.

The committee appointed to consider some measures for making provision for the poor of the town of Charlestown, reported. The report was recommitted.

Ordered, That Col. Grout, and Mr. Woodbridge, be added to the committee appointed to consider the accounts which the committee of safety may transmit to this Congress.

Ordered, That the committee appointed to inspect the letters brought by Capt. Jenkins, be a committee to consider what is best to be done with them ; and that Mr. Dickinson be of that committee, in the room of Mr. Phillips.

The committee appointed to inquire where safe and convenient stores for securing gunpowder might be had, reported. The report was accepted, and is as follows :

The committee appointed to look out for a place, or places, for the safe keeping the powder that is, or may be lodged in this town, have attended that service, and beg leave to report, as their opinion, that some part of the powder be kept in the middle school-house, and some part in the east school-house, also, some part in a building belonging to Mr. Josiah Capen, near the great bridge; also, that a building be erected, as soon as possible, within the limits of the said Capen's land, not far from the great bridge in said Watertown, which place was proposed sometime since, to build a provincial magazine at, agreeably to a law of this colony. All which is humbly submitted.

JONATHAN BROWN, *per order*.

The same committee [were directed] to see that the powder is well guarded, and to consider and report what sort of a building shall be erected.

The committee directed to prepare instructions to the committee who were appointed to procure powder from the counties of Worcester and Hampshire, reported. The report was accepted, and is as follows, viz. :

To the several towns in the county of Hampshire, on the easterly side of Connecticut river, and the towns in the county of Worcester.

This Congress, taking into their most serious consideration the great want of powder in our public magazines, and considering how much depends on that important and most necessary article, which, under God, if provided, may prove the salvation of America; and, as your towns lay the least exposed to the ravages of our enemy: therefore, it is most earnestly recommended by this Congress to the selectmen of each town and district in the county of Worcester, that they deliver the whole of the towns' stock of powder, in said county of Worcester, to John Caldwell, Esq., Mr. Amos Singletary, and Mr. Israel Nichols, or either of them, a committee appointed by this Congress to receive the same, except so much as is allowed to be kept in each town, which will appear by the schedule hereunto annexed; and that it be replaced so soon as the state of the colony magazines will admit thereof, or otherwise will be paid for in money.

And it is likewise recommended to the selectmen of each town and district in the county of Hampshire, except those on the westerly side of Connecticut river, to deliver the respective town stocks of powder to Mr. Noah Goodman, who is appointed by this Congress to receive the same from the county of Hampshire, agreeably to the annexed schedule: therefore, *Resolved*, that the said committees, appointed by this Congress to collect the powder from the counties of Worcester and Hampshire, be directed to give a receipt to the selectmen of such towns as they shall receive powder from, in the form following :

The —— day of ——, 1775. Received of A. B., selectmen of the town of ——, the town stock of powder, containing —— weight, to the use of the Massachusetts' Bay; which powder is to be replaced again, as soon as the state of the colony magazine will admit of it, or paid for in money.

And the committee appointed to receive the powder are hereby, severally, empowered and directed, to employ such wagoners, or teamsters, as shall be necessary, with great despatch, to convey the same to the committee of supplies; for which service, said wagoners and teamsters, when they have delivered said powder to the committee of supplies, and shall produce a certificate from either of the committee men appointed to collect said powder, setting forth the sum agreed for the conveyance of said powder, then the committee of supplies shall give orders to the receiver general of the colony, for the sum so agreed for, to be paid in cash; and the receiver general is hereby directed to pay the same accordingly.

The schedule is as follows, viz.:

Towns' names.	Town's stock of powder.	Supplied already.	To be left in town.
COUNTY OF WORCESTER.			
Worcester,	2½ barrels,	1 barrel,	½ barrel.
Lancaster,	2½ do.	1 do.	½ do.
Mendon,	5½ do.	2 do.	½ do.
Brookfield,	6 do.	3 do.	½ do.
Oxford,	3½ do.	1 do.	½ do.
Charlton,	1⅔ do.	½ do.	¼ do.
Sutton,	4½ do.	- - -	½ do.
Leicester,	2 do.	1 do.	½ do.
Spencer,	½ do.	- - -	¼ do.
Paxton,	- -	- - -	½ do.
Rutland,	- -	- - -	½ do.
Oakham,	- -	- - -	¼ do.
Hubbardston,	- -	- - -	¼ do.
New Braintree,	1 do.	- - -	¼ do.
Southborough,	1¾ do.	- - -	½ do.
Northborough,	2 do.	1 do.	½ do.
Shrewsbury,	5 do.	- - -	½ do.
Lunenburg,	2 do.	- - -	½ do.
Fitchburg,	- -	- - -	¼ do.
Uxbridge,	2 do.	- - -	½ do.
Harvard,	2½ do.	- - -	½ do.
Dudley,	- -	- - -	½ do.
Hutchinson,	2 do.	½ do.	½ do.
Bolton,	2 do.	- - -	½ do.
Upton,	1¾ do.	- - -	¼ do.
Sturbridge,	3½ do.	- - -	½ do.
Leominster,	1 do.	- - -	½ do.
Hardwick,	2 do.	- - -	½ do.
Western,	- -	- - -	¼ do.
Holden,	½ do.	- - -	¼ do.
Douglas,	- -	- - -	¼ do.
Grafton,	2½ do.	- - -	½ do.
Petersham,	3 do.	- - -	½ do.
Royalston,	- -	- - -	¼ do.
Westminster,	½ do.	- - -	¼ do.
Athol,	- -	- - -	¼ do.
Templeton,	2 do.	- - -	½ do.
Princeton,	1½ do.	- - -	¼ do.
Ashburnham,	- -	- - -	½ do.
Winchendon,	- -	- - -	¼ do.
Westborough,	3 do.	½ do.	½ do.
Northbridge,	- -	- - -	¼ do.
COUNTY OF HAMPSHIRE.			
Springfield,	1¼ do.	- - -	¼ do.
Wilbraham,	1 do.	- - -	¼ do.
Hadley,	¾ do.	- - -	¼ do.
South Hadley,	1¼ do.	- - -	¼ do.

SCHEDULE—*Continued.*

Towns' names.	Town's stock of powder.	Supplied already.	To be left in town.
Amherst,	- -	- - -	¼ barrel,
Granby,	½ barrel,	- - -	¼ do.
Montague,	- -	- - -	¼ do.
Northfield,	1½ do.	- - -	¼ do.
Brimfield,	1 do.	- - -	¼ do.
South Brimfield,	- -	- - -	¼ do.
Monson,	½ do.	- - -	¼ do.
Pelham,	- -	- - -	¼ do.
Palmer,	- -	- - -	¼ do.
New Salem,	1 do.	- - -	¼ do.
Belchertown,	1 do.	- - -	¼ do.
Warwick,	1 do.	- - -	¼ do.
Shutesbury,	- -	- - -	¼ do.

Ordered, That Capt. Brown make provision for the two poor women, late of the town of Charlestown, now at the door, till to-morrow morning.

Ordered, That Mr. Kollock, Col. Grout, and Mr. Dickerson, be a committee to examine the accounts of Major Barber, agreeably to his letter.

A letter from the committee of inspection of the town of Biddeford, was read, and committed to Col. Richmond, Capt. Stone, and Mr. Langdon, who are directed to examine the prisoner, Thomas Neat, brought from Biddeford, and report.[1]

Adjourned to 8 o'clock, to-morrow morning.

SATURDAY, JULY 1, 1775.

[The committee appointed to bring in a resolve for the purpose of making provision for the poor of the town of Charlestown, reported the following, which was accepted, viz :]

Whereas, the distressed circumstances of the inhabitants of the town of Charlestown, calls for the charitable aid of this colony: therefore, *Resolved*, that such of those inhabitants as are unable to remove or support themselves, be removed to the several towns in the county of Worcester, mentioned in the schedule hereunto annexed.

And it is further recommended to the selectmen of the aforesaid towns to provide for, and employ said inhabitants, in the best and most prudent manner that may be, and render their accounts to this or some

(1) A suspicious person, named Thomas Neat, a deserter from one of the king's ships, was arrested in Biddeford, and sent as prisoner to Watertown.

future Congress, or House of Representatives, which reasonable accounts shall be paid out of the public treasury of said colony.

And it is further *Resolved*, that Deacon Cheever, Capt. Brown, and Major Fuller, of Newton, be a committee to agree with teamsters, not exceeding the rate of nine pence per ton per mile, for transporting such inhabitants as are unable to travel, with their effects, and give certificates to such teamsters, expressing that they are the poor of the town of Charlestown, and the sum they are to receive for such service; and upon said teamsters producing said certificate to the committee of supplies, endorsed with the test of the selectmen of the town where such poor and their effects are lodged, that said teamster has done the service agreed for, per said certificate, the committee of supplies are hereby directed to draw, on the receiver general of said colony, for the payment of said teamster; and the said receiver general is hereby ordered to pay the same.

County of Worcester. Lancaster, 30; Mendon, 30; Brookfield, 20; Oxford, 15; Charlton, 10; Sutton, 30; Leicester, 12; Spencer, 10; Paxton, 7; Rutland, 15; Oakham, 6; Hutchinson, 20; New Braintree, 15; Southborough, 6; Westborough, 20; Northborough, 10; Shrewsbury, 10; Fitchburg, 10; Uxbridge, 10.

The committee appointed to consider what methods would be proper to try and punish crimes which may be committed by the soldiers stationed on the sea coasts, reported. The report was recommitted, and Major Hawley and Mr. Greenleaf added to the committee.

Two letters from Rev. John Murray were read, and committed to Col. Grout, Major Fuller, of Newton, and Major Goodwin.

An account of Jabez Matthews [for a journey to Quebec] was read, and committed to Major Fuller, Col. Mitchell, and Mr. Ingalls.

Ordered, That Mr. Lothrop, Mr. Dickenson, and Mr. Nye, be a committee to consider a resolve of the committee of safety, respecting whaleboats.

A resolve of the committee of safety, proposing that electrical points should be erected over the powder magazines, was read, and committed to the committee who were appointed to build a store for depositing gunpowder therein, and seeing that it is well guarded.

A petition from eighteen Stockbridge Indians was read, and committed to Mr. Kollock, Mr. Crane, and Major White.

The committee appointed to examine Thomas Neat, reported. The report was accepted, and is as follows: The committee appointed to examine Thomas Neat, have attended that service, and are humbly of opinion, that he ought to be discharged, and set at liberty, and do recommend him for a pass, to be signed by the secretary, to go to New York, there to apply for a further pass, as he proposes to go to Virginia. Submitted.   EZRA RICHMOND, *pr. order.*

Resolved, That the following persons be appointed deputy commissaries in the Massachusetts army, being one to each regiment:

Mr. Samuel Norton, recommended by Col. Lincoln.

Capt. Ebenezer Craft, of Sturbridge, recommended by Col. Learned, Rev. Mr. Paine, &c.

Mr. Jedediah Easterbrooks, Lunenburg, recommended by Mr. Gill and Dr. Taylor.

Mr. Ezekiel Cheever, Boston, recommended by ª[Col. Pigeon.]

Mr. Samuel Russell Gerry, Marblehead, recommended by   do.

Mr. Ebenezer Warren, Boston, recommended by the hon. committee of supplies.

Mr. John Fenno, Boston, recommended by Secretary Ward.

Mr. Alexander Sheppard, Newton, recommended by ª[Col. Pigeon.]

Mr. Ephraim Russell, Stow, recommended by Col. Doolittle, and the paymaster general.

Mr. Daniel Bell, Boston, recommended by Mr. Pitt.

Mr. William Mollineaux, Boston, recommended by do.

Mr. Daniel Henshaw, Jr.,   "   "   by Doct. Church.

Mr. John Checkley,   "   "   by do. and others.

Mr. Jabez Brown, Stow, recommended by the paymaster general.

Mr. Joseph Clark, Boston, recommended by Gen. Warren, Doct. Church, &c.

Mr. Gillam Taylor, Boston, recommended by Gen. Warren and others.

Mr. Andrew Newell, Charlestown, recommended by Mr. Cheever.

Capt. James Littlefield, Wells, recommended by Col. Scammon and others.

Mr. Waterman Thomas, Marshfield, recommended by Gen. Thomas.

Mr. Peter Clark, Newfoundland, recommended by Col. Palmer & Son.

Mr. Timothy Newell, Sturbridge, recommended by Capt. Timothy Parker.

Mr. John Story, Ipswich, recommended by Col. Farley.

Mr. Eliakim Atherton, Bolton, recommended by Col. Whitecomb.

Mr. Abraham Tuckerman, Boston, recommended by Col. Palmer and Col. Brewer.

Mr. William Holmes, Boston, recommended by his father.

Mr. Enoch Woodbridge, Stockbridge, recommended by Col. Porter for Col. Paterson's regiment.

a [myself.]

Resolved, That the commissary general be directed to see that a sufficient number of deputy commissaries be placed at or near Prospect Hill, for the more convenient supply of the forces stationed there.

The president, by leave of Congress, brought in a resolve, directing General Ward to order two companies to Plymouth, which was accepted, and is as follows, viz:

Whereas, the town of Plymouth appears to be in danger of being attacked by the enemy: therefore, *Resolved*, that General Ward be and hereby is directed, immediately to issue his orders, that two full companies, from Col. Cotton's regiment, under proper officers, march, without delay, to Plymouth, and there remain for the guard and defence of the inhabitants, till they can be relieved by such companies as are to be raised for the defence and protection of the sea coasts, and to be stationed there for that purpose.

Ordered, That Col. Palmer bring in a resolve, directing that the rules and regulations of the army be frequently read to the soldiers.

The committee appointed to consider some method of trying criminals on the sea coast, reported again. The report was accepted, and is as follows, viz.:

Resolved, That all offences committed by any of the forces raised for the defence of the sea coast, shall be tried by a court martial, consisting of the field officers of the regiment of militia within which, that company to which the offender belongs is stationed, together with the commissioned officers of that company, according to the rules and regulations for the Massachusetts army, agreed upon by a former Congress, excepting those offences and causes which are punishable with death, which are to be tried, agreeably to the laws of the land, by the civil authority.

Also *Resolved*, That in case any of the soldiers shall lose, destroy, or unnecessarily fire away any of his powder, ammunition, or cartridges, without giving reasonable satisfaction to his commanding officer therefor, the captain shall deduct four [ªtimes] the value thereof out of his wages, to be applied as is directed in the first article of the rules and regulations abovementioned.

Also [*Resolved*,] That each of the officers of which these courts martial shall consist, shall be supplied with a pamphlet, containing said rules and regulations, with these resolves annexed thereto, which shall be read, once a week, by the captain or commanding officer of each company to their respective companies.

By order of Congress,   —— ——, *President.*

Attest,   —— ——, *Secretary.*

a [double.]

55

Ordered, That the committee who brought in the foregoing resolves get a number of them printed; and that they also procure as many pamphlets, containing rules and regulations of the army, as they think proper.

A petition from James Fry, requesting that his son might be appointed a deputy commissary, was read: whereupon, *Ordered,* that the petitioner have leave to withdraw his petition.

Ordered, That Mr. Kollock, Mr. Ellis, and Mr. Fox, be a committee to consider a petition and account of Mr. Josiah Stearns.[1]

A petition from the committee of correspondence for the town of Sandwich was read, and committed to Col. Richmond, Col. Grout, and Col. Mitchell.[2]

A number more of letters from London were laid upon the table, and committed to the secretary, Mr. Langdon, and Col. Richmond.

The committee to whom were committed a number of letters, reported, that, in a letter directed to John Rowe, Esq., was enclosed a number of blank bills of exchange, designed for the use of the army at Boston: whereupon, *Ordered,* that said committee draw up a true state of this matter, and keep the blank bills as vouchers thereof.

Col. Palmer, agreeably to order, reported the following resolve, which was accepted, viz.: Whereas certain rules and regulations for

(1) Josiah Stearns prayed for compensation for services in bringing letters written in London, from the island of Nantucket, where they had been received on the arrival of a vessel commanded by Capt. Seth Jenkins.

(2) The committee of Sandwich requested the advice of Congress in relation to vessels owned by Simeon Wing and Jesse Barlow, captured by the British cruiser Falcon, Capt. Linsey, and retaken by a schooner from Dartmouth, commanded by Capt. Egery. They state these facts:

" Mr. Wing's vessel, commanded by his son Thomas, hath been plying, as a wood boat, between Sandwich and Nantucket for some years, and it hath been the usual practice to settle with the custom house once a year, the officer always giving them their choice of paying twelve pence per trip, or the whole at the year's end: and this hath been, we find, on examining, the common practise with other vessels which have followed the same business at the same place. Upon Captain Wing's returning from Nantucket through the Vineyard Sound, his sloop was taken by a barge from Capt. Linsey's brig. An Indian fellow, on board of Wing's vessel, informed Capt. Linsey of said Barlow's vessel, which had brought a cargo lately from the West Indies, and was laden with provisions, in Buzzard's Bay. Captain Linsey employed Captain Wing's vessel, putting fourteen men on board, to proceed up the bay and take said Barlow's vessel, which they carried off. The master of the latter vessel was taken with Wing, being then on board as a passenger, so that both vessels, with all the crews and passengers, were taken, and proceeded to the cove to Captain Linsey. Mr. Barlow made application to some people at Dartmouth, who went with a sloop, one half of which Barlow ventured, and retook the vessels and men, with their arms, and carried them into Dartmouth. Messrs. Wing and Barlow applied to the Dartmouth people, who took the vessels, for them again: the people offered them their vessels, upon Wing's paying them eight dollars, and Barlow ten dollars, with which they complied, and Wing paid the money ; after which, the Dartmouth people detained the vessels until the orders of Congress could be known, and refuse to give them up, without Barlow and Wing paying forty-five dollars, and giving bonds to indemnify the Dartmouth people."

the Massachusetts army, were resolved and agreed upon by a former Congress of this colony, but no provision was therein made for the regular reading the same to the several corps in said army : therefore, *Resolved*, that said rules and regulations be read, at least, once every month, at the head of each regiment, or other corps in said army, and that the general be directed to order his officers to see that this resolve be duly observed.

The committee appointed to prepare a letter to the governor and company of Connecticut, reported. The report was accepted, and is as follows, viz. :

May it please your honors :

The distressed situation of the eastern parts of this province, calling for the serious attention of the humane, this Congress beg leave to address you in their behalf. By reason of a number of our friends removing from the sea ports into the interior towns, and a large army before Boston, to support the rights of the colonies, this colony is unable to spare the necessary supplies of grain and provisions to our friends in the province of Maine; by which means, and an embargo laid upon grain and provisions in your colony, they are reduced to the alternative of starving, or supplying the ministerial troops with lumber, either of which they deprecate.

We would therefore suggest to your honors the expediency of taking off the embargo, so far as to permit the inhabitants of the eastern parts of this province to purchase grain and provisions for themselves, they producing a certificate from any of the committees mentioned in the enclosed list, and giving bonds to your officers, that they will deliver it to such committee.

We are, with the greatest sincerity,

Your honors' most obedient humble servants.

To the honorable the Governor and Company
of the colony of Connecticut.

[List enclosed in the foregoing letter.]

Machias; James Lyon, George Stillman, Jeremiah O'Brian, Benjamin Foster, Samuel Scott, Manwaring Beal, Nathaniel Sinclair : *Number four;* John Stevens, Phineas Whitten : *Goldsborough;* Benjamin Glasher, William Shaw : *Narraguagus;* Joseph Wallis, Alexander Campbell : *St. Georges;* [blank] : *Penobscot;* [blank] : *Bristol;* [blank] : *Boothbay;* David Reed, [Joseph] Emerson : *Pownalborough;* Timothy Langdon, Ebenezer Whittier, John Getchell, John

Huse, Timothy Parsons: *Georgetown;* Dummer Sewall, John Wood: *Brunswick;* Aaron Hinckley, Esq., Benjamin Stone: *North Yarmouth;* Samuel Stanwood: *Falmouth, Casco Bay;* Hon. Jedediah Prebble, Esq., Hon. Enoch Freeman, Esq., Mr. Richard Codman, Capt. John Waite, Mr. John Butler, Mr. Samuel Freeman, Mr. Benjamin Winslow: *Berwick;* Hon. Benjamin Chadburn, Mr. John Hill, Mr. Robert Furnass.

The committee on the account of Mr. Jabez Matthews, reported. The report was accepted, and is as follows, viz.:

[*Resolved*, That the receiver general be, and he is hereby directed to pay Mr. Jabez Matthews or order, the sum of thirty pounds nine shillings and eleven pence, lawful money, in colony notes or bills of credit of this or the other governments, which are, by a resolve of this Congress, made payable on the said treasury, in discharge of an account exhibited by him to this Congress, for the time and expense of himself and three persons on an embassy to Canada. And the committee of supplies are hereby ordered to furnish Mr. Jabez Matthews with four pounds of powder, for himself and associates.]

The committee appointed to consider the resolve of the committee of safety, relative to whale boats, reported. The report was recommitted.

Afternoon.

Mr. Kollock was appointed, in the room of Major Goodwin, on the committee for making provision for the reception of Generals Washington and Lee.

Ordered, That Col. Mitchell deliver the 215 spears, which he has procured for the use of the army, to General Thomas, at Roxbury.

Ordered, That Doct. Taylor, Mr. Fox, and Capt. Bragdon, be a committee to bring in a resolve, directing how the sick and wounded shall be removed to the hospitals.

Thomas Rice, Esq. was appointed to swear the soldiers in the county of Lincoln, in the room of David Fales, Esq. John Lee, Esq. was appointed to swear the soldiers in the county of Essex, and Rushworth Jordan for the county of York, in addition to those already appointed.

A petition from the selectmen of Mendon was read, and the petitioners had leave to withdraw their petition.

The committee appointed to consider how the soldiers shall be supplied with coats, reported, and Tuesday next, at 9 o'clock, A. M., was assigned to consider the report.

The committee appointed to take into consideration the memorial from the committee of correspondence of the town of Sandwich, reported. The committee were directed to bring in a resolve to recommend to the parties in said petition mentioned, to leave the matters in dispute to arbitration.

Major Hawley, by leave of Congress, brought in a resolve, directing the receiver general to pay out of the treasury, the bills of credit of the other colonies. The resolve was accepted, and is as follows:

Resolved, That the receiver general of this colony, be, and he hereby is directed, as far as shall be in his power, to pay and satisfy any drafts and orders of this Congress, or of any person or persons, who are, or shall be empowered by this Congress to draw on him for any sum or sums whatsoever, in such notes or bills of credit of any of the American colonies, which, by a resolution of this Congress, passed on the 28th day of June last, are made payable into the treasury of this colony, where such orders do not expressly direct the payment of silver or gold.

The committee appointed to devise means for the better accommodation of the sick and wounded of the colony army, reported. The report was accepted, and is as follows, viz.: In order that all the sick and wounded in the army may be provided for, and taken care of, in the best way and manner possible, *Resolved*, and it is hereby *Ordered*, that when any person in the army is so ill, either by a wound or otherwise, that the surgeon of the regiment, to which the sick or wounded person belongs, finds the sick or wounded as abovesaid cannot be properly taken care of in the regiment to which he belongs, said surgeon shall send the sick or wounded as abovesaid, to the hospital provided for the use of the camps to which they belong, and a certificate of the man's name, and the company and regiment to which he belongs; and in that case, the surgeon of the said hospital shall receive said sick or wounded under his care; and in case said hospital shall become too full, in that case, the surgeon of said hospital shall send such of his patients as may with safety be removed, to the hospital in Watertown, and a certificate setting forth the man's name, what company and regiment each belongs to; and in that case the surgeons of the Watertown hospital shall receive said sick or wounded under his care.

Ordered, That a copy of the last mentioned resolve be sent to Generals Ward and Thomas.

The report of the committee upon the account of Mr. Paul Revere, was considered and not accepted.

Ordered, That Major Hawley, Mr. Dexter, and Mr. Pickering, be a committee to draw up a resolve to be prefixed to the addresses to Generals Washington and Lee, which are as follow.

To His Excellency George Washington, Esq., general and commander in chief of the continental army:

May it please your excellency:—The Congress of the Massachusetts colony, impressed with every sentiment of gratitude and respect, beg leave to congratulate you on your safe arrival, and to wish you all imaginable happiness and success in the execution of your elevated station.

While we applaud that attention to the public good, manifested in your appointment, we equally admire that disinterested virtue, and distinguished patriotism, which alone could call you from those enjoyments of domestic life, which a sublime and manly taste, joined with a most affluent fortune can afford, to hazard your life, and to endure the fatigues of war, in the defence of the rights of mankind and the good of your country.

The laudable zeal for the common cause of America, and compassion for the distresses of this colony, exhibited by the great despatch made in your journey hither, fully justify the universal satisfaction we have with pleasure observed on this occasion, and are promising presages, that the great expectations formed from your personal character and military abilities, are well founded.

We wish you may have found such regularity and discipline already established in the army, as may be agreeable to your expectations. The hurry with which it was necessarily collected, and the many disadvantages, arising from a suspension of government, under which we have raised and endeavored to regulate the forces of this colony, have rendered it a work of time; and though, in great measure effected, the completion of so difficult, and at the same time so necessary a task, is reserved to your excellency, and we doubt not will be properly considered and attended to.

We would not presume to prescribe to your excellency, but supposing you would choose to be informed of the general character of the soldiers who compose the army, beg leave to represent, that the greatest part of them have not before seen service; and although naturally brave, and of good understanding, yet, for want of experience in military life, have but little knowledge of divers things most essential to the preservation of health and even life. The youth of the army are not possessed of the absolute necessity of cleanliness in their dress and lodging, continual exercise, and strict temperance, to preserve them from diseases frequently prevailing in camps, especially among those, who, from their childhood, have been used to a laborious life.

We beg leave to assure you, that this Congress will, at all times, be ready to attend to such requisitions as you may have occasion to make to us; and to contribute all the aid in our power, to the cause of America, and your happiness and ease in the discharge of the duties of your exalted office.

We most fervently implore Almighty God, that the blessings of Divine Providence may rest on you; that your head may be covered in the day of battle; that every necessary assistance may be afforded, and that you may be long continued, in life and health, a blessing to mankind.

[The following answer was returned by General Washington:]

Gentlemen :—Your kind congratulations on my appointment and arrival, demand my warmest acknowledgments, and will ever be retained in grateful remembrance.

In exchanging the enjoyments of domestic life for the duties of my present honorable, but arduous station, I only emulate the virtue, and public spirit of the whole province of the Massachusetts Bay, which, with a firmness and patriotism without example in modern history, has sacrificed all the comforts of social and political life in support of the rights of mankind, and the welfare of our common country. My highest ambition is, to be the happy instrument of vindicating those rights and to see this devoted province again restored to peace, liberty and safety.

The short space of time which has elapsed since my arrival, does not permit me to decide upon the state of the army. The course of human affairs forbids an expectation, that troops formed under such circumstances, should, at once, possess the order, regularity, and discipline of veterans. Whatever deficiencies there may be, will, I doubt not, soon be made up by the activity and zeal of the officers, and the docility and obedience of the men. These qualities, united with their native bravery and spirit, will afford a happy presage of success, and put a final period to those distresses which now overwhelm this once happy country.

I most sincerely thank you, gentlemen, for your declaration of readiness, at all times, to assist me in the discharge of the duties of my station. They are so complicated and extended, that I shall need the assistance of every good man and lover of his country; I therefore repose the utmost confidence in your aids. In return for your affectionate wishes to myself, permit me to say, that I earnestly implore that divine being, in whose hands are all human events, to make you and your constituents, as distinguished in private and public happiness, as you have been by ministerial oppression, by private and public distress.

GEORGE WASHINGTON.

To the Honorable Charles Lee, Esq., major general of the continental army :

Sir :—The Congress of the Massachusetts colony, possessed of the fullest evidence of your attachment to the rights of mankind and regard to the distresses, which America in general, and this colony in particular, are involved in, by the impolitic, wicked, and tyrannical system adopted by administration, and pursued with relentless and savage fury, do, with pleasure, embrace this opportunity to express the great satisfaction and gratitude they feel on your appointment as a major general in the American army. We sincerely congratulate you on your safe arrival here, and wish you all possible happiness and success in the execution of so important a trust.

We admire and respect the character of a man, who, disregarding the allurements of profit and distinction his merit might procure, engages in the cause of mankind, in defence of the injured, and relief of the oppressed. From your character, from your great abilities, and military experience, united with those of the commander in chief, under the smiles of providence, we flatter ourselves with the prospect of discipline and order, success and victory.

Be assured, sir, that it will give us great pleasure to be able to contribute to your happiness. May the favors and blessings of Heaven attend you. May Divine Providence guard and protect you, conduct you in the paths of honor and virtue, grant you the reward of the brave and virtuous here, the applause of mankind, and the approbation of your own conscience and eternal happiness hereafter.

[The following answer was returned by General Lee :]

To the Gentlemen of the Provincial Congress of the Massachusetts :

Gentlemen :—Nothing can be so flattering to me, as the good opinion and approbation of the delegates of a free and uncorrupted people. I was educated in the highest reverence for the rights of mankind, and have acquired, by a long acquaintance, a most particular regard for the people of America. You may depend, therefore, gentlemen, on my zeal and integrity ; I can promise you nothing from my abilities. God Almighty grant us success equal to the righteousness of the cause. I thank you, gentlemen, for an address which does me so much honor, and shall labor to deserve it.

Ordered, that the sum of fifty pounds be paid to Mr. Paul Revere, in full, for engraving four plates, and printing 14,500 impressions, and that Mr. Langdon bring in a resolve for that purpose.

Ordered, That Mr. Phillips, Col. Grout, and Mr. Crane, be a committee to devise means for supporting the poor of the towns of Boston and Charlestown to the places of their destination.

Ordered, That the committee for procuring and furnishing a house for Generals Washington and Lee, be directed to purchase what things are necessary, that they cannot hire.

Ordered, That Mr. Goodwin and Col. Richmond be added to the committee last mentioned.

Ordered, That the last mentioned committee be directed to procure some refreshment for the Generals, Washington and Lee.

Mr. Langdon, agreeably to order, brought in the following resolve, which was accepted, viz. :

Resolved, That there be paid, out of the public treasury of this colony, to Mr. Paul Revere, or order, the sum of fifty pounds, in full, for procuring and engraving four plates, and printing 14,500 impressions of colony notes; and the receiver general is hereby directed to pay the same sum accordingly.

The committee appointed to consider of means for securing sundry whale boats, procured for the use of this colony, and now lying at Weymouth and Braintree, beg leave to report: That Capt. Edmund Soper, of Braintree, be empowered to take charge of the same, and with the assistance of Capt. Seth Turner's and Capt. Vinton's companies, now posted in Braintree, to convey and secure them in some safe and convenient place, where they will not be exposed, either to the enemy, or the weather, and there to remain till the further order of this or some future Congress, or House of Representatives.

Adjourned till eight o'clock, tomorrow morning.

SABBATH DAY, JULY 2, 1775.

Ordered, That Mr. Bliss and Mr. Cutt, be of the committee for devising means for the support of the poor of the towns of Boston and Charlestown, to the places of their destination, in the room of Mr. Phillips and Mr. Crane.

The report of the committee for securing the lamps of the light houses, was read, accepted, and is as follows, viz. :

The committee appointed to consider the expediency of removing and securing the lamps, with the oil, &c., from the several light houses within this colony, have attended that service, and beg leave to report as follows, viz.:

That it be recommended to the committee of correspondence, or selectmen of the town of Chelsea, to remove and secure, if practicable, the lamps and oil from the light house at the entrance of Boston harbor, with all the appurtenances thereto belonging; also, that it be recommended to the committee of safety of the town of Gloucester, that the same measures be taken with respect to the light houses on Thatcher's Island, so called, and that the keeper of said lights, with the several boats, cattle, &c., be also removed from thence.

Furthermore, that it be recommended to the committee of correspondence for the town of Plymouth, to remove and secure the lamps, oil, &c., from the light house at the Gurnet, so called, with all the appurtenances thereto belonging; and, that the keepers of the several light houses as above specified, be discharged from the service of this colony, till the further order of this or some future Congress, or House of Representatives.

Ordered, That three copies of the last mentioned report be sent to the places in said report mentioned, and that the committee, who drew the report, forward the copies.

Ordered, That Doct. Taylor, Mr. Pickering, and Mr. Greenleaf, be a committee to write to Mr. Russell, desiring him to pay the money due from him to the treasury, immediately.

The petition of Joseph Barrell for himself and others, [was] read, and ordered to lie upon file.[1]

(1) This petition bears date June 30, 1775, and is as follows:

"The petition of Joseph Barrell, late of Boston, humbly sheweth, that in the fire in Boston, which began in the soldiers' barracks, on the evening of the 17th of May last, his store, together with his effects to a very considerable amount, were consumed. Your petitioner humbly apprehends, that this loss is entirely occasioned by the cruel oppression of the British administration; as, at the general desire of the friends of the country, he removed with his family from Boston, that scene of distress, and, by the chicanery of General Gage, was prevented from carrying his effects with him; as he, with his distressed townsmen, were shamefully deceived by the fairest promises of a speedy removal, with their effects, without molestation, until the end of the capitulation on the side of the general was fully answered, and then they were insulted, by the most cruel perversion of that comprehensive, plain English word *effects*, confining it to a few trifles, which, when they were suffered to depart, was clogged with such restrictions as will forever disgrace him. But, notwithstanding all this, still your petitioner had been safe, in all probability, had not the General, by an order, as extraordinary as it was new, secured from the inhabitants the fire engines, and given the use of them to his troops; whereby, as your petitioner is informed, it was a very considerable time before they were in use at all, and then were conducted with such consummate ignorance as to be of no service; in which time, the flames raged to that degree, that no human help could prevent them; and your petitioner is further informed, that some of his effects, saved from the fire by his friends, were afterwards wantonly destroyed by the savage order of the officer of the army.

The letter of Mr. Alexander Sheppard, Jun., to the committee of safety [was] read.[1]

The report of the committee for devising means for the support of the poor of Boston and Charlestown, to the places of their destination, was read, and accepted, and is as follows:

Whereas, it is necessary, that further provision be made for the suffering poor of the towns of Boston and Charlestown, therefore, *Resolved*, that such person or persons as shall produce a certificate from any or either of the selectmen or overseers of the poor of the said towns, that they are of the poor of the town to which the said selectmen or overseers do, or did in March last, belong, that then the commissaries, in the towns of Watertown and Roxbury, are hereby directed to deliver, out of the province stores, to them, a sufficiency of provisions to carry them to the place of their destination, the commissary to take a receipt from such selectmen or overseers therefor.

And it is recommended to the inhabitants of this province, to treat such poor with humanity, by affording them shelter in their houses from the weather, and, if desired, to exchange such provisions with them as said poor may have occasion for on their way.

Ordered, That the foregoing resolve be published in the Watertown, Cambridge, and Worcester newspapers.

Adjourned to four o'clock, P. M.

At four o'clock, P. M., the Congress met, and adjourned to Monday morning, eight o'clock.

MONDAY, JULY 3, 1775.

Ordered, That the committee of safety, who were appointed a committee to take into consideration the expediency of a new emission of notes or bills of credit, be directed to sit, and report as soon as possible.

Resolved, That the resolve of the first instant, ordering the rules and regulations of the army to be read monthly, be reconsidered.

Resolved, That the receiver general be directed to pay to Mr. Josiah

Wherefore, your petitioner humbly hopes, that his case, together with the case of his fellow sufferers, may, by the honorahle Congress, be represented to the grand Continental Congress, that they, in their great wisdom, may take such measures as to them shall seem fit, to alleviate their sufferings, and that what is thus destroyed in the general cause, may not fall so very heavily on any individual."

(1) The letter of Alexander Sheppard, Jun., related to compensation for surveys of lands in the province, now the state, of Maine.

Stevens, the sum of two pounds, in colony notes or bills of credit, payable to said receiver, for his services in bringing a number of letters to this Congress, taken out of a vessel from London.

Afternoon.

A vote of the Congress of New Hampshire [was] read, and Messrs. Child and Ashley, the bearers thereof, [were] admitted on the floor.[1] They produced a letter from Messrs. Bucknam and Wales, to Col. Bayley, of New Hampshire, and his answer.

Ordered, That Messrs. Dexter, Col. Lincoln, Doct. Church, Mr. Pitts, and Capt. Bragdon, be a committee to confer with Messrs. Child and Ashley, from the province of New Hampshire.

Ordered, That the addition of the words " overseers of the poor," be added to the resolve of yesterday, respecting the poor of the towns of Boston and Charlestown.

Ordered, That Mr. Cutt, Col. Farley, and Col. Dwight, be a committee to take into consideration the petition of Thomas Morton, [for leave to export fish.]

Ordered, That a letter for Thomas Irving, Esq., be opened, and ordered to be committed to the committee who were to take under consideration, what should be done with the letters from London.

The petition of the selectmen of Abington, [relating to donations for the poor of Boston,] was read, and committed to Col. Mitchell, Mr. Lothrop, and Mr. Ellis.

Major Goodwin, who was appointed to bring in a resolve for directing the committee of supplies to furnish the non-commissioned officers, who lost their clothes and blankets, in the late engagement, with clothes and blankets, reported. The report was accepted, and is as follows:

Whereas, in consequence of a letter from General Ward, provision was made, by a resolve of this Congress, for private soldiers who had lost their clothes and blankets in a late engagement, but no provision was made for non-commissioned officers in similar circumstances, therefore, *Resolved*, that the committee of supplies be, and they hereby are directed, to furnish said non-commissioned officers with clothes and blankets, in such manner and form as they were directed by said resolve to supply said privates.

Adjourned to Tuesday morning, eight o'clock.

(1) The communication from New Hampshire related to the establishment of friendly intercourse and union with the people of Canada.

TUESDAY, JULY 4, 1775.

Ordered, That the honorable the president, Hon. Major Hawley, and Mr. Greenleaf, be a committee to prepare a letter to Governor Trumbull, desiring him to forward to this colony, as soon as may be, whatever flour may arrive at Connecticut for the use of the army.

A letter from Col. Gridley was read, [relating to the commissions of officers,] and ordered to lie on the table.

Ordered, That Mr. Pickering, Mr. Partridge, and Mr. Goodwin, be a committee to prepare a letter to General Washington, informing him of the provision this Congress has made for the sick and wounded of the army.

An account of Ephraim Fenno was read, and committed to Mr. Wheeler, Mr. Jewett, and Col. Dwight.

Ordered, That Asa Barns, and other officers of Col. Woodbridge's regiment, recommended by the committee of safety, be commissioned, agreeably to the recommendation of said committee.

The committee on the petition of the selectmen of Abington, reported, verbally, that the matter respecting the donations for the poor of Boston, be considered at large.

Ordered, That Col. Mitchell, Capt. Stone, Mr. Kollock, Col. Jones, and Mr. Crane, be a committee for that purpose.

Ordered, That Mr. Johnson, Mr. Fairfield, and Mr. Crane, be a committee to examine the accounts of those persons who were empowered to procure arms for the use of the colony army.

The committee on the petition of Thomas Morton, reported. The report was ordered to lie on the table for the present.

A resolve of the committee relative to the goods of Thomas Hutchinson, Esq., and others, hid in and about Milton, was read, and committed to Major Bliss, Col. Grout, and Mr. Crane.

Resolved, That three o'clock, P. M., be assigned for the choice of some gentleman to serve on the committee of supplies, in the room of Mr. Vose, who declines serving.

Ordered, That Mr. Jewett, Mr. Lothrop, Capt. Thatcher, Col. Jones, Mr. Wheeler, Col. Farley, and Mr. Cross, be a committee to consider the expediency of making a draw bridge of the bridge at Cambridge, agreeably to the request of General Washington, and that said committee be directed to sit forthwith.

At the request of General Washington, communicated by Mr. Gill, *Resolved*, that no more commissions, for the present, be delivered to any officers of the colony army, those employed, more particularly, for the protection of the sea coasts excepted.

The resolve relative to furnishing the soldiers with coats, was considered, and recommitted for amendment.

Ordered, That Mr. Partridge, Mr. Pickering, and Doct. Taylor, be a committee, to consider in what manner the late inhabitants of the town of Boston, may choose members to represent that town in the next General Assembly of this colony.

Resolved, That the committee of supplies be, and hereby are directed, to supply the Rev. Mr. Gordon with a good horse to use during his service as a chaplain to this Congress.

Ordered, That Doct. Taylor, Doct. Church, and Mr. Johnson, be a committee to bring in a resolve appointing Doct. [Andrew] Craigie, a commissary of medical stores, and that said committee be directed to consider what is a proper establishment for his pay.

Afternoon.

A recommendation of the committee of safety relative to an Indian's having a horse, was read, and committed to Doct. Taylor, Mr. Partridge, and Mr. Glover.

Ordered, That Capt. Brown, Capt. Parker, and Mr. Richmond, be a committee to sort and count the votes for a member of the committee of supplies, in the room of Major Vose, and Capt. Partridge was chosen in the room of Major Vose.

Ordered, That the committee for making out commissions, be directed to make out a commission for Samuel Brewer, as adjutant general, and date it the day of his appointment.

The committee appointed to write a letter to Governor Trumbull, reported. The report was read, and ordered to be recommitted for additions and amendments.

Ordered, That any three of the committee of supplies, of which Mr. Gill is to be one, in the absence of Mr. Cheever, be a quorum to do business.

The committee upon the letter relative to the Indian's having a horse, reported. The report was accepted, and is as follows, viz. :

Resolved, That a small horse, taken by Henries Vomhavi, from Noddle's Island, be granted to the said Henries for his own use, to encourage his further brave conduct and good behaviour in camp.

Ordered, That Col. Spalding, Mr. Woodbridge, and Mr. Johnson, be a committee to take under consideration the sufferings of Abraham Ninham.[1]

Ordered, That Mr. Glover, Doct. a[Taylor,] and Col. Groat, be on

(1) This person met with some pecuniary loss, while employed in the public service, in bearing a letter to the Western Indians.

a [Glover.]

the committee of conference with the members from New Hampshire, in the room of Mr. Pitts, Col. Lincoln, and Capt. Bragdon.

Ordered, That Mr. Bent be on the committee for the Abington petition, in the room of Doct. Jones.

Ordered, That the President, Mr. Langdon, and Major Bliss, be a committee to take into consideration the conduct of the people of Nantucket, and report what is expedient to be done with respect to them.

Ordered, That Mr. Wheelock, with letters from the Congress of New Hampshire, be admitted upon the floor.

Ordered, [That] Doct. Church, Mr. Hopkins, and Major Bliss, be a committee to introduce Mr. Wheelock, and also to deliver a copy of the letter from New Hampshire to his excellency General Washington, and also to draw an answer to the letter from New Hampshire.

The report of the committee upon the account of Mr. White was accepted, and is as follows, viz. :

The committee appointed to consider accounts, transmitted to this Congress by the committee of safety, beg leave to report, by way of resolve, that William White be paid the sum of six pounds, lawful money, for service done by said William White, by order of the committee of safety, and that the receiver general be directed to pay said sum to the said William White.

The committee appointed to write to Governor Trumbull, reported. The report was read, accepted, and is as follows, viz. :

May it please your honor :

Your favor of the 27th June, we received, and heartily thank you for the information therein given us. The arrival of the flour from New York to Norwich, gives us great pleasure, as we stand in need of large supplies of that commodity. We request your honor to give orders that the same may be forwarded, as soon as possible, to our committee of supplies at Watertown; and any further quantities that may arrive hereafter, we desire may be sent, immediately upon its arrival, to the same committee; almost all the grain in this colony being already brought in, and our stock not equal to the demands for bread.

We have the pleasure to be able to acquaint your honor, that Generals Washington and Lee, with Mr. Mifflin, aid-de-camp to General Washington, arrived at Cambridge, last Sabbath, in good health, a little after 12 o'clock, at noon, and have great reason to expect, from their known characters, and their activity, and vigilance, already discovered, that their presence in the army will be attended with most happy consequences. Our camps at Cambridge and Roxbury are daily putting on a more defensible appearance; the health in our army is as general as we could expect. Several privates in the Cambridge camp were last week taken down with the small pox, but we have great reason to hope, that the precautions taken on this occurrence, will, by the divine blessing, prevent the spreading of that distemper in the camp.

We are, with the greatest respect, your honor's
Most obedient humble servants.

Ordered, That Col. Grout, Mr. Langdon, and Doct. Taylor, be a committee to take into consideration the letter from Mr. Sheppard, relative to the eastern plans of the sea coasts.

The committee appointed to bring in a resolve for appointing Mr. Craigie, medical commissary, reported. [The report] was read, and is as follows, viz. :

Resolved, That Mr. Andrew Craigie be, and he is hereby appointed a medical commissary and apothecary for the Massachusetts army, and that said Craigie be allowed five pounds per month, for his services as abovesaid.

Ordered, That the committee for making out commissions make out a warrant for Mr. Craigie, medical commissary.

The committee appointed to take into consideration the loss of Indian Nimham, reported. The report was read, accepted, and is as follows, viz. :

The committee appointed to consider the losses of Abraham Nimham, in his journey to Cagnawauga, in carrying a message to the Indians, beg leave to report by way of resolve : That the said Abraham Nimham be paid the sum of thirty-six shillings, lawful money, and that the receiver general be directed to pay the said sum to Jahleel Woodbridge, Esq., and he to account with the said Abraham Nimham.

Resolved, That this Congress will attend to matters of the greatest importance, that they may finish the business and dissolve, sometime before the sitting of the General Court.

Ordered, That the matter contained in a resolve of the committee of safety, relating to the effects of refugees, being before provided for by this Congress, subside.

Adjourned to Wednesday morning, 8 o'clock.

WEDNESDAY, JULY 5, 1775.

A letter from William Tollman, of Dartmouth, was read, and committed to the committee appointed to consider at large of the donations for the poor of Boston.

The report of the committee on the petition of Thomas Morton was read, and accepted, and is as follows, viz.: The committee appointed to consider the memorial of Thomas Morton, beg leave to report by way of resolve:

Resolved, That the prayer of the memorial be granted, and that William Powell, Esq., late of Boston, have leave to export one thousand quintals of Jamaica old codfish, to the West Indies, and that the committee of correspondence in Newburyport see that the said William Powell, Esq. strictly complies with the resolutions of the continental and provincial Congresses.

Ordered, That Mr. Greenleaf, Col. Richmond, Doct. Taylor, Mr. Glover, and Capt. Holmes, be a committee to wait upon General Washington, to inform him that this Congress have it in contemplation to rise this week, and to know if he has any matter to lay before the Congress.

A list of surgeons who have been examined and approved of, by a committee of this Congress, was laid before the Congress, and read, and is as follows:

Doct. David Jones, surgeon; Samuel Blanchard, mate, in Col. Gerrish's regiment; Aaron Putnam, mate, in Col. Fry's regiment; Joseph Hunt, mate to Doct. Joseph Foster, in Cambridge hospital; Jacob Bacon, mate in Col. Scammon's regiment; Harris Clary Fridges, mate; Edward Durant, surgeon, Col. Mansfield's regiment; Josiah Harvey, mate, Col. Fellow's regiment; Abraham Watson, Jr., surgeon, William Vinal, mate, Col. Gardner's regiment; Doct. John Georges, mate, General Heath's regiment; Doct. Isaac Spafford, surgeon, Col. Nixon's [regiment]; Doct. John Crooker, surgeon in Col. Scammon's regiment; Doct. Walter Hastings, surgeon in Col. Bridges' [regiment]; Doct. Timothy Child, surgeon, in Col. Patterson's [regiment]; Doct. Levi Willard, surgeon, in Col. Reed's [regiment]; Doct. Daniel Parker, surgeon, in Col. Walker's [regiment]; and Doct. Thomas Kittridge, surgeon, in Col. Fry's regiment.

Thereupon, *Ordered*, That warrants be made out for them agreeably thereto.

Resolved, That the order of Congress relative to the date of the warrants for the staff officers, be so far reconsidered, as that the warrants for the surgeons be dated the 28th June, ultimo.

Ordered, That the committee who were appointed to deliver out commissions to the officers of the army, be a committee to prepare, and lay before this Congress, a list of such as have been commissioned.

A form of a warrant for a medical commissary, was read and accepted, and is as follows, viz.:

The Congress of the Colony of the Massachusetts Bay, to ———
———,   *Greeting.*

We, being informed of your skill in medicine, and reposing especial trust and confidence in your ability and good conduct, do, by these presents, constitute and appoint you the said ——— ———, to be medical commissary and apothecary to the army raised by this Congress, for the defence of this colony.   You are, therefore, carefully and diligently to discharge the duty of a medical commissary and apothecary in all things appertaining thereto, observing such orders and instructions as you shall, from time to time, receive from any your superior officers, according to the rules and discipline established by said Congress, for which this shall be your sufficient warrant.

By order of Congress,

——— ———, *President.*

Ordered, That Col Smith, Mr. Plympton, Mr. Ellis, Mr. Bigelow, Deacon Stone, Capt. Brown, Major Fuller, and Capt. Stone, be a committee to procure two hundred axes with helves, immediately, for the use of the army, and when procured, to forward them immediately to General Washington, or his order, and lay before the Congress a list of the persons of whom they shall be procured, with the price agreed on, and that the committee assure the persons of whom they may procure said axes, that they shall be paid for, as soon as the Congress can make provision therefor.

The committee appointed to consider in what manner the late inhabitants of the town of Boston, should choose representatives, reported.   The report was accepted, and is as follows, and was ordered to be sent immediately to Mr. William Cooper; viz.:

As it appears to this Congress, fit and reasonable, that the good people of the town of Boston, though at present in a dispersed state, should have a just and equal representation in the great and general assembly of this colony; and as the choice of representatives for that purpose, in legal town meeting, convened, in the common and ordinary way, is, at present, utterly impracticable, therefore, *Resolved*, that Mr. William Cooper, town clerk of Boston, be, and he hereby is empowered and directed, by notifications, under his hand, in the several newspapers, immediately to notify and give warning to the freeholders and others who were inhabitants of the said town of Boston, and were qualified according to law, to vote for representatives in May, 1774, and are now dispersed, to assemble and meet at the meeting-house in Concord, on Tuesday, the 18th day of July, instant, at three o'clock, in the afternoon, then and there, to elect and depute one or more freeholders in said town, according to the numbers limited by a law of this colony, to serve for, and represent them in a great and general court or assembly, to be convened, held, and kept, for the service of said colony, until the day next preceding the last Wednesday of May next, if necessary, and no longer, at the meeting-house in Watertown, upon Wednesday the 19th instant, by nine o'clock, in the forenoon, and so, from day to day, during their session or sessions. Hereof he is desired not to fail, and make return of this resolve, with the name or names of the person and persons elected or deputed by a major part of the electors present, unto the great and general assembly, at the time and place above mentioned for its meeting.

The committee appointed the 2d instant, to prepare a letter to the Hon. James Russell, Esq., reported. The draft prepared, was accepted, ordered to be signed by the president, and forwarded, and is as follows, viz.:

Sir :—The present necessity for cash is such, that it is necessary for this Congress to direct you to pay in to Henry Gardner, Esq., receiver general of this colony, all the public money in your hands or care, belonging to said colony, without further delay.

By order of Congress,

———— ————, President.

To the Hon. James Russell, Esq., of Dunstable.

Ordered, That Capt. Holmes, Capt. Carpenter, Mr. Glover, Mr. Jewett, and Mr. Parker, be a committee to consider some method to prevent conveying intelligence to our enemies, and also to put a stop to supplying them with provisions.

The committee appointed to consider the request of General Washington, relative to making a draw bridge of the bridge at Cambridge, reported. The report was accepted, and is as follows, viz.:

The committee appointed to wait on his excellency General Washington, relative to making the bridge over Charles river, in Cambridge, a draw bridge, have attended that service, and beg leave to report, that his excellency suggested, that he apprehends it to be of great importance, that this business be immediately entered upon; also, he mentioned, that he did not intend the passing and repassing should be impeded. His excellency recommends to the Congress the doing it, as they are the best judges of proper persons to be employed. His excellency hinted, that it would be agreeable to him, to be consulted as to the manner of its being done.   *Per order*, DUMMER JEWETT.

[The same committee, being directed to bring in a resolve relative to said bridge, reported the following, which was accepted, viz.:]

Whereas, his excellency General Washington, has signified to this Congress his desire, that the bridge over Charles river, in Cambridge, should be made a draw bridge, and that the Congress would see to the doing of it, immediately, therefore, *Resolved*, that Capt. Thatcher, Mr. Whittemore, Mr. Temple, Mr. Cross, and Capt. Parker, be a committee to procure materials, and employ a suitable number of artificers, for accomplishing the aforementioned business, agreeably to the direction of his excellency General Washington; the same to be done at the immediate expense of this colony; and, that the committee render to this Congress or some future House of Representatives, their account of said expense.

Resolved, That three o'clock, in the afternoon, be assigned for the choice of some person to serve on the committee of supplies, in the room of Mr. Partridge, who, at his request, has been excused, and that in such choice, the members of the Congress may have liberty to vote for any person who may not belong to the Congress.

The committee appointed to consider of the donations for the poor of Boston, reported. The report was recommitted.

A petition of Jonathan Brewer, [relating to recruits for his regiment,] was read, and committed to Deacon Stickney, Doct. Taylor, and Col. Spaulding.

Ordered, That Doct. Taylor, Mr. Lothrop, and Mr. Jewett, be a committee to distribute the pamphlets which contain depositions relative to the battle of Lexington.

Ordered, That Col. Glover be of the committee for stationing the soldiers in the county of Essex, in the room of Mr. Gerry, excused.

The committee appointed to examine the accounts of the committee appointed to procure fire-arms, reported. The report was accepted, and is as follows, viz.:

Whereas, Messrs. John Bliss, William Page, Abiel Sadler, and Lemuel Kollock, were appointed by this Congress to collect a number of fire-arms, for the use of the colony, and have delivered said arms to the committee of safety, at Cambridge, as appears by receipts from said committee, and have exhibited their accounts for said service, which accounts appear to be reasonable: therefore, *Resolved*, that there be paid by the receiver general, to the several persons aforesaid, the following sums, viz.: to John Bliss, the sum of £5 11s.; to William Page, £6 17s.; to Abiel Sadler, £5 10s.; to Lemuel Kollock, £3 10s. 8d.; being £21 18s. 8d., in full of the aforesaid account.

Ordered, That the list of persons of whom the arms were procured, be lodged with the receiver general.

Ordered, That Mr. Partridge, Col. Bowers, and Mr. Jewett, be a committee to consider a letter from General Ward.[1]

The committee appointed to consider the petition of the eighteen Stockbridge Indians, reported. The report was accepted, and is as follows, viz.:

Whereas, it appears to this Congress, by a petition from the Stockbridge Indians enlisted in the American army, that they, in their more serious hours, being sensible of their want of prudence in disposing of their money, are desirous that this Congress, in their wisdom, would devise some method to prevent their getting too much strong drink, and they also request that all their wages, that are now due, or shall hereafter be due to them for their services, be paid to Timothy Edwards, and Jahleel Woodbridge, Esq., or to their order: therefore, *Resolved*, that Timothy Edwards, or Jahleel Woodbridge, Esqrs. be, and are hereby empowered, to draw the wages of the aforesaid Indians, and deal out the same as they shall find said Indians have need thereof, according to any order or orders of this Congress, that have been, or shall hereafter be made, for paying all or any part of the wages due to the soldiers, and render an account of their doings to this, or some future Congress, or House of Representatives, when required. And the receiver general is accordingly directed to pay the same to the said Timothy Edwards, or Jahleel Woodbridge, Esqrs., as aforesaid, and take their receipt therefor. And it is also recommended and enjoined by this Congress, that all persons who sell spirituous liquors, be particularly careful not to let said Indians have too much strong drink, as that wholly unfits them for any service.

The committee appointed to consider a letter of Mr. Alexander Sheppard, reported. The report was accepted, and is as follows, viz.:

The committee appointed to take under consideration the letter from Mr. Sheppard, beg leave to report, by way of resolve, as follows, viz.: *Resolved*, that it be, and it hereby is recommended to Mr. Alexander Sheppard, jun., that he retain in his hands all the plans he hath of the

---

(1) The letter of General Ward related to supplies of arms and provisions for the soldiers in camp.

province of Maine, and that he do not suffer them to go out of his possession, to any person, upon any consideration, until the further order of this, or some future Congress, or House of Representatives.

Ordered, That part of the resolve, relative to the light-houses, which empowered the selectmen and committees of correspondence to remove and secure the lamps and oil from the light-house at the entrance of Boston harbor, be reconsidered, and that Mr. Crane, Capt. Holmes, and Deac. Washburn, be a committee to consider at large, on some measures for removing and securing the lamps and oil aforesaid.

Ordered, That Mr. Bancroft, Mr. Fox, and Mr. Lothrop, be a committee to consider a letter from Mr. James Lyon, dated Machias, June 17, 1775.[1]

Afternoon.

The committee appointed to consider the state of the donations for the poor of Boston, reported. The report was recommitted, and Mr. Batchelder added to the committee, in the room of Capt. Stone, absent.

The committee appointed to bring in a resolve, for the purpose of calling the general assembly together, at any time sooner than the 19th instant, if occasion should require, [reported.] The report was accepted, and is as follows, viz. :

Whereas, this Congress, pursuant to the recommendation of the General Congress of this continent, have sent out their letters to the several towns in this colony, desiring that representatives might be elected and returned by them, to serve in a great or general court, or assembly, to be convened, held, and kept, for the service of this colony, at Watertown, on the 19th day of July current; and whereas, such unforeseen events may take place, between this time and the said 19th day of July, as may render the convening of such general court or assembly, at Watertown aforesaid, at the time aforesaid, very improper and unsafe; therefore, *Resolved*, that Henry Gardner, Esq., Mr. Gill, Deacon Cheever, Mr. White of Brookline, and Capt. Thatcher, be a committee, in case they, or the major part of them should judge it improper and unsafe, that such general assembly should be convened at the said Watertown, at the time aforesaid, to agree upon, and determine, at what other place in this colony, the said general assembly should be convened; and the said committee, or the major part of them, are hereby fully empowered to determine at what place it shall be most expedient, that the said general assembly should be convened,

(1) James Lyon, chairman of the committee of safety, informs Congress, that the people of the town had determined to arm a sloop, captured from the enemy, to defend their harbor, and expressing deep sense of " their own weakness," applied " for advice and support."

and to give notice thereof to the several persons who have been, or may be chosen to serve in such assembly, in such way and manner as they shall judge most expeditious and effectual.

Ordered, That Doct. Church, Col. Bowers, and Mr. Bayley, be a committee to confer with General Washington, on the subject of furnishing his table, and know what he expects relative thereto, and that they sit forthwith.

Ordered, That the committee appointed to procure necessary furniture for the house provided for General Washington, complete the business of their commission by purchase, or by borrowing.

Ordered, That Mr. Wheeler, Col. Grout, and Mr. Durfee, be a committee to consider a letter from Mr. James Winthrop.[1]

A letter from Benjamin Greenleaf, Esq. of Newburyport, was read, accompanying sundry letters brought by Capt. Folger, from London,[2] a jacket enclosed to Major Sill, of the 63d regiment; also, three maps enclosed to said Major Sill, viz.: one of New England, one of Virginia and Maryland, and one of New York; whereupon, *Ordered*, that the jacket be committed to the care of the secretary, till further orders of Congress, and that the maps be put into the hands of the committee of supplies, and they are directed to get them framed for the use of the colony.

The committee appointed to prepare a letter to General Washington, enclosing a resolution of Congress relative to the sick and wounded, reported.   The report was accepted, and is as follows, viz.:

[*To his Excellency General Washington:*]

This Congress ordered the enclosed resolution to be prepared, and sent to Generals Ward and Thomas; but by the agreeable event of your excellency's appointment to the chief command of the American army, and arrival at camp, the propriety of that step ceases.   We mean not to dictate to your excellency, but presume, that to secure the health of the army, and [to afford] relief for the sick, will naturally engage your attention.   Every thing in the power of this Congress [to do] to enable you to discharge, with ease, the duties of your exalted and important station, will be, by us, attended to, with the greatest

(1) James Winthrop, Esq., Postmaster of Cambridge, represented that the income of the office was insufficient for his support, that he had no other business to add by its profits to his revenue, and tendered his resignation.

(2) The letters enclosed in the communication of Benjamin Greenleaf, Esq., were principally of domestic character, from the relatives, connexions, and friends of soldiers and officers of the royal troops in Boston.

alacrity. If the enclosed resolution has that tendency, we attain the end intended by transmitting to you the same, and are, with respect, Your Excellency's most humble servants.

Ordered, That Doct. Taylor, Mr. Pitts, and Mr. Lothrop, be a committee to count and sort the votes for a member of the committee of supplies in the room of Mr. Partridge. The committee having attended that service, reported, that Mr. Lothrop was chosen.

Resolved, That the resolve, directing the committee of supplies to get the three maps framed, be reconsidered, and that the secretary be directed to take care of them, as they are for the use of the colony.

The report of the committee appointed to consider how the soldiers should be provided with coats, was again read and accepted, and is as follows, viz. :

Resolved, That thirteen thousand coats be provided, as soon as may be, and one thereof given to each non-commissioned officer and soldier in the Massachusetts forces, agreeably to the resolve of Congress, on the 23d day of April last; and in order to facilitate their being procured :

Resolved, That the said thirteen thousand coats be proportioned immediately on all the towns and districts in this colony, except the towns of Boston and Charlestown, [in proportion] as they paid to the last provincial tax; which towns and districts are desired to cause them to be made of good plain cloth, preference to be given to the manufactures of this country, and to be delivered to the committee of supplies, without buttons, on or before the first day of October next, and sooner if possible. That for every yard of such cloth of seven-eighths of a yard wide, they shall be allowed and paid the sum of five shillings four pence, and in that proportion for cloth of a greater or less width, and the sum of four shillings for making each and every coat; and the selectmen of each town and district, respectively, are directed to lay their accounts before the committee of supplies, who are ordered to draw on the receiver general for the payment thereof.

Resolved, That each coat be faced with the same kind of cloth of which it is made; that the coats be made in the common plain way, without lappels, short, and with small folds, and that the selectmen cause a certificate to be sewed to the inside of each coat, purporting from what town it came, and by whom the coat was made, and if the cloth was manufactured in this country, by whom it was manufactured.

Resolved, That the committee of supplies be, and they are hereby directed, immediately, to proportion the coats on the several towns and districts as aforesaid, inform them of their proportion, and assure them that the coats they supply shall be delivered to the men of their town respectively, so far as circumstances will admit, and enclose to them a sample of the goodness of the cloth of which the coats are to be made, with a copy of this and the foregoing resolves, and to desire those towns and districts who cannot supply the whole of their proportion of the coats as aforesaid, and also those who can supply more than their proportion, to give them information what number they can supply, on, or before the tenth day of August next.

Resolved, That the committee of supplies be, and they are hereby directed to provide all the coats proportioned on such towns and districts as give information to them as aforesaid, that they cannot supply them, and they are to cause all the coats to be buttoned with pewter buttons, and that the coats for each regiment, respectively, have buttons of the same number stamped on the face of them.

[The committee reported the following schedule of the apportionment of coats, which was accepted.][1]

[*Suffolk County.*—Roxbury, 182; Dorchester, 96; Milton, 56; Braintree, 108; Weymouth, 66; Hingham, 88; Dedham, 104; Medfield, 42; Wrentham, 105; Brookline, 43; Needham, 43; Stoughton, 82; Stoughtonham, 37; Medway, 43; Bellingham, 29; Hull, 21; Walpole, 33; Chelsea, 31; Cohasset, 30.

Essex County.—Salem, 380; Danvers, 116; Ipswich, 204; Newbury, 177; Newburyport, 184; Marblehead, 265; Lynn, 93; Andover, 189; Beverly, 112; Rowley, 89; Salisbury, 77; Haverhill, 113; Gloucester, 163; Topsfield, 43; Boxford, 54; Almsbury, 69; Bradford, 63; Wenham, 41; Middleton, 34; Manchester, 33; Methuen, 54.

Middlesex County.—Cambridge, 118; Watertown, 49; Woburn, 81; Concord, 73; Newton 66; Reading, 77; Marlborough, 89; Billerica, 61; Framingham, 71; Lexington, 49; Chelmsford, 55; Sherburne, 36; Sudbury, 95; Malden, 45; Weston, 45; Medford, 60; Littleton, 44; Hopkinton, 45; Westford, 51; Waltham, 44; Stow, 41; Groton, 69; Shirley, 25; Pepperell, 37; Townsend, 30;

---

(1) The schedule of apportionment omitted in the journal, was printed in connexion with the resolves, in handbills, and is copied from the publication made at the time of its acceptance.

Ashby, 12; Stoneham, 16; Natick, 23; Dracut, 39; Bedford, 31; Holliston, 38; Tewksbury, 31; Acton, 37; Dunstable, 33; Lincoln, 33; Wilmington, 29.

Hampshire County.—Springfield, 71; Wilbraham, 36; Northampton, 81; Southampton, 29; Hadley, 33; South Hadley, 25; Amherst, 38; Granby, 17; Hatfield, 37; Whately, 13; Williamsburg, 9; Westfield, 57; Deerfield, 41; Greenfield, 26; Sherburne, 16; Conway, 17; Sunderland, 25; Montague, 20; Northfield, 30; Brimfield, 48; South Brimfield, 30; Monson, 26; Pelham, 27; Greenwich, 27; Blanford, 20; Leverett, 5; Palmer, 28; Granville, 47; New Salem, 25; Belchertown, 31; Colrain, 17; Ware, 14; Warwick, 12; Bernardston, 16; Murrayfield, 17; Charlemont, 12; Ashfield, 14; Worthington, 7; Shutesbury, 16; Chesterfield, 26: Southwick, 23; West Springfield, 72; Ludlow District, 23.

Plymouth County.—Plymouth, 100; Scituate, 125; Duxbury, 44; Marshfield, 54; Bridgewater, 188; Middleborough, 160; Rochester, 86; Plympton, 56; Pembroke, 66; Kingston, 38; Hanover, 37; Abington, 46; Halifax, 24; Wareham, 30.

Barnstable County.—Barnstable, 94; Sandwich, 74; Yarmouth, 66; Eastham, 49; Harwich, 60; Wellfleet, 38; Chatham, 26; Truro, 33; Falmouth, 53.

Bristol County.—Taunton, 105; Rehoboth, 147; Swanzey with Shawamet, 67; Dartmouth, 244; Norton, 55; Mansfield, 35; Attleborough, 88; Dighton, 49; Freetown, 58; Raynham, 37; Easton, 41; Berkley, 29.

York County.—York, 114; Kittery, 125; Wells, 89; Berwick, 134; Arundel, 41; Biddeford, 46; Pepperellborough, 34; Lebanon, 9; Sanford, 10; Buxton, 10.

Dukes County.—Edgartown, 36; Chilmark, 44; Tisbury, 32.

Nantucket County.—Sherburne, 174.

Worcester County.—Worcester, 93; Lancaster, 116; Mendon, 88; Brookfield, 112; Oxford, 41; Charlton, 41; Sutton, 111; Leicester, 41; Spencer, 37; Paxton, 24; Rutland, 53; Oakham, 16;

Rutland District, 46; Hubbardston, 8; New Braintree, 37; Southborough, 54; Westborough, 43; Northborough, 30; Shrewsbury, 79; Lunenburgh, 57; Fitchburg, 13; Uxbridge, 55; Harvard, 56; Dudley, 37; Bolton, 55; Upton, 23; Sturbridge, 51; Leominster, 43; Hardwick, 61; Holden, 30; Western, 38; Douglass, 24; Grafton, 42; Petersham, 43; Royalston, 9; Westminster, 37; Athol, 23; Templeton, 28; Princeton, 24; Ashburnham, 12; Winchendon, 10.

Cumberland County.—Falmouth, 146; Cape Elizabeth, 53; North Yarmouth, 54; Scarborough, 52; Brunswick, 27; Harpswell, 26; Gorham, 27; Windham, 10; Piersontown, 5; New Boston, 3; New Gloucester, 20.

Lincoln County.—Pownalborough, 25; Georgetown, 50; Woolwich, 15; Newcastle, 13; Topsham, 13; Booth-Bay, 14; Bristol, 20; Bowdoinham, 3; Medumcook, 3; Hallowell, 4; Broad-Bay, 10; Vassalborough, 3; St. Georges, 10; Winthrop, 3; Winslow, 3; Gardinerston, 7.

Berkshire County.—Sheffield, 61; Great Barrington, 37; Stockbridge, 29; Pittsfield, 37; New Marlborough, 34; Egremont, 14; Richmond, 26; Lenox, 16; Tyringham, 14; Lanesborough, 37; Sandisfield, 26; Williamstown, 23; Becket, 10; Gageborough, 12; Partridgefield, 7; East Hoosuck, 11; Jericho, 5; Plantation, No. 5, 7; Plantation, No. 7, 7.

Suffolk, 1189; Essex, 2553; Middlesex, 1778; Hampshire, 1204; Plymouth, 1054; Barnstable, 493; Bristol, 953; York, 612; Dukes County, 112; Nantucket, 174; Worcester, 1846; Cumberland, 423; Lincoln, 196; Berkshire, 413;   .   .   .   .   .   .   13,000]

Resolved, That Mrs. Dorothy Coolidge be allowed and paid out of the public treasury of this colony, the sum of £7 15s 8d, in full of her account, and the receiver general of this colony, is hereby ordered to pay the aforesaid sum of £7 15s 8d, to the said Dorothy Coolidge, or order, accordingly.

Adjourned to eight o'clock, tomorrow morning.

THURSDAY, JULY 6, 1775.

Ordered, That Mr. Johnson and Doct. Jones, be of the committee to answer the letter from the Congress of New Hampshire, in the room of Doct. Church and Mr. Hopkins.

Ordered That the committee of safety be directed to supply General Washington with some faithful, expeditious person, to go on express to Philadelphia.

Ordered, That the committee of safety be a committee to desire General Washington to let them know if there is any house at Cambridge, that would be more agreeable to him and General Lee than that in which they now are; and in that case, the said committee are directed to procure such house, and put it in proper order for their reception.

The committee of safety, by Col. Palmer, reported a resolve relative to a new emission of bills of credit, the consideration whereof was referred to 3 o'clock, P. M.

Ordered, That Col. Farley, Mr. Durfee, and Capt. Holmes, be a committee to consider a letter from Mr. Joseph Hallett, dated New York, June 26, 1775, relative to a quantity of flour forwarded to Norwich, &c., for the army.

Resolved, That the committee of supplies be, and hereby are empowered and directed, to impress, for the service of the colony, the saw mill at said Watertown, belonging to Mr. John Cook, or any other mill which they have occasion for, for the public service.

Ordered, That Col. Tyng and Mr. Fox, be added to the committee who were appointed to consider the accounts that might be transmitted to Congress by the committee of safety, in the room of Mr. Lothrop and Deacon Fisher.

Ordered, That the committee of supplies, be directed to forward to Newport, the letter to Lieut. Governor Cook, received by this Congress in a letter from the Continental Congress.

A letter from John Fenton, Esq., was read [and] ordered to subside.[1]

Ordered, That Major Hawley, Doct. Taylor, and Col. Grout, be a committee to prepare a vote of thanks to the committee of this Congress this day returned from their embassy to Ticonderoga.

Ordered, That Mr. Baker be added to the committee to examine Major Barber's account.

(1) Mr. Fenton, a prisoner at Medford, desired to be removed to head quarters, and to have a trial.

Ordered, That Col. Tyng, Doct. Taylor, and Mr. Bliss, be a committee to consider an account exhibited by Doct. Church and Mr. Gill, of the expense of entertaining and escorting Generals Washington and Lee, from Springfield to head quarters.

Ordered, That Mr. Langdon, Major Bliss, and Mr. Jewett, be a committee to consider the report of the committee this day returned from Ticonderoga, and the papers accompanying it, and also the rolls made up by Capt. Noble and Capt. Herrick.

Afternoon.

A letter from General Green was read, and committed to Col. Davis, Col. Tyng, and Mr. Reed.[1]

Ordered, That Col. Davis, Mr. Fessenden, and Capt. Page, be a committee to consider a petition of Josiah Capen.

Ordered, That Mr. Whittemore, Major Bliss and Col. Dwight, be a committee to consider the account of Mr. Allen Gray, and report.

Ordered, That Mr. Gill, Mr. Wheeler and Mr. Sullivan, be a committee to consider the services of the secretary, and report what grant they think is adequate thereto.

Ordered, That the Hon. Major Hawley, Mr. Sullivan and Doct. Taylor, be a committee to bring in a resolve explanatory of the sense of Congress expressed in a resolve of the 31st ultimo, relative to the estates of refugees.

The committee appointed to consider the account of Doct. Church and Mr. Gill, reported verbally, that they had examined the account, and found it well vouched, and thought it ought to be allowed.

Thereupon, *Resolved,* that the receiver general be, and he hereby is directed, to pay Doct. Benjamin Church and Mr. Moses Gill, or their order, the sum of twenty-eight pounds, five shillings, ten pence, lawful money, in discharge of an account by them exhibited, of the expenses of escorting and entertaining Generals Washington and Lee from Springfield to the camp at Cambridge.

Resolved, That the committee appointed by a resolve of this Congress of the first instant, to agree with such teamsters as they may employ to convey the poor of the town of Charlestown to certain towns in the county of Worcester, be directed to pay them a sum not exceeding one shilling per ton, per mile, for such service, instead of nine pence, the price fixed in said resolve, and that said committee be

---

(1) General Green requested, that Congress would interfere to restrain the sale of spirituous liquors in the camp, the health, discipline, and morals of the troops being impaired by unlicensed indulgence.

likewise directed and empowered to remove the inhabitants of the town of Boston in like manner.

The report of the committee of safety, relative to a new emission of bills of credit, was taken into consideration, and recommitted to Mr. Spooner, Major Hawley, Doct. Taylor, Capt. Stone and Mr. Wheeler, who are directed to consider the sum of the bills already impressed and the propriety of striking off more from the same plates.

Resolved, That the committee of supplies be directed to pay the selectmen of the several towns and districts in the colony, for the blankets they have respectively furnished the soldiers with, any resolve of Congress to the contrary notwithstanding.

The committee appointed to consider the report of the committee [sent on an embassy] to Ticonderoga, reported. The report was recommitted, and the last mentioned committee are directed to lay before the committee first mentioned, a state of their account, debt and credit.

The committee appointed to prepare a vote of thanks to the committee who have been on an embassy to Ticonderoga, reported. The report was accepted, and is as follows, viz.: Whereas, Walter Spooner, Jedediah Foster and James Sullivan, Esquires, a committee of this Congress, lately ordered on a commission to the important posts of Ticonderoga and Crown Point, for divers purposes expressed in their instructions, have this day returned and made their report in writing, and it appearing upon full consideration thereof, that the said committee have executed the various branches of their instructions, with ability, fidelity and despatch, and that their services had been attended with much fatigue and danger, therefore, *Resolved*, that the services of said committee do merit the express approbation and thanks of Congress, and they do hereby testify and render the same to them, and each of them.

Ordered, That Mr. Hemmenway, Mr. Whittemore and Capt. Parker, be a committee to consider what allowance is proper to be made to Mr. Edmund Fowle, for the use of his house by the committees of this and the former Congress.

The committee appointed to consider the accounts transmitted to Congress by the committee of safety, reported on the account of Ebenezer White and others. The report was accepted, and is as follows, viz.:

Whereas, Messrs. Ebenezer White, Daniel Hemmenway, Col. Simeon Spaulding and Benjamin Ely, were appointed to collect a number of fire-arms for the use of this colony, and have delivered said arms, as appears by receipt from the committee of safety, or clerk of the ordnance stores, and have exhibited their accounts to Congress, which accounts appear to be reasonable: Therefore, *Resolved*, that there be paid out of the public treasury, to the several persons employed in collecting arms as aforesaid, the following sums, and the receiver general is accordingly ordered to pay the said sums, viz.: to Ebenezer White, the sum of £1 19s.; to Daniel Hemmenway, £4 8s.; to Col. Simeon Spauding, £4 7s.; to Benjamin Ely, £13 10s. 11d.—£24 4s. 11d.

Ordered, That Capt. Holmes be added to the committee last mentioned.

Adjourned to eight o'clock, to-morrow morning.

FRIDAY, JULY 7, 1775.

Capt. Stone, of Framingham, was appointed, in the room of Major Bliss, on the committee, which were chosen to prepare an answer to the letter from the Congress of New Hampshire.

Resolved, That Mr. Shillaber have leave to bring in a resolve, recommending to the committee of the city of Philadelphia to permit him to export from thence a quantity of flour.

Ordered, That Deacon Bayley, Major Brooks, Mr. Baker, Col. Grout and Doct. Taylor, be a committee to consider a resolve of the committee of safety, recommending to this Congress the seizing the crown officers.

In compliance with a resolve of the committee of safety, recommending that a committee be appointed to draw up, and transmit to Great Britain, a fair and impartial account of the late battle at Charlestown, as soon as possible: *Ordered*, that the said committee of safety be a committee for that purpose, and that they likewise be a standing committee for that and the like purposes.

Ordered, That Mr. Wheeler, Capt. Batchelder and Doct. Taylor, be a committee to consider the petition of Mr. Daniel Murray, and a letter from Mr. Joseph Reed, secretary to General Washington, on the subject thereof.[1]

Ordered, That Deacon Nichols, Mr. Glover and Col. Mitchell, be a committee to consider a resolve of the committee of safety, relative to the appointment of a master workman for the blacksmiths.

(1) Daniel Murray, son of Col. Murray, of Rutland, in Worcester county, applied to General Washington for permission to join his refugee friends in Boston, with the females of his father's family. Mr. Secretary Reed transmitted the request to Congress, with the opinion of General Washington, that the subject was more peculiarly within the jurisdiction of that body than in his own discretion.

The committee appointed to consider the services of the secretary, reported. The report was recommitted, and the committee directed to consider, in particular, his extra services to this time, and the expense of his clerks, and the said secretary is directed to lay before this Congress, or some future assembly of this colony, an account of his future services.

Ordered, That a warrant be made out for Doct. Isaac Foster, as surgeon of the hospital at Cambridge, and another to Doct. Isaac Rand, as surgeon of the hospital at Roxbury.

Mr. Shillaber, agreeably to order, presented the following resolve, which was accepted, viz.: Mr. William Shillaber, of Danvers, a member of this Congress, having represented to this Congress, that he has a vessel now at Philadelphia, having there disposed of her cargo, a schooner called the William, commanded by Samuel Tucker, and that he apprehends, from such instructions as he has [given] and will give the said master, that the vessel, if laden with flour, or partly so, might arrive safe at some port in this colony, and having applied for the approbation of this Congress, and set forth that he is willing to risk the same: therefore, *Resolved*, that this Congress do approve thereof, and it is hereby recommended to the committee of inspection at Philadelphia, that they permit the said Capt. Tucker to lade his vessel as above desired, and sail from that port: provided the same be not against the resolution of the American Congress, or any resolution formed in that colony.

The committee appointed to consider the resolve of the committee of safety relative to a new emission of bills of credit, reported. The report was accepted, and is as follows, viz.: Whereas, several persons have been employed in the service of this colony, and several have supplied small articles, whose accounts amount severally to small sums only, and it appearing to this Congress, that the plates engraved for impressing or striking off the bills for the payment of the soldiers in the service of this colony are still sufficient for the striking off a number of impressions on each plate; therefore, *Resolved*, that there be impressed, or struck off, on the plate containing the engraving for notes of ten shillings, eighteen shillings and twelve shillings, six hundred and sixty-seven sheets, and no more; and that there be impressed, or struck off, on the plate for notes of sixteen shillings, fifteen shillings and nine shillings, six hundred and sixty-seven sheets, and no more; and also on the plate for twenty shillings, fourteen shillings, and six shillings, that there be impressed, or struck off, five hundred and forty sheets, and no more: which last number, together with one hundred and twenty-seven sheets, or impressions, already struck off on that plate, and not signed, make the like number of six hundred and sixty-seven sheets, or impressions, which, together, amount to two thousand and one sheets, or impressions, each sheet containing forty shillings, amounting to the sum of £4002, which, together with the sum of £25,998, already perfected of those notes, make the sum of £30,000.

We also report, that a committee be appointed to agree with Mr. Revere, or some other suitable person, for the striking off the above number of sheets. Also, that a committee be appointed to authenticate said sheets, when they are struck off.

Ordered, That Deacon Mitchell, Capt. Holmes, and Capt. Stone, of Framingham, be a committee to agree with some persons to strike off the bills, agreeably to the foregoing report.

Ordered, That the chairman of the committee of supplies be directed to attend this Congress with a copy of such resolves as constitute their commission.

The committee appointed to consider the petition of Daniel Murray, &c. reported. The report was accepted, and is as follows, viz.: The committee appointed to take into consideration the letter from his excellency General Washington, to the committee of safety, respecting the petition of Daniel Murray of Rutland, who has requested leave for his sister, and two of his brothers, to go into Boston, which petition the committee of safety have referred to the consideration of this Congress, beg leave to report, that it is their opinion, that the aforementioned petition ought not to be granted. That the committee of safety be directed to acquaint his excellency the General, of the resolution of this house, of the 24th of June last, respecting the permitting of persons to go into Boston, and that it is their opinion, that said resolution ought not to be receded from in the present case.

Walter Spooner, Esq. was appointed in addition to Col. Richmond, to swear the soldiers to be stationed in the county of Bristol.

The committee appointed to consider the report of the committee, who have been on an embassy to Ticonderoga, reported. The report was accepted, and is as follows, viz.:

The committee appointed to take under consideration the report of the committee from Crown point, &c., beg leave to report by way of resolve, as follows, viz.:

Whereas, it appears to this Congress, that the sum of four hundred pounds, received by Walter Spooner, Jedediah Foster, and James Sullivan, Esqrs., of the receiver general, the 14th of June last, for the use of this colony, has been expended by them for the purpose for which it was designed by this Congress; therefore, *Resolved*, that the said Walter Spooner, Jedediah Foster, and James Sullivan, Esqrs., be, and they are hereby discharged, from all demands, the said colony at any time had upon them for the same, and that the receipts produced by them be filed in the treasurer's office.

Resolved, That there be paid, out of the public treasury of this colony, to Walter Spooner, Jedediah Foster, and James Sullivan, Esquires, the sum of twenty-six pounds three shillings and nine pence, for the balance due to them, from this colony, for their time, and expenses to Crown point, &c., and the receiver general is hereby directed to pay the same sum accordingly.

Resolved, That there be paid, out of the public treasury of this colony, to Mr. Abijah Merril, the sum of four hundred pounds, to be by him delivered to Col. Easton, for advance pay to two hundred men at Crown point and Ticonderoga, and the said Merril to take a receipt of said Easton therefor, and the receiver general is hereby directed to pay the same sum accordingly.

Resolved, That there be paid, out of the public treasury of this colony, the sum of two hundred and fifty-two pounds eleven shillings and one penny half penny, to Lieut. William Satterlee, or order, being the balance of the pay roll of Capt. Herrick's company, from the 3d of May to the 25th June last, and the receiver general is hereby directed to pay the same sum accordingly. And the said Herrick and Satterlee are hereby discharged from all demands which Col. Arnold, or this province had, for the sum of twenty-three pounds twelve shillings, received by said Herrick and Satterlee of said Arnold, for the use of the company of said Herrick.

Col. Grout was appointed to accompany Mr. Merril to the receiver general, to know of him if he can pay him the £400, agreeably to the above resolve.

Ordered, That Mr. Shillaber, Capt. White, and Mr. Crane, be a committee to consider the account of Mr. Edward Mitchell, and any other accounts that may be rendered of the expense of procuring spears for the army.

Ordered, That Col. Robinson, Major Brooks, and Deacon Bayley, be a committee to procure a steward for his excellency General Washington.

Afternoon.

Leave of absence was granted to the receiver general, till the beginning of next week.

The committee appointed to consider the letter of Mr. Joseph Hallet, dated New York, June 26, 1775, reported verbally, that the same be referred to the committee of supplies.[1] The report was accepted.

Mr. Batchelder was appointed in the room of Mr. Sullivan, to consider what grant was proper to be made for the services of the secretary.

Ordered, That Mr. Johnson, Major Perly, and Mr. Hemmenway, be a committee to procure stores for depositing the fish, which the committee of supplies may purchase for the use of the colony, either by hire, or by building new stores, as they may think best.

Ordered, That Mr. Phillips, Mr. Kollock, and Deacon Gould, be a committee to consider the subject of a letter, this day received from General Ward, and to inquire of the committee of supplies what provision is made for supplying the army with the articles [of clothing] therein mentioned.

Col. Grout informed the Congress that he had accompanied Mr. Merril to the receiver general's office, and that the receiver general informed them, that there was not money in the treasury, sufficient to pay said Merril the sum which the Congress have directed the said receiver general to pay him.

Ordered, That Col. Dwight, Col. Robinson, and Deacon Williams, be a committee to prepare a letter to Col. Easton, informing him, that the state of the treasury is such, that Mr. Merril cannot, at present, be supplied with the sum of £400, which this Congress has this day directed the receiver general to pay him.

Ordered, That Capt. Holmes be directed to inquire of Mr. Revere, how many sheets of notes or bills of credit can be struck off, from the plates he now has by him, more than six hundred and sixty-seven, which were directed to be struck off, by a resolve of this Congress, this day passed.

Resolved, That to-morrow morning, eight o'clock, be assigned for the consideration of a request made by Col. Danielson, in behalf of the officers of the army, that they might have a month's pay advanced.

The committee appointed to consider the letters from General Green, reported. The report was recommitted, and Mr. Robinson added to the committee.

Leave of absence was granted to Mr. Langdon.

Ordered, That the committee appointed to procure a steward for General Washington, be directed to procure him likewise two or three women, for cooks.

---

(1) The letter was in relation to flour, sent from the southern colonies for the army.

Ordered, That the committee appointed to inquire how General Washington's table should be furnished, be a committee to bring in a resolve for the purpose of complying with the requisition of General Washington relative thereto, and that Mr. Hopkins be added to this committee in the room of Col. Bowers.

Ordered, That the Hon. Major Hawley, Col. Grout and Col. Robinson, be a committee to wait upon General Lee, to know of him what provision he expects should be made by this Congress for the furnishing his table.

The committee who were appointed to consider what sum should be granted the secretary for his services, again reported. The report was accepted, and is as follows, viz.: The committee appointed to take into consideration the allowance that ought to be made Mr. Samuel Freeman, for his services as secretary of the Congress, to the present time, beg leave to report, that they find there has been much business done by the said Freeman in the service of the colony, and the said Freeman has been obliged to employ several clerks to assist him, which he agrees to pay; he has also been at considerable expense to be furnished with books, paper, ink, quills, and house to hold his office in, as secretary; for all which they beg leave to report the following resolution, viz.:

Resolved, That the receiver general of this colony be, and he hereby is directed, to pay Mr. Samuel Freeman, out of the public money of said colony, the sum of thirty pounds eight shillings and six pence, for his services as secretary to the Congress, and that those further services, which he may have to perform, in recording the proceedings of this Congress, when performed, be exhibited to some future house of representatives of this province, for their consideration and allowance.

The committee appointed to prepare a letter to Col. Easton, reported the following, which was accepted :

Sir: The committee appointed by the Congress to settle matters at Ticonderoga, having given you encouragement, that they would send, by the first opportunity, the £400 due from this colony, on advance pay, to the men under your command, it gives us pain that we are obliged to say, we have not the whole of the money in the treasury; but you may depend, Sir, that so soon as the notes can be struck off, and properly authenticated, the same will be immediately remitted to you. The embarrassments under which the province labors, will, we [trust,] apologize for our not being ready by the first opportunity. We rely upon you, Sir, that you will do all in your power to make the troops under your command easy, as the good of the colony so much depends thereon.

To Col. Easton, at Ticonderoga.

The committee appointed to consider some method to prevent supplying our enemies with provisions, &c., reported. The report was accepted, and ordered to be printed in the newspapers, and is as follows, viz. :

Whereas, complaints have been made to this Congress, of the inhabitants of some of the sea port towns frequently supplying our enemies with butter and cheese, fresh provisions, &c., also, [it is] suspected, that intelligence has been given them, therefore, *Resolved*, that it be, and hereby is recommended, to the committees of safety, correspondence and inspection, and where there are no such committees, to the selectmen of the sea port towns and districts in this colony, that they, forthwith, exert themselves to prevent any person or persons from supplying our enemies with any kind of provision whatsoever, or intelligence. And it is further recommended to the committees or selectmen as aforesaid, of each town and district, not to suffer any vessel or boat of any kind, to go from the shore on board any vessel or vessels of any size whatsoever, in the service of our enemies, without first obtaining a permit, in writing, of the committees or selectmen aforementioned, for that purpose, and that no boats be suffered to land from men of war, tenders, or any other vessels employed to distress the sea coasts and trade of this country, without permit obtained as aforesaid.

The committee appointed to consider the account of Col. Mitchell, relative to the expense of providing spears, reported. The report was ordered to lie on the table till Col. Mitchell produced a receipt from General Thomas, or the committee of safety, for the delivery of them.

The committee appointed to inquire of the committee of supplies what provision they had made for shirts, breeches, &c., reported. The report was accepted, and is as follows, viz. : The committee appointed to make inquiry of the committee of supplies, what provision they have made of the articles of shirts, breeches, stockings and shoes, and consider whether it is requisite to take any further care to procure those articles, have attended the service, and beg leave to recommend, that persons be immediately despatched to the neighboring counties, to collect such a proportion of the above mentioned articles from the several towns in said counties, as may be judged proper.

Ordered, That the committee who brought in the above report, be a committee to bring in a list of those towns from whence the articles above mentioned ought to be procured, and the proportion each town shall supply.

[The committee appointed to consider the subject of supplying the island of Nantucket with provisions, reported. The report was accepted, and is as follows, viz. :]

Whereas, by the act of parliament called the restraining act, the inhabitants of Nantucket are exempted from the restrictions in said act mentioned. And whereas, the Continental Congress, on the 17th of May last, took the matter under consideration, and thought it expedient, to prevent the Newfoundland fishery from being supplied with provisions through Nantucket, to prohibit the exportation of provisions from any of the colonies to that island, excepting from this : And whereas, the inhabitants of Nantucket have by them, large quantities of provisions in their stores, and are fitting out a large fleet of whaling vessels, whereby they intend to avail themselves of the act aforementioned, and the provisions they have by them may be unnecessarily expended, in foreign and not domestic consumption : therefore, *Resolved*, that no provisions or necessaries of any kind be exported from any part of this colony to the island of Nantucket, until the inhabitants of said island shall have given full and sufficient satisfaction to this Congress, or some future house of representatives, that the provisions they have now by them, have not been, and shall not be, expended in foreign, but for domestic consumption. And the several committees of correspondence, inspection and safety, in their respective towns, are required to see that this resolve be not contravened.

Adjourned to eight o'clock, to-morrow morning.

SATURDAY, JULY 8, 1775.

A list of surgeons examined by a committee appointed for that purpose, was exhibited to Congress, and warrants ordered to be made out agreeably thereto.

Ordered, That Major Hawley, Major Bliss, and Col. Gerrish, be a committee to inspect the commissions of the committee of safety and the committee of supplies, and report to this Congress, what is expedient to be done relative thereto, more especially in the recess of the Congress.

Ordered, That Capt. Stone be appointed in the room of Mr. Sullivan, on the committee who were directed to bring in a resolve, explanatory to the resolve of Congress relative to the refugees.

A petition of several field officers in the army, was read, relative to the appointment of commissaries for the regiment from the county of Essex.

Ordered, That the petitioners have leave to withdraw their petition.

Ordered, That Capt. Holmes, Mr. Fox, and Mr. Perry, be a committee to consider a petition from a number of the inhabitants of Frenchman's Bay, [for supplies of provisions.]

Ordered, That Mr. Fessenden, Mr. Walker, and Capt. White, be a committee to examine and consider all accounts that may be rendered to this Congress, relative to the expenses of procuring axes and shovels for the use of the army.

A committee of this Congress, agreeably to their appointment, reported the following resolve, which was accepted, and ordered to be printed in the several newspapers.[1]

Ordered, That Mr. Hayward, repair to the receiver general, at Stow, and direct him to attend this Congress, immediately.

Ordered, That Capt. Carpenter be, and hereby is, appointed to desire Col. Timothy Walker to pay what public monies he has in his hands, into the treasury, immediately, and the committee of supplies are directed to employ some person to be sent express to Col. Walker, for this purpose.

Ordered, That Mr. Woodbridge, Col. Robinson, and Deacon Nichols, be a committee to consider a proposal of exempting the soldiers in the army from paying the postage of letters, and to report thereon.

Ordered, That Doct. Taylor, Major Brooks, and Mr. Hall, be a committee to examine and consider an account of Major Bliss; and also, an account of Doct. Church.

Ordered, That Major Fuller, Mr. Hall, and Col. Robinson, be a committee to countersign and number the new emission of bills, who are likewise empowered and directed to superintend the impression of said bills.

The committee appointed to bring in a resolve for the purpose of complying with the requisitions of General Washington, reported the following order, which was accepted, viz.:

Ordered, That Col. Robinson, Major Brooks, and Deacon Bailey, be a committee to make inquiry forthwith, for some ingenious, active, and faithful man, to be recommended to General Washington, as a steward; likewise, to procure and recommend to him some capable

(1) No resolve corresponding to that mentioned in the record is preserved on file, or was published in the newspapers of Cambridge, Watertown, or Worcester. The entry on the journal is probably intended to refer to the resolve for restraining the sale of spirituous liquors, passed on the same day.

woman, suitable to act in the place of a house-keeper, and one or more good female servants.

The report of the committee on the account of Mr. Daniel Taylor, was read, and ordered to lie upon the table.

The committee on the petition of Col. Jonathan Brewer, reported. The report was accepted, and is as follows, viz. :

Resolved, That the prayer of Col. Brewer's petition be so far granted, that said Col. Brewer be allowed to recruit men sufficient to complete his regiment, or so far as he can complete his said regiment in twenty days, he not to enlist any person as a soldier who shall not furnish himself with a good and sufficient fire-arm.

Resolved, That three o'clock, in the afternoon, be assigned, to consider the expediency of appointing a surgeon general for the Massachusetts forces.

The committee appointed to consider the artificers' accounts, reported the following resolve on Mr. Clark's account.

Resolved, That the receiver general be, and he hereby is directed to pay to Mr. Matthew Clark, or order, the sum of nine pounds six shillings and six pence, in full discharge of his account for time and materials, in repairing boats for the use of this colony.

[The] order of the day [was] moved for.

Ordered, That Major Hawley bring in a resolve for the payment of a month's pay to the officers of the army, as soon as provision can be made therefor.

The committee on the account of Major Bliss, reported. The report was accepted, and is as follows, viz. :

Resolved, That Major John Bliss be allowed, and paid out of the public treasury of this colony, the sum of £5 7s, in full discharge of the above account, and the receiver general of this colony, is hereby ordered to pay the aforesaid sum of £5 7s, to the said John Bliss, or order, accordingly.

Major Fuller, agreeably to order, brought in the following resolve.

Resolved, That there be paid out of the public treasury, the sum of twelve shillings to Mr. John Cook, for the use that Mr. Paul Revere made of his house, whilst he was striking off the colony notes therein.

The committee appointed to consider a proposal for exempting the soldiers of the army from the postage of letters, reported. The report was ordered to subside.

Major Fuller brought in a resolve, directing what notes each of the committee should sign, which was accepted, and is as follows, viz. :

Resolved, That Abraham Fuller, Mr. Stephen Hall, Jun., and Col.

Robinson, the committee appointed to countersign the colony notes, now ordered to be struck off, countersign and number said notes of the following denominations, viz.: said Abraham Fuller countersign and number the notes of eighteen shillings, twelve shillings, and ten shillings; said Stephen Hall countersign and number the notes of sixteen shillings, fifteen shillings, and nine shillings; said Col. Robinson countersign and number the notes of twenty shillings, fourteen shillings, and six shillings.

Afternoon.

The report of the committee on the letter of General Green was read, and recommitted to Col. Robinson, Major Brooks, and Col. Gerrish.

Major Hawley, agreeably to appointment, reported the following resolve, relative to advance pay to the officers of the army, which was accepted.

Whereas, application has been made lately to this Congress, in behalf of the commissioned officers of that part of the continental army before Boston, raised by this colony, that, for the relief of the present necessities of the said officers, there might be immediately advanced and paid to them, one full month's pay, according to the establishment lately made by Congress for the army; and the Congress, having taken the said application into due consideration, do *Resolve*, that it is expedient and proper, that there should be advanced and paid unto the said commissioned officers, one month's pay, in notes or bills of credit of this colony, as soon as provision can be made therefor by a further emission of notes or bills of credit, than has been already ordered by Congress.

The committee appointed to consider how stores may be procured for the reception of fish, reported. The report was ordered to subside.

The committee appointed to agree with Mr. Paul Revere, for striking off a new emission of colony notes, reported. The report was accepted, and is as follows, viz.:

Resolved, That there be eighteen hundred seventy-four sheets impressed and struck off, according to the resolve of this Congress, passed the 7th instant. And that Mr. Paul Revere be employed to do said service, at the rate of six shillings for each hundred sheets so struck off, provided said Revere find ink, and house room, and procure suitable paper, the colony paying only the prime cost of said paper.

[The] committee [was] instructed to direct Mr. Revere to alter the date of the notes to July 8th, if it can be done.

Ordered, That Mr. Hall, Capt. Batchelder, and Mr. Ellis, be a committee to consider a resolve of the committee of safety, recommending to this Congress to make an establishment for four master armorers.

Ordered, That Mr. Samuel Sanger, Mr. Johnson, and Deacon Wyman, be added to the committee who were appointed to give passes for removing the poor of Boston, and Charlestown, to the towns in the county of Worcester, and that Major Fuller be excused from serving on said committee.

Ordered, That Capt. Stone, Capt. Brown, and Col. Smith, be a committee to revise the resolves of Congress relative to the poor of Boston and Charlestown, and report what they think proper to be done thereon.

Agreeably to the recommendation of the committee of safety, *Resolved,* that Mr. Jonathan Hastings be, and he hereby is appointed, postmaster for the town of Cambridge, in the room of Mr. James Winthrop.

The committee appointed to examine several accounts of the expense of procuring axes and shovels, reported. The reports were accepted, and Mr. Woodbridge was appointed to bring in a proper resolve for the paying of the several accounts, agreeably thereto.

The committee appointed to prepare an answer to the letter from the New Hampshire Congress, reported the following, which was accepted, and ordered to be transcribed, authenticated, and sent foward, viz. :

Gentlemen: We received your favor of the 3d instant, by Mr. Wheelock and Col. Beetle, and much rejoice to find, that the honorable Congress of New Hampshire, and the good people of your government in general, are so warmly attached to the common cause.

We highly approve of Mr. Dean's being sent to the Continental Congress, more especially as he is so well acquainted in Canada, and lately came from thence, and we think it is a matter of great importance to New York, and all the New England colonies in particular, and to America in general, to satisfy our friends in Canada, that we are truly friendly to them, and also effectually to prevent our inveterate enemies there from making depredations on our frontiers: and as we have the greatest confidence in the wisdom and vigilance of that honorable body, therefore, we think it most advisable to wait their determination. We are, with great respect, gentlemen,

Your friends in the common cause.

Hon Congress of the Colony of New Hampshire.

The committee appointed to consider the subject of a letter from General Green, reported. The report was accepted, and is as follows, viz. :

The Congress having taken into consideration the difficulties and troubles which have [arisen] and daily are arising in our camps, by reason of divers evil-minded persons selling spirituous liquors, by which means, it is not in the power of the officers, although a constant exertion has been hitherto made, to prevent the same, in order to keep that steady government in camp so absolutely necessary; therefore, *Resolved*, that if any licensed person shall, after the 15th instant, presume to sell any spirituous liquors to any soldier, without a permit from the captain, or commanding officer of the company he belongs to, specifying the quantity, he shall, for the first offence, forfeit his license, and for the second, suffer such punishment as shall be inflicted on him or her, by a court martial; and any person who is not a licensed person, or whose license is without the limits of said camp, [who] shall presume to retail any spirituous liquor to any of the troops, shall suffer for the first offence, the penalties inflicted by a court martial : this resolve not to extend to any person who shall have a license or permit from the general or commanding officer.

The committee appointed to bring in a list of such towns as might supply the army with shirts, breeches, &c., reported. The report was recommitted for introducing the form of a receipt.

The committee appointed to consider the petition of the inhabitants of Frenchman's Bay, reported. The report was accepted, and is as follows, viz. :

The committee appointed to consider the petition of Thomas Donnell and others, of Frenchman's Bay, have attended that service, and beg leave to report by way of resolve.

Whereas, Mr. Philip Hodgkins has applied to this Congress for a supply of provisions for the inhabitants of Frenchman's Bay, and being at a great distance from the committees of correspondence of that place, therefore, *Resolved*, that it be recommended, and it is, by this Congress, accordingly recommended, to the governor and company of the colony of Connecticut, that they suffer the inhabitants of Frenchman's Bay to purchase such provisions in said colony as they stand in need of.

Major Hawley, who was appointed to bring in a resolve explanatory of the resolve of this Congress relative to the refugees, reported. The report was accepted, and is as follows, viz. :

Whereas, a certain resolve was made and passed, on the 21st day of

June last, respecting the improvement of the estates of several persons who have fled to General Gage, in manner as is expressed in the said resolve, and it being made to appear to this Congress that the said resolve is taken in such a sense, in divers parts of this colony, as to make it necessary, that some explanation of the said resolve should be made by this Congress, it is therefore, *Resolved,* that henceforward the said resolve ought not to be construed to extend to any estates of such persons, excepting such estates as are left unimproved and void of any occupant, or possessor, and that no other estate of such person ought to be treated in the manner prescribed in the said resolve, until they shall be regularly indicted and tried for their supposed offences.

Ordered to be printed in the several papers.

Resolved, That eight o'clock to-morrow morning be assigned for the consideration of the expediency of appointing a surgeon general of the Massachusetts army.

Ordered, That the account books of Major Barber be committed to the care of the committee of supplies.

Adjourned to Sunday morning, eight o'clock.

SUNDAY, JULY 9, 1775.

The committee appointed to consider a resolve relative to seizing the crown officers, reported by way of resolve. The report was re-committed, and the secretary was added to the committee, and the committee [were] directed to report by way of letter, and to insert a clause relative to the desire of this Congress, that the Continental Congress would adjourn nearer the seat of action.

The committee appointed to consider a resolve of the committee of safety, recommending the appointment of four master armorers, reported. The report was ordered to lie on the table, till the committee for revising the commission of the committee of safety, and the commission of the committee of supplies, reported.

Ordered, That Mr. Gill, Mr. Pickering and Mr. Woodbridge, be a committee to consider a letter from Mr. John Scollay, relative to the poor of the town of Boston.[1]

(1) The letter of Mr. John Scollay, with the paper enclosed, follows :

" BOSTON, JULY 8TH, 1775.

" SIR :—His excellency the governor having, by Mr. Secretary Flucker, sent a message to the selectmen, overseers of the poor, and committee of donations, respecting the removal of the poor, and other inhabitants of the town of Boston, they attended the same, and, after deliberating on the matter, presented to Mr. Secretary their doings thereon, a copy of which is here enclosed, to which his excellency has been pleased to accede."

As there has, of late, been an interruption of the inhabitants, with their effects, passing out of the town into the country, perhaps the matter may have dropped with you, and proper accommoda-

Ordered, That the Secretary, Doct. Taylor and Major Brooks, be a committee to confer with Mr. John Lane, on the difficulties which attend the supplying the Indians at Falmouth, Casco Bay.

Resolved, That the Hon. Jedediah Preble, and the Hon. Enoch Freeman, Esq., be, and hereby are empowered, to supply the Indians of the Penobscot tribe, with any quantity of goods, not exceeding the value of three hundred pounds, and to draw on the receiver general for the same, who is hereby directed to pay such drafts, in three months after the date of this resolve, and to take furs and skins of the said Indians, in exchange, on the account of this colony, they to be accountable for their proceedings.

Ordered, That Deacon Cheever be a committee to bring in a resolve, empowering the committee of supplies to furnish General Washington with such articles of household furniture, as he has wrote to said committee for.

tions may not have been provided for the reception of any more of the poor of the town than have already left it; and as the state of the inhabitants is really distressing, we shall be glad that immediate attention be given to the above, and that we, as soon as may be, know your resolutions thereon. As many of these poor unhappy people are not in a condition to be removed by land carriage, therefore, we should think that the place of their destination might be as near water carriage as may be convenient: if it would not be thought assuming, we would beg leave to suggest the towns of Salem or Marblehead, as proper places for the above purpose.

His excellency does expect, that whatever vessels or other carriages may be employed in this business, ample security be given that they shall be safe from any detention, and that they, with the persons that occupy them, be permitted to return without hindrance or molestation."

"I am, in behalf of the committee, Sir, your most humble servant,

JOHN SCOLLAY, *Chairman."*

JAMES WARREN, Esq.

"The selectmen, overseers of the poor, and committee of donations, having received a message from his excellency the governor, by Mr. Secretary Flucker, respecting the removal of the poor, and other inhabitants of the town, and attended the same, with all proper deference and respect, beg leave to represent: That the number of the poor in the alms-house, amounts to about two hundred, of which they suppose that one hundred and sixty or one hundred and seventy, may be removed, for which the selectmen, overseers, and committee aforesaid, will make all proper provision, his excellency providing boats and carriages for transportation by water or land, as may be thought best, and allowing such quantities of provisions, bedding, clothing and medicine as may be necessary and proper. The few unhappy persons that may be unable to be removed must be left, and are earnestly recommended to his excellency's well known humanity."

"As to the poor, and other inhabitants of the town, who, if not already, will soon be reduced to the greatest distress, the selectmen, overseers and committee apprehend, that by far the greatest part, if not the whole, would immediately remove themselves, with the small assistance they might receive from the committee of donations, provided they could obtain his excellency's permission."

"The selectmen, overseers and committee, previous to their removal, beg for leave to write to such persons in the country as may be empowered to take care of, and provide for the poor, that these destitute persons may find such assistance and relief as their particular circumstances may require."

Afternoon.

Resolved, That the consideration of the allowance proper to be made to Mr. Fowle for the use of his house, by several committees of this Congress, be referred to the general assembly.

The committee on the letter of Mr. John Scollay, of Boston, reported. The report was ordered to lie, for further consideration.

The committee appointed to prepare a list of such towns, as it would be expedient to apply to, for shirts, breeches, &c., again reported. The report was accepted, and is as follows, viz. :

Whereas, there is now a very pressing demand for some articles of clothing, more especially of shirts, breeches, stockings and shoes, in the army raised by the colony of the Massachusetts Bay, and there is danger of very mischievous consequences, from a delay of supplying the same: *Resolved*, that the inhabitants of the respective towns and districts in the counties specified in a list hereunto annexed, be most earnestly desired, as soon as possible, to procure such a number of each of the articles of shirts, breeches and stockings, as are affixed to their said towns and districts respectively, of a serviceable quality, and as many good shoes, as they can obtain, and deliver the same to the person or persons now to be appointed by this Congress to collect them, who are directed to give receipts to the owners, at the prices for which they shall mutually agree, keeping an account thereof, in the form following :

The ——— day of ——— 1775. Received of ———, — shirts, at —; — pair of breeches at —; — pair of stockings at —; —pairs of shoes at —: amounting to the sum of ———, for the service of the colony of the Massachusetts Bay; which the receiver general is directed, in forty days after the date hereof, to pay to the said ———, or order, in notes, or bills of credit of this colony, and the receiver general is hereby required to pay the same accordingly. And that this business may be effected with the greatest expedition, the selectmen and committees of correspondence in the several towns and districts beforementioned, are hereby most earnestly requested, to afford the utmost aid in their power, to the person or persons appointed as aforesaid, in collecting said articles. And those persons are further directed to take such measures, as will enable them to ascertain the price of each article, on its arrival, and to contract, at a reasonable rate, with suitable waggoners and teamsters to transport the effects, when procured, with great despatch, to the committee of supplies, at Watertown, giving them a certificate of the sums to be paid for such service, for which sum, said committee are hereby directed to draw on the public treasury, in favor of any thus contracted with, or their orders, and the receiver general is accordingly directed to pay the same.

Committee.—Suffolk : Mr. Daniel Vose, *Milton;* Mr. Abner Ellis, *Dedham;* Deacon Jabez Fisher, *Wrentham.*

Essex : Major Asa Perley, *Boxford;* Col. Daniel Thurston, *Bradford;* Major A. Fuller, *Middleton.*

Middlesex : Mr. Peter Bent, *Marlborough;* Capt. Timothy Walker, *Wilmington;* Mr. Israel Hobart, *Townshend;* Mr. Samuel Sprague, *Stoneham.*

Plymouth : Mr. Ebenezer Thompson, *Halifax;* Col. Joseph Cushing, *Hanover;* Mr. George Partridge, *Duxbury.*

Bristol : Mr. Thomas Durfee, *Freetown ;* Capt. Benjamin King, *Raynham;* Benjamin Aikin, Esq., *Dartmouth.*

Worcester : Mr. David Bancroft, *Worcester ;* Mr. Joseph Wheeler, *Harvard;* Col. Jonathan Grout, *Petersham.*

Barnstable : Col. Joseph Otis, *Barnstable;* Col. N. Freeman, *Sandwich;* Col. Elisha Cobb, *Wellfleet.*

Dukes County : James Athorne, Esq.

Resolved, That the receiver general be, and he hereby is directed, to pay Doct. Benjamin Church, Jr., or order, the sum of £34 5s. 2d. in full discharge of his account of expenses of himself and servant, on a journey to Philadelphia, in May last.

Ordered, That Mr. Gill, Mr. Phillips and Doct. Taylor, be a committee to provide a dinner on the 19th instant, for themselves and the clergy.

Ordered, That Mr. Kollock, Doct. Taylor and Deacon Nichols, be a committee to get the resolves relative to procuring shirts, breeches, &c., printed, and dispersed, one to each town mentioned in the schedule, and one to each of the committee.

The committee appointed to bring in an additional resolve relative to the poor of Boston, reported. The report was accepted, and is as follows, viz. :

Whereas, it appears that some towns in this colony have a larger number of the poor of the towns of Boston and Charlestown, than has been heretofore assigned them, and more than they are willing to retain :

Resolved, That it be recommended to the selectmen of those towns, to cause such poor to be removed to some town, that shall not have the proportion heretofore assigned, or shall be willing to receive them, and, if convenient, to those of such towns that said poor may choose; provided said poor are possessed of a certificate from either of the selectmen, or overseers of the poor, of the towns of Boston or Charlestown, showing that they were inhabitants of either of those towns, on the first of March last; and the selectmen, or overseers of the poor of the towns qualified as aforesaid, to which the before mentioned poor may be conveyed, with a certificate as above prescribed, are requested to receive, and make provision for the same, as has been before directed : all reasonable charges attending such removal to be paid by this colony.

Ordered, That Mr. Kollock, Mr. Batchelder and Deacon Plympton, be a committee to bring in a resolve, for the purpose of supplying the Penobscot Indians with a small quantity of gunpowder.

Resolved, That the selectmen of the town of Watertown be, and hereby are empowered and directed, to take into their custody one Daniel Green, now in this town, who was wounded and taken a prisoner the 19th of April last, and convey him to the jail in Concord, there to be confined till the further order of this Congress, or some future house of assembly of this colony.

Adjourned to Monday morning, eight o'clock.

MONDAY, JULY 10, 1775.

[The committee appointed to bring in a resolve for supplying the Penobscot Indians with gunpowder, reported. The report was accepted, and is as follows, viz. :]

Whereas, application has been made to this Congress, by Capt. John Lane, agent for the Penobscot tribe of Indians, for a small quantity of powder, for supplying said Indians: therefore, *Resolved*, that the committee of supplies is hereby directed to deliver, out of the public stores of this colony, to the said John Lane, twenty-five pounds of powder, for the use aforesaid, taking said Lane's receipt therefor, to deliver the same to General Preble and Col. Enoch Freeman, on account of this colony; and said committee are hereby directed to replace the same again, as soon as may be, from some town in this colony, (if they judge it necessary,) that can best spare the same.

Ordered, That the warrants for surgeons, adjutant generals and quarter master generals, be committed to the committee of safety to be delivered.

Ordered, That Deacon Baker bring in a resolve, directing the receiver general to pay Mr. Hastings, for his services, as door-keeper.

Ordered, That the letter from John Scollay, Esq , [relating to the poor] of Boston, and the paper accompanying it, be put into the hands of the committee of safety.

Ordered, That the President, Doct. Church and Mr. Gerry, be a committee to prepare an answer to a letter this day received from General Lee, and that 11 o'clock be assigned for the choice of some person to attend General Lee, on an interview with General Burgoyne.[1]

Ordered, That Mr. Pickering, Mr. Spear and Mr. Phillips, be a committee to examine a number of letters this day laid before the Congress, brought from London by Capt. Folger.

Resolved, That it be, and it is hereby ordered, that the committee of supplies immediately furnish General Washington with ten good horses, with saddles and bridles, for the public use.

Ordered, That Mr. Batchelder count and sort the votes for a person to attend General Lee on an interview with General Burgoyne.   Mr.

(1) The following is the letter from Gen. Lee :

HEAD QUARTERS, JULY THE 10TH, 1775.

"General Lee presents his respects to the president and gentlemen of the Provincial Congress of Massachusetts, and submits to their perusal a letter which he yesterday received from General Burgoyne, in answer to one which was read and approved of by the delegates of this province and other members of the Continental Congress. He begs leave to receive their commands with respect to the proposed interview. If they approve of it, he shall be glad to accept of it; if they disapprove, he shall reject it; but if they approve of it, he must request that they will depute some one gentleman of their body to accompany General Lee, and be witness of the conversation. He desires their answer immediately, as he has engaged to inform Gen. Burgoyne by four o'clock this afternoon, whether the interview is to take place. He shall likewise be much obliged to the gentlemen, if they will return the letter—but if they choose to take a copy, he can have no objection."

On the arrival of General Burgoyne in Boston, General Lee addressed a letter to that officer, expressing warm feelings of personal regard for his former companion in arms, and explaining his views of the rights of the Americans, and their determination and power to maintain them. General Burgoyne, in reply, proposed a meeting. "Above all," he says, " I should find an interview happy if it should induce such explanations as might tend in their consequences to peace. I feel, in common with all around me, for the unhappy people of this country : they foresee not the distress that is impending over them. I know Great Britain is ready to open her arms upon the first overture of accommodation. I know she is equally resolute to maintain her original rights, and if the war proceeds, your one hundred and fifty thousand men will not be a match for her power."

The proposed interview was declined in the following note :

CAMBRIDGE, HEAD QUARTERS, JULY 11, 1775.

" General Lee's compliments to General Burgoyne—would be extremely happy in an interview he so kindly proposed—but as he perceives that General Burgoyne has already made up his mind on this great subject ; and as it is impossible that he, General Lee, should ever alter his opinion, he is apprehensive that the interview might create those jealousies and suspicions so natural in a people struggling in the dearest of all causes, that of their liberty, property, wives, children, and future generations. He must, therefore, defer the happiness of embracing a man whom he most sincerely loves, until the subversion of the present tyrannical ministry and system, which he is persuaded must be in a few months, as he knows Great Britain cannot stand the contest. He begs General Burgoyne will send the letters which his aid de camp has for him. If Gardiner is aid de camp, he desires his love to him."

Batchelder having attended that service, reported, that Mr. Elbridge Gerry was chosen.

Ordered, That Col. Porter, Doct. Taylor and Major Brooks, be a committee, whose business it shall be, in conjunction with the committee of safety, to make thorough inquiry into the subject matter of a letter this day received from General Washington, [relating to reenforcements for the army.] And that the committee be directed to confer with General Washington on the subject of his letter, and particularly inform him of the number of men we had generally estimated in the Massachusetts forces, from the returns of the general officers, from the money paid out of the treasury, for a month's advance pay to the soldiers, and from the provision made for billeting the said forces.[1]

(1) The following is the letter of General Washington mentioned in the text, addressed to the President of Congress :

HEAD QUARTERS, CAMBRIDGE, JULY 9, 1775.

" SIR :—After much difficulty and delay, I have procured such returns of the state of the army as will enable us to form a judgment of its strength. It is with great concern I find it far inadequate to our general expectations and the duties which may be required of it. The number of men fit for duty in the forces raised in this province, including all the out posts and artillery, does not amount to nine thousand. The troops raised in the other colonies are more complete ; but yet fall short of their establishment. So that upon the whole, I cannot estimate the present army at more than fourteen thousand five hundred men capable of duty."

" I have the satisfaction to find the troops, both in camp and quarters, very healthy ; so that the deficiency must arise from the regiments never having been filled up to the establishment, and the number of men on furlough : but the former is much most considerable. Under all these circumstances I yesterday called a council of war ; and, enclosed, I send you an extract of our determinations, so far as they respect the province of Massachusetts Bay."

"Your own prudence will suggest the necessity of secrecy on this subject, as we have the utmost reason to think the enemy suppose our numbers much greater than they are : an error which it is not our interest to remove."

" The great extent of our lines, and the uncertainty which may be the point of attack, added to the necessity of immediate support, have induced me to order that horses, ready saddled, should be kept at several posts, in order to bring the most speedy intelligence of any movement of the enemy."

" For this purpose I should be glad that ten horses might be provided as soon as possible."

"I have the honor to be, Sir, your most obedient and very humble servant,

GEORGE WASHINGTON."

" P. S. As I am informed the Congress proposes to rise immediately, I should be glad to know what committees are left, or upon whom the executive business devolves.   G. W——N."

"AT A COUNCIL OF WAR, held at Head Quarters, July 9, 1775.—Present : His excellency General Washington, Generals Ward, Lee, Putnam, Thomas, Heath, Green, Gates."

" His excellency proposed to the consideration of the council—What number of troops may be necessary for the present service in and near Boston, to defend the posts already occupied, against the force supposed to be employed against us ?"

" Upon which it was agreed, that the army for the above purpose ought to consist of at least 22,000 men."

" As it appears by the returns now made, that the number of effective men is far short of the above estimate, a question was proposed, viz. :"

" In what manner this deficiency should be supplied ?"

"And it was unanimously agreed, that it ought to be done by sending an officer from each company

The committee appointed to prepare a letter to General Lee, reported. The report was accepted, and ordered to be authenticated, and sent forward to General Lee, by Doct. Church, Doct. Taylor and Mr. Gerry, a committee for that purpose.

SIR :—The Congress have perused the letter from General Burgoyne, which you was kind enough to submit to their inspection. They can have no objection to the proposed interview, from a want of the highest confidence in the wisdom, discretion and integrity of General Lee, but beg leave to suggest, that, as the confidence of the people in their General, is so essentially necessary, to the well conducting the enterprize in which we are engaged, and as a people contending for their liberties are naturally disposed to jealousy, and not inclined to make the most favorable constructions of the motives of conduct which they are not fully acquainted with, whether such an interview might not have a tendency to lessen the influence, which the Congress would wish to extend, to the utmost of their power, to facilitate and succeed the operations of war.

The Congress, agreeably to your request, have, to prevent, as far as we are able, any disagreeable consequences, which may arise from the jealousy of the people on such an occasion, appointed Mr. Elbridge Gerry to attend you at the proposed interview, if you shall think proper to proceed in it ; and as they do not think themselves authorized to counteract the general's inclination, they would submit it to his opinion, whether the advice of the council of war might not be taken in a matter of such apparent delicacy.

To the honorable General Lee.

Ordered, That Col. Mitchell, Capt. Batchelder, and Deacon Nichols, be a committee to consider the circumstances of the town of Hull, and report what is best to be done.

Ordered, That Mr. Phillips, Deacon Nichols, and Capt. Stone, be a committee to consider the situation of the public stock of powder, and report what shall be done with it.

in the forces raised in Massachusetts Bay, to recruit the regiments to which they respectively belong, to the establishment fixed by the Provincial Congress, the colonies of Rhode Island and Connecticut being already engaged in recruiting. And that, in the mean time, his excellency the General do apply to the Provincial Congress of this province, for their assistance, in procuring a temporary reenforcement, subject to the same military rules as the army now raised, inasmuch as the present extent of lines, and great probability of an early attack, render such reenforcement indispensably necessary."

Resolved, That the resolve which passed yesterday, relative to Daniel Green, be reconsidered, and that Capt. Stone be appointed to bring in a resolve with regard to him.

Ordered, That Mr. Baker, Mr. Kollock, and Capt. Parker, be a committee to consider an account of Mr. John Gill.

Ordered, That Capt. Vose, Mr. Jewett, and Mr. Bigelow, be a committee to consider an account of Mr. Moses Lammon, for a gun sold Barnabas Evans.

Ordered, That the committee for signing the bills, &c., be directed to sit, and despatch the business, that the soldiers may be paid off, according to the order of Congress.

Ordered, That Capt. Stone, Mr. Bigelow, and Capt. Harnden, be a committee to consider the account of Mr. Isaac Bissell.

Resolved, That the committee of supplies, be directed to write to the selectmen of Charlestown and Walpole, in the government of New Hampshire, and desire them to inform them, what cannon there are in those towns belonging to this colony, and the said committee are to take into their custody such as they shall find to be the property of this colony.

Resolved, That Mr. Stephen Hall be on the committee in the room of Doct. Gunn, to sign the colony notes.

Mr. Israel Nichols' account was passed upon, and *Ordered*, that the receiver general be, and he is hereby directed, to pay Mr. Israel Nichols, the sum of eighteen shillings, in full of his account.

Capt. Stone, agreeably to order, brought in the following resolve, respecting Daniel Green, which was accepted :

Resolved, That the selectmen of Watertown be, and hereby are directed, to take Daniel Green, a prisoner, taken in the late battle on the 19th of April last, who is now in this town, and safely convey him to Mr. Jones, prison keeper at Concord; and said prison keeper is hereby directed safely to keep, and properly support the said Green, until further order of the Congress or House of Representatives.

The committee on Capt. Lane's account, reported. The report was accepted, and is as follows, viz. :

Resolved, That the receiver general be, and he is hereby directed, to pay John Lane, the sum of three pounds six shillings, for horse hire, and expenses, from Falmouth to Watertown, and back again, in behalf of the Penobscot tribe of Indians.

Resolved, That the receiver general be, and he is hereby directed, to pay to Mr. Simon Hastings, the sum of eight pounds four shillings, for attending this Congress as a door-keeper, for forty-one days, the present session.

Adjourned to Tuesday morning, eight o'clock.

TUESDAY, JULY 11, 1775.

A letter from ———— ————, of New York, to the committee of donations for the town of Boston, was read; upon which, the Congress assumed the consideration of a report relative to such donations, which was accepted, and ordered to be printed in the newspapers, and is as follows, viz:

Whereas, the poor of Boston and Charlestown, who have been assigned to the several towns in this colony, and have been, and still are supported at the public expense, for reasons that are obvious; therefore, *Resolved*, that the money, grain, flour, &c. that have, or shall be generously given for the support of said poor, and lodged within this colony, ought to be considered as belonging to the public stock of this colony, for the use aforesaid; and the committee of supplies are hereby directed to take care of such donations accordingly, till the further order of this Congress, or House of Representatives; and when any town shall, by order of said committee, or otherwise, receive or make use of such donations, or any part thereof, the selectmen of such town are hereby ordered to exhibit an exact account thereof, to this Congress, or some future House of Representatives, as credit to their accounts of charges for the support of the poor abovesaid.

A resolve of the committee of safety, relative to soldiers who had enlisted a second time, was read, and committed to the committee who were yesterday appointed to inquire into the subject of General Washington's letter.

Resolved, That if this committee is not ready to report to the Congress at its present session, that they be directed to report to the next General Assembly or House of Representatives.

Ordered, That Doct. Church, Capt. Stone, and Mr. Woodbridge, be a committee to inquire into the subject of a resolve of the committee of safety, relative to Mr. Winslow's employing one William Lightly, to carry a load of molasses from Connecticut to New York.

Resolved, That this Congress has no objection to Mrs. Mary Greenwood having a permit to go into Boston.

The committee appointed to consider the circumstances of the town of Hull, reported. The report was accepted, and is as follows, viz.:

The committee appointed by this Congress to consider of a request of a committee from the town of Hull, setting forth that they are now invested by an armed vessel, and expect that the communication between them, and their neighbors, will soon be cut off, beg leave to report the following resolve, viz. :

Resolved, That it be, and it is hereby accordingly recommended to the selectmen and committees of correspondence of the town of Hingham, and district of Cohasset, that they cause all convenient assistance to be given to the inhabitants of Hull, in removing their effects from that place, and securing and removing the crops of grain, and other produce, from said town, to some secure place for the use of the present proprietors of the same.

Mr. Pickering, by leave of Congress, presented the following resolve in behalf of Capt. Samuel Williams, which was accepted :

On an application made to this Congress, setting forth that a number of gentlemen at Salem, in this colony, have employed Capt. Samuel Williams of that town, to procure for them, at their cost, a number of barrels of powder, at New York, or elsewhere to the southward : *Resolved*, that the intention of those gentlemen is agreeable to this Congress, and that Capt. Samuel Williams appears to be a friend to his country, and possesses the confidence of his townsmen, and that if he executes his commission, it will be of great service to this, and the other colonies.

Resolved, That the persons employed in cutting the grass on the land of the refugees, be allowed half a pint of rum, each, per day.

Afternoon.

Ordered, That Mr. Gerry, Mr. Phillips, and Col. Porter, be a committee to repair immediately to General Washington, and know of him what number of men he would have this Congress raise, for a temporary reinforcement of the army; and to inform the General of the powers vested by this Congress, in the committee of safety, and to confer with the General, at large, on the state of the army, and in particular, with respect to some soldiers of the army who have enlisted twice.

Ordered, That the president, Col. Palmer, Mr. Jewett, Capt. Stone, and Col. Farley, be a committee to devise some means of raising speedily a temporary reenforcement of the army, and to bring in an establishment.

Ordered, That Capt. Brown, Mr. Glover, and Major Fuller, be a committee to procure three couriers by ten o'clock tomorrow morning.

Resolved, That the receiver general be empowered and directed to employ some person to number the colony notes.

Ordered, That Mr. Fox, and Mr. Bigelow, be added to the committee, who were appointed to consider what was proper to be done with the public stock of powder.

Ordered, That Col. Lincoln bring in a resolve, determining what is best to be done with the whale-boats.

Ordered, That Mr. Shillaber, Mr. Johnson, and Mr. Brown, be a committee to see that the fish, procured by the committee of supplies for the use of this colony, be properly taken care of.

A memorial of William Hunt was read, and ordered to lie on the table.

Major Barber's account was allowed, and the receiver general directed to pay it.

Col. Lincoln, agreeably to appointment, brought in the following resolve, relative to whale-boats, which was accepted:

Whereas, the Congress, sometime past, directed and empowered, in the absence of Capt. Joshua Davis, Capt. Edmund Soper to take care of a number of whale-boats, then lying in the river at Braintree, purchased by said Davis for the use of the colony, and as he hath procured and brought there, a very considerable number more, which require his care and inspection; and as one person is sufficient to have the care of the whole of them: therefore, *Resolved*, that, as Capt. Davis is now returned, Capt. Edmund Soper be excused from any care of said boats, until further orders; that he give information to said Davis, where they are lodged, and if he hath delivered any of them to the order of the officers in the army, to whom they were delivered, in order to his receiving them into his possession, as soon as the public service will admit of it.

Adjourned to eight o'clock tomorrow morning.

WEDNESDAY, JULY 12, 1775.

The committee appointed to consider a resolve of the committee of safety, relative to Mr. Winslow's employing one William Lightly to carry a load of molasses to New York, &c., reported the following letter to Governor Trumbull, which was accepted, and ordered to be authenticated, and sent forward:

May it please your honor:

The brigantine Nancy, now in the harbor of Stonington, in Connecticut, being laden with molasses, the property of the late Joshua Winslow of Boston, a noted, and active friend to administration; which, as we are well informed, is now directed to be conveyed to New

York, and from thence as we conjecture, from sundry suspicious circumstances, to be sent to Boston; the master who has undertaken this business, being now in custody, having given the information before-mentioned, the Congress of the Massachusetts Bay beg leave to observe to your honor, whether prudence and good policy do not suggest to detain said ship and cargo, or such part of it as belongs to said Winslow, for the use of the colonies, rather than to suffer them to fall into the hands of General Gage, where they will be improved to the support of our enemies, and to augment the distress of these colonies.

We have the honor to be, &c.

To the Hon. Governor Trumbull.

Resolved, That said William Lightly be confined in Concord jail, and that Mr. Davis be dismissed, and that Mr. Woodbridge bring in a resolve for this purpose.

Ordered, That Mr. Crane, and Mr. Fox, make out warrants for several surgeons and surgeons' mates, agreeably to a list this day exhibited by Doct. Taylor, and that such warrants, when made out, be transmitted to the committee of safety.

Mr. Glover, by leave of Congress, brought in a resolve, recommending to such able-bodied men as have left their sea-port towns to return; which resolve was accepted, and is as follows, viz.:

Whereas, many able-bodied men, who were inhabitants of the sea-port towns of the colony, have removed their families into the country, and have themselves left said towns, and carried with them their arms and ammunition; therefore, *Resolved,* that this Congress do approve of the conduct of such persons, so far as it respects the removing the women, and children, and valuable effects. It is recommended to the male inhabitants, fit to bear arms, that they return to their respective towns, and there continue with that dignity and firmness which ought ever to distinguish an American, and to defend them from the ravages of the enemy, until it shall be judged by the inhabitants of such towns, at a meeting for that purpose, expedient to vacate the same.

Ordered, That Doct. Taylor, Capt. Stone, and Col. Moseley, be a committee to consider the subject of a letter from Capt. Noble, dated Pittsfield, July 3, 1775, and report.[1]

Mr. Woodbridge, agreeably to appointment, brought in the following resolves, which were accepted.

---

(1) Capt. Noble asked the allowance of the pay roll of his company engaged in the public service, under Col. Benedict Arnold.

Resolved, That the receiver general be, and hereby is directed, to pay to Mr. Jacob Biglow, the sum of £13, for sundry axes, shovels, and spades, and for procuring and carting the same, for the use of the army, agreeably to the directions of this Congress.

Resolved, That the receiver general be, and he is hereby directed to pay Jonathan Brown, the sum of £5 2s. for sundry axes, and for collecting the same for the use of the army, agreeably to the direction of this Congress.

Resolved, That the receiver general be, and he is hereby directed to pay Major A. Fuller, £7 2s. 8d. for axes, &c., as above.

Resolved, That the receiver general be, and he is hereby directed to pay Deacon Jonas Stone, the sum of £18 12s. 8d. for axes, &c., as above.

Resolved, That the receiver general be, and he is hereby directed to pay Mr. Enoch Ellis, the sum of £8 3s. 7d. for axes, &c., as above.

The committee appointed to confer with the General, relative to the number of men necessary to be raised for a temporary reenforcement, reported a letter from him, which was committed to the committee appointed to devise means of raising such reenforcement, to which committee Col. Porter, Mr. Glover, and Capt. Parker, were added.

Resolved, That Doct. Church, Doct. Taylor, and Doct. Whiting, be a committee to take into their custody all the medicines, medical stores and instruments, which are, or may be provided for the use of the army, by this colony, and to distribute them at their best discretion, so that no peculation or needless waste be made of the medicinal stores belonging to the public.

Resolved, That the president have leave to go home in the afternoon. Adjourned to three o'clock, P. M.

Afternoon.

The committee appointed to consider the situation of the public stock of powder, reported. The report being amended, was drawn anew, accepted, and is as follows, viz. :

This Congress taking into consideration the situation of the public stock of powder that is now in Watertown : *Resolved*, that it be recommended to the committee of supplies, to make a division of said powder into two or more parcels, as they shall judge requisite; that they deposite one part in this town, and the remainder in such other town or towns as they shall think most expedient.

Ordered, That Col. Lincoln, Mr. Gill, and Capt. Stone, be a committee to examine fifteen persons, taken prisoners at Long Island, and sent to this Congress by the committee of safety.

Ordered, That Doct. Taylor, Mr. Phillips, and Major Fuller, be a committee to enlarge the commission of the committee of safety.

A letter from the committee of safety, requesting this Congress to appoint a special committee to make provision for the poor of Boston and Charlestown, was read. The matter, after debate, was ordered to subside.

The report of the committee for devising means of raising a temporary reenforcement, was taken into consideration, and after much debate was recommitted; and Col. Palmer, and Mr. Phillips, were added to the committee.

The committee appointed to examine the fifteen prisoners, sent to the Congress by the committee of safety, reported, verbally, facts as they found them: whereupon, *Ordered*, that Jonathan Winship, and Jacob Whipple, two of the prisoners, be discharged immediately; that Jacob Davis, another of the prisoners, be sent to the main guard at Cambridge, the Congress having great reason to suspect, that he enlisted in, and deserted from the army raised by this colony, and that the officers of the guard be certified, in writing, of what crime the said Jacob now stands charged; that John Freeman, a negro man, said to be the servant of Mr. Joseph Howett of Newburyport, be sent to the jail at Cambridge, there to continue till further orders; that the other prisoners, with the said Jacob and John, be committed to Capt. Crafts, to be kept under guard, until further orders.

Ordered, That Capt. Brown cause suitable provision to be made for the said prisoners.

Ordered, That Mr. Learned be directed to charge the expense of keeping Mr. Lightly, and the guard that attend him, to this colony.

Ordered, That Major Fuller, Mr. Kollock, and Mr. Crane, be a committee to consider what is a proper establishment of salt for the army, and report.

The committee appointed to consider a letter from Capt. James Noble to Walter Spooner, Esq., reported a resolve, and a letter, which were accepted, and are as follow, viz.: *Resolved*, that Henry Gardner, Esq., receiver general, be, and he is hereby ordered to pay to Capt. James Noble, or order, £100, as part of his pay roll, as captain in Col. Benedict Arnold's regiment, in the late expedition against the posts of Ticonderoga and Crown point, for the use of said company.

SIR: We received yours of the 3d instant, by Mr. William Barber, together with your account of expenses, and a muster roll of your company, whilst in the service of this colony, under the command of

Col. Benedict Arnold, but before your account can be passed with propriety, it must be examined, and adjusted by indifferent persons. Therefore, it is *Ordered*, that the committee of correspondence for the town of Pittsfield, be a committee for that purpose; and it is further *Ordered*, that you make oath to the truth and justness of your muster roll, and see that the same be right cast; then charge yourself with the £27 7s. 1d., which you received of Col. Arnold, as advance pay for your company; also with the £100 now sent you by Mr. Barber, agreeably to your order; then return said roll and account, and when you comply with the above, you will receive the balance due.

To Capt. James Noble.

Lieut. Zachariah Gurney having conducted fifteen persons who were taken at Long Island, to this Congress, and the Congress having ordered eleven of them, under a guard of this town, and dismissed the other two, the said Gurney is discharged from further attendance.

The report of the committee on Mr. John Gill's account was taken up, and accepted, and is as follows, viz. :

The committee on the account of John Gill, beg leave to report by way of resolve, as follows : *Resolved*, that the receiver general be, and he is hereby directed, to pay to the within named John Gill, the sum of £6 17s 8d, in full, of his services on several journeys, horse hire, expenses, &c.

The committee appointed to devise means for raising a temporary reenforcement, again reported. The report was amended, accepted, and is as follows, viz. :   Whereas, a speedy augmentation of the army is wanted, and has been requested by the general, to serve as a temporary reenforcement until the new levies now raising to fill up the regiments in the field, can come in, and until they shall be discharged by the general of the army, or the assembly of this colony, therefore, *Resolved*, that it be, and hereby is most earnestly recommended to the inhabitants of ———— town, that they immediately raise and send to the camp at Cambridge, —— men, provided with a good fire-lock, ammunition, and a blanket, each, who shall be detained not longer than one month, at farthest, from the beginning of their march, and shall be honorably paid for their service by the colony, all due regard being had to the present urgency of farming business, and the inconvenience of complying with such a requisition at this juncture. And the military officers, selectmen, and committees of correspondence, are desired to see this resolve executed without delay, and that they be paid according to the following establishment :

N. B. The above is copied from the original report on file, which has been altered and still appears to be incorrect. The following is a copy of the printed one on file:

To the military officers, selectmen, and committees of correspondence in the town of ———.

Gentlemen:—You are hereby most earnestly requested to procure the execution of the subsequent resolve, with the greatest possible expedition.

In Provincial Congress, *Watertown*, July 12, 1775.

Whereas a very speedy augmentation of the army is indispensably necessary, and has been requested by his excellency General Washington, to serve as a temporary reenforcement until the new levies now raising to fill up the regiments in the field may be completed: Therefore, *Resolved*, that it be, and it is hereby most earnestly recommended to the commanding officer of every company in the town of ——, that they immediately raise, and send to the camp at Cambridge, —— able bodied men, each provided with a good fire-lock, ammunition, and blanket, who shall be detained not longer than one month, at farthest, from the beginning of their march, and be paid honorably for their service; all due regard in the pay being had to the difficulty of complying with this requisition in the present urgency of the business of husbandry. Those who are required from ——— together with others who are called from ———, will form one company, under the command of such officers as the field officers of that regiment from which the greatest number of said company is taken, shall appoint. And the field officers above mentioned, or the major part of them, are desired accordingly, without delay, to appoint one captain, and two lieutenants, of persons who now are, or have been in command, well calculated to serve the public in these departments.

By order of Congress.

A true copy. Attest.

Resolved, That the resolve passed this forenoon, recommending to all able bodied men, who have left their sea-port towns to return, be reconsidered.

Adjourned to eight o'clock, to-morrow morning.

THURSDAY, JULY 13, 1775.

A letter from General Washington's secretary, dated nine o'clock, P. M., July 12, 1775, was read; whereupon, *Resolved*, that the resolve passed yesterday, for raising a temporary reenforcement, be reconsidered.[1]

A petition from the selectmen and committee of Harpswell, was read, and committed to Mr. Johnson, Mr. Perry, and Deacon Baker.

The instructions reported to be given Capt. Davis, were considered, and, after debate, the report was ordered to be dismissed.

Ordered, That Capt. Stone, Capt. Baker, and Mr. Learned, be a committee to consider what towns the ten prisoners now under guard in this town, shall be sent to.

Ordered, That Michael Edwards, now under guard in this town, be immediately discharged.

Ordered, That Mr. Phillips, Col. Farley, and Mr. Kollock, be a committee to examine and consider an account of Mr. Solomon Lothrop, [for the entertainment of General Washington.]

Ordered, That Col. Lincoln, Col. Porter, and Mr. Perry, be a committee to consider some method of supplying the recruiting officers with money for the purpose.

[The committee reported the following resolve, which was accepted, viz. :]

Resolved, That the committee of safety be, and they hereby are empowered and directed, to give orders on the receiver general in favor of such officer or officers as are, or shall be appointed as recruiting officers, not exceeding the sum of four pounds to any one of them, and take their receipts for the sum they shall order to them respectively, which sum is to be deducted from their wages on the rolls being made up, unless otherwise ordered by a house of representatives of this colony ; and the receiver general is hereby directed to pay said order accordingly.

Resolved, That the resolve passed yesterday, directing the receiver general to pay Capt. James Noble, or order, the sum of one hundred pounds, be reconsidered, and that a resolve be drawn by Capt. Stone,

---

(1) The following is the letter mentioned in the text :

HEAD QUARTERS, CAMBRIDGE, JULY 12, 1775.

" SIR:—Upon a conference with the other generals respecting the militia, it has been concluded, that one thousand men to be stationed in and about Medford, will be sufficient for the present service."

" His excellency has also directed me to request of the Congress, in his name, that they would urge the committees in the several towns, to forward and promote the new levies as much as possible, and that they would exert themselves to send to the camp, such soldiers as have staid beyond their furloughs, or have left the service, and may be returned to their former homes.

" I am sir, with much respect, Your most obedient humble servant,

JOS. REED, *Secretary.*"

directing the said receiver general, to pay Mr. William Barber, the said sum of one hundred pounds, for the use of Capt. Noble.

Resolved, That Capt. Stone be appointed to the office of president of this Congress in the absence of Col. Warren.

Capt. Stone, agreeably to his request, being excused from the office of president :

Resolved, That Col. Benjamin Lincoln be appointed to officiate as president of this Congress in the absence of the Hon. James Warren, Esq.

The committee appointed to consider the petition of the selectmen and committee of safety of the district of Harpswell,[1] reported, that the consideration of said petition be referred to the general assembly. The report was accepted.

Resolved, That Lieut. Zachariah Gurney be, and he hereby is directed, to take into his custody John Davis, and John Freeman a negro man, and convey them to Cambridge, and deliver them according to the resolves of this Congress respecting them; copies of which are to be delivered him, together with this resolve.

Capt. Stone, agreeably to the direction this day of Congress, brought in the following resolve, which was accepted :

(1) " *To the honorable the Provincial Congress of Massachusetts Bay, convened at Watertown, July —, 1775.*"

" The petition of the selectmen and committee of safety, at the desire, and in behalf of the inhabitants of the district of Harpswell, humbly sheweth ; that your petitioners have, at all times, exerted themselves in prosecuting those measures recommended by the Continental and Provincial Congresses ; that it is their fixed determination to continue thus to do ; that some of said inhabitants cheerfully enlisted for the public safety, and to ward off that despotic and arbitrary power with which administration is aiming to govern the colonies ; that said district, on the account of its situation, being an *isthmus,* or neck of land, about ten miles in length, with many adjacent islands, navigable on each side, upwards of seven miles for ships of the navy, and abounding with cattle, sheep, &c., is peculiarly exposed to the ravages of the British troops ; that the inhabitants of said district, did, at their own cost, station guards every night, at sundry places most exposed, lest the troops should be benefited by their provision ; that the enlisted men were, upon the 20th of June last, put upon duty by order of their superior officers, to guard said district from the plundering of troops which were daily expected with cutters, &c. ; that the inhabitants of said district are in low circumstances, and are unable to enlist any more men, unless their husbandry employment greatly suffers, which must be an additional distress to that which they already feel ; that, should the men already enlisted be called away to join the army, said district is liable to fall an easy prey to the ravages of troops which may attack it for fresh provisions. Your petitioners therefore, humbly pray, that this honorable Congress in their great wisdom, would allow said district the number of men already enlisted, with such additional number, as the Congress may judge proper ; and your petitioners, as in duty bound, shall ever pray."

"JOHN RODICK,   }   *Selectmen*
WILLIAM SYLVESTER. } *of said District.*

PAUL KENDALL,   } *Committee of Safety*
WILLIAM SYLVESTER. } *for said District.*"

Harpswell, 8 July, 1775.

Resolved, That Henry Gardner, Esq., receiver general, be, and he is hereby ordered, to pay to Mr. William Barber, for the use of Capt. James Noble, £100, as part of said Noble's pay roll as captain in Col. Benedict Arnold's regiment, in the late expedition against the posts of Ticonderoga and Crown Point, for the use of said Noble's company.

The committee appointed to consider an account of Mr. Solomon Lothrop, reported. The report was accepted, and is as follows, viz.:

Resolved, That the receiver general be, and hereby is directed, to pay Mr. S. Lothrop, the sum of £24 6s. 9d. in full of his account exhibited this day, for entertainment provided for General Washington.

Resolved, That the resolve passed yesterday, directing the receiver general to pay Mr. John Gill £6 17s. 8d. be reconsidered.

Resolved, That John Davis, one of the persons taken from Long Island, and brought under guard to this Congress, be remanded to the commander in chief of the American forces, at Cambridge, being suspected to have deserted from Capt. Foster's company in the artillery, and engaged in the service of our enemies: that he be delivered, together with a copy of this resolve, to such officer as the general shall appoint.

Resolved, That John Freeman a negro man, one of the persons taken from Long Island, and brought under guard to this Congress, be committed to the jail in Cambridge; there to remain until he be discharged by order of this Congress, or some future house of representatives, or by order of the committee of safety, in case there is no Congress or house of representatives then sitting, and the jail keeper is hereby directed to receive, detain, and provide for the said John accordingly.

Ordered, That Mr. Crane, Major Fuller and Mr. Jewett, be a committee to consider a resolve of the committee relative to horses, this day presented to Congress.

The resolve of the committee of safety, relative to such soldiers as have enlisted twice, was read, and again recommitted to Col. Porter, Col. Mosely and Capt. Stone.

Ordered, That Mr. Phillips, Mr. Kollock and Mr. Robinson, be a committee to bring in a resolve, recommending to the inhabitants of this colony not to kill any more sheep, till the general assembly shall take some order hereon.

The committee appointed to make an establishment of salt, for the soldiers, reported. The report was accepted, and is as follows: Whereas, complaints have been made to this Congress, that there is now great want of salt in the camps; therefore, *Resolved*, that the commissary be, and hereby is directed, when application is made by any of the officers for the above said article, to deal out one gill per week to each person, for which said application is made, and no more.

The committee appointed to consider a resolve of the committee of safety, relative to several horses taken from the enemy, reported. The report was accepted, and is as follows, viz. : Whereas, four horses were taken by Capt. Brown, of Salem, and a party with him at or near Charlestown neck, and some disputes having arisen whose property said horses should be, therefore, *Resolved*, that the said horses be delivered into the hands of Capt. Brown aforesaid, until the further order of this Congress, or some future house of representatives of this colony, to whom he is to be accountable for the same.

The committee appointed to bring in a resolve recommending to the inhabitants of this colony, not to kill any more sheep, &c., reported. The report was accepted, and ordered to be printed in the newspapers, and in handbills to be issued for procuring coats, &c.

Whereas, there is the highest probability of a very large demand for the article of wool, and inconceivable mischief may ensue from delaying a speedy provision for its increase; therefore, *Resolved*, that it be earnestly recommended to the inhabitants of this colony, that they refrain from killing any sheep, or lambs, excepting in cases of absolute necessity, till the further order of this Congress, or some future assembly of this colony, and it is expected of every person who regards the advice of this body, the decisions of the Continental Congress, or the welfare of this people, that they grant a strict compliance herewith.

A resolve was brought in on the account of Alexander Gray, and accepted, and is as follows, viz. :

Resolved, That the receiver general be, and hereby is directed, to pay Mr. Alexander Gray, or order, £2 7s. 8d. in full for the balance of his account of time, and expenses, on a journey to Philadelphia, as an express to the Continental Congress.

A resolve for payment of Mr. Nathaniel Barber's account was brought in, accepted, and is as follows, viz. :

Resolved, That the receiver general be, and hereby is directed, to pay Mr. Nathaniel Barber, or order, £4 14s. 4d. in full for one month's service as store keeper of the ordnance, and expenses of horse hire, &c., agreeably to an account exhibited to this Congress, by said Barber.

The committee appointed to consider a resolve of the committee of safety, relative to soldiers who had enlisted twice, reported. The report was accepted, and is as follows, viz. : Whereas, many inconveniences have arisen by reason of divers soldiers of the forces raised by this colony enlisting a second time into other companies than those which they first enlisted into, which ought to be remedied; therefore, *Resolved*, that every soldier, who, before the second day of July instant, has enlisted into other companies than those with whom he at first enlisted, unless the second enlistment was made with the consent of the officer with whom he at first enlisted, or by consent of the committee of safety, or order of Congress, in either of which cases the first enlistment shall be void, shall return to the company with whom he first enlisted, if requested by the commanding officer of such company, otherwise to remain in the company he next enlisted into. And in case any dispute shall arise, whether any such second enlistment was made by consent, or order, as above expressed, the committee of safety are hereby empowered and directed fully and finally to settle and determine the same.

The committee appointed to consider what towns the ten prisoners shall be sent to, reported. The report was accepted, and is as follows, viz. :

Resolved, That ten persons, taken from Long Island, be sent to the towns in the county of Worcester hereafter named, viz. : John Hayes and Thomas Bibby to the town of Lunenburg; James Griffin and John Reed to Rutland; Perez Merren and Michael Malony to Shrewsbury; Patrick Hickey and Richard Nash to Brookfield; Michael Mellows and John Fleming to Sutton : to be received, employed and provided for, by the selectmen of those respective towns, in the best way and manner they can, till the further order of this colony. And it is further *Resolved*, that the prisoners shall not be at liberty to pass over the line of the town, where they are respectively stationed, without a pass from the selectmen of such town, after they have arrived therein.

Further *Resolved*, That a copy of the foregoing, so far as relates to each town, be by them carried to the selectmen of such town, and that each of the above named persons be informed, that any attempt to make an escape, or evade the execution of the above resolve, shall be deemed full evidence of his being engaged in the service of the enemies of this country, and that he shall be treated as such.

Further *Resolved*, that each of the said persons be furnished with two days' provisions, to enable them to repair to the several places of

63

their destination; which provision shall be delivered to them by Captain Brown, out of the colony stores in this place.

Ordered, That the president, Mr. Phillips, and Col. Porter, Mr. Gerry, and Capt. Stone, be a committee to revise and explain the commission of the committee of safety.

Afternoon.

[The committee appointed to revise the commission of the committee of safety, reported. The report was accepted, and is as follows, viz.:]

Resolved, That the Hon. John Hancock, Esq., Doct. Benjamin Church, Capt. Benjamin White, Col. Joseph Palmer, Mr. Richard Devens, Mr. Abraham Watson, Col. Azor Orne, Hon. Benjamin Greenleaf, Esq., Nathan Cushing, Esq., Doct. Samuel Holten, and Hon. Enoch Freeman, Esq., be, and hereby are appointed a committee of safety for this colony, with the powers and authorities hereafter expressed, and no other, that is to say; that the said committee shall have full power, at any time during the recess of this Congress, if they shall judge it necessary, in the shortest and most effectual manner, to summon and cause to come together a quorum of this Congress, forty at the least to be accounted a quorum, at such place as the said committee shall judge most proper; and in assembling such quorum the said committee are hereby strictly enjoined to notify such members as may be most expeditiously assembled. Also, that the said committee be, and they hereby are invested with full power, until the thirtieth day of July instant, or until their commission shall be abrogated by the representative body of the inhabitants of this colony, upon application made to them therefor, by the general and commander in chief of the continental army in this colony, for the time being, or whenever the said committee, without such application, shall judge the safety of the lives and property of the inhabitants of this colony, or of any of them, shall absolutely require it, to warn, and cause to be assembled, such and so many of the militia thereof, as they shall judge necessary, at such place or places within the colony as they shall judge proper, and such militia to retain and discharge as to the said committee shall seem meet. Also, that the said committee are hereby empowered, during the time last mentioned, to procure, and employ for that part of the said continental army raised by this colony, all such armorers and other tradesmen and artificers, as they shall suppose and judge to be needed, to further and promote the operations of the said army, and them, as also all such tradesmen and artificers as are now retained, and employed for that part of the said army, to regulate, arrange, remove, dismiss, and discharge, for unskilfulness, unfaithfulness, or whenever the service may not require the further retaining them, or any of them. And the said committee are hereby desired to be attentive to the behavior and performances of such tradesmen and artificers as are now, or shall be in the service and employ of this colony in the said army, that the colony be not defrauded by unfaithful, and incompetent persons.

And the said committee are hereby authorized to execute all the commissions, and perform all the services which have been given them, and to which they have been appointed in and by any special resolves of this Congress, made and passed at this session, which they have not yet executed and performed.

And furthermore, the said committee are hereby empowered to make such further provision for the reception, sustenance, and support of the poor of Boston and Charlestown as have, or may come out of said towns, as may appear to be necessary for their comfortable subsistence, according to the intention of Congress, taking all imaginable care to guard against the infection of the small pox, by persons coming out of the town of Boston, and any other means whatever.

And it is hereby *Resolved*, and *Ordered*, that any five of said committee, if a majority are not present, be a quorum, with full powers to act in the same manner as if the whole were present. And the whole of said committee are desired, notwithstanding, to give their punctual, and constant attendance on said committee.

Resolved, That the said committee be, and they hereby are fully empowered, until the thirtieth of July instant, or until their commission shall be abrogated by the representative body of the inhabitants of this colony, to receive, examine, and discharge, or cause to be confined, according to their wisdom, any person or persons taken captive, that may properly come under the cognizance of the representative body of this people, and to receive, and duly secure, any interests, or effects, the conduct whereof is not already provided for, that shall be at the disposal of this colony. And all the powers with which the committee of safety were vested by the resolve of the eighteenth of May last, except such as are contained in the above resolves, are hereby revoked, and declared null and void.

Ordered, That Major Fuller of Newton, Col. Farley, Mr. Crane, Capt. Stone, and Major Fuller, be a committee to examine the prisoners brought from Machias, and report what is best to be done with them.

Ordered, That Col. Mosely, Mr. Woodbridge, and Mr. Kollock, be a committee to consider Lieut. Ely Styles' [account of the] expense of bringing ten prisoners from Machias.

The committee last mentioned, having attended the service to which they were appointed, reported the following resolve, which was accepted, viz.:

Resolved, That the receiver general be, and he is hereby directed to pay Lieut. Ely Styles the sum of six pounds twelve shillings, in full discharge of the money he expended in bringing a number of prisoners from Machias to Watertown.

The committee appointed to consider what is best to be done with the ten prisoners brought from Machias, reported: whereupon, *Resolved*, that the commanding officer of the town of Watertown be desired to appoint some officer, with a guard of not more than eight men, to conduct the said prisoners to the jail in Worcester, tomorrow morning: that Captain Crafts be desired to take care of the said prisoners, till that time; and that the officer who may be appointed to conduct said prisoners to Worcester, be empowered to draw on Capt. Brown, the commissary in this town, for so much provisions as may be necessary for their support to Worcester; and Capt. Brown is directed to supply them accordingly.

The report above mentioned was [reconsidered, amended, and] accepted, as follows, viz.:

Resolved, That Thomas Skinner, a seaman, William Nurse, a marine, John Burrows, a seaman, Nicholas Durham, a marine, Peter Larcher, a sailor, Thomas Crispo, Joseph Temple, sailors, William Bishop, a sailor, and John Pardra, a marine, prisoners, all taken on board the armed schooner, called the Margaretta, commanded by Matthew Moor, near Machias, be all sent under a proper guard to the common jail in the county of Worcester, and the jail keeper is hereby directed to receive them therein, and provide for them, and detain them there till the further order of this Congress or [the] House of Representatives of this colony.

Ordered, That Mr. Phillips be appointed to acquaint General Washington with the proceedings of this Congress, with regard to Daniel Green, lately conveyed to Concord jail, and the reasons thereof; and desire his excellency to take such further order concerning him as his wisdom may direct.

Ordered, That the president, Mr. Gill, and Mr. Gerry, be a committee to return the thanks of this Congress to the Rev. Mr. Gordon, for his attendance and acceptable services to this Congress as their chaplain.

Ordered, That the president, Mr. Gill, and Mr. Gerry, be a committee to return the thanks of this Congress to the proprietors of the meeting-house for the use of it, during the session of this Congress.

Ordered, That the present president, (Col. Lincoln,) Mr. Gill, and Mr. Gerry, be a committee to return the thanks of this Congress to the Hon. James Warren, Esq., for his faithful services as president of the Congress.

Resolved, That the committee of supplies be, and hereby are directed, on application made by any of the inhabitants of the eastern parts of the colony, to grant them such relief, out of the public stores, as they may think proper, consistent with the general interest, during the recess of the Congress.

Whereas, the Hon. Jedediah Preble, and the Hon. Enoch Freeman, Esq., have employed some persons to build a number of whale-boats for the service of the public, therefore, *Resolved,* that the committee of supplies be, and hereby are directed, to deliver to Capt. Briant Morton, or order, to be by said Morton delivered to said Preble and Freeman, such a quantity of nails and provisions as they think will be necessary to complete the building said boats.

The Congress then adjourned to Wednesday next, at eight o'clock, A. M.

WEDNESDAY, JULY 19, 1775.

Col. Easton being admitted, requested that a committee be appointed to consider the necessity of drawing on the treasury for the sum of twelve hundred pounds, said to be due to his regiment at Ticonderoga.

On a motion made, *Ordered,* that Deacon Fisher, Doct. Taylor, and Mr. Gill, be a committee for that purpose, and that they be directed, in case they cannot report to this Congress, to make report to the next House of Representatives.

On a motion made and seconded, that the Congress be dissolved, the question was put, and it passed in the affirmative.

The Congress was accordingly dissolved.

SAMUEL FREEMAN, *Secretary.*

JOURNALS

OF

THE COMMITTEE OF SAFETY

AND OF

THE COMMITTEE OF SUPPLIES

OF

THE PROVINCIAL CONGRESS

OF

𝕸𝖆𝖘𝖘𝖆𝖈𝖍𝖚𝖘𝖊𝖙𝖙𝖘.

1774—1775.

JOURNAL.

NOVEMBER 2, 1774.

At a meeting of the committee of safety, at the house of Capt. Stedman, in Cambridge, November 2, 1774, Wednesday :

Present—Hon. John Hancock, Esq., chairman, Col. Orne, Mr. Watson, Col. Palmer, Mr. Devens, Capt. Heath, Doct. Warren, Doct. Church, Capt. White, John Pigeon :

Voted, That John Pigeon be clerk of this committee.

Voted, That it be recommended to the committee of supplies, to procure, as soon as may be, 355 barrels of pork, 700 barrels of flour, 20 tierces of rice, 300 bushels of pease ; and that there be deposited of them, in Worcester, 200 barrels of pork, 400 barrels of flour, 150 bushels of pease ; and, at Concord, 155 barrels of pork, 300 barrels of flour, 50 tierces of rice, and 150 bushels of pease.

Adjourned to meet next Tuesday, ten o'clock, at Capt. Stedman's.

NOVEMBER 8, 1774.

At a meeting of the committees of safety and of supplies at the house of Capt. Stedman, Tuesday the 8th of November, 1774 :

Present—Doct. Warren, Doct. Church, Capt. White, Capt. Heath, Mr. Devens, Col. Palmer, Mr. Watson, J. Pigeon, *committee of safety :* Col. Lee, Deacon Cheever, Mr. Gill, Mr. Hall, Col. Lincoln, *committee of supplies :*

Voted, unanimously, by the committee of safety, that the committee of supplies be advised to procure all the arms and ammunition they can, at the neighboring provinces on the continent ; and, that it is recommended, that the committee of supplies do, and may with safety, engage to pay for the same, on the arrival here of said arms and ammunition.

Voted, That the committees adjourn to Mrs. Whittemore's, in Charlestown, to meet next Tuesday, at ten o'clock.

64

NOVEMBER 15, 1774.

At a meeting of the committees of safety and supplies, at Mrs. Whittemore's, in Charlestown, on Tuesday, 15th November, 1774:

Present—Doct. Warren, Doct. Church, Col. Palmer, Mr. Devens, Mr. Watson, Col. Orne, Mr. White, J. Pigeon, *committee of safety:* Col. Lee, Col. Lincoln, Deacon Cheever, Mr. Gill, *committee of supplies:*

Voted, unanimously, that Mr. Gill be desired to apply to Mr. William Powell, to get seven large pieces of cannon, on the best terms he can; and, that said Gill and Mr. Benjamin Hall be desired to get them out of Boston to some place in the country, in such manner as they may think most prudent.

DECEMBER 20, 1774.

At a meeting of the committees of safety and supplies, at the house of Mrs. Whittemore, of Charlestown, on Tuesday, the 20th of December, 1774:

Present—John Hancock, Esq., Col. Orne, Col. Heath, Capt. White, Doct. Church, Doct. Warren, Mr. Watson, Col. Palmer, J. Pigeon, *committee of safety:* Col. Lee, Deacon Cheever, Mr. Gill, Mr. Hall, *committee of supplies:*

Voted, That the committee of supplies endeavor to procure the following articles, viz.: 200 spades, 150 iron shovels, 150 pick-axes, 1000 six quart iron pots, 200 bill hooks, 1000 wooden mess bowls, 1 tenant saw, sieves, cartridge paper, tin cases, tubes, drills, hand mallets, drawing knives, gunner's quadrants, and fuses, as much as they think necessary of each of those articles, to which the quantity is not annexed.

Voted, unanimously, that Doct. Warren, Doct. Church, and the Hon. John Hancock, Esq., be a committee to inspect the commissaries' stores, in Boston, and report what surgeon's stores and stores of other kind are there.

Voted, unanimously, that the Hon. John Hancock, Esq., Doct. Warren, and Mr. Gill, be a committee to write a letter to Henry Gardner, Esq., directing him to draft a letter to the collectors and constables, requesting them to make immediate payments of the taxes for 1773 and 1774, and all other province money in their hands.

Voted, That the committees adjourn to meet next Wednesday, at eleven o'clock, at Mrs. Whittemore's, in Charlestown.

JANUARY 5, 1775.

At a meeting of the committees of safety and supplies, at the house of Mrs. Whittemore, of Charlestown, on Thursday, the 5th of January, 1775 :

Present—John Hancock, Esq., Doct. Warren, Mr. Watson, Col. Heath, J. Pigeon, *committee of safety :* Col. Lee, Mr. Gill, Deacon Cheever, Mr. Hall, Col. Lincoln, *committee of supplies :*

Voted, That the last vote at the meeting on the 20th ultimo, wherein a committee was appointed to write a letter to Henry Gardner, Esq., directing him to write to the collectors and constables, requesting immediate payment of the taxes for 1773 and 1774, and all other province debts, be reconsidered, which was done, and, *Voted,* that it subside, and that said Gardner receive the taxes, &c., when brought to him.

Voted, That Doct. Warren be desired to wait on Col. Robinson, to desire him to deliver to any person Deacon Cheever shall send, two brass cannon, and two seven inch mortars and beds, and, that Mr. William Dawes be desired to deliver to said Cheever, one pair of brass cannon, and, that the said Cheever procure carriages for said cannon, or any other cannon that require them; that the battering cannon carriages be carried to the cannon at Waltham, and, that the cannon and carriages remain there till further orders.

Voted, That the committees adjourn, and meet at this place on the last Wednesday in this month, eleven o'clock, but if stormy, the next fair day.

JANUARY 25, 1775.

At a meeting of the committees of safety and supplies, at the house of Mrs. Whittemore, of Charlestown, on Wednesday, the 25th of January, 1775 :

Present—Doct. Warren, Mr. Watson, Deacon Palmer, Mr. Devens, Capt. White, Col. Orne, J. Pigeon, *committee of safety :* Mr. Gill, Deacon Cheever, Mr. Hall, Col. Lincoln, *committee of supplies :*

Voted, That all the cannon, mortars, cannon balls and shells, be deposited at the towns of Worcester and Concord, in the same proportion as the provisions are to be deposited.

Voted, unanimously, that two ten inch mortars be provided, and also, two howitzers be provided, together with a suitable quantity of shells, by the committee of supplies.

Voted, unanimously, that the committee of supplies endeavor to procure the following articles, viz. :   200 axes handled and ground complete, 50 wheelbarrows.

Voted, unanimously, that Deacon Cheever settle the account with Mrs. Whittemore, for charges of entertainment at her house, pay the same, and exhibit his account to the next Congress.

Voted, That the two committees adjourn, and meet next Friday week, at one o'clock, at Capt. Stedman's, of Cambridge, and dine together, and, that Mr. Watson bespeak a dinner and room.

FEBRUARY 3, 1775.

At a meeting of the committee of safety and committee of supplies, at the house of Capt. Ebenezer Stedman, on Friday, the 3d of February :

Present—The Hon. John Hancock, Mr. Watson, Col. Palmer, Capt. White, Col. Orne, Col. Heath, Mr. Devens, *committee of safety :* Col. Lee, Col. Lincoln, Deacon Cheever, Mr. Gill, and Mr. Hall, *committee of supplies :*

Voted, unanimously, that the six pounders that were formerly voted to be procured, be passed by.

Voted, unanimously, that the two pieces of brass cannon in the care of Capt. Robinson, and the two pieces of [cannon] that were taken out of Boston, be included in the sixteen that were voted.

Voted, unanimously, that the chairman of [the committee of] supplies be directed to report to the Congress their transactions, since their appointment, and, that this report be made to-morrow forenoon.[1]

FEBRUARY 13, 1775.

At a meeting of the committee of safety and the committee of supplies, at Capt. Stedman's, at Cambridge, on Monday, February 13, 1775 :

Present—Hon. John Hancock, Mr. Palmer, Deacon Fisher, Capt. White, Mr. Watson, Col. Heath, Mr. Devens, of the *committee of safety :* Col. Lincoln, Mr. Gill, Elbridge Gerry, of the *committee of supplies :*

Voted, That the committee of supplies be desired to purchase all the powder they can, upon the best terms they can.

Voted, That Capt. White and Col. Lincoln, be a committee to wait on Col. Robinson, and receive from him the four brass field pieces, and three brass mortars, now in his hands, the property of the province, and as soon as may be, remove them to the town of Concord,

(1) The records of this meeting, and of that held February 13, are subscribed by Richard Devens, as clerk *pro tempore.*

and they are to inform him that the committee agree, in case of a rupture with the troops, that the said field pieces shall be for the use of the artillery companies in Boston and Dorchester, and if matters are settled without, said field pieces are to be returned to said Robinson.

FEBRUARY 21, 1775.

At a meeting of the committee of safety, and committee of supplies, at the house of Capt. Nathan Adams, in Charlestown, Tuesday, February 21, 1775:

Present—Hon. John. Hancock, Doct. Joseph Warren, Doct. Church, Mr. Watson, Col. Heath, Mr. Devens, Col. Orne, *committee of safety :* Mr. Gill, Mr. Cheever, Mr. Gerry and Col. Lincoln, *committee of supplies :*

Voted, unanimously, by both committees, that the committee of supplies do procure ten tons of brimstone, provided, it can be had on this condition ; that the committee of supplies engage to pay therefor, when the present owner shall have opportunity to sell the same, or that it shall be returned in six months if not used, and if used, that it shall then be paid for.

Voted, unanimously, by the committee of safety, that the committee of supplies purchase all kinds of warlike stores, sufficient for an army of fifteen thousand men to take the field.

Voted, unanimously, that the powder that is now at Concord be removed to Leicester.

Voted, unanimously, that the committee of supplies get fifteen thousand canteens.

Voted, That Docts. Warren and Church be a committee to bring in an inventory of what is necessary in the way of their profession, for the above army to take the field.

Voted, That these committees adjourn to to-morrow morning, at nine o'clock, in this place.

FEBRUARY 22, 1775.

At a meeting of the committee of safety, and the committee of supplies, Wednesday morning, February 22, 1775:

Present—Hon. John Hancock, Col. Orne, Col. Heath, Capt. White, Mr. Watson, Mr. Devens, Mr. Pigeon, Doct. Warren and Doct. Church, *committee of safety :* Col. Lincoln, Mr. Cheever, Mr. Gerry and Mr. Gill, of the *committee of supplies :*

Voted, That the committee of supplies procure one hundred bell tents, for arms.

Voted, That the committee of supplies procure one thousand field tents complete, for the soldiers.

Voted, That the committee of supplies procure ten tons of lead balls, in addition to what were formerly voted.

Voted, That said committee employ a number of men to make cartridges for fifteen thousand men, for thirty rounds.

Voted, That said committee purchase three hundred bushels of beans or peas, more than formerly ordered. Also, that they purchase twenty hogsheads of molasses: also, 150 quintals of salt fish: also, two carpenters' chests of tools complete.

Voted, That Mr. John Pigeon be the commissary of stores.

Voted, That Mr. Abraham Watson, on the arrival of more troops, take possession of the province arms, now at the college, and send them to Worcester.

Voted, That the province arms, now at Boston and Roxbury, be removed by Moses Gill, Esq., to Worcester.

Voted, unanimously, by both committees, that, on certain intelligence, or such as appears to the committee to be such, of the arrival of the reenforcements coming to General Gage, that then the committee appointed to assemble the Congress, be desired to despatch couriers to assemble the Congress immediately.

Voted, That the committees adjourn to this place, to meet to-morrow morning, at forty-five minutes after 7 o'clock: and that when the committees meet to transact business after the arrival of the reenforcements to General Gage, it be at Capt. Stedman's at Cambridge.

FEBRUARY 23, 1775.

At a meeting of the committee of safety and the committee of supplies, February 23, 1775:

Present—Hon. John Hancock, Col. Orne, Capt. White, Doct. Church, Mr. Devens, Mr. Watson, Doct. Warren, Mr. Pigeon, *committee of safety:* Col Lincoln, Mr. Gerry, Mr. Cheever and Mr. Gill, *committee of supplies:*

Voted, That Doct. Church, Mr. Gerry and John Pigeon, be a committee to draft a letter to the commanding officers of the militia, and the commanding officers of the minute men through the province, to assemble one fourth part of the militia through the province on receipt of this letter.

Voted, That one hundred of each of the letters be printed, and two hundred of the resolves of Congress, relating to the committee of safety assembling the militia.

Voted, That Moses Gill, Esq., and Doct. Church, be a committee to draft a letter to each member of Congress, to require his attendance directly on receipt of said letters.

Voted, by the two committees, that the following colonels have each two field pieces put into their hands, by the committee of supplies, viz. : Col. Gardner of Cambridge, Col. Mitchel of Bridgewater, Col. Warren of Plymouth, Col. Heath of Roxbury, Col. Ward of Shrewsbury, Col. Foster of Brookfield, Col. Robinson of Dorchester, and two for the use of the artillery company of Boston, lately commanded by Major Paddock.

Voted, That Mr. Gerry and Doct. Church, be a committee to draft a letter to the above colonels, relative to the above cannon.

Voted, That the committee of supplies purchase twenty hogsheads of rum, and send them to Concord.

Voted, That Doct. Warren be desired to apply to the company formerly under the command of Major Paddock, and know how many of them may be depended on, officers and men, to form an artillery company, when the constitutional army of the province shall take the field, and that report be made without loss of time.

Voted, That Mr. Cheever and Mr. Devens procure couriers to carry letters to the several colonels who are appointed to have the care of the sixteen field pieces, and get an answer, and bring to the committee of supplies.

Voted, That Cols. Gardner and Heath be desired to procure, by borrowing, field pieces to learn their companies the exercise of them.

FEBRUARY 24, 1775.

At a meeting of the committee of safety, and the committee of supplies, February 24, 1775 :

Present—Hon. John Hancock, Col. Orne, Mr. Devens, Capt. White, Mr. Watson, J. Pigeon, Doct. Warren, Col. Heath, *committee of safety :* Col. Lincoln, David Cheever, Esq., Mr. Gerry and Mr. Gill, *committee of supplies :*

Voted, That what artillery companies are formed in the regiments, shall consist of thirty-two privates.

Voted, That the committee of supplies procure the following articles, and send the same to Concord, viz. : 1000 candles; 100 hhds. salt; a suitable supply of wooden spoons; 20 casks of raisins; 20 bushels of oatmeal; 1500 yards Russia linen; also 2 barrels Lisbon oil; 6 casks of Malaga wine, and 9 casks of Lisbon wine, to be lodged at Stow.

Voted, That Doct. Warren, Doct. Church, Mr. Gerry, Mr. Cheever, Col. Orne and Mr. Devens, make inquiry where fifteen doctor's chests can be got, and on what terms, and report at the next meeting.

Voted, unanimously, that the clerk of the committee of safety, in behalf of said committee, sign the letters to Col. Warren, Col. Ward, Col. Mitchell and Col. Foster, relating to two pieces of cannon to be put under the care of each of those gentlemen.

Voted, unanimously, that Mr. John Goddard, of Brookline, be waggon master for the army, and that Capt. White inform him of his choice by the province.

Voted, That Mr. Pigeon, Capt. White and Mr. Watson, be a committee to consider how many couriers shall be chosen to go to the several colonels through the province for returns of militia men, and the minute men, and report what road each courier shall go.

Voted, That eight field pieces, with the shot and cartridges, and two brass mortars with their bombs, be deposited at Leicester, with Col. Henshaw.

Voted, That these committees adjourn to Tuesday, the 7th of March, [to meet] at the house of Capt. Stedman of Cambridge, at ten o'clock.

MARCH 7, 1775.

At a meeting of the committee of safety, and the committee of supplies, at the house of Capt. Stedman of Cambridge, on Tuesday, the 7th of March, 1775 :

Present—Hon. John Hancock, Doct. Church, Doct. Warren, Mr. Watson, Mr. Palmer, Capt. White, Mr. Devens, Col. Heath, Mr. Pigeon, Mr. Adams, Hon. Thomas Cushing, Esq., *committee of safety :* Col. Lee, Mr. Gill, Deacon Cheever, Col. Lincoln, *committee of supplies :*

Voted, That the committee of supplies be directed to make a draft on Henry Gardner, Esq., the receiver general, in favor of Doct. Joseph Warren and Doct. Benjamin Church, for five hundred pounds. lawful money, to enable them to purchase such articles for the provincial chests of medicine as cannot be got on credit, to be deducted from the provincial tax payable by the town of Boston.

Voted, That what the seven hundred barrels of flour formerly voted, fall short of two hundred weight each, be made up to the quantity of fourteen hundred weight of flour.

Voted, That the committees adjourn, to meet at Capt. Stedman's in Cambridge, at nine o'clock on Tuesday next.

MARCH 14, 1775.

At a meeting of the committees of safety and supplies, at the house of Capt. Stedman, Tuesday, 14th March, 1775:

Present—Hon. John Hancock, Col. Heath, Capt. White, Col. Palmer, Mr. Devens, Col. Orne, Mr. Watson, Mr. Pigeon, Hon. Thomas Cushing and Mr. Samuel Adams, *committee of safety:* Deacon Cheever, Mr. Gerry and Mr. Gill, *committee of supplies:*

Voted, That watches be kept constantly at places where the provincial magazines are kept, and that the clerk write on the subject to Col. Barrett of Concord, Henry Gardner, Esq. of Stow, and Capt. Timothy Bigelow of Worcester, leaving it to them how many the watches shall consist of.

Voted, That the members on these committees, belonging to the towns of Charlestown, Cambridge and Roxbury, be desired, at the province expense, to procure at least two men for a watch every night, to be placed in each of those towns, and that said members be in readiness to send couriers forward to the towns where the magazines are placed, when sallies are made from the army by night.[1]

Voted, That the committees adjourn to [meet on] the 22d of this month, at Concord.

MARCH 23, 1775.

At a meeting of the committees of safety and supplies, at the house of Mr. Taylor, at Concord, the 23d March, 1775:

Present—Hon. John Hancock, Esq., Col. Orne, Col. Heath, Capt. White, Deacon Palmer, Mr. Watson, Mr. Devens, Mr. Pigeon, *committee of safety:* Deacon Cheever, Col. Lincoln, Col. Lee, Mr. Gerry, Mr. Gill, *committee of supplies:*

Voted, That a ton of musket bullets now arrived at Concord, be there lodged with Col. Barrett.[2]

---

(1) On the fifteenth of March, the committees directed Col. Barrett of Concord, to engage a sufficient number of faithful men to guard the colony magazines in that town, to keep a suitable number of teams in constant readiness, by day and night, on the shortest notice, to remove the stores, and to provide couriers to alarm the neighboring towns, on receiving information of any movements of the British troops.

(2) The following letter from Plymouth is preserved on the files of the committees:

" PLYMOUTH, MARCH 27, 1775."

" The selectmen and committee of correspondence of the town of Plymouth, beg leave to represent the peculiar circumstances of this town, and to desire such aid and protection as you, in your wisdom, shall think proper to direct. We have an open harbor, on which lie the towns of Plymouth, Kingston and Duxborough, extending twelve or thirteen miles, in almost every part of where it is extremely easy for troops to land, commit ravages, and retreat, unless a sufficient force is continually on duty to watch and repel them. Ever since the late alarm, the inhabitants of this

APRIL 1, 1775.

At a meeting of the committee of safety, at Concord, April 1, 1775, *Voted*, that the stores at Concord, and elsewhere, shall not be removed without written orders from the committee of safety.

APRIL 5, 1775.

At a meeting of the committee of safety, at the house of Mr. Taylor, of Concord, on Wednesday, April 5, 1775 :

Present—Hon. John Hancock, Esq., Col. Palmer, Col. Heath, Capt. White, Mr. Watson, J. Pigeon, Mr. Devens :

Voted, unanimously, that the committee of supplies do directly furnish this committee with an exact account, in writing, of all the provisions and stores, and the places of their disposition.

Voted, That one piece of cannon be sent to Col. Mitchell of Bridgwater.

APRIL 14, 1775.

At a meeting of the committee of safety at Concord, at the house of Mr. Taylor, on Saturday, April 14, 1775 :

Present—Hon. John Hancock. Esq., Col. Heath, Capt. White, Mr. Devens, Col. Gardner, Mr. Watson, Mr. Palmer :

Voted, That the cannon now in the town of Concord, be immediately disposed of within said town, as the committee of supplies may direct.

Voted, That the cannon powder now at Leicester be removed, one load at a time, to this town, and made into cartridges, under the direction of the committee of supplies.

N. B. Mr. Devens acted as clerk pro tempore. Col. Gardner this day was chosen as one of the committee of safety, instead of Deacon Fisher, who resigned, in consequence of the distance he lives.

town, apprehensive of danger, have been on almost constant duty, without being able to attend to their private affairs : the consequence of which must produce great distress, if not ruin, unless they can be relieved. Another very peculiar circumstance attending us is, that in case we should be attacked, no immediate aid can come to our assistance from the back country, we being surrounded by a wilderness, extending several miles, without any inhabitants at all, and several more miles with very few and scattering ones. We, therefore, pray your consideration of these matters, and that you would order the minute regiment under the command of Col. Cotton, to be posted here, and that proper provision be made for them."

    " We are, gentlemen, with great respect,"

        " Your very humble servants,"

            "JOHN TORREY, *Chairman, per order of*
                the committee and selectmen of the town of Plymouth."

" *To the honorable the committee of safety for the province of the*
    Massachusetts Bay, now sitting at Cambridge or elsewhere."

APRIL 17, 1775.

At a meeting of the committees of safety and supplies, at Mr. Taylor's house, in Concord, on Monday, April 17, 1775 :

Present—Hon. John Hancock, Esq., Col. Heath, Col. Palmer, Capt. White, Mr. Devens, Col. Gardner, Mr. Watson, Col. Orne and J. Pigeon, *committee of safety :* Col. Lee, Mr. Gill, Mr. Cheever, Mr. Gerry and Col. Lincoln. *committee of supplies :*

Voted, unanimously, that application be made to Capt. Hatch, for captain of the artillery company for Boston, and if he refuses, to offer it to Mr. Crafts, and so on in order as they stand in the company ; also, that Capt. Robinson of Dorchester be applied to as captain of the company of Dorchester ; and that Mr. Newhall of Charlestown be applied to ; that the captain for the Marblehead company be not appointed until the Marblehead members make inquiry and report; that Capt. Timothy Bigelow be applied to as captain of the Worcester company ; that Mr. Thomas Wait Foster of Hadley, be applied to as captain of the company at Hadley.

Voted, That two four pounders, now at Concord, be mounted by the committee of supplies, and that Col. Barrett be desired to raise an artillery company, to join the army when raised, they to have no pay until they join the army; and also that an instructer for the use of the cannon be appointed, to be put directly in pay.

Voted, unanimously, that six pounds, lawful money, a month, be a captain's pay in an artillery company, that the first and second lieutenant have four pounds, the lieutenant of fireworks to have three pounds, five shillings, that the sergeants have forty-two shillings per month ; the corporals thirty-eight shillings per month, the common men thirty-six shillings per month, the drummers and fifers thirty-eight shillings per month ; also, that four shillings per week be allowed for their board.

Voted, That when these committees adjourn, it be to Mr. Wetherby's, at the Black Horse, Menotomy, on Wednesday, at ten o'clock.

Voted, That the four six pounders be transported to Groton, and put under the care of Col. Prescott.

Voted, That two seven inch brass mortars be transported to Acton.

Voted, That the two committees adjourn to Mr. Wetherby's, at Menotomy, [at] ten o'clock.

APRIL 18, 1775.

At a meeting of the committees of safety and supplies, on Tuesday, the 18th of April, 1775 :

Present—Col. Orne, Col. Palmer, Col. Heath, Col. Gardner, Mr.

Devens, Mr. Watson, Capt. White, J. Pigeon, *committee of safety :*
David Cheever, Esq., Mr. Gerry, Col. Lee, Col. Lincoln, *committee of
supplies :*

Voted, That the two brass two pounders, and two brass three pounders, be under the care of the Boston company of artillery, and of Capt.
Robinson's [company.]

[The following letter was sent to Capt. Timothy Bigelow.]

NEWTON, APRIL 17, 1775.

Capt. Timothy Bigelow :

SIR :—The committee desired me to write you, to desire the favor
of your company, next Wednesday, the 19th instant, at Mr. Wetherby's, at the Black Horse, in Menotomy, on business of great importance.

Sir, your most humble servant,

J. PIGEON, *Clerk.*

P. S. The committee meet at ten o'clock.

Voted, That all the ammunition be deposited in nine different towns
in this province; that Worcester be one of them; that Lancaster be
one, (N. B. Col. Whitcomb is there;) that Concord be one; and, that
Groton, Stoughtonham, Stow, Mendon, Leicester, and Sudbury, be the
others.[1]

Voted, That part of the provisions be removed from Concord, viz. :
50 barrels of beef, from thence to Sudbury, with Deacon Plympton;
100 barrels of flour, of which what is in the malt-house in Concord be
part; 20 casks of rice; 15 hogsheads of molasses; 10 hogsheads of
rum; 500 candles.

Voted, That there be, by the committee of supplies, provided, six
ammunition carts, one to be in each town where a company of matrosses is fixed.

Voted, That one company of matrosses be stationed at Worcester;
one at Concord; one at Stoughtonham; one at Stoughton; one at
Stow; and, one at Lancaster.[2]

Voted, That thirty-three rounds of round shot, thirty-three rounds of
grape shot, and, thirty-three canisters of langrage, be provided and
lodged with each of the twelve field pieces belonging to the province,

(1) In the original journal the words " be another," are added to the name of each town.

(2) The word " ditto" is inserted in the original, before the place designated for the station of the
company.

together with one hundred cartridges of powder, one hundred and sixteen tubes, one hundred wads, together with all necessary materials.

Voted, That the towns of Worcester, Concord, Stow, and Lancaster, be provided with two iron three pound cannon each.

Voted, That four hundred and fifty four-pound-cannon ball be carried from Stoughtonham to Sudbury.

Voted, That one ton of grape shot be carried from Stoughtonham to
Sudbury.

Voted, That one ton of three pound cannon ball be carried from
ditto to ditto.

Voted, That one half of the two pound cannon ball, now at Stoughtonham, exclusive of what is for the use of the matrosses, be carried to
Sudbury.

Voted, That the vote of the fourteenth instant, relating to the powder being removed from Leicester to Concord, be reconsidered, and,
that the clerk be directed to write to Col. Barrett, accordingly, and to
desire he would not proceed in making it up in cartridges.

Voted, That one half of the musket cartridges be removed from Stow
to Groton.

Voted, That the muskets balls under the care of Col. Barrett, be
buried under ground, in some safe place, that he be desired to do it,
and to let the commissary only be informed thereof.

Voted, That the spades, pick-axes, bill-hooks, shovels, axes, hatchets, crows, and wheelbarrows, now at Concord, be divided, and one
third remain in Concord, one third at Sudbury, and one third at Stow.

Voted, That five hundred iron pots be deposited at Sudbury, five
hundred at Concord, and one thousand at Worcester.

Voted, That the two thousand wooden bowls be deposited [in those
towns in the same proportion] as the pots; and the spoons in the same
manner.

Voted, That the fifteen thousand canteens be deposited [in the same
manner]as the above.

Voted, That the weights and measures be put into the commissary's
hands.

Voted, That two medicinal chests still remain at Concord, at two different parts of the town; three of said chests at Sudbury, in different
parts of the town; six do. at Groton, Mendon, and Stow, two in each
town, and in different places; two ditto in Worcester, one in each part
of the town; and, two in Lancaster, ditto; that sixteen hundred yards
of Russia linen be deposited in seven parts, with the doctor's chests;

that the eleven hundred tents be deposited in equal parts in Worcester, Lancaster, Groton, Stow, Mendon, Leicester, and Sudbury.

Voted, That these committees adjourn to nine o'clock instead of ten.

Voted, That the papers belonging to the committees be lodged with Mr. Abraham Watson.

[The following letter was sent to Col. Barrett :]

NEWTON, APRIL 19, 1775.

Col. Barrett ;

SIR :—The committee have directed me to inform you, that the cannon powder, which last Saturday you were desired to have removed from Leicester, one load at a time, and to make up into cartridges, they would not have you send for, unless you have already ; but, if sent for, take care of it ; but do'nt make it into cartridges.

I am, Sir, your humble servant,

J. PIGEON, *Clerk.*

[APRIL 20, 1775.]

[The following circular letter was sent to the several towns :]

[GENTLEMEN :—The barbarous murders committed upon our innocent brethren, on Wednesday, the 19th instant, have made it absolutely necessary, that we immediately raise an army to defend our wives and children from the butchering hands of an inhuman soldiery, who, incensed at the obstacles they meet with in their bloody progress, and enraged at being repulsed from the field of slaughter, will, without the least doubt, take the first opportunity in their power, to ravage this devoted county with fire and sword. We conjure you, therefore, by all that is sacred, that you give assistance in forming an army. Our all is at stake. Death and devastation are the certain consequences of delay. Every moment is infinitely precious. An hour lost may deluge your country in blood, and entail perpetual slavery upon the few of our posterity who may survive the carnage. We beg and entreat, as you will answer to your country, to your own consciences, and above all, as you will answer to GOD himself, that you will hasten and encourage by all possible means, the enlistment of men to form the army, and send them forward to head quarters at Cambridge, with that expedition, which the vast importance and instant urgency of the affair demands.][1]

(1) The following letter was addressed by the committee of safety to the governments of the colonies of New Hampshire and Connecticut.

"CAMBRIDGE, APRIL 20, 1775."

" On Wednesday, the 19th instant, early in the morning, a detachment of General Gage's army

APRIL 21, 1775.

At a meeting of the committee of safety, April 21, 1775, [the following] form of enlistment [was adopted :]

I, A. B. do hereby solemnly engage and enlist myself as a soldier in the Massachusetts service, from the day of my enlistment to the last day of December next, unless the service should admit of a discharge

marched into the country to Lexington, about thirteen miles from Boston, where they met with a small party of minute men exercising, who had no intention of doing any injury to the regulars; but they fired upon our men, without any provocation ; killed eight of them the first onset ; then marched forward to Concord, where they destroyed the magazines and stores for a considerable time. Our people however, mustered, as soon as possible, and repulsed the troops, pursuing them quite down to Charlestown, until they reached a place called Bunker's Hill, although they received a very large reenforcement at Lexington from General Gage. As the troops have now commenced hostilities, we think it our duty to exert our utmost strength to save our country from absolute slavery. We pray your honors would afford us all the assistance in your power, and shall be glad that our brethren who come to our aid, may be supplied with military stores and provisions, as we have none of either more than is absolutely necessary for ourselves. We pray God to direct you to such measures as shall tend to the salvation of our common liberties.

Per order of the committee of safety."

A letter was addressed to General Gage, by Doct. Joseph Warren, of the same date, which follows :

"CAMBRIDGE, APRIL 20, 1775."

" SIR :—The unhappy situation into which this colony is thrown, gives the greatest uneasiness to every man who regards the welfare of the empire, or feels for the distresses of his fellow-men, but even now, much may be done to alleviate those misfortunes which cannot be entirely remedied, and I think it of the utmost importance to us, that our conduct be such as that the contending parties may entirely rely upon the honor and integrity of each other, for the punctual performance of any agreement that shall be made between them. Your excellency, I believe, knows very well the part I have taken in public affairs. I ever scorned disguise. I think I have done my duty ; some may think otherwise ; but be assured, Sir, as far as my influence goes, every thing which can reasonably be required of us to do, shall be done, and every thing promised shall be religiously performed. I should now be very glad to know from you, Sir, how many days you desire may be allowed for such as desire to remove to Boston, with their effects ; and what time you will allow the people in Boston for their removal. When I have received that information, I will repair to Congress, and hasten, as far as I am able, the issuing a proclamation. I beg leave to suggest, that the condition of admitting only thirty waggons at a time into the town, appears to me very inconvenient, and will prevent the good effects of a proclamation intended to be issued for encouraging all waggoners to assist in removing the effects from Boston with all possible speed. If your excellency will be pleased to take the matter into consideration, and favor me, as soon as may be, with an answer, it will lay me under a great obligation, as it so nearly concerns the welfare of my friends in Boston. I have many things which I wish to say to your excellency, and most sincerely wish I had broken through the formalities which I thought due to your rank, and freely have told you all I knew or thought of public affairs, and I must ever confess, whatever may be the event, that you generously gave me such opening, as I now think I ought to have embraced, but the true cause of my not doing it, was the knowledge I had of the vileness and treachery of many persons around you, who I supposed had gained your entire confidence.

I am, &c."

"JOSEPH WARREN."

His Excellency General Gage.

of a part or the whole sooner, which shall be at the discretion of the committee of safety; and, I hereby promise, to submit myself to all the orders and regulations of the army, and faithfully to observe and obey all such orders as I shall receive from any superior officer.

Resolved, That there be immediately enlisted out of the Massachusetts forces, eight thousand effective men, to be formed into companies to consist of a captain, one lieutenant, one ensign, four sergeants, one fifer, one drummer, and seventy rank and file; nine companies to form a regiment, to be commanded by a colonel, lieutenant colonel, and major; each regiment to be composed of men suitable for the service, which shall be determined by a muster master or muster masters to be appointed for that purpose; said officers and men to continue in the service of the province for the space of seven months from the time of enlistment, unless the safety of the province will admit of their being discharged sooner; the army to be under proper rules and regulations.

Voted, That the field pieces be removed from Newburyport, and deposited, for the present, in the hands of Capt. Dexter, of Malden.

Voted, that a courier be immediately despatched to Stoughton, to require the immediate attendance of Col. Richard Gridley, and his son Scarborough Gridley, upon this committee.

Voted, That a courier be sent to command the attendance of David Mason, now upon furlough in Salem.

Voted, That Mr. Mason be ordered to provide one field piece, with every implement necessary for action, and proceed forthwith to provide for the remainder, till the whole are in a thorough state of preparation, unless otherwise ordered: the cannon to be provided for are eight three-pounders, and three six-pounders.

Voted, That orders be given to Capt. Dexter to conceal the cannon committed to his care, which was accordingly done.

Voted, That the resolve above written be so far reconsidered, as that the companies, rank and file, consist of fifty men each, and that no further obligation be required of those companies who are adjudged to be firmly enlisted by their respective officers.

Voted, That an establishment be proposed for the troops at an early day after the meeting of Congress.

Ordered, That Mr. Pigeon, the commissary general, be directed to carry thirty-five barrels of pork, and an half barrel of hog's fat, from the town of Salem to the town of Cambridge, by virtue of an order from Mr. William Bond.

Voted, That the general officers be forthwith desired to make a return of such officers and soldiers as are already under sufficient engagements to serve in the Massachusetts army.

Voted, That the general officers be desired, with all possible speed, to give in a list of such officers as they shall judge duly qualified to serve as colonels, lieutenant colonels, and majors, for such a number of regiments as shall, with the officers and soldiers already engaged, make up an army of eight thousand men.

Voted, That Major Bigelow be applied to, to furnish a man and horse to attend the surgeons, and convey medicines agreeably to their directions.

APRIL 22, 1775.

Voted, That the commissary general be directed to have the stores belonging to the colony removed from all the sea port towns with all possible speed.

Voted, That Capt. Foster be ordered to take the care of the cannon and intrenching tools at Mr. Richardson's tavern.

Voted, That the commissary general be directed to inspect the intrenching tools, and, if any are out of order, to see them, with all possible speed, repaired.[1]

APRIL 24, 1775.

Resolved, That General Ward be desired, immediately, to direct all the field officers of the regiments of minute men now in Cambridge, to attend the committee of safety at their chamber at Mr. Steward Hasting's house.[2]

(1) Letter from the committee of safety to the committee of the inhabitants of Boston.

"CAMBRIDGE, APRIL 22, 1775."

"GENTLEMEN:—The committee of safety being informed, that General Gage has proposed a treaty with the inhabitants of the town of Boston, whereby he stipulates, that the women and children, with all their effects, shall have safe conduct without the garrison, and their men also, upon condition that the male inhabitants within the town, shall, on their part, solemnly engage, that they will not take up arms against the king's troops, within the town, should an attack be made from without. We cannot but esteem those conditions to be just and reasonable, and as the inhabitants are in danger of suffering from the want of provisions, which, in this time of general confusion, cannot be conveyed into the town, we are willing you shall enter into and faithfully keep the engagement aforementioned, said to be required of you, and to remove yourselves, and your women, children, and effects, as soon as may be."

"We are, &c."

(2) The committee forwarded the following letter to the Congress of New Hampshire:

"CAMBRIDGE, APRIL 24, 1775."

"Our friends from New Hampshire having shown their readiness to assist us in this day of distress, we therefore thought it best to give orders for enlisting such as were present in the service of

Resolved, That the inhabitants of Chelsea and Malden be, and hereby are, absolutely forbidden, to fire upon, or otherwise injure any seamen belonging to the navy under the command of Admiral Graves, unless fired upon by them, until the said inhabitants of Chelsea and Malden receive orders from this committee or the general of the provincial forces so to do.

APRIL 25, 1775.

Resolved, That the three cannon now at Marlborough, be brought to the town of Waltham, and mounted on the carriages prepared for them, till further orders.

Resolved, That Col Freeman, of Sandwich, be directed to take such a number of men as may be sufficient for the purpose, and secure the whale and such other boats at Cape Cod, as may be of use to this colony.

Resolved, That Col. Paul Dudley Sergeant, of New Hampshire, be desired, forthwith, to recommend ten persons belonging to the colony of New Hampshire, to receive beating orders for the enlistment of persons belonging to said colony, until they are discharged by this colony, or taken into the service of the colony of New Hampshire.

Resolved, That it be recommended to the Provincial Congress, to reduce the regiments so far, as that the companies consist of fifty-nine men, including officers ; and also, that they allow only two lieutenants to a company.

Resolved, That ———— ———— be ordered, with the troop of horse under his command, to proceed forward, as an escort to the honorable members of the Continental Congress on their way to Philadelphia, until they are met by an escort from the colony of Connecticut.

APRIL 26, 1775.

Voted, That an express be sent to General Preble, at Falmouth, desiring his attendance at Cambridge, as a general officer, or in his private capacity.

Ordered, That fifteen of the prisoners at Concord, be removed from thence to Worcester gaol immediately.

Upon a motion made, *Voted,* that the secretary of this committee

this colony, as many desired something may be done to hold them together, until the resolve of your Congress is known, when we are ready and desirous they should be discharged from us, and put under such command as you shall direct. Colonel Sergeant has been so kind as to afford his utmost assistance in concluding this matter."

" We are, &c. &c."

be directed and empowered to sign any papers or writings in behalf of this committee.

Voted, That Mr. Ephraim Jones, the gaol keeper of Worcester, be directed to receive fifteen prisoners from the gaol in Concord.

Voted, That this committee recommend it to the Provincial Congress, that they make an establishment for such a number of armorers as they may judge necessary for the forces belonging to this colony.

Resolved, That as many men as are not already enlisted, and incline to remain in the army, immediately enlist, in order that it may be ascertained what number may be still necessary to be raised in each town to complete the complement of troops for this colony, and to forward to each town their remaining quotas; and the men that may now enlist may be assured, that they shall have liberty to be under the command of such officers as may be appointed by the committee of safety, until the particular regiment and companies are completed; and the utmost care will be taken to make every soldier happy in being under good officers.

Resolved, That the resolve of the twenty-fourth instant, respecting the inhabitants of Chelsea and Malden, be reconsidered, and *Ordered,* that it be immediately remanded; also,

Resolved, That the inhabitants of Chelsea and Malden be hereby desired, to put themselves in the best state of defence, and exert the same in such manner, as under their circumstances, their judgments may direct.

APRIL 27, 1775.

Resolved, That Capt. Derby be directed, and he hereby is directed, to make for Dublin, or any good port in Ireland, and from thence to cross to Scotland or England, and hasten to London. This direction is, that so he may escape all cruisers that may be in the chops of the channel to stop the communicating of the provincial intelligence to the agent.

Voted, That it is the sense of this committee, that it would promote the service, if two majors were appointed to each of the general officers' regiments; and that it be recommended accordingly to the Provincial Congress.

A letter, dated twenty-sixth instant, was sent to the colony of Rhode Island, and another of the same tenor was sent to the colony of Connecticut, [which are as follow:]

[CAMBRIDGE, APRIL 26, 1775.]

[The distressed situation in which we are, and the dangers to which the liberties of all America, and especially the New England colonies are exposed, will be the best apology for our importunate application to you for immediate assistance. We pray, as you regard the safety of your country, that as large a number of troops as you can spare, may immediately march forward, well stocked with provisions and ammunition: that they come under proper officers, enlisted for such a time as may be necessary; and, that as large a train of artillery as can be procured be sent down to our aid. We rely greatly upon you, as we know the bravery of your men. Our men have behaved with the utmost resolution; but as many of them came from home without any preparation, it is impossible to keep them in the field without allowing many of them time to return to their families for one or two days, during which time, we may all, possibly, be cut off, as we have a powerful and watchful enemy to deal with. We are far from despairing. We firmly trust, that, by the blessing of Heaven on us, we shall deliver our country. We are determined, at all events, to act our part with firmness and intrepidity, knowing that slavery is far worse than death. We pray, that our sister Rhode Island would immediately put in for a share of honor in saving the liberties of America; as a moment lost may never be recalled. May God direct you and us at this important moment, on which the fate of us and posterity depends.]

[We are, gentlemen, with great affection and respect,

Your most obedient servants.]

Ordered, That Col. John Glover take such effectual methods for the prevention of such intelligence being carried on board the Lively, ship of war, Capt. Bishop commander, now lying in the harbor of Marblehead, or any other, as may have a tendency to injure the most important cause we are engaged in, and, that he take such effectual methods for carrying this order into execution, as shall appear best calculated to effect this purpose.[1]

(1) The following letters were forwarded by the committee to the selectmen of Boston:

"CAMBRIDGE, APRIL 27, 1775."

" It is here currently reported, that General Gage gives out publicly, that the provincials fired upon his detachment before the troops fired upon the provincials. Such a report occasions astonishment and resentment, as there is the clearest evidence, not only that the troops fired first at Lexington and killed eight men there, before our people fired one gun, but then marched several miles further to Concord, and killed two men and wounded several others, before one gun was fired in that place by our men. He is a man, we trust, of too much honor to propagate such a false account, and has been scandalously deceived by his officers. We think it probable, that ten days may suffice for removing your persons and most valuable effects. We hope you will take care, that your

APRIL 28, 1775.

Voted, To recommend to the colony Congress, now sitting in Watertown, and it is recommended accordingly, to make an establishment for post riders, between the Massachusetts forces and the town of Worcester.

Also, that the said Congress take such order as they may think proper to prevent any town or district taking any notice of his excellency General Gage's precepts for calling a general assembly.

Doct. Warren was appointed to give the sentiments of this committee on Lord Dartmouth's circular letter to the other governments.

Voted, That Mr. President Langdon be, and he hereby is appointed, chaplain of the army in Cambridge pro tempore, and that he be furnished with a copy of this vote.

Major Brown [was] appointed to give such repairs to the cannon, at Waltham, as may be judged proper.

Ordered, That the commissary general be directed to provide quarters for about one hundred and fifty men from Connecticut, under the command of Major Brown.

Voted, That it is the sense of this committee, that no enlisting order be hereafter given out, unless a written order is received from the respective colonels.

Voted, That for the future, no order go out, to any men that live in New York or any other government, for the enlisting of men for the service of this province.

Ordered, That the cannon, now in Medford, be immediately brought to this town, under the direction of Capt. Foster.

agreement is expressed in the most unequivocal terms. We take it, that it is not expected that we suffer any persons to remove into town besides such as mean to take up their residence there."

" We are, &c."

Selectmen of Boston.

Another letter bears date on the same day.

GENTLEMEN :—Your letter of the 25th instant, came to hand late last evening, or you should have had an answer sooner. We feel for you with the keenest sensibility. Nothing on our part shall be wanting. Our wish is to know, when you are to be permitted to come out, and at what time. We shall encourage the waggoners to go in. We have no desire to injure or molest the person or property of any one who inclines to take refuge in Boston, and so soon as we know the day appointed for you to come out, and the time limited therefor, we shall take care that our part is performed with that punctuality which we are determined ever to observe in all cases where the honor of our country or the safety of our beloved countrymen is concerned. We desire that we may, without delay, be furnished with an authenticated copy of your engagements with the general, and such other information as is necessary for us."

" We are, Gentlemen, &c."

Voted, That General Thomas be desired to distribute the orders which he has received, some time since, for enlisting a regiment, to such captains as he thinks proper.

Mr. Henderson Inches, who left Boston this day, attended, and informed the committee, that the inhabitants of Boston had agreed with the general, to have liberty to leave Boston with their effects, provided that they lodged their arms with the selectmen of that town, to be by them kept during the present dispute, and that, agreeably to said agreement, the inhabitants had, on yesterday, lodged 1778 fire-arms, 634 pistols, 973 bayonets, and 38 blunderbusses, with their selectmen.

Voted, That Doct. Warren, Col. Palmer and Mr. Watson, be a subcommittee, to take the state of Boston into consideration, and report as soon as may be.

APRIL 29, 1775.

A vote of the Provincial Congress was read, respecting the removal of the inhabitants of Boston, whereupon, Col. Orne, Mr. Devens and Capt. White, were appointed a sub-committee, to take the matter into consideration, and report as soon as may be.

[The following circular was addressed to the several towns:]

[CAMBRIDGE, APRIL 29, 1775.]

[Gentlemen : As many of the persons now in camp, came from their respective towns, without any expectation of tarrying any time, and are now under the necessity of returning; this is to desire, you would, with the utmost haste, send other persons to supply their places, for a few days, until the enlistments are completed, and the men sent down to us.

We pray you, immediately, to set about this business, as the most fatal consequences must follow, if we should be reduced to so weak a state, as that the army, under General Gage, may be able to issue out of the town, and spread destruction through this country, and we think none can be unwilling to come for a few days, to relieve their brethren, who have been so long absent from their families.]

Voted, That orders be sent into the neighboring towns, requiring one half of the militia to be immediately sent to Roxbury and Cambridge, as a reenforcement to our army, and that the rest of the inhabitants hold themselves in readiness to march at a minute's warning.

Also, *Voted*, That Mr. Watson, Capt. White and Col. Gardner, be a sub-committee, to report the towns to be sent to, the destination of the reenforcements, and the expresses to be despatched.

Voted, That the secretary be directed to empower expresses to press as many horses as they may have occasion for.

Voted, That the committee of supplies, at Watertown, be directed to attend this committee immediately, and that the secretary write them accordingly.

Upon information that the supplies of powder and ball, at Watertown, were in the keeping of the commissary general, *Voted*, that General Ward be desired to apply to the commissary for such a quantity of said stores as he may have occasion for.

Voted, That Doct. Isaac Foster be directed and empowered to remove all the sick and wounded, whose circumstances will admit of it, into the hospital, and to supply proper beds and bedding, clothing, victuals, and furniture, with every other article he shall judge proper for said hospital, and that this be a sufficient order for him to draw on the commissary for such articles as he can supply, and to draw orders upon the commissary for the payment of whatever expenses are necessary for procuring the above mentioned articles.

Voted, That the secretary desire Messrs. Halls, printers, at Salem, to print three hundred letters, to be sent to the several towns in the province.

Capt. Benedict Arnold, with a company, being arrived here from Connecticut, *Ordered*, that the commissary general be directed to provide suitable quarters for said company.

Upon a motion made, *Voted*, that orders be given to General Thomas for seizing Governor Hutchinson's papers.

A letter from General Thomas, respecting some companies of minute men at Dartmouth, was read, whereupon, *Voted*, that Col. Orne, Col. Palmer and Col. Gardner, be a sub-committee, to consider and give directions relative to the general's request.

Letters from Col. Hancock, now at Worcester,[1] were read; whereupon, *Voted*, that four reams of paper be immediately ordered to Worcester, by Mr. Barber, for the use of Mr. Thomas, printer, he to be accountable.

(1) The Hon. John Hancock, on his journey to Philadelphia, to attend the Continental Congress, was detained at Worcester two days, awaiting the arrival of his colleagues, delegates from Massachusetts, and the attendance of an escort. One of his letters to the committee is printed on page 170. An application was made for paper to supply the press of Isaiah Thomas. The following recommendations for appointments were made during the same visit:

" WORCESTER, APRIL 24, 1775."

" GENTLEMEN:—From a conviction of your disposition to promote the general good, I take the freedom to request your countenance and good offices in favor of Mr. Edward Crafts, of this place, that he may be appointed to the command of a company. I know him well; he is capable. I beg

A letter from Medford was read; whereupon, *Voted,* that the company now raised there, hold themselves in readiness to march at a minute's warning, remaining in Medford till further orders.

The sub-committee on General Thomas' letter, reported, that it be ordered that Capt. Nathaniel Richmond, with any other captain that can bring into the camp fifty-six men, including sergeants, that will enlist into the service of this colony, shall have the encouragement given by the Provincial Congress, and shall immediately enter into pay upon their enlistment; [that] the critical situation of our public affairs demands the utmost exertions of the friends of America; and should remissness now appear, the consequences may be fatal.

Voted, That Mr. Watson be desired to make inquiry with respect to the colony arms not in use, and that Capt. Goodridge, of the Indian company, have such a number as is desired.

Voted, That Col. Gerrish be desired to send Major Dunbar, now a prisoner at head quarters, to Woburn, under a strong guard, and order him to be there kept in safe custody, till further orders from this committee.

Voted, That Capt. Hill and company be furnished with provisions at any tavern they see fit to call at, in conveying Major Dunbar to a place of safety, at the expense of the province.

Voted, That Capt. Brown, of Watertown, be desired, upon any advice of the troops coming out, to order the cannon to a place of safety, and, for that purpose, be empowered to press horses, cattle, &c.

your attention to this. It will give great satisfaction to Mr. Adams and myself, and to the people of this county: do gratify us. I also beg leave, you would recommend to the notice of General Heath, in my name, Mr. Nathaniel Nazro, of this town, who is desirous of being noticed in the army. He is lively, active, and capable. My respects to Heath, and all friends. Pray General Heath to take notice of this recommendation. God bless you. Adieu."

            " I am your real friend,

                   JOHN HANCOCK."

" *To the Committee of Safety.*"

               " WORCESTER, APRIL 26, 1775."

" GENTLEMEN:—Having had the honor to command the Cadet company at Boston, and knowing the ability of those who composed that corps, I cannot withhold mentioning, and recommending to the notice of you and the general officers, Mr. John Smith, and Mr. John Avery, two excellent good soldiers, and gentlemen, who will advance the reputation of the province in that department of command where they may be placed. I therefore most strongly recommend them, and earnestly pray they may be noticed. I will be answerable for their conduct. There are several other gentlemen of that corps, who may be useful, particularly Mr. Brent and Mr. Cunningham. Do notice Messrs. Smith and Avery. They will be useful. I set out to-morrow morning. God bless you. Why don't you send to Mr. Crafts. Pray improve him. He is a good man, and one on whom you may depend. Don't miss him."

            " I am your real friend,

                   JOHN HANCOCK."

" *To the Committee of Safety.*"

APRIL 30, 1775.

Capt. Benedict Arnold, captain of a company from Connecticut, attended, and reported, that there are at Ticonderoga, 80 pieces of heavy cannon, 20 pieces of brass cannon, from 4 to 18 pounders, 10 to 12 mortars; at Skeenborough, on the South Bay, 3 or 4 pieces of brass cannon; the fort, in a ruinous condition, is supposed to have about 40 or 45 men, a number of small arms and considerable stores; and that there is a sloop of 70 or 80 tons on the lake.

Voted, That an order be given to Major Bigelow, desiring him to have the province arms, either in Worcester or Concord, immediately brought to this town.

Voted, That Mr. John Chandler Williams be directed to attend this committee, that he may be employed as an express.

Voted, That the committee appointed yesterday, to consider the state of the town of Boston, be now desired to sit, and form a plan for the liberation of the inhabitants.

The sub-committee on the removal of the inhabitants from Boston, reported, which report was accepted, and Doct. Warren, Col. Palmer and Col. Orne, were appointed to wait upon the Congress with the proposals.

Voted, That two offices be opened to deliver permits for such persons as desire to enter Boston with their effects.

Voted, That Col. Samuel Gerrish be appointed to the office [of granting permits,] at the house of Mr. John Greaton of Roxbury.

Voted, That Col. William Henshaw be appointed to the office of granting permits, at the sign of the sun, in Charlestown.

Whereas, proposals have been made by General Gage to the inhabitants of the town of Boston, for the removal of their persons and effects into the country, excepting their arms and ammunition: *Resolved,* that any of the inhabitants of this colony, who may incline to go into the town of Boston with their effects, fire-arms and ammunition excepted, have toleration for that purpose, and that they be protected from any injury or insult whatsoever. This resolve to be immediately published.

The following orders were delivered to Col. Samuel Gerrish:

You are hereby empowered, agreeably to a vote of the Provincial Congress, to grant liberty, that any of the inhabitants of this colony, who may incline to go into Boston with their effects, fire-arms and ammunition excepted, have toleration for that purpose; and that they be protected from any injury or insult whatsoever, in their removal to

67

Boston. The following form of a permit is for your government, the blanks in which you are to fill up with the names and number of the persons, viz. :

Permit A. B., the bearer hereof, with his family, consisting of —— persons, with his effects, fire-arms and ammunition excepted, to pass unmolested into the town of Boston, between sunrise and sunset.

By order of the Provincial Congress.

JOSEPH WARREN, *clerk pro tem.*

Voted, That Andrew Craigie be appointed to take care of the medical stores, and to deliver them out as ordered by this committee; and that the secretary make out his commission accordingly.

Voted, That it be recommended by this committee to the council of war, that Mr. Joseph Pierce Palmer be appointed to the post of quarter master general of the army.

MAY 1, 1775.

Voted, That the quarter master general be directed to clear that chamber in Stoughton College, occupied by S. Parsons, Jr., for a printing office for Messrs. Halls.

Whereas, many of our brethren of the colonies of Connecticut and Rhode Island are now with us, to assist in this day of public and general distress, in which we are all deeply concerned : and, whereas, our brethren of said colonies have brought with them some of the paper currencies of their respective colonies, which have not, of late, had a currency with us, and for want of which, our common interests may greatly suffer :

Resolved, That said paper currencies shall, from and after the date hereof, be paid and received within this colony, in all payments, to all intents and purposes, in the same proportion to silver, as the same are paid and received within the respective colonies by which the same have been issued.

Resolved, That Col. Palmer be a committee to inquire into the matter, [to find] what colonies have such currencies, to alter this resolve agreeably thereto, and to present the same to the honorable Congress for their consideration.

[*Voted,* That the Rev. Mr. Gordon have free access to the prisoners detained at Worcester and elsewhere, and that all civil magistrates and others be aiding and assisting him in examining and taking depositions of them and others.]

MAY 2, 1775.

Doct. Warren, Col. Palmer and Col. Gardner, [were appointed] a sub-committee, to confer with General Ward, relative to the proposal made by Col. Arnold of Connecticut, for an attempt upon Ticonderoga.

A number of recantations, from the town of Marblehead, having been laid before the committee, for their opinion, as to the propriety of receiving them:

Voted, That it is the opinion of this committee, that said recantations be received, and that the persons making them, be made acquainted with the proclamation lately issued by Congress, respecting those [who] may incline to get into Boston ; and that it be recommended to the inhabitants of this province, that they be protected from all injuries or insults whatsoever, so long as they adhere to their several recantations, now before this committee, and continue to assist and abide by their country, and the inhabitants of Marblehead in particular, in the important dispute between Great Britain and America.

Voted, That two muster masters be appointed, one at the camp in Cambridge, and one at the camp in Roxbury.

Voted, That General Thomas be desired to give such orders, respecting the whale boats at Falmouth, and other ports southward, as he may judge proper.

Voted, That the Massachusetts Congress be desired to give an order upon the treasurer, for the immediate payment of one hundred pounds in cash; and also to order 200 pounds of gunpowder, 200 pounds of lead balls, and 1000 flints, and also ten horses, to be delivered unto Capt. Benedict Arnold, for the use of this colony, upon a certain service approved of by the council of war : said Arnold to be accountable for the same, to this or some future Congress, or house of representatives of this colony.

Voted, That two companies be raised in Braintree, for the immediate defence of the sea coast of said town ; the said companies to be joined to such regiment in future as they may be ordered to, should there be occasion, or discharged from service, as soon as the public good would admit of it : and that Col. Thayer be furnished with two sets of enlisting papers for this purpose.[1]

Voted, That General Thomas be, and he hereby is directed and empowered to stop the trunks mentioned to be in Col. Taylor's hands, until this committee send some proper persons to examine their contents.[2]

(1) This vote was reconsidered May 4th.

(2) The following is a letter from General Thomas, dated May 2, 1775 :

"GENTLEMEN :—In consequence of directions from the committee of safety, I sent an officer,

Resolved, That agreeably to a vote of Congress, General Thomas be directed and empowered to appoint suitable persons, to accompany such people into the country as may be permitted to bring their effects into Boston, upon the conditions mentioned in the proclamations posted up, and that General Thomas give such general orders as he may judge the common safety requires.

Voted, That Col. Arnold, appointed to a secret service, be desired to appoint two field officers, captains, &c., to be allowed the same pay during their continuance in service as is established for officers and privates of the same rank, who are ordered by the Congress of Massachusetts Bay to be raised for the defence of the rights and liberties of America; the officers and privates to be dismissed by Col. Arnold, or the committee of safety, whenever they shall think proper.

Voted, That the committee of supplies be desired to procure ten horses for Col. Arnold, to be employed on a special service.

Voted, That Mr. Isaac Bradish, keeper of the prison in Cambridge, be supplied with provisions out of the colony stores, for the support of the prisoners under his care, who have or may be committed by the orders of the council of war or of this committee.

The quarter master general having informed that some persons unknown had made spoil of liquors in the cellars of General Brattle, and Mr. Borland, and others, whereupon, *Voted,* that he be directed to take possession of those liquors, and other stores, immediately, in all the houses which are deserted, and that a particular account of such stores be taken, and that they be then committed to the care of the commissary general.

[A letter to the governor and company of the colony of Connecticut was reported, accepted, and is as follows :]

[CAMBRIDGE, MAY 2, 1775.]

[We yesterday had a conference with Doct. Johnson and Col. Wol-

on whom I could depend, to the house of Governor Hutchinson, who brought off all the papers he could find in that house ; but I was informed that Colonel Taylor, of Milton, had lately taken several trunks out of the governor's house, not many days ago, in order to secure them from being plundered. I immediately sent another messenger to Col. Taylor, for all the papers that belonged to Governor Hutchinson which he had in his possession ; he sent me for answer, he did not know of any papers that belong to said Hutchinson, but just now comes to inform me that there are several trunks in his house, which he took as aforesaid, which he expects will be sent for very soon. I suspect there may be papers in said trunks, and if it is thought proper, two or three judicious persons be sent to break open and search for papers, he will give them his assistance. This, gentlemen, is submitted to the consideration of the honorable committee."

"I have, gentlemen, the honor to subscribe myself, your most obedient humble servant,

JOHN THOMAS."

"ROXBURY CAMP, MAY 2, A. D. 1775."

cot, who were appointed by your assembly to deliver a letter to, and hold a conference with General Gage. We feel the warmest gratitude to you for those generous and affectionate sentiments which you entertain toward us. But you will allow us to express our uneasiness on account of one paragraph in your letter, in which a cessation of hostilities is proposed. We fear that our brethren in Connecticut are not even yet convinced of the cruel designs of administration against America, nor thoroughly sensible of the miseries to which General Gage's army have reduced this wretched colony. We have lost the town of Boston, and we greatly fear for the inhabitants of Boston, as we find the general is perpetually making new conditions, and forming most unreasonable pretensions for retarding their removal from that garrison. Our sea posts on the eastern coasts are mostly deserted : our people have been barbarously murdered by an insidious enemy, who, under cover of the night, have marched into the heart of the country, spreading destruction with fire and sword. No business but that of war is either done or thought of in this colony. No agreement or compact with General Gage will, in the least, alleviate our distress, as no confidence can possibly be placed in any assurances he can give to a people whom he has first deceived, by taking possession of and fortifying the town of Boston, and whom he has suffered his army to attack in the most inhuman and treacherous manner. Our relief now must arise from driving General Gage with his troops out of the country, which, by the blessing of God, we are determined to accomplish, or perish in the attempt, as we think it better to meet an honorable death in the field, whilst fighting for the liberties of all America, and far preferable to be butchered in our own houses, than to be reduced to an ignominious slavery. We must entreat, that our sister colony Connecticut, will afford, immediately, all possible aid ; as, at this time, delay will be attended with all that fatal train of events, which would follow from an absolute desertion of the cause of American liberty. Excuse our earnestness on this subject, as we know that upon the success of our present contest depend the lives and liberties of our country and succeeding generations.]

[We are, &c.]

[*To the Governor and Company of Connecticut.*]

MAY 3, 1775.

Voted, That two companies be raised in the towns of Malden and Chelsea, for the defence of the sea coast of said towns, the said companies to be joined to such regiments in future, as they may be ordered to, should there be occasion, or discharged from service as soon as the public good will admit of it.

Voted, That the quarter master general be directed to pay the strictest attention, that the household furniture of those persons, who have taken refuge in the town of Boston, may be properly secured, and disposed of in places of safety.

The following orders were given Col. Arnold, relative to an attempt upon Ticonderoga, viz. :

To Benedict Arnold, Esq., commander of a body of troops on an expedition to reduce and take possession of the fort of Ticonderoga:

SIR :—Confiding in your judgment, fidelity, and valor, we do, by these presents, constitute and appoint you, colonel and commander in chief over a body of men not exceeding four hundred, to proceed, with all expedition, to the western parts of this and the neighboring colonies, where you are directed to enlist those men, and with them, forthwith, to march to the fort at Ticonderoga, and use your best endeavors to reduce the same, taking possession of the cannon, mortars, stores, &c., upon the lake ; you are to bring back with you, such of the cannon, mortars, stores, &c., as you shall judge may be serviceable to the army here, leaving behind what may be necessary to secure that post, with a sufficient garrison.   You are to procure suitable provisions and stores for the army, and draw upon the committee of safety for the amount thereof, and to act in every exigence, according to your best skill and discretion, for the public interest, for which this shall be your sufficient warrant.

                    BENJAMIN CHURCH, JUN.,
                              [*For the*] *committee of safety.*

              By order,
                    WILLIAM COOPER, *Secretary.*
Cambridge, May 3, 1775.

                                        MAY 4, 1775.

[*Moved and Voted*, That the vote passed the second of May, respecting the raising of two companies in Braintree, be reconsidered, and that the copy of said vote together with the two enlisting papers, be ordered to be returned into the hands of said committee of safety ; and whereas, a petition from the towns of Braintree, Weymouth, and Hingham, hath this day been presented to this committee, setting forth the exposed situation of those towns, and praying for such relief and protection as may be thought proper,[1] therefore, *Voted*, that the town of Braintree be hereby empowered to raise one company, the town of Hingham another company, and the town of Weymouth half of one company, for the immediate defence of the sea coasts of said towns; the said two companies and a half to be joined to such regiment in future as they may be ordered to, should there be occasion, or discharged from service on the last day of December next, or sooner if

(1) The petition of the selectmen of Braintree, Weymouth, and Hingham, follows:

" *To the honorable Committee of Safety now sitting at Cambridge:*

"The petition of the selectmen of Braintree, Weymouth, and Hingham, humbly sheweth: that the several towns to which they respectively belong, are in a defenceless state, and as we apprehend, in great danger of an attack from the troops now in Boston, or from the ships in the harbor; more especially, as they are now, or will soon be, in want of fresh provisions; that we have been at the trouble and expense of keeping up a military watch in each town for this fortnight past, at an expense which we are by no means able to bear, which is no real defence unto us. Besides all that has been said, the inhabitants of the said towns have been, and are still likely to be, in our present situation, almost constantly kept in tumult and disorder, and unable to keep about their business, to their great damage."

"Your petitioners therefore, humbly pray your honors, to take our distressed state into your wise and serious consideration, and grant us, at least, the return of those men that have enlisted into the service from our several towns, or such other relief and protection as in your wisdom you shall think fit, and your petitioners, as in duty bound, shall ever pray."

$$\left.\begin{array}{l}\text{"JAMES PENNIMAN,}\\\text{NORTON QUINCY,}\\\text{EDMUND SOPER,}\\\text{JONATHAN BASS,}\end{array}\right\} \textit{Selectmen of Braintree.}$$

$$\left.\begin{array}{l}\text{JAMES HUMPHREY,}\\\text{SAMUEL KINGMAN,}\\\text{EBEN'R COLSON,}\end{array}\right\} \textit{Selectmen of Weymouth.}$$

$$\left.\begin{array}{l}\text{BENJA. CUSHING,}\\\text{JOSEPH ANDREWS,}\end{array}\right\} \textit{Selectmen of Hingham.}"$$

Weymouth, May 3, 1775.

A petition for powder and arms was received from the committee of Brunswick:

BRUNSWICK, MAY 3, 1775.

"GENTLEMEN:—We, whose names are hereunto subscribed, beg liberty to inform you of our situation, as we are chosen by this town to examine into the circumstance of it, which we have done, and find the town very deficient as to arms and ammunition, and have sent by water to Salem, but have just had our money returned back without arms or ammunition; at present, we have not more than one quarter of a pound of powder to a man throughout the town, nor more than one firelock to two men; and in this defenceless state, we are obliged to apply to you to assist our trusty friend whom we have sent, Capt. Nathaniel Larrabee; and as we think it would be unsafe to transport powder by water, we have ordered him to take only one hundred weight, and for him to consult with you how and in what way it would be safest to get arms and more powder down to us. We should esteem it as a favor, to be informed from you, by way of letter, at every convenient opportunity, of our public affairs."

"We are, gentlemen, yours, ever to be commanded,

AARON HINKLEY,
BENJA. STONE,
SAMUEL STANDWOOD,
JAMES CURTIS."

the public safety will admit of it, and that the selectmen of said towns be furnished with a copy of this vote and one set of beating orders, respectively.]

Resolved, As the opinion of this committee, that the public good of this colony requires, that government in full form ought to be taken up immediately, and that a copy of this resolution be transmitted to the Congress now sitting at Watertown.

[The] sub-committee reported the draught of a letter to the governor and company of the colony of Connecticut, requesting the speedy march of three or four thousand of their men, which was accepted, and ordered, that a fair copy be transmitted immediately. [It is as follows:]

[CAMBRIDGE, MAY 4 1774.]

[The distressed situation in which a wicked and despotic administration have involved this colony, will justify us in your eyes, as we presume, in our present most earnest and pressing desire, that you will immediately send us three or four thousand men of your establishment, in order to enable us to secure a pass of the greatest importance to our common interest, and which the enemy will certainly possess themselves of as soon as their reenforcements arrive; and if they once get possession, it will cost us much blood and treasure to dislodge them; but it may now be secured by us, if we had a force sufficient, without any danger; therefore, we earnestly repeat our request for three or four thousand men for this present purpose, with all possible despatch, and supported with all necessary stores of ammunition and provisions; and we would beg, that they may be forwarded in companies or regiments as fast as they can be got ready; this will make it easier to the troops, and to the country through which they may pass, and may, probably, be of more essential service to our common cause.]

[*To the Governor and Company of Connecticut.*]

Voted, That William Cooper, Jun., be appointed a clerk to this committee in the room of Mr. Palmer, appointed quarter master general; Samuel Cooper was added as an assistant.

Voted, That a chest of medicines be removed from hence to Roxbury, under the care of General Thomas.

There having been eight guns sent in for the use of the colony, Col. Whitcomb and General Heath were appointed to appraise the same, who reported as follows, viz.: one gun taken of Capt. How, appraised at £2; one ditto of Joel Brigham, £2; one ditto of John Baker,

£1 8s.; one ditto of Aaron Agar, £2 8s.; one ditto of James Stone, £1 4s.; one ditto of Asa Fay, £1 10s.; one ditto of Aaron Fay, £1 1s. 4d.; one ditto of William Bethank, 18s.; total, £8 9s. 4d.

Memorandum, Col. Jonathan Ward gave a receipt for the above guns, for which he made himself accountable, which receipt is entered in the minute book.

A letter was reported for the inhabitants of New York, which was accepted, and a copy of the same [put] on file, [and is as follows :]

[CAMBRIDGE, MAY 4, 1775.]

[It is with great satisfaction this committee received your letter of the second instant, expressive of your tender care, and sympathy with this colony under our alarming situation. All we can write on this occasion is, that the exigency of our affairs requires all the assistance which your better judgment shall dictate. We rest assured, that your zeal for the common safety will inspire you to do every thing that is proper for the safety and preservation of the unalienable rights of America.]

A draught of a letter to the governor and company of Rhode Island, respecting the sending a number of troops immediately, was reported, whereupon, *Voted*, that the same be accepted, and transmitted by an express.[1]

Voted, That a sub-committee be appointed to wait upon the council of war to recommend their giving orders for a return of the enlisted men, and that they will take order, that such men as are enlisted, may be admitted to join the camp with all expedition, that so such men as are far from home, and do not intend to enlist, may have leave to depart as soon as it can be done with safety to the colony.

Voted, That Col. Gardner be appointed to lay this vote before the council of war.

Voted, That it be recommended to the council of war, that six companies of each of the two regiments to be raised in the county of Plymouth, be ordered to join the army at Roxbury, as soon as they are completed; and that the four other companies of each of said regiments, which may be raised most contiguous to the sea coast of said county, be retained for the immediate defence of said sea coast, to be regulated by the colonels of said regiments until further orders.

(1) The letter to Rhode Island was in the same words with that sent to Connecticut.

Voted, That Col. Palmer and Col. Cushing be appointed to lay the foregoing vote before said council.

Advice being received, that a number of transports with troops are just arrived at Boston from England, Doct. Church, Col Palmer, and Mr. Devens, were appointed to confer with the council of war, upon the occasion.

Voted, That Col. Bricket be desired to take possession of all the arms and ammunition that he shall find in Mr. Borland's house, and bring them to head quarters.

MAY 7, 1775.

Whereas, it appears to this committee, that great uneasiness may arise in the army, by the appointment of surgeons who may not be agreeable to the officers and soldiers in their respective regiments, therefore, *Voted*, that it be recommended to the Congress, to allow the colonel of each regiment to nominate the surgeon for his regiment; said surgeon to nominate his mate; and unless there is some material objection made against them, that they be accordingly appointed.

Mr. George Babcock, charged with the care of a house, having complained that certain persons had come to said house, and taken from thence considerable furniture, *Voted*, that this complaint be referred to Congress, and that Mr. Cushing be desired to accompany said Babcock there, and that the above vote be sent to the council of war for their approbation; which vote being sent, it was approved of accordingly.

Resolved, That it be, and hereby is recommended to the selectmen and committee of correspondence for the town of Sudbury, that they use their utmost influence, that the effects of Col. Ezra Taylor of that town, be secured from any injury whatsoever.

Ordered, That the selectmen and the committee of correspondence for the town of Chelsea, be desired to take such effectual methods for the prevention of any provisions being carried into the town of Boston, as may be sufficient for that purpose.

[The following letter to the chairman of the committee of safety and protection of Albany, was accepted, and ordered to be forwarded.]

[SIR:—We have received your important and very agreeable letter of May current, by the worthy gentleman, Captain Barent Ten Eyck. While we lament the effusion of the blood of our friends and fellow countrymen, shed by more than brutal cruelty, urged on by the corrupt administration of a British minister of state; yet, amidst all our sorrows on that mournful occurrence, we rejoice greatly, at the bright prospect lying before us, in the unanimity of the colonies on this extended continent. We have the highest satisfaction in the assurance from you, that the citizens of Albany continue firmly and resolutely to cooperate with their brethren in New York and with the several colonies on the continent, in their opposition to the ministerial plan now prosecuting against us, and that the city have unanimously appointed a committee of safety, protection and correspondence, which we esteem as a necessary measure to bind us all in one indissoluble bond of union in the common cause of the American colonies.]

[Be assured, Sir, that we shall ever esteem it as our honor and interest to correspond with you, at all times, on matters tending to promote the common good. Suffer us to say, that we have the greatest pleasure in your information, that the extensive county of Albany will follow your laudable example, and in the important aid the general cause will receive from our sister colony, New York. The enclosed, you may depend upon it, is a well authenticated account of the late engagement in this colony, and supported by a great number of affidavits.][1]

[Permit us to say, Sir, that you may rely upon the resolution of the people of this colony to exert themselves, in every possible way, and that they have, long since, devoted their lives and fortunes in the glorious cause of liberty and their country; and that they never can give up their stand, to oppose despotism and tyranny, while they have such full assurances from their sister colonies, that they are equally engaged in the defence of the natural and constitutional rights of Americans. The blood of our neighbors, repeatedly and untimely poured out, cries aloud to the survivors to defend the American rights for which they bled and died. We have their wounds fresh in mind, and while the colonies are united, we have the fullest assurance, under God, of the salvation of our country.]

[We are, Sir, affectionately,

Your very humble servants.]

[*In Committee of Safety, Cambridge, May 7, 1775.*]

MAY 9, 1775.

Moved and Voted, That the Congress be desired to direct their secretary to furnish this committee with copies of all such resolves as have passed the Congress in any ways relative to the duty enjoined this committee, and as the circumstances of this colony are very different from

___

(1) The narrative will be found in the Appendix.

what they were at their first appointment, the committee would represent to the Congress, that they apprehend it is necessary, that the whole of their duty may be comprised in a new commission.

The council of war having determined that two thousand men are necessary to reenforce the army now at Roxbury, and that, if possible, the reenforcement be brought into camp the ensuing night; this committee took the vote of the council of war into consideration; thereupon, *Ordered*, that the commanding officers of the towns of Dorchester, Dedham, Newton, Watertown, Waltham, Roxbury, Milton, Braintree, Brookline, and Needham, immediately muster one half of the militia, and all the minute men under their command, and march them forthwith to the town of Roxbury, for the strengthening of the camp there.

A firelock of Mr. Borland was appraised by Col. Palmer and Col. Orne, at forty shillings, and delivered Col. Sergeant, for which he is to be accountable.

A vote passed, recommending it to the Provincial Congress, that a court of inquiry be appointed, for the trial of accused persons.

Voted, That Daniel Taylor, of Concord, be desired to send down to Cambridge, about sixty oars for boats, from twelve to sixteen feet in length.

MAY 10, 1775.

Voted, That one company of men be raised by the district of Cohasset, for the immediate defence of the sea coast of said district: the said company to be joined to such regiment in future, as it may be ordered to, should there be occasion, or discharged from service as soon as the public good will permit.

Voted, That Nathan Cushing, Esq. be desired forthwith to engage four armorers, for the service of this colony, and order them immediately to repair to the town of Cambridge, with their tools and other matters necessary for that purpose.

Whereas, the council of war are of opinion, that many batteaux, whale boats, and other vessels, will immediately, or very soon, be wanted in Charles river and other places; and as there is not a sufficient number of such vessels to be now obtained, it is therefore *Resolved*, that it would be of public utility to have one or more master carpenters immediately engaged in that service; and that this resolve be immediately sent to Congress for their consideration.

Mr. Daniel Taylor, of Concord, [was] empowered to impress a carriage or carriages, for the bringing down oars from that town to Cambridge.

Voted, That orders be issued to the colonels of the several regiments, to repair with the men they have enlisted, to Cambridge, immediately.[1]

The Provincial Congress having resolved, that the general officers be directed forthwith to call in all the soldiers who are enlisted in the service of this colony, and that they give immediate orders to all the enlisted soldiers, and all others now in the camps at Cambridge and Roxbury, that they do not depart till the further orders of the Congress, whereupon, *Voted,* that the following letter be immediately sent to the respective colonels of the army, viz. :

CAMBRIDGE, MAY 10, 1775.

SIR :—As we are meditating a blow against our restless enemies, we therefore enjoin you, as you would evidence your regard to your country, forthwith, upon the receipt of this order, to repair to the town of Cambridge, with the men enlisted under your command.

We are, &c.

Voted, That the following letter, signed by Benjamin Church, Jr., as chairman of this committee, be transmitted to Joseph Warren, Esq. president of the Congress, to be communicated, viz. :

SIR :—Conformable to the order of Congress, the committee of safety, with the council of war, have issued orders to the several colonels, a copy of which we enclose you : upon receiving the return, those who have completed their regiments will be commissioned, agreeably to the direction of Congress ; those who find it impracticable to fill their companies, must be incorporated into other defective regiments, which is the only plan the committee find themselves able

(1) The orders appear to have been founded, in part, on some communications like the following, sent from Boston :

"MONDAY, 8 MAY, 1775."

"An old campaigner says, he knows by the movements, that there is a stroke meditated somewhere, and likely to be to-night ; he thinks a feint [will be made] at the neck to divert, and a large body [sent] to take the ground on Dorchester neck."

"He advises to send a large body on Dorchester neck, so as not to be discovered from the town, every night, and have a strong body in Roxbury : if they should observe the troops landing on Dorchester neck, to have force sufficient to cut them off entirely. We, in town, know nothing, nor are able to communicate, as the tories and troops are very vigilant."

MAY 10, 1775.

"Elijah Shaw declares, that Gen. Gage's officers have said in his hearing, that they shall soon come out, and that a soldier requested him to convey him into the country, for the troops would soon make a push either towards Dorchester neck or Chelsea ; but he refused. He further declares, that Earl Percy swears he will be revenged on some of our men : and further says, that the troops have robbed him of 11 cows, 3 calves, a yearling heifer, 48 sheep, 61 lambs, 4 hogs, and poultry, hay 5 tons, and almost all his furniture."

to suggest on this emergency, but should there finally be a deficiency, enlisting orders must be given to others.

Yours, &c.

On a motion made and seconded, *Ordered*, that William Goodwin have orders to fetch a number of boats from Charlestown, and likewise orders to press teams for the same purpose.

Mr. William Goodwin, of Charlestown, was directed and empowered to take possession of a number of boats now at Charlestown, and likewise to press teams, wherever they may be found, to convey said boats to Cambridge; directing the owners of such teams to transmit their accounts to this committee.

Voted, That Mr. Watson be directed and empowered to remove to Cambridge the boats now in Menotomy river, and to impress what carriages may be necessary.

The commanding officers of the neighboring regiments, were directed forthwith to repair to the town of Cambridge, with the men enlisted under their command.

MAY 11, 1775.

Voted, That Mr. William Cooper, Jr., be, and he hereby is appointed, a clerk to Doct. Warren, president of the Congress.

MAY 12, 1775.

Voted, That Mr. Charles Miller be, and he hereby is appointed, deputy commissary to Mr. Pigeon, the commissary general.

Voted, That orders be given to Mr. Clark, boat-builder, that he give such repairs to the boats as may be judged necessary.

Voted, That Mr. Isaiah Thomas have sixty reams of printing crown paper, and eight reams of printing demy paper, supplied him, by the committee of supplies, they taking his obligation to be accountable to the colony for the amount thereof.

Ordered, That Mr. Charles Miller be, and he hereby is empowered and directed, to impress any horse he may have occasion for on the service of the province.

Voted, That Mr. Joseph Branch be, and he hereby is appointed, one of the armorers for the colony forces.

The following is the report of a joint committee, appointed by the committee of safety and the council of war, for the purpose of reconnoitering the highlands in Cambridge and Charlestown, viz. :

We have carefully examined the lands, and their situation, in regard of annoying and preventing the enemy from passing into the country from Boston, [and] are of opinion, that the engineers be directed to cause a breast work to be raised near the bridge, by the red house, at the head of the creek, near the road from Cambridge to Charlestown, on the south side of said road; also a breast work [to be] raised at the north side of the road, opposite the said red house, and to run in the same line as the fence now stands, upon the declivity of the hill there; also a redoubt on the top of the hill where the guard house now stands; and three or four nine pounders [to be] planted there: also a strong redoubt [to be] raised on Bunker's Hill, with cannon planted there, to annoy the enemy coming out of Charlestown, also to annoy them going by water to Medford. When these are finished, we apprehend the country will be safe from all sallies of the enemy in that quarter: all which is humbly submitted.

BENJAMIN CHURCH, *chairman*
of the sub-committee from the committee of safety.
WILLIAM HENSHAW, *chairman*
of the sub-committee from the council of war.

The committee of safety having taken the foregoing report into consideration, apprehend the matter not to belong to them officially; and although they are persuaded that the high lands above mentioned are important, yet not being the proper judges what works are necessary to be constructed, to make said posts tenable, are of opinion that the determination of this matter rests solely with the council of war.

BENJAMIN CHURCH, Jr., *Chairman.*

Ordered, That this report be sent up to the council of war.

The council of war having sent in to this committee, a proposal respecting the suspending the orders of Congress respecting the removal of the persons and effects of the tories, and ordering the crown officers through the continent to be apprehended:

Resolved, That the recommendation of the council of war, respecting the seizure of the servants and friends of government, improperly so called, and keeping them in custody, until General Gage shall have complied with the condition proposed by him to the town of Boston, and accepted by them, be referred to Congress, for their determination thereon.

Voted, That this committee adjourn to Congress, upon matters of great importance.

MAY 13, 1775.

Voted, That Capt. Isaac Foster be recommended to the council of war, as a suitable person to carry such provisions into the town of Charlestown, for the use of the inhabitants, as the general shall think proper to permit to be carried in.

Voted, That General Thomas be desired to deliver out medicines to such persons as he shall think proper, for the use of the sick soldiers at Roxbury, until the surgeons for the respective regiments are regularly appointed.

Voted, That the provisions and chest of medicines belonging to Madam Vassal, now under the care of Col. Starks, be stored as Col. Starks may direct, till further orders: and that the other packages may pass into Boston or elsewhere.

Ordered, That the commissary general or his deputy be, and he hereby is directed, to supply Col. Rosseter with provisions for thirteen men for eight days, said men being discharged by recommendation of the council of war, and order of this committee.

Whereas the committee are informed, that a number of men enlisted into the colony army, under Col. Jonathan Brewer, are now posted at Waltham, and are receiving provisions from the public stores: *Resolved,* that the commanding officer of the colony forces be desired to order said enlisted men at Waltham, immediately to repair to head quarters, and in case of refusal, that orders be given for the prevention of their being supplied with provisions of any kind from the public magazines.

One Thomas Nicholas, a negro, brought before this committee on account of his suspicious behavior for some time past, having been examined, *Resolved,* that it be recommended to the council of war to commit said negro, until there be further inquiry into his conduct.

Mr. Solomon Shaw was appointed one of the armorers for the army, and General Thomas was desired to accommodate him with a suitable place at Roxbury, for carrying on his business.

Ordered, That Mr. Isaac Bradish, keeper of the jail in Cambridge, be directed and empowered to confine one Thomas Nicholas, negro, till further orders.

MAY 14, 1775.

Ordered, That the commissary general supply with provisions, for six days, four men of Capt. Williams' company, and three men of

Capt. Noble's company :—these men came down with Col. Patterson, and are returning home, being dismissed.

Voted, That Capt. John Currier have one set of beating orders for Col. Fry's regiment; and in case it should not be consented to by the colonel, he agrees to join that regiment which shall be thought most convenient.

Mr. Andrew Craigie, commissary of the medicinal stores, &c., was directed and empowered to impress beds, bedding, and other necessaries for the sick, as they may be wanting, giving the owners a receipt for such articles as he may take for the purpose aforesaid.

Resolved, That it be recommended to the committee of supplies, to engage ninety-seven barrels of tar, in the sloop Adventure, Samuel Foot, master, just arrived at Salem from Virginia, it being apprehended, that the service of the colony requires said tar being secured.

A vote of the council of war, desiring a supply of hoes and brooms, was recommended to the committee of supplies by this committee.

The following was sent to the gentlemen, the selectmen of the town of Lynn :

Whereas Josiah Martin has, under guard, been brought before this committee to be inquired of touching his conduct, respecting his appearing in favor of carrying into execution the tyrannical designs of administration for the enslaving of this province : upon examination of the evidences produced, *Resolved,* that the said Martin's conduct has, in some instances, been unfriendly to his country; but that, on his being charged with the same, he has promised, with his life and fortune, to stand forth for the defence of his country, and that so long as he evinces this disposition, by his conduct, and does not any more attempt to go into the town of Boston, that he be received with the favor of his countrymen, and that no insult nor injury be offered him or his property.

The following resolve, relative to the live stock on the islands near Boston, passed this committee, viz :

Resolved, as the opinion of this committee, that all the live stock be taken from Noddle's island, Hog island, Snake island, and from that part of Chelsea near the sea coast, and be driven back; and that the execution of this business be committed to the committees of correspondence and selectmen of the towns of Medford, Malden, Chelsea and Lynn, and that they be supplied with such a number of men as they shall need, from the regiment now at Medford.

Resolved, That Col. Palmer and Col. Orne be directed to apply to the committee of supplies, at Watertown, for a particular account of the ordnance and military stores, and where the same are deposited, agreeably to the request of the council of war.

Voted, That it is the opinion of this body, that all persons escaping from their imprisonment in the town of Boston, ought to be received and protected in the several towns in this and the neighboring colonies, except such as are of principles inimical to the liberties of their country, who are not to be received, but on their first recanting their said principles, and making their peace with their countrymen to the satisfaction of the selectmen, committees of inspection, &c., in the town to which they shall apply : and that the wives and children of such persons, who shall choose to remain in Boston with General Gage, may and ought to be treated with humanity and tenderness in the several towns they may go to dwell in, during the present troubles, and, by no means, to suffer the least injury, or meet with the smallest mark of disrespect upon account of their said husbands or fathers.

The council of war having recommended that forty persons of the regiment commanded by Col. Fellows, have liberty to return to their several homes. *Resolved*, that they be dismissed accordingly, and that the commissary general be directed to supply said persons with six days' provisions to serve them on their return home.

This committee, having been informed by the committee of supplies, that they had secured as many naval stores as Col. Gridley of the train had indented for, *Voted*, that Capt. Foot be permitted to deliver his cargo, naval stores not excepted, agreeably to the bills of lading he had signed for the same.

Voted, That Mr. William Haskins be, and he hereby is appointed, first clerk to the deputy commissary general.

The council of war having recommended that Capt. Joseph Foster, Thomas Jenkins, James Lammans, John Rutherford, Jonathan March, J. Mensh, J. Simmins, J. Crost, of Col. Porter's regiment, who are not enlisted, may be dismissed, they were accordingly dismissed, and had an order on the commissary general for four days' provisions each.

Voted, That Matthew Clark and five other persons, who are repairing the boats brought to this town, be supplied with provisions while they are at work for the colony.

MAY 15, 1775.

The sub-committee, appointed to apply to the committee of supplies for a particular account of the ordnance and military stores, reported, and handed in to the committee the following list, viz. :

A List of Military Stores under the care of Capt. Foster, viz. :

At *Cambridge ;*—pick axes, 460 : hatchets, 23 : seven-inch shells, 298 : spades, 190 : pieces of cannon, 24 : axes, 156 : boxes of grape shot, 41 1-4 : hogsheads of flints containing 75,000, 2 : carpenter's tool chests, 2 : boxes of axes, 4 : 4 barrels 1 cask leaden balls : boxes small arm cartridges, 18 : barrels of bomb fuses, 1 : barrels of matches, 1 : chests of tin cannisters, 2 : boxes of paper for cartridges, 1 : nine pound ball, 607 : six-pound balls, 1123 : four-pound ditto, 200 : two-pound ditto, 800 : seven-inch shells, 298 : twenty-four pound ball, 122 : three-pound ball, 620 : No. 1 and 2 paper cartridges for cannon boxes, 2 : one barrel containing four tube cannisters, 16 straps, 4 packs, 4 powder horns, 5 skeins dry matches : 1 barrel cannisters filled with langrage, but no cartridges affixed to them, for 6 pounders : 4 casks, marked, paper cartridges filled : 1 barrel, marked, 84 two pound cartridges.

Under the care of Col. Barrett and Capt. Heywood.

Musket balls, 9,000 : grape shot, 1,600 : bar lead, 700 : musket cartridges, about 3,000 weight : 3 barrels of bandages.

More at Cambridge, under the care of Capt. Foster.

2 casks of tubes : 1 barrel, marked, 60 cases with flannel cartridges for three pair single fortified guns : 2 barrels containing case shot, part fuses and tubes : 1 barrel containing a number of paper cartridges not filled : 2 casks of cases with flannel cartridges, marked I. T. T.

Attest, ALEXANDER SHEPHERD, Jr.,

By order of the Committee.

Moved and *Voted*, That the original list of military stores be handed in to the council of war, and it was handed in accordingly.

Voted, That the Hampshire companies, now at Medford, if enlisted into this colony's service, under Col. Stark or Col. Sargent, and properly equipped, shall be provided with barracks : those of them, if any, who are not, and do not choose to be enlisted, and are not equipped, are to be furnished with provisions for their return.

Voted, That Capt. John Walker of Worcester, who came down to this committee for liberty to go into Boston, upon the proclamation issued by Congress, be apprehended and confined as a prisoner of war, he being an half pay officer, and under the orders of General Gage; and so not included in said proclamation.

Upon a motion made, the question was put, whether Col. Phipps be permitted to have a cow, calf, and a load of hay, to go into the town of Boston : passed in the negative.

Voted, That Capt. Naler Hatch [with the] Malden company be assigned to Col. Gardner's regiment, but they are to remain in Malden until the special order of Col. Gardner shall be received for their attendance elsewhere.

Voted, That nine indians, of Col. Porter's regiment, have liberty to return home, and that the commissary general be directed to furnish them with six days' provisions for that purpose, the same having been recommended by the council of war.

Upon the application of Lady Frankland, *Voted*, that she have liberty to pass into Boston with the following goods and articles for her voyage, viz. :

6 trunks : 1 chest : 3 beds and bedding : 6 wethers : 2 pigs : 1 small keg of pickled tongues : some hay : 3 bags of corn : and such other goods as she thinks proper.

The following permit was granted :

To the Colony Guard :

Permit Lady Frankland of Hopkinton, with her attendants, goods, and the provisions above mentioned, to pass to Boston, by express order of the committee of safety.

                    BENJAMIN CHURCH, Jr., *Chairman.*

HEAD QUARTERS, May 15, 1775.

Voted, That the letters and writings from New York, via New London, relative to the establishing a post office and riders for the service of the colony be sent to the Congress.

Voted, That John Tucker of Col. Porter's regiment be dismissed from the service, and that he be furnished by the commissary with seven days' provisions.

Voted, That Jonathan Blaisdel of Amesbury, be appointed an armorer for the army.

Resolved, That Mr. Borland's house be appropriated for the use of the committee of safety, and the quarter master general is directed to provide quarters for the troops now lodged at said house.

Voted, That the quarter master general be directed to remove as many of the three companies now at Mr. Borland's, to the house of Doct. Kneeland, as the house can accommodate, and that the three companies at Mr. Vassal's house, be placed at Mr. Foxcroft's house, and that Mr. Borland's house be cleared and cleansed as soon as possible.

Resolved, That it be recommended to the honorable Congress, that the records of the probate office for the county of Middlesex, supposed to be at Mr. Danforth's and Doct. Kneeland's houses, be removed to Doct. Minot's, at Concord, and, that the records of the county at Mr. Foxcroft's office, be removed to said Minot's house.

The following certificate was delivered Mr. Goddard, viz.:

This is to certify, that Mr. John Goddard, has been appointed by the joint committees of safety and supplies as waggon master to this colony, to convey such articles of stores from one part of this colony to another as the public exigency may require, under the direction of the commissary general and the ordnance store keeper, and, that such other waggoners or drivers are to be employed, as he shall recommend for that purpose.

The following permit was given to Capt. Walker.

Permit Capt. John Walker, now on his parole of honor, to pass unmolested to his family at Worcester.

Mr. John Goddard, waggon master, was directed and empowered, in case of emergency, to impress such waggons and cattle as shall be requisite for the public service.

Voted, That the clearing Mr. Borland's and Mr. Vassal's houses be suspended till further orders.

Voted, That Thomas Austin, of Charlestown, be, and hereby is appointed an armorer for the army.

Voted, That the above vote, appointing Mr. Thomas Austin one of the armorers for the army, be, and hereby is reconsidered.

MAY 16, 1775.

In a letter from Col. James Barrett, of this day, it is represented, that a prisoner now at Worcester, is a paper-maker, and that Mr. James Boice, of Milton, is in want of such a person in his paper manufactory; therefore, *Resolved*, that Col. Barrett, be, and he hereby is directed and empowered, to remove said prisoner from Worcester to said Boice's manufactory in Milton.

Voted, That Capt. Hill, and four men, with four prisoners, have an order for supplies on the taverners and innholders in the towns they pass through.

Whereas, it is recommended by the council of war, that fifty-four whale-boats be immediately provided for the use of this colony: *Resolved*, that a copy of said vote of the council of war, be transmitted to the committee of supplies, and that they be desired to procure and place said boats, agreeably to the recommendation of the council of war.

Voted, That Capt. Butler be desired to furnish those men of his own company with arms, who are destitute thereof.

By a resolve of the Provincial Congress, the following is the establishment for ten companies of matrosses :

Captain, £6 10*s*. per month; captain lieutenant, £5 10*s*. per month; first lieutenant, £4 10*s*. per month; 2 second lieutenants, each, £3 12*s*. per month; sergeants, each, £2 10*s*. per month; corporals, each, £2 6*s*. per month; six bombadiers, each, £2 4*s*. 6*d*. per month ; six gunners, each, £2 4*s*. per month ; 32 matrosses, £2 3*s*. per month.

Voted, That Col. Gridley have one set of beating orders, for a company of matrosses.

Voted, That Col. Azor Orne have one of the college arms, he giving a receipt for the same.

MAY 17, 1775.

Whereas, it is determined, in council of war, that ten swivels be immediately provided for the use of the army, and delivered in camp, at Cambridge :

Resolved, That a copy of the foregoing vote be transmitted to the committee of supplies, and that they be desired to procure said swivel guns immediately.

Resolved, That the three pieces of cannon, with the stores, now at Waltham, be immediately removed to Watertown, near the bridge, by advice of the general, and that Mr. Elbridge Gerry, one of the committee of supplies, be desired and empowered to remove the same.

Ordered, That Col. Orne, Doct. Church and Col. Palmer, be a committee to repair to the Provincial Congress, and request, that forthwith, the duty of the committee of safety be precisely stated, and that said committee be empowered by Congress to conduct in such manner as shall tend to the advantage of the colony; and to justify the conduct of said committee, so far as their proceedings are correspondent with the trust reposed in them ; and to inform [the Congress] that until the path of their duty is clearly pointed out, they must be at a total loss how to conduct, so as to stand justified in their own minds, and in the minds of [the people of] this colony.

Mr. William Beman, in Col. Fellows' regiment, is appointed by this committee to act as an armorer for the forces posted at Roxbury.

Resolved, That Mr. Joseph Austin, of Charlestown, be directed to attend upon this committee of safety, immediately.

Voted, That Col. Fellows be directed to procure a shop and tools, and every material necessary for an armorer, at Roxbury, to work immediately in the colony service.

Voted, That the commissary deliver Mr. Matthew Clark sixty oars, for the use of this colony.

Voted, That the carrying any hay into the town of Boston, on account of John Borland, Esq., be suspended until further order from this committee.

Voted, That Mr. Stephen Hall be appointed to inspect the college walls, and see that they are kept in proper repair.

Voted, That the selectmen of Cambridge be directed to supply General Ward with four half barrels of powder, for the use of this colony.

Whereas, General Gage has not kept his agreement with the inhabitants of the town of Boston, but, notwithstanding his said agreement, has prevented, and even refused, said inhabitants, with their effects, from removing into the country ; therefore, *Resolved*, that it be recommended to the Congress, that they rescind their resolution of the 30th ultimo, permitting the inhabitants of this colony to remove, with their effects, into the town of Boston, which resolution was founded upon said agreement.

Resolved, That Col. Orne and Col. Palmer be directed to attend the Congress, with the above resolve.

Resolved, That in case of an alarm, this committee will repair to Coolidge's tavern, in Watertown.

Upon a motion made, *Voted*, that Capt. How be directed to restore the six sets of enlisting papers, which he this day took out without the consent of the committee, by a fraud practised upon the chairman.

Voted, That application be made to his Excellency General Ward, that he would order Edward How under guard, until this committee can have a full hearing of his case.

[Whereas, one Mr. Mellicant, of Waltham, who is an officer in his majesty's service, under half pay, is suspected, by means of his, said Mellicant's wife having free access into and out from the town of Boston, of communicating such intelligence to our enemies as may have a tendency to injure the important cause we are engaged in, and, in some degree, defeat the plans forming for the salvation of this colony and continent : therefore, *Resolved*, that the selectmen and committee of correspondence of the town of Waltham be, and hereby are directed and empowered, to take such effectual methods, for the preventing any intelligence going into the town of Boston, by means of the abovesaid Mr. Mellicant, or any of his family, as to them, in their wisdom, shall seem meet.]

MAY 19, 1775.

Voted, That Capt. John Lane have enlisting papers delivered him, for raising a company of indians at the eastward.

The following certificate was delivered Col. Gerrish, for the Provincial Congress :

Col. Samuel Gerrish having satisfied this committee that his regiment is full, we recommend to the Congress that said regiment be commissioned accordingly.

Ordered, That Mr. Newall proceed to Watertown, and lodge the ten swivel guns he has under his care, at Edward Richardson's, innholder in said Watertown; it being recommended by General Ward.

The committee of correspondence of the town of Northborough, having sent a certain Ebenezer Cutler to this committee for trial, upon complaint of his being an enemy to this country, and this committee not having authority to act in the case, as they apprehend, do refer the matter to Congress.

Col. Ebenezer Learned having satisfied this committee that his regiment is full, it was recommended to the Congress that said regiment be commissioned accordingly.

The following letter of direction to the several colonels, was forwarded, viz. :

SIR :—The necessity of completing the colony army, and the suspicions entertained by some of the officers who have been engaged in recruiting men, oblige us to request your immediate return, to this committee, of the number of men enlisted in your regiment, with the names of the officers of said regiment, as the Congress have urged for said returns, that commissions may be issued, and due subordination take place.

Voted, That Mr. John Wood, of Roxbury, be, and hereby is appointed, an armorer for the army.

Voted, That Mr. Dike, of Bridgwater, be, and he hereby is appointed, an armorer for the army.

General Thomas was informed, by letter, that the committee had appointed Messrs. Beman, Shaw, Wood and Dike, as armorers for the forces posted at Roxbury, and [was] desired to acquaint the committee if any further appointments were necessary.

Voted, That Doct. Church have an order for a horse and sulky, and a single horse, for his journey to Philadelphia upon the province account.

[Whereas, some persons have hinted that Samuel Barrett, Esq., of Boston, has, in some instances, been unfriendly to his country, and the common cause of liberty, for which this colony now suffers and bleeds, and as such suggestions may have a tendency to injure him, we have inquired into the conduct of the said Samuel Barrett, Esq., during the unnatural contest between Great Britain and the colonies, and from his acts and explicit declarations, we have reason to think that he is friendly to the rights and liberties of this, his native country, and we recommend him accordingly.]

MAY 20, 1775.

Voted, That Capt. Edward How, Ebenezer Cutler, and Nicholas, a black fellow, now under guard, be sent up to Congress for examination and trial, and Capt. White is appointed to attend Congress, with the above named persons.

Voted, That the general be desired to furnish a guard for the occasion.

Voted, That for the future, no person having orders to impress horses, shall impress the horse of Deacon Timothy Winn, of Woburn, he and his horse being employed in the colony service.

Resolved, That it is the opinion of this committee, as the contest now between Great Britain and the colonies respects the liberties and privileges of the latter, which the colonies are determined to maintain, that the admission of any persons, as soldiers, into the army now raising, but only such as are freemen, will be inconsistent with the principles that are to be supported, and reflect dishonor on this colony, and that no slaves be admitted into this army upon any consideration whatever.

Col. Joseph Read having satisfied this committee, that his regiment is full, a certificate was given him of the same, and it was recommended to the honorable the Provincial Congress, that his regiment might be commissioned accordingly.

70

Col. Read had thirteen sets of regulations for the army delivered him by order.[1]

MAY 23, 1775.

Whereas, our enemies make frequent excursions to the islands and sea coasts, from whence they plunder hay, cattle, and sheep; which not only greatly injures many individuals, but also the public, and strengthens the hands of our enemies; therefore, *Resolved*, that it be recommended to the honorable Congress, to take some effectual measure to secure the stock on the islands and sea coasts, to prevent its falling into the hands of our enemies.

The following orders relative to furnishing one of the expresses with provisions, horses, &c., were issued, viz. :

(1) The following letter was addressed to General Preble.

CAMBRIDGE, MAY 20, 1775.

Honorable General Preble,

SIR:—This committee, received your favor of the fifteenth instant, touching the raising men, for the service of this colony, and note your just observations on the subject.

The committee, after the resolutions of the Congress for establishing an army of thirteen thousand six hundred men, thought the exigencies of the times and the exposed situation of the several towns near Boston, made it absolutely necessary, that the army should be immediately raised, and, that for the facilitating of this important business it was expedient that orders should be issued to such men as were recommended as proper persons for such important trusts. Accordingly, orders were issued to as many colonels as were sufficient to complete said army; but from the delay which appeared in the army's being formed, by the slow progress made in the enlisting men, and the exposed situation of the colony camp, by the going off of numbers from time to time, it was rendered necessary, that further orders should be issued for completing the army with all possible speed; and in consequence of that determination, among others, Col. March received orders for the enlisting of a regiment for the service of this colony, and, we understand, has made some considerable progress in enlisting men for said service. We are also informed by your honor, that Col. Phinney has received enlisting orders from you, and has engaged in the business of enlisting men to complete a regiment; and we are further informed by your honor, that it is impracticable that two regiments should be raised in the county of Cumberland, and being told by Col. Phinney, that many of the men that would be raised in your county, could not be supplied by the towns from which they are enlisted, with fire-arms and blankets, this committee, taking into consideration the exposed situation of your county and the probability of the army's being completed without drawing men from those parts of the colony which are more immediately exposed, would recommend, Sir, that you would use your influence, that a stop be put to the raising any men in your county until it may be known by the returns from the several colonels authorized for the raising regiments, whether it may be necessary to take any men from your county, and should this necessity take place, this committee will endeavor to give you such early intelligence as may be necessary. The request of this committee to your honor, we flatter ourselves, will not be conceived by you as carrying in it the least disrespect to Col. March or Col. Phinney, but solely from the probability of the army's being complete without taking men from those parts of the colony which are more immediately exposed. We should be glad to see your honor at head quarters, which we hope your health will soon admit, and with you we join in the hope of soon seeing a speedy end to the great difficulties this distressed colony now labors under.

We are, Sir, with the great respect, your honors humble servants,

P. S. Please to inform the within mentioned colonels, of this determination.

Yours, &c.

To all innkeepers, taverners, and other persons whom it may concern:

You are desired to furnish the bearer, Mr. John Chandler Williams, with all necessaries upon his journey and return, as also with horses, if necessary, and to exhibit the accounts to the committee of safety for this colony, as he is now upon the country service.

MAY 26, 1775.

The following warrant, for supplying an express on the colony service, was issued:

To all innkeepers, taverners, and other persons whom it may concern:

You are desired to furnish the bearer, Mr. John Gill, with all necessaries upon his journey to, and return from Rhode Island, as also with horses, if necessary, and to exhibit your account to the committee of safety for this colony, he being an express on the colony service.

The following certificate was given Dr. Bond:

Doct. Nathaniel Bond, of Marblehead, having been charged before this committee, with having acted an unfriendly part to this colony, said committee appointed Joseph Warren, Esq., Col. Thomas Gardner, and Lieut. Col. Joseph Palmer, as a court of inquiry to examine witnesses in the case, and hear and determine the same; and upon full inquiry into the case, they are clearly of opinion, that said Bond's general behavior has been friendly to American liberties, and though he may have discovered an imprudent degree of warmth in some instances, yet we do not find any proof of an inimical temper or disposition to this country, and therefore, recommend him to the esteem and friendship of his country[men], hoping, that, as the error which occasioned his being brought before this committee, appears to have been altogether involuntary, and was such as several of our most firm friends were led into by false rumors spread of the transactions of the nineteenth instant, no impressions to the doctor's disadvantage may remain on the minds of any person whatsoever.[1]

(1) The commission given to the committee of safety by the Provincial Congress, May 18, 1775, is entered in the original record at length. It will be found in the preceding journals, page 240.

The Hon. Benjamin Greenleaf having been elected a member of the committee of safety, declined the acceptance of the office, by the following letter to Mr. Secretary Freeman.

" NEWBURYPORT, MAY 26, 1775."

" Sir:—I yesterday received your letter of the nineteenth instant, informing me, that the Provin-

This committee have taken into their most serious consideration, the state of the New England army, proposed to be raised for the defence and security of the lives, liberties, and property of the Americans; and find that the several colonies have not, collectively, raised more than 24,500 men; whereas, 30,000 were supposed to be necessary; and said committee also find a considerable number of officers of minute men now at head quarters, who, with their men, cannot find room for employment in the army upon the present establishment of this colony; and as our enemies have determined to distress us upon our sea coasts, by taking our vessels, with provisions, salt, molasses, &c., as well as by plundering our islands and coasts of live stock, which will require a greater number of men to guard said coasts, than was at first estimated; and as said army, or any part thereof, may be disbanded at any future time, when the public safety will admit thereof, and as the public military spirit now runs high, it is therefore, *Resolved*, that the consideration of these premises be recommended to the honorable Congress; and that Col. Palmer be directed to attend said Congress with this resolve, in order to know whether they will make any addition to their present establishment.

MAY 21, 1775.

[This committee have often contemplated the mode of ascertaining the completion of the several regiments, and find no clear and explicit rule to their satisfaction, and therefore, beg leave to suggest to the honorable Congress of this colony, whether, a return from a muster-master, that such or such a regiment had such a number of privates who had passed muster, would not be a good rule for ascertaining when a regiment may be said to be full; and submit the consideration of the same to said honorable Congress.]

cial Congress had done me the honor of choosing me a member of the committee of safety, and that they requested my attendance without delay. I readily exert myself on every occasion that presents, as far as I am able, to promote such measures as have a tendency to relieve the country from its present difficulties and embarrassments; but my ill state of health forbids my attending closely to business, and therefore, disqualifies me to act in that department, with advantage to the public or myself, for which reason, I have to entreat the indulgence of the Congress, while I ask to be excused from that service; assuring them I cannot be an indifferent observer of the scene that is now acting; but, as I have hitherto attended to our public affairs, as far as my health would permit, almost to the total neglect of my own personal concerns, I shall continue to do so, if my life is spared until this land obtains a complete deliverance from the hands of tyranny and oppression; but then it must be in a sphere wherein I shall not be liable to so much confinement and solicitude as I must necessarily submit to, as a member of that committee."

"I am, with respect, Sir, your most humble servant,

B. GREENLEAF."

MAY 22, 1775.

Whereas, it appears to this committee, that no immediate service renders it necessary, that riders should be kept in pay at present, therefore, *Voted*, that all such riders as have been employed by this committee, be from this day discharged from said service.[1]

MAY 24, 1775.

Voted, That the commissary general be directed to supply John Carter, and three others, with provisions as armorers and coopers, now in the province service.

Col. Scammon having satisfied the committee, that his regiment was nearly full, a certificate was given him thereof, and it was recommended to the Provincial Congress, that his regiment be commissioned accordingly.

Resolved, That it be recommended to Congress, immediately, to take such order respecting the removal of the sheep and hay from Noddle's island as they may judge proper, together with the stock on the adjacent islands.

Voted, That the commissary general be directed to supply twenty-five men of Capt. Sprague's company, who are stationed at Chelsea.

MAY 26, 1775.

The Congress having passed a resolve, that the house of John Vassal, Esq., be appropriated for the use of the committee of safety, there-

---

(1) General Ward, having represented to Congress, that the army were deficient of arms, and that a supply of plank was needed for the artificers, and complained of the delay in furnishing these articles, the letters were transmitted to the committee of supplies. The answer shows, that the wants of the troops were not occasioned by defect of diligence, and indicates the feeling excited by any suspicion of neglect.

IN COMMITTEE OF SUPPLIES, MAY 22, 1775.

To the Honorable Provincial Congress:

The letters which we have this day received from General Ward, through your honorable Congress, carry with them an impression which the committee cannot conceive they deserve. We are conscious to ourselves of having discharged the heavy duty of our office, to the utmost of our power with fidelity, and we think, the general, on consideration, must acknowledge it ; nevertheless, after we had issued an advertisement in the Essex Gazette, for collecting all the colony arms, the Congress are troubled with the affair, as if the committee had not used every proper exertion in the transaction of the affair. But, what we think most hardly of, is the matter of the plank. We received a memorandum and ordered it to be provided immediately. The owner of the mill had not procured them yesterday, but engaged to have them in readiness by Tuesday morning, and we directed the boatmen to apprise the general of this.

We shall, in justice to ourselves, expect an explanation of this matter, whenever the affairs of the colony can be a little settled, from the general ; and, in the interim, we think it necessary to remove any unfavorable impression from the minds of the members of the honorable Congress.

With respect, your humble servant,

DAVID CHEEVER, *per order.*

fore, *Resolved*, that the quarter master general be directed to clear the said house, immediately, of the soldiers now lodged there, that it may be improved for that purpose.

Colonels Ward and Gardner having satisfied this committee, that their regiments were in a good [state of] forwardness, a certificate to that purpose was given them; and it was recommended to the honorable Provincial Congress, that said regiments be commissioned accordingly.

Colonels Patterson and William Prescott having satisfied this committee, that their respective regiments are nearly full, a certificate was given them of the same; and it was recommended to the Provincial Congress, that said regiments be commissioned accordingly.

Colonels Cotton and Bridge having satisfied this committee, that their respective regiments are full, a certificate was given them thereof; and it was recommended to the Provincial Congress, that said regiments be commissioned accordingly.

Colonels Asa Whitcomb, Frye, and Doolittle having satisfied this committee, that their respective regiments were nearly full, a certificate was given them thereof; and it was recommended to the honorable the Provincial Congress, that said regiments be commissioned accordingly.

Col. Walker having satisfied this committee, that his regiment was complete, a certificate was given him thereof; and it was recommended to Congress, that said regiment be commissioned accordingly.

Col. Donaldson having satisfied this committee, that his regiment is in good forwardness, a certificate was given him thereof; and it was recommended to the honorable Congress, that said regiment be commissioned accordingly.

MAY 27, 1775.

Col. Mansfield having satisfied this committee, that his regiment is in good forwardness, he had a certificate thereof, and a recommendation to Congress, that the regiment be commissioned accordingly.

Mr. Wesson, keeper of Thomas Oliver, Esquire's farm, had orders to secure any creatures that might be put into his inclosures by ill-disposed persons, and to inform the committee thereof.

Voted, That agreeably to the recommendation of General Ward, Jacob Rhodes, of Charlestown, be empowered to impress such cattle as may be necessary for the removal of two boats from that town to Cambridge.

Joseph Smith, keeper of John Vassal, Esq's farm, had orders to secure any creatures that might be put into his inclosures by ill-disposed persons, and to inform the committee thereof.

[The following letter was sent to the Provincial Congress :]

[GENTLEMEN :—This committee having received information from sundry persons, selectmen of the town of Waltham, respecting the conduct of Major Abijah Browne, of said Waltham, informing, that he, the said Browne, at sundry times and in sundry places, did utter many things disrespectful and reflecting on the conduct of the honorable Congress, the several committees, and upon the general of the colony army, this committee, apprehending that any determination on this case is out of the department of this committee, beg leave to refer the matter, with the evidence respecting the same, to your honors, that you may be furnished with such light as may enable you to determine thereon, as to you in your wisdom shall seem meet.

We are, your honors, most obedient humble servants.]

MAY 28, 1775.

A number of guns taken from some persons in Grafton, were appraised by a sub-committee appointed for that purpose, and delivered Luke Drury, for the use of his company, and a receipt taken in the rough minutes; as, reference thereto being had, will particularly appear.

MAY 29, 1775.

A number of letters taken from Robert Temple, Esq., by the committee of safety of Cohasset, were sent to this committee for examination, and though the committee think that the matter is not strictly within their commission, yet considering that the present Congress must be dissolved this day, and the good and safety of this colony may be effected by an immediate examination of said letters, therefore, *Resolved*, that the matter be immediately taken up by the committee, and as Mr. Temple is now attending, that he be so directed respecting said letters, as shall, after examination, appear necessary to promote the greatest good of this colony.

Voted, That a committee be chosen to draw up a certificate for Mr. Temple, and an order for his receiving the goods taken from him.

The committee appointed for that purpose, reported a certificate, which was accepted, and is as follows, viz. :

Whereas, the committee of inspection of the district of Cohasset, have transmitted to us, a number of letters found in the possession of

Robert Temple, Esq., and this committee have carefully inspected said letters, and had the said Mr. Temple before them, and examined him, both with regard to his principles and conduct in the present controversy between Great Britain and the colonies in America; and whereas, we think it the duty of this committee, at the same time that we applaud the vigilance of the committee of Cohasset, who have stopped those letters, and that of the town of Plymouth, who have sent two of their members with Mr. Temple to this committee, to do justice to individuals, in consequence of which, we *Resolve*, that it be recommended to the committee at Cohasset, to deliver Mr. Temple, such articles of his as are now in their possession, and likewise, that they and all others consider and treat him as a friend to the interest of this country, and the rights of all America.[1]

Col. Quincy, of Braintree, having proposed to this committee the erecting of a small defensive work against the depredations of our enemies upon the farms in his neighborhood, [they] do refer the matter to the council of war.

Col. Fellows having satisfied this committee that his regiment is full, he had a certificate thereof; and a recommendation that said regiment be commissioned accordingly, was given him for the honorable Congress.

It being expected that the present Congress will be dissolved this night, and hearing that one volume of copies of Mr. Hutchinson's letters, are in the hands of Capt. McLane, at the upper paper mills, in Milton, which volume may be of use to this colony, if in the hands of the Provincial Congress; therefore, *Resolved*, that the Rev. Mr. Gorden, of Roxbury, be desired and empowered to receive from said Capt. McLane, all such copies as are in his hands, or in any other hands,

---

(1) Robert Temple, Esq., subsequently, presented the following representations to the committee.

"I, Robert Temple, of Ten Hills, near Charlestown, New England, do declare, that I have received no injury to my property, nor have I been under any apprehensions of danger to either my person or property from the troops that are under the command of General Ward. But, it is a fact, that I have been so threatened, searched for, attacked by the names of tory and enemy to this country, and treated in such a manner, that not only my own judgment, but that of my friends, and of almost the whole of the town where I lived, made it necessary or prudent for me to fly from my home. I am confident, that this is owing to the wickedness of a few, very few, who have prejudiced some short sighted people against me, who live too far from my abode, to be acquainted with my proper character. I am confirmed in this opinion, from the kind protection that my wife and family have received, and continue to receive from General Ward, as well as from the sentiments which the committee of safety have been pleased to entertain of me.

                                                                            R. TEMPLE."

"*Plymouth, May* 31, 1775."

and to be accountable to the present or some future Congress for the same.

MAY 30, 1775.

Elisha Lettinwell was directed to proceed with two teams to Chelsea, and bring up from thence the cannon and other stores saved from the schooner which has been burned by our people, and to lodge said stores in this town.

MAY 31, 1775.

The committee met, by adjournment, at Watertown, being the day appointed by charter for the election of councillors, when the Congress convened, and had a suitable discourse delivered [before] them by Mr. President Langdon, at the meeting-house, where the committee attended in the afternoon. Afterwards they met, and adjourned, to meet at Cambridge, on Tuesday morning, at eight o'clock.

JUNE 1, 1775.

On a motion made by Mr. Samuel Whittemore, of Gloucester, that the forces now raised in said town, and in Manchester, should remain there for the present, for the security of the sea ports : *Voted*, that there be returns immediately required of the number of men now in camp, and if it shall then appear that the safety of the whole will permit of it, the request will be granted.

JUNE 2, 1775.

A gun taken from Samuel Flagg, of Grafton, for the use of the colony, was appraised by a committee, appointed for that purpose, at forty shillings, lawful money; which gun was delivered Capt. Luke Drury, for the use of his company, and a receipt taken from him in the rough minutes.

Col. John Nixon having satisfied this committee that his regiment is in good forwardness, he had a certificate thereof, and a recommendation to the Provincial Congress that said regiment be commissioned accordingly.

JUNE 3, 1775.

Voted, That Mr. Devens be a committee, to join Col. Putnam, from the council of war, as a committee to wait upon the committee of supplies for a conference, and to desire their attendance at head quarters.

Voted, That Col. Gridley be required to make immediate return of the regiment of artillery.

JUNE 5, 1775.

A number of officers belonging to Col. John Nixon's regiment, were

71

recommended to the Congress to be commissioned; and a list of said officers ordered to be put on file.

Col. Glover having satisfied this committee that he has about four hundred and sixty men in his regiment, a certificate was given him to that purpose, and it was recommended to the honorable Congress that said regiment be commissioned accordingly.

The honorable the Provincial Congress having, by their committee, inquired of this committee what progress has been made in raising a regiment for the train: *Resolved*, that the honorable Congress be informed that this committee have given out enlisting orders to raise nine companies, and that they will immediately procure a return, and forward it to the Congress.

JUNE 9, 1775.

A number of officers, belonging to Col. Whitcomb's regiment, were recommended to the Congress to be commissioned; as by copy of the list on file.

Two small arms, taken from General Brattle's house, were appraised by Capt. White and Mr. Devens, a committee appointed for that purpose, at one pound six shillings and eight pence; which guns were delivered Capt. Joseph Stebbins, for the use of his company, and a receipt taken for the same in the rough minute book.

Resolved, That the armorers repair no fire-arms for any soldier, without a certificate from his commanding officer, and that they keep an exact account of what arms they repair, and the soldiers' names to whom they belong; also what regiment they belong to; and also that the arms that first come be first repaired; and that this vote be transmitted to the several armorers in the colony service.

Capt. Hall, of Mistick, having informed the [committee] that a parcel of spars were brought on this side [of] Mistick bridge, *Voted*, that Mr. Hall be desired to remove them to such a place of security as he shall judge proper, till the further order of this committee.

Voted, That Capt. Ebenezer Winship have the recommendation of this committee to the honorable Congress, for being commissioned, with his subalterns, in Col. Nixon's regiment.

JUNE 10, 1775.

Whereas, a return has been made by Col. John Glover, of the state of his regiment, now at Marblehead, and it appearing to be for the safety of this colony [that] said regiment should continue for the present at said Marblehead, therefore, *Resolved*, that Col. John Glover be, and he hereby is directed, to continue said regiment, under his command, at Marblehead, until further orders, and that he hold them in readiness to march, at a minute's warning, to any post where he may be directed; and that he fill up said regiment as soon as possible.

Whereas, sundry pieces of mowing land, belonging to persons who have left this town, have upon them considerable quantities of grass, which, if not cut soon, must diminish much in quantity, and as hay will be wanted for the use of this colony, therefore, *Resolved*, that it be recommended to the honorable Provincial Congress, that they appoint a committee of Congress to view said pieces of land, and act thereon as to them, in their wisdom, shall seem meet.

Voted, That Col. Learned be empowered to appoint one armorer and an assistant, for the army at Roxbury, provided he can obtain tools and accommodation for them.

A list of the gentlemen who have been commissioned, or who have received any encouragement for commissions, was sent to Congress, a copy of which is on file, [and is as follows :]

The following return was sent in to the Provincial Congress.

In obedience to a resolve of the honorable the Provincial Congress, "that the committee of safety certify to the Congress the names of such gentlemen as are candidates for the command of a regiment, with the number of privates, &c." This committee now report, that besides twenty gentlemen to whom they have given certificates, viz. : Col. Asa Whitcomb, General Ward, Lieut. Col. Ward, Col. Glover, Col. Fry, Col. Learned, Col. Read, Col. Nixon, Col. Fellows, General Thomas, Lieut. Col. Bayley, Col. Bridge, Col. Cotton, Col. Walker, Col. Prescott, Col. Scammon, Col. Donaldson, Col. Patterson, Col. Gardner, Col. Mansfield, Col. Gerrish; General Heath took out ten sets of orders, and has raised a full regiment, which has done duty in the army for several weeks, as he has informed this committee, but has made no return in writing, nor applied for a certificate : Col. David Brewer has received ten sets of orders, but has made no returns, though we hear he has enlisted a number of men as rangers : Col. Robinson has applied to this committee for a recommendation, in consequence of a petition signed by ten companies, the copy of which petition accompanies this report. The committee promised Col. Robinson that they would recommend him, if there should be a vacancy. Col. Woodbridge informs this committee, and it appears, that 360 men stand ready to go under him. The committee would observe, that Col. Woodbridge has been in the camp, with his minute men, doing duty ever since the battle, but did not apply to this committee for enlisting orders, until the committee had issued orders sufficient to complete the army, and therefore the committee did not give him orders, but promised they would recommend him, if there should be a vacancy.

Col. Porter, now in conjunction with Col. Patterson, and, by agreement with Col. Patterson, to have the chief command in the regiment, officiated some time in that capacity, waiting for the men raised by Col. Porter's orders to arrive; but they not arriving so soon as expected, another officer with several companies arrived, and offering to join Col. Porter's regiment, Col. Porter said he was willing to resign, rather than the public service should be hindered. Since this, we are informed by Col. Porter, that the men raised by his order are upon their march to Cambridge.

Col. Henshaw expected to have the command of a lieutenant colonel in General Ward's regiment, but the dispute between him and Col. Ward having been already laid before the Congress, and acted upon; we would further represent, that he has signified to this committee, that a number of companies incline to go under him, as by his return which accompanies this report.

About five or six weeks past, Mr. Greenleaf applied to this committee, desiring that the men raised in and about Newbury might not be annexed to Col. Gerrish's regiment, or any other where it would be disagreeable to them. He afterwards applied to this committee respecting said men, and desired that the eight companies enlisted upon orders issued by this committee, through Col. Gardner's hand, who have since petitioned in favor of Col. Little's taking the command of them, might be put under him as colonel of a regiment. We then found we had given orders for as many regiments as would complete the establishment made by this colony, and therefore did not give Col. Little any orders to raise a regiment, but promised that if any vacancy should happen he should have the preference. We find said companies were early in the field, and have done duty ever since, and are very well equipped.

Early after the 19th of April, this committee sent two sets of beating orders to the Hon. General Preble, desiring him to give out such orders to such persons as were suitable for commissions, in order to form a regiment; and Col. March was also supplied with ten sets of orders, for the purpose of raising a regiment, to be commanded by him. Soon after, it was represented to us, by the committee of correspondence of Falmouth, that it would be inconvenient to that county, in their exposed situation, to raise men for the army, and the same was agreed to by Colonels Phinney and March, and this committee : on which we wrote to General Preble, informing him of the same, but heard nothing further, until about six days past, we received a return from Col. Phinney of about five hundred men enlisted in a regiment to go under his command, and Col. March certified that he agreed to come in as his second, a copy of which letter to General Preble accompanies this report.

Col. Sergeant's case having been represented to Congress, the copy of said representation accompanies this report.

The committee beg leave further to represent, that the reason why more enlisting orders were delivered out than were sufficient to enlist the number of men established by Congress, was an apprehension that the province was in the utmost danger for want of men; the committee not being able to prevail on the militia and minute men to tarry in camp, and there being but few men enlisted at that time, obliged us to issue further orders.

JUNE 12, 1775.

The committee not apprehending that it was necessary to detain Eliphalet Hill, of Newbury, any longer, as a rider in the colony service, he was dismissed therefrom yesterday.

Shubael and Joseph Sever, of Framingham, entered into the colony service, as armorers, the 10th instant.

Capt. Lawrence, in Col. Prescott's regiment, offering to act as an armorer without any pay for his labor, and to return home for some tools which are necessary to effect the repairs of the muskets, it was consented to by the committee, and the said Lawrence was desired to procure his tools as soon as may be.

JUNE 13, 1775,

Jonathan Stickney, in Col. Woodbridge's regiment, received a small arm of one Guillam, a scholar, for which he gave a receipt in the rough minute book, to deliver the same again to this committee, when so required.

Whereas, it is daily expected, that General Gage will attack our army now in the vicinity of Boston, in order to penetrate into the country, it is of the utmost importance, that said army be, in every respect, prepared for action as soon as possible, therefore, *Resolved*, that the general be desired, to order each colonel in the army, to make immediate return to him of the state and equipment of the respective regiments, setting forth what number of men are destitute of arms, and what arms are fit for immediate service; and, that this vote be laid before the general as soon as may be.

Mr. Devens was appointed a committee, to inquire of the committee of supplies, relative to the quantity of powder in their possession, and where the same is.[1]

On a motion made, *Resolved*, that the debates and determinations of this committee be kept in profound secrecy by its members and their attendants, until further order of this committee.

Whereas, Daniel Adams, of Boston, a lunatic, now in camp at Cambridge, occasions great disorders in said camp, therefore, *Resolved*, that the selectmen of the town of Woburn be, and they hereby are directed and empowered, to take into their custody and care the above mentioned Daniel Adams, and make such provision for him, at the expense of this colony, as his circumstances, being peculiar, may require, and also for the guards while there.

Whereas, frequent complaints have been made to this committee, of the waste and destruction of the property of some persons who have left their habitations in sundry towns in this colony, and taken refuge in the town of Boston, therefore, *Resolved*, that it be recommended to the honorable Congress now sitting at Watertown, that they take the above into their consideration, and act thereon, as to them in their wisdom shall seem meet.

The committee earnestly recommended to the honorable Congress, that the representations from the quarter master general, be taken into immediate consideration, especially as the committee, from their own knowledge, find the rooms too much crowded, and the healths and lives of the soldiers thereby greatly exposed; and if tents cannot be immediately furnished, that some barracks be forthwith erected.[2]

JUNE 14, 1775.

Whereas, this committee are informed, that Doct. How, of Andover, is prepared to receive [insane patients,] and is well skilled in such disorders as Daniel Adams, of Boston, sent on the 13th instant, to the town of Woburn, is affected with, therefore, *Resolved*, that the selectmen of the town of Woburn, be, and they hereby are released from keeping said Daniel Adams in the town of Woburn, and they are required to provide a horse and carriage, with provisions, to forward the said Adams to Andover, the expense of which will be paid by this colony.

(1) Forty-six half barrels of powder were in the magazine at Watertown; four half barrels of cartridges had been sent to Cambridge ; and thirty-five half barrels of powder were expected from Worcester county.

(2) The quarter master general represented, that there was great want of tents and barracks, and that the least delay in making provision for the shelter of the troops, would be attended with injurious consequences.

Resolved, That Daniel Adams, a lunatic, now at Woburn, be carried to the town of Andover, and committed to the care of Doct. How, and the said Doct. How is hereby desired to take proper care of the said lunatic, at the expense of this colony.

A number of men belonging to the company of Capt. Drury, having petitioned that they might be permitted to join, some, the regiment commanded by Col. Gardner, and others, the regiment commanded by Col. Nixon; and the committee having considered their several requests, *Voted,* as the opinion of this committee, that said company be joined to such regiment as it shall appear the major part of said company are in favor of, when called upon for that purpose.

Resolved, That Capt. White, and Mr. Devens, be a committee to proceed to the house of Thomas Ireland, of Charlestown, and find out whether a certain infamous woman, who calls herself ——— Jackson, be there, and if she can be found, order her to head quarters, they being sent furnished with an order from the general, for a file of men for that purpose.

General Heath having satisfied this committee, that his regiment is near full, a certificate was given him thereof; and it was recommended to the honorable Congress, that his regiment be commissioned accordingly.

Mr. Nathaniel Mulliken having represented to this committee, that on the 19th of April last, his house was plundered and burned by the soldiery ; at which time he lost a pair of silver shoe buckles, which he says he is well informed are in the possession of a sergeant of the 52d regiment, now in Concord jail; it is the desire of this committee, that the committee of correspondence for said town, with whom they think it properly belongs, would make inquiry into this matter, and if they find it to be as has been represented, that they would use their endeavors, that the said Mulliken may have justice done him by the delivery of said buckles,

Two guns taken from John Borland, Esq's house, for the colony service, were appraised by Messrs. Devens, Watson, and Orne, at twenty-seven shillings and thirty-three shillings, which guns were delivered William Hudson Ballard, for the use of his company, and a receipt taken for the same in the rough minute book.

Upon reading a letter from General Thomas, in favor of Capt. Israel Henrick, *Resolved,* that this committee, do not think the matter contained in said letter comes within the commission of this committee, and therefore, refer it to the honorable Congress.

JUNE 15, 1775.

The following resolve respecting the allowance for provisions to the soldiers in the Massachusetts army, passed at the Congress, June 10, 1775.

Resolved, That each soldier in the Massachusetts army shall have the following allowance per day, viz. :

Article 1.　One pound of bread.

Art. 2.　Half a pound of beef, and half a pound of pork, and if pork cannot be had, one pound and a quarter of beef; and one day in seven they shall have one pound and a quarter of salt fish instead of one day's allowance of meat.

Art. 3.　One pint of milk, or if milk cannot be had, one gill of rice.

Art. 4.　One quart of good spruce or malt beer.

Art. 5.　One gill of peas or beans, or other sauce equivalent.

Art. 6.　Six ounces of good butter per week.

Art. 7.　One pound of good common soap for six men per week.

Art. 8.　Half a pint of vinegar per week per man, if it can be had.

Ordered, That Capt. Benjamin White, and Col. Joseph Palmer, be a committee to join with a committee from the council of war, to proceed to Roxbury camp, there to consult with the general officers on matters of importance, and to communicate to them a resolve this day passed in this committee, respecting Bunker hill in Charlestown, and Dorchester neck.

Whereas, this committee lately applied to the honorable the Congress of this colony, for an augmentation of the army now in the vicinity of Boston, and as some circumstances have since taken place, which strengthen the arguments then used in favor of the said augmentation, particularly, that many of the then expected reenforcements for General Gage's army have arrived; that General Gage has issued a very extraordinary proclamation, in which the inhabitants of Massachusetts Bay are in the most explicit manner declared rebels[1]; and various accounts have been brought to this committee of the movements of Mr. Gage's army, and that he intends soon to make another attempt to penetrate into the country; from the consideration of all which premises together with that of our army :

Resolved, That the good and welfare of the colony requires, that there be an immediate augmentation of said army; that such soldiers

(1) The proclamation of General Gage is printed in the journals of Congress, page 330.

in the army as are destitute of arms be immediately supplied therewith; that such regiments of militia as are in any degree destitute of officers be immediately filled up in such manner as the honorable Congress may direct; and, that all the militia in the colony be ordered to hold themselves in readiness to march on the shortest notice, completely equipped, having thirty rounds of cartridges per man; all which is earnestly recommended to the immediate consideration of the honorable Congress now sitting at Watertown; to which the committee would beg leave to add, a general recommendation to the people to go to meeting armed, on the Lord's day, in order to prevent being thrown into confusion.

Whereas, it appears of importance to the safety of this colony, that possession of the hill called Bunker's hill in Charlestown, be securely kept and defended, and also, some one hill or hills on Dorchester neck be likewise secured, therefore, *Resolved*, unanimously, that it be recommended to the council of war, that the above mentioned Bunker's hill be maintained by sufficient forces being posted there, and as the particular situation of Dorchester neck is unknown to this committee, they desire that the council of war take and pursue such steps respecting the same, as to them shall appear to be for the security of this colony.

Ordered, That Capt. Benjamin White, and Col. Joseph Palmer, be a committee to join with a committee from the council of war, to proceed to Roxbury camp, there to consult with the general officers on matters of importance, and to communicate to them a resolve this day passed in this committee respecting Bunker's hill in Charlestown, and Dorchester neck.

JUNE 16, 1775.

The committee took into consideration the resolves of Congress, relative to barracks; whereupon, *Voted*, that Mr. Watson, Mr. Cushing and Doct. Holten, be a committee to make inquiry whether any houses or tents are to be obtained for the troops that want cover.

The commissary general was directed to furnish Messrs. Joseph and Thomas Austin, armorers in the colony service, with provisions as wanted.

Col. Gridley's captains and subalterns for the train, were this day recommended to Congress to be commissioned.

Mr. Burbeck was recommended as lieutenant colonel in Col. Gridley's train of artillery, Mr. Scarborough Gridley as first major, and Mr. David Mason as second major, in said regiment of artillery.

JUNE 17, 1775.

Colonels David Brewer and Jonathan Brewer, having made returns of the field officers, and officers of nine companies of their respective regiments, it was recommended to the Provincial Congress, that they might be commissioned accordingly.

[The following order was issued to the towns in the vicinity of Boston.]

[*To the Selectmen of the Town of* ———]

[GENTLEMEN :—You are ordered instantly to send all the town stock of powder you have to the town of Watertown, saving enough to furnish one pound to each soldier.]

The following was voted to be sent Mr. John Badger, viz. :

SIR :—As the safety of the colony army demands that any person or persons suspected of having the small pox, be immediately placed in such place as may prevent its spreading in said army, and your house is thought proper for that purpose, you are directed immediately to quit said house, that the person now suspected may be placed therein.

The following vote was laid before the committee of supplies, viz. :

As, in consequence of our late movements, a constant fire is kept up on the colony troops, we think it necessary that there should be quick intelligence brought to head quarters from the scene of action : we therefore desire that this committee may be immediately furnished with four of the best riding horses for the service aforesaid.[1]

JUNE 18, 1775.

A letter was forwarded to the commanding officers of the militia in the neighboring towns, for the march of their respective regiments, as per copy on file, [which is as follows :]

(1) The committee of supplies inform the committee of safety, that they are unable to furnish horses to send the summons for the militia by express. They add, " we are sensibly concerned for the expenditure of powder, and as any great consumption by cannon may be ruinous, on our side, we think it proper to inform you, that exclusive of thirty-six half barrels of powder received from the governor and council of Connecticut, there are only in the magazine twenty-seven half barrels, and that no more can be drafted from the towns without exposing them more than they will consent to."

The following circular was addressed to the towns :

CHAMBER OF SUPPLIES, WATERTOWN, JUNE 18, 1775.

GENTLEMEN :—The welfare of our country again induces us to urge your exertions in sending to the magazine in this place, what can be procured of the following articles ; salt pork, beans, peas,

CAMBRIDGE, JUNE 18, 1775.

[*To the Commanding Officer of the Militia of the Town of* ————.]

[SIR :—As the troops under General Gage are moving from Boston into the country, you are, on the receipt of this, immediately to muster the men under your command, see them properly equipped, and march them forthwith to Cambridge.

By order of the Committee of Safety.

BENJA. WHITE, *Chairman.*]

A letter countermanding the above orders, was forwarded to the several colonels in the neighboring towns, as per copy on file, [which is as follows :]

[It is thought best by this committee, that those companies of the militia which have not been called into the camp, at Cambridge, by written orders, should remain at their respective towns, and that those companies of them which have been so called, and are on their march, should return, and hold themselves in complete readiness to give us their assistance when called upon.]

JUNE 19, 1775.

Resolved, That the house of the Rev. Samuel Cook, of Menotomy, be improved as a hospital for the colony army; and that Mr. William Eustis be, and hereby is appointed, to the care of the sick and wounded in said hospital, till the further order of this committee.

Ordered, That Doct. Isaac Foster be, and he hereby is directed, to take up and improve as hospitals, so many houses in Menotomy, as he may find necessary for the safety of the sick and wounded of the colony army, and that he employ such person or persons as may be necessary to carry such provisions and other necessaries as may be wanted for the use of the aforesaid sick and wounded ; and further, that

vinegar, and blankets, the prices whereof, as well as the carting, shall be allowed according to the custom of your place, which we desire you to certify. It is of the utmost importance that the army should be supplied agreeably to the resolve of the Congress, more especially with these articles ; the four first of which are necessary for the subsistence as well as the health of the men, and the others for their comfort. The occasion of the deficiency in blankets is mostly owing to a number of men enlisted from Boston and other towns, which have been vacated, and they all must be procured immediately, or our worthy countrymen will suffer.

As the country affords every thing in plenty necessary to subsist the army, and we cannot, at present, obtain many things but by your assistance, we assure ourselves that you will act your parts as worthily as you have done, and hope that the event of all our exertions will be the salvation of our country.

DAVID CHEEVER, *per order of Committee of Supplies.*

To the Selectmen and Committee of Correspondence of the Town of he take such precautions, respecting the small pox hospital, as may be necessary for the prevention of the spreading of that epidemical disorder in the camp or elsewhere.

Pursuant to a resolve of the Provincial Congress sent to this committee, respecting the nomination of four conductors, two clerks, and one overseer, for a company of artificers in the regiment of artillery; the committee beg leave to recommend the following persons to the offices affixed to their names, viz.: Mr. John Ruddock, Mr. John Austin, Mr. John Kneeland, Mr. Thomas Uran, *Conductors;* Mr. Nathaniel Barber, Jr., Mr. Isaac Pierce, *Clerks;* Joseph Airs, *Overseer of the Artificers.*

It being very desirable to obtain the most certain accounts of the names and places of abode of the persons who have been killed or wounded in the battle of Lexington, so called, on the 19th of April past, and at any time since; and also of all such as may be killed or wounded at any future time, during the present unnatural contest between Great Britain and the American colonies, in order to transmit to future generations the names of such as have gloriously suffered in the cause of liberty and their country, to effect which, *Resolved,* that it be recommended to the honorable Congress to order, that the selectmen of the several towns and districts in this colony, transmit, from time to time, to this or some future Congress or house of representatives, the names and addition of all such persons, who have been or may be killed or wounded as above, within their respective towns and districts; and that they severally cause the same to be fairly entered upon their town and district books.

JUNE 20, 1775.

The following was sent to the Provincial Congress, viz.:

This committee being informed that Capt. John Wiley, who was recommended as a proper person for the command of a company, in the train, has not skill for such a trust, and that the company will leave the army, unless some other person is appointed to said command, your honors will please to take this matter into consideration, and act thereon, as you in your wisdom shall judge necessary.

Resolved, That no more of the militia of this colony march, than are called for by express orders from this committee, on any alarm that may take place.

Ordered, That Mr. Abner Graves, who came down as a minute man on the 20th of April, to defend his country, be discharged, and he is accordingly discharged.

Voted, That a certificate be given Samuel Pool, of Boston, to pass the guard to the town of Littleton.

The following receipt was taken from Benjamin Lincoln, Esq., viz. :

Received of the honorable the committee of safety, thirty-seven blankets, which they received into their hands, and give their receipt for them to Mr. William Vance. Received by me,

BENJAMIN LINCOLN.

JUNE 21, 1775.

Resolved, That Joseph Adams, driver of the stage from Newbury, be, and he hereby is directed, to transport back to Newbury, Elizabeth Royal and her child, who, as she says, is wife to William Royal, first sergeant in the 63d regiment of foot, now in Boston, and deliver her to the care of the selectmen of said Newbury, who are hereby directed to provide for her and her child, at the expense of the colony.

Voted, That the quarter master general be directed to order nine horses in the colony service, to be stabled at Mr. Hastings' barn this night.

Mr. Thomas Williams, on the colony service to Marblehead, had an order on the taverners and innholders, for the necessary supply of provisions for man and horse.

Col. Woodbridge, having satisfied this committee that eight companies, belonging to this regiment, were in good forwardness, it was recommended to the honorable Congress, that they be commissioned accordingly.

Ordered, That Mr. James Munroe, an armorer in the provincial service, take into his keeping a [quantity] of old iron, saved out of the cutter burned at Winnesimit ferry, he to be accountable to the committee for the same.

Stephen Frost, ensign in Capt. Locke's company of Col. Gardner's regiment, was recommended to the honorable Congress for a commission.

Two half barrels of powder were received from Billerica, for which Col. Palmer gave a receipt. Said powder was delivered to Major Barber of the train.

Whereas, a great number of horses have been, from time to time, put into the stables and yard at Mr. Hastings', at head quarters, not belonging to the colony, to the committee of safety, or the general officers, their aids de camp, or post riders, to the great expense of the public, and inconvenience of the committee, generals, &c., therefore,

Resolved, that no horses be hereafter admitted into said stables or yard, or be taken from thence, but only by order of said committee or general officers.

As it is thought of great importance, that intelligence of the state and situation of the army, or any part thereof, should, at all times, be known to the general officers, and that such orders as may be sent by the generals, be communicated, with all speed, therefore, *Resolved,* that it be recommended to the honorable Congress, that they make such establishment for aid de camps, to the generals, as to them, in their wisdom, shall seem meet.

JUNE 22, 1775.

Samuel Patch, in Col. William Prescott's regiment, was recommended to the honorable Congress, to be commissioned as a captain; and Zachary Walker and Joshua Brown, as lieutenants in said regiment.

Resolved, That it be, and it hereby is recommended to the town of Medford, that they immediately supply Major Hale with as many spades and shovels as they can spare, as it is of importance for the safety of this colony, that the works begun on Winter hill be finished, and that they will be retarded unless soon supplied with tools of that kind.

A number of Col. Donaldson's officers were recommended to the honorable Congress to be commissioned, as by copy on file.

JUNE 23, 1775.

Agreeably to a resolve of the Provincial Congress, orders were issued to the colonels of the several regiments, that they forthwith make return of the officers in their respective regiments who are not commissioned, [that they] may immediately receive their commissions, and that the vacancies, if any such there are, may be filled up.

A letter from General Thomas, recommending a supervisor for the armorers at Roxbury, is referred over to Congress.

The following was voted to be sent the Provincial Congress, viz.:

This committee beg leave to represent to the honorable the Provincial Congress, that they apprehend it [to be] absolutely necessary for the safety of the colony, that two persons of ability and prudence be appointed to superintend the regular supply of our two camps; one of them to be placed in the camp near this place, and the other at Roxbury, whose duty it shall severally be, constantly to attend said camps, and examine into the supplies of each regiment, to see that such supplies are properly delivered out in time, quantity and quality, and seasonably to advise the commissary general when, and what articles of supplies, are wanted at the respective camps : All which is humbly submitted.

Col. Palmer and Col. Orne appointed a committee, to join a committee from the council of war, to view the encampment on Prospect hill, and the works carrying on there.

This day was lodged with this committee, by Capt. Cyprian Howe, thirty arms, sent by Capt. Josiah Stone, of Framingham, for which a receipt was given by the secretary of this committee.

Voted, That Mr. Joseph Jones, of Lancaster, be supplied with provisions, till the further orders of this committee, he being well skilled in the train.

The following fire-arms were received from the town of Attleborough, viz. :

1 gun from Henry Richardson, -	No. 1, -	appraised at £1 16
1 " Jacob Perry, - - -	" 2, -	" " 1 13
1 " George Stanley, - -	" 3, -	" " 2 00
1 " Amos Stanley, - - -	" 4, -	" " 1 10
1 " Samuel Freeman, Jr.,	" 5, -	" " 2 00
1 " Benjamin Allen, - -	" 6, -	" " 1 16
1 " Ditto, - - - - - - -	" 7, -	" " 1 4
1 " David Richardson, -	" 8, -	" " 2 2
1 " Ebenezer Lane, - -	" 9, -	" " 1 7
1 " Elisha Gay, - - - -	" 10, -	" " 2 14
1 " Daniel Dagget, - -	" 11, -	" " 2 2

£20 4

The following fire-arms were received from the town of Rehoboth, viz. :

1 gun from James Dagget, - - -	No. 11, -	appraised at £2 8
1 " Benjamin Ridge, - -	" 12, -	" " 2 14
1 " Elisha Carpenter, - -	" 13, -	" " 1 4
1 " Nathan Round, - -	" 14, -	" " 2 8
1 " Richard Whittaker, -	" 15, -	" " 1 19
1 " James Dagget, - - -	" 16, -	" " 2 2
1 " Benjamin Ridge, - -	" 17, -	" " 1 13
1 " John Wheeler, - - -	" 18, -	" " 1 13
1 " William Cole, - - -	" 19, -	" " 1 13
1 " Stephen Bullock, - -	" 20, -	" " 2 8

£20 2

JUNE 24, 1775.

Ordered, That the commanding officer who has the charge of the hay on John Vassal, Esq.'s estate, be directed to supply Mr. Seth Brown, who has the care of the colony horses, with as much hay as they may need for their consumption.

A gun taken after the late action was appraised by this committee at thirty shillings, and delivered Col. Brewer for the use of his regiment; for which he gave his receipt to be accountable to this committee in the rough minute book.

A gun, appraised at two pounds fourteen shillings, was delivered Elisha Frizel, of Capt. Robert Oliver's company, in Colonel Doolittle's regiment, he having had his gun split in the late engagement. A receipt was taken for the same in the rough minute book.

A number of Col. Prescott's officers were recommended to the honorable Congress, to be commissioned as by the captain's return on file.

Capt. Ezra Badlam, of a company in the train, and four lieutenants, were recommended to the honorable Congress, to be commissioned, as by the captain's return on file.

Capt. Samuel McCobb, of Col. Nixon's regiment, had twenty firearms delivered him, appraised by the towns which sent them at thirty-seven pounds twelve shillings, for which he gave his receipt in the rough minute book, to be accountable to this committee.

Ordered, That Mr. Brown, the keeper of the colony horses, do not admit any horses into the stables of John Vassal, Esq., but such as are the property of this colony.

Resolved, That the overseer, and such a part of the company of artificers under his direction as may be necessary, be posted in Newton, in buildings of Mr. John Pigeon, for the purpose of carrying on their business, and what loss said Pigeon shall sustain, in consequence of said artificers being posted there, this committee will use their influence that the damage so sustained be reimbursed by this colony.

Resolved, That the cannon in this and the town of Watertown, not mounted, and all other military stores not wanted for present use, be removed forthwith to the town of Newton, where the artificers are to carry on their works.

Voted, That Mr. Pigeon, the commissary general, have the care and direction of removing the spare military stores to Watertown.

A gun, said to have belonged to James Boynton, was delivered to Eliphalet Cole, in Capt. Parley's company, in Col. Fry's regiment.

A gun was delivered to Aaron Cromby, in Capt. Gridley's company, of the train.

Eighty-four fire-arms, collected from several towns, were received of Mr. Thomas Cowden, for the use of this colony, for which a receipt was given him by Mr. Watson, of this committee.

JUNE 25, 1775.

Whereas, Mr. Pigeon, the commissary general, has represented to this committee, that the public service will be promoted by a faithful person being appointed as a supervisor of the camp, for reasons offered; upon consideration of which, and for other reasons, this committee beg leave to represent to the honorable Congress, that they apprehend it to be absolutely necessary for the safety of this colony, that two persons, of known ability and prudence, be appointed, to superintend the regular supply of our two camps; one of them to be placed in the camp near this place, and the other at or near Roxbury; whose duty it shall severally be, constantly to attend said camps, and examine into the supplies of each regiment, to see that such supplies are properly delivered out, in time, quantity and quality, and seasonably to advise the commissary general when, and what articles of supplies are wanted at the respective camps, and also to take care that the empty casks are saved and returned to the commissary general's office for farther service, and in general to do all the service to the public which such appointment requires.

JUNE 26, 1775.

Twenty small arms were delivered Capt. Lemuel Trescott, of Col. Jonathan Brewer's regiment, for the use of his company, for which he gave a receipt in the minute book, to be accountable when called upon therefor.

Six small arms were delivered Capt. William Hudson Ballard, for the use of his company in Col. Fry's regiment, for which he gave a receipt, to be accountable when called upon therefor.

Col. Moses Little, having made a return to this committee of a lieutenant colonel, major, ten captains, and twenty lieutenants, it was recommended to the honorable Congress, that they be commissioned accordingly.

Three small arms were delivered Capt. John Nutting, for the use of his company in Col. Prescott's regiment, amounting, by appraisement, to seven pounds ten shillings, for which he gave a receipt in the minute book, to be accountable when called upon therefor.

Six small arms were delivered Lieutenant Whitney, for the use of Capt. Farwell's company in Col. Prescott's regiment, amounting, as by appraisement, to thirteen pounds twelve shillings, for which a receipt was given by the lieutenant in the minute book.

Six small arms were delivered Capt. Joshua Parker, of Col. Prescott's regiment, for the use of his company, amounting, as by appraisement, to thirteen pounds eight shillings, for which he gave a receipt to be accountable to the committee when called upon therefor.

Ten small arms were delivered Capt. Asa Lawrence, for the use of his company in Col. Prescott's regiment, appraised at nineteen pounds three shillings, for which he gave a receipt to be accountable to this colony, which receipt is on file.

Three small arms, for the use of Capt. Wyman's company in Col. Prescott's regiment, appraised at five pounds, were delivered to his lieutenant, for which he gave a receipt in the minute book, to be accountable when called upon therefor.

Three small arms, for the use of Capt. Oliver Parker's company in Col. Prescott's regiment, were delivered said Parker, amounting, as by appraisement, to four pounds nine shillings and four pence, for which a receipt was taken in the minute book.

Whereas, this committee find the public hospital in this town has been much neglected, to the great injury of the patients in said hospital, occasioned by the want of some suitable person being placed there as surgeon, therefore, *Resolved*, that Doct. John Warren, be, and he hereby is appointed, to the oversight of said hospital, and that he take proper care such provision be made as may be necessary for the comfortable support of the patients in said hospital until further orders.

Fifty-eight small arms, amounting, by appraisement, to one hundred and nine pounds fifteen shillings, were delivered Col. Asa Whitcomb, for the use of his regiment, and a receipt taken for the same in the minute book.

June 27, 1775.

Passed upon John Chandler Williams' account, who was employed as a rider in the service of this colony, amounting to £4 4s 6d, as by the copy thereof on file.

It was recommended to the honorable the Provincial Congress, that William Dana be commissioned as captain lieutenant; Mr. Treadwell as first lieutenant; Jonas Simmons and William Stevens as second lieutenants; in Capt. Edward Craft's company of the train, in Col. Gridley's regiment.

A gun was taken for the use of this colony, which was owned by Aaron Bar, of Mansfield, who died of the wounds he received in the battle of Bunker hill, which gun has been valued by this committee, at thirty-six shillings lawful money.

One hundred and twenty-four small arms were received of Mr. Abiah Sadler, and ten of Capt. Stone, collected by them for the service of this colony, amounting, by appraisement, to two hundred and fifty-one pounds fourteen shillings and eight pence, for which receipts were given by Mr. Watson.

JUNE 28, 1775.

Two small arms were delivered Col. Samuel Gerrish, for the use of his regiment, amounting, as by appraised value, to three pounds three shillings, for which a receipt was taken in the minute book.

The following is a resolve of the Provincial Congress, relative to supplying the army with small arms, viz. :

IN PROVINCIAL CONGRESS, WATERTOWN, JUNE 26, 1775.

Whereas, this Congress has ordered a number of fire-arms to be furnished from several towns and districts in this colony, to be forwarded to the army, to supply those who are destitute of arms; but no provision is made for delivering them out, and taking proper receipts for the same, therefore, *Resolved*, that all the small arms that are or may be procured by the above order, be delivered to the committee of safety, at Cambridge, they to give their receipts for the same to the person from whom they receive them; that the same be delivered out to such officers as shall produce orders therefor from the Hon. General Ward, they giving receipts for the same to the said committee of safety, to be returned in good order, unless lost in the service of the colony ; and every soldier who shall receive any such fire-arms, shall give his receipt for the same to the officer from whom he shall receive it, to be returned as aforesaid ; and the officer shall return said receipts to the committee of safety; and in case the same shall not be returned at the close of the campaign, or sooner, the value of the said fire-arms shall be deducted out of the wages of the person receiving the same; and that the committee of safety shall appraise all such arms as have not already been appraised, and take an account of the whole.

By order of Congress,

JOSEPH WARREN, *President.*

The following was received from General Ward, in consequence of the above vote of Congress, viz. :

Head Quarters, Cambridge, June 28, 1775.

The general orders, that the commanding officer of each regiment make application to the committee of safety for so many fire-arms as their respective regiments stand in need of; each commanding officer to give his receipt for the fire-arms he may receive, and the committee of safety are hereby ordered to deliver out arms to such commanding officers as make application to them for the same.

Per order, SAMUEL OSGOOD, *Major of Brigade.*

In consequence of the above order of the council of war, the following protest was entered, and a copy of the same, together with the other proceedings, was, by a vote of this committee, laid before the honorable Congress, viz.:

Whereas, the Provincial Congress did, on the 26th instant, pass a resolve, "that all the small arms that are or may be procured by the above order (mentioned in said resolve,) be delivered to the committee of safety, at Cambridge, they to give their receipt for the same, to the person from whom they receive them; *that the same be delivered out to such officers,* as shall produce orders therefor from the Hon. General Ward:" and whereas, the Hon. General Ward, in consequence of that part of the above quotation which is scored, has this day issued general orders, in which are these words, "*and the committee of safety are hereby ordered to deliver out arms to such commanding officers as make application to them for the same:*" and whereas, this committee apprehend, that said resolve does not empower the general to *order them* to deliver said arms, but only to *order his officers* to receive from the committee such arms as they are ordered by the honorable Congress to deliver on the *general's orders to his officers:* and whereas, the committee apprehend, that it is of vast importance that no *orders* are issued by the military, or obeyed by the civil power, but only such as are *directed* by the honorable representative body of the people, from whom all military and civil power originates; and, though this committee are satisfied, that General Ward has misunderstood said resolve, and does not mean or intend to set up the *military* power above the *civil,* yet, lest this order of the general, should be adduced as a precedent in future, we think it our indispensable duty to protest against the general's said order; notwithstanding which protest, we also think it our indispensable duty to deliver said arms agreeably to the spirit of said resolve, and as the exigency of the public requires; and submit our conduct to the honorable Congress.

Forty-three small arms, amounting, as by appraisement, to seventy-nine pounds two shillings and four pence, were delivered to Col. Gardner, for the use of his regiment, and a receipt taken for the same in the minute book, from Lieutenant Colonel Bond.

Thirty small arms were delivered Major Brooks, for the use of Col. Bridge's regiment, amounting, as by appraisement, to fifty-five pounds nineteen shillings and six pence, for which he gave a receipt to be accountable to this colony, which receipt is on the files of the committee.

Nine small arms were delivered Col. William Prescott, for the use of his regiment, amounting, as by appraisement, to seventeen pounds nine shillings, for which a receipt was given in the minute book.

Twenty-five small arms were delivered Col. Fry, for the use of his regiment, amounting, as by appraisement, to forty-nine pounds eight shillings and two pence, for which he gave a receipt to be accountable to the colony, which receipt is on the minute book.

Twenty-five small arms were delivered Col. John Glover, for the use of his regiment, amounting, as by appraisement, to forty-six pounds twelve shillings and eight pence, for which he gave a receipt in the minute book to be accountable to this colony.

Received of Major Barber, store-keeper for the trains, by order of the Provincial Congress, thirty-two small arms, amounting, as by appraisement, to £———.

Mr. Devens and Col. Orne, appointed to draw up a vote relative to Capt. Trevet and company, reported the following, which was accepted, viz :

Whereas, from a mistake made by one of the general officers, Capt. Samuel Russel Trevet has been put under arrest, which mistake is set forth in a certificate by order of the general, and upon examination it appears that said Trevet has approved himself a good officer, but said mistake has unhappily operated to the dispersion of his company; therefore, *Resolved*, that Capt. Trevet be directed to collect his said company, as soon as possible, and then apply to this committee, in order to be commissioned.[1]

(1) A committee was formed from members of the Provincial Congress, of the council of war, and of the committee of safety, to inquire into the alleged misconduct of some of the officers of the American army in the battle of the 17th of June. The investigation appears to have been founded on the statement of General Putnam, that as he was riding up the hill, during the engage-

This committee being greatly alarmed at the danger of the small pox spreading in the American army, which, should it take place, we fear may be attended with very fatal consequences to this colony and continent: therefore, *Resolved*, that it be earnestly recommended to the honorable Congress, to take such speedy and effectual measures, to prevent a communication of that very dangerous and distressing distemper, from the small pox hospital, to the army, or to the inhabitants of this colony, as to them in their wisdom may seem meet.

Whereas, sundry persons, who, in the exigency of our public affairs, have been employed in the service of this colony, are, from time to time, exhibiting their accounts to this committee, in order for payment, therefore, *Resolved*, that said accounts be transmitted to the honorable Congress, that this matter be taken into their consideration, and that such orders pass thereon as their wisdom may dictate.

JUNE 30, 1775.

One hundred and fifty-two small arms were received of Capt. William Page, collected by him for the use of this colony, amounting, as by appraised value, to £———, for which a receipt was given him by Mr. Watson

Mr. Samuel West was recommended to the honorable Congress, to be commissioned as second lieutenant in Capt. Abner Cranson's company, in Col. Asa Whitcomb's regiment.

Forty small arms were delivered Col. John Paterson, for the use of his regiment, amounting, as by appraisement, to seventy-eight pounds sixteen shillings and four pence, for which a receipt was given in the minute book.

Fifty-one small arms were delivered Col. James Scammon, for the use of his regiment, amounting, as by appraisement, to ninety-seven pounds eighteen shillings and eight pence, for which guns a receipt was taken in the minute book.

Three small arms, for the use of this colony, were received of Col. Simeon Spalding, amounting, as by appraisement, to five pounds four shillings.

---

ment, he met an officer of artillery drawing a cannon down, who alleged as the cause of his movement, that he had expended his ammunition. General Putnam dismounted, and finding some cartridges unexpended, ordered the officer to return to his post. Another captain left the field, under similar circumstances. It was in evidence, that the balls were too large for the service of the guns, and that it was necessary to break the cartridges before they could be used. The officers appear to have left the hill for the purpose of preserving the guns from capture. The examination subsided, without further proceedings. Capt. Trevet was in no way implicated in any suspicion of misconduct, and his arrest resulted from an unfortunate mistake.

Whereas, the honorable Provincial Congress has this day passed a resolve, appointing this committee to be a committee to consider of a further emission of notes or bills of credit, as mentioned in said resolve; but this committee, finding themselves unable to proceed in the business without a more perfect knowledge of the emissions lately made, both in quantity and circumstances of payment; and also for want of sufficient knowledge of the demands made, or to be made, upon the colony, do *Resolve*, that Col. Palmer attend the honorable Congress to-morrow, in order to obtain all necessary light in the premises.

Whereas, a considerable number of whale boats have been procured for the service of this colony, and many of them are said to be now in the towns of Braintree and Weymouth, and, unless proper care be taken of said boats, they will probably sustain great damage: therefore, *Resolved*, that it be recommended to the honorable Congress, that such order be taken respecting said boats, as their wisdom may direct.

This committee beg leave to suggest to the honorable Congress, whether the magazine wherein gunpowder is deposited, ought not to be guarded by electrical points; as any considerable loss in that article would deeply affect the public, which is humbly submitted.

Twenty-seven small arms, for the use of this colony, were received of Mr. Benjamin Ely, for which a receipt was given by the secretary of this committee, which guns were collected by order of Congress, and amount, by appraisement, to £————.

Forty-four small arms, for the use of this colony, were received of Mr. John Bliss, for which a receipt was given him by the secretary of this committee, which guns were collected by order of Congress, and amount, by appraisement, to £————.

Voted, That the commissary general be directed to supply head quarters with provisions as usual, till the further order of this committee.

JULY 1, 1775.

Forty-nine small arms, for the use of the colony, were received from the Rev. Mr. Lemuel Kollock, for which a receipt was given by Mr. Devens; which guns were collected by order of Congress, and amount, by appraisement, to £————.

Fifteen small arms were delivered Col. Ruggles Woodbridge, for the use of his regiment, amounting, as by appraisement, to twenty-nine pounds sixteen shillings and eight pence, for which guns a receipt was taken in the minute book.

Voted, That two thirds of the hay under the care of Mr. David Sanger, be brought to head quarters, and one third carried to the committee of supplies, at Watertown.

Six small arms were received of Mr. Abner Ellis, for the use of this colony, amounting, by appraisement, to £———, for which a receipt was given by the secretary of this committee.

Forty-four small arms were received of Benjamin Ely, by the hands of Mr. Solomon Edwards, for the use of this colony, for which a receipt was given by the secretary, which arms were collected by order of Congress, and amount, as by appraisement, to £———.

Eight small arms were received of Col. John Dickinson, by the hands of Benjamin Scott, Jun., for the use of this colony, amounting, by appraisement, to £———, for which a receipt was given by the secretary.

Capt. Jacob Miller was recommended to the honorable Congress, as a captain in Col. Doolittle's regiment, in the room of Capt. Leland, who has resigned.

Seventy-one small arms were delivered Col. David Brewer, for the use of his regiment, amounting, as by appraisement, to one hundred thirty-eight pounds six shillings, which guns he engaged should be returned in good order, unless lost in the service of this colony, as by his receipt in the minute book.

Thirteen small arms were delivered Col. Jonathan Brewer, for the use of his regiment, amounting, as by appraisement, to twenty-six pounds seven shillings, for which a receipt was taken in the minute book.

J<small>ULY</small> 2, 1775.

One hundred small arms were delivered Col. Glover, for the use of his regiment, amounting, as by appraisement, to one hundred ninety-two pounds eleven shillings, which guns he engaged should be returned in good order, unless lost in the service of this colony, as by his receipt in the minute book.

One hundred and seven small arms were received of Mr. Daniel Hemmenway, by the hands of Mr. John Elder, for the use of this colony, for which a receipt was given by Mr. Abraham Watson.

J<small>ULY</small> 3, 1775.

Twenty-six small arms were delivered Col. James Fry, for the use of his regiment, amounting, as by appraisement, to fifty-five pounds four shillings, for which a receipt was given in the minute book.

Ten small arms were delivered Col. Ephraim Doolittle, for the use of his regiment, amounting, as by appraisement, to twenty-two pounds eighteen shillings, for which a receipt was taken in the minute book.

One gun, for the use of Col. Gardner's regiment, was delivered to Lieut. Col. Bond, amounting, by appraisement, to two pounds fourteen shillings, for which a receipt was taken in the minute book.

Ten small arms were delivered Col. Moses Little, for the use of his regiment, amounting, as by appraisement, to twenty-two pounds one shilling and four pence, for which a receipt was given in the minute book.

Two small arms were delivered Col. Moses Little, for the use of his regiment, amounting, as by appraisement, to four pounds four shillings, for which a receipt was taken in the minute book.

Thirteen guns were received of Mr. Benjamin Ely, by the hands of Mr. John Eaton, collected by order of Congress, for which a receipt was given him.

Fifteen small arms were delivered Col. William Prescott, for the use of his regiment, amounting, by appraisement, to twenty-nine pounds sixteen shillings, for which a receipt was given in the minute book.

A number of officers in Col. Woodbridge's regiment, were recommended to the honorable Congress, to be commissioned, as by return on file.

Whereas, Mr. Edmund Quincy, of Stoughtonham, has represented to this committee, that sundry household goods and other effects, now or late the property of Thomas Hutchinson, Esq., and other persons publicly known to be also enemies to the rights and liberties of America, are hid in several places in and near Milton, which property will probably be lost or wasted, unless proper care is taken of the same, for such persons as may hereafter justly claim the same, therefore, *Resolved*, that said Quincy, be, and he hereby is empowered, to receive and convey to this committee, at Cambridge, all such goods and effects as aforesaid, for the use of such person or persons as the honorable Congress or some future Congress, or House of Representatives of this colony may order; he also producing to this committee, the Congress or House of Representatives, an account of all the articles he may so receive, the names of the persons from whom he may receive the same, and an account of the charges that may arise from such salvage and removal; and he also is hereby empowered, to press, if necessary, such teams as may be needed for removing such effects.

Also, *Resolved*, That this be immediately transmitted by the hands

74

of said Quincy, to the honorable Congress now sitting at Watertown, for their approbation or disapprobation.

Henries Vomhavi, an Indian, having represented to this committee, that he had taken two horses at Noddle's island, one a little horse, which he is desirous of retaining as some recompense for his fatigue and risk in that action, in which, it is said he behaved with great bravery; it is the opinion of this committee, that said Indian should be gratified in his request, which will be an encouragement to others in the service, provided, the honorable Congress should approve thereof.

Passed upon Mr. William White's account, a person employed by this committee as a rider in the colony service, which account amounted to six pounds thirteen shillings four pence, and a certificate was given him accordingly.

Thirty-nine small arms were delivered Col. Jonathan Brewer, for the use of his regiment, amounting, by appraisement, to sixty-eight pounds eighteen shillings and eight pence, for which a receipt was taken in the minute book.

JULY 4, 1775.

Mr. George Armstrong, who brought in a company of minute men, and has been in the army since the first alarm, having desired leave of absence from the camp, for some time, it was accordingly granted him; and an order was given the said Armstrong, on the taverners and innholders on the road to Murraysfield, to supply him with necessary provisions on his return home.

Mr. Eleazer Wier, was directed to deliver Benjamin Willing, one dozen and a half of files, for the use of the armorers now working at Mr. Gideon Frost's shop.

Voted, That Mr. David Sanger be directed to fill the widow Vassal's barn with hay.

Nine small arms were delivered Col. Joseph Read, for the use of his regiment, amounting, as by appraisement, to seventeen pounds fourteen shillings, for which guns a receipt was taken in the minute book.

Four guns were delivered Col. Moses Little, for the use of his regiment, amounting, as by appraisement, to nine pounds two shillings, for which a receipt was taken in the minute book.

JULY 5, 1775.

Thirty-seven fire-arms were received from Major Ebenezer White, which guns were collected by order of Congress, and amount, as by appraisement, to eighty-five pounds seven shillings.

Thirty-seven small arms, valued at eighty-five pounds seven shillings, were delivered General Thomas, for the use of his regiment, as by his receipt on file.

Six small arms were delivered Col. William Prescott, for the use of his regiment, amounting, by appraisement, to eleven pounds six shillings, for which a receipt was taken in the minute book.

Four small arms were delivered Col. William Prescott, for the use of his regiment, amounting, as by appraisement, to eight pounds fourteen shillings, for which a receipt was taken in the minute book.

Ten small arms were delivered Col. Moses Little, for the use of his regiment, amounting, as by appraisement, to eighteen pounds seven shillings and four pence, for which a receipt was taken in the minute book.

Passed upon John Bullfinch's, and twelve other persons' accounts, who worked with Jeremiah Russell, amounting in the whole to forty-four pounds eight shillings and eight pence, for which a certificate was given them, for the committee of accounts.

Voted, That Joseph Bates have liberty to cut thirty hundred of hay, on John Vassal, Esq's estate in Cambridge, he to be accountable therefor, and that Samuel Sanger, who has the care of the hay, be directed accordingly.

Eight guns, collected in Princeton, were received of Mr. Ephraim Woolson, by the hands of Sylvanus Oakes, amounting, by appraisement, to fourteen pounds seven shillings, for which a receipt was given him by the secretary.

JULY 6, 1775.

Voted, That Joseph and Parsons Smith, be allowed to cut, each, one ton of English hay, and one ton of black grass, on the estate of John Vassal, Esq., in Cambridge, they to be accountable therefor : and that Mr. David Sanger be directed accordingly.

A hand vice, screw plate, and pins, were purchased of Mr. Richard Estes, for the use of the armorers, amounting, as by receipt in the minute book, to eight shillings.

Mr. Seth Brown was directed and empowered to clear the widow Vassal's barns, for the reception of hay and horses for the colony service ; and also to prevent horses feeding in the pastures owned by said widow.

Mrs. Elizabeth Hicks was paid four shillings, by Mr. Devens, for bringing up a boat from Charlestown, as by receipt on file.

Voted, That Mr. Fisk, who has the care of Jonathan Sewall's farm, have liberty to cut on said farm one ton of English hay and two tons of salt hay, and that Mr. David Sanger be directed accordingly.

[*Voted*, That it be recommended to the honorable Provincial Congress to pass the following resolve :]

Whereas, the exigencies of the colony require that there should be, as soon as possible, an emission of bills of credit : therefore, *Resolved*, that there be immediately issued on the credit of this colony, and deposited in the treasury, a sum not exceeding one hundred thousand pounds, lawful money, in bills of credit of the following denominations, viz. : of one shilling, of two shillings, of two shillings and six pence, of four shillings, of five shillings, of seven shillings and six pence, of eight shillings, of eleven shillings, of thirteen shillings, of seventeen shillings, of nineteen shillings, of thirty shillings, of forty shillings, of sixty shillings, of eighty shillings, and of one hundred shillings; to be five thousand of each denomination, and no more, and to be of the form following, viz. :

COLONY OF THE MASSACHUSETTS BAY. } 　JULY ——, 1775.　　No. 109.

The possessor of this bill shall be paid, by the treasurer of this colony, two shillings and six pence, lawful money, by the 18th day of July, 1777, and [it] shall be received in all payments at the treasury at all times.

By order of Congress.

A. D. ⎫
B. E. ⎬ *Committee.*
C. F. ⎭

which said bills shall be paid and received in the public treasury, and in all payments in this colony, without any abatement or discount, upon any pretence whatsoever, under penalty of treble damages to both the payer and receiver, which penalty shall be applied to the discharge of the public debts of this colony.

And said bills shall also be printed on the back, with the colony seal, the value of the bill, and its date, and round the seal, these words : *Issued in defence of American Liberty.* Also, *Resolved*, that A. B. and C. be a committee to sign or authenticate all said bills, from one shilling to eleven shillings, inclusively; and that D. E. and F. be another committee to sign or authenticate all other the said bills, which are of from thirteen shillings to one hundred shillings, inclusively.

5000 bills of	1s.	-	-	-	£250
5000	" 2s.	-	-	-	500
5000	" 2s. 6d.	-	-	-	625
5000	" 4s.	-	-	-	1,000
5000	" 5s.	-	-	-	1,250
5000	" 7s. 6d.	-	-	-	1,875
5000	" 8s.	-	-	-	2,000
5000	" 11s.	-	-	-	2,750
5000	" 13s.	-	-	-	3,250
5000	" 17s.	-	-	-	4,250
5000	" 19s.	-	-	-	4,750
5000	" 30s.	-	-	-	7,500
5000	" 40s.	-	-	-	10,000
5000	" 60s.	-	-	-	15,000
5000	" 80s.	-	-	-	20,000
5000	"100s.	-	-	-	25,000——£100,000

[The following letter was sent to General Washington :]

MAY IT PLEASE YOUR EXCELLENCY :—The bearer, Capt. Brown, is the officer who took the horses that came off from Bunker's hill; you'll please to direct said horses being delivered to his care.

To His Excellency General Washington.

This committee have, with great concern, considered the advantages our enemies will derive from General Gage's misrepresentations of the battle of Charlestown, unless counteracted by the truth of that day's transactions being fairly and honestly represented to our friends, and others, in Great Britain: therefore, *Resolved*, that it be humbly recommended to the honorable Congress, now sitting at Watertown, to appoint a committee to draw up and transmit to Great Britain, as soon as possible, a fair, honest and impartial account of the late battle of Charlestown, on the 17th ultimo, so that our friends, and others, in that part of the world, may not be, in any degree, imposed upon by General Gage's misrepresentations of that day's transactions; and that they also be a standing committee for that purpose.

With hearts deeply affected by the sufferings of our friends in the town and harbor of Boston, now under the cruel hand of tyrannic power; and reflecting upon the advice of the late Continental Congress, respecting our enemies seizing any of our friends, it is *Resolved*, by this committee, that it be recommended to the honorable Provincial Congress, now sitting at Watertown, to recommend to the grand American Congress, that every crown officer, within the united colonies, be immediately seized, and held in safe custody until our friends who have been seized by General Gage are set at liberty, and fully recompensed for their loss and imprisonment.

Voted, That Mr. John Steel and his two sons be appointed armorers for this colony's forces.

Eight small arms were delivered Col. Ebenezer Bridge, for the use of his regiment, amounting, as by appraisement, to seventeen pounds six shillings, for which a receipt was taken in the minute book.

Whereas, the honorable Congress have made an establishment for a company of artificers, which consists of carpenters, blacksmiths, and wheelwrights; and a captain is appointed for the carpenters, but no provision is made for captains or master workmen for the blacksmiths and wheelwrights, therefore, *Resolved*, that the premises be recommended to the consideration of the honorable Congress, now sitting at Watertown.

JULY 7, 1775.

Two guns were received from Capt. Josiah Stone, of Framingham, for the use of this colony, amounting, by appraisement, to three pounds sixteen shillings, for which a receipt was given by Mr. Devens.

Forty small arms were delivered Col. Scammon, for the use of his regiment, amounting, by appraisement, to seventy-four pounds thirteen shillings and four pence, for which a receipt was taken in the minute book.

One small arm was delivered Col. Gridley, for the use of his regiment, amounting, by appraisement, to two pounds four shillings, for which a receipt was taken in the minute book.

Passed upon Matthew Clark's account, amounting to nine pounds three shillings and six pence; and a certificate was delivered him for the committee on accounts.

Whereas, Mr. Seth Brown, who has had the care of horses for the cannon, has resigned that employment, and as Thomas Organ, who was in the service of the late General Warren, is willing to undertake that service, looking upon him to be a person well qualified for that trust, we desire he may be appointed accordingly.

The above was directed to the gentlemen of the committee of supplies.

Passed upon Mr. Isaac Bissel, a post rider's account, amounting, as by copy on file, to two pounds one shilling; and a certificate was given him for the committee on accounts.

[Whereas, a number of soldiers in the American army, are from time to time, observed to be much disguised with spirituous liquors, and should not some effectual measures be taken to put a stop to this disorder, not only the morals and health, but also the lives and liberties of this people will be endangered ; therefore, *Resolved*, that it be, and it is hereby recommended to his Excellency General Washington, that an order be issued to suppress retailers of spirituous liquors within and near the camps, in such manner as to him may seem meet.]

Upon application made to this committee by Capt. Rogers, and due examination into the matter, the following was voted to be sent the selectmen, &c., of the town of Reading, to be communicated to the adjacent towns.

GENTLEMEN :—Whereas, Capt. Jacob Rogers, late an inhabitant of Charlestown, but who, through the necessity of the times, has been obliged to quit Charlestown, has since taken up his residence in the town of Reading ; but some licentious persons of the town of Stoneham, as is represented to us, have threatened to raise a mob, and drive him out of said Reading, to the great terror of his family, and this, without any cause that we can find, evidence having appeared of his good behavior while in Charlestown ; in order to put a stop to such disorderly conduct, it is *Resolved*, that all the inhabitants of this colony be desired, as they regard the peace and welfare of the country, to behave peaceably and quietly towards the said Capt. Rogers ; and if his conduct should hereafter be unworthy a friend to American liberty, he is then to be orderly complained of, to such authority as may then exist within this colony, but by no means to be proceeded against in any disorderly manner.

Twenty-eight guns, for the use of the colony, collected by order of Congress, were received of Mr. John Ingraham, July 7th.

Passed upon Mr. John Barber's account, amounting to seven pounds thirteen shillings and eight pence ; and a certificate was given him for the committee on accounts.

JULY 8, 1775.

Two small arms were received of Col. Simeon Spaulding, for the use of this colony, amounting, by appraisement, to two pounds twelve shillings.

Two small arms, appraised at four pounds four shillings, were delivered Capt. Job Cushing, of Col. Ward's regiment, as by receipt on file.

Fifteen small arms [were delivered,] for the use of Col. Sergeant's regiment, amounting, as by appraisement, to twenty-seven pounds three shillings, for which a receipt has been taken in the minute book.

The honorable the Provincial Congress having acquainted this committee, that Mr. James Winthrop, post master in Cambridge, had declined serving any longer in that office, and desired that another might be recommended to them for that place :

Voted, That Mr. Jonathan Hastings, Jun., be recommended to the honorable Congress, as a suitable person for the trust aforesaid.

Two small arms were received of Mr. Seth Stone, of Cambridge, for the use of this colony, amounting, as by appraisement, to three pounds eighteen shillings, for which a receipt was given him by the secretary.

Passed upon John Gill, Jun., a post rider's account, amounting to six pounds seventeen shillings and eight pence, for which a certificate was given.

[Whereas, many complaints have been made to this committee, that the armorers frequently deliver the arms out of their shops unfit for service, and delay the work unnecessarily ; in order to prevent occasion for such complaints in future, and to hasten the public service in an orderly manner, which has not yet been provided for, it is *Resolved*, that it be, and it hereby is, recommended to the honorable Congress, to make an establishment for, at least, four master armorers, each one of whom shall work and superintend one shop, each of which shops, as we apprehend, may well accommodate eight men, including the master.]

[*Resolved*, That the instructions to be given to the officers of the regiments, be sent to the council of war, and if approved, be forwarded : they are as follow :]

[*Instructions for the officers of the several regiments of the Massachusetts Bay forces, who are immediately to go upon the recruiting service.*]

[You are not to enlist any deserter from the ministerial army, nor any stroller, negro, or vagabond, or person suspected of being an enemy to the liberty of America, nor any under eighteen years of age.]

[As the cause is the best that can engage men of courage and principle to take up arms, so it is expected that none but such will be accepted by the recruiting officer ; the pay, provision, &c., being so ample, it is not doubted but the officers sent upon this service, will, without delay, complete their respective corps, and march the men forthwith to camp.]

[You are not to enlist any person who is not an American-born, unless such person has a wife and family, and is a settled resident in this country.]

[The persons you enlist, must be provided with good and complete arms.]

One small arm was received of Mr. Samuel Haynes, of Sudbury, for the use of this colony, amounting, by appraisement, to thirty shillings, for which a receipt was given him by the clerk.

Whereas, considerable uneasiness has arisen in some part of the army, from some of the soldiers enlisting a second time into other companies than those which they first enlisted into, and if not prevented will be attended with great inconvenience, therefore, *Resolved*, that it be recommended to the honorable Provincial Congress, to pass such an order as may cause those soldiers who have conducted as above, to return to their respective companies into which they were first enlisted, or otherwise order, as to them in their wisdom shall seem meet.

Whereas, it is necessary [that] the house of Mr. John Vassal, ordered by Congress for the residence of his excellency General Washington, should be immediately put in such condition as may make it convenient for that purpose, therefore, *Resolved*, that Mr. Timothy Austin be, and hereby is empowered and authorized, to put said house in proper order for the purposes above mentioned, and that he procure such assistance and furniture as may be necessary to put said house in proper condition for the reception of his excellency and his attendants.

(NOTE.)—The following letter was sent to the towns required to furnish clothing by the committee of supplies.

"WATERTOWN, JULY 10, 1775."

"GENTLEMEN:—In obedience to the order of Congress, we have proportioned thirteen thousand coats on all the towns and districts in this colony, excepting Boston and Charlestown; and have inclosed you the proportion, with their resolves, and a sample as a direction to you both as to the color and quality of the cloth which shall be manufactured by you, and of the quality of the imported cloths of which the coats shall be made; we are to assure you, that the coats you supply shall be delivered to the men of your town so far as circumstances will admit

"We are, gentlemen, respectfully, your most humble servants,

DAVID CHEEVER, *Chairman.*

P. S. A large number of shirts, stockings, and summer breeches are wanted immediately for the use of the army, you are therefore, earnestly requested, as you value the lives and health of your countrymen, to furnish this committee as soon as possible, with a large number of the said articles, not less than two shirts, two pair of stockings, and two pair of summer breeches to each coat, apportioned as the share of your town, and send them, as soon as procured, to Mr. William Hunt, at Watertown. We shall be ready to order payment for the same as soon as received, according to the prices which you shall certify, relying on your judgment to prevent impositions upon the soldiers.

JULY 11, 1775.

The commission from the honorable Congress to this committee, was this day received from said Congress.

His excellency General Washington having signified to this committee, that they send Monsieur Viart to the town of Worcester; *Resolved*, that a post immediately proceed with said Viart, to Worcester, and that Mr. Devens provide a horse for that purpose.

Two small arms were delivered Col. Mansfield, for the use of his regiment, amounting to five pounds eight shillings four pence, for which a receipt was taken in the minute book.

Resolved, That the committee of correspondence in the town of Worcester, be hereby required and directed to take into their custody, Monsieur Viart, a Frenchman; that they suffer him, on his parole, to have the liberty to walk for his health to a convenient distance about the town, but to guard against his escape, till they shall receive further orders on this subject, either from the general or this committee.

The following order was issued.

CAMBRIDGE, JULY 11, 1775.

To the Taverners and Innholders on the road between Cambridge and Worcester.

You are hereby required to supply with necessary provisions, Mr. ———, and a Frenchman with him, (he being on public service,) and charge the same to this colony.

The honorable the Congress of this colony, having passed a resolve that this committee be appointed to draw up and transmit to Great Britain, a fair and impartial account of the late battle of Charlestown, as soon as possible; and this committee being exceedingly crowded with business, therefore, *Resolved*, that the Rev. Doct. Cooper, Rev. Mr. Gordon and the Rev. Mr. Peter Thatcher, be desired to draw up a true statement of said action, as soon as may be, and lay it before this committee.

The committee of safety of Marblehead, were advised by this committee, that five ships sailed this day from Boston, their destination unknown.

The taverners and innholders on the road to Marblehead, were required to supply Mr. Thomas Williams, an express in the colony service, with necessary provisions, and to transmit an account of the charge thereof, to this committee.

Whereas, a number of horses have been taken from the enemy by our soldiers, and a difficulty arises whose property the horses in justice ought to be : therefore, *Resolved*, that it be, and it is hereby recommended, to the honorable Congress, to take such order respecting the same, as to them, in their wisdom, shall seem meet.

[Whereas, his excellency General Washington, by his secretary Mr. Reed, has sent to this committee fifteen persons, taken at Long Island, this committee apprehending, that by their commission, they have no power to dispose of said persons: therefore, *Resolved*, that the above fifteen persons be immediately sent to the honorable the Congress, at Watertown, and that Mr. Richard Devens and Col. Orne, be a committee to go to the Congress with this resolve.]

JULY 12, 1775.

[Whereas, frequent complaints have been made to this committee, that many of the arms returned from the armorers have not been sufficiently repaired, which error may have arisen from ignorant or careless persons being employed as armorers, or for want of a master workman or superintendent in each shop, therefore, *Resolved*, that Benjamin Guillam, an armorer in the shop belonging to Gideon Frost, be, and he hereby is directed, to work as a master armorer in said shop, and to superintend the other armorers in that shop, whose duty it shall be to receive into said shop such arms as may, at any time, be sent there, by any of the colonels in that part of the American army belonging to this colony, in order to be repaired ; to see that such arms are properly repaired ; to deliver the same, when so repaired, to the persons from whom they were received; to see that no persons employed in said shop, as armorers, are either ignorant of said business, or careless, or idle ; and if any such should be employed in the shop, said Guillam shall, without delay, inform this committee thereof; and that he suffer no more than eight armorers, including himself, to be employed at any one time, in said shop.]

JULY 13, 1775.

[Mr. Benjamin Guillam, an armorer, had an order on the committee of supplies for two hundred pounds of iron, and what files and old brass he has occasion for, for himself and others that work in his shop.]

[Mr. Monroe recommended Seth Johnston, of Old Rutland, and Enoch Putnam, of Granby, as proper persons for armorers.]

[Thomas Organ was this day commissioned to take the care of the colony horses, and from time to time to attend to such orders as he shall receive from this committee.]

[His excellency General Washington having this day ordered, to the direction of this committee, ten prisoners taken some time past, at Machias, on board an armed cutter, the committee, apprehending from their commission of the 8th instant, that they are altogether restricted from acting as a committee but only in the recess of Congress, except in conformity to certain special resolves of Congress, or for making provision for the poor of Boston and Charlestown, and guarding against the small pox; as mentioned in said commission, have *Resolved*, that the said prisoners be sent to Congress for their orders, and that Doct. Church be directed to attend Congress with this resolve.]

[Whereas, Lieut. Ely Stiles has represented to this committee, that he has been at considerable expense in conducting the prisoners from Machias to head quarters, and desires to be repaid, but this matter not being within the powers with which this committee is vested, they beg leave to recommend the consideration of this case to the honorable Congress.]

[Whereas, some evil minded persons, taking advantage of the confusion occasioned by the battles of Lexington and Charlestown, have plundered and carried off, into several parts of this and the neighboring colonies, sundry goods and household furniture belonging to some of the unhappy sufferers of Boston and Charlestown : therefore, *Resolved*, that it be recommended to the honorable Congress, that the several selectmen and committees of correspondence in the several towns and districts within this colony, be directed and ordered, and also the town officers in the neighboring colonies be, and they hereby are severally and earnestly requested, to inspect their several towns and districts, and if they observe any such goods or household furniture, such officers are directed or desired to send all such effects to the office of Mr. Joseph Pierce Palmer, quarter master general, in Cambridge, for the benefit of the true and rightful proprietors, or that the Congress may take such other measures as in their wisdom may seem meet.]

JULY 14, 1775.

[Whereas, Mr. Seth Brown, who lately had the care of the artillery horses, at Cambridge, resigned that employment : upon which this committee recommended to the committee of supplies to appoint Mr. Thomas Organ to the care of said horses, instead of said Brown, but said committee of supplies having signified to this committee that such appointment was not within their commission, but was, as they apprehended, within ours, and accordingly returned said recommendation, with their reply upon the back thereof: and whereas, the public safety requires that said horses should be taken proper care of, and always kept in readiness for use upon the shortest notice, therefore, *Resolved*, that although said appointment is not within, but contrary to the commission of this committee, yet apprehending that it is absolutely necessary for the public service, that an hostler should be appointed for that employment, and no other mode of appointment appearing, in this time of the recess of Congress, this committee do, for the reasons assigned, appoint said Organ to the care of said horses, for the purpose aforesaid, until further orders.]

JULY 15, 1775.

[*Ordered*, That Mr. Sanger put as much hay into the general's barns, in this town, as they will receive, any order to the contrary notwithstanding.]

[Complaint having been made to this committee by the honorable General Ward, and other officers in the army, that several men are dangerously sick, and their lives would be greatly hazarded, except immediate application of medicine be made to them, and that the surgeons of some of the regiments had applied, but could not obtain any; a sub-committee was therefore chosen to visit the hospital, and to see the surgeons, and, upon inquiry, found that there were no such medicines as are immediately wanted: therefore, *Resolved*, that as the lives of some part of the army are in great danger, for want of medicines, notwithstanding the commission of the committee of safety does not admit of direction in this matter, that Mr. Commissary Craigie be desired to procure, at the expense of the colony, such medicines as may be immediately and absolutely necessary; in consequence of which, the following order was given Mr. Commissary Craigie:

SIR:—You are hereby desired immediately to supply the store under your care, with such medicines as are absolutely necessary for the present relief of the sick in the army.][1]

(1.) Although the sessions of the committee continued after the fifteenth day of July, 1775, the journal is not preserved to a later date.

APPENDIX.

PROCEEDINGS

OF THE

CONVENTIONS OF THE PEOPLE

IN THE

COUNTIES OF MASSACHUSETTS.

CONVENTION OF SUFFOLK COUNTY.

AT a meeting of the delegates of every town and district in the county of Suffolk, held on Tuesday, the sixth of September, 1774, at the house of Mr. Richard Woodward of Dedham, and, by adjournment, at the house of Mr. Daniel Vose of Milton, on Friday, the ninth instant, Joseph Palmer, Esq. being chosen moderator, and William Thompson, Esq., clerk, a committee was chosen to bring in a report to the convention, and the following, being several times read, and put paragraph by paragraph, was unanimously voted, viz. :

Whereas, the power, but not the justice; the vengeance, but not the wisdom of Great Britain, which of old persecuted, scourged, and exiled our fugitive parents from their native shores, now pursues us, their guiltless children, with unrelenting severity : and whereas this, then savage and uncultivated desert, was purchased by the toil and treasure, or acquired by the valor and blood of those, our venerable progenitors, who bequeathed to us the dear bought inheritance. who consigned it to our care and protection ; the most sacred obligations are upon us to transmit the glorious purchase, unfettered by power, unclogged with shackles, to our innocent and beloved offspring. On the fortitude, on the wisdom, and on the exertions of this important day, is suspended the fate of this new world, and of unborn millions. If a boundless extent of continent, swarming with millions, will tamely submit to live, move, and have their being at the arbitrary will of a licentious minister, they will basely yield to voluntary slavery, and future generations shall load their memories with incessant execrations. On the other hand, if we arrest the hand which would ransack our pockets, if we disarm the parricide who points the dagger to our bosoms, if we nobly defeat that fatal edict, which proclaims a power to frame laws for us in all

76

cases whatsoever, thereby entailing the endless and numberless curses of slavery upon us, our heirs and their heirs forever; if we successfully resist that unparalleled usurpation of unconstitutional power, whereby our capital is robbed of the means of life; whereby the streets of Boston are thronged with military executioners; whereby our coasts are lined, and the harbors crowded with ships of war; whereby the charter of the colony, that sacred barrier against the encroachments of tyranny, is mutilated, and in effect annihilated; whereby a murderous law is framed, to shelter villains from the hands of justice; whereby that unalienable and inestimable inheritance which we derived from nature, the constitution of Britain, which was covenanted to us in the charter of the province, is totally wrecked, annulled, and vacated; posterity will acknowledge that virtue which preserved them free and happy; and while we enjoy the rewards and blessings of the faithful, the torrent of panegyric will roll down our reputations to that latest period, when the streams of time shall be absorbed in the abyss of eternity.

Therefore, we have resolved and do resolve:

1. That whereas, his majesty, George the third, is the rightful successor to the throne of Great Britain, and justly entitled to the allegiance of the British realm, and, agreeably to compact, of the English colonies in America; therefore, we, the heirs and successors of the first planters of this colony, do cheerfully acknowledge the said George the third to be our rightful sovereign, and that said covenant is the tenure and claim on which are founded our allegiance and submission.

2. That it is an indispensable duty which we owe to God, our country, ourselves, and posterity, by all lawful ways and means in our power, to maintain, defend, and preserve those civil and religious rights and liberties, for which, many of our fathers fought, bled, and died; and to hand them down entire to future generations.

3. That the late acts of the British parliament, for blocking up the harbor of Boston, and for altering the established form of government in this colony, and for screening the most flagitious violators of the laws of the province from a legal trial, are gross infractions of those rights, to which we are justly entitled by the laws of nature, the British constitution, and the charter of the province.

4. That no obedience is due from this province, to either or any part of the acts abovementioned; but that they should be rejected as the attempts of a wicked administration to enslave America.

5. That so long as the justices of our superior courts of judicature, court of assize, and general gaol delivery, and inferior courts of common pleas in this county, are appointed, or hold their places by any other tenure than that which the charter and the laws of the province direct, they must be considered as under undue influence, and are, therefore, unconstitutional officers, and as such, no regard ought to be paid to them by the people of this county.

6. That if the justices of the superior court of judicature, court of assize, &c., justices of the court of common pleas, or of the general sessions of

the peace, shall sit and act during their present disqualified state, this county will support and bear harmless all sheriffs and their deputies, constables, jurors, and other officers, who shall refuse to carry into execution the orders of said courts; and, as far as is possible, to prevent the inconveniences that must attend the suspension of the courts of justice, we do earnestly recommend it to all creditors to exercise all reasonable and generous forbearance to their debtors; and to all debtors to discharge their just debts, with all possible speed; and if any disputes concerning debts or trespasses should arise, which cannot be settled by the parties, we recommend it to them to submit all such causes to arbitration; and if the parties, or either of them, shall refuse so to do, they ought to be considered as cooperating with the enemies of this country.

7. That it be recommended to the collectors of taxes, constables, and all other officers, who have public moneys in their hands, to retain the same, and not to make any payment thereof to the province or county treasurers, until the civil government of the province is placed upon a constitutiona. foundation, or until it shall otherwise be ordered by the proposed provincial congress.

8. That the persons who have accepted seats at the council board, by virtue of a mandamus from the king, in conformity to the late act of the British parliament, entitled an act for regulating the government of the Massachusetts bay, have acted in direct violation of the duty they owe to their country, and have thereby given great and just offence to this people. Therefore,

Resolved, That this county do recommend it to all persons who have so highly offended by accepting said department, and have not, already, publicly resigned their seats at the council board, to make public resignations of their places at said board, on or before the twentieth day of this instant September; and that all persons neglecting so to do, shall, from and after that day, be considered by this county as obstinate and incorrigible enemies to this colony.

9. That the fortifications began and now carrying on upon Boston neck, are justly alarming to this county, and give us reason to apprehend some hostile intention against that town; more especially as the commander in chief has, in a very extraordinary manner, removed the powder from the magazine at Charlestown, and has also forbidden the keeper of the magazine at Boston, to deliver out to the owners, the powder which they lodged in said magazine.

10. That the late act of parliament, for establishing the roman catholic religion and the French laws in that extensive country now called Canada, is dangerous in an extreme degree, to the protestant religion, and to the civil rights and liberties of all America; and therefore, as men and protestant christians, we are indispensably obliged to take all proper measures for our security.

11. That, whereas, our enemies have flattered themselves that they shall make an easy prey of this numerous, brave, and hardy people, from an ap-

prehension that they are unacquainted with military discipline; we, therefore, for the honor, defence, and security of this county and province, advise, as it has been recommended, to take away all commissions from the officers of the militia: that those who now hold commissions, or such other persons, be elected in each town as officers in the militia, as shall be judged of sufficient capacity for that purpose, and who have evidenced themselves to be inflexible friends to the rights of the people: and that the inhabitants of those towns and districts, who are qualified, do use their utmost diligence to acquaint themselves with the art of war as soon as possible, and do for that purpose appear under arms at least once every week.

12. That during the present hostile appearances on the part of Great Britain, notwithstanding the many insults and oppressions which we most sensibly resent; yet, nevertheless, from our affection to his majesty, which we have at all times evinced, we are determined to act merely on the defensive, so long as such conduct may be vindicated by reason and the principles of self-preservation, but no longer.

13. That as we understand it has been in contemplation to apprehend sundry persons of this county, who have rendered themselves conspicuous in contending for the violated rights and liberties of their countrymen, we do recommend, should such an audacious measure be put in practice, to seize and keep in safe custody every servant of the present tyrannical and unconstitutional government, throughout the county and province, until the persons so apprehended be liberated from the hands of our adversaries, and restored safe and uninjured to their respective friends and families.

14. That until our rights are fully restored to us, we will, to the utmost of our power, (and we do recommend the same to the other counties,) withhold all commercial intercourse with Great Britain, Ireland, and the West Indies, and abstain from the consumption of British merchandize and manufactures, and especially of East India teas and piece goods, with such additions, alterations, and exceptions, only as the grand Congress of the colonies may agree to.

15. That under our present circumstances, it is incumbent on us to encourage arts and manufactures amongst us, by all means in our power; and that Joseph Palmer, Esq., of Braintree, Mr. Ebenezer Duer, of Roxbury, Mr. James Boice and Mr. Edward Preston, of Milton, and Mr. Nathaniel Guild, of Walpole, be, and hereby are appointed a committee, to consider of the best ways and means to promote and establish the same, and report to this convention as soon as may be.

16. That the exigencies of our public affairs demand that a provincial congress be called, to concert such measures as may be adopted and vigorously executed by the whole people; and we do recommend it to the several towns in this county, to choose members for such a provincial congress, to be holden at Concord, on the second Tuesday of October next ensuing.

17. That this county, confiding in the wisdom and integrity of the Continental Congress, now sitting at Philadelphia, will pay all due respect and submission to such measures as may be recommended by them to the colo-

nies, for the restoration and establishment of our just rights, civil and religious, and for renewing that harmony and union between Great Britain and the colonies, so earnestly wished for by all good men.

18. Whereas, the universal uneasiness which prevails among all orders of men, arising from the wicked and oppressive measures of the present administration, may influence some unthinking persons to commit outrages upon private property: we would heartily recommend to all persons of this community, not to engage in any routs, riots, or licentious attacks upon the property of any persons whatsoever, as being subversive of all order and government; but by a steady, manly, uniform, and persevering opposition, to convince our enemies, that in a contest so important, in a cause so solemn, our conduct shall be such as to merit the approbation of the wise, and the admiration of the brave and free of every age and of every country.

19. That should our enemies, by any sudden invasion, render it necessary for us to ask the aid and assistance of our brethren in the country, some one of the committee of correspondence, or a selectman of such town, or the town adjoining where such hostilities shall commence, or shall be expected to commence, shall despatch couriers with written messages to the selectmen or committees of correspondence of the several towns in the vicinity, with a written account of such matters, who shall despatch others to committees or selectmen more remote, till proper and sufficient assistance be obtained; and that the expense of said couriers be defrayed by the county, until it shall be otherwise ordered by the provincial congress.

Voted, That Joseph Warren, Esq. and Doct. Benjamin Church, of Boston, Deacon Joseph Palmer and Col. Ebenezer Thayer, of Braintree, Capt. Lemuel Robinson, William Holden, Esq. and Capt. John Homans, of Dorchester, Capt. William Heath, of Roxbury, Col. William Taylor and Doct. Samuel Gardner, of Milton, Isaac Gardner, Esq., Capt. Benjamin White and Capt. Thomas Aspinwall, of Brookline, Nathaniel Sumner, Esq. and Mr. Richard Woodward, of Dedham, be a committee to wait on his excellency the governor, to inform him that this county are alarmed at the fortifications making on Boston neck, and to remonstrate against the same, and the repeated insults offered by the soldiery to persons passing and repassing into that town, and to confer with him upon those subjects.

WILLIAM THOMPSON, *Clerk.*

The committee appointed at the convention, accordingly prepared, and on Monday, September 12th, 1774, presented the following address, viz. :

To his Excellency Thomas Gage, Esq., Captain General and Commander in Chief of his Majesty's province of Massachusetts Bay.

May it please your Excellency :—The county of Suffolk, being greatly, and in their opinion, justly alarmed, at the formidable appearances of hostility, now threatening his majesty's good subjects of this country, and more particularly of the town of Boston, the loyal and faithful capital of this province, beg leave to address your excellency, and to represent, that the apprehensions of the people are more especially increased by the dangerous design now carrying into execution, of repairing and mantling the fortification at the south entrance of the town of Boston, which, when completed, may, at any time, be improved to aggravate the miseries of that already impoverished and distressed city, by intercepting the wonted and necessary intercourse between the town and country, and compel the wretched inhabitants to the most ignominious state of humiliation and vassallage, by depriving them of the necessary supplies of provisions, for which they are chiefly dependant on that communication.

We have been informed, that your excellency, in consequence of the application of the selectmen of Boston, has, indeed, disavowed any intention to injure the town in your present manœuvres, and expressed your purpose to be for the security of the troops and his majesty's subjects in the town. We are at a loss to guess, may it please your excellency, from whence your want of confidence in the loyal and orderly people of this country could originate. A measure so formidable, carried into execution from a preconceived though causeless jealousy of the insecurity of his majesty's troops and subjects in the town, deeply wounds the loyalty, and is an additional injury to the faith-ful subjects of this country, and affords a strong motive for this application. We therefore entreat your excellency, to desist from your design, assuring your excellency, that the people of this county are by no means disposed to injure his majesty's troops; they think themselves aggrieved and oppressed by the late acts of parliament, and are resolved, by divine assistance, never to submit to them; but have no inclination to commence a war with his majesty's troops; and beg leave to observe to your excellency, that the ferment now excited in the minds of the people, is occasioned by some late transactions, by seizing the powder in the arsenal at Charlestown, by withholding the powder lodged in the magazine of the town of Boston from the legal proprietors, insulting, beating, and abusing passengers to and from the town by the soldiery, in which they have been encouraged by some of their officers, putting the people in fear, and menacing them in their nightly patrols into the neighboring towns, and more particularly, by fortifying the sole avenue by land to the town of Boston. In duty, therefore, to his majesty, and to your excellency, and for the restoration of order and security in this county, we, the delegates from the several towns in this county, being commissioned for this purpose, beg your excellency's attention to this our humble and faithful address, assuring you, that nothing less than an immediate removal of the ordnance, and restoring the entrance into that town to its former state, and an effectual stop of all insults and abuses in future, can place the inhabitants of this county in that state of peace and tranquillity, in which every free subject ought to live.

By order of the committee,

JOSEPH WARREN, *Chairman.*

Boston, Sept. 10, '774.

To which address, his excellency was pleased to make the following answer:

GENTLEMEN :—I hoped the assurances I gave the selectmen of Boston, on the subject of your address to me, had been satisfactory to every body. I cannot possibly intercept the intercourse between the town and the country; it is my duty and interest to encourage it; and it is as much inconsistent with my duty and interest to form the strange scheme you are pleased to suggest, of reducing the inhabitants to a state of humiliation and vassallage, by stopping their supplies; nor have I made it easier to effect this, than what nature has made it. You mention the soldiers insulting, beating, and abusing passengers as a common thing; an instance, perhaps, may be given of the bad behavior of some disorderly soldiers; but I must appeal to the inhabitants of both town and country, for their general good behavior, from their first arrival to this time. I would ask, what occasion there is for such numbers going armed in and out of the town, and through the country, in an hostile manner? Or, why were the guns removed, privately, in the night, from the battery at Charlestown?

The refusing submission to the late acts of parliament, I find general throughout the province; and I shall lay the same before his majesty.

                                    THOMAS GAGE.

                                            Sept. 12, 1774.

The committee of the delegates from the several towns in the county of Suffolk, who presented the address to the governor, on receiving his answer, met together, and having carefully perused the same, were of opinion, that his excellency's answer could not be deemed satisfactory to the county. And further thought, his excellency, in his reply, had been pleased to propose several questions, which, if unanswered by the committee, would leave on the minds of persons not fully acquainted with the state of facts, some very disagreeable impressions concerning the conduct and behavior of the people in this county and province. And the following address was unanimously voted to his excellency.

May it please your Excellency:—The answer you have been pleased to favor us with, to the address this day presented to you, gives us satisfaction so far as it relates to your own intentions; and we thank your excellency, for the declaration which you have made, that it is your duty and interest to encourage an intercourse between town and country; and we entreat your indulgence, while we modestly reply to the questions proposed in your answer. Your excellency is too well acquainted with the human heart not to be sensible, that it is natural for the people to be soured by oppression, and jealous for their personal security, when their exertions for the preservation of their rights are construed into treason and rebellion. Our liberties are invaded by acts of the British parliament; troops are sent to enforce those acts; they are now erecting fortifications at the entrance of the town of Boston; upon the completing those, the inhabitants of the town of Boston will be in the power of a soldiery, who must implicitly obey the orders of an administration, who have hitherto evinced no singular regard to the liberties of America. The town is already greatly impoverished and distressed by the operation of the barbarous port-bill. Your excellency, we are persuaded, from principles of humanity, would refuse to be an actor in the tragical scene that must ensue upon shutting up the avenues to the town, and reducing the inhabitants by distress and famine, to a disgraceful and slavish submission; but that cruel work may possibly be reserved for a successor, disposed and instructed thereto. Daily supplies of provisions are necessary for the subsistence of the inhabitants of the town. The country, disgusted and jealous at the formidable operations now carrying on, survey with horror, a plan concerted, whereby the inhabitants of the town of Boston may be imprisoned and starved, at the will of a military commander. They kindly invite them to abandon the town, and earnestly solicit them to share the homely banquet of peace in the country. Should their refusal involve them in miseries hitherto unheard of, and hardly conceived of, the country must stand acquitted, and will not hold their liberties so loosely, as to sacrifice them to the obstinacy of their brethren in Boston.

Your excellency has been pleased to order the powder from the magazine in Charlestown; to forbid the delivery of the powder in the magazine of Boston to the legal proprietors; to seize the cannon at Cambridge; and to bring a formidable number from Castle-William, which are now placed at the entrance of the town of Boston; and has, likewise, in addition to the troops now here, been pleased to send for reenforcements to Quebec, and other parts of the continent. These things, Sir, together with the dispositions of the ships of war, we humbly think, sufficiently justify the proceedings for which your excellency seems to be at loss to account.

Your excellency has suggested, that nature has made it easy to cut off the communication between town and country. Our only request is, that the entrance into the town may remain as nature has formed it. If security to his majesty's troops is the only design in the late manœuvre, we beg leave to assure your excellency, that the most certain, and by far the most honorable method of making them secure and safe, will be to give the people of the province, the strongest proof that no design is forming against their liberties. And we again solicit your excellency, with that earnestness which becomes us on this important occasion, to desist from every thing which has a tendency to alarm them, and particularly from fortifying the entrance into the town of Boston. We rely on your excellency's wisdom and candor, that in your proposed representation to our common sovereign, you will endeavor to redeem us from the distresses which we apprehend were occasioned by the grossest misinformation, and that you will assure his majesty, that no wish of independence, no adverse sentiments or designs towards his majesty or his troops now here, actuate his good subjects in this colony; but that their sole intention is, to preserve pure and inviolate those rights to which, as men and English Americans, they are justly entitled, and which have been guarantied to them by his majesty's royal predecessors.

A copy of the foregoing was delivered to Mr. Secretary Flucker, by the chairman, with a desire, that he would, as soon as was convenient, present it to the governor, and request his excellency to appoint a time for receiving it in form. The secretary informed the chairman the ensuing day, that he had seen the governor, and had given him the copy of the address, but, that he declined receiving it in form. The chairman mentioned to him the importance of the business, declaring his belief, that the troops were not in any danger, and that no person had, so far as he had been informed, taken any steps which indicated any hostile intention, until the seizing and carrying off the powder from the magazine in the county of Middlesex; and that if any ill consequences should arise, that should affect the interest of Great Britain, the most candid and judicious, both in Europe and America, would consider the author of the ferment now raised in the minds of the people, as accountable for whatever consequences might follow from it.

He therefore desired the secretary, once more to make application to his excellency, and to state the affair to him in that serious manner which the case seemed to require. The secretary accordingly made a second application to the governor, but received for answer, that he had given all the satisfaction in his power, and he could not see that any further argumentation upon the subject would be to any purpose. Upon this, the committee were again convened, and it was unanimously *Resolved*, that they had executed the commission intrusted to them by the county, to the utmost of their ability. And after voting that the reply to his excellency's answer should be inserted in the public papers as soon as possible, they adjourned without day.

Every vote passed by the delegates of the county, and by the committee appointed to wait on the governor, was unanimous.

CONVENTION OF MIDDLESEX COUNTY.

At a meeting of the following gentlemen, being committees from every town and district in the county of Middlesex, and province of Massachusetts Bay, held at Concord, in said county, on the 30th and 31st days of August, 1774, to consult upon measures proper to be taken at the present very important day, viz.:

Capt. Thomas Gardner, Doct. Samuel Blodget, Capt. Samuel Whittemore, Mr. Loammi Baldwin, Mr. Abraham Watson, Capt. Ezekiel How, Mr. Samuel Thatcher, Mr. John Maynard, Capt. Eliphalet Robbins, Mr. Phinehas Gleason, Capt. Ephraim Frost, Mr. Samson Belcher, Mr. Joseph Wellington, Mr. Thomas Plympton, Mr. Nathaniel Sparhawk, Mr. Hezekiah

77

Maynard, Capt. Isaac Foster, Doct. Samuel Curtis, Mr. Peter Edes, Mr. Alpheus Wood, Mr. William Wyer, Mr. Edward Barnes, David Cheever, Esq., Mr. William Boyd, Mr. Richard Devens, Mr. Ebenezer Bridge, Jr., Mr. John Frothingham, Mr. Joshua Abbot, Mr. John Codman, Capt. Ralph Hill, Doct. Isaac Foster, Mr. William Thompson, Mr. Samuel White, Doct. Timothy Danforth, Mr. Josiah Capen, Capt. Josiah Bowers, Mr. David Beamis, Mr. Solomon Pollard, Mr. David Sanger, Capt. Thaddeus Bowman, Mr. Elijah Bond, Mr. Jonas Stone, Mr. Ephraim Wood, Jr., Mr. Joseph Loring, Mr. John Flint, Mr. Benjamin Brown, Mr. Nathan Merriam, Joseph Haven, Esq., Mr. William Clark, Capt. Josiah Stone, Mr. Joshua Hammond, Mr. William Brown, Capt. Jonas Stone, Mr. David Haven, Mr. Edward Durant, Mr. Ebenezer Marshall, Capt. Samuel Wyman, Mr. Jonathan Williams Austin, Mr. Robert Douglass, Mr. Simeon Spaulding, Mr. Samuel Stevens, Jr., Mr. Jonathan Stow, Mr. Benjamin Walker, Capt. Daniel Taylor, Capt. Francis Harris, Mr. James Hussey, Mr. Asa Holden, Mr. James Locke, Mr. Obadiah Sawtell, Henry Gardner, Esq., Mr. Benjamin Brown, Mr. John Marble, Mr. Jonathan Flint, Doct. Charles Whitman, Mr. Joseph Parker, Capt. Phinehas Taylor, Capt. John Dexter, Mr. Joseph Bryant, Capt. Ebenezer Harnden, Mr. James Hay, Mr. Thomas Hill, Mr. Edward Buckman, Mr. Samuel Sprague, James Prescott, Esq., Mr. James Kettell, Oliver Prescott, Esq., Mr. Benjamin Pierce, Capt. Josiah Sawtell, Mr. Thomas Rand, Capt. Benjamin Jaquith, Mr. Josiah Smith, Mr. Timothy Walker, Mr. Joshua Symonds, Mr. Edward Kendall, Mr. Ebenezer Brooks, Jr., Mr. William Borden, Capt. Josiah Hartwell, Mr. Thomas Upham, Mr. Oliver Hoar, Mr. Abel Perry, Mr. Daniel Rogers, Jr., Mr. Hezekiah Broad, Mr. Samuel Park, Mr. Peter Colburn, Capt. Thomas Mellen, Mr. Ephraim Colburn, Capt. Roger Dench, Mr. Stephen Davis, Mr. Jacob Gibbs, John Read, Esq., Capt. Jonathan Minot, Mr. Joseph Hartwell, Mr. John Abbot, Mr. John Moore, Doct. Asaph Fletcher, Capt. John Webber, Mr. Nathaniel Boynton, Mr. Daniel Mellen, Mr. Zacheus Wright, Mr. Aaron Phipps, Capt. Richard Sanger, Mr. Joshua Hemenway, Mr. Benjamin Fassett, Mr. Francis Falkner, Mr. Samuel Bullard, Mr. John Heywood, Capt. William Coolidge, Mr. Ephraim Hapgood, Mr. Jonathan Hammond, Capt. William Prescott, Mr. Samuel Harrington, Mr. Henry Woods, Mr. Jacob Bigelow, Mr. William Green, Capt. Abijah Brown, Mr. Nehemiah Hobart, Mr. Charles Witherell, Mr. Joseph Danforth, Capt. Edmund Bancroft, Mr. Lemuel Perham, Mr. Josiah Fisk, Mr. Jonathan Brown, Mr. Samuel Farrar, Mr. Aaron Beard, Capt. Abijah Pierce, Mr. David Bayley, Capt. Eleazer Brooks, Mr. Ebenezer Stone, Capt. Joseph Butterfield, Mr. Jonathan Locke.

The Honorable James Prescott, Esq., was chosen chairman.

After having read the late act of the British parliament, entitled an act for the better regulating the government of the province of Massachusetts Bay in New England, and debated thereon:

Voted, That a committee be appointed to take into consideration the said act, and report to this meeting.

Voted, That Mr. Jonathan Williams Austin of Chelmsford, Capt. Thomas

Gardner of Cambridge, Doct. Isaac Foster of Charlestown, Capt. Josiah Stone of Framingham, Mr. Richard Devens of Charlestown, Doct. Oliver Prescott of Groton, Henry Gardner, Esq. of Stow, Mr. William Brown of Framingham, and Mr. Ebenezer Bridge, Jr. of Billerica, be the committee, who reported as follows:

It is evident to every attentive mind, that this province is in a very dangerous and alarming situation. We are obliged to say, however painful it may be to us, that the question now is, whether, by a submission to some late acts of the parliament of Great Britain, we are contented to be the most abject slaves, and entail that slavery on posterity after us, or by a manly, joint, and virtuous opposition, assert and support our freedom. There is a mode of conduct, which in our very critical circumstances, we would wish to adopt; a conduct, on the one hand, never tamely submissive to tyranny and oppression, on the other, never degenerating into rage, passion, and confusion. This is a spirit which we revere, as we find it exhibited in former ages, and will command applause to the latest posterity.

The late acts of parliament pervade the whole system of jurisprudence, by which means, we think, the fountains of justice are fatally corrupted. Our defence must, therefore, be immediate in proportion to the suddenness of the attack, and vigorous in proportion to the danger.

We must now exert ourselves, or all those efforts, which, for ten years past, have brightened the annals of this country, will be totally frustrated. Life and death, or, what is more, freedom and slavery, are, in a peculiar sense, now before us, and the choice and success, under God, depend greatly upon ourselves. We are therefore bound, as struggling not only for ourselves, but future generations, to express our sentiments in the following resolves; sentiments which, we think, are founded in truth and justice, and therefore sentiments we are determined to abide by.

Resolved, That as true and loyal subjects of our gracious sovereign, George the third, king of Great Britain, we by no means intend to withdraw our allegiance from him; but, while permitted the free exercise of our natural and charter rights, are resolved to expend life and treasure in his service.

Resolved, That when our ancestors emigrated from Great Britain, charters and solemn stipulations expressed the conditions, and what particular rights they yielded; what each party had to do and perform; and which each of the contracting parties were equally bound by.

Resolved, That we know of no instance, in which this province has transgressed the rules on their part, or any ways forfeited their natural and charter rights to any power on earth.

Resolved, That the parliament of Great Britain have exercised a power contrary to the abovementioned charter, by passing acts, which hold up their absolute supremacy over the colonists; by another act blocking up the port of Boston; and by two late acts, the one entitled, an act for better regulating the government of the province of Massachusetts Bay, the other entitled, an act for the more impartial administration of justice in said province; and by enforcing all these iniquitous acts with a large armed force, to dragoon and enslave us.

Resolved, That the late act of parliament, entitled an act for the better regulating the government of the province of the Massachusetts Bay in New England, expressly acknowledges the authority of the charter, granted by their majesties king William and queen Mary, to said province; and that the only reasons suggested in the preamble to said act, which is intended to deprive us of the privileges confirmed to us by said charter, are, the inexpediency of continuing those privileges, and the charge of their having been forfeited, to which charge the province has had no opportunity of answering.

Resolved, That a debtor may as justly refuse to pay his debts, because it is inexpedient for him, as the parliament of Great Britain deprive us of our charter privileges, because it is inexpedient to a corrupt administration for us to enjoy them.

Resolved, That in all free states there must be an equilibrium in the legislative body, without which constitutional check, they cannot be said to be a free people.

Resolved, That the late act, which ordains a council to be appointed by his majesty, his heirs and successors, from time to time, by warrant under his or their signet or sign manual, and which ordains that said councillors shall hold their offices respectively for and during the pleasure of his majesty, his heirs and successors, effectually alters the constitutional equilibrium, renders the councillors absolute tools and creatures, and entirely destroys the importance of the representative body.

Resolved, That no state can long exist free and happy, where the course of justice is obstructed, and that, when trials by juries, which are the grand bulwarks of life and property, are destroyed or weakened, a people falls immediately under arbitrary power.

Resolved, That the late act, which gives the governor of this province a power of appointing judges of the superior and inferior courts, commissioners of oyer and terminer, the attorney general, provosts, marshals, and justices of the peace, and to remove all of them, the judges of the superior court excepted, without consent of council, entirely subverts a free administration of justice; as the fatal experience of mankind, in all ages, has testified, that there is no greater species of corruption, than when judicial and executive officers depend, for their existence and support, on a power independent of the people.

Resolved, That by ordaining jurors to be summoned by the sheriff only, which sheriff is to be appointed by the governor, without consent of council, that security which results from a trial by our peers is rendered altogether precarious, and there is not only an evident infraction upon our charter, but a subversion of our common rights as Englishmen.

Resolved, That every people have an absolute right of meeting together to consult upon common grievances, and to petition, remonstrate, and use every legal method for their removal.

Resolved, That the act which prohibits these constitutional meetings, cuts away the scaffolding of English freedom, and reduces us to a most abject state of vassallage and slavery.

Resolved, That it is our opinion, these late acts, if quietly submitted to, will annihilate the last vestiges of liberty in this province, and therefore we must be justified by God and the world, in never submitting to them.

Resolved, That it is the opinion of this body, that the present act, respecting the government of the province of Massachusetts Bay, is an artful, deep-laid plan of oppression and despotism, that requires great skill and wisdom to counteract. This wisdom we have endeavored to collect from the united sentiments of the county. And although we are grieved that we are obliged to mention any thing that may be attended with such very important consequences, as may now ensue, yet a sense of our duty as men, as freemen, as christian freemen, united in the firmest bonds, obliges us to *Resolve,* that every civil officer now in commission in this province, and acting in conformity to the late act of parliament, is not an officer agreeably to our charter, therefore unconstitutional, and ought to be opposed, in the manner hereafter recommended.

Resolved, That we will obey all those civil officers, now in commission, whose commissions were issued before the first day of July, 1774, and support them in the execution of their offices according to the manner usual before the late attempt to alter the constitution of this province ; nay, even although the governor should attempt to revoke their commissions. But, that, if any of said officers shall accept a commission under the present plan of arbitrary government, or in any way or manner whatever, assist the governor or administration in the assault now making on our rights and liberties, we will consider them as having forfeited their commissions, and yield them no obedience.

Resolved, That whereas the Hon. Samuel Danforth and Joseph Lee, Esq's. two of the judges of the inferior court of common pleas for the county, have accepted commissions under the new act, by being sworn members of his majesty's council, appointed by said act, we therefore look upon them as utterly incapable of holding any office whatever. And whereas, venires on the late act of parliament, have issued from the court of sessions, signed by the clerk, we think they come under a preceding resolve, of acting in conformity to the new act of parliament. We therefore *Resolve,* that a submission to courts thus acting, and under these disqualifications, is a submission to the act itself, and of consequence, as we are resolved never to submit in one iota to the act, we will not submit to courts thus constituted, and thus acting in conformity to said act.

Resolved, That as, in consequence of the former resolve, all business at the inferior court of common pleas and court of general sessions of the peace, next to be holden at Concord, must cease ; to prevent the many inconveniences that may arise therefrom, we *Resolve,* that all actions, writs, suits, &c., brought to said court, ought to remain in the same condition, as at present, unless settled by consent of parties, till we know the result of a provincial and continental congress. And we *Resolve*, that no plaintiff, in any cause, action, or writ, aforesaid, ought to enter said action in said court, thus declared to be unconstitutional. And we *Resolve*, if the court shall sit, in defiance to the voice of the county, and default actions and issue executions accordingly, no officer ought to serve such process. And we are also determined to support all constables, jurors, and other officers, who, from these constitutional principles, shall refuse obedience to courts which we have resolved are founded on the destruction of our charter.

Resolved, That it is the opinion of this body of delegates, that a Provincial Congress is absolutely necessary in our present unhappy situation.

These are sentiments which we are obliged to express, as these acts are intended immediately to take place. We must, now, either oppose them, or tamely give up all we have been struggling for. It is this that has forced us so soon on these very important resolves. However, we do it with humble deference to the provincial and continental congress, by whose resolutions we are determined to abide; to whom and the world we cheerfully appeal for the uprightness of our conduct.

On the whole, these are "great and profound questions." We are grieved to find ourselves reduced to the necessity of entering into the discussion of them. But we deprecate a state of slavery. Our fathers left a fair inheritance to us, purchased by a waste of blood and treasure. This we are resolved to transmit equally fair to our children after us. No danger shall affright, no difficulties intimidate us; and if, in support of our rights, we are called to encounter even death, we are yet undaunted, sensible that he can never die too soon, who lays down his life in support of the laws and liberties of his country.

Which report being maturely deliberated,

Voted, That the sense of the whole body, respecting the same, be collected by yeas and nays; which being done, there were one hundred and forty-six yeas, and four nays.

Voted, That it be recommended to the several towns and districts in this county, that each appoint one or more delegates to attend a provincial meeting, to be holden at Concord, on the second Tuesday of October next.

Voted, That a fair copy of the proceedings of this meeting, be made out, and forwarded to the grand Continental Congress, and also to the town clerk of each town in this county.

Voted, That the thanks of this meeting be given to the Hon. James Prescott, Esq, for his faithful services as chairman.

Voted, That this meeting be dissolved, and it was accordingly dissolved.

EBENEZER BRIDGE, *Clerk.*

CONVENTION OF ESSEX COUNTY.

At a meeting of delegates from every town in the county of Essex, in the province of Massachusetts Bay, held at Ipswich, in the said county, on the 6th and 7th days of September, 1774, viz.: for

Salem—Hon. Richard Derby, Jun. Esq., Mr. John Pickering, Jun., Capt. Jonathan Gardner, Jun., Capt. Richard Manning, Capt. Timothy Pickering, Jun.

Danvers—Doct. Samuel Holten, Capt. William Shillaber.

Ipswich—Capt. Michael Farley, Mr. John Patch, 3d, Mr. Daniel Noyes, Mr. Jonathan Cogswell, Jun., Mr. Nathaniel Farley.

Newbury—Hon. Joseph Gerrish, Esq., Capt. Joseph Hale, Capt. Moses Little, Samuel Gerrish, Esq.

Newburyport—Capt. Jonathan Greenleaf, Tristam Dalton, Esq., Mr. Stephen Cross, Mr. John Bromfield.

Marblehead—Jeremiah Lee, Esq., Azor Orne, Esq., Mr. Elbridge Gerry, Mr. Joshua Orne, Mr. William Dolliber.

Lynn—Capt John Mansfield, Mr. Daniel Mansfield.

Andover—James Frye, Esq., Mr. Joshua Holt, Mr. Samuel Osgood.

Beverly—Capt. Benjamin Lovet, Mr. Samuel Goodridge, Mr. Joseph Wood.

Rowley—Mr. Nathaniel Mighill, Daniel Spafford, Esq.

Salisbury—Nathaniel Currier, Esq., Mr. Samuel Smith, Mr. Henry Eaton.

Haverhill—Samuel White, Esq., Mr. Jonathan Webster, Mr. Isaac Reddington, Mr. Joseph Haynes.

Gloucester—Daniel Witham, Esq., Capt. Peter Coffin, Mr. Samuel Whittemore, John Low, Esq., Mr. Solomon Parsons.

Topsfield—Capt. Samuel Smith, Mr. John Gould, Mr. Enos Knight.

Almsbury—Mr. Winthrop Merrill, Mr. Caleb Pilsbury.

Bradford—Capt. Daniel Thurston, Mr. Peter Russell.

Wenham—Mr. Benjamin Fairfield, Capt. Jacob Dodge, Doct. Tyler Porter.

Manchester—John Lee, Esq., Capt. Andrew Masters, Mr. Andrew Woodbury.

Methuen—Mr. John Bodwell, Mr. John Sergeant.

Boxford—Capt. Asa Perley, Mr. Thomas Perley, Mr. Joseph Hovey.

Middleton—Capt. Archelaus Fuller, Mr. Ephraim Fuller, Doct. Silas Meriam.

Voted, That Jeremiah Lee, Esq., be chairman.

Several papers relative to the situation of our public affairs, and the alteration of our constitution and laws, intended by the late act of Parliament, for regulating the government of this province, as also the said act, being read; after consultation and debate had thereon, a committee of nine persons were appointed to consider and report on the same. The committee reported a number of resolves, which they thought necessary to be entered into by the county at this time; which resolves, after being read several times, debated on, and amended, were unanimously accepted, the delegates one by one, declaring their assent.

The report is as follows:

The delegates appointed by the several towns in this county, to meet together at this alarming crisis, to consider and determine on such measures as shall appear to be expedient for the county to adopt; deeply impressed with a sense of the importance of this delegation, of the abilities and qualifications necessary for conducting our public affairs with wisdom and prudence, but with the firmness and resolution becoming freemen, with the respect and deference due to the sentiments of our brethren in the other counties of the province, with submission to the future determinations of a provincial assembly, and the decisions of the grand American Congress, do, in the name of the county, make the following *resolves*, viz.:

1. That the several acts of parliament which infringe the just rights of the colonies, and of this province in particular, being subjects of deliberation before the Continental Congress, renders it expedient for this county to suspend their determinations respecting them; except so far as their immediate operation requires immediate opposition. That the act of parliament, entitled an act for the better regulating the government of the province of the Massachusetts Bay, in New England, being a most dangerous infraction of our constitutional and charter rights, and tending to a total subversion of the government of the province, and destruction of our liberties; and having been, with uncommon zeal, with arbitrary exertions, and military violence, attempted to be carried into execution; and this zeal, these exertions, and this violence still continuing: from the sacred regard, and the inviolable attachment we owe to those rights which are essential to and distinguish us as Englishmen and freemen; and from a tender concern for the peace of this county, we are bound to pursue all reasonable measures, by which any attempts to enforce immediate obedience to that act may be defeated.

2. That the judges, justices, and other civil officers in this county, appointed agreeably to the charter and the laws of the province, are the only civil officers in the county whom we may lawfully obey; that no authority whatever, can remove these officers, except that which is constituted pursuant to the charter and those laws; that it is the duty of these officers to continue in the execution of their respective trusts, as if the aforementioned act of parliament had never been made; and, that while they thus continue, untainted by any official conduct in conformity to that act, we will vigorously support them therein, to the utmost of our power, indemnify them in their persons and property, and to their lawful doings yield a ready obedience.

3. That all civil officers in the province, as well as private persons, who shall dare to conduct in conformity to the aforementioned act, for violating the charter and constitution of the province, are, and will be considered by this county, as its unnatural and malignant enemies; and in the opinion of this body, such men, while they persist in such conduct, and so contribute to in-

volve the colonies in all the horrors of a civil war, are unfit for civil society; their lands ought not to be tilled by the labor of any American, nor their families supplied with clothing or food.

4. The fourth resolve, which respected Peter Frye, Esq., was omitted by the direction of the delegates of Salem, Marblehead, and Danvers, they supposing his frank and generous declaration inserted in the papers would give full satisfaction to the county, and render a publication of this resolve superfluous and improper.

5. That a committee be raised to wait on the honorable William Browne, Esq, of Salem, and acquaint him, that with grief this county has viewed his exertions for carrying into execution acts of parliament, calculated to enslave and ruin his native land; that while the county would continue the respect for several years paid him, it firmly resolves, to detach from every future connection with all such as shall persist in supporting, or in any way countenancing the late arbitrary edicts of parliament; that the delegates, in the name of the county, request him to excuse them from the painful necessity of considering and treating him as an enemy to his country, and therefore, that he would resign his office as councillor on the late establishment, and decline as a judge, and in every other capacity, to execute the late acts of parliament, and all others deemed by the province unconstitutional and oppressive.

6. That in the opinion of this body, all town meetings in this county, ought to be called agreeably to the laws of the province and the ancient usage of the county.

7. That it is the opinion of this body of delegates, that a provincial congress is absolutely necessary in our present unhappy situation; and, that as writs are now issued for the election of representatives for a general assembly, to be held at Salem, on the fifth day of October next, the representatives so elected will properly form such provincial congress. And it is further our opinion, that these representatives should be instructed by their several towns, to resolve themselves into a provincial congress accordingly; if when assembled, they shall deem it necessary or expedient; in order to consult and determine on such measures as they judge will tend to promote the true interest of his majesty, and the peace, welfare, and prosperity of the province.

8. Deeply affected with a sense of the miseries and calamities now impending over the colonies, and this province in particular, we are compelled to form these resolutions; which, as we apprehend, being founded in justice and necessity, on the principles of our natural, essential, and unalienable rights, we are determined to abide by. At the same time, we frankly, and with sincerity declare, that we still hold ourselves subjects of his majesty king George the third; as such, will bear him true allegiance; and are ready with our lives and fortunes, to support and defend his person, crown, and dignity, and his constitutional authority over us. But, by the horrors of slavery, by the dignity and happiness attending virtuous freedom, we are constrained to declare, that we hold our liberties too dear to be sported with,

and are therefore, most seriously determined to defend them. This, in the present dispute, we conceive may be effected by peaceable measures. But, though above all things, slavery excepted, we deprecate the evils of a civil war; though we are deeply anxious to restore and preserve harmony with our brethren in Great Britain; yet, if the despotism and violence of our enemies should finally reduce us to the sad necessity, we, undaunted, are ready to appeal to the last resort of states; and will, in support of our rights, encounter even death, "sensible that he can never die too soon, who lays down his life in support of the laws and liberties of his country."

Voted, That Jeremiah Lee, Esq., Doct. Samuel Holten, and Mr. Elbridge Gerry, be a committee to wait on the Hon. William Browne, Esq., agreeably to the fifth resolve.

Voted, That a committee be chosen to notify the members of this body to assemble again when they shall think it necessary; and that the members from Salem and Marblehead, be this committee; and that they, or the major part of them, be and they are hereby empowered to issue notifications accordingly.

JOHN PICKERING, Jun., *Clerk*.

Salem, Friday, September 9, 1774.

Jeremiah Lee, Esq., Doct. Samuel Holten, and Mr. Elbridge Gerry, waited on the honorable William Browne, Esq., at Boston, with the fifth resolve of the delegates of this county, and received the following answer, viz.:

Gentlemen:—I cannot consent to defeat his majesty's intentions, and disappoint his expectations, by abandoning a post to which he has been graciously pleased to appoint me; an appointment made without my solicitation or privity, and accepted by me from a sense of duty to the king, and the hopes of serving my country. I wish therefore, to give him no cause to suspect my fidelity, and I assure you, I will do nothing without a true regard to its interest. "As a judge, and in every other capacity," I intend to act with honor and integrity, and to exert my best abilities; and be assured, that neither persuasions can allure me, nor shall menaces compel me to do any thing derogatory to the character of a councillor of his majesty's province of the Massachusetts Bay.

WILLIAM BROWNE.

Boston, September 9th, 1774.

To Jeremiah Lee, Esq., Doct. Samuel Holten, and Mr. Elbridge Gerry.

CONVENTION OF HAMPSHIRE COUNTY.

At a Congress of committees from every town and district within the county of Hampshire, and province of the Massachusetts Bay, excepting

Charlemont and Southwick, held at the court house, in Northampton, within the said county, on the 22d and 23d days of September, 1774, to consult upon measures proper to be taken at this time of general distress in the province, occasioned by the late attacks of the British parliament on the constitution of the said province, whereby they have endeavored to sap and destroy its most fundamental rights, and reduce the inhabitants thereof to a state of vassallage and slavery:

Mr. Ebenezer Hunt, Jun., of Northampton, was chosen clerk of said congress, and Mr. Timothy Danielson, of Brimfield, chairman.

After divers observations made upon the late acts of the British parliament, for taxing the American colonies, and for subverting the constitution of this province, a committee of nine persons, members of the said congress, were appointed to consider and report thereon; which committee reported as follows:

The committees appointed by the several towns in this county, to meet together at this alarming crisis, to consider and determine on measures expedient for the county to adopt, with the respect and deference due to the future determinations of a provincial congress, and the decisions of the grand American Congress, as they are not able to make any resolves respecting the rights and liberties of the people of this province, more agreeable to their own sentiments than such as have been made by their brethren in the other counties, do, on mature deliberation, make the following, for the most part similar to theirs, viz.:

1. That as true and loyal subjects of George the third, king of Great Britain, &c., we by no means intend to withdraw our allegiance from him, so long as he will defend and protect us in the free and full exercise and enjoyment of our charter rights and liberties.

2. That the charter of this province is a most solemn stipulation and compact between the king and the inhabitants thereof; and that it ought to be kept sacred and inviolate by each party, and that it cannot, in any respect, be varied or altered by one party only, without a most criminal breach of faith, and that they know of no instance, wherein the inhabitants of this province, on their part, have violated the said compact.

3. That the several acts of the British parliament, which infringe the just rights of the colonies, and of this province in particular, being subjects of deliberation before the Continental Congress now sitting, renders it expedient for this county to suspend their determination respecting them, except so far as their immediate operation requires our immediate resolutions thereon.

4. That whereas, his excellency Thomas Gage, Esq., lately appointed by his majesty, governor of this province, did, at the last session of the great and general court, wholly decline and refuse to accept the grant for his support, then made him by both houses of assembly; and has since, by his proclamation, bearing date 23d of August last, and otherwise, manifested and declared his full resolution and determination to execute a late act of the British

parliament, entitled an act for the better regulating the government of the province of the Massachusetts Bay, in New England, whereby they have attempted to sap the foundation of the constitution of this province, and annihilate the most important rights of the inhabitants thereof; and has also, actually, at Salem, by an armed force, endeavored to execute the said acts; we are obliged therefore, to declare, that our minds are so deeply impressed with the abovesaid conduct of his excellency Thomas Gage, Esq., as to excite in us very great doubts whether he can any longer be considered as the constitutional governor of this province; and consequently, whether any writs issued by him for convening a general assembly, or any other acts whereby he shall attempt to exercise the office of a governor of this province, have any force or validity, and whether any obedience or respect thereto can be paid, without a degree of submission to and acknowledgment of the force and validity of said acts; but in case any towns within the province should judge it safe and expedient so far to regard the writs lately issued by his excellency Thomas Gage, Esq., for the convening a general court or assembly of this province, to be held at Salem, on the 5th day of October next, as to elect and depute any persons as their representatives to repair to Salem, at the time aforesaid, we cannot but declare it as our clear opinion, that they ought, and our full expectation is that they will, most maturely and deliberately consider, whether any such representatives can do any one act in concert with his excellency Thomas Gage, Esq., and his mandamus council, without an implied acknowledgment of the authority and force of the abovesaid acts of parliament.

5. That it is the opinion of this congress, that a provincial congress is absolutely necessary in our present unhappy situation, and that we approve of the proposal made by a late Middlesex congress, that the said provincial congress should be holden at Concord, on the second Tuesday of October next, and we accordingly recommend to the several towns and districts within this county, that each appoint one or more delegates to attend the same.

6. That the collectors, constables, and all other officers, who have or shall have by them moneys collected upon the province assessments, delay making payment of the same to the honorable Harrison Gray, Esq., until the civil government of this province is placed upon a constitutional foundation, but that they deposit the same in the treasuries of their respective towns and districts.

7. Whereas, the universal uneasiness which prevails among all orders of men in this county, arising from the unjust and oppressive measures of the present administration, may influence some persons inconsiderately to commit outrages upon particular persons or their property, we would heartily recommend to all the inhabitants of this county, not to engage in any routs, riots, or licentious attacks upon the person or property of any one, as being subversive of all order and government; but, by a steady, manly, uniform, and persevering opposition to the said measures, to convince our enemies,

that in a contest so important and solemn, our conduct shall be such as to merit the approbation of all sober and wise men.

8 That in the opinion of this Congress, all town meetings ought to be called agreeably to the laws and ancient usage of the province.

9. That the inhabitants of the several towns and districts within this county, be advised, for their own honor, and for the defence of their country, that they use the utmost diligence, forthwith, to acquaint themselves with the military art, under the command and direction of such persons as they shall choose, and that they furnish themselves with the full lawful quantity of ammunition, and good effective arms, as soon as may be, for that purpose.

Attest, EBENEZER HUNT, Jun., *Clerk.*

CONVENTION OF PLYMOUTH COUNTY.

At a meeting of the delegates of every town in the county of Plymouth, in the province of Massachusetts Bay, held at Plimpton, in said county, on Monday, the 26th day of September, 1774, and then by adjournment, at the county court house in Plymouth, on Tuesday, the 27th day of September, 1774, present:

Plymouth—Hon. James Warren, Esq., Mr. John Torrey, Capt. Theophilus Cotton, William Watson, Esq., Mr. Thomas Lothrop.

Scituate—Nathan Cushing, Esq., John Cushing, Jun., Esq., Capt. Israel Vinal, Jun., Mr. Barnebas Little, Mr. William Turner, Capt. Joseph Tolman.

Wareham—Mr. Ebenezer Briggs, Mr. Barnabas Bates.

Marshfield—Capt. Anthony Thomas, Capt. William Thomas.

Abington—Doct. David Jones, Capt. Woodbridge Brown, Mr. William Reed, Jun.

Bridgewater—Capt. Edward Mitchell, Mr. Nathaniel Reynolds, Mr. Nathan Mitchell, Mr. Thomas Hooper.

Kingston—John Thomas, Esq., Capt. John Gray, Mr. William Drew.

Hanover—Capt. Joseph Cushing, Mr. Joseph Ramsdell, Mr. Joshua Simmons, Capt. Robert Eells, Doct. Lemuel Cushing.

Pembroke—Capt. John Turner, Doct. Jeremiah Hall, Mr. Seth Briggs, Capt. Edward Thomas, Capt. Elijah Cushing.

Duxborough—Capt. Wade Wadsworth, Mr. George Partridge, Mr. Peleg Wadsworth.

Halifax—Mr. Barnabas Thompson, Moses Inglis, Mr. Ebenezer Thomas.

Middleborough—Capt. Ebenezer Sprout, Mr. John Miller, Mr. Ebenezer Wood, Mr. Benjamin Tucker, Mr. Nathaniel Foster.

Rochester—Capt. Ebenezer White, Mr. Nathaniel Hammond, Mr. Nathan Nye.

Plimpton—Mr. William Ripley, Mr Samuel Lucas, Mr. Seth Cushing.

Voted, That the Hon. James Warren, Esq., be chairman.

A committee of nine, viz.: James Warren, Esq., William Cushing, Esq., Capt. Joseph Cushing, John Thomas, Esq., Doct. Jones, Mr. John Torrey, Mr. Thomas Lothrop, Mr. George Partridge, and Doct. Jeremiah Hall, were chosen to bring in, at the adjournment, a report to this body, and the following being several times read, and put paragraph by paragraph, was unanimously voted, viz.:

Whereas, the British administration, instead of cultivating that harmony and affection, which have so long subsisted, to the great and mutual advantage of both Britain and the colonies, have, for a series of years, without provocation, without justice, or good policy, in breach of faith, the laws of gratitude, the natural connections and commercial interests of both countries, been attacking with persevering and unrelenting injustice, the rights of the colonists; and have added, from one time to another, insults to oppressions, till both have become, more especially in this colony, intolerable, and every person who has the feelings of a man, and any sense of the rights of mankind, and the value of our happy constitution, finds it now necessary, to exert himself to the utmost of his power, to preserve them: we, who are returned from the several towns in the county of Plymouth, and now met on the ground first trod by our venerable ancestors, and at the place Providence directed them to, as an asylum from the persecuting rage and oppression of their cotemporaries in Britain; feeling the same spirit, and actuated in defence of our rights, by the same principles which animated them in acquiring and transmitting them to us and succeeding posterity, in a manner which will ever distinguish the heroism and virtue of their characters, do resolve:

1. That the inhabitants of the American colonies are entitled to all the natural rights of mankind, and are, by right, subject to the control of no power on earth, but by their own consent.

2. That the inhabitants of this province have no other political connection with, or dependence on Britain, than what was, originally, by our ancestors, for themselves and posterity, stipulated with the king, and in the form of a grant from him expressed in the charter.

3. That the interposition of any other power on earth in our affairs, and more especially, in attempts to tax or even legislate for us, and that of the king himself, in other manner than is expressed and provided for in the original compact, is an infraction of our natural and constitutional rights.

4. That the people of this province have, at all times, been loyal and dutiful subjects to the king of Great Britain, have observed all the conditions of their original compact, borne great affection to his other subjects in all parts of his dominions, and are ready, at all times, to render him that allegiance which his protection of our rights entitles him to, and to sacrifice our lives and fortunes in defence of his person and constitutional government.

5. That the parliament of Great Britain has not only assumed, but exer-

cised with unexampled severity, a power over these colonies, to legislate for, and tax them without their own consent, and by several acts passed in the late session of parliament, for blocking up the port of Boston, the better regulating the government of the province of the Massachusetts Bay, the securing the most flagitious violators of the laws of the province from a legal trial, and the establishing the roman catholic religion in that extensive country, called Canada, has shewn their determination to deprive us of both our civil and religious rights.

6. That it is a duty every man and body of men owes to posterity, as well as to God and our country, to oppose with all their power, the execution of said acts, and that we strongly recommend it to the inhabitants of the province, never to submit to them in any instance whatever.

7. That the provision made in one of said acts for the appointment of a council and of civil officers in this province and the tenure of their several offices, together with the manner of returning jurors, at once destroys every idea of free legislation, and an impartial administration of justice, and breaks down that inestimable barrier of liberty, and security of life and property, a trial by our peers, by rendering the whole of them a set of ministerial tools and hirelings.

8. That those persons who have accepted seats at the council board, by mandamus from the king, in conformity to a late act of the British parliament, have violated the fundamental rights of the society they belonged to; have traitorously attempted to destroy the constitution of their country, which they were bound by the laws of God and man to defend; and have, by their persevering obstinacy, against the entreaties of their fellow countrymen, exposed themselves to their just resentment and indignation.

9. That the judges, justices, sheriffs, and other civil officers in the province, who are appointed to their several offices agreeably to the charter and laws of the same, and refuse to act in conformity to the acts of parliament, or to assist the administration in the execution of them, are the only proper persons who are entitled to the obedience of the people; and that we will aid and support them in the execution of their offices, in the manner usual before the attempt to alter the constitution of the province; and will indemnify their persons and property; and that no legal authority can remove them from their respective offices, except that which is constituted pursuant to the charter, and the laws of this province.

10. That all officers and private persons, who shall presume to conform to or by any means aid and assist the execution of the late acts of parliament, do, by such conduct, forfeit that protection and friendship good men in society are entitled to, and are and ought to be considered and treated as our inveterate enemies, as men lost to every sense of virtue, and the obligations due to God and man.

11. That every people have a right to meet together when they please, to consult upon their grievances, and the proper methods to be taken for their removal; and that any act which prohibits such meetings, strikes at the foundation of freedom, and will reduce to slavery and misery such as submit to it.

12. That the present exigencies of our public affairs, render it absolutely necessary that there be a provincial congress; and we do recommend it to the several towns in this county, to instruct their representatives to form themselves into such a congress, agreeably to the seventh resolve of the delegates for the county of Essex, for the purposes there mentioned.

13. That our enemies may be disappointed, and we be the better enabled to make that last appeal, which the law of God and nature will justify, we recommend it to the people of this county, to apply themselves with all diligence, and in the most effectual manner, to learn military discipline, and to equip themselves immediately with arms and ammunition according to law.

14. That whereas, the present circumstances of the province are such, that if the public moneys now raised should be paid into the public treasuries, they may be misapplied, perhaps to purposes detrimental to the interest of the people: we therefore recommend to the collectors of taxes, sheriffs, and other officers in this county, to retain the same in their hands, and not to make any payment thereof to the province treasurer, until the civil government of the province is placed upon a constitutional foundation, or until it shall otherwise be ordered by the proposed provincial congress; and that they be indemnified in their persons and property for so doing.

15. That the fortification erected on Boston neck, the seizing the powder in the magazine at Charlestown, the prohibiting the keeper of the magazine at Boston to deliver the powder, which is private property, and many other instances of the conduct of the army and commander in chief, are justly alarming, and give us the strongest reasons to apprehend hostile intentions against the town of Boston in particular, and the province in general.

16. That if any persons who have distinguished themselves by virtuously contending for the violated rights and liberties of this country, should be seized, in order to be transported to England, or in any way subjected to the tyrannical power of administration now prevailing, we do recommend, that the good people of this county immediately make reprisals, by seizing and keeping in safe custody, every servant of the present tyrannical government, and all such as are known to have favored and abetted their measures, and detain them till our friends are restored safe and uninjured to their respective families.

17. That it is highly proper and necessary for the towns to continue to meet and transact their affairs as usual, and we recommend to the selectmen of the several towns in this county, to issue their warrants for calling town meetings, agreeably to the laws of the province and former usages, and to the constables to warn the same, whenever their circumstances require it, and to the people in the county to support each other in the exercise of a privilege and a right, by long experience found so beneficial to their interest and happiness.

18. That it is justifiable and proper for the people, at such a time as is this, to prevent any courts sitting and proceeding to business, or any officers

of any court executing their office, who shall refuse, when requested, to make and sign a full and ample declaration, expressing their abhorrence of the late innovations attempted in our constitution, and that they do not now, nor will at any time hereafter, hold their commissions in any other way than what is prescribed by the charter and well known constitution of this province, and that they will not, in any way, countenance, aid, or support the execution of the late acts of parliament.

19. That the circumstances of the country require, and make it necessary, that we should, until our rights are fully restored, withhold all commercial intercourse with Great Britain and Ireland, and refrain from the consumption of British manufactures and merchandize, especially East India teas, and other goods, subject to such additions, alterations, and exceptions only, as the grand Congress of the colonies may agree to.

20. We recommend to the several towns in this county, to make provision for, and to order the payment of their several representatives out of their town treasuries, in order to do justice to them, and at the same time defeat one of the machinations of our enemies.

21. That those justices of the courts of general sessions of the peace and common pleas for this county, who, at the last term, in the name of the whole, addressed his excellency governor Gage, have, therein, wantonly, without reason, and without provocation, aspersed the clergy, the committees of correspondence, and other good people of this county, and thereby shown that they have no tender feelings for the distresses of their country, and can rejoice at their calamities.

22. That this county should entertain a high sense of gratitude for the benevolent alacrity and readiness, shown by our brethren in the other colonies, to aid and support this province under our present distresses, and to come to our relief, whenever the blood-thirsty malice of our enemies shall make it necessary.

23. That Edward Winslow, Jr. one of the two clerks of the court of general sessions of the peace and court of common pleas for this county, has, by refusing this body a copy of an address made at the last term in this county to Thomas Hutchinson, Esq., betrayed the trust reposed in him, and by refusing his attendance when requested, treated the body of this county with insult and contempt, and by that means rendered himself unworthy to serve the county in said office.

24. That it be earnestly recommended to the inhabitants of this county, that they carefully avoid all riots, routs, tumults, and disturbances, under our present distressed circumstances, and that they maintain all that peace and good order that the nature of our present situation will admit.

THOMAS LOTHROP, *Clerk.*

79

CONVENTION OF BRISTOL COUNTY.

At a meeting of the gentlemen, delegates from the following towns in the county of Bristol, viz.: Taunton, Dartmouth, Rehoboth, Freetown, Dighton, Swansey, Norton, Mansfield, Raynham, Berkeley and Easton, held at the court house, in Taunton, on the 28th and 29th days of September, 1774, to consult upon proper measures to be taken at the present alarming crisis of our public affairs:

Zephaniah Leonard, Esq., was chosen chairman.

After having read the act of parliament for regulating the government of this province, and the resolves of the counties of Suffolk, Middlesex, &c., the following resolutions were unanimously adopted:

Whereas, our ancestors, of blessed memory, from a prudent care for themselves, and a tender concern for their descendants, did, through a series of unparalleled dangers and distresses, purchase a valuable inheritance in this western world, and carefully transmitted the same to us, their posterity; and whereas, for many years past, we have quietly enjoyed certain rights and privileges, stipulated by charter, and repeatedly confirmed by royal engagements, which rights and privileges are now unjustly invaded by the pretended authority of a British parliament, under pretext that it is inexpedient for us any longer to enjoy them; and as the same persons who found out this inexpediency, will, no doubt, in time, discover that it is inexpedient for us to enjoy any rights, and even any property at all; we cannot, in justice to ourselves and posterity, and in gratitude to our revered ancestors, tamely stand by, and suffer every thing that is valuable and dear to be wrested from us; but are resolutely determined, at the risk of our fortunes and lives, to defend our natural and compacted rights, and to oppose, to our utmost, all illegal and unconstitutional measures, which have been, or may be hereafter, adopted by a British parliament or a British ministry. And though we deprecate the evils which are naturally consequent upon a breach of that mutual affection and confidence which has subsisted betwixt Great Britain and her colonies, yet we think it better to suffer those evils, than voluntarily submit to perpetual slavery. We are sensible that the important crisis before us demands the exercise of much wisdom, prudence, and fortitude, and we sincerely hope, that all our deliberations and actions will be guided by the principles of sound reason, and a hearty desire to promote the true interest of the British empire. Accordingly, we resolve in the following manner, viz.:

Resolved, That we freely recognize George the third, king of Great Britain, &c., as our rightful sovereign, and as allegiance and protection are reciprocal, we are determined faithfully to yield the former as long as we are allowed the enjoyment of the latter.

Resolved, That the late acts of the British parliament, relating to the continent in general, and this province in particular, are contrary to reason and the spirit of the English constitution, and, if complied with, will reduce us to the most abject state of servitude.

Resolved, That all civil officers in this province, considered as holding their respective offices by the tenure specified in a late act of the British parliament, deserve neither obedience nor respect; but we will support all civil authority that is agreeable to the charter of the province granted by king William and queen Mary.

Resolved, That it is our opinion, that the several towns of this county should regulate themselves in all their public proceedings, agreeably to the laws of this province.

Resolved, That we will use our utmost endeavors to discountenance and suppress all mobs, riots, and breaches of the peace, and will afford all the protection in our power to the persons and properties of our loyal fellow subjects.

Resolved, That, in all things, we will regulate ourselves by the opinion and advice of the Continental Congress, now sitting at Philadelphia; and as we place great confidence in the abilities of the gentlemen, members of that congress, we will cheerfully subscribe to their determinations.

Resolved, That our brethren of the town of Boston, who are now suffering under the cruel hand of power in the common cause of America, are justly entitled to all that support and relief which we can give, and are now ready to afford them.

Resolved, That whereas, our brethren of the county of Suffolk have, by their spirited and noble resolutions, fully made known our sentiments, we therefore think it unnecessary for us to be more particular, as we most cheerfully adopt their measures and resolutions.

Voted, That the above proceedings be inserted in the public papers.

Voted, That the committee for the town of Taunton, be empowered to call a meeting of this body, whenever they think it necessary.

Voted, That the thanks of this body be given to the chairman, for his faithful services.

Voted, That this assembly be adjourned, and it was accordingly adjourned.

DAVID COBB, *Clerk*.

CONVENTION OF WORCESTER COUNTY.

JOURNAL of a convention of the committees of correspondence and delegates, of the several towns in the county of Worcester.

TUESDAY, AUGUST 9, 1774.

At a meeting of the committees of correspondence for the county of Worcester, in county Congress assembled, on the 9th day of August, A. D. 1774, at the house of Mrs. Mary Sternes, in Worcester, there were present:

Worcester—William Young, Esq., Mr. Joshua Bigelow, Capt. Timothy Bigelow, Lieut. John Smith.

Lancaster—Doct. William Dunsmore, Deacon David Wilder, Mr. Aaron Sawyer, Capt. Samuel Ward, Capt. Asa Whitcomb, Capt. Hezekiah Gates, Mr. John Prescott, Mr. Ephraim Sawyer.

Mendon—Capt. Nathan Tyler, Deacon Edward Rawson, Mr. James Sumner, Elder Nathaniel Nelson, Mr. Benoni Benson.

Rutland District—Mr. Asa Hapgood, Lieut. Nathan Sparhawk, Deacon John Mason, Lieut. Andrew Parker.

Brookfield—Jedediah Foster, Esq., Capt. Jeduthan Baldwin, Capt. Phinehas Upham.

Oxford—Capt. Ebenezer Learned, Doct. Alexander Campbell.

Charlton—Mr. Caleb Curtis, Capt. Jonathan Tucker.

Sutton—Mr. Amos Singletary, Capt. Henry King, Rev. Ebenezer Chaplin.

Leicester, Spencer and Paxton—Col. Thomas Denny, Capt. William Henshaw, Capt. Joseph Henshaw, Rev. Benjamin Conklin.

Westborough—Capt. Stephen Maynard.

Shrewsbury—Hon. Artemas Ward, Mr. Phinehas Heywood.

Lunenburg—Doct. John Taylor.

Harvard—Rev. Joseph Wheeler.

Bolton—Capt. Samuel Baker, Mr. Jonathan Holman.

Petersham—Capt. Ephraim Doolittle, Col. Jonathan Grout.

Southborough—Capt. Jonathan Wood.

Hardwick—Capt. Paul Mandell, Mr. Stephen Rice, Lieut. Jonathan Warner, Deacon John Bradish.

Holden—Mr. John Child.

Douglas—Mr. Samuel Jennison.

Princeton—Mr. Moses Gill.

A committee was appointed to sort and count the votes given in, for a chairman or president, and clerk, who reported that William Young, Esq., of Worcester, was elected chairman, and William Henshaw, Esq., of Leicester, clerk.

The Rev. Benjamin Conklin, being invited, opened the meeting with very earnest and solemn prayer.

Voted, To choose a committee of ten, to draw up some proper resolves to lay before the convention for their consideration.

Voted, That Mr. Timothy Bigelow, Capt. Joseph Henshaw, Capt. Ephraim Doolittle, Capt. Samuel Ward, Mr. John Smith, Mr. Luke Drury, Mr. Joshua Bigelow, Deacon Edward Rawson, Capt. Paul Mandell, Lieut. Jonathan Holman, be the committee.

The committee retired, and again returned, after some time, and reported that they had drafted a number of resolves, which were read.

After debate thereon, it was voted to lay the resolves upon the table for further consideration.

Voted, To adjourn to to-morrow morning, at 7 o'clock, to meet at the same place.

WEDNESDAY, AUGUST 10, 1774.

Met according to adjournment. In the absence of the president, Deacon Baker was chosen chairman *pro tempore.*

Voted, That the committee chosen yesterday, be a committee to write a letter to the gentlemen chosen by this province to attend the Continental Congress, to inform them of the sense of the county respecting our public affairs.

A letter being reported, was considered and accepted.

Voted, That the committee chosen yesterday, be a committee to send a letter to all of the towns and districts in this county, who have not chosen committees of correspondence, desiring them to choose such committees, or send delegates to represent them at the adjournment of this convention.

The committee chosen to write to the several towns, after some time, reported, that they were ready to read a letter; which was done, and the same was accepted, and is as follows:

WORCESTER, AUGUST 9, 1774.

FRIENDS AND BRETHREN:—The committees of correspondence from a majority of towns in this county, have now convened at Worcester, in order to consult and determine upon the most regular steps to be taken and recommended to the several towns in this county, at this truly critical and alarming crisis, when it no longer remains a doubt, that the acts, annihilating our once free constitution, are actually come authenticated, attended with three more transports and a ship of war, and the council, appointed by his majesty, are about taking the oaths required for that office. In the first place, we beg leave to observe, that a considerable number of respectable towns in this county have not yet chosen committees, and by that means, may not have received the letters notifying this convention; therefore, we earnestly recommend, as brethren and fellow sufferers, when all that is valuable in this life is at stake, that you choose committees of correspondence, or such other delegates as you may think proper, to meet this convention at their adjournment, when the united wisdom and aid of the whole are wanting, to oppose the torrent of tyranny rushing upon us. In order to avoid a second disappointment, by having our letters fall into unfriendly hands, and you thereby be deprived of a proper notification, we shall be careful to have them transmitted by such of our members as live nearest those towns which have not sent their committees.

The convention stands adjourned to the last Tuesday of August instant, at the house of Mrs. Mary Sternes, innholder, at Worcester, at 10 o'clock, before noon.

By order of the committees of correspondence in convention,

TIMOTHY BIGELOW.

The consideration of the resolves reported yesterday, was resumed: the same were severally read, considered, debated, and each accepted without one dissentient vote : and it was *Ordered,* that the same be signed by the chairman and clerk, and printed, and circulated in handbills.   They are as follow :

1. *Resolved,* That we bear all true allegiance to his majesty king George the third, and that we will, to the utmost of our power, defend his person, crown, and dignity, but at the same time, we disclaim any jurisdiction in the commons of Great Britain over his majesty's subjects in America.

2. *Resolved,* That the charter of this province is the basis of our allegiance to his majesty, wherein, on his part, the royal faith is plighted, to protect and defend us, his American subjects, in the free and full enjoyment of each and every right and liberty enjoyed by his subjects in Great Britain ; his American subjects likewise bear him true allegiance.

3. *Resolved,* That we have, within ourselves, the exclusive right of originating each and every law respecting ourselves, and ought to be on an equal footing with his majesty's subjects in Great Britain.

4. *Resolved,* That an attempt to vacate said charter, by either party, without the consent of the other, has a tendency to dissolve the union between Great Britain and this province, to destroy the allegiance we owe to the king, and to set aside the sacred obligations he is under to his subjects here.

5. *Resolved,* That the right lately assumed, by the parliament of Great Britain, over this province, wherein they claim a disposal of our lives and properties, and to alter and disannul our charter without our consent, is a great and high-handed claim of arbitrary power.

6. *Resolved,* That as parliament have not only adopted the aforementioned principle, but have actually put it into practice, by taxing the Americans, and most cruelly blocking up the harbor of Boston, in order to force this province to submission to such power, and have farther proceeded to pass several acts to change our free constitution in such manner, which, if effected, will render our lives and properties wholly insecure :   Therefore,

7. *Resolved,* That it is the indisputable duty of every American, and more especially in this province, to unite in every virtuous opposition that can be devised, in order to save ourselves and posterity from inevitable ruin.   And, in the first place, we greatly approve of the agreement entered and entering into through this and the neighboring provinces, for the non-consumption of British goods.   This, we apprehend, will have a tendency to convince our brethren in Britain, that more is to be gained in the way of justice, from our friendship and affection, than by extortion and arbitrary power. We apprehend that the balance of our trade with Britain has been greatly in their favor; that we can do much better without it than they can ; and that the increase of such trade heretofore, was greatly occasioned by the regard and affection borne by the Americans to their brethren in Britain. Such an agreement, if strictly adhered to, will greatly prevent extravagance, save our money, encourage our own manufactures, and reform our manners.

8. *Resolved,* That those justices of the court of general sessions, and common pleas, for this county, who, in a late address to his excellency Gover-

nor Gage, aspersed the good people of this county, have thereby discovered that they were destitute of that tender regard which we might justly expect in our present distressed situation.

Voted, That we most earnestly recommend it to the several towns in this county, (and if it should not be thought too arrogant,) to every town in the province, to meet and adopt some wise, prudent, and spirited measures, in order to prevent the execution of those most alarming acts of parliament, respecting our constitution.

Voted, That the meeting be adjourned to the last Tuesday of August instant, to meet at the house of Mrs. Mary Sternes, innholder, in Worcester, at 10 o'clock of the forenoon, and it was adjourned.

TUESDAY, AUGUST 30, 1774.

At a meeting of the committees of correspondence from each and every town and district within the county of Worcester, convened in Congress, at Worcester, on Tuesday, the 30th day of August, A. D. 1774, there were present one hundred and thirty members, together with a number of delegates and gentlemen from several towns.

William Young, Esq. was president.

Voted, That the Rev. Mr. Chaplain be desired to attend this meeting, and to pray: who came in, and the meeting was opened with prayers.

Voted, By reason of the straitness of the place, and the many attending, to adjourn to the county court house.

The Congress met in the county court house, according to adjournment; debated on many things, and adjourned to 3 o'clock, P. M.

Afternoon.

Met according to adjournment, at the court house.

Voted, To choose a committee of nine persons, to take into consideration the state of public affairs, and prepare resolves to lay before the convention.

Voted, That Capt. Joseph Henshaw, Mr. Phinehas Heywood, Capt. Ephraim Doolittle, Capt. Henry King, Mr. Timothy Bigelow, Mr. Samuel Jennison, Capt. Samuel Ward, Mr. Luke Drury, and Capt. Joseph Gilbert, be a committee for the purpose aforesaid.

Voted, That the Rev. Mr. Chaplain be desired to attend the Congress tomorrow.

Voted, That this meeting be adjourned till to-morrow, at 7 o'clock, A. M. to this place.

The meeting was closed with prayer.

WEDNESDAY, AUGUST 31, 1774.

The Congress met according to adjournment.

Voted, That the Rev. Mr. Chaplain open the meeting with prayer; which was done.

Voted, That every person who speaks in this meeting shall rise up, and, after he is done speaking, shall sit down, and not speak more than twice on the same subject, without obtaining leave, and shall not speak irrelevantly.

The committee appointed yesterday, returned, and informed that they were ready to report resolutions.

The resolves prepared by the committee were read.

Voted, To adjourn to 2 o'clock, P. M.

Afternoon.

Met according to adjournment.

Voted, To accept of the introduction of the resolves brought in by the committee, and the same were amended.

Voted, The first resolve in the affirmative :

Voted, The second resolve in the affirmative :

Voted, The third resolve in the affirmative :

Voted, The fourth resolve in the affirmative :

Voted, The fifth resolve in the affirmative :

Voted, The sixth resolve in the affirmative :

Voted, The seventh resolve in the affirmative :

Voted, The eighth resolve in the affirmative :

Voted, That the whole of the resolves be accepted, which are as follow :

Whereas, the charter of this province, as well as laws enacted by virtue of the same and confirmed by royal assent, have been, by the parliament of Great Britain, without the least color of right or justice, declared in part null and void ; and in conformity to an act of said parliament, persons are appointed to fill certain offices of government, in ways and under influences, wholly unknown before in this province, incompatible with its charter, and forming a complete system of tyranny : and whereas, no power on earth hath a right, without the consent of this province, to alter the minutest title of its charter, or abrogate any act whatsoever, made in pursuance of it, and confirmed by royal assent, or to constitute officers of government in ways not directed by charter, and as we are assured that some officers of the executive courts in this county, have officially conducted in compliance with and in conformity to the late acts of parliament altering our free constitution ; and as the sittings of such courts may have a tendency to affect the good people of this county, in such manner as may insensibly lead them to submit to the chains of slavery forged by our enemies ; therefore,

1. *Resolved*, That it is the indispensable duty of the inhabitants of this county, by the best ways and means, to prevent the sitting of the respective courts under such regulations as are set forth in a late act of parliament, entitled, an act for regulating the civil government of the Massachusetts Bay.

2. *Resolved*, That in order to prevent the execution of the late act of parliament, respecting the courts, that it be recommended to the inhabitants of this county, to attend, in person, the next inferior court of common pleas and general sessions, to be holden at Worcester, in and for said county, on the sixth day of September next.

3. *Resolved*, That it be recommended to the several towns, that they choose proper and suitable officers, and a sufficient number, to regulate the

movements of each town, and prevent any disorder which might otherwise happen; and that it be enjoined on the inhabitants of each respective town, that they adhere strictly to the orders and directions of such officers.

4. And whereas, the courts of justice will necessarily be impeded by the opposition to the said acts of parliament, therefore, *Resolved*, that it be recommended to the inhabitants of this province in general, and to those of this county in particular, that they depute fit persons to represent them in one general provincial convention, to be convened at Concord, on the second Tuesday of October next, to devise proper ways and means to resume our original mode of government, whereby the most dignified servants were, as they ever ought to be, dependant on the people for their existence as such; or some other which may appear to them best calculated to regain and secure our violated rights. The justice of our complaints and the modes of redress, we submit to the determination of our sister colonies, being, in our opinion, the only just tribunal we can appeal to on earth.

5. *Resolved,* That it be recommended, that such innholders and retailers, who shall be approbated by the selectmen in their respective towns, continue and exercise their respective functions; provided, they strictly adhere to the law of this province respecting innholders and retailers.

6. *Resolved,* That it be recommended to the several towns, that they indemnify their constables for neglecting to return lists of persons qualified to serve as jurors.

7. *Resolved,* That as the ordinary course of justice must be stayed, in consequence of the late arbitrary and oppressive acts of the British parliament, we would earnestly recommend to every inhabitant of this county, to pay his just debts as soon as may be possible, without any disputes or litigation.

8. *Resolved,* That as the dark and gloomy aspect of our public affairs has thrown this province into great convulsions, and the minds of the people are greatly agitated with the near view of impending ruin; we earnestly recommend to every one, and we engage ourselves, to use the utmost influence in suppressing all riotous and disorderly proceedings in our respective towns.

It was *Moved,* That whereas, it is generally expected, that the governor will send one or more regiments to enforce the execution of the acts of parliament, on the 6th of September, that it be recommended to the inhabitants of this county, if there is intelligence, that troops are on their march to Worcester, to attend, properly armed, in order to repel any hostile force which may be employed for that purpose.[1]

The motion, after some debate being withdrawn;

(1) That the expectation of the visit of the royal troops was not without foundation, will appear by the following extracts of the official despatch of General Gage to the Earl of Dartmouth, dated, Salem, August 27, 1774.

" Since the unwarrantable impeachment of the chief justice [Oliver,] I understand he has never

Voted, That if there is an invasion, or danger of an invasion, in any town in this county, then such town as is invaded, or being in danger thereof, shall, by their committees of correspondence, or some other proper persons, send letters, by express posts, immediately, to the committees of the adjoining towns, who shall send to other committees in the towns adjoining them, that they all come properly armed and accoutred to protect and defend the place invaded.

Voted, That it be recommended to the towns in this county, to pay no regard to the late act of parliament, respecting the calling town meetings, but, to proceed in their usual manner ; and also, that they pay no submission to any acts altering our free constitution.

Voted, That it be recommended to each town of the county, to retain in their own hands, what moneys may be due from them severally to the province treasury, till public tranquillity be restored, and more confidence can be reposed in the first magistrate and his council.

Voted, To postpone the consideration of the petition of Doct. William Paine, respecting the establishment of a hospital for the small pox, to the adjournment of this meeting.

Voted, That each member will purchase at least two pounds of powder in addition to any he may have on hand, and will use all his exertions to supply his neighbors fully.

Voted, That the members and delegates endeavor to ascertain what number of guns are deficient to arm the people in case of invasion.

---

taken his seat upon the bench, but he has promised me to attend the superior court at Boston, towards the end of the month, and I hope also, he will preside in said court to be held at Worcester, in September, notwithstanding the threats thrown out against him. I have engaged to meet him at Boston, to prevent violence, which, from the present system, I dont expect to meet with there ; I believe, that I must attend him also at Worcester, where I am to expect it."

" By the plan lately adopted, forcible opposition and violence is to be transferred from the town of Boston to the country."

" In Worcester, they keep no terms ; openly threatening resistance by arms ; have been purchasing arms ; preparing them ; casting balls ; and providing powder ; and threaten to attack any troops who dare to oppose them. Mr. Ruggles, of the new council, is afraid to take his seat as judge of the inferior court, which sits at Worcester, on the 6th of next month ; and, I apprehend, that I shall soon be obliged to march a body of troops into that township, and perhaps into others, as occasions happen, to preserve the peace."

In reference to the mandamus councillors, General Gage writes, " your lordship judged right, that art would be practised on this occasion, to intimidate and prejudice ; even force was attempted on Mr. Ruggles, by a number of people collected on the road, near Worcester, with intent to stop him, but he made his way through them."

On the second of September following, Gov. Gage writes to the Earl of Dartmouth, as follows :

" I came here to attend the superior court, and with the intention to send a body of troops to Worcester, to protect the court there ; and if wanted, to send parties to the houses of the councillors who dwell in that county ; but finding, from undoubted authority, that the flames of sedition had spread universally throughout the country, beyond conception ; the councillors already driven away ; and that no court would proceed on business ; I waited the event of the sitting of the superior court here, on the 30th ultimo ; the judges met, but could get neither grand nor petit jury."

Voted, That the resolves accepted in this convention, and the vote about town meetings, be signed by the chairman and clerk, and printed.

Voted, That the Rev. Mr. Chaplain be requested to close the meeting with prayer.

Voted, To adjourn this meeting to the first Tuesday of September next, then to meet at the house of Mr. Timothy Bigelow, in Worcester, at 10 o'clock, A. M.

TUESDAY, SEPT. 6, 1774.

The committees of correspondence and delegates of the several towns, met in convention, at the house of Mr. Timothy Bigelow, according to adjournment.

The Rev. Mr. Chaplain opened the meeting with prayer.

Voted, As the opinion of this convention, that the court should not sit on any terms.

Voted, That the several committees inform the people of their respective towns, of this vote of the convention, and, that they choose one man from each company, as a committee to wait on the judges to inform them of the resolution to stop the courts sitting, if the people concur therein.

Voted, That the body of the people in this county now in town, assemble on the common.[1]

Voted, To choose a committee of three persons to inquire of the committees of the towns, how long it will be before they make the determination of the body of the people respecting the courts, known to the judges, and to inform the convention thereof.

Voted, To adjourn to the green beyond Mr. Salisbury's, where the convention proceeded.

Voted, That a committee of three, viz.: Capt. Mandell, Deacon Rawson, and Mr. Samuel Jennison, be a committee to inform the grand jurors of the determination of the county as to the courts being held.

Voted, to adjourn to the court house at two o'clock, P. M.

Afternoon.

Met according to adjournment, and again adjourned to the green, to attend the body of the people.

Voted, To choose a committee of three persons to proceed to wait on the committees of the towns, to inquire the occasion of the delay of the judges in making their appearance before the body of the people.

Voted, That three persons be chosen a committee, to acquaint John Chandler, Esq., and the other protesters, that they must follow after the judges

(1) On the invitation of the convention, the people of the county had assembled to the number of about six thousand. The companies of the several towns were under officers of their own election, and marched in military order. Having been formed in two lines, when the arrangements were completed, the royalist justices, and officers, were compelled to pass through the ranks, pausing, at intervals, to read their declarations of submission to the public will. At evening, finding that no troops were on their way to sustain the judicial tribunals, whose constitution had been corrupted by the act of parliament, the great assembly dispersed peacefully.

through the ranges of the body of the people; that they go immediately after the judges, and read their recantations.[1]

Voted, That the thanks of the convention be given to the Rev. Mr. Chaplain, for his attendance with them.

Voted, That it be recommended to the military officers in this county, that they resign their commissions to the colonels of the respective regiments.

Voted, That the field officers resign their offices, and publish their resignations in all the Boston newspapers.

Voted, That it be recommended to the several towns of the county, to choose proper officers for the military of the town, and a sufficient number.

Voted, That it be recommended to the several towns and districts of this county, that they provide themselves, immediately, with one or more field pieces, mounted and fitted for use; and also a sufficient quantity of ammunition for the same; and that the officers appoint a suitable number of men, out of their respective companies, to manage said field pieces.

Voted, To take notice of those justices of the inferior court of common pleas and general sessions of the peace of this county, who aspersed the people in a late address to Gov. Gage.[2]

---

(1) Forty-three of the royalist inhabitants of Worcester, had made their protest against the patriotic resolutions of that town. This protest having been entered on the municipal records, by the clerk, without authority, he was subsequently compelled, in open meeting, to obliterate the document; the work of the pen not being effectual in destroying its former traces, his fingers were dipped in ink, and drawn over the page, which still remains in the town book, entirely illegible. Most of the subscribers of the loyal paper were forced to sign recantations of their expressed opinion. To these persons the vote in the text refers.

(2) The address of the justices of the county of Worcester, was presented June 21, 1774, and with the answer of Governor Gage, follows:

To his Excellency Thomas Gage, Esq., Captain General and Governor in Chief in and over the province of Massachusetts Bay, in New England.

May it please your Excellency :—The justices of the court of general sessions of the peace, and justices of the inferior court of common pleas, held at Worcester, on the second Tuesday of June, 1774, beg leave, at our first session, after your safe arrival, to congratulate your excellency thereon, and also, on your appointment to the most important office of first magistrate in this province; in full confidence, from the amiable character your excellency has obtained in your other important departments in America, you will ever delight in promoting the good of this government. We find a peculiar difficulty in expressing the distress of our minds relating to the unhappy circumstances of this province at this time; and can, with sincerity, say, that we have no doubt, from your well known character, you will do all that is in your power, to extricate us out of our distresses, in every way consistent with the true interest of Great Britain and her colonies, which we hold inseparable. And we do bear our testimony against all riots, routs, combinations, and unwarrantable resolves, which, we apprehend, have been the unhappy occasion of many of our troubles. And as there are now circulating through this province, certain inflammatory pieces, signed by order of the committee of correspondence of the town of Boston; and in this county, by order of certain persons, calling themselves a committee of correspondence of the town of Worcester, directed to the several towns in the county, stimulating the people to break off all connexion with Great Britain, which have still a tendency to alienate the affections of the people of this province and county from the mother country, and create discord and confusion, we do assure your excellency, that we will do every thing in our power, to discountenance such proceedings, and support the execution of the laws, and render your excellency's administration successful and prosperous.

To which his Excellency was pleased to return the following answer:

Voted, That three persons be a committee to require the committee of the day, to make report to the convention, of their proceedings with the judges.

Voted, That the principals in the protest reading their recantation, shall be accepted for all those who signed the recantation.

Voted, That four men be desired to attend, in addition to those who are to walk with Col. Gardner Chandler, sheriff of the county, through the ranges of the people.

Voted, That it be recommended to the officers of each company of the people assembled, to keep good order: enjoin it on their men not to do the least damage to any person's property: but to march quietly home: and that the convention have nothing further to lay before them.

Voted, That Deacon Rawson, Mr. Asa Whitcomb, and Doct. Crosby, be a committee to wait on a number of justices, to give them an opportunity to sign the declaration, which has been signed by the justices and officers of the inferior court, and is as follows:

WORCESTER, SEPT. 6, 1774.

Worcester, ss. The justices of the inferior court, and justices of the court of general sessions of the peace, for the county of Worcester, to the people of the county, now assembled at Worcester:

GENTLEMEN:—You having desired, and even insisted upon it, that all judicial proceedings be stayed by the justices of the court appointed this day, by law, to be held at Worcester, within and for the county of Worcester, on account of the unconstitutional act of the British parliament, respecting the administration of justice in this province, which, if effected, will reduce the inhabitants thereof to mere arbitrary power; we do assure you, that we will stay all such judicial proceedings of said courts, and will not endeavor to put said act into execution.

THOMAS STEEL,	EZRA TAYLOR,
JOSEPH WILDER,	JOHN CALDWELL,
ARTEMAS WARD,	EPHRAIM WILSON,
TIMOTHY PAINE,	SAMUEL WILDER,
JOHN CHANDLER,	JOSHUA UPHAM,
DANIEL HENSHAW,	JOHN CHANDLER, JR.,
ABEL WILLARD,	DANIEL OLIVER,
CHARLES BRIGHAM,	JOSEPH DORR,
ROBERT GODDARD,	EZRA HOUGHTON,
FRANCIS WHIPPLE,	NATHAN TYLER,
JOSHUA WILLARD,	*Justices.*

GENTLEMEN:—I return you my most sincere and hearty thanks for your very affectionate and truly patriotic address.

Your disavowal of the malevolent labors of a desperate faction, who, by raising groundless fears and jealousies, and using every sort of artifice and fraud, endeavor to delude and intimidate the people, and to create in them an aversion and enmity towards their brethren in Great Britain, is a proof that you hold sentiments the most friendly to your country.

May your designs to discountenance such proceedings, meet with all the success that every real patriot must hope and wish for; and I will, at all times, be ready to advance so laudable a work, which alone can give peace and happiness to the province, and restore the union so necessary to be cemented with the kingdom of Great Britain.

We, the officers of the court, do, for ourselves, give the people the same assurances above.

> GARDNER CHANDLER, *Sheriff.*
> RUFUS CHANDLER,
> JOHN SPRAGUE,
> NATHANIEL CHANDLER, *Attorneys.*

Voted, To choose a committee of nine persons, to draw up a form of a vote for administering justice, and to protect the justices in the execution of their offices.

Voted, That Capt. Ward, Capt. Henshaw, Deacon Rawson, Joseph Wheeler, Samuel Jennison, Lieut. Joseph Baker, Capt. Mandell, Timothy Bigelow, and Lieut. Jonathan Holman, be the committee for that purpose.

Voted, That the above committee be appointed to confer with the justices of the county, to-morrow morning.

Voted, That the consideration of the justices' address to Governor Gage, be committed to the same committee.

Voted, To adjourn till to-morrow, at 8 o'clock, A. M.

WEDNESDAY, SEPTEMBER 7, 1774.

The convention met according to adjournment.

Voted, To accept of the acknowledgment made by Thomas Steel, Joseph Wilder, Timothy Paine, John Chandler, Abel Willard, and Joshua Upham, Esquires, for aspersing the people of this county in a late address to Governor Gage.

Voted, That the justices who addressed Governor Gage at the last session of the court, be brought before the convention, and make and sign a declaration, in writing, of the inadvertence of their proceedings: which is done, and the declaration is as follows:

Whereas, the committees in convention have expressed their uneasiness to a number of the justices of the common pleas and general sessions, now present in the convention, who, in an address to Governor Gage, at their session in June last, aspersed the people of this county; those justices, in the presence of the convention, frankly declare that they precipitately entered into the measure; they are sorry for it; and they disclaim an intention to injure the character of any; and were the same measure again proposed, they should reject it.

THOMAS STEEL,	DUNCAN CAMPBELL,
JOSEPH WILDER,	JEDEDIAH MARCY,
TIMOTHY PAINE,	FRANCIS WHIPPLE,
JOHN CHANDLER,	EZRA HOUGHTON,
ABEL WILLARD,	ISAAC BARNARD,
JOSHUA UPHAM,	

The committee on the administration of justice, and respecting the offices of probate and sheriff, made a report, which was accepted, and is as follows:

Whereas, the late act of parliament respecting the province, is evidently designed to prevent any civil officers holding their places by virtue of the charter of this province, thereby interrupting the course of justice, and it is necessary to have civil officers till further provision can be made: therefore,

Resolved, That the justices of the peace for this county, who were in said office on the last day of June past, except Timothy Ruggles, John Murray, and James Putnam, Esquires, be hereby desired to act in said offices, as single justices, except in judicial proceedings merely civil: also, that the judge of probate, sheriffs, and coroners, who were in office on the last day of June past, exercise their respective offices till the rising of the Provincial Congress, proposed to sit at Concord, on the second Tuesday of October next, notwithstanding any proposed supersedeas that may be sent to them, or any of them, or any proclamation designed to prevent them from holding and exercising their said offices. And we, hereby, also recommend, to the people of this county, that they consider and treat them as being in their said offices, and support and defend them in the execution thereof, according to the laws of this province.

Voted, To put the laws in execution respecting pedlars and chapmen.

Voted, That the Norfolk exercise be adopted.

Voted, To take notice of Mr. Samuel Paine, assistant clerk, for sending out venires.

Voted, That Mr. Samuel Jennison go to Mr. Samuel Paine forthwith, and desire his immediate attendance before this body, to answer for his sending venires to the constables, commanding their compliance with the late act of parliament.

Mr. Paine appeared, and stated that he felt bound by the duty of his office to comply with the act.

Voted, That Mr. Paine has not given satisfaction, and that he be allowed to consider till the adjournment of this meeting.

Voted, To adjourn till the 20th of September instant, to meet at the court house, in Worcester, at 10 o'clock, A. M.[1]

(1) On the day following the adjournment of the county convention, a meeting of the blacksmiths of the county of Worcester was held. Their resolutions, which were published in a handbill, and subscribed by forty-three persons, follow:

Whereas, at a meeting of the delegates from the counties of Worcester, Middlesex, and Essex, with the committee of correspondence of the town of Boston, in behalf of the county of Suffolk, holden at Boston the 26th day of August, 1774, it was resolved—That all such officers or private persons as have given sufficient proof of their enmity to the people and constitution of this country, should be held in contempt, and that those who are connected with them ought to separate from them: laborers to shun their vineyards; merchants, husbandmen, and others, to withhold their commerce and supplies:

In compliance, therefore, to a resolution of so respectable a body as aforesaid, so reasonable in its contents, and so necessary at this distressing day of trial, we, the subscribers, being deeply impress-

SEPTEMBER 20, 1774.

The convention met, according to adjournment, and was opened with prayers.

Voted, To defer the consideration of the expediency of adjourning to the superior court, for the present.

Voted, That the sheriff send out precepts to the towns for the choice of representatives.

Voted, That Capt. Joseph Henshaw, Capt. Thomas Denny, Capt. Whitcomb, Mr. Timothy Bigelow, and Capt. Tyler, be a committee, to report in relation to giving instructions to the representatives.

Voted, That the same committee take into consideration the choice of field officers.

Voted, As the opinion of this convention, that the sheriff adjourn the superior court appointed by law to be held this day, and that he retain such as are, or may be committed as criminals, in his custody, until they have a trial.

Voted, That the plan for military organization be recommitted to the same committee who have reported, to make further additions and amendments.

Adjourned till to-morrow morning, at 8 o'clock, A. M.

ed with a sense of our duty to our country, paternal affection for our children and unborn millions, as also for our personal rights and liberties, solemnly covenant, agree and engage to and with each other, that from and after the first day of December, 1774, we will not, according to the best of our knowledge, any or either of us, nor any person by our directions, order or approbation, for or under any or either of us, do or perform, any blacksmith's work, or business of any kind whatever, for any person or persons whom we esteem enemies to this country, commonly known by the name of tories, viz. : all councillors in this province appointed by mandamus, who have not publicly resigned said office, also every person who addressed Governor Hutchinson on his departure from this province, who has not publicly recanted : also every officer exercising authority by virtue of any commission tending to carry any of the late oppressive acts of parliament into execution in America : and, in particular, we will not do any work for Timothy Ruggles of Hardwick, John Murray of Rutland, and James Putnam of Worcester, Esquires : nor for any person or persons cultivating, tilling, improving, dressing, hiring, or occupying any of their lands or tenements. Also, we agree to refuse our work of every kind, as aforesaid, to all and every person or persons who shall not have signed the non-consumption agreement, or have entered into a similar contract or engagement, or that shall not strictly conform to the association or covenant agreed upon and signed by the *Continental Congress* lately convened at Philadelphia.

We further agree, that we will not do any work for any mechanic, tradesman, laborer, or others, that shall work for, or in any ways, or by any means whatever, aid, assist, or promote the business, or pecuniary advantage, pleasures or profits of any the said enemies to this country.

Resolved, That all lawful ways and means ought to be adopted by the whole body of the people of this province, to discountenance all our inveterate political enemies in manner as aforesaid. Therefore, we earnestly recommend it to all denominations of artificers, that they call meetings of their respective craftsmen in their several counties, as soon as may be, and enter into associations and agreements for said purposes : and that all husbandmen, laborers, &c. do the like : and that whoever shall be guilty of any breach of any or either of the articles or agreements, be held by us in contempt, as enemies to our common rights.

ROSS WYMAN, *Chairman*,

TIMOTHY BIGELOW, *Clerk*.

The convention met according to adjournment, and was opened with prayer.

A paper was sent by Mr. Samuel Paine, clerk of the inferior court, which is as follows:

To the several gentlemen of the committees of correspondence for the county of Worcester, now convened in Worcester.

GENTLEMEN:—I thought I gave you all the satisfaction, relative to my issuing the warrants, at your last meeting, which could reasonably be expected: still, you have demanded of me more. As I considered myself, in that matter, as acting merely officially, and, as such, had no right to judge of the propriety or impropriety of the act of parliament, and my issuing the warrants gave the people, who were the only judges, an opportunity to determine for themselves whether they should be complied with or not, upon this representation, I hope I shall stand fair in the eye of my countrymen. Should not this be a sufficient excuse for me, you must know, gentlemen, that I was regularly appointed clerk of the peace for this county, by the justices, in September last, and, as the said justices of the court of general sessions of the peace, as well as the inferior court of common pleas for this county, whose servant I am, on the sixth day of September current, did give assurance to the body of the people of this county, then assembled at Worcester, that they would not endeavor to put said act in execution, so, gentlemen, I give you the same assurance.

Your devoted servant,

SAMUEL PAINE.

Voted, That the paper sent by Mr. Paine is not satisfactory, and that the same be committed to Mr. Joseph Henshaw, Mr. Bigelow and Mr. Doolittle, who reported, after some time, as follows:

The committee to whom the convention referred the consideration of a letter addressed to them, signed Samuel Paine, have had the same before them, and beg leave to report:

The letter appears to have been written by a young man, who, by his connections, has lately started into the office of clerk of the sessions and inferior court, through the indulgence of the bench of justices. The letter is affrontive to the convention, and in no respect answers their reasonable requisitions. Considering the person who wrote it, the committee are of opinion, it is of too small importance to be noticed any further by the convention, and therefore recommend, that said letter be dismissed, and the person treated with all neglect.

By order of the committee,

JOSEPH HENSHAW, *Chairman.*

Voted, To take notice of Mr. Sheriff Chandler, for carrying an address to Governor Gage, and that a committee wait on him, and request his attendance before this body, forthwith.

Voted, That Doct. Dunsmore, Mr. Drury, and Mr. Clapp, be a committee to inform the sheriff of this vote of the convention respecting his conduct. Mr. Sheriff came in, and presented the following declaration, which was accepted:

Whereas, the convention of committees have expressed their uneasiness to the sheriff of this county, now present before the convention, for presenting, with others, an address to Governor Gage, he frankly declares it was precipitately done by him: that he is sorry for it: and disclaims an intention to do any thing against the minds of the inhabitants of this county: and, had he known it would have given offence, he would not have presented said address.

GARDINER CHANDLER.

Resolved, That as the ordinary courts of justice will be stayed, in consequence of the late arbitrary and oppressive acts of the British parliament, we would earnestly recommend to every inhabitant of this county, to pay his just debts, as soon as possible, without any dispute or litigation, "and if any disputes concerning debts or trespasses should arise, which cannot be settled by the parties, we recommend it to them to submit all such causes to arbitration; and if the parties, or either of them, shall refuse to do so, they ought to be considered as co-operating with the enemies of the country."

The committee on instructions submitted their report, which was accepted, and is as follows:

Resolved, That it be recommended to the several towns and districts, that they instruct their representatives, who may be chosen to meet at Salem, in October next, absolutely to refuse to be sworn by any officer or officers, but such as are or may be appointed according to the constitution, or to act as one branch of the legislature in concert with any others, except such as are, or may be appointed, according to the charter of this province: and that they refuse to give their attendance at Boston, while the town is invested with troops and ships of war: and should there be any thing to prevent their acting with such a governor and council as is expressly set forth in the charter, that they immediately repair to the town of Concord, and there join in a provincial congress, with such other members as are or may be chosen for that purpose, to act and determine on such measures as they shall judge to be proper to extricate this colony out of the present unhappy circumstances.

Voted, That it be again recommended to the several towns and districts in this county, that they provide themselves immediately with one or more field pieces, mounted and fitted for use, and also, a sufficient quantity of ammunition for the same, and that the officers appoint a suitable number of men, out of their respective companies, to manage said field pieces.

Whereas, the people of this county are under solemn obligations not to purchase any goods imported from Great Britain, after the last day of August, 1774, which they determine sacredly to adhere to, until our many grievances be redressed, therefore, *Resolved*, that it be recommended, and we do earnestly recommend it to the committees of correspondence or selectmen, in the several seaport towns in this province, to appoint, or cause to be appointed, committees to inspect the imports that have been, or shall be made, since the last day of August, aforesaid, and publish all such in the Boston newspapers, with the names of the importers, that so we may carefully avoid all such persons in our dealings for the future.

Voted, To choose a standing committee for the county, to correspond with the committees of correspondence for the several counties, and elsewhere, as they shall think proper ; also, to prepare matter to lay before this body at their several meetings; to give the earliest intelligence to the several committees of any new attack upon the liberties of the people, and call a county congressional convention at any time, as occasion may require.

Voted, That the committees of correspondence for the towns of Worcester and Leicester, be a committee for the above purpose, and that Messrs. Thomas Denny, Joseph Henshaw, and Joshua Bigelow, be added to the committee.

As the several regiments in this county are large and inconvenient, by the increase of its inhabitants since the first settlement of said regiments, therefore, *Voted,* that the county be divided into seven distinct regiments, in the following manner, to wit:

First—Worcester, Leicester, Holden, Spencer, Paxton.

Second—Sutton, Oxford, Sturbridge, Charlton, Dudley.

Third—Lancaster, Bolton, Harvard, Lunenburg, Leominster, Fitchburg, Ashburnham, Westminster.

Fourth—Brookfield, Western, Braintree, Hardwick, Oakham.

Fifth—Rutland, Hutchinson, Petersham, Athol, Templeton, Winchendon, Royalston, Hubardston, Princeton.

Sixth—Southborough, Westborough, Northborough, Shrewsbury, Grafton.

Seventh—Mendon, Uxbridge, Northbridge, Upton, Douglas.

Voted, That it be recommended to the several towns in this county, to choose proper military officers, and a sufficient number for each town, and that the captains, lieutenants, and ensigns, who are chosen by the people in each regiment, do convene, on or before the tenth day of October next, at some convenient place in each regiment, and choose their field officers to command the militia until they be constitutionally appointed, and that it be recommended to the officers in each town of the county, to enlist one third of the men of their respective towns, between sixteen and sixty years of age, to be ready to act at a minute's warning; and that it be recommended to each town in the county, to choose a sufficient number of men as a committee to supply and support those troops that shall move on any emergency.

Voted, That it be recommended to the company officers of the minute men, to meet at Worcester, on the 17th of October next, at ten o'clock of the forenoon, to proportion their own regiments, and choose as many field officers as they shall think necessary.

Voted, That it be recommended to the justices of the county, that they liberate any persons confined in jail for debt, who are entitled to such liberation by the laws of the province.

Voted, That Capt. Joseph Henshaw, Colonel Thomas Denny, and Capt. Willard Moore, be a committee to present the following remonstrance, in behalf of this convention, to his Excellency General Gage.

To his Excellency Thomas Gage, Esq., &c. &c.

The people of the county of Worcester, being earnestly solicitous for the peace and welfare of the province in general, cannot view the measures now pursuing by your excellency, but with increasing jealousy, as they apprehend there has not existed, and does not at present exist, any just occasion for the formidable hostile preparations making on the neck leading to our distressed capital.

It is a matter of such notoriety, that your excellency must be sensible, there was not the least opposition made to obstruct the introduction of the king's troops at their first landing, nor have the people, since that time, discovered any intention to disturb them, till your excellency was pleased to order the seizure of the powder in the arsenal at Charlestown, in a private manner, which occasioned the report that a skirmish had happened between a party of the king's troops and the people at Cambridge, in which several of the latter fell. This caused the people to form and march from divers parts of the country; but no sooner had the report proved false, than they returned peaceably to their homes.

The inhabitants of the province in general, and of the town of Boston, have never given cause for those cruel and arbitrary acts, for blockading their harbor and subverting the charter by altering the civil government of the province, which, however, this people are determined, by the divine favor, never to submit to, but with their lives, notwithstanding they are aggrieved at the king's displeasure against them, through the instigation of traitorous and designing men.

This county finds it difficult to comprehend the motives for the present hostile parade, unless it be in consequence of some preconcerted plan to subject the already distressed town of Boston to mean compliances or military contributions. They are equally at a loss to account for your excellency's conduct towards the county of Suffolk, as in your answer to their address, remonstrating against fortifying the only avenue to the town, which, by that means, may, in some future time, be improved to cut off the communication between town and country, and thereby reduce the miserable inhabitants to the greatest straits; your excellency is pleased in answer to observe, that you had not made it easier to effect this, than what nature has made it; if so, the county cannot conceive, why this expense and damage of the town to no purpose; your excellency is likewise pleased to take notice of the general good behavior of the soldiers, but at the same time pass over that part complaining of the detention of private property, and proceed to answer by way of quere, to which you would not permit a reply. This county are constrained to observe, they apprehend the people justifiable in providing for their own defence, while they understood there was no passing the neck without examination, the cannon at the north battery spiked up, and many places searched, where arms and ammunition were suspected to be, and if found, seized; yet, as the people have never acted offensively, nor discovered any disposition so to do, till as above related, the county apprehends this can never justify the seizure of private property.

It is with great anxiety this county observes the wanton exercise of power in the officers of the customs at Salem, and on board the king's ships, respecting the article of fuel, destined for the use of the inhabitants of Boston, who are obliged to have it with the additional charge of landing and relading at Salem, before it can proceed; when your excellency must be sensible, the act, which is the professed rule of conduct, expressly excepts fuel and victuals, which may be brought to Boston by taking on board one or more officers, without the aforesaid charge, while that destined for the troops proceeds direct, free from the same. There are many other things which bear extremely hard on the inhabitants, while they are prohibited from transporting the smallest articles from one part of the town to another, water-borne, without danger of a seizure, or to get hay, cattle, &c., from any of the islands, notwithstanding there is no other way of transportation.

Your excellency, we apprehend, must have been greatly misinformed of the character of this people, to suppose such severities tend either to a submission to the acts, or reconciliation with the troops; and the county are sorry to find the execution of the acts attempted with an higher hand than was intended, unless the acts themselves should be thought too lenient.

Bringing into the town a number of cannon from Castle-William; sending for a further reinforcement of troops, with other concurring circumstances, strongly indicating some dangerous design; have justly excited in the minds of the people, apprehensions of the most alarming nature, and the authors must be held accountable for all the blood and carnage made in consequence thereof. Therefore, this county, in duty to God, their country, themselves, and posterity, do remonstrate to, and earnestly desire your excellency, as you regard the service of the king, and the peace and welfare of the province, to desist from any further hostile preparations, and give the people assurance thereof, by levelling the entrenchments and dismantling the fortifications, which will have a tendency to satisfy their doubts, and restore that confidence so essential to their quiet, and his majesty's service.

By order of the convention of committees for the county of Worcester.

JOSEPH HENSHAW, *Chairman.*

Attest, WILLIAM HENSHAW, *Clerk.*

Voted, That this meeting be adjourned to the first Tuesday of December next, at 10 o'clock, of the forenoon, to meet at the court house in Worcester.

DECEMBER 6, 1774.

The convention of committees met according to adjournment, and after prayer by the Rev. Mr. Maccarty, proceeded to business.

The committee appointed to present the remonstrance to General Gage, reported, that they offered the same to Mr. Secretary Flucker, who kept the address some days, and returned it to them, with the following answer:

Boston, Oct. 6, 1774.

GENTLEMEN:—His excellency the governor is ever ready to receive any address of his majesty's subjects, properly laid before him; but that from the county of Worcester, which you were appointed to present, not being directed to him as governor of the province, and there being an article in it injurious to his majesty, the governor declines receiving it at present, as he wishes to have an alteration in those two points before it is presented.

I am, Gentlemen, your humble servant,

THOMAS FLUCKER.

To Messrs. Thomas Denny, Joseph Henshaw, Willard Moore.

The committee being afterwards informed, that if the address were directed to General Gage, with his official titles, it would be received, they waited on the governor, on Friday, October 14th, and presented the address, entitled as follows:

"*To his Excellency Thomas Gage, Esq., Governor of his Majesty's Province of the Massachusetts Bay, and Commander in Chief of the King's forces in North America.*"

The governor returned the following answer to the same:

GENTLEMEN:—I have repeatedly given the strongest assurances, that I intended nothing hostile against the town or country, and therefore, desire you to ease the minds of the people against any reports that may have been industriously spread amongst them to the contrary; my wish is to preserve peace and tranquillity.

With respect to the execution of the port-bill, it is a matter belonging to other departments; and if any thing is done not warranted by said act, the law is open for redress.

THOMAS GAGE.

Voted, To request the Provincial Congress to establish the Norfolk exercise, with such alterations as they shall think proper, instead of the exercise of 1764.

Voted, To recommend the raising an artillery company in this county, to exercise and manage the field pieces, and that the persons chosen for that purpose in each town, meet at Worcester, on the 17th of January next, at eleven o'clock, A. M., to form themselves into a company, and to choose officers.

Voted, That Timothy Bigelow, Mr. Bancroft, William Henshaw, Mr. Sawyer, and Mr. Jonathan Stone, be a committee to draft a petition and remonstrance to the Provincial Congress, against the sixty-four exercise, and put the votes of this convention in order.

Voted, That William Henshaw, Capt. Timothy Bigelow, and Col. Joseph Henshaw, be a committee to present the petition and remonstrance to the Provincial Congress.

Voted, To recommend to the several towns in this county, to give it in charge to their constables and collectors, on their peril, not to pay any public moneys to Harrison Gray, Esq., late treasurer of this province, and to indemnify them for paying it where the towns shall order them to pay.

Voted, That the inhabitants of each town in this county, order their assessors not to return any certificates of the lists of assessments made by them, to Harrison Gray, Esq., late treasurer of the province, and that they indemnify them therefor.

Whereas, we are informed there is a covenant circulating through this province, wherein the signers have combined against the liberties of the people, therefore, *Voted,* that William Henshaw, Capt. Timothy Bigelow, and Col. Joseph Henshaw, be a committee humbly to request the advice of the Provincial Congress, what measures this county shall take in that affair.[1]

Voted, To choose a committee of nine persons, any two of whom to go to the field officers of the county of Worcester, to know the reason why they have not resigned their commissions to the governor, and published such resignation in the Boston newspapers, agreeably to a vote of this convention at a former meeting, and demand a categorical answer, whether they will comply or not with said requisition, and make report to this body at their next meeting.

Capt. Gates, Capt. Timothy Bigelow, Mr. Joshua Bigelow, Major Willard Moore, Col. Sawyer, Mr. Dodge, Capt. Joseph Gilbert, and Mr. Hezekiah Ward, were chosen a committee for the above purpose.

Voted, That it be recommended to the inhabitants of each town in this county, to choose committees of inspection to carry into effect the resolves and proceedings of the Continental Congress.

Voted, That we will encourage a printing office to be set up in this county, and recommend to every town herein, to give all proper encouragement to such undertaking.

Voted, That Capt. Timothy Bigelow, Mr. Joshua Bigelow, and William

(1) This vote relates to the royalist covenant, drawn by Gen. Ruggles, inserted in the note to the journal of the Provincial Congress, *ante* page 68.

Henshaw, be a committee to consult with Mr. Isaiah Thomas, and endeavor to procure a printing office to be set up.

Voted, That the convention be adjourned, to meet on the 26th of January next, at ten o'clock, A. M., at Worcester, at the court house.

JANUARY 26, 1774.

The convention met at the court house in Worcester.

In the absence of the chairman, Col. Artemas Ward was chosen chairman pro tempore.

Voted, That Col. William Henshsw, Col. Ward, Mr. David Bancroft, Capt. Timothy Bigelow, Doct. Dunsmore, Mr. Longley, Capt. Job Cushing, Capt. Page, and Col. Sparhawk, be a committee to take into consideration a plan for this county to adopt respecting the non-consumption covenants of the Continental and Provincial Congress, and to report thereon.

Voted, That it be recommended to the selectmen in each town and district in the county, to insert in the warrants for the next March meetings, an article to choose a county treasurer agreeably to law.

Voted, To adjourn till to-morrow morning, at nine o'clock, A. M.

JANUARY 27, 1774.

The convention met according to adjournment.

The committee chosen yesterday, being ready to report,

Voted, That the convention sit with closed doors, during the disputes on the covenants.

The committee on the covenant reported as follows:

Resolved, That it be recommended to the inhabitants of this county that have not signed this or a similar covenant, that they do it as soon as may be with convenience. The covenant is as follows:

We, the subscribers, having seen the association and covenant drawn up by the grand Continental Congress, respecting the non-importation, non-consumption, and non-exportation of goods, signed by our delegates, and also the delegates of the other colonies on the continent, and also the addition thereto, made by the delegates in Provincial Congress, dated Cambridge, December 5, 1774, for carrying into execution the said association, and having attentively considered, do heartily approve of said association, and the addition, and of every part thereof; and in order to make the same association our own personal act, we do, by these presents, associate under the sacred ties of virtue, honor, and love of our country, strictly to observe and keep all and every article and clause in said association, and addition contained with respect to the importation, exportation, and consumption, according to the true intent, meaning, and letter thereof, and will duly inform, and give notice of every evasion or contravention of said agreement, so far as we are able. All and every of which clauses aforesaid, to remain firm and in force until overruled by a continental and provincial body duly assembled.

The above was accepted by the convention, and signed by the members thereof.

Voted, That Col. Ward, Capt. Newhall, and Col. Holman, be a committee to wait on the Rev. Mr. Fish, and desire him to preach a sermon before the convention, at the next meeting, and in case of failure, to wait upon the Rev. Mr. Paine, for that purpose.

Voted, That Mr. Chairman, Mr. Bancroft, and Mr. Stone, be a committee to wait on the Rev. Mr. Maccarty, and obtain leave to use his pulpit, and to make provision for the reverend clergy who may attend.

Voted, That Col. Ward, Capt. Bigelow, Capt. Willard, Capt. Fay, and Capt. Newhall, be a committee to take into consideration the misbehavior of innholders, retailers, and persons selling liquors without a license.

Voted, To adjourn to three o'clock, P. M.

Afternoon.

The convention met according to adjournment.

Voted, That Col. Ward, Doct. Dunsmore, Capt. Bigelow, William Henshaw, Capt. Willard, Capt. Fay, and Capt. Newhall, be a committee to take into consideration, the conduct of certain persons inimical to their country.

Their report thereon was made, accepted, and is as follows:

Whereas, the convention of committees for the county of Worcester, did, on the 31st of August, 1774, resolve; that it be recommended to such innholders and retailers in said county, who may be approbated by the selectmen in their respective towns, to continue and exercise their respective functions, provided they strictly adhere to the laws of this province, respecting innholders and retailers, and it was the sense of the convention, that no person or persons, ought to sell spirituous liquors in said county, but such as are, or shall be approbated by the selectmen of their respective towns or districts: and as complaint has been made to the convention now sitting, that a number of persons in this county do practise the selling strong liquors without the approbation as aforesaid, which is not only counteracting a resolve of said convention, but is against the law of the province, is of dangerous consequence, and has a tendency to corrupt the morals of the people: for preventing the same, and promoting peace and good order, it is *Resolved,* that it be recommended to the committees of correspondence, inspection, and selectmen in every town and district in this county, carefully to inquire into such illegal practices, and disorders, and not only discountenance, but discourage and put a final stop to such breaches of good order; but, provided any person will not be reclaimed, he or they ought to be held up to the public view, and treated not only with neglect, but contempt, as enemies of the public as well as of private good, until they reform.

And, whereas, Isaac Jones of Weston, in the county of Middlesex, innholder and trader, has, by his conduct of late years, in various instances,

82

manifested a disposition inimical to the rights and privileges of his country-men : therefore,

Resolved, That it be earnestly recommended to all the inhabitants of this county, not to have any commercial connections with said Isaac Jones, but to shun his house and person, and treat him with that contempt he deserves : and should any persons in this county be so lost to a sense of their duty, after this recommendation, as to have any commercial connections or deal-ings with said Jones, we do advise the inhabitants of this county to treat such persons with the utmost neglect.

Voted, That Mr. Willard Moore, Mr. Nathaniel Longley, and Capt. Wil-liam Page, be a committee to take under consideration a motion made re-specting Messrs. Mills and Hicks, and Draper's newspapers, who made re-port, which was accepted, as follows :

Whereas, the enemies of these united colonies are indefatigable in their endeavors to create divisions among the inhabitants, and as there are seve-ral printers on the continent, viz.: Rivington and Gaines of New York, Draper, Mills and Hicks of Boston, that incessantly assist them in their en-deavors, by publishing their scandalous performances in their several news-papers : therefore,

Resolved, That it be recommended to the good people of this county, not to take any more of the aforesaid papers, but that they encourage those printers who have invariably appeared friendly to the country.

Voted, That Col. Ward, Capt. Newhall, Capt. Page, Capt. Bigelow, and Major Moore, be a committee to take the affairs of trade into consideration, and to remonstrate against riots and routs.

The report of this committee was accepted, and is as follows :

Resolved, That it be strongly recommended by this body to the commit-tees of inspection in the several towns in this county, that they be very as-siduous in the discharge of the trust reposed in them, with respect to trade; to see that all traders keep strictly to the rules laid down by the Continen-tal and Provincial Congress : and also, that they make strict inquiry of eve-ry person that purchases goods abroad, who they trade with, and when the goods were imported ; and that it be also recommended to the inhabitants of this county, whenever they purchase goods as abovesaid, that they be very careful not to break covenant : and that they take bills of parcels of every article, and lay the same before the committee for their inspection, that no person may be imposed upon by those villains that are inimical to the cause of liberty.

Whereas, we are fully sensible that our enemies are assiduously endeav-oring to provoke us to acts of violence, not only with those whom we esteem inimical to our liberties, who are natives of this province, but also with General Gage, and the king's troops ; endeavoring thereby, as we ap-prehend, to exceed the bounds of our patience, that they may have a pre-tence to represent us as the aggressors : therefore,

Resolved, That we are diposed to conduct ourselves in a friendly manner towards his majesty's troops, agreeably to the recommendation of the Continental Congress, so long as they behave peaceably towards us.

Resolved, That it be recommended to the inhabitants of this county, to be very careful in discountenancing and suppressing all acts of violence, except so much as is necessary to carry the resolves of the Continental and Provincial Congress into execution; and being fully convinced of the justice of our cause, we are determined firmly and religiously to support and maintain our rights, *even to the loss of our lives and fortunes*, before we will dastardly and impiously give up and submit to an arbitrary power.

Voted, That the standing committee fit and prepare the votes and resolves of the convention for the press, and get such a number of handbills, containing the same, struck off as they shall think proper, for circulation.

Voted, To adjourn to the twenty-eighth day of March next, to meet at 10 o'clock, A. M. at the court house in Worcester.

MARCH 28, 1775.

The convention met according to adjournment.

Voted, That the Rev. Mr. Chaplain be requested to open this convention with prayer.

Voted, That the convention do now proceed to the meeting house, to attend the sermon by the Rev. Elisha Fish, and the other exercises.

The convention being again met in the afternoon:

Voted, That the thanks of the convention be presented to the Rev. Mr. Fish, for the discourse preached before them, and that the standing committee wait upon him and request a copy thereof for the press.

Voted, That the standing committee print as many copies of said discourse as they judge fit, for circulation.

MAY 31, 1775.

The convention met according to adjournment, at the court house, in Worcester.

Mr. William Young was elected chairman pro tempore, and Jeduthan Baldwin clerk pro tempore.

Voted, That the Rev. Mr. Chaplain be desired to open this convention with prayer.

Voted, To pass over counting the votes for county treasurer.

Voted, That Col. Hezekiah Ward, Mr. Padleford, and Mr. Joshua Bigelow, be a committee to draw up a remonstrance to the Provincial Congress, that no man be allowed to have a seat therein who does not vote away his own money for public purposes, in common with the other members, and with his constituents.

Resolved, That a committee be appointed, to take into consideration the subject of allowing those who are inimical to the country, to exercise the right of voting in town meetings.

Resolved, That the erecting of a paper mill in this county would be of great public advantage; and if any person or persons will undertake the erecting of such mill and the manufacture of paper, that it be recommended to the people of the county to encourage the undertaking by generous contributions and subscriptions.[1]

CONVENTION OF BERKSHIRE COUNTY.

AT a meeting of sixty gentlemen, deputies of the several towns in the county of Berkshire, appointed to consult and advise what was necessary and prudent to be done by the inhabitants of this county, in the present alarming situation of our public affairs, met at Stockbridge, July 6th, 1774:

John Ashley, Esq. was unanimously chosen chairman, and Mr. Theodore Sedgwick, clerk.

Mr. Williams, Mr. Sedgwick, Mr. Curtis, Mr. Brown, and Mr. Hopkins, being appointed, reported the following resolves, viz.:

Resolved, That king George the third is our rightful king, and that we will bear true allegiance to him.

Resolved, That the inhabitants of his majesty's colonies in America, are justly entitled to all the rights and liberties that the inhabitants of Great Britain are entitled to, which rights and liberties have been particularly confirmed to the inhabitants of this province, by charter.

Resolved, That it is one of the grand rights and liberties of said inhabitants of Great Britain, that they cannot, constitutionally, be deprived of their property but by their own consent.

Resolved, That the late act of the British parliament, for giving and granting to his majesty, a duty upon all teas imported from Great Britain into America, which duty, by said act, is made payable here, for the purpose of raising a revenue, was made without the consent of the inhabitants of America, whereby their property is taken from them without their consent, and therefore ought to be opposed in all legal and prudent ways.

Resolved, That it is an undoubted right of the inhabitants of said colonies, in all actions, to be tried by their peers of the vicinity; and, therefore, that all those acts of the British parliament, that any way respect the collecting the duties aforesaid, whereby the trial by jury is taken away, or whereby the ancient trial by jury is in any way altered, are unconstitutional and oppressive.

Resolved, That whenever any franchises and liberties are granted to a corporation or body politic, those franchises and liberties cannot legally be taken from such corporations and bodies politic, but by their consent or by forfeiture: that the inhabitants of this province have many great and invaluable franchises and liberties granted to them by charter; which franchises

---

(1) Although meetings of the Worcester County Convention were held at a later date, no regular journal of the subsequent proceedings can be recovered.

and liberties have not been forfeited or resigned by said inhabitants; that by the late acts of the British parliament, some of the most valuable of those franchises and liberties of the said inhabitants are taken from them, without even the form of a trial: therefore,

Resolved, That it is the indispensable duty of every person, who would preserve to himself and posterity the inestimable blessings of liberty, by all constitutional ways and means in his power, to endeavor to avert the much dreaded consequences of these arbitrary and oppressive acts; and that, for that purpose, it is prudent for the inhabitants of the said colonies to enter into an agreement not to purchase or consume the manufactures of Great Britain, under such limitations and exceptions as shall be agreed upon; and that such a non-consumption agreement is neither unwarrantable, hostile, traitorous, nor contrary to our allegiance due to the king; but tends to promote the peace, good order, and safety of the community.

Which said report being maturely considered, it was put to vote, paragraph by paragraph, and each and every paragraph thereof was unanimously accepted.

A committee being appointed to make a draught of a form of a solemn league and covenant, to be recommended to be signed by the inhabitants of this county, to prevent the consumption of the merchandize of Great Britain; the following draught was reported, viz.:

Whereas, the parliament of Great Britain have, of late, undertaken to give and grant away our money, without our knowledge or consent; and in order to compel us to a servile submission to the above measures, have proceeded to block up the harbor of Boston; also have vacated, or are about to vacate the charter, and repeal certain laws of this province, heretofore enacted by the general court, and confirmed by the king and his predecessors: therefore, as a mean to obtain a speedy redress of the aforesaid grievances, we do hereby, solemnly and in good faith, covenant and engage with each other:

1. That we will not import, purchase, or consume, or suffer any person by, for, or under us, to import, purchase, or consume, in any manner whatever, any goods, wares, or merchandize, which shall arrive in America from Great Britain, from and after the first day of October, one thousand seven hundred and seventy-four, or such other time as shall hereafter be agreed upon by the American Congress; nor any goods, which shall be ordered from thence, after this day, until our charter and constitutional rights shall be restored, or until it shall be determined, by the major part of our brethren in this and the neighboring colonies, that a non-importation and non-consumption agreement will not have a tendency to effect the desired end, or until it shall be apparent that a non-importation or non-consumption agreement will not be entered into by the majority of this and the neighboring colonies; except such articles as the said General Congress of North America shall agree to import, purchase, and consume.

2. We do further covenant and agree, that we will observe the most strict

obedience to all constitutional laws, and authority, and will, at all times, exert ourselves to the utmost, for the discouragement of all licentiousness, and suppression of all mobs and riots.

3. We will all exert ourselves, as far as in us lies, in promoting love, peace, and unanimity among each other; and for that end we engage to avoid all unnecessary lawsuits whatever.

4. As a strict and proper adherence to this present agreement will, if not seasonably provided against, involve us in many difficulties and inconveniences; we do promise and agree, that we will take the most prudent care for the raising and preserving sheep, for the manufacturing all such cloths as shall be most useful and necessary; for the raising of flax and manufacturing linens. Further, that we will, by every prudent method, endeavor to guard against all those inconveniences which may otherwise arise, from the foregoing agreement.

5. That if any person shall refuse to sign this or a similar covenant, or, after having signed it, shall not adhere to the real intent and meaning thereof, he or they shall be treated by us with all that neglect justly deserved.

6. That if this or a similar covenant shall, after the first day of August next, be offered to any trader or shop-keeper in this county, and he or they shall refuse to sign the same, for the space of forty-eight hours, that we will not, from thenceforth, purchase any articles of British manufactures, from him or them, until such time as he or they shall sign this or a similar covenant.

Witness our hands, this ———— day of July, Anno Domini, 1774.

Which being several times distinctly read, it was put paragraph by paragraph, and accepted.

This Congress, in deference to the resolves of the late house of representatives, in imitation of the pious example of the reverend pastors of the associated churches in the town of Boston, and from a sense of their dependence on God for every mercy, do earnestly recommend to all denominations of christians in this county, to set apart and observe Thursday, the fourteen day of July current, as a day of public fasting and prayer, to implore the divine assistance, that he would in mercy interpose and avert all those evils with which we are threatened.

And each and all the members of this Congress are enjoined to inform the several ministers of the several religious assemblies to which they belong, hereof.

Voted, That the several members of this Congress, do recommend to the charity of the inhabitants of the several towns and places to which they belong, the distressed circumstances of the poor of the towns of Boston and Charlestown, and that whatever shall be collected for them, be remitted in fat cattle in the next fall, by such ways and means as shall be hereafter agreed upon.

Voted, unanimously, That thanks be given Col. Ashley, for his constant attendance, uprightness, and impartiality, as chairman.

Voted, That the clerk be enjoined to make a fair copy of the proceedings of this meeting, and transmit the same to the committee of correspondence of the town of Boston.

Voted, To dissolve this meeting; and it was dissolved accordingly.

THEODORE SEDGWICK, Clerk.

N. B.—The proceedings aforesaid were preceded by an animated prayer, made by the Rev. Mr. West.

CONVENTION OF CUMBERLAND COUNTY.

AT a meeting of the following gentlemen, chosen by the several towns in the county of Cumberland, held at Falmouth, in said county, on the 21st day of September, 1774, at the house of Mrs. Greele, viz.:

Falmouth—Hon. Enoch Freeman, Esq., Stephen Longfellow, Esq., Mr. Richard Codman, Capt. John Waite, Mr. Enoch Ilsey, Mr. Samuel Freeman.

Scarborough—Capt. Timothy McDaniel, Capt. Reuben Fogg, Mr. Joshua Fabyan.

North Yarmouth—Mr. John Lewis, David Mitchel, Esq., Mr. Jonathan Mitchel, Mr. John Gray, Mr. William Cutter.

Gorham—Solomon Lombard, Esq., William Gorham, Esq., Capt. Edmund Phinney, Capt. Briant Morton, Mr. Joseph Davis.

Cape Elizabeth—Doct. Clement Jordan, Mr. Peter Woodbury, Mr. Samuel Dunn, Capt. Jeduthan Dyer, Doct. Nathaniel Jones, Mr. George Strout.

Brunswick—Mr. Samuel Thompson, Mr. Samuel Stanwood, Capt. Thomas Moulton.

Harpswell—Mr. Joseph Ewing, Capt. John Stover, Mr. Andrew Dunning.

Windham—Mr. Zerubabel Honeywell, Mr. Thomas Trott, Mr. David Barker.

New Gloucester—Mr. William Harris, Mr. Isaac Parsons.

The Hon. Enoch Freeman, Esq., was chosen chairman, and Mr. Samuel Freeman, clerk.

A committee from the body of the people, who were assembled at the entrance of the town, waited on this convention, to see if they would choose a committee of one member out of each town, to join them, to wait upon Mr. Sheriff Tyng, to see whether he would act in his office, under the late act of parliament for regulating the government. On a motion made, *Voted*, that a messenger be sent to the said Sheriff Tyng, to desire his attendance at this convention. A messenger then waited upon Mr. Tyng, with the following billet, viz.:

Mr. Sheriff Tyng's company is desired at the convention of the county now sitting at Mrs. Greele's.

SAMUEL FREEMAN, Clerk.

Wednesday, Sept. 21st, 1774, 11 o'clock, A. M.

Mr. Tyng accordingly attended, and, after some interrogations, subscribed the following declaration, viz.:

COUNTY OF CUMBERLAND, FALMOUTH, SEPT. 21, 1774.

Whereas, great numbers of the inhabitants of this county are now assembled near my house, in consequence of the false representations of some evil minded persons, who have reported that I have endeavored, all in my power, to enforce the late acts of parliament, relating to this province: I do hereby solemnly declare, that I have not, in any way whatever, acted or endeavored to act, in conformity to said acts of parliament; and, in compliance with the commands of the inhabitants so assembled, and by the advice of a committee from the several towns in this county, now assembled in Congress, I further declare I will not, as sheriff of said county, or otherwise, act in conformity to, or by virtue of, said acts, unless by the general consent of the said county. I further declare, I have not received any commission inconsistent with the charter of this province, nor any commission whatever, since the first day of July last.

WILLIAM TYNG.

COUNTY OF CUMBERLAND.—At the convention of committees from the several towns in the said county, held at the house of Mrs. Greele, in Falmouth, in said county, September 21st, 1774, *Voted*, that the foregoing, by William Tyng, Esq., subscribed, is satisfactory to this convention.

Attest: SAMUEL FREEMAN, *Clerk.*

The convention then formed themselves into a committee, to accompany Mr. Tyng to the body of the people, to present the above declaration, and adjourned to the old town house, at three o'clock, P. M., the deliberation to be in public.

The committee accordingly went with Mr. Tyng, who read the declaration to the people, which they voted to be satisfactory, and after refreshing themselves, returned peaceably to their several homes.

Afternoon.

Met according to adjournment.

Voted, That Mr. Samuel Freeman, Solomon Lombard, Esq., Stephen Longfellow, Esq., David Mitchel, Esq., Mr. John Lewis, Capt. John Waite, Mr. Samuel Thompson, Capt. Timothy McDaniel, Doct. Nathaniel Jones, Mr. Isaac Parsons, Enoch Freeman, Esq., Mr. David Barker, and Capt. John Stover, be a committee to draw up the sentiments of this convention, and report the same at the adjournment.

Then adjourned to Thursday morning, eight o'clock, September 22.

THURSDAY, SEPTEMBER 22, 1774.

Met according to adjournment, when the committee presented the following report, which, after being read paragraph by paragraph, was unanimously accepted, viz.:

The great concern with which the people of this county view the increasing differences, which now subsist between the mother country and the colonies, and the dark prospect which some late acts of the British parliament have, in particular, opened to them, have occasioned the several towns herein to choose committees for this convention, "to consider what measures it would be thought expedient to adopt for the general interest of the county, in the present alarming situation of our public affairs." We, therefore, the said committees, pursuant to the request of our respective towns, guided by a strong attachment to the interest of our oppressed country, think it proper, with respect and deference to our brethren in the other counties, to make known our minds as follows:

We think it the indispensable duty of every subject of the English constitution, for his own sake, as well as that of future generations, to use his utmost care, and endeavor, according to the station he is in, to preserve the same inviolate and unimpaired ; for we regard it, not only as the foundation of all our civil rights and liberties, but as a system of government the best calculated to promote the people's peace and happiness: and we lament, that in the present administration, there are men so lost to all the principles of honor, equity, and justice, as to attempt a violation of the rights which we have long enjoyed, and which, while we profess ourselves, as we now declare we do, faithful subjects to George the third, our rightful sovereign, we have a right still to enjoy entire and unmolested : and it is a melancholy consideration, that the acknowledged head of this respected state should be induced to pass his sanction to such laws as tend to the subversion of that glorious freedom, which preserves the greatness of the British empire, and gives it reputation throughout all the nations of the civilized world. It is too apparent, that the British ministry have long been hatching monstrous acts to break our constitution, and some they have at length brought forth. We think the colonies deserve a better treatment from his majesty than this which he assents to. We are his loyal subjects, and merit his regard, and cannot help thinking that if he would pursue his own unbiassed judgment, and lay aside the selfish counsel of wicked and designing men, he and his subjects would be mutually happy, and provocations on both sides cease. But since the ministry have borne their tyranny to such a length, as to endeavor to execute their wicked designs, by military force, in our metropolis, we fear it is their aim to introduce despotic monarchy. But though their tyranny and fell oppression seem now, with hasty strides, to threaten all the colonies with ruin and destruction, we hope no vengeance will affright, or wiles allure us to give up our dear bought liberty, that choicest boon of Heaven, which our fathers came into these regions to enjoy, and which we therefore will retain while life enables us to struggle for its blessings. We believe our enemies supposed we must submit, and tamely give up all our rights. It is true, a vigorous opposition will subject us to many inconveniences, but how much greater will our misery be, if we relinquish all we now enjoy, and lay our future earnings at the mercy of despotic men? We cannot bear the thought. Distant posterity would have cause to curse our folly, and the rising generation would justly execrate our mem-

83

ory. We, therefore, recommend a manly opposition to those cruel acts, and every measure which despotism can invent to abridge our English liberties, and we hope that patience will possess our souls till Providence shall dissipate the gloomy cloud, and restore us to our former happy state. The late act for regulating the government of this province, we consider, in particular, as big with mischief and destruction, tending to the subversion of our charter and our province laws, and in its dire example, alarming to all the colonies. This, through the conduct of some enemies among ourselves, will soon bring us into difficulties, which will require some able counsel to remove. We therefore recommend to each town in this county, to instruct their several representatives to resolve themselves, with the other members of the house, at their approaching session, into a provincial congress, for this purpose.

To this congress we shall submit the general interest of the province, but for the particular benefit of this county, we do advise and recommend:

1. That the justices of the sessions, and court of common pleas, and every other civil officer in this county, whom no authority can remove but that which constituted them, agreeably to charter and our own provincial laws, would religiously officiate in their several departments, as if the aforesaid act had never been invented, and that every private person would pay a strict obedience to such officers, be always ready to protect and to support them, and promote a due observance of our own established laws; and if any persons whatsoever should, henceforth, in any manner, dare to aid the operation of the said tyrannical act, they should be considered as malignant enemies to our charter rights, unfit for civil society, and undeserving of the least regard or favor from their fellow countrymen.

2. That every one should do his utmost to discourage lawsuits, and likewise compromise disputes as much as possible.

3. That it be recommended to the honorable Jeremiah Powell, Esq., and Jedediah Preble, Esq., constitutional councillors of this province, residing in this county, that they should take their places at the board the ensuing session as usual.

4. We cannot but approve of the recommendation given by the convention of Suffolk county, to the several collectors of province taxes, not to pay one farthing more into the province treasury, until the government of the province is placed on a constitutional foundation, or until the Provincial Congress shall order otherwise, and we recommend the same to the several collectors in this county; but we think it the duty of the several collectors of county, town, and district taxes, to perfect their collections, and pay the same into their several treasuries as soon as possible. And here we think it proper to observe, that though we do not coincide in every instance with our Suffolk brethren, which may be owing to a want of knowing all the circumstances of affairs, yet we highly applaud their virtuous zeal and determined resolution.

5. We recommend to every town in this county, charitably to contribute to the relief of our suffering brethren in our distressed metropolis.

6. Lest oppression, which maketh even wise men mad, should hurry some people into tumults and disorders, we would recommend, that every individual in the county use his best endeavors to suppress, at all times, riots, mobs, and all licentiousness, and that our fellow subjects would consider themselves, as they always are, in the presence of the great God, who loveth order, not confusion.

7. That when a general non-importation agreement takes place, we shall look upon it to be the duty of every vender of merchandize, to sell his goods at the present rates; and if any person shall exhorbitantly enhance the prices of his goods, we shall look upon him as an oppressor of his country. And in order to prevent imposition in this respect, we recommend that a committee be chosen in each town, to receive complaints against any who may be to blame herein: and if he shall refuse to wait on such committee, on notice given, or be found culpable in this respect, his name shall be published in the several towns of the county, as undeserving of the future custom of his countrymen.

8. That every one who has it in his power, would improve our breed of sheep, and, as far as possible, increase their number; and also encourage the raising of flax, and promote the manufactures of the country.

9. As the very extraordinary and alarming act for establishing the Roman catholic religion, and French laws, in Canada, may introduce the French or Indians into our frontier towns, we recommend that every town and individual in this county, should be provided with a proper stock of military stores, according to our province law, and that some patriotic military officers be chosen in each town, to exercise their several companies, and make them perfect in the military art.

10. Our general grievances being the subject of deliberation before the Continental Congress, renders it inexpedient to consider them particularly; on their wisdom we have a great dependence, and we think it will be our duty to lay aside every measure to which we have advised, that may be variant from theirs, and pay a due regard to their result.

And now we think it proper to declare, that as we have been recounting the hardships we endure by the machinations of our enemies at home, we cannot but gratefully acknowledge our obligation to those illustrious worthies, our friends of the minority, who constantly opposed those wicked measures, and would heartily wish, some great and good men would invent and mark out some plan that will unite the parent state to these, its colonies, and thereby prevent the effusion of christian blood.

Then, *Voted,* That every member of this convention be severally interrogated, whether he now has, or will hereafter, take any commission under the present act of parliament, for regulating the government of this province.

The members were accordingly interrogated, and each and every one of them answered in the negative.

Voted, That the several committees which compose this convention, or the major part of each, be, and hereby are, desired to interrogate the civil officers, and other persons whom they may think fit, in their respective towns, whether they now have, or will hereafter take, any commission under the aforesaid act.

Voted, That the whole proceedings of this convention be, by the clerk, transmitted to the press, and also to the town clerks of the respective towns in this county, as soon as may be.

Voted, That this convention be continued, and that the committee of Falmouth, or the major part of them, be, and hereby are empowered, on any occasion that in their opinion requires it, to notify a meeting of the delegates thereof, at such time and place as they may think proper, setting forth the occasion thereof.

Voted, That the thanks of this convention be given to the Hon. Enoch Freeman, Esq., for his faithful services as chairman.

SAMUEL FREEMAN, *Clerk.*

NARRATIVES

OF THE

EXCURSION OF THE KING'S TROOPS,

APRIL 19, 1775.

IN PROVINCIAL CONGRESS, WATERTOWN, MAY 22, 1775.

Resolved, That the following narrative of the excursion and ravages of the king's troops, under the command of General Gage, on the nineteenth of April last, together with the depositions taken by order of the Congress, to support the truth of it, be sent to the press for publication.

SAMUEL FREEMAN, *Secretary*.

A NARRATIVE OF THE EXCURSION AND RAVAGES OF THE KING'S TROOPS, UNDER THE COMMAND OF GENERAL GAGE, ON THE NINETEENTH OF APRIL, 1775: TOGETHER WITH THE DEPOSITIONS TAKEN BY ORDER OF CONGRESS TO SUPPORT THE TRUTH OF IT. PUBLISHED BY AUTHORITY.[1]

ON the nineteenth day of April, one thousand seven hundred and seventy-five, a day to be remembered by all Americans of the present generation, and which ought, and doubtless will be handed down to ages yet unborn, the troops of Britain, unprovoked, shed the blood of sundry of the loyal American subjects of the British king in the field of Lexington. Early in the morning of said day, a detachment of the forces under the command of General Gage, stationed at Boston, attacked a small party of the inhabitants of Lexington and some other towns adjacent, the detachment consisting of about nine hundred men, commanded by Lieutenant Colonel Smith: The inhabitants of Lexington and the other towns were about one hundred, some with and some without fire-arms, who had collected upon information that the detachment had secretly marched from Boston the preceding night, and landed on Phipps's Farm in Cambridge, and were proceeding on their way with a brisk pace towards Concord, as the inhabitants supposed, to take or destroy a quantity of stores deposited there for the use of the colony; sundry peace-

---

(1) This narrative reported by a committee of which Doct. Church was chairman, and the depositions taken by the committee of which Mr. Gerry was first named, with those subsequently collected, were printed, at Worcester, by Isaiah Thomas, in May, 1775.

able inhabitants having the same night been taken, held by force, and otherwise abused on the road, by some officers of General Gage's army, which caused a just alarm, and a suspicion that some fatal design was immediately to be put in execution against them. This small party of the inhabitants were so far from being disposed to commit hostilities against the troops of their sovereign, that unless attacked, they were determined to be peaceable spectators of this extraordinary movement; immediately on the approach of Colonel Smith with the detachment under his command, they dispersed; but the detachment, seeming to thirst for blood, wantonly rushed on, and first began the hostile scene by firing on this small party, by which they killed eight men on the spot and wounded several others before any guns were fired upon the troops by our men. Not contented with this effusion of blood, as if malice had occupied their whole souls, they continued the fire, until all of this small party who escaped the dismal carnage were out of the reach of their fire. Colonel Smith, with the detachment, then proceeded to Concord, where a part of this detachment again made the first fire upon some of the inhabitants of Concord and the adjacent towns, who were collected at a bridge upon this just alarm, and killed two of them and wounded several others, before any of the provincials there had done one hostile act. Then the provincials, roused with zeal for the liberties of their country, finding life and every thing dear and valuable at stake, assumed their native valor and returned the fire, and the engagement on both sides began. Soon after, the British troops retreated towards Charlestown, having first committed violence and waste on public and private property, and on their retreat were joined by another detachment of General Gage's troops, consisting of about a thousand men, under the command of Earl Percy, who continued the retreat; the engagement lasted through the day; and many were killed and wounded on each side, though the loss on the part of the British troops far exceeded that of the provincials. The devastation committed by the British troops on their retreat, the whole of the way from Concord to Charlestown, is almost beyond description; such as plundering and burning of dwelling-houses and other buildings, driving into the street women in child-bed, killing old men in their houses unarmed. Such scenes of desolation would be a reproach to the perpetrators, even if committed by the most barbarous nations, how much more when done by Britons famed for humanity and tenderness: And all this because these colonies will not submit to the iron yoke of arbitrary power.

_____

The following depositions were taken and authenticated as soon as possible after the action, to prove and elucidate the truth of facts relative thereto.

We, Solomon Brown, Jonathan Loring, and Elijah Sanderson, all of lawful age, and of Lexington, in the county of Middlesex and colony of the Massachusetts Bay, in New England, do testify and declare, that on the evening of the eighteenth of April, instant, being on the road between Lexington and Concord, and all of us mounted on horses, we were, about ten of the clock, suddenly surprized by nine persons, whom we took to be regular officers, who rode up to us, mounted and armed, each holding a pistol in his hand, and after putting pistols to our breasts, and seizing the bridles of our horses, they swore, that if we stirred another step we should be all dead men, upon which we surrendered ourselves. They detained us until two o'clock the next morning, in which time they searched and greatly abused us; having first inquired about the magazine at Concord, whether any guards were posted there, and whether the bridges were up; and said four or five regiments of regulars would be in possession of the stores soon; they then brought us back to Lexington, cut the horses' bridles, and girths, turned them loose, and then left us.

SOLOMON BROWN,
JONATHAN LORING,
ELIJAH SANDERSON.

Lexington, April 25th, 1775.

MIDDLESEX, ss. APRIL 25TH, 1775.

Jonathan Loring, Solomon Brown, and Elijah Sanderson, being duly cautioned to testify the whole truth, made solemn oath to the truth of the above deposition by them subscribed: before us,

WILLIAM READ,
JOSIAH JOHNSON,   } *Justices of the Peace.*
WILLIAM STICKNEY, }

I, Elijah Sanderson, above named, do further testify and declare, that I was on Lexington common the morning of the nineteenth of April, aforesaid, having been dismissed by the officers above mentioned, and saw a large body of regular troops advancing towards Lexington company, many of whom were then dispersing, I heard one of the regulars, whom I took to be an officer, say, "damn them—we will have them," and immediately the regulars shouted aloud, run and fired on the Lexington company, which did not fire a gun before the regulars discharged on them; eight of the Lexington company were killed, while they were dispersing, and at a considerable distance from each other, and many wounded, and although a spectator, I narrowly escaped with my life.

ELIJAH SANDERSON.

Lexington, April 25th, 1775.

MIDDLESEX, ss. APRIL 25TH, 1775.

Elijah Sanderson, above named, being duly cautioned to testify the whole truth, made solemn oath to the truth of the above deposition by him subscribed: before us,

WILLIAM READ,
JOSIAH JOHNSON,   } *Justices of thr Peace.*
WILLIAM STICKNEY, }

I, Thomas Rice Willard, of lawful age, do testify and declare, that being in the house of Daniel Harrington, of Lexington, on the nineteenth instant, in the morning, about half an hour before sunrise, I looked out at the window of said house and saw, as I suppose, about four hundred regulars in one body, coming up the road and marching toward the north part of the common back of the meeting-house of said Lexington: and as soon as said regulars were against the east end of the meeting-house, the commanding officer said something, what I know not: but upon that, the regulars ran till they came within about eight or nine rods of about an hundred of the militia of Lexington, who were collected on said common, at which time the militia of Lexington dispersed; then the officers made an huzza, and the private soldiers succeeded them; directly after this, an officer rode before the regulars, to the other side of the body, and hollowed after the militia of said Lexington, and said " lay down your arms—damn you—why don't you lay down your arms ?" and that there was not a gun fired till the militia of Lexington were dispersed : and further saith not,

THOMAS RICE WILLARD.

MIDDLESEX, ss. APRIL 23D, 1775.

The within named Thomas Rice Willard, personally appeared, and after due caution to testify the whole truth, and nothing but the truth, made solemn oath to the truth of the within deposition, by him subscribed : before us,

WILLIAM READ,
JONATHAN HASTINGS, } *Justices of the Peace.*
DUNCAN INGRAHAM,

Lexington, 25th of April, 1775.

Simon Winship, of Lexington, in the county of Middlesex, and province of the Massachusetts Bay in New England, being of lawful age, testifieth and saith, that on the nineteenth of April, instant, about four o'clock in the morning, as he was passing the public road in said Lexington, peaceably and unarmed, about two miles and a half distant from the meeting-house in said Lexington, he was met by a body of the king's regular troops, and being stopped by some officers of said troops, was commanded to dismount; upon asking why he must dismount, he was obliged by force to quit his horse, and ordered to march in the midst of the body, and being examined whether he had been warning the minute men, he answered no, but had been out and was then returning to his father's. Said Winship further testifies, that he marched with said troops until he came within about half a quarter of a mile of said meeting-house, where an officer commanded the troops to halt, and then to prime and load ; this being done, the said troops marched on till they came within a few rods of Capt. Parker and company, who were partly collected on the place of parade, when said Winship observed an officer at the head of said troops, flourishing his sword, and with a loud voice giving the word *fire!* which was instantly followed by a discharge of arms from said regular troops; and said Winship is positive, and in the most solemn manner declares, that there was no discharge of arms on either side, till the word fire was given by said officer as above.

SIMON WINSHIP.

MIDDLESEX, SS. APRIL 25TH, 1775.

Simon Winship, above named, appeared, and after due caution to testify the whole truth, and nothing but the truth, made solemn oath to the truth of the above deposition, by him subscribed: before us,

WILLIAM READ, } Justices of the Peace.
JOSIAH JOHNSON, }

Lexington, April 25th, 1775.

I, John Parker, of lawful age, and commander of the militia in Lexington, do testify and declare, that on the nineteenth instant, in the morning, about one of the clock, being informed, that there were a number of the regular officers riding up and down the road, stopping and insulting people as they passed the road, and also informed that a number of the regular troops were on their march from Boston, in order to take the province stores at Concord, I ordered our militia to meet on the common in said Lexington, to consult what to do, and concluded not to be discovered, nor meddle, or make with said regular troops, if they should approach, unless they should insult or molest us; and upon their sudden approach, I immediately ordered our militia to disperse and not to fire. Immediately, said troops made their appearance, and rushing furiously on, fired upon and killed eight of our party, without receiving any provocation therefor from us.

JOHN PARKER.

MIDDLESEX, SS. APRIL 25TH, 1775.

The above named John Parker, personally appeared, and after being duly cautioned to declare the whole truth, made solemn oath to the truth of the above deposition, by him subscribed: before us,

WILLIAM READ,
JOSHUA JOHNSON, } Justices of the Peace.
WILLIAM STICKNEY, }

Lexington, April 24th, 1775.

I, John Robbins, being of lawful age, do testify and say, that on the nineteenth instant, the company under the command of Captain John Parker, being drawn up sometime before sunrise, on the green or common, and I being in the front rank, there suddenly appeared a number of the king's troops, about a thousand as I thought, at the distance of about sixty or sev-

84

enty yards from us, huzzaing, and on a quick pace towards us, with three officers in their front on horseback, and on full gallop towards us; the foremost of which cried, "throw down your arms!—ye villains!—ye rebels!" upon which, said company dispersing, the foremost of the three officers ordered their men saying, "*fire!—by God!—fire!*" at which moment we received a very heavy and close fire from them; at which instant, being wounded, I fell, and several of our men were shot dead by me. Capt. Parker's men I believe, had not then fired a gun: and further the deponent saith not,

JOHN ROBBINS.

MIDDLESEX, ss. APRIL 24TH, 1775.

John Robbins, within named, appeared, and being duly cautioned to testify the truth, and nothing but the truth, made solemn oath to the truth of the within deposition, subscribed by his special order, he being so maimed and wounded, that he thought he could neither write his name, nor make his mark: before us,

WILLIAM READ,   }
 JOSIAH JOHNSON, } *Justices of the Peace.*

We, Benjamin Tidd, of Lexington, and Joseph Abbot, of Lincoln, in the county of Middlesex, and colony of the Massachusetts Bay, in New England, of lawful age, do testify and declare, that on the morning of the nineteenth of April, instant, about five o'clock, being on Lexington common and mounted on horses, we saw a body of regular troops marching up to the Lexington company, which was then dispersing; soon after, the regulars fired, first a few guns, which we took to be pistols, from some of the regulars who were mounted on horses; and then the said regulars fired a volley or two, before any guns were fired by the Lexington company. Our horses immediately started and we rode off: and further say not,

BENJAMIN TIDD,
 JOSEPH ABBOTT.

Lexington, April 25th, 1775.

MIDDLESEX, ss. APRIL 25TH, 1775.

Benjamin Tidd, and Joseph Abbott, above named, being duly cautioned to testify the whole truth, made solemn oath to the truth of the above deposition, by them subscribed: before us,

WILLIAM READ,   }
 JOSIAH JOHNSON, } *Justices of the Peace.*
 WILLIAM STICKNEY, }

We, Nathaniel Mulliken, Phillip Russell, Moses Harrington, Jun., Thomas and Daniel Harrington, William Grimer, William Tidd, Isaac Hastings, Jonas Stone, Jun., James Wyman, Thaddeus Harrington, John Chandler,

Joshua Reed, Jun., Joseph Simonds, Phineas Smith, John Chandler, Jun., Reuben Lock, Joel Viles, Nathan Reed, Samuel Tidd, Benjamin Lock, Thomas Winship, Simeon Snow, John Smith, Moses Harrington, 3d, Joshua Reed, Ebenezer Parker, John Harrington, Enoch Willington, John Hosmer, Isaac Green, Phineas Stearns, Isaac Durant, and Thomas Headley, Jun, all of lawful age, and inhabitants of Lexington, in the county of Middlesex, and colony of the Massachusetts Bay, in New England, do testify and declare, that on the nineteenth of April, instant, about one or two o'clock in the morning, being informed, that several officers of the regulars, had, the evening before, been riding up and down the road, and had detained and insulted the inhabitants passing the same ; and also understanding, that a body of regulars were marching from Boston, towards Concord, with intent, as it was supposed, to take the stores belonging to the colony in that town, we were alarmed, and having met at the place of our company's parade, were dismissed by our captain, John Parker, for the present, with orders to be ready to attend at the beat of the drum. We further testify and declare, that about five o'clock in the morning, hearing our drum beat, we proceeded towards the parade, and soon found, that a large body of troops were marching towards us; some of our company were coming up to the parade, and others had reached it ; at which time, the company began to disperse ; whilst our backs were turned on the troops, we were fired on by them, and a number of our men were instantly killed and wounded. Not a gun was fired by any person in our company on the regulars, to our knowledge, before they fired on us, and they continued firing until we had all made our escape.

NATHANIEL MULLIKEN,	JOEL VILES,
PHILLIP RUSSELL,	NATHAN REED,
MOSES HARRINGTON, JUN.,	SAMUEL TIDD,
THOMAS HARRINGTON,	BENJAMIN LOCK,
DANIEL HARRINGTON,	THOMAS WINSHIP,
WILLIAM GRIMER,	SIMEON SNOW,
WILLIAM TIDD.	JOHN SMITH,
ISAAC HASTINGS,	MOSES HARRINGTON, 3D.,
JONAS STONE, JUN.,	JOSHUA REED,
JAMES WYMAN,	EBENEZER PARKER,
THADDEUS HARRINGTON,	JOHN HARRINGTON,
JOHN CHANDLER,	ENOCH WILLINGTON,
JOSHUA REED, JUN.,	JOHN HOSMER,
JOSEPH SIMONDS,	ISAAC GREEN,
PHINEAS SMITH,	PHINEAS STEARNS,
JOHN CHANDLER, JUN.,	ISAAC DURANT,
REUBEN LOCK,	THOMAS HEADLEY, JUN.

Lexington, April 25th, 1775.

MIDDLESEX, ss. APRIL 25TH, 1775.

Nathaniel Mulliken, Phillip Russell, Moses Harrington, Jun., Thomas

Harrington, Daniel Harrington, William Grimer, William Tidd, Isaac Hastings, Jonas Stone, Jun., James Wyman, Thaddeus Harrington. John Chandler, Joshua Reed, Jun., Joseph Simonds, Phineas Smith, John Chandler, Jun., Reuben Lock, Joel Viles, Nathan Reed, Samuel Tidd, Benjamin Lock, Thomas Winship, Simeon Snow, John Smith, Moses Harrington, 3d, Joshua Reed, Ebenezer Parker, John Harrington, Enoch Willington, John Hosmer, Isaac Green, Phineas Stearns, Isaac Durant, and Thomas Headley, Jun., above named, being duly cautioned to testify the whole truth, made solemn oath to the above deposition, as containing nothing but the truth, as subscribed by them: before us,

> WILLIAM REED,
> JOSIAH JOHNSON,   } *Justices of the Peace.*
> WILLIAM STICKNEY,

We, Nathaniel Parkhurst, Jonas Parker, John Munroe, Jun., John Winship, Solomon Peirce, John Muzzy, Abner Meads, John Bridge, Jun., Ebenezer Bowman, William Munroe, 3d, Micah Hagar, Samuel Sanderson, Samuel Hastings, and James Brown, of Lexington, in the county of Middlesex, and colony of the Massachusetts Bay, in New England, and all of lawful age, do testify and say, that on the morning of the nineteenth of April, instant, about one or two o'clock, being informed, that a number of regular officers had been riding up and down the road the evening and night preceding, and that some of the inhabitants as they were passing, had been insulted by the officers and stopped by them, and being also informed, that the regular troops, were on their march from Boston, in order, as it was said, to take the colony stores then deposited at Concord, we met on the parade of our company in this town. After the company had collected we were ordered by Capt. John Parker, who commanded us, to disperse for the present, and be ready to attend the beat of the drum, and accordingly the company went into houses near the place of parade. We further testify and say, that about five o'clock in the morning, we attended the beat of our drum, and were formed on the parade. We were faced towards the regulars then marching up to us, and some of our company were coming to the parade, with their backs towards the troops, and others on the parade began to disperse, when the regulars fired on the company before a gun was fired by any of our company on them; they killed eight of our company and wounded several, and continued their fire until we had all made our escape.

NATHANIEL PARKHURST,	JOHN BRIDGE, JUN.,
JONAS PARKER,	EBENEZER BOWMAN,
JOHN MUNROE, JUN.,	WILLIAM MUNROE, 3D.,
JOHN WINSHIP,	MICAH HAGAR,
SOLOMON PEIRCE,	SAMUEL SANDERSON,
JOHN MUZZY,	SAMUEL HASTINGS,
ABNER MEADS,	JAMES BROWN.

Lexington, 25th April, 1775.

MIDDLESEX, ss. APRIL 25TH, 1775.

Nathaniel Parkhurst, Jonas Parker, John Munroe, Jun., John Winship, Solomon Peirce, John Muzzy, Abner Meads, John Bridge, Jun., Ebenezer Bowman, William Munroe, 3d., Micah Hagar, Samuel Sanderson, Samuel Hastings, and James Brown, above named, being duly cautioned, to testify the whole truth, made solemn oath to the truth of the above deposition, by them subscribed: before us,

WILLIAM READ,
JOSIAH JOHNSON, } *Justices of the Peace.*
WILLIAM STICKNEY,

I, Timothy Smith, of Lexington, in the county of Middlesex, and colony of Massachusetts Bay, in New England, being of lawful age, do testify and declare, that on the morning of the nineteenth of April, instant, being at Lexington common, as a spectator, I saw a large body of regular troops, marching up towards the Lexington company then dispersing, and likewise, saw the regular troops fire on the Lexington company before the latter fired a gun; I immediately ran, and a volley was discharged at me, which put me in imminent danger of losing my life; I soon returned to the common, and saw eight of the Lexington men, who were killed and lay bleeding at a considerable distance from each other, and several were wounded, and further saith not,

TIMOTHY SMITH.

Lexington, April 25th, 1775.

MIDDLESEX, ss. APRIL 25TH, 1775.

Timothy Smith, above named, being duly cautioned to testify the truth, made solemn oath to the truth of the above deposition, by him subscribed: before us,

WILLIAM READ,
JOSIAH JOHNSON, } *Justices of the Peace.*
WILLIAM STICKNEY,

We, Levi Mead and Levi Harrington, both of Lexington, in the county of Middlesex, and colony of the Massachusetts Bay, in New England, and of lawful age, do testify and declare, that on the morning of the nineteenth of April, being on Lexington common, as spectators, we saw a large body of regular troops marching up towards the Lexington company, and some of the regulars on horses, whom we took to be officers, fired a pistol or two on the Lexington company, which was then dispersing; these were the first guns that were fired, and they were immediately followed by several volleys from the regulars, by which eight men belonging to said company were killed, and several wounded.

LEVI MEAD,
LEVI HARRINGTON.

Lexington, April 25th, 1775.

MIDDLESEX, ss. APRIL 25TH, 1775.

Levi Mead and Levi Harrington, above named, being duly cautioned to testify the whole truth, made solemn oath to the truth of the above deposition, by them subscribed: before us,

> WILLIAM READ,
> JOSIAH JOHNSON, } *Justices of the Peace.*
> WILLIAM STICKNEY,

Lexington, April 25th, 1775.

I, William Draper, of lawful age, and an inhabitant of Colrain, in the county of Hampshire, and colony of the Massachusetts Bay, in New England, do testify and declare, that being on the parade at said Lexington, April nineteenth, instant, about half an hour before sunrise, the king's regular troops appeared at the meeting-house of Lexington. Captain Parker's company, who were drawn up back of said meeting-house on the parade, turned from said troops, making their escape by dispersing. In the mean time, the regular troops made an huzza, and ran towards Captain Parker's company who were dispersing, and immediately after the huzza was made, the commanding officer of said troops, as I took him to be, gave the command to the troops, "*fire!—fire!—damn you, fire!*" and immediately they fired, before any of Captain Parker's company fired, I then being within three or four rods of said regular troops: and further saith not,

> WILLIAM DRAPER.

MIDDLESEX, ss. APRIL 25TH, 1775.

William Draper, above named, being duly cautioned to testify the whole truth, made solemn oath to the truth of the above deposition by him subscribed: before us,

> WILLIAM READ,
> JOSIAH JOHNSON, } *Justices of the Peace.*
> WILLIAM STICKNEY,

Lexington, April 23d, 1775.

I, Thomas Fessenden, of lawful age, testify and declare, that being in a pasture near the meeting-house, at said Lexington, on Wednesday last, at about half an hour before sunrise, I saw a number of regular troops pass speedily by said meeting-house, on their way towards a company of militia of said Lexington, who were assembled to the number of about an hundred in a company, at the distance of eighteen or twenty rods from said meeting-house: and after they had passed by said house, I saw three officers on horseback advance to the front of said regulars, when one of them, being within six rod of said militia, cried out, "disperse you rebels immediately;" on which he brandished his sword over his head three times; mean while, the second officer, who was about two rods behind him, fired a pistol point-

ed at said militia, and the regulars kept huzzaing till he had finished brandishing his sword; and when he had thus finished brandishing his sword, he
pointed it down towards said militia, and immediately on which, the said
regulars fired a volley at said militia, and then I ran off as fast as I could,
while they continued firing till I got out of their reach. I further testify,
that as soon as ever the officer cried " disperse you rebels," the said company of militia dispersed every way as fast as they could, and while they were
dispersing, the regulars kept firing at them incessantly: and further saith
not,

THOMAS FESSENDEN.

MIDDLESEX, ss. APRIL 23D, 1775.

The within named Thomas Fessenden appeared, and after due caution to
testify the whole truth, and nothing but the truth, made solemn oath to the
truth of the within deposition by him subscribed: before us,

WILLIAM READ, } Justices of the Peace.
JOSIAH JOHNSON, }

———

Lincoln, April 23d, 1775.

I, John Bateman, belonging to the fifty-second regiment, commanded by
Colonel Jones, on Wednesday morning, on the nineteenth day of April instant, was in the party marching to Concord. Being at Lexington, in the
county of Middlesex, being nigh the meeting-house in said Lexington, there
was a small party of men gathered together in that place, when our said
troops marched by; and I testify and declare, that I heard the word of command given to the troops to fire, and some of said troops did fire, and I saw
one of said small party lie dead on the ground nigh said meeting-house;
and I testify, that I never heard any of the inhabitants so much as fire one
gun on said troops.

JOHN BATEMAN.

MIDDLESEX, ss. APRIL 23D, 1775.

The above named John Bateman voluntarily, being previously cautioned
to relate nothing but the truth, made solemn oath to the deposition by him
subscribed: before us,

JOHN CUMMINGS,   } Justices of the Peace.
DUNCAN INGRAHAM, }

———

Lexington, April 23d, 1775.

We, John Hoar, John Whitehead, Abraham Garfield, Benjamin Munroe,
Isaac Parks, William Hosmer, John Adams, and Gregory Stone, all of Lincoln, in the county of Middlesex, Massachusetts Bay, all of lawful age, do
testify and say, that on Wednesday last we were assembled at Concord, in the
morning of said day, in consequence of information received, that a brigade
of regular troops were on their march to the said town of Concord, who
had killed six men at the town of Lexington. About an hour afterwards,

we saw them approaching, to the number, as we apprehended, of about twelve hundred; on which, we retreated to a hill about eighty rods back, and the said troops then took possession of the hill where we were first posted; presently after this, we saw the troops moving towards the north bridge, about one mile from the said Concord meeting-house. We then immediately went before them and passed the bridge, just before a party of them, to the number of about two hundred, arrived. They there left about one half of their two hundred at the bridge, and proceeded with the rest towards Colonel Barrett's, about two miles from the said bridge. We then, seeing several fires in the town, thought the houses in Concord were in danger, and marched towards the said bridge, and the troops who were stationed there, observing our approach, marched back over the bridge, and then took up some of the planks. We then hastened our march towards the bridge, and when we had got near the bridge they fired on our men, first three guns one after the other, and then a considerable number more, and then, and not before, having orders from our commanding officers not to fire till we were fired upon, we fired upon the regulars, and they retreated. On their retreat through this town, and Lexington, to Charlestown, they ravaged and destroyed private property, and burned three houses, one barn, and one shop.

John Hoar,	Isaac Parks,
John Whitehead,	William Hosmer,
Abraham Garfield,	John Adams,
Benjamin Munroe,	Gregory Stone.

MIDDLESEX, SS. APRIL 23D, 1775.

The within named John Hoar, John Whitehead, Abraham Garfield, Benjamin Munroe, Isaac Parks, William Hosmer, John Adams, and Gregory Stone, appeared, and made oath solemnly to the truth of the above deposition: before us,

William Read,
John Cummings,   } Justices of the Peace.
Jonathan Hastings,
Duncan Ingraham,

Lexington, April 23d, 1775.

We, Nathan Barrett, captain; Jonathan Farrer, Joseph Butler and Francis Wheeler, lieutenants; John Barrett, ensign; John Brown, Silas Walker, Ephraim Melvin, Nathan Buttrick, Stephen Hosmer, Jr., Samuel Barrett, Thomas Jones, Joseph Chandler, Peter Wheeler, Nathan Pierce, and Edward Richardson, all of Concord, in the county of Middlesex, in the province of the Massachusetts Bay, of lawful age, testify and declare, that on Wednesday, the nineteenth instant, about an hour after sunrise, we assembled on a hill near the meeting-house in Concord aforesaid, in consequence of information that a number of regular troops had killed six of our countrymen at Lexington, and were on their march to said Concord: and about an hour after we saw them approaching, to the number, as we imagine, of about twelve hundred; on which, we retreated to a hill about eighty rods back, and the aforesaid troops then took possession of the hill where we were first posted. Presently after this we saw them moving towards the north bridge, about one mile from said meeting-house; we then immediately went before them, and passed the bridge just before a party of them, to the number of about two hundred, arrived. They there left about one half of those two hundred at the bridge, and proceeded with the rest towards Colonel Barrett's, about two miles from the said bridge. We then, seeing several fires in the town, thought our houses were in danger, and immediately marched back towards said bridge; and the troops who were stationed there, observing our approach, marched back over the bridge, and then took up some of the planks. We then hastened our steps towards the bridge, and when we had got near the bridge, they fired on our men; first three guns, one after the other, and then a considerable number more; upon which, and not before, having orders from our commanding officers not to fire till we were fired upon, we fired upon the regulars, and they retreated. At Concord, and on their retreat through Lexington, they plundered many houses, burnt three at Lexington, together with a shop and a barn, and committed damage, more or less, to almost every house from Concord to Charlestown.

NATHAN BARRETT,	NATHAN BUTTRICK,
JONATHAN FARRER,	STEPHEN HOSMER,
JOSEPH BUTLER,	SAMUEL BARRETT,
FRANCIS WHEELER,	THOMAS JONES,
JOHN BARRETT,	JOSEPH CHANDLER,
JOHN BROWN,	PETER WHEELER,
SILAS WALKER,	NATHAN PEIRCE,
EPHRAIM MELVIN,	EDWARD RICHARDSON.

Lexington, April 23d, 1775.

We, Joseph Butler and Ephraim Melvin, do testify and declare, that when the regular troops fired upon our people at the north bridge, in Concord, as related in the foregoing depositions, they shot one, and we believe two of our people, before we fired a single gun at them.

JOSEPH BUTLER,
EPHRAIM MELVIN.

MIDDLESEX, ss. APRIL 23D, 1775.

The within named Nathan Barrett, Jonathan Farrer, Joseph Butler, Francis Wheeler, John Barrett, John Brown, Silas Walker, Ephraim Melvin, Nathan Buttrick, Stephen Hosmer, Samuel Barrett, Thomas Jones, Joseph Chandler, Peter Wheeler, Nathan Peirce, and Edward Richardson, appeared, and made solemn oath to the truth of the above depositions by them subscribed: before us,　　JONATHAN HASTINGS,
JOHN CUMMINGS, } *Justices of the Peace.*
DUNCAN INGRAHAM,

Concord, April 22d, 1775.

I, Timothy Minot, Jr., of Concord, on the nineteenth day of this instant April, after I had heard of the regular troops firing upon the Lexington men, and fearing that hostilities might be committed at Concord, thought it my incumbent duty to secure my family. After I had secured my family, sometime after that, returning towards my own dwelling, and finding that the bridge on the northern part of said Concord was guarded by regular troops, being a spectator of what had happened at said bridge, I declare that the regular troops stationed on the bridge, after they saw the men that were collected on the westerly side of said bridge marched towards said bridge, then the troops returned towards the easterly side of said bridge, and formed themselves, as I thought for a regular fight. After that, they fired one gun, then two or three more, before the men that were stationed on the westerly part of said bridge fired upon them.

TIMOTHY MINOT, JR.

MIDDLESEX, ss. APRIL 23D, 1775.

Doct. Timothy Minot, Jr. personally appeared, and after due caution to testify the truth, and nothing but the truth, made solemn oath to the truth of the above deposition by him subscribed : before us,

WILLIAM READ,
JONATHAN HASTINGS,
JOHN CUMMINGS,
DUNCAN INGRAHAM,
} *Justices of the Peace.*

Lexington, April 23d, 1775.

I, James Barrett, of Concord, colonel of a regiment of militia in the county of Middlesex, do testify and say, that on Wednesday morning last, about day break, I was informed of the approach of a number of the regular troops to the town of Concord, where were some magazines belonging to this province : when there were assembled some of the militia of this and the neighboring towns, then I ordered them to march to the north bridge, so called, which they had passed, and were taking up. I ordered said militia to march to said bridge, and pass the same, but not to fire on the king's troops unless they were first fired upon. We advanced near said bridge, when the said troops fired upon our militia, and killed two men dead on the spot, and wounded several others, which was the first firing of guns in Concord. My detachment then returned the fire, which killed and wounded several of the king's troops.

JAMES BARRETT.

MIDDLESEX, ss. APRIL 23D, 1775.

The above named James Barrett personally appeared, and after due caution to testify the whole truth, and nothing but the truth, made solemn oath to the truth of the above deposition by him subscribed : before us,

WILLIAM READ,
JONATHAN HASTINGS,
DUNCAN INGRAHAM,
} *Justices of the Peace.*

Lexington, April 23d, 1775.

We, Bradbury Robinson, Samuel Spring, Thaddeus Bancroft, all of Concord, and James Adams, of Lincoln, all in the county of Middlesex, all of lawful age, do testify and say, that on Wednesday morning last, near ten of the clock, we saw near one hundred of regular troops, being in the town of Concord, at the north bridge in said town, so called, and having passed the same they were taking up said bridge, when about three hundred of our militia were advancing towards said bridge, in order to pass said bridge, when, without saying any thing to us, they discharged a number of guns on us, which killed two men dead on the spot, and wounded several others, when we returned the fire on them, which killed two of them, and wounded several; which was the beginning of hostilities in the town of Concord.

BRADBURY ROBINSON,
SAMUEL SPRING,
THADDEUS BANCROFT.

MIDDLESEX, ss. APRIL 23D, 1775.

The within named Bradbury Robinson, Samuel Spring, Thaddeus Bancroft and James Adams, made solemn oath to the truth of the within deposition by them subscribed: before us,

WILLIAM READ,
WILLIAM STICKNEY,   } Justices of the Peace.
JONATHAN HASTINGS,

Concord, April 23d, 1775.

I, James Marr, of lawful age, testify and say, that in the evening of the eighteenth instant, I received orders from George Hutchinson, adjutant of the fourth regiment of the regular troops stationed in Boston, to prepare and march: to which order I attended, and marched to Concord, where I was ordered by an officer, with about one hundred men to guard a certain bridge there. While attending that service, a number of people came along, in order, as I supposed, to cross said bridge, at which time a number of regular troops first fired upon them.

JAMES MARR.

MIDDLESEX, ss. APRIL 23D, 1775.

The above named James Marr appeared, and after due caution to testify the truth, and nothing but the truth, made solemn oath to the truth of the above deposition by him voluntarily subscribed: before us,

DUNCAN INGRAHAM,   } Justices of the Peace.
JONAS DIX,

I, Edward Thornton Gould, of his majesty's own regiment of foot, being of lawful age, do testify and declare, that on the evening of the eighteenth instant, under the order of General Gage, I embarked with the light infantry and grenadiers of the line, commanded by Colonel Smith, and landed on the marshes of Cambridge, from whence we proceeded to Lexington. On our arrival at that place, we saw a body of provincial troops armed, to the number of about sixty or seventy men. On our approach, they dispersed, and soon after firing began, but which party fired first I cannot exactly say, as our troops rushed on, shouting and huzzaing, previous to the firing, which was continued by our troops so long as any of the provincials were to be seen. From thence we marched to Concord. On a hill near the entrance of the town, we saw another body of the provincials assembled. The light infantry companies were ordered up the hill to disperse them. On our approach they retreated towards Concord. The grenadiers continued on the road under the hill towards the town. Six companies of light infantry were ordered down to take possession of the bridge which the provincials retreated over. The company I commanded was one of the three companies of the above detachment, and went forward about two miles. In the mean time, the provincial troops returned, to the number of about three or four hundred. We drew up on the Concord side of the bridge. The provincials came down upon us; upon which we engaged and gave the first fire. This was the first engagement after the one at Lexington. A continued firing from both parties lasted through the whole day. I myself was wounded at the attack of the bridge, and am now treated with the greatest humanity, and taken all possible care of, by the provincials at Medford.

EDWARD THORNTON GOULD.

Medford, April 20th, 1775.

Province of the Massachusetts Bay,

MIDDLESEX COUNTY, APRIL 25TH, 1775.

Lieutenant Edward Thornton Gould, aforenamed, personally made oath to the truth of the foregoing declaration, by him subscribed: before us,

THADDEUS MASON,
JOSIAH JOHNSON,   } *Justices of the Peace.*
SIMON TUFTS.

Province of the Massachusetts Bay.

CHARLESTOWN, ss.

I, Nathaniel Gorham, Notary and Tabellion Public, by lawful authority, duly admitted and sworn; hereby certify to all whom it doth or may concern, that Thaddeus Mason, Josiah Johnson, and Simon Tufts, Esq'rs, are three of his majesty's justices of the peace, quorum unus, for the county of Middlesex, and that full faith and credit is and ought to be given to their transactions as such, both in court and out. In witness whereof, I have hereunto affixed my name and seal, this twenty-sixth day of April, Anno Domini, one thousand seven hundred and seventy-five.

NATHANIEL GORHAM.

N. B.   A certificate was made out under the signature of the notary public, that all the other justices who administered the oaths to the several deponents, were his majesty's justices of the peace, in the counties where such certificates were made, and were legally appointed to that office, and that full faith and credit is and ought to be given to their transactions.

A paper having been printed in Boston, representing, that one of the British troops killed at the bridge at Concord, was scalped, and the ears cut off from the head, supposed to be done in order to dishonor the Massachusetts people, and to make them appear to be savage and barbarous, the following deposition was taken that the truth might be known.

We, the subscribers, of lawful age, testify and say, that we buried the dead bodies of the king's troops that were killed at the north bridge in Concord, on the nineteenth day of April, 1775, where the action first began, and that neither of those persons were scalped, nor their ears cut off, as has been represented.

ZACHARIAH BROWN,
THOMAS DAVIS, JUN.

Concord, May 11th, 1775.

Zachariah Brown, Thomas Davis, Jun., personally appeared before me, and made oath to the above declaration.

DUNCAN INGRAHAM, *Justice of the Peace.*

Hannah Adams, wife of Deacon Joseph Adams, of the second precinct in Cambridge, testifieth and saith, that on the nineteenth day of April last past, upon the return of the king's troops from Concord, divers of them entered our house, by bursting open the doors, and three of the soldiers broke into the room in which I then was, laid on my bed, being scarcely able to walk from my bed to the fire, not having been to my chamber door from my being delivered in child-birth to that time.   One of said soldiers immediately opened my curtains with his bayonet fixed, pointing the same to my breast. I immediately cried out, "for the Lord's sake do not kill me?" he replied, "damn you."   One that stood near said, "we will not hurt the woman, if she will go out of the house, but we will surely burn it."   I immediately arose, threw a blanket over me, went out and crawled into a corn-house near the door, with my infant in my arms, where I remained until they were gone.   They immediately set the house on fire, in which I had left five children, and no other person; but the fire was happily extinguished, when the house was in the utmost danger of being utterly consumed.

HANNAH ADAMS.

MIDDLESEX, SS. CAMBRIDGE, SECOND PRECINCT, 16TH MAY, 1775.

Hannah Adams, the subscriber of the above deposition, personally appeared, and made oath to the truth of the same : before me,

JONATHAN HASTINGS, *Justice of the Peace.*

Cambridge, May 19th, 1775.

We, Benjamin Cooper and Rachel Cooper, both of Cambridge, aforesaid, of lawful age, testify and say, that in the afternoon of the nineteenth day of April last, the king's regular troops under the command of General Gage, upon their return from the blood and slaughter which they had made at Lexington and Concord, fired more than a hundred bullets into the house where we dwelt, through doors, windows, &c. Then a number of them entered the house, where we and two aged gentlemen were, all unarmed. We escaped for our lives into the cellar. The two aged gentlemen were, immediately, most barbarously and inhumanly murdered by them : being stabbed through in many places, their heads mauled, skulls broke, and their brains dashed out on the floor and walls of the house ; and further say not,

BENJAMIN COOPER,
RACHEL COOPER.

MIDDLESEX, SS, MAY 10TH, 1775.

The above named Benjamin Cooper and Rachel Cooper, appeared, and after due caution, made solemn oath to the truth of the above deposition, by them subscribed : before me,

JONAS DIX, *Justice of the Peace.*

The following is a list of those provincials who were killed, wounded, and missing in the action of the nineteenth of April, 1775, and the towns to which they respectively belonged : including all that were lost on that day.

CAMBRIDGE.—*Killed :* William Marcy, Moses Richardson, John Hicks, Jason Russell, Jabish Wyman, Jason Winship. *Wounded :* Capt. Samuel Whittemore. *Missing :* Samuel Frost, Seth Russell.

CHARLESTOWN.—*Killed :* James Miller, and a son of Captain William Barber.

WATERTOWN.—*Killed :* Joseph Cooledge.

SUDBURY.—*Killed :* Deacon Josiah Haynes, Asahel Reed. *Wounded :* Joshua Haynes, Jun.

ACTON.—*Killed :* Capt. Isaac Davis, Abner Hosmer, James Hayward.

BEDFORD.—*Killed :* Capt. Jonathan Wilson. *Wounded :* Job Lane.

WOBURN.—*Killed :* Asa Parker, Daniel Thomson. *Wounded :* George Read, Jacob Bacon.

MEDFORD.—*Killed*: Henry Putnam, William Polly.

NEWTON.—*Wounded*: Noah Wiswall.

LEXINGTON.—*Killed*: Jonas Parker, Robert Munroe, Jedediah Munroe, John Raymond, Samuel Hadley, Jonathan Harrington, Jun., Isaac Muzzy, Caleb Harrington, Nathaniel Wyman, John Brown. *Wounded*: Francis Brown, John Robbins, Solomon Peirce, John Tidd, Joseph Comie, Ebenezer Munroe, Jun., Thomas Winship, Nathaniel Farmer, Prince, a negro.

BILLERICA.—*Wounded*: John Nichols, Timothy Blanchard.

CHELMSFORD.—*Wounded*: Deacon Aaron Chamberlain, Capt. Oliver Barron.

CONCORD.—*Wounded*: Abel Prescott, Jun., Capt. Charles Miles, Capt. Nathan Barrett.

FRAMINGHAM.—*Wounded*: Daniel Hemenway.

STOW.—*Wounded*: Daniel Conant.

DEDHAM.—*Killed*: Elias Haven. *Wounded*: Israel Everett.

NEEDHAM.—*Killed*: Lieut. John Bacon, Serjeant Elisha Mills, Amos Mills, Nathaniel Chamberlain, Jonathan Parker. *Wounded*: Capt. Eleazer Kingsbury, and a son of Doct. Tolman.

ROXBURY.—*Missing*: Elijah Seaver.

BROOKLINE.—*Killed*: Isaac Gardner, Esq.

SALEM.—*Killed*: Benjamin Peirce.

DANVERS.—*Killed*: Henry Jacobs, Samuel Cook, Ebenezer Goldthwait, George Southwick, Benjamin Deland, Jun., Jotham Webb, Perly Putnam. *Wounded*: Nathan Putnam, Dennis Wallis. *Missing*: Joseph Bell.

BEVERLY.—*Killed*: Mr. Kinnym. *Wounded*: Nathaniel Cleaves, Samuel Woodbury, William Dodge.

LYNN.—*Killed*: Abednego Ramsdell, Daniel Townsend, William Flynt, Thomas Hadley. *Wounded*: Joshua Felt, Timothy Munroe. *Missing*: Josiah Breed.

BRITISH OFFICIAL ACCOUNT.

A CIRCUMSTANTIAL ACCOUNT OF AN ATTACK THAT HAPPENED ON THE NINETEENTH OF APRIL, 1775, ON HIS MAJESTY'S TROOPS, BY A NUMBER OF THE PEOPLE OF THE PROVINCE OF MASSACHUSETTS BAY. DRAWN UP BY ORDER OF HIS EXCELLENCY GOVERNOR GAGE, AND ENCLOSED IN A LETTER TO GOVERNOR TRUMBULL, OF CONNECTICUT.

On Tuesday, the eighteenth April, about half past ten at night, Lieutenant Colonel Smith, of the 10th regiment, embarked from the common, at

Boston, with the grenadiers and light infantry of the troops there; and landed on the opposite side; from whence he began his march towards Concord, where he was ordered to destroy a magazine of military stores, deposited there for the use of an army to be assembled, in order to act against his majesty and his government. The colonel called his officers together, and gave orders, that the troops should not fire, unless fired upon; and after marching a few miles, detached six companies of light infantry, under the command of Major Pitcairn, to take posssssion of two bridges, on the other side of Concord. Soon after, they heard many signal guns, and the ringing of alarm bells repeatedly; which convinced them, that the country was rising to oppose them, and that it was a preconcerted scheme to oppose the king's troops whenever there should be a favorable opportunity for it. About three o'clock the next morning, the troops being advanced within two miles of Lexington, intelligence was received, that about five hundred men in arms, were assembled and determined to oppose the king's troops; and on Major Pitcairn's galloping up to the head of the advanced companies, two officers informed him, that a man, advanced from those that were assembled, had presented his musket and attempted to shoot them, but the piece flashed in the pan; on this, the major gave directions to the troops to move forward, but on no account to fire, nor even attempt it, without orders. When they arrived at the end of the village, they observed about two hundred armed men, drawn up on a green, and when the troops came within one hundred yards of them, they began to file off towards some stone walls on their right flank. The light infantry observing this, ran after them; the major instantly called to the soldiers not to fire, but to surround and disarm them. Some of them, who had jumped over a wall, then fired four or five shots at the troops; wounded a man of the 10th regiment, and the major's horse in two places, and at the same time several shots were fired from a meeting-house on the left: upon this, without any order or regularity, the light infantry began a scattered fire, and killed several of the country people, but were silenced as soon as the authority of their officers could make them.

After this, Colonel Smith marched up with the remainder of the detachment, and the whole body proceeded to Concord, where they arrived about nine o'clock, without any thing further happening; but vast numbers of armed people were seen assembling on all the heights. While Colonel Smith with the grenadiers and part of the light infantry remained at Concord, to search for cannon, &c. there, he detached Captain Parsons with six light companies, to secure a bridge at some distance from Concord, and to proceed from thence to certain houses where it was supposed there were cannon and ammunition. Captain Parsons, in pursuance of these orders, posted three companies at the bridge, and on some heights near it, under the command of Captain Laurie, of the 43d regiment, and with the remainder went and destroyed some cannon, wheels, powder, and ball. The people still continued increasing on the heights, and in about an hour after, a large body of them began to move towards the bridge; the light companies of the 4th and 10th then descended and joined Captain Laurie. The people continued to advance in great numbers, and fired upon the king's troops, killed three men, wounded four officers, one sergeant, and four private men; upon which, after returning the fire, Captain Laurie and his officers, thought it prudent to retreat towards the main body at Concord, and were soon joined by two companies of grenadiers. When Captain Parsons returned with the three companies over the bridge, they observed three soldiers on the ground, one of them scalped, his head much mangled and his ears cut off, though not quite dead;[1] a sight which struck the soldiers with horror. Captain Parsons marched on and joined the main body, who were only waiting for his coming up to march back to Boston. Colonel Smith had executed his orders without opposition, by destroying all the military stores he could find: both the colonel and Major Pitcairn, having taken all possible pains to convince the inhabitants that no injury was intended them, and that, if they opened their doors when required, to search for said stores, not the slightest mischief should be done; neither had any of the people the least occasion to complain; but they were sulky, and one of them even struck Major Pitcairn. Except upon Captain Laurie, at the bridge, no hostilities happened, from the affair at Lexington until the troops began their march back. As soon as the troops had got out of the town of Concord, they received a heavy fire, from all sides, from walls, fences, houses, trees, barns, &c., which continued without intermission, till they met the first brigade with two field pieces, near Lexington, ordered out under the command of Lord Percy, to support them: advices having been received, about seven o'clock next morning, that signals had been made, and expresses gone out to alarm the country, and that the people were rising to attack the troops under Colonel Smith. Upon the firing of the field pieces, the people's fire was, for a while, silenced; but, as they continued to increase greatly in numbers, they fired again as before, from all places where they could find cover, upon the whole body, and continued so doing, for the space of fifteen miles. Notwithstanding their numbers, they did not attack openly during the whole day, but kept under cover on all occasions. The troops were very much fatigued, the greater part of them having been under arms all night, and made a march of upwards of forty miles, before they arrived at Charlestown, from whence they were ferried over to Boston.

The troops had above fifty killed, and many more wounded. Reports are various about the loss sustained by the country people; some make it very considerable; others not so much.

Thus this unfortunate affair has happened, through the rashness and imprudence of a few people, who began firing on the troops at Lexington.

(1) See the Journal of Congress, May 9, 1775, *ante* page 209; and the depositions of Zachariah Brown, and Thomas Davis, Jun., *ante* page 677.

INTERCEPTED LETTERS.

THE following extracts of letters, written by British officers and soldiers in Boston, and intercepted, relating to the events of the 19th of April, 1775, were communicated to the Provincial Congress.[1]

BOSTON, APRIL 28, 1775.

I am well, all but a wound I received through the leg by a ball from one of the Bostonians. At the time I wrote you from Quebec, I had the strongest assurance of going home, but the laying the tax on the New England people caused us to be ordered for Boston, where we remained in peace with the inhabitants, till, on the night of the 18th of April, twenty-one companies of grenadiers and light infantry were ordered into the country, about eighteen miles; where, between four and five o'clock in the morning, we met an incredible number of the people of the country in arms against us. Col. Smith, of the 10th regiment, ordered us to rush on them with our bayonets fixed; at which time, some of the peasants fired upon us, and our men returning the fire, the engagement began; they did not fight us like a regular army, only like savages, behind trees and stone walls, and out of the woods and houses, where, in the latter, we killed numbers of them, as well as in the woods and fields. The engagement began between four and five in the morning, and lasted till eight at night. I cannot be sure when you will get another letter from me, as this extensive continent is all in arms against us. These people are very numerous, and full as bad as the Indians for scalping and cutting the dead men's ears and noses off, and those they get alive, that are wounded and cannot get off the ground.

BOSTON, APRIL 28, 1775.

The grenadiers and light infantry marched for Concord, where were powder and ball, arms, and cannon mounted on carriages; but before we could destroy them all, we were fired on by the country people, who are not brought up in the military way as ourselves: we were surrounded always in the woods; the firing was very hot on both sides; about two in the afternoon the second brigade came up, which were four regiments and part of the artillery; which were of no use to us, as the enemy were in the woods; and when we found they fired from houses, we set them on fire, and they ran to the woods. We were obliged to retreat to Boston again, over Charles river, our ammunition being all fired away. We had one hundred and fifty wounded and killed, and some taken prisoners. We were forced to leave some behind, who were wounded. We got back to Boston about two o'clock next morning; and they that were able to walk were forced to mount guard and lie in the field. I never broke my fast for forty-eight hours, for we carried no provisions, and thought to be back next morning.

(1) See the Journal of May 1, *ante* page 173. Neither the address nor signature of any letter has been preserved.

I had my hat shot off my head three times, two balls through my coat, and my bayonet carried away by my side, and near being killed. The people of Boston are in great trouble, for General Gage will not let the town's people go out. Direct for me to Chatham's division of marines.

BOSTON, APRIL 30, 1775.

Before this reaches you, you may hear that our regiment has been engaged with the provincials. The grenadiers and light infantry marched about nine at night. At six next morning, four hundred and twenty-three soldiers and forty-seven marines, in all fifteen hundred, marched to reenforce the grenadiers and light infantry: we joined about one o'clock, and found them not engaged, which they had been eight hours before; for we had two pieces of cannon, which made us march very slow. As soon as we came up we fired the cannon, which brought them from behind the trees, for we did not fight as you did in Germany; for we did not see above ten in a body, for they were behind trees and walls, and fired at us, and then loaded on their bellies. We had but thirty-six rounds, which obliged us to go home that night; and as we came along, they got before us, and fired at us out of the houses, and killed and wounded a great number of us, but we levelled their houses as we came along. It was thought there were about six thousand at first, and at night double that number. The king's troops lost, in killed and wounded, one hundred and fifty, and the Americans five hundred, men, women, and children; for there was a number of women and children burnt in their houses. Our regiment had five killed and thirty-one wounded, particularly Col. Bernard in the thigh, which all the regiment is sorry for. I got a wounded man's gun, and killed two of them, as I am sure of. We have been busy in fortifying the town ever since we engaged, and in a few days we expect a good many more troops from England, and then we shall surely burn the whole country before us if they do not submit, which I do not imagine they will do, for they are an obstinate set of people. They have formed an army, and keep guard close to our works, so that our sentries can talk together at ease. We were engaged from six to six. The whole country are in arms against us, and they are headed by two of the generals that headed our army last war; their names are Black and Putnam. We have a great deal of shipping, but they are of little service, only to cover the town, cannon and troops, except the small schooners that go up the creek and destroy them, which they have done, many of them. There is no market in Boston: the inhabitants are all starving: the soldiers live on salt provisions, and the officers are supplied by the men of war cutters, who go up the creeks and take live cattle and sheep wherever they find them We vex the Americans very much by cutting down their liberty poles and alarm posts. We have had a great many died in our regiment last winter, so that what with wounded men, and what have deserted, we have not three hundred men, and duty is so hard that we come off guard in the morning and mount picket at night.

BOSTON, APRIL 25, 1775.

The rebels, when we came to Concord, burnt their stores, fired upon the king's troops, and a smart engagement ensued. About two o'clock, our brigade came up to them, when we engaged, and continued fighting and retreating towards Boston. The rebels were monstrous numerous, and surrounded us on every side; when they came up we gave them a smart fire, but they never would engage us properly. We killed some hundreds and burnt some of their houses. I received a wound in my head. The troops are in Boston, and surrounded on the land side by the rebels, who are very numerous, and fully determined to lose their lives and fortunes, rather than be taxed by England. We had thirty-four killed and wounded. I suppose the king's troops, lost in all about one hundred and sixty. In case they should take Boston, the troops will retire on board the men of war, and then the men of war will burn the town, and remain till more troops come from England, and then conquer them, so their estates and lives will be forfeited. There are only four thousand soldiers, and about fifty or sixty thousand of them.

BOSTON, MAY 2, 1775.

The 19th of April the engagement happened, and my husband was wounded and taken prisoner; but they use him well, and I am striving to get to him, as he is very dangerous, but it is almost impossible to get out or in, or to get any thing, for we are forced to live on salt provisions entirely, and they are building batteries round the town, and so are we, for we are expecting them to storm us. Are expecting more troops every day. My husband is now lying in one of their hospitals, at a place called Cambridge, and there are now forty or fifty thousand of them gathered together, and we are not four thousand at most. It is a very troublesome time; for we are expecting the town to be burnt down every day, and I believe we are sold, and I hear my husband's leg is broke, and my heart is almost broken.

RAVAGES OF THE BRITISH TROOPS.

STATEMENTS OF THE LOSSES SUSTAINED BY THE INHABITANTS FROM THE RAVAGES OF THE BRITISH TROOPS, APRIL 19, 1775.

The committee appointed to estimate the damages done at Cambridge, Lexington, and Concord, by the king's troops, on the nineteenth of April, 1775, have attended that duty, and beg leave to report:

That the destruction made by fire and robbery on said day, by said troops, is as follows, viz. :

The damages to the buildings in Cambridge, estimated according to the best skill and judgment of your committee, after viewing the same, amount to £76 5 6

The value of the goods and chattels that were destroyed, or taken out of the houses, or near the same, by the estimation of those persons who left the same, according to their several accounts exhibited on oath, and annexed, amounts to £1036 6 3

The value of the goods and chattels that were destroyed, or taken out of the said houses, or near the same, by the estimation of those persons who left the same, by their several accounts exhibited, who were not sworn, by reason of some being absent, or some other inconvenience that attended the same, amounts to £72 6 10

The damage done to the meeting-house and school-house in the north-west precinct in said Cambridge, as estimated by your committee, amounts to £0 13 4

The vessels, linen, and cash, belonging to the church of said precinct, taken out of the house of Joseph Adams, deacon of said church, as by his account, exhibited on oath, amount to   .   .   .   £16 16 8

The whole losses suffered in Cambridge, amount to   .   £1202 8 7

The damages sustained in Lexington, are as follow, viz. :

The buildings destroyed by fire, with the cash, utensils, and moveables, either burnt in the same, or carried away, estimated by the owners of the property, as by their accounts, exhibited on oath, amount to   £891 8 6

The damages to other buildings in said town, estimated as were those in Cambridge, amount to £32 18 7

Damages sustained from the robberies of said troops, by sundry inhabitants, as by their several accounts on oath,   .   .   .   £760 18 2

Damages sustained by other inhabitants, as by their several accounts exhibited, but not on oath, for the reason before mentioned, amount to the sum of £74 4 2

Damages to the meeting-house in said town,   .   .   £1 12 0

The whole amount in Lexington, ...   £1761 1 15

The damages sustained in Concord, were as follow, viz. :

The damages to the buildings, estimated as above, are   .   £2 12 0

The damages sustained by sundry inhabitants, estimated in manner aforesaid, under oath, amount to £209 16 10

The damages to other inhabitants, not under oath, for reasons before mentioned, amount to £59 1 9

The damage to sundry door locks broke in his majesty's jail in said town, by account exhibited, on oath, by the under keeper of said jail,   £3 6 0

The whole amount in Concord, ...   £274 16 7

> ABRAHAM FULLER,
> ICHABOD GOODWIN,
> OLIVER WHITNEY,
> *Committee.*

ACCOUNTS OF DAMAGES.

The original accounts of the injuries done to individuals, not having been preserved on the files, the following returns were made, by order of the Legislature, in 1783.

JOSEPH LORING.

An account of the real and personal estate belonging to Joseph Loring, of Lexington, destroyed and carried off by the British troops in their ravages in said town, on the nineteenth of April, 1775, viz. :

A large mansion-house, and a barn seventy feet long, and a corn-house, all burnt, ...   £350 0 0

Household goods and furniture, viz : eight good feather beds and bedding; a large quantity of pewter and brass ware; three cases of drawers; two mahogany tables; with the furniture of eight rooms, ...   230 0 0

All the wearing apparel of my family, consisting of nine persons, ...   60 0 0

All my husbandry tools and utensils, with a cider mill and press, with about five tons of hay, and two calves,   .   .   72 0 0

About two hundred rods of stone wall thrown down, .   .   5 0 0

£3 in specie, ...   3 0 0

    £720 0 0

N. B. The above mentioned buildings were the first that were destroyed in the town, and near the ground where the brigade commanded by Lord Percy met the detachment retreating under Lt. Col. Smith. It does not appear that any of the militia were in or near these buildings, neither could they, in any way, either expose or retard the British troops in their operations : therefore, the destruction must be considered as brutal, barbarous, and wanton.

> JOSEPH LORING.

JONATHAN HARRINGTON.

Account of things I lost on the nineteenth of April, 1775, by the British troops.

One eight day clock, carried off, almost new,   .   .   .   £15 0 0

One fine India dark gown, ...	£2 8 0
One striped English cotton gown, ...	1 10 0
Two dozens of cotton and linen and two sheets, . .	10 0 0
Six shirts, six shifts, to the value of	7 0 0
One lawn apron; one do. cambric; one do. linen, . .	2 10 0
Four new check aprons, ...	1 10 0
One dozen of handkerchiefs, part check, part printed, . .	1 10 0
One bed blanket, ...	0 18 0
Fifteen pairs stockings, part worsted, part thread and yarn, .	4 0 0
Six large diaper table cloths, ...	4 10 0
One dozen fine diaper cloths, ...	2 8 0
One dozen cotten linen do.	1 4 0
One dozen of napkins, diaper, ...	1 10 0
One scarlet riding hood, ...	2 0 0
One pair of new boots and two pairs of shoes, . .	2 4 0
One new razee great coat; one do. blue, . . .	6 0 0
Two new beaver hats, ...	4 0 0
Five yards of cotton and linen cloth, . . .	0 14 0
A number of women's caps, ...	1 10 0
One muff and tippet, ...	0 12 0
Three looking glasses, all large, ...	6 0 0
Two large moose skins, ...	4 0 0
Three cartridge boxes; three bridles and straps, all new, .	3 0 0
Three and a half yards of ratteen, ...	1 15 0
Two cans, one trimmed with silver, one do. pinchbeck, .	0 18 0
One dozen of stone plates, mugs, bowls, tea pots, &c., .	1 12 0
Two good razors; a number of books; Latin history, &c., .	2 0 0
One dozen of spoons, porringers, &c., to the value of .	1 16 0
One damask cloth. New buckskin breeches, . .	2 8 0
Damage to my house, ninety-four squares of glass, . .	4 0 0
Forty-two wooden sashes broke to pieces, . . .	2 0 0
Two desks broke, clock, cans, &c., ...	1 0 0
	£103 7 0

The above is a true copy from the original that was taken in and sworn to by Major Fuller and others, with some additional things.

JONATHAN HARRINGTON.

LYDIA WINSHIP.

Lexington, January 23d, 1783.

This may certify, to whom it may concern, that I, the subscriber, lost, on the nineteenth of April, 1775, by the British troops, in household furniture, wearing apparel, and in money, more than I can replace with the sum of sixty-six pounds, thirteen shillings and four pence. £66 13 4

LYDIA WINSHIP.

JOHN MASON.

The loss and damage I sustained by the British troops, on the nineteenth of April, 1775, in sundry articles of clothing and household furniture, &c. &c., was £14 13 4

JOHN MASON.

Lexington, January 23d, 1783.

———

MATTHEW MEAD.

The account of the loss that I sustained by the British troops, on the nineteenth of April, 1775, amounts to one hundred and one pounds, agreeably to the present value of those things that I lost. £101 0 0

MATTHEW MEAD.

———

BENJAMIN MERRIAM.

The following is a true and just account of the damage sustained by Benjamin Meriam, by the ravages of the British troops, in the town of Lexington, on the nineteenth day of April, 1775.

Real Estate, ... £6 0 0
Personal Property, ... 217 4 0

BENJAMIN MERRIAM.

———

NATHANIEL FARMER.

The following is a just and true account of what damages and losses I sustained, by the wanton ravages and depredations of the troops of his British majesty, under the command of Lord Percy, on their return from Concord, on the nineteenth of April, 1775, viz.:

To the wearing apparel of my family, consisting of seven persons, together with my bedding, ... £26 0 0
To the furniture of three rooms, much damaged and carried off, ... 16 0 0
To damage done my house and shop windows, .   . 4 10 0

£46 10 0

NATHANIEL FARMER.

———

THOMAS FESSENDEN.

The following is a just and true account of the damages I sustained, by the wanton ravages of the British troops, under the command of Lord Percy, on the nineteenth of April, 1775, in their return from Concord, viz.:

To damage done my house and windows, and fences, .   . £6 0 0

To the wearing apparel of my whole family, consisting of seven persons, ...   25 0 0

To the bedding and furniture of four rooms, with several articles of plate, ...   75 0 0

To one horse and chaise stolen and carried to Boston, .   38 0 0

To sundry pieces of broadcloth, and many other articles in my trading shop, ...   20 0 0

£164 0 0

THOMAS FESSENDEN.

Lexington, January 23, 1783.

_____

BENJAMIN FISKE.

The losses that I sustained, April 19th, 1775:

Four fine Holland shirts, ...	£3 13 0
One sash window, ...	0 18 0
One black silk apron, ...	0 15 0
One gold ring, ...	0 15 0
One stone ear ring, ...	0 12 0
One pair stone sleeve buttons, ...	0 12 0
One black gauze handkerchief, ...	0 9 0
One black barcelona do.	0 6 0
Two pair cotton hose, ...	0 18 0
To cash, ...	0 6 0
One quart pewter basin, ...	0 2 0

£9 7 0

BENJAMIN FISKE.

_____

JEREMIAH HARRINGTON.

I lost on the nineteenth of April, 1775, the following articles:

One broadcloth great coat, ...	£3 6 0
One pair goatskin breeches, ...	0 19 0
One pair cotton and linen sheets, ...	1 6 8
Three yards calico, at 6s per yard, . . .	0 18 0
One yard and a quarter tow cloth, . . .	0 1 10
Four linen handkerchiefs, ...	0 8 0
Two diaper towels, ...	0 2 0
Ten yards tow cloth, ...	0 15 0
One pewter platter, ...	0 2 5
Eight pewter plates, ...	1 4 0
Six pint porringers, ...	0 16 0

Six spoons,	.	.	.	.	.	.	.	0	4	0
One pair hose,	.	.	.	.	.	.	.	0	3	0
One pair shoes,	.	.	.	.	.	.	.	0	9	0

£11 13 11

JEREMIAH HARRINGTON.

ROBERT HARRINGTON.

An account of the damage done by the British troops, on the nineteenth of April, 1775:

To clothing and linen to the amount of £12 0 0

ROBERT HARRINGTON.

JOSHUA BOND.

The following is a true and just account of the damages sustained by Joshua Bond, by the ravages of the British troops, in the town of Lexington, on the 19th day of April, 1775.

| One dwelling-house and shop, | . | . | . | . | . | £54 | 0 | 0 |
| Personal property, | . | . | . | . | . | . | 135 | 16 | 7 |

JOSHUA BOND.

BENJAMIN BROWN.

A true and just account of the loss and damage sustained by the wanton cruelty and barbarity of the British troops, on the 19th of April, 1775, in real property, and in household furniture and wearing apparel, &c. &c.

| Real property, | . | . | . | . | . | . | . | £7 | 0 | 0 |
| Personal estate, | . | . | . | . | . | . | . | 35 | 0 | 0 |

N. B. Having delivered to a committee, sent by the great and general court or convention, a list of the articles valued separately and distinctly, the subscriber has nothing more to deliver in now, than the total of the whole as above.

BENJAMIN BROWN.

Lexington, January 20, 1783.

HEPZIBETH DAVIS.

Lost at Concord fight:

One pair of sheets,	.	.	.	.	.	.	£0	18	0
Two pair of pillow cases,	.	.	.	.	.	.	0	8	0
Three napkins,	.	.	.	.	.	.	0	4	0
Two table cloths,	.	.	.	.	.	.	0	4	0
Three smocks,	.	.	.	.	.	.	0	13	6

| Three aprons, | . | . | . | . | . | . | 0 | 6 | 0 |
| Shoes, caps and other articles, | . | | . | . | . | . | 2 | 8 | 0 |

$$£5 \quad 1 \; 6$$

her
HEPZIBETH ✕ DAVIS.
mark.

BENJAMIN ESTABROOK.

Lexington, January 27, 1783.

This may certify, that I, the subscriber, lost, on the 19th of April, 1775, by the British troops, in damages to my buildings and furniture, and provisions carried away, more than I can replace now for twelve pounds.

BENJAMIN ESTABROOK.

SAMUEL BEMIS.

An account of damages, and plundering from me, by the king's troops, on their return from Concord, on the 19th of April, 1775:

About twelve panes of window glass,	.	.	.	.	£0	12	0
One pair of sheets and pillow cases,	.	.	.	.	1	7	0
Part of a timepiece,	.	.	.	.	.	1	16	0
A looking glass,	.	.	.	.	.	0	6	8
Two boxes, with sundries,	.	.	.	.	0	7	0

$$£4 \quad 8 \; 8$$

SAMUEL BEMIS.

Lexington, January 23d, 1783.

NATHAN BLODGET.

This is to certify, that the following is a just and true account of the damages and waste I sustained, by the ravages of the troops, under the command of Lord Percy, on the 19th of April, 1775, viz.:

My wearing apparel, namely: two coats, one pair of breeches, one beaver hat, and sundry other articles, . . . £18 0 0

NATHAN BLODGET.

Lexington, January 22, 1783.

ELIZABETH SAMSON.

This may certify, to whom it may concern, that I, the subscriber, lost, on the 19th of April, 1775, by the British troops, in wearing apparel, more than I can replace with the sum of . £10 0 0

ELIZABETH SAMSON.

JONATHAN SMITH, JR.

The account of the things that I lost by the British troops, on the 19th of April, 1775:

Three silver spoons,	.	.	.	.	.	£0 12 0
One pair of silver buckles,	.	.	.	.	.	0 18 0
One pair of sleeve buttons,	.	.	.	.	.	0 6 8
One satin bonnet and cloak,	.	.	.	.	.	3 12 0
One hat and one pair of shoes,	.	.	.	.	.	1 10 0
Two pewter porringers,	.	.	.	.	.	0 2 0
One block-tin tea pot,	.	.	.	.	.	0 12 0
One blanket,	.	.	.	.	.	0 18 0
To a number of other articles,	.	.	.	.	.	2 2 0
Damage done to the house,	.	.	.	.⁙	.	3 0 0

£13 12 8

JONATHAN SMITH, JR.

___

JOHN WILLIAMS.

A true and just account of the damages received by the British king's troops, under the command of Lord Percy, April 19, 1775:

To damage done to my house and fence,	.	.	.	£3 10 0
To wearing apparel and household furniture,	.	.	.	33 5 0

Sum total, . . .£36 15 0

JOHN WILLIAMS.

Lexington, January 23, 1783.

___

JOHN WINSHIP.

Taken by the British troops the 19th of April, 1775:

Two suits of clothes, valued at twelve pounds, lawful money, . £12 0 0

JOHN WINSHIP.

Lexington, January 23, 1783.

___

MARGARET WINSHIP.

This is to certify, that the following is a just and true account of the damages and waste I sustained, by the ravages of the troops under the command of Lord Percy, on the 19th of April, 1775, viz.:

My wearing apparel and bedding, with sundry articles of plate, £15 0 0
Also the furniture of two rooms, much damaged and carried off, 6 0 0

Damages done to my house and windows,   .   .   .   1 10 0

$$\overline{\text{£22 10 0}}$$

MARGARET WINSHIP.

Lexington, January 22, 1783.

MARRETT MUNROE.

Damage done by the British troops, the 19th of April, 1775, to my property carried off, to the amount of five pounds and six pence,   .   £5   0 6

MARRETT MUNROE.

WILLIAM MUNROE.

The account of things taken away and destroyed by the British troops, April 19, 1775:

Household furniture and clothing, ...	£83 11 9
In the retail shop, ...	90 0 0
	£173 11 9
Damage of real property, ...	30 0 0

WILLIAM MUNROE.

AMOS MUZZY.

April 19, 1775.

An account of what damage the British troops did me that day:

To breaking glass windows, ...	£6 14 0
To one looking-glass, ...	7 10 0
To crockery ware, ...	2 0 0
To damage to real estate, ...	2 0 0
	£18 4 0

AMOS MUZZY.

LYDIA MULLIKEN.

An account of the real and personal property belonging to the widow Lydia Mulliken and her son, destroyed and carried off by the British troops, in their ravages in said town, on the 19th of April, 1775:

One mansion house and shop, ...	£128 0 0
Household furniture, ...	106 12 0
My wearing apparel, and that of five of my family, .	98 18 8
A number of valuable clocks and clockmaker's tools, .	105 10 0
	£431 0 0

The above account is computed at the lowest rate that things can be purchased at this day.

LYDIA MULLIKEN.

WILLIAM MUNROE.

An account of the loss and damage sustained by William Munroe, late of Lexington, destroyed by the ravages of the British troops, on the 19th of April, 1775, viz.:

Household goods and furniture, ... £9 0 0

ISAAC REED, *one of the heirs to said estate.*

Lexington, January 24, 1783.

PAPERS

TICONDEROGA AND CROWN POINT.

Benedict Arnold to the Committee of Safety.

Cambridge, April 30, 1775.

GENTLEMEN:—You have desired me to state the number of cannon, &c., at Ticonderoga. I have certain information, that there are at Ticonderoga, eighty pieces of heavy cannon; twenty brass guns from four to eighteen pounders; and ten or twelve large mortars. At Skenesborough, on the south bay, there are three or four brass cannon. The fort is in a ruinous condition, and has not more than fifty men, at the most. There are large numbers of small arms, and considerable stores, and a sloop of seventy or eighty tons on the lake. The place could not hold out an hour against a vigorous onset.

Your most obedient servant,

BENEDICT ARNOLD.

Hon Joseph Warren, and the honorable Committee of Safety.

Committee of Safety to the Congress of New York.

Cambridge, April 30, 1775.

GENTLEMEN:—It has been proposed to us to take possession of the fortress of Ticonderoga. We have a just sense of the importance of that fortification, and the usefulness of the fine cannon, mortars, and field pieces which are there. But we would not, even on this emergency, infringe upon the rights of our sister colony of New York; but we have desired the gentleman who will carry this letter, to represent the matter to you, that you may give such orders as are agreeable to you.

We are, with the greatest respect and affection,

Your most obedient servants,

JOSEPH WARREN, *Chairman.*

To Alexander McDougall, Esq.

Edward Mott to the Provincial Congress.

To the honorable Provincial Congress, or to the Council of War for the Province of Massachusetts Bay:

Shoreham, May 11, 1775.

GENTLEMEN:—I would congratulate you on the surrender of the garrison of Ticonderoga to the American forces. The affair was planned and conducted after the following manner: a number of the provincial gentlemen of the assembly at Hartford, on Friday the 28th of April, conversing on the distressed condition of the people of Boston, and the means necessary to relieve them, fell on the scheme to take that fortress, that we might have the advantage of the cannon that were there, to relieve the people of Boston. I told the gentlemen, that in my opinion, it might be taken by surprise with a few men, if properly conducted; on which, they desired me, if I was willing to serve my country in that way, to join Capt. Noah Phelps, of Simsbury, and Mr. Bernard Romans, on that design; and furnished us with £300 in cash from the treasury, and desired us to go forward to the upper towns and search into the situation of said garrison, and if I thought proper, to proceed to take possession of the same. On which, we collected to the number of sixteen men in Connecticut, and proceeded forward till we came to Col. Easton's, at Pittsfield; and there we consulted with Col. Easton, and John Brown, Esq., who, after they heard our plan of operation, agreed to join us, and after informing them that we intended raising our men on the Grants for the aforesaid purpose, as it would be difficult to raise and march a number of men through the country any distance without our plans being discovered, Col. Easton and Mr. Brown told us, that the people on the Grants were poor, and at this time of year it would be difficult to raise a sufficient number of men there to take and hold said garrison; whereon Col. Easton offered to raise men in his own regiment for the aforesaid purpose, to join with the green mountain boys; on which I set out with him for the town of Jericho, where Col. Easton raised between forty and fifty men, and proceeded to Bennington, at which place the men arrived the next day. At this place a council of war was called, Col. Easton being chairman, and it was voted, that Col. Allen should send forward parties to secure the roads to the northward, to prevent all intelligence from arriving before us. On Sunday evening, the 7th of this instant May, we arrived at Castleton, where, on the next day, was held a council of war by a committee chosen for that purpose, of which committee I had the honor to be chairman. After debating and consulting on different methods of procedure in order to accomplish our designs, it was concluded and voted, that we would proceed in the following manner, viz.: that a party of thirty men under the command of Capt. Herrick, should, on the next day, in the afternoon, proceed to Skenesborough, and take into custody, Major Skene and his party, and take possession of all the boats that they should find there, and in the night proceed up the lake to Shoreham, with the remainder of our men, which were about one hundred and forty, who were under the command of Col. Ethan Allen, and Col. James Easton as his second, and Capt. Warner, the third in command; as these three men were the persons who raised the men they were chosen to the command, and to rank according to the number of men that each one raised. We also sent off Capt. Douglas, of Jericho, to proceed directly to Panton, and there consult his brother in law, who lived there, and send down some boats to Shoreham, if possible, to help our people over to the fort. All this it was concluded should be done or attempted, and was voted universally. After this affair was all settled, and the men pitched on to go in each party, all were preparing for their march, being then within about nine miles of Skenesborough, and about twenty-five miles on the way we went, from Ticonderoga.

Col. Arnold arrived to us from you with his orders. We were extremely rejoiced to see that you fully agreed with us, as to the expediency and importance of taking possession of the garrisons. But we were shockingly surprised when Col. Arnold presumed to contend for the command of those forces that we had raised, whom we had assured, should go under the command of their own officers, and be paid and maintained by the colony of Connecticut; but Mr. Arnold, after we had generously told him our whole plan, strenuously contended and insisted, that he had a right to command them and all their officers; which bred such a mutiny amongst the soldiers, as almost frustrated our whole design. Our men were for clubbing their firelocks and marching home, but were prevented by Col. Allen and Col. Easton, who told them, that he should not have the command of them, and if he had, their pay would be the same as though they were under their command; but they would damn the pay, and say they would not be commanded by any others but those they engaged with. After the garrison was surrendered, Mr. Arnold again assumed the command, although he had not one man there, and demanded it of Col. Allen; on which, we gave Col. Allen his orders in writing, as follow, viz.:

To Col. Ethan Allen :

SIR:—Whereas, agreeably to the power and authority to us given by the colony of Connecticut, we have appointed you to take the command of a party of men and reduce and take possession of the garrison at Ticonderoga, and the dependencies thereto belonging; and as you are now in actual possession of the same, you are hereby required to keep the command and possession of the same for the use of the American colonies, until you have further orders from the colony of Connecticut, or the Continental Congress.

Signed, per order of the committee of war,

EDWARD MOTT, *Chairman of said Committee.*

Col James Easton, was of great service both in council and action, and in raising men for the above expedition, and appeared to be well qualified to be not only a colonel of the militia at home, but to command in the field. Also, John Brown, Esq., of Pittsfield, we recommend as an able counsellor, and full of spirit and resolution, as well as good conduct. We wish they may both be employed in the service of their country in a situation equal to their merits.

I have the pleasure to add, that on Wednesday morning last, the 10th of this instant May, about the break of day, our men entered the gate; till then they were undiscovered, and in the most courageous and intrepid manner darted like lightning upon the guards, so that but two had time to snap their firelocks at us, and in a few minutes, the fortress and its dependencies were delivered into our hands. There are about forty soldiers taken prisoners of war, including officers, and excluding those taken at Skenesborough. Not one life was lost in these noble acquisitions.

I am, Gentlemen, in haste, your most obedient humble servant,

EDWARD MOTT, *Chairman of the Committee of War.*

Certificate of Col. Easton, and others.

Ticonderoga, May 11, 1775.

To the Provincial Congress now sitting at Watertown:

This is to certify, that previous to Col. Benedict Arnold's arrival to the forts Ticonderoga and Crown Point, a committee sent from the colony of Connecticut, furnished with money for the purpose of reducing and garrisoning said forts, had, with the assistance of eighty men from Massachusetts, and one hundred and forty men from the New Hampshire Grants, marched within a few miles of Ticonderoga, and this morning, at day break, took possession of said fort, and gave the command thereof into the hands of Col. Ethan Allen. Col. Arnold refuses to give up his command, which causes much difficulty; said Arnold not having enlisted one man, neither do we know that he can do so. As said committee have raised the men, and are still raising supplies for the purpose of repairing said fort, taking the armed sloop, and defending the country and the fort, we think said Arnold's further proceeding in the matter, highly inexpedient both in regard to expense and dispute.

JAMES EASTON,	*Committee of War for the*
EPAPHRUS BALL,	*expedition against Ti-*
EDWARD MOTT,	*conderoga and Crown*
NOAH PHELPS,	*Point.*

Benedict Arnold to the Committee of Safety.

Ticonderoga, May 11, 1775.

GENTLEMEN:—I wrote you yesterday,[1] that arriving in the vicinity of this

(1) The letter of the 10th of May, was not received by the Committee of Safety.

place, I found, one hundred and fifty men, collected at the instance of some gentlemen from Connecticut, designed on the same errand on which I came, headed by Col. Ethan Allen; and that I had joined them, not thinking proper to wait the arrival of the troops I had engaged on the road, but to attempt the fort by surprise; that we had taken the fort at four o'clock yesterday morning, without opposition, and had made prisoners, one captain, one lieutenant, and forty odd privates and subalterns; and that we found the fort in a most ruinous condition, and not worth repairing; that a party of fifty men were gone to Crown Point, and that I intended to follow with as many more, to seize the sloop, &c.; and that I intended to keep possession here, until I had further advice from you. On and before our taking possession here, I had agreed with Col. Allen, to issue future orders jointly, until I could raise a sufficient number of men to relieve his people; on which plan, we proceeded, when I wrote you yesterday; since which, Col. Allen, finding he had the ascendency over his people, positively insisted I should have no command, as I had forbid the soldiers' plundering and destroying private property. The power is now taken out of my hands, and I am not consulted, nor have I a voice in any matters. There are here, at present, near one hundred men, who are in the greatest confusion and anarchy, destroying and plundering private property, and committing every enormity, paying no attention to the public service. The party I advised were gone to Crown Point, have returned, having met with head winds; and that expedition, and taking the sloop, mounted with six guns, are entirely laid aside. There is not the least regularity among the troops; but every thing is governed by whim and caprice; the soldiers threatening to leave the garrison on the least affront. Most of them must return home soon, as their families are suffering. Under our present situation, I believe one hundred men could retake the fort, and there seems no prospect of things being in a better situation. I have, therefore, thought proper to send an express, advising you of the state of affairs, not doubting you will take the matter into your serious consideration, and order a number of troops to join those I have coming on here; or that you will appoint some other person to take the command of them and this place, as you shall think most proper. Col. Allen is a proper man to head his own wild people, but entirely unacquainted with military service; and as I am the only person who has been legally authorized to take possession of this place, I am determined to insist on my right, and think it my duty to remain here, against all opposition, until I have further orders. I cannot comply with your orders in regard to the cannon, &c., for want of men. I have written to the governor and general assembly of Connecticut, advising them of my appointment, and giving them an exact detail of matters as they stand at present. I should be extremely glad to be honorably acquitted of my commission, and that a more proper person might be appointed in my room; but, as I have, in consequence of my orders from you, gentlemen, been the first person who entered and took possession of the fort, I shall keep it, at every hazard, until I have further advice and orders from you, and the general assembly of Connecticut.

I have the honor to be, Gentlemen,

Your most obedient, humble servant,

BENEDICT ARNOLD.

P. S. It is impossible to advise you how many cannon are here and at Crown Point, as many of them are buried in the ruins; there are a large number of iron and some brass cannon and mortars, &c., lying on the edge of the lake, which, as the lake is high, are covered with water. The confusion we have been in, has prevented my getting proper information, further than that there are many cannon, shells, mortars, &c., which may be very serviceable to our army at Cambridge.[1]

B. A.

To the Committee of Safety, Cambridge.

Benedict Arnold to the Committee of Safety.

TICONDEROGA, MAY 14, 1775.

GENTLEMEN :—My last was of the 11th instant, per express ; since which, a party of men have seized on Crown Point, in which they took eleven prisoners, and found sixty-one pieces of cannon serviceable, and fifty-three unfit for service. I ordered a party to Skenesborough, who have made Major Skene prisoner, and seized a small schooner, which has just arrived here. I intend setting out in her directly, with a batteau and fifty men, to take possession of the sloop, which we are advised this morning, by the post, is at St. Johns, loaded with provisions, &c., waiting a wind for this place. Inclosed is a list of cannon, &c. here, though imperfect, as we have found many pieces not included, and some are on the edge of the lake covered with water. I am, with the assistance of Mr. Bernard Romans, making preparation at Fort George, for transporting to Albany those cannon that will be serviceable to our army at Cambridge. I have about one hundred men here, and expect more every minute. Mr. Allen's party is decreasing, and the dispute between us subsiding. I am extremely sorry matters have not been transacted with more prudence and judgment. I have done every thing in my power, and put up with many insults to preserve peace, and serve the public. I hope soon to be properly released from this troublesome business, and that some proper person may be appointed in my room, till which

I am, very respectfully, Gentlemen,

Your most obedient humble servant,

BENEDICT ARNOLD.

(1) The answer to this letter is inserted in the Journal of the Provincial Congress, *ante* page 250.

P. S. Since writing the above, Mr. Romans concludes on going to Albany to forward carriages for the cannon, &c., and provisions, which will be soon wanted. I beg leave to observe, he has been of great service here, and I think him a very spirited, judicious gentleman, who has the service of the country much at heart, and hope he will meet proper encouragement.

B. A.

List of Cannon, Mortars, and Stores, taken at Crown Point and Ticonderoga, May 11, 1775:

At Crown Point—Two iron twenty-four pounders: one iron twenty-four, useless: one brass twenty-four, serviceable: four iron eighteens, and fourteen iron twelves, not examined, but appearing good: four French iron twelves, useless: eight French twelves and eighteens, not examined, but appearing good: seven long nines, double fortified, and good: twelve long nines, serviceable: two long nines, mounted: thirty-three long sixes and nines, useless: seven long nines and twelves, useless: two long sixes, good: two short sixes, bad: three short sixes, not examined: three short sixes, useless: one English thirteen inch mortar: one French thirteen inch, two French eight inch, and two eight inch howitzers, all serviceable.

At Ticonderoga—Three long eighteen pounders, good: two French eighteens, bad: two French twelves, bad, and two good: six French twelves, double fortified, good, and two bad: twelve long nines, good, and five bad: eighteen sixes, bad: nine fours, good: one six, good: nineteen swivels, good: two wall pieces, good: two French twelves, bad: one thirteen inch mortar and bed, good: one seven inch and bed, good: one seven inch howitzer, good: twenty-eight iron truck wheels: ten carriages, fit for use: forty-two port fires: five copper ladles, with staves: twelve copper ladles without staves: seventeen lintstocks: one hundred, eighteen pound shot: five hundred and fifty, twelve pound shot: two hundred and forty, nine pound shot: one thousand four hundred and thirty, six pound shot: one hundred and sixty eight, quilted grape shot: nine tons lead balls: three thousand seven hundred pounds iron balls: twenty-eight barrels powder, damaged: nine hundred and six shells: thirty thousand flints.

Benedict Arnold to the Committee of Safety.

CROWN POINT, MAY 19, 1775.

GENTLEMEN:—My last was of the 14th instant, by Mr. Romans, via New Haven. I then acquainted you of the occasion of delay in not carrying your orders into execution. The afternoon of the same day, being joined by Captains Brown and Oswald, with fifty men enlisted on the road, they having taken possession of a small schooner at Skenesborough, we immediately proceeded on our way to St. Johns, and at eight o'clock, P. M. the 17th instant, arrived within thirty miles of St. Johns. The weather proving calm, we manned out two small batteaux with thirty-five men, and the next morning, at six o'clock, arrived at St. Johns, surprised and took a sergeant and his party of twelve men, the king's sloop of about seventy tons, with two brass six pounders and seven men, without any loss on either side. The captain was gone to Montreal, and was hourly expected, with a large detachment for Ticonderoga, a number of guns and carriages for the sloop, which was just fixed for sailing; add to this, there were a captain and forty men at Chamblée, twelve miles distant from St. Johns, who were expected there every minute with the party: so that it seemed to be a mere interposition of Providence that we arrived in so fortunate an hour. We took such stores on board as were valuable, and the wind proving favorable, in two hours after our arrival, weighed anchor for this place, with the sloop and four of the king's batteaux, having destroyed five others: so that there is not left a single batteau for the king's troops, Canadians or Indians, to cross the lake in, if they have any such intention. I must, in justice to Col. Allen, observe, that he left Crown Point soon after me for St Johns, with one hundred and fifty men, and on my return I met him five leagues this side, and supplied him with provisions, his men being in a starving condition. He informed me of his intention of proceeding on to St. Johns with eighty or one hundred men, and keeping possession there. It appeared to me a wild, impracticable scheme, and provided it could be carried into execution, of no consequence, so long as we are masters of the lake; and of that I make no doubt, as I am determined to arm the sloop and schooner immediately.

I wrote you, gentlemen, in my former letters, that I should be extremely glad to be superseded in my command here, as I find it next to impossible to repair the old fort at Ticonderoga, and am not qualified to direct in building a new one. I am really of opinion, it will be necessary to employ one thousand or fifteen hundred men here this summer, in which I have the pleasure of being joined in sentiment by Mr. Romans, who is esteemed an able engineer. I am making all possible provision for wheel carriages, &c., to carry such cannon, &c. to Albany, as can be spared here and will be serviceable to our army at Cambridge.

I must refer you for particulars to the bearer, Capt. Jonathan Brown, who has been very active and serviceable, and is a prudent and good officer, and beg leave to observe, I have had intimations given me, that some persons had determined to apply to you and the Provincial Congress, to injure me in your esteem, by misrepresenting matters of fact. I know of no other motive they can have, only my refusing them commissions, for the very simple reason, that I did not think them qualified. However, gentlemen, I have the satisfaction of imagining I am employed by gentlemen of so much candor, that my conduct will not be condemned until I have the opportunity of being heard.

I am, with the greatest respect, Gentlemen,

Your most devoted and very humble servant,

BENEDICT ARNOLD.

P. S. Enclosed is a memorandum of such cannon, &c. as I intend sending to Cambridge: also of such as are here.

By a return from Montreal to General Gage, I find there are seven hundred and seventeen men in Canada, of the 7th and 26th regiments, including seventy, whom we have taken prisoners.

To the Committee of Safety, Cambridge.

Benedict Arnold to the Committee of Safety.

CROWN POINT, MAY 23, 1775.

GENTLEMEN:—My last was of the 19th instant, by Capt. Jonathan Brown. I then advised you of my taking possession of the king's sloop, &c., and that, on the 18th instant, on my return from St. Johns, Colonel Allen, with about eighty or one hundred men, passed me, with the intention of making a stand at St. Johns, and not being able to dissuade him from so rash a purpose, I supplied him with provision, &c. Yesterday he arrived at Ticonderoga with his party, and says, that on the evening of the 18th instant, he arrived with his party at St Johns, and hearing of a detachment of men on the road from Montreal, he laid an ambush for them: but his people being so much fatigued, when the party was about one mile distant, he thought proper to retreat, and crossed the lake at St. Johns, where they continued through the night: at dawn the next day, they were, when asleep, saluted with a discharge of grape shot from six field pieces, and a discharge of small arms from about two hundred regulars. They made a precipitate retreat and left behind three men.

Immediately on this advice, I proceeded here with the sloop and schooner, as well armed as possible under our circumstances, and eighty men, which, with the party here before, make near one hundred and fifty men, with whom I am determined to make a stand here to secure the cannon, it being impossible to remove them at present. I am in hourly expectation of two or three hundred men more. Most of those here have enlisted. Colonel Allen's men are, in general, gone home. As the regulars have good information of our strength and movements, I am apprehensive of their paying us a visit, provided they can get batteaux from Montreal to St. Johns. I shall make every possible preparation to give them a warm reception. I have commissioned Capt. John Stone in the sloop, and Capt. Isaac Mathews in the schooner, and have written to New York for a number of gunners and seamen, to man the two vessels, being in great want of them at present, and obliged to stay on board one of them myself.

As soon as a sufficient number of men arrive, I shall lose no time in carrying your orders into execution, in regard to the cannon. This morning, very luckily, an escort of provisions, five barrels of pork, and thirty barrels of flour, arrived here, as a present from Albany, under the care of Capt. Elijah Phelps, the last barrel of our pork being broached. I have ordered fifty barrels of pork, and one hundred barrels of flour, from Albany, which I expect soon. Prior to which, I bought five oxen and thirty barrels of flour, which is all the provision purchased yet. The people enlisted have been promised the same bounty as is given in the Massachusetts Bay. A sum of money will be requisite to carry matters into execution. I have £160, found in the sloop: but as it was the property of the captain, I don't choose to make use of it at present. I have sent to Albany repeatedly for powder, and can get none there: only one hundred and fifty pounds here, which I brought from Concord; and I beg you will order a quantity to be sent forward here immediately. I have written to Connecticut, but can have no dependence from that quarter, as it is very scarce there. I hope some gentleman will soon be appointed in my room here, who is better able to serve the public than I am. In the interim,

I am, Gentlemen, your most obedient humble servant,

BENEDICT ARNOLD.

P. S. Since writing the above, one of Col. Allen's party, who was taken prisoner at St. Johns, has made his escape, and says, that on the 19th instant, there were about four hundred regulars at St. Johns, who expected to be reenforced by more men, and were making all possible preparations to cross the lake, and retake Crown Point and Ticonderoga. I have sent expresses to Fort George and Skenesborough, to rally the country. You may depend, gentlemen, these places will not be given up, unless we are overpowered with numbers, or deserted by Providence, which has, hitherto, supported us.

I am yours, &c.

B. ARNOLD.

———

Gov. Trumbull to the Provincial Congress.

HARTFORD, MAY 25, 1775.

GENTLEMEN:—Your letter of the 17th instant, with the enclosed resolve of the Provincial Congress of Massachusetts Bay, was delivered to me by Col. Easton, and communicated to the general assembly, who have desired me to return their congratulations on the reduction of Ticonderoga, a fortress truly important, and to assure you they entertain a proper sense of the merit of those officers and soldiers by whose bravery and good conduct it was achieved. As this advantage was gained by the united councils and enterprise of a number of private gentlemen in your province, New Hampshire, New York, and this colony, prompted only by a zeal for the liberty of their country, without public authority to our knowledge, and is of great and general importance to the united colonies, it was thought best to take the advice of the Continental Congress upon the manner of treating it in future, both by the general assembly of this colony and the committee of New York, as well as by you. Despatches were accordingly sent to Philadelphia, and the sentiments of the Continental Congress thereon have been received this day, by express, with a letter from the committee of New York, copies of which, enclosed, are herewith sent you.

By them you will see, the present custody of that fortress is committed to the province of New York, with the assistance of the New England colonies, if needed. The general assembly of this colony behold your situation with concern, and a fixed resolution to contribute every thing in their power to your defence and preservation, and as far as pertains to them, are willing and desirous you should have the benefit of such artillery as may be spared from the fortresses of Crown Point and Ticonderoga; but, as they do not consider themselves as entitled to the command of those places, they cannot take upon themselves to give orders for the removal of the heavy cannon that may be spared, without the concurrence of the other colonies interested in them.

The necessity of securing and maintaining the posts on the lakes, for the defence of the frontiers, becomes daily more evident, from the reiterated intelligence we receive, of the plan formed by our enemies to distress us, by inroads of Canadians and savages, from the province of Quebec, upon the adjacent settlements. The enclosed copy of a letter from our delegates attending at New York, to communicate measures with the Provincial Congress in that city, throws an additional light on this subject, and is thought worthy to be communicated to you. Whilst the designs of our enemies against us, fill us with concern, we cannot omit to observe the smiles of Providence upon us, in revealing their wicked plans, and hitherto prospering the attempts of the colonies to frustrate them. With a humble reliance on the continuance of divine favor and protection in the cause, of the justice of which a doubt cannot be entertained, the general assembly of this colony are ready to cooperate with the other colonies, in every exertion for their common defence, and to contribute their proportion of men and other necessaries, for maintaining the posts on the frontiers, or defending or repelling invasions in any other quarter, agreeably to the advice of the Continental Congress.

I am, Gentlemen, in behalf of the general assembly of this colony,

Your most obedient humble servant,

JONATHAN TRUMBULL.

To the Provincial Congress of Massachusetts.

Committee of New York to Gov. Trumbull.

NEW YORK, MAY 22, 1775.

HONORED SIR:—I am directed by the general committee of association for this city and county, to transmit to your honor the enclosed authentic copy of a resolution of the Continental Congress, received by express, and

89

to inform your honor, that in consequence thereof, we immediately shipped to Albany one hundred barrels of pork, and that a select committee has been appointed to purchase and forward, without delay, cordage, oakum, pitch, guns, and every other necessary that may be wanted from hence, to carry into execution the aforesaid resolution.

We have also, by express, desired our brethren of Albany to give their aid and assistance.

I have the honor to be, most respectfully,

Your honor's most obedient and humble servant,

HENRY REMSEN, *Deputy Chairman.*

Hon. Gov. Trumbull.

Resolution of the Continental Congress.

IN CONTINENTAL CONGRESS, THURSDAY, MAY 18, 1775.

Whereas, there is indubitable evidence that a design is formed by the British ministry, of making a cruel invasion, from the province of Quebec, upon these colonies, for the purpose of destroying our lives and liberties, and some steps have actually been taken, to carry the said design into execution: and whereas, several inhabitants of the northern colonies residing in the vicinity of Ticonderoga, immediately exposed to incursions, impelled by a just regard for the defence and preservation of themselves and their countrymen from such imminent dangers and calamities, have taken possession of that post, in which was lodged a quantity of cannon and military stores, that would certainly have been used in the intended invasion of these colonies: this Congress earnestly recommend it to the committees of the cities and counties of New York and Albany, immediately to cause the said cannon and stores to be removed from Ticonderoga to the south end of Lake George, and, if necessary, to apply to the colonies of New Hampshire, Massachusetts Bay, and Connecticut, for such an additional body of forces as will be sufficient to establish a strong post at that place, effectually to secure the said cannon and stores, or so many of them as it may be judged proper to keep there; and that an exact inventory be taken of all such cannon and stores, in order that they may be safely returned, when the restoration of the former harmony between Great Britain and the colonies, so ardently wished for by the latter, shall render it prudent and consistent with the overruling law of self-preservation.

A true copy from the minutes.

CHARLES THOMPSON, *Secretary.*

Committee of Connecticut to the General Assembly.

NEW YORK, MAY 23, 1775.

SIR:—We arrived in this city last evening, and have the satisfaction to inform you, that the committee of New York have complied with the directions of the Continental Congress, as to furnishing our forces at Ticonderoga with provisions.

The Provincial Convention of this province are now sitting, but have not got through the business of examining certificates, &c. We have not, therefore, as yet, laid our appointment before them. We have had a personal conference with Mr. Price, an eminent English merchant of Montreal, who is sent by the English merchants of that place, express to the Continental Congress, with intelligence of a most interesting nature. He informs us, that all the French officers of Canada are now in actual pay under General Carlton ; that St. Luke La Corne, who was superintendent of all the Indians in Canada, while it was in the hands of the French, and is father in law of Mr. Campbell, who is superintendent under his majesty, has sent belts to the northern tribes, as far up as the falls of St. Mary and Michilimakinak, to engage them to take up arms against the New England colonies, but the event of that embassy is not yet known : that a similar application had been made to the tribes nearer to the frontiers of the English settlements, but with little success, as not more than forty Indians could be found that would engage in the measures : that the plan of operations in Canada is, to procure the savages to join with the Canadians in hostilities against the rebels of New England.

Mr. Price gives it as his opinion, that the Canadian peasants will not, but with the utmost reluctance, engage against the colonists, but that the noblesse are our bitter enemies : he also says, that General Carlton was expected at Montreal in a day or two after he left that place, which was the 11th of May instant, and that he was to take up his residence there for this summer.

We are now about to take up lodgings in the heart of the city, where we shall have an opportunity of conversing with the citizens, and of learning their true spirit.

The Provincial Convention of New Jersey meet this day : we propose to wait on them sometime this week.

We can, at present, give you no just account of the state of the cause of liberty in this city, but hope, from the little information we have already had, that there will not be so general a defection as was apprehended.

We are, Sir, with due respect, your most obedient humble servants,

NATHANIEL WALES, JR.,
THADDEUS BURR,
PIERPONT EDWARDS.

To the Hon. William Williams, Esq.,
Speaker of the House of Assembly, Connecticut.

Congress of New York to the Committee of Safety.

In Provincial Congress, New York, May 26, 1775.

BRETHREN:—Having received a minute of the grand Continental Congress, of which we send you a copy herewith; we wrote a letter to the governor and company of the colony of Connecticut, of which we also send you a copy.

We do not doubt of your ready concurrence in the measures recommended by that august body, in which we do entirely acquiesce.

We pray you to act on this occasion with prudence and expedition, especially as we have received intimations from our brethren in Connecticut, that they cannot send a sufficient force for the purposes mentioned to them in our letter. And we beg leave to assure you, that we are affectionately your friends and brethren in the general cause of freedom.

We are, Gentlemen, your humble servants,

P. V. B. LIVINGSTON, *President.*

*To Joseph Warren, Esquire, and others, the Committee of Safety
for the Colony of Massachusetts Bay.*

Benedict Arnold to the Committee of Safety.

Crown Point, May 26, 1775.

GENTLEMEN:—My last was of the 23d instant; I then advised you of the situation of matters here; since which, there has been no material alteration. Very few men have arrived; we have fixed the sloop with six carriage and twelve swivel guns; the schooner with four carriage and eight swivel; both vessels are in good order, and tolerably well manned, eight gentlemen having arrived from Hartford, who are seamen. I have sent two ten inch iron mortars, two eight inch brass mortars, and two eight inch howitzers to Ticonderoga, to be forwarded to Fort George. You may depend on my sending the cannon from this place as soon as possible. There are three thirteen inch iron mortars here. I beg to know what I shall do with them. I have received large donations of flour, pork, peas, &c., from Albany, near seventy barrels, and I am informed, there is a large quantity on the road from that place, and a quantity supplied from Connecticut. The advices I received from Butterfield, and communicated in the postscript of my last of the 23d instant, prove to be premature. I have good intelligence from a batteau immediately from St. Johns, which place she left the 19th instant, that the regulars were returned to Chamblee.

I am, with great respect, Gentlemen, your obedient servant,

BENEDICT ARNOLD.

To the Committee of Safety, Cambridge.

General Assembly of Connecticut to the Provincial Congress.

Hartford, May 27, 1775.

GENTLEMEN:—You have, doubtless, received the advice of the Continental Congress, relative to the important fortresses and posts of Ticonderoga and Crown Point. We esteem it necessary to be guided by their opinion in every important transaction, and have great satisfaction in their approbation of the capture made of those posts; and their advice relating to the removing the cannon, &c., to the south end of Lake George, and making a stand there, must probably be complied with, unless they, upon further consideration, shall alter their opinion, and advise to making the stand at one or both the aforesaid forts, which this house and assembly judge to be much more expedient, on many obvious accounts, and have, several days since, signified their opinion to our delegates at said Congress, and from thence, and for other reasons, hope for their concurrence.

The bearer, Capt. Phelps, who has been very active and useful in the captures, is just arrived with important advices from Col. Arnold, of an expected attack, speedily from Governor Carlton, and is charged with the same advices from Mr. Arnold to you. In consequence of them, and the imminent danger the people there are exposed to, our assembly have just ordered five hundred pounds of our pittance of powder, to be forthwith sent them; and also, have ordered four companies to march, for their present relief, and have advised the New York Provincial Congress of this step; and also, are now despatching advices of the same to the Continental Congress, again setting forth the advantage of maintaining a post at Ticonderoga or Crown Point, and suggesting our wishes, that they reconsider their advice.

In the mean time, you may be assured that we have no such claim to the acquisition or the command of them as in the least degree to interfere with any measures you may think proper to adopt relating to them, and consider what we have done as a small and temporary relief.

I am, Gentlemen, in the name and behalf of the house of representatives, your most obedient and humble servant, by their order,

WILLIAM WILLIAMS, *Speaker.*[1]

Governor Trumbull to the Provincial Congress.

Hartford, May 29, 1775.

GENTLEMEN:—I am desired to inclose to you, a copy of a letter from the Congress of New York to this assembly, dated 25th instant, which you will receive herewith, per Mr. Brown, who is on his return from the Continental Congress. The contents of the above mentioned letter were immediately taken into consideration by this assembly; in consequence whereof, they

(1) The answer to this letter is printed in the Journals of the Provincial Congress, page 288.

came into the following resolutions. That one thousand men, including four hundred which we had before ordered, under command of Col. Hinman, should march, as soon as possible, to Ticonderoga and Crown Point, for the support and defence of those fortresses. That they continue there until they are relieved by the province of New York, or are otherwise ordered by this assembly. That Col. Hinman take the command of our troops on those stations. That the troops be furnished with one pound of powder and three pounds of bullets to each soldier. That Col. Hinman be ordered to keep up the strictest vigilance, to prevent any hostile incursions from being made into the settlements of the province of Quebec. And, that the Provincial Congresses of New York and Massachusetts Bay, be advised of these measures; and the New York Congress be requested to forward the necessary supplies for said troops, and such other supplies of ammunition as they shall judge necessary.

Advice of these resolutions is already sent forward to New York, per Mr. Colton, your express to Philadelphia.

It is matter of doubt with us, whether the above mentioned detachment of troops ordered by this colony, will be sufficient for the important purposes for which they are destined. But we recollect that Col. Arnold is now on the spot with a commission, as we understand, to raise a regiment in the pay of your province. We are not informed how far he has proceeded in that design. If he meets with success, we flatter ourselves that his regiment, joined with the troops we have sent, will be able to maintain their ground and keep possession of those important posts.

We take the liberty to recommend to your consideration, the furnishing such additional supply of powder from you, as you shall think necessary to be sent forward for the support of those northern posts. I am very sorry to have it to say, that we are credibly informed there are not five hundred pounds of powder in the city of New York: but at the same time, are advised, that means are taking to supply them with that very important article.

I am, with great truth and regard, Gentlemen,

Your most obedient humble servant,

JONATHAN TRUMBULL.

The honorable Provincial Congress of Massachusetts Bay.

———

The Congress of New York to the Assembly of Connecticut.

In Provincial Congress, New York, May 25, 1775.

To the honorable the Governor and Company of the English Colony of Connecticut :

BRETHREN:—By a minute of the grand Continental Congress of the 18th of May, in the year of our Lord one thousand seven hundred and seventy-five, a copy of which we do herewith transmit you, we are informed, that Ticonderoga hath been taken by sundry inhabitants of the northern colonies; and from the minute aforesaid, we are assured that this measure was for the common safety of the American colonies. In pursuance of the directions contained in that minute, we have given the necessary orders for removing the cannon and stores, taken at that important fortress, to the south end of Lake George, and for securing them there; and we have appointed Messrs. John N. Bleeker, Henry I. Bogert, George Palmer, Dirk Swart, and Peter Lansing, superintendents of this business. There is no doubt but that our brethren of Connecticut will feel great reluctance at the idea of ordering any of their troops to march within the bounds of this colony, for the purpose of defending the fort at Ticonderoga, and the cannon and stores above mentioned at Fort George. But we pray you to cast away all fears of offending us upon this occasion. We shall be happy to hear that you have placed a part of your forces in these posts, with intent to defend them until they shall be relieved by troops from this colony.

In further pursuance of the directions of the grand Congress, we have ordered provisions to be conveyed to Ticonderoga and Lake George, and we shall continue to furnish such supplies as we shall deem necessary.

You will be pleased, gentlemen, to appoint trusty commanders over your forces destined for the purposes above mentioned; and we do assure you of our willingness that they shall take the command at those places while garrisoned by your troops.

We beg leave to assure you, that in this and all other matters, we will pay the highest attention to every recommendation of the grand Continental Congress, and that we have the honor to be,

Gentlemen, your most obedient humble servants,

P. V. B. LIVINGSTON, President.

By order of the Congress,

JOHN McKISSON,   } Secretaries.
ROBERT BENSON, }

P. S. We pray you to use every effort to preserve and improve the present peaceable dispositions of the Canadians and Indians, for which purpose we think it will be necessary to keep up the strictest vigilance to prevent any incursions from being made into the province of Quebec.

P. V. B. LIVINGSTON, President.

Benedict Arnold to the Committee of Safety.

Crown Point, May 29, 1775.

GENTLEMEN:—I was equally surprised and alarmed this day, on receiving

advice, via Albany, that the Continental Congress had recommended the removing of all the cannon, stores, &c:, at Ticonderoga to Fort George, and
evacuating Ticonderoga entirely, which being the only key of this country,
leaves our very extensive frontiers open to the ravages of the enemy, and if
put into execution, will be the entire ruin of five hundred families to the
northward of Ticonderoga. I have written to the Congress and given my
sentiments very freely, with your instructions to me, as I fancy they have had
no intelligence of my appointment or orders. Col. Allen has entirely given
up the command. I have one hundred and fifty men here, and expect, in two
or three weeks, to have my regiment completed, and believe they will be
joined by a thousand men from Connecticut and New York. I have sent to
Lake George, six large brass and iron mortars and howitzers, and one brass
and three iron twelve pounders; and shall pursue your orders with all the
despatch in my power.

I am, Gentlemen, with great respect,

Your most obedient and humble servant,

BENEDICT ARNOLD.

———

Col. Easton to the Provincial Congress.

PITTSFIELD, MAY 30, 1775.

*To the honorable Provincial Congress, now sitting at Watertown, and to the
honorable Committee of Safety, at Cambridge.*

MAY IT PLEASE YOUR HONORS :—When I arrived express from Ticonderoga, to the honorable Provincial Congress and Committee of Safety, at Watertown and Cambridge, I represented to those two honorable boards, that the
reduction of that important fortress had taken its rise in the general court
of the colony of Connecticut, as it was also mentioned in the letter from
Capt. Mott to those two honorable boards aforesaid; upon which, the Congress passed a resolve, and the president of the Congress was ordered to
write to the said general assembly, desiring them to garrison and fortify
those late acquisitions, and also to bring down some of the cannon to our
head quarters at Cambridge. When I arrived at the assembly, and delivered the letter to the governor, his honor told me, that the assembly had not,
as an assembly, taken the matter up, but that it had its original in private
persons belonging to the assembly. However, it was immediately attended
to, and a committee of both houses was appointed to take the matter under
consideration, and did so; but did not report till Capt. Mott came from the
Continental Congress, with the approbation of that honorable body for the
taking and maintaining the fortress aforesaid. The council have detained
me till farther intelligence can be had from the Congress at New York, and
Mr. Sheppard is sent in my stead. I am, however, sent on my way, with all
haste, for Ticonderoga, without receiving said intelligence, on account of

the great danger that fortress is in of being besieged in a short time. By order of the aforesaid assembly, I have sent forward five hundred pounds of powder, under a proper guard, and shall, this day, hasten after it with all expedition.

I expect no provision from Connecticut will be made for me, and the men that were with me from this province at the taking of said fort, which were about fifty, and about one hundred who have gone as a reenforcement, except the paying them till about this time. Though Connecticut will raise men and assist in the defence of that fortress, yet they expect that our congress will properly officer and organize the men they send, and also pay them.

It is agreed, on all hands, the fortress must be maintained, as it is of infinite importance to the general cause. I have no doubt but very violent attempts will soon be made to wrest it out of our hands. As I have about one hundred and fifty men now at that fort, and shall be able to fill up a regiment in a few days time, I would just hint to your honors, that I should be willing to serve my country in the capacity I stand in at home, as the head of a regiment on this northern expedition. Should you see fit to gratify me with the command of a regiment for the fortifying and garrisoning said fortress, you may depend on my most faithful exertions to defend it, to the last extremity, against the whole weight of Canada, and on the most punctual observance of all your orders. And I shall be ready to make such farther acquisitions as shall be in my power, consistent with wisdom and prudence for the safety of what are already made, that you in your wisdom shall direct.

As to other regimental officers, Capt. Israel Dickinson and John Brown, Esq., have distinguished themselves very highly, both in council and action, and, in my humble opinion, are well qualified to command in the field. In a word, gentlemen, what is now wanted, is, that you put that fortress into the best posture of defence, in conjunction with Connecticut: that you properly officer one or more regiments: as there must be order and command in all armies, that you nominate a commander in chief: and forward pay with all expedition. I hope to receive an answer to this without any unnecessary delay. Should you see fit to appoint a chaplain to attend us, I recommend to you the Rev. Thomas Allen of this place, as a suitable person, who is well known to General Pomeroy.

I am, Gentlemen, your humble servant,

JAMES EASTON.

N. B. 'Tis necessary that provisions for the troops be provided immediately, and also a number of the military laws lately made by the Congress.

J. EASTON.

Governor Trumbull to the Provincial Congress.

Hartford, June 1, 1775.

GENTLEMEN:—Your letter of the 29th May, by Mr. Sheppard, is received, and I observe your agitation occasioned by the resolution of the General Congress, touching Ticonderoga and Crown Point. It was looked on in the same light here, and hath been repeatedly mentioned to the delegates from Connecticut, that removing from Ticonderoga to the south end of Lake George, would expose great part of the frontiers to invasion and distress, and a fort at the latter could scarcely be tenable. The expressions of the resolution are not clear. The Provincial Congress at New York, take them to mean no more than the removing the supernumerary cannon and stores from those two fortresses to the south end of Lake George; but, not to leave or abandon those two important posts. Mine of the 29th of May, by Mr. Brown, informs what hath been resolved here, which is fully approved by the Provincial Congress at New York. They express their concern to keep and maintain " the important posts of Ticonderoga and Crown Point." We have received intelligence from Albany, of the readiness of that city and county to afford their utmost assistance for securing those important posts, for the common defence of our rights and liberties. Our general assembly was closed last evening. I shall be attentive to your intelligence, and will communicate to you all that appears important, that shall come first to my knowledge: please to direct for me at Lebanon. I congratulate you on the union and increasing harmony of these North American colonies, and the wonderful concurrence and coincidence of counsels amongst them. May our hearts be united in humble thankfulness therefor.

I am, with great truth and regard, Gentlemen,

Your most obedient humble servant,

JONATHAN TRUMBULL.

The honorable Provincial Congress of Massachusetts Bay.

———

Col. Easton to the Provincial Congress.

Crown Point, June 6, 1775.

RESPECTABLE GENTLEMEN:—It is of the utmost importance to the united colonies to cultivate harmony and friendship with the Canadians and their Indians. I have painfully exerted myself to procure and secure it. I have sent you a copy of a letter Col. Allen and myself wrote to the Canadians. It appears to me of importance, that your honors should be acquainted with the state of policy and of facts. You will discover, by perusing the enclosed, that a party of Canadians made an attack upon our reconnoitering party. Since that, Mr. Ferris, an inhabitant of the New Hampshire Grants, has been at Montreal, and returned to this place; he is a man I can confide in, and he informs that Saint Luke La Corne, who acted many barbarities towards our people the last war, for which he was sainted, has been using his utmost influence to excite the Canadians and Indians to take part in the war against the united colonies; and that he, and Capt McCoy who commanded the Canadian attack, have made but little proficiency. Most of the said party of Canadians were appointed officers, but could procure but very few soldiers and not one Indian. Saint Luke advises, that some in every parish be immediately executed, except they will join the king's troops. There are lately come to Saint Johns, near two hundred regulars, and joined Capt. McCoy's party of about fifty Canadians, who have been mentioned as assailants on the reconnoitering party, and they are there fortifying. I still retain my sentiments that policy demands that the colonies advance an army of two or three thousand men into Canada and environ Montreal. This will inevitably fix and confirm the Canadians and Indians in our interest. Nothing gives me so much concern, as the mistaken policy in our worthy Congress and assemblies, who, for want of the real knowledge of certain facts, imagine, that to push an army thither would offend the Canadians and incense them against the colonies. The armed vessels are advanced to the north part of the lake to command it, and, consequently, to guard the frontier settlements thereon. We hear that Col. Hinman is appointed commander in chief of this department, and is marching hither with a thousand men. These are joyful tidings to us. We hope they will prove true; for we cannot long conduct our army without it be regularly organized with officers and under pay.

I am, Gentlemen, your most obedient humble servant,

JAMES EASTON.

To the honorable the Gentlemen of the Provincial Congress, or,
Committee of Safety, at Watertown and Cambridge.

————

Proclamation of Cols. Allen and Easton.

Ticonderoga, June 1, 1775.

To our worthy and respectable friends and countrymen, the French people of Canada, Greeting :

FRIENDS, FELLOW SUBJECTS, AND COUNTRYMEN :—You are, undoubtedly, more or less acquainted with the unnatural and unhappy controversy subsisting between Great Britain and her colonies, the particulars of which, in this letter, we do not pretend to expatiate upon ; but refer you to the consideration of the justice and equitableness of our cause from your former acquaintance with the merits of it. We need only observe, that the inhabitants of the colonies viewed the controversy on their part to be justifiable in the sight of God and all unprejudiced and honest men, that have or may have opportunity and ability to examine into the ground of it. Fixed in this principle, those inhabitants are resolved to vindicate their cause at the hazard of their lives and fortunes, but have not the least disposition to injure, molest, or, in any way, deprive our fellow subjects, the Canadians, of either liberty or property; nor have they any design to wage war with them; and, on the other hand, from all the intelligence that the inhabitants of the said colonies have received from the Canadians, it has appeared that they were alike disposed for friendship, or at least neutrality, and not at all disposed to take part with the king's troops in the present civil war against the colonies. We were, nevertheless, surprised to hear, that a number of about thirty Canadians, attacked our reconnoitering party, consisting of four men; fired on and pursued them until they returned the fire. This is the account of the party who have all arrived at head quarters. We desire to know of any gentleman of the Canadians, the facts of the case, if they be different: as one story must be allowed to be good till another is told. Our general orders to the soldiers were, that they should not, on pain of death, molest or kill any of your people. But if it shall appear, upon examination, that the reconnoitering party commenced hostilities against you, they shall suffer, agreeably to the sentence of a court martial: for our special orders from the colonies were, to befriend and protect you, if need be, so that if you desire their friendship, you are invited to embrace it: for nothing can be more undesirable to the inhabitants of these colonies, than a war with their fellow subjects, the Canadians, or with the Indians. You are, undoubtedly, very sensible that a war has already commenced between Great Britain and the colonies: hostilities have already begun. To fight the king's troops has become inevitable. The colonies cannot avoid it. But pray, is it necessary the people of your country and ours should butcher each other? God forbid. There are no controversies subsisting between us. Pray let old England and the colonies fight it out, and the Canadians stand by and see what the arm of flesh can do. We are apprehensive, that the conduct of your people before complained of, had not a general approbation, and are still confident, that your country, as such, will not wage war with the colonies, or approve of the aforesaid hostile conduct of your people; as we conceive it impolitic, to the last degree, for the Canadians to enter into a bloody war with the English colonies, without either provocation or motive; but every motive of interest, virtue, and honor, to dissuade you from it. To conclude, we apprehend St. Luke La Corne, Monsieur Ronvelo, and Capt. McCoy, the last of whom commanded the Canadian party aforesaid, and probably some others, whose interest it is to irritate and excite your people to take up arms against the colonies, have inveigled some of the baser sort already to attack the said four men as before related. We expect, gentlemen, as to these particulars, you will, in good time, favor us with an answer, and in the interim, we subscribe ourselves your unfeigned friends,

ETHAN ALLEN, } *At present, the principal Command-*
JAMES EASTON, } *ing Officers of the Army.*

A copy of the letter that we sent to the Canadians, to be communicated to them in print, translated into French by the favor of Mr. Walker, our friend at Montreal. This we submit to your honor's consideration.

Yours, at command,

ETHAN ALLEN,
JAMES EASTON.

Report of the Committee sent to Ticonderoga.

Cambridge, July 6, 1775.

The committee appointed to proceed to the posts of Ticonderoga and Crown Point, &c.,[1] beg leave to report, that they proceeded through the new settlements called the New Hampshire Grants, and carefully observed the road through the same, and find that there is a good road from Williamstown to the place where the road crosseth the river called Paulet river, which is about fifteen miles from Skenesborough; from thence to the falls at Wood Creek near Major Skene's house, the road is not feasible, and is unfit for carriages, but cattle may be driven that way very well.

Your committee, having taken with them the copies of the commission and instructions from the committee of safety to Col Benedict Arnold, and informed themselves, as fully as they were able, in what manner he had executed his said commission and instructions, have found that he was with Col. Allen, and others at the time the fort was reduced; but do not find that he had any men under his command at the time of the reduction of those fortresses; but find that he did, afterwards, possess himself of the sloop on the lake. At Saint Johns we found the said Arnold, claiming the command of said sloop, and a schooner, which is said to be the property of Major Skene; and also all the posts and fortresses at the south end of Lake Champlain and Lake George, although Col. Hinman was at Ticonderoga, with near a thousand men under his command at the several posts.

Your committee informed the said Arnold of their commission, and, at his request, gave him a copy of their instructions; upon reading of which, he seemed greatly disconcerted, and declared he would not be second in command to any person whomsoever; and after some time contemplating upon the matter, resigned his post, and gave your committee his resignation under his hand, dated the 24th of June; which is submitted, and, at the same time, he ordered his men to be disbanded, which he said were between two and three hundred. Your committee, not finding any men regularly under said Arnold, by reason of his so disbanding them, appointed Col. Easton, who was at Ticonderoga, to take the command under Col. Hinman, who was the principal commanding officer, at those posts, of the Connecticut forces, and endeavored to give the officers and men who had served under

----

(1) The instructions to Walter Spooner, Jedediah Foster, and James Sullivan, Esquires, the committee, are entered in the Journals of Congress, June 13, 1775, *ante* page 327.

said Arnold, an opportunity to reenlist; of whom, numbers enlisted and several of the officers agreed to hold their command under the new appointment.

Your committee, having taken a critical survey of the garrison and posts of Ticonderoga and Crown Point, found them in a very defenceless state, and after consulting with Col. Hinman, were of opinion, upon the whole, that it is necessary to retain in the service of this colony, for the present, the number of four hundred men, as the committee were informed from intelligence from Canada, that great preparations were making and all endeavors used to bring over the Canadians and savages to be inimical to these colonies.

Your committee having found Capt. Noble at the Point, with a number of men who had been under said Arnold, willing to engage in the service, we paid to said Noble, one hundred pounds, to be delivered to the men, as advance pay; and appointed Mr. William Satterly, a worthy man, to muster them and inspect their arms; and took Capt. Noble's and Satterly's receipt for the same, and their promise to apply it for that purpose.

Your committee returning to Ticonderoga, and Col. Easton being there, they paid into his hands the sum of two hundred and eighty pounds, to be applied for the purpose aforesaid, and took his receipt and promise so to do; and appointed Mr. Jonas Fay, a respectable person, to muster the men and their arms, all except Capt. Noble's company. We also paid into the hands of one Remember Baker, said to be a good officer, who engaged a certain number of men under Col. Easton, the sum of twenty pounds, and took his receipt and promise to apply said money as advance pay to said men; which completes the whole of the money delivered to said committee for the purposes aforesaid.

Your committee have engaged to Col. Easton, that the remaining part of the advance pay should be immediately sent to him.

Your committee found, that as soon as Col. Arnold had disbanded his men, some of them became dissatisfied and mutinous, and many of them signified to the committee, that they had been informed that they were to be defrauded of their pay for past services. The committee, in order to quiet them, engaged, under their hands, in behalf of the colony of the Massachusetts Bay, that as soon as the rolls should be made up and properly authenticated, they should be paid for their past services, and all those who should engage anew, should have the same bounty and wages as is promised to those who serve within said colony.

Your committee inquired of Mr. Henry Bleeker, of Albany, how the men at those posts were supplied with provisions; who informed us, that he acted under his brother, who was commissioner of supplies from New York; that all the men at those stations, of whatsoever colony, were supplied by him, without distinction, and that he should continue so to supply, until otherwise directed.

Your committee appointed Timothy Edwards, and Samuel Brown, Esq'rs, a committee to supply the men under Col. Easton's command, with such necessaries as should not be supplied from New York; and appointed Capt. Elisha Phelps, to act as commissary under them, to deal out to the men whatsoever should be supplied by the said Edwards and Brown.

Your committee, being of opinion, that a major should be appointed under Col. Easton, and one surgeon to the battalion, and having inquired into the disposition of the officers and men who have engaged, have appointed John Brown, Esq., as major, and Mr. Jonas Fay, as surgeon.

Your committee, when they had received Col. Arnold's resignation, directed him to return to Congress and render an account of his proceedings, agreeably to their instructions, a copy of which order is herewith submitted.

Your committee made an examination of the military stores at those posts, a schedule whereof is herewith delivered, excepting some lead and iron balls, and old chains, which have been dug out of the ruins of Crown Point fort.

Your committee, finding that the men at those stations had not a sufficiency of gunpowder to defend the posts, and upon a careful inquiry not finding any at Albany, have directed said committee of supplies to supply two hundred weight from some of the town stocks in the county of Berkshire, on the credit of the colony.

Your committee are of opinion, that the maintaining of those posts is of the utmost importance to the security of the colony of New York and the New England colonies, which was a sufficient inducement to the committee to continue in the pay of this colony the number of men before mentioned. The fortresses not being at present tenable, then there must be a sufficient number of men to command the lake, and prevent the enemy from landing.

Your committee are of opinion, that the best security of those posts in there present state, is by armed vessels of various construction, to be kept constantly cruising on the lake, and small boats with swivel guns to act as scouts, which will effectually prevent the army from sudden surprise.

Your committee have, agreeably to their instructions, advised the Hon. American Congress, the Hon. Convention of the colony of New York, and the governor of Connecticut, by respectfully signifying to them, their opinion of the importance of the maintaining those posts, and the measures for effecting the same.

All which is humbly submitted,

WALTER SPOONER, *by order.*

Return of Ordnance Stores at Crown Point.

Seven punches for vents of guns; three scoops for shells; one pair brass scales; fourteen mallets; one set of measures for powder; three hundred and ten pounds of slow match; one hundred, eighteen-pound shot; five hundred and eighty, twelve-pound shot; five hundred and eighty, nine-pound shot; five hundred and eighty, six-pound shot; one thousand four hundred and thirty grape shot; sixty-eight, eight-inch shells; three hundred and seventy, six-inch shells; six sponges with ramrods; six waggon bodies; nine hundred and six wheels; twenty-two wadhooks with ramrods; one cross-cut saw; one whip saw.

Stores at Ticonderoga.

Three guns and triangles; six gages for twelve-pound shot; three copper hoops; six copper ladles; twelve iron ladles; shells, shot, &c., in vast quantities.

June 23, 1775.

The Committee to Benedict Arnold.

CROWN POINT, JUNE 23, 1775.

SIR:—You having signified to the committee who are appointed and directed by the Provincial Congress of Massachusetts Bay, to inquire into the state of the fortresses of Crown Point, Ticonderoga, &c. and the appendages thereof, your resolution to resign all your command of the said fortresses, and the vessels and stores thereunto belonging, for reasons under your hand expressed, this is to inform you, that it is the expectation of the Provincial Congress aforesaid, that the chief officer of the Connecticut forces at those stations, will command the same for the present: and the committee accordingly expect that you will conform yourself to the directions of said Congress in that behalf, and deliver the same to such chief officer of the Connecticut forces, or his order, for which this shall be your authority. The committee expect that you will, as soon as may be, lay an account of your disbursements before the Provincial Congress, agreeably to our instructions, a copy whereof is lodged with you.

By order of the committee.

WALTER SPOONER, *Chairman.*

Col. Benedict Arnold.

The Committee to the Continental Congress.

TICONDEROGA, JUNE 23, 1775.

To the honorable the President, and the members of the American Congress, now sitting at Philadelphia.

MAY IT PLEASE YOUR HONORS:—The Congress of the colony of the Massachusetts Bay, on the fourteenth day of June last, appointed Walter Spooner, Jedediah Foster, and James Sullivan, a committee to repair to the fortresses of Ticonderoga and Crown Point, on Lake Champlain, to inquire into the importance of holding those posts, and also into the method by which they may be maintained; to establish there, in the pay of said colony, so many men to defend the same posts as they should judge necessary, not exceeding four hundred; and the said committee were also, by said Congress directed, when they should have made themselves fully acquainted with the situation and importance of said posts, respectfully to signify their thoughts thereon to your honors.

Wherefore, by order of said committee, I take leave to inform you, that it is the opinion of said committee, such is the importance of those fortresses, that should they once be in the hands of the enemies to America, the colony of New York, together with the New England colonies, would be in continual danger of having depredations committed on them, by the regular forces, who would be possessed of those garrisons; and should the Canadians and savages, who, we hope, are not yet at enmity with us, be inclined to take part with the ministerial army, the distress of the colonies, before mentioned, must be extremely great.

A garrison at the south end of Lake George, however tenable, could be of but little service to the New England colonies: because the most easy route for an army from Quebec into New England, would be through Lake Champlain to South Bay, from whence they might travel by land through the new settlements of New York into the New England governments, destroy the frontier towns in their march, drive the farmers from their fields, prevent the large supplies of wheat and other necessaries which may soon be expected from these new settlements, and send distress and famine into the heart of the country: and this all without being, on a right line, within many miles of the south end of Lake George.

I am also directed, by said committee, to signify to your honors, that it is the opinion of the committee, that the defence of those fortresses must be supported by holding command of Lake Champlain, which, they conceive, may be most easily done, by having vessels, of various constructions, well manned and armed, floating there: for which purpose, the committee have stationed four hundred men there, which are all that the embarrassed circumstances of our colony can at present admit of, to co-operate with near a thousand, under the command of Col. Hinman, who is sent to those posts by the government of Connecticut; but whether the forces now on the lake are sufficient for the purposes aforementioned, your honors will judge.

I am, in behalf of the committee,

Your honors' most humble servant,

WALTER SPOONER, *Chairman.*

To the honorable Continental Congress.

91

The Committee to Gov. Trumbull.

SPRINGFIELD, JULY 3, 1775.

MAY IT PLEASE YOUR HONORS:—When the Congress of the colony of the Massachusetts Bay were informed that your government had sent Col. Hinman to Lake Champlain, with a thousand men, to defend the important posts there, it was with the deepest concern that they saw he was not commander in chief of the fortresses and their appendages : and immediately despatched a committee, whereof I had the honor to be chairman, to let the commander of their forces know that it was the expectation of our Congress, that the commander in chief of the Connecticut forces should be over our officers and privates : the committee was also ordered respectfully to signify to your honor, their opinion of the necessity of holding those fortresses, as also of the most expedient method to do it.

Whereupon, they proceeded, and at Crown Point let Col. Arnold know, that it was expected that he should give up the command of the garrison, &c. to Col. Hinman, and be under him as officer there : but he declined it : declared he would not be second to any man : disbanded his forces, and resigned his commission. A majority of his men engaged anew under Col. James Easton, who the committee appointed under the commander of the forces of your government, on Lake Champlain, and to be regulated by your martial laws; and the committee left the garrison and appendages in peace, with much satisfaction, commanded by Col. Hinman, who, they are confident, is fully equal to the appointment.

The committee also order me to inform your honor, that it is their opinion, that the abandoning the posts on Lake Champlain, would probably prove the utter ruin of the New England governments, and that they apprehend armed vessels, floating batteries, &c. will be the surest means of commanding the lakes. The committee would write your honor more fully on the subject, but they are convinced, from the letters you have favored our Congress with, that you are fully possessed of the importance of holding those fortresses.

Justice compels the committee to let your honor know, that on Col. Arnold's refusing to serve under Col. Hinman, a mutiny arose among some of Arnold's men, who would not engage anew in our service, which seemed to be attended with dangerous symptoms, but by the noble exertions of the officers of your government, with those of Judge Duer, of Charlotte county, in the colony of New York, and the ample support by them rendered to the committee, in the most difficult situation, it was happily quelled; the particulars of it are too tedious and disagreeable to trouble your honor's attention, while you have constantly business of the last importance before you.

But thus much the committee order me to take leave to say, that from the polite, generous and manly disposition of Col. Hinman, and the officers in the Connecticut forces under him, we may gather the most happy prospects of a campaign in the northward replete with honor and interest to the colonies.

I am, in behalf of the committee,

Your honor's most obedient servant,

WALTER SPOONER, *Chairman.*

Hon. Jonathan Trumbull.

———

The Committee to the Congress of New York.

SPRINGFIELD, JULY 3, 1775.

To the honorable the President and Members of the Convention of the Colony of New York.

GENTLEMEN :—Notwithstanding the many calamities that the colony of the Massachusetts Bay now struggles under, the Congress there are resolutely determined to leave nothing within their power undone, which may have even a probable tendency to preserve the rights and property of the American colonies. In pursuance of this resolution, they, on the 14th day of June, appointed a committee, whereof I have the honor to be chairman, to proceed to Ticonderoga and Crown Point, to inquire into the importance of holding those posts, and, among other things, respectfully to signify to you their thoughts on the subject. The committee have made such inquiries as they were directed to prosecute, and have ordered me to take leave to inform you, that it is their opinion, should the fortresses on Lake Champlain fall into the hands of our enemies, the colony of New York, with the New England colonies, must be in the utmost insecurity, for the enemy might land at the southern end of a part of the waters of Lake Champlain, called South Bay, from whence, as Fort Edward is razed to the foundation, there is nothing to check them, or prevent their spreading fire and devastation down to Albany, and over all the frontier towns eastward, in New York and the New England colonies: wherefore, it is the opinion of the committee, that all possible care ought to be taken to keep the command of Lake Champlain, which, perhaps, may be more easily effected by armed vessels of various constructions, than otherwise.

The committee has established on the lakes, in the pay of the Massachusetts colony, four hundred effective men, with proper officers, which are all that the distressed state of the colony, at present, admit of: which regiment, from the peculiar embarrassments which that colony is now laboring under, must look for present supplies of provisions to the colony of New York.

While the committee was at the posts above mentioned, there was a dangerous mutiny set on foot by some persons, employed by Col. Arnold, an officer of our colony, who had their own interest more at heart than the public good, which, had it not been for the influence and well timed exertions of Judge Duer, a gentleman of the county of Charlotte, in your colony, and the principal officers of the Connecticut forces, might have been attended with fatal consequences. As the committee suppose the colony to be under great obligations to that worthy gentleman, they cannot but inform his own government of his zealous exertions for the public good.

We are, Gentlemen, with great respect,

Your obedient humble servants,

WALTER SPOONER, *Chairman.*

Hon. Provincial Congress of New York.

Provincial Congress of New York to the Committee of Safety.

IN PROVINCIAL CONGRESS, NEW YORK, JUNE 7, 1775.

GENTLEMEN:—The multiplicity of business brought before us by the Continental Congress, and a short adjournment of our body, from Saturday till Tuesday morning, have rendered it impossible for us to give a more early attention to your favor.

We have little to say upon the principal subject of your letter, as we conceive that the Provincial Congresses of both colonies are concluded from any discretionary provision relative to the ordnance and other stores taken at Crown Point and Ticonderoga, of which you must be fully convinced by the acts of the Continental Congress on that subject, copies of which are enclosed.

We are fully apprised of the dangerous consequences, that would await this capital of our colony, either from supineness, or a confidence in the honor of those, who being the avowed instruments of ministerial vengeance, we cannot expect will hold any faith with us. Whatever articles we are now possessed of, that may be used to the injury of this city in particular, or of the continent in general, we shall be studious to prevent, if possible, from falling into the hands of our enemies. In sympathizing with you for the unhappy town of Boston, we shall do every thing in our power to prevent this city from being reduced to the same deplorable situation, and shall watchfully attend to every means of defence which our present or future circumstances may enable us to improve.

We are, Gentlemen and Brethren,

With great respect and sincere affection,

Your most obedient humble servants,

P. V. B. LIVINGSTON, *President.*

To Joseph Warren, Esq., and the
    Committee of Safety for the colony of Massachusetts Bay, Watertown.

Resolves of the Continental Congress.

MAY 30, 1775.

A letter from Col. Arnold, dated Crown Point, May 23, 1775, was laid before the Congress, informing that he had certain intelligence, that "on the 19th there were then four hundred regulars at St. John's, making all possible preparation to cross the lake, and expected to be joined by a number of Indians, with a design of retaking Crown Point and Ticonderoga," and earnestly calling for a reenforcement and supplies. This letter being taken into consideration,

Resolved, That the governor of Connecticut be requested immediately to send a strong reenforcement to the garrisons of Crown Point and Ticonderoga, and that so many of the cannon and other stores be retained, as may be necessary for the immediate defence of those posts, until further order from this Congress, and that the provincial convention of New York be informed of this resolve, and desired to furnish those troops with provisions and other necessary stores, and to take effectual care that a sufficient number of batteaux be immediately provided for the lakes.

Ordered, That the above resolve be immediately transmitted in a letter by the president, to Gov. Trumbull, and the convention at New York.

Ordered, That the president in his letter acquaint Gov. Trumbull, that it is the desire of Congress, that he should appoint a person, in whom he can confide, to command the forces at Crown Point and Ticonderoga.

JUNE 1, 1775.

Upon motion, *Resolved,* That it be recommended to the government of Connecticut, or the general of the forces of that colony, to appoint commissaries to receive at Albany and forward the supplies of provisions, for the forces on Lake Champlain, from the provincial convention of New York, and that the said convention use their utmost endeavors in facilitating and aiding the transportation thereof, from thence to where the said commissaries may direct.

JUNE 8, 1775.

The Congress being informed that a Major Skene, with some other officers, who arrived last evening, in a vessel from London, were, with their papers, in the custody of the troops of this city; that the said Skene had lately been appointed governor of the forts of Ticonderoga and Crown Point; that one of the officers with him is a lieutenant in the regulars, now in the province of Quebec; and moreover, that the said Skene had declared that he has authority to raise a regiment in America; from all this, apprehending that the said Skene is a dangerous partizan of administration, and that his papers may contain intelligence of ministerial designs against America, very important to be known,

Resolved, That a committee be appointed to examine the papers of the said Skene and lieutenant, in their presence.

That the committee consist of Mr. J. Adams, Mr. Deane, and Mr. Mifflin.

That the said committee be upon honor to conceal whatever, of a private nature, may come to their knowledge by such examination; and that they communicate, to this Congress, what they shall discover relative to the present dispute, between Great Britain and America.

JUNE 10, 1775.

The committee for examining Gov. Skene's letters, &c., having communicated to Congress what they found relative to the dispute between Great Britain and these colonies:

Upon motion, *Resolved*, That Gov. Philip Skene, Lieutenant Moncrief, and Mr. Lundy, be released from their present confinement, and permitted to go at large any where within eight miles of the city, between Delaware and Schuylkill, on their parole of honor, not to pass those limits, and that they will hold no correspondence with any person whatsoever, on any political subject.

JUNE 19, 1775.

The president laid before the Congress, sundry letters he had received from Massachusetts Bay and New York, which were read.

The letters from Massachusetts Bay being taken into consideration, the Congress came to the following resolve:

That the governor of Connecticut be requested to direct all the forces raised in that colony, not employed at Ticonderoga and Crown Point, or recommended by this Congress to be marched towards New York, to be immediately sent to join the combined army before Boston. And it is earnestly recommended to the colony of Rhode Island, and to the provincial convention of New Hampshire, to send immediately to the army before Boston, such of the forces as are already embodied, towards their quotas of the troops agreed to be raised by the New England colonies.

JUNE 22, 1775.

A letter from Crown Point, dated June 10, was laid before the Congress and read. Information being given, that two officers who brought the letter were at the door, and had some things of importance to communicate,

Ordered, That they be introduced, and they were introduced. After they withdrew, the Congress came to the following resolutions:

Resolved, That it be recommended to the officer commanding in the New York department, to procure, as soon as possible, a list of the men employed in taking and garrisoning Crown Point and Ticonderoga, and keeping possession of the lakes, and also of their disbursements, in order that they may be paid.

Resolved, That their pay be the same as that of the officers and privates in the American army; the highest of the officers not to exceed that of a captain, and that the pay commence the third day of May last, and continue till they are discharged.

Resolved, That it be recommended to the convention of New York, that they, consulting with General Schuyler, employ in the army to be raised for the defence of America, those called Green Mountain Boys, under such officers as the said Green Mountain Boys shall choose.

EXTRACTS

JOURNALS OF THE CONTINENTAL CONGRESS

RELATING TO MASSACHUSETTS.

Sept. 14, 1774.

THE delegates from the province of Massachusetts Bay, agreeable to a request from the joint committees of every town and district in the county of Middlesex, in the said province, communicated to the Congress the proceedings of those committees at Concord, on the 30th and 31st days of August last, which were read.

Sept. 17, 1774.

The resolutions entered into by the delegates from the several towns and districts in the county of Suffolk, in the province of the Massachusetts Bay, on Tuesday, the 6th of September, and their address to his excellency governor Gage, dated the 9th, were laid before the Congress.

The Congress taking the resolutions into consideration,

Resolved, unanimously, That this assembly deeply feels the suffering of their countrymen in the Massachusetts Bay, under the operation of the late unjust, cruel, and oppressive acts of the British parliament—that they most thoroughly approve the wisdom and fortitude, with which opposition to these wicked ministerial measures has hitherto been conducted, and they earnestly recommend to their brethren, a perseverance in the same firm and temperate conduct, as expressed in the resolutions determined upon at a meeting of the delegates for the county of Suffolk, on Tuesday, the 6th instant, trusting that the effect of the united efforts of North America in their behalf, will carry such conviction to the British nation, of the unwise, unjust, and ruinous policy of the present administration, as quickly to introduce better men and wiser measures.

NOTE.—Several resolutions of the Continental Congress, closely connected with the proceedings of the Provincial Congress, or its committees, have been inserted in their appropriate places: May 17, 1775, relating to exportations to the British dominions, *ante* page 313: May 29, 1775, respecting exportations to the island of Nantucket, page 313; June 9, 1775, for furnishing flour; and June 10, 1775, for encouraging the manufacture of gunpowder, page 354 ; June 9, 1775, for assuming government, page 359; May 18, 1775, relating to the stores at Ticonderoga, page 706; and other resolves relating to Ticonderoga and Crown Point, pages 724—5—6.

Resolved, unanimously, That contributions from all the colonies for supplying the necessities, and alleviating the distresses of our brethren at Boston, ought to be continued, in such manner, and so long as their occasions may require.

Ordered, That a copy of the above resolutions be transmitted to Boston by the president.

Ordered, That these resolutions, together with the resolutions of the county of Suffolk, be published in the newspapers.

OCTOBER 6, 1774.

The Congress resumed the consideration of the means proper to be used for a restoration of American rights. During this debate, an express from Boston arrived with a letter from the committee of correspondence, dated the 29th of September, which was laid before the Congress.

In this the committee of correspondence inform the Congress, that they "expected some regard would have been paid to the petitions presented to their governor, against fortifying their town in such a manner as can be accounted for only upon the supposition, that the town and country are to be treated by the soldiery as declared enemies—that the entrenchments upon the Neck are nearly completed—that cannon are mounted at the entrance of the town—that it is currently reported, that fortifications are to be erected on Copp's hill, Beacon hill, Fort hill, &c., so that the fortifications, with the ships in the harbor may absolutely command every avenue to the town both by sea and land—that a number of cannon, the property of a private gentleman, were a few days ago seized and taken from his wharf by order of the general—that from several circumstances mentioned in the letter, there is reason to apprehend, that Boston is to be made and kept a garrisoned town; —that from all they can hear from Britain, administration is resolved to do all in their power to force them to a submission—that when the town is inclosed, it is apprehended the inhabitants will be held as hostages for the submission of the country—they apply therefore to the Congress for advice how to act—that, if the Congress advise to quit the town, they obey—if it is judged that by maintaining their ground they can better serve the public cause, they will not shrink from hardship and danger—finally, that as the late acts of parliament have made it impossible that there should be a due administration of justice, and all law therefore must be suspended—that as the governor has by proclamation prevented the meeting of the general court, they therefore request the advice of the Congress."

OCTOBER 7, 1774.

The Congress resumed the consideration of the letter from the committee of correspondence in Boston, and after some debate—

Resolved, That a committee be appointed to prepare a letter to his excellency General Gage, representing "that the town of Boston and province of Massachusetts Bay, are considered by all America as suffering in the common cause, for their noble and spirited opposition to oppressive acts of parliament calculated to deprive us of our most sacred rights and privileges." 2d. Expressing our concern, that, while the Congress are deliberating on the most peaceable means for restoring American liberty, and that harmony and intercourse, which subsisted between us and the parent kingdom so necessary to both, his excellency, as they are informed, is raising fortifications round the town of Boston, thereby exciting well grounded jealousies in the minds of his majesty's faithful subjects therein, that he means to cut off all communication between them and their brethren in the country, and reduce them to a state of submission to his will, and that the soldiers under his excellency's command, are frequently violating private property, and offering various insults to the people, which must irritate their minds, and if not put a stop to, involve all America in the horrors of a civil war —To entreat his excellency, from the assurance we have of the peaceable disposition of the inhabitants of the town of Boston and the province of the Massachusetts Bay, to discontinue his fortifications, and that a free and safe communication be restored and continued between the town of Boston and the country, and prevent all injuries on the part of the troops, until his majesty's pleasure shall be known, after the measures now adopting shall have been laid before him.

Mr. Lynch, Mr. S. Adams, and Mr. Pendleton, are appointed a committee to draught a letter agreeable to the foregoing resolution.

OCTOBER 8, 1774.

The Congress resumed the consideration of the letter from Boston, and upon motion,

Resolved, That this Congress approve the opposition of the inhabitants of the Massachusetts Bay, to the execution of the late acts of parliament; and if the same shall be attempted to be carried into execution by force, in such case, all America ought to support them in their opposition.

OCTOBER 10, 1774.

The Congress resuming the consideration of the letter from Boston;

Resolved unanimously, That it is the opinion of this body, that the removal of the people of Boston into the country, would be, not only extremely difficult in the execution, but so important in its consequences, as to require the utmost deliberation before it is adopted; but in case the provincial meeting of that colony should judge it absolutely necessary, it is the opinion of the Congress, that all America ought to contribute towards recompensing them for the injury they may thereby sustain; and it will be recommended accordingly.

Resolved, That the Congress recommend to the inhabitants of the colony of Massachusetts Bay, to submit to a suspension of the administration of justice, where it cannot be procured in a legal and peaceable manner, under the rules of their present charter, and the laws of the colony founded thereon.

Resolved unanimously, That every person and persons whomsoever, who shall take, accept, or act under any commission or authority, in any-wise derived from the act passed in the last session of parliament, changing the form of government, and violating the charter of the province of Massachusetts Bay, ought to be held in detestation and abhorrence by all good men, and considered as the wicked tools of that despotism, which is preparing to destroy those rights, which God, nature, and compact, have given to America.

The committee brought in a draught of a letter to General Gage, and the same being read and amended, was ordered to be copied, and to be signed by the president in behalf of the Congress.

OCTOBER 11, 1774.

A copy of the letter to General Gage, was brought into Congress, and agreeable to order, signed by the president, and is as follows:

Philadelphia, October 10, 1774.

SIR :—The inhabitants of the town of Boston have informed us, the representatives of his majesty's faithful subjects in all the colonies from Nova Scotia to Georgia, that the fortifications erecting within that town, the frequent invasions of private property, and the repeated insults they receive from the soldiery, have given them great reason to suspect a plan is formed very destructive to them, and tending to overthrow the liberties of America.

Your excellency cannot be a stranger to the sentiments of America, with respect to the acts of parliament, under the execution of which, those unhappy people are oppressed, the approbation universally expressed of their conduct, and the determined resolution of the colonies, for the preservation of their common rights, to unite in their opposition to those acts.—In consequence of these sentiments, they have appointed us the guardians of their rights and liberties, and we are under the deepest concern, that whilst we are pursuing dutiful and peaceable measures to procure a cordial and effectual reconciliation between Great Britain and the colonies, your excellency should proceed in a manner that bears so hostile an appearance, and which even those oppressive acts do not warrant.

We entreat your excellency to consider what a tendency this conduct must have to irritate and force a free people, hitherto well disposed to peaceable measures, into hostilities, which may prevent the endeavors of this Congress to restore a good understanding with our parent state, and may involve us in the horrors of a civil war.

In order therefore to quiet the minds and remove the reasonable jealousies of the people, that they may not be driven to a state of desperation, being fully persuaded of their pacific disposition towards the king's troops, could they be assured of their own safety, we hope, Sir, you will discontinue the fortifications in and about Boston, prevent any further invasions of private property, restrain the irregularities of the soldiers, and give orders that the communication between the town and country may be open, unmolested and free.

Signed by order and in behalf of the General Congress,

PEYTON RANDOLPH, *President.*[1]

As the Congress have given General Gage an assurance of the peaceable disposition of the people of Boston and the Massachusetts Bay;

Resolved unanimously, That they be advised still to conduct themselves peaceably towards his excellency General Gage, and his majesty's troops now stationed in the town of Boston, as far as can possibly be consistent with their immediate safety, and the security of the town; avoiding and discountenancing every violation of his majesty's property, or any insult to his troops, and that they peaceably and firmly persevere in the line they are now conducting themselves, on the defensive.

Ordered, That a copy of the foregoing resolve, and of that passed on Saturday, and the three passed yesterday, be made out, and that the president

---

(1) The following is the answer of General Gage to the letter of the Continental Congress.

BOSTON, OCTOBER 20, 1774.

To Peyton Randolph, Esq.:

SIR:—Representations should be made with candor, and matters stated exactly as they stand. People would be led to believe, from your letter to me of the 10th instant, that works were raised against the town of Boston, private property invaded, the soldiers suffered to insult the inhabitants, and the communication between the town and country shut up and molested.

Nothing can be farther from the true situation of this place than the above state. There is not a single gun pointed against the town, no man's property has been seized or hurt, except the king's, by the people's destroying straw, bricks, &c., bought for his service. No troops have given less cause for complaint, and greater care was never taken to prevent it; and such care and attention were never more necessary from the insults and provocations daily given to both officers and soldiers. The communication between the town and country has been always free and unmolested, and is so still.

Two works of earth have been raised, at some distance from the town, wide off the road, and guns put in them. The remainder of old works, going out of the town, have been strengthened, and guns placed there likewise. People will think differently, whether the hostile preparation throughout the country, and the menaces of blood and slaughter, made this necessary; but I am to do my duty.

It gives me pleasure that you are endeavoring at a cordial reconciliation with the mother country, which, from what has transpired, I have despaired of. Nobody wishes better success to such measures than myself. I have endeavored to be a mediator, if I could establish a foundation to work upon, and have strongly urged it to people here to pay for the tea, and send a proper memorial to the king, which would be a good beginning on their side, and give their friends the opportunity they seek to move in their support.

I do not believe that menaces, added to unfriendly proceedings, will have the effect which too many conceive. The spirit of the British nation was high when I left England, and such measures will not abate it. But I should hope that decency and moderation here would create the same disposition at home; and I ardently wish that the common enemies to both countries may see, to their disappointment, that these disputes between the mother country and the colonies have terminated like the quarrels of lovers, and increased the affection which they ought to bear to each other.

I am, Sir, your most obedient humble servant,

THOMAS GAGE.

inclose them in a letter to the committee of correspondence for the town of Boston, being the sentiments of the Congress on the matters referred to them by the committee, in their letter of the 29th of September last.

Resolved unanimously, That a memorial be prepared to the people of British America, stating to them the necessity of a firm, united, and invariable observation of the measures recommended by the Congress, as they tender the invaluable rights and liberties derived to them from the laws and constitution of their country.

OCTOBER 14, 1774.

The Congress met according to adjournment, and resuming the consideration of the subject under debate, made the following declaration and resolves:

Declaration of Rights.

Whereas, since the close of the last war, the British parliament, claiming a power, of right, to bind the people of America by statutes in all cases whatsoever, hath in some acts expressly imposed taxes on them, and in others, under various pretences, but in fact for the purpose of raising a revenue, hath imposed rates and duties payable in these colonies, established a board of commissioners, with unconstitutional powers, and extended the jurisdiction of courts of admiralty, not only for collecting the said duties, but for the trial of causes merely arising within the body of a county:

And whereas, in consequence of other statutes, judges, who before held only estates at will in their offices, have been made dependant on the crown alone for their salaries, and standing armies kept in times of peace: And whereas, it has lately been resolved in parliament, that by force of a statute, made in the thirty-fifth year of the reign of king Henry the eighth, colonists may be transported to England, and tried there upon accusations for treasons and misprisions, or concealments of treasons committed in the colonies, and by a late statute, such trials have been directed in cases therein mentioned:

And whereas, in the last session of parliament, three statutes were made; one entitled, "an act to discontinue in such manner and for such time as are therein mentioned, the landing and discharging, lading, or shipping of goods, wares, and merchandise, at the town, and within the harbor of Boston, in the province of Massachusetts Bay in North America;" another entitled, "an act for the better regulating the government of the province of Massachusetts Bay in New England;" and another entitled, "an act for the impartial administration of justice, in the cases of persons questioned for any act done by them in the execution of the law, or for the suppression of riots and tumults, in the province of the Massachusetts Bay in New England:" And another statute was then made, "for making more effectual provision for the government of the province of Quebec, &c." All which statutes are impolitic, unjust, and cruel, as well as unconstitutional, and most dangerous and destructive of American rights:

And whereas, assemblies have been frequently dissolved, contrary to the rights of the people, when they attempted to deliberate on grievances; and their dutiful, humble, loyal, and reasonable petitions to the crown for redress, have been repeatedly treated with contempt, by his majesty's ministers of state:

The good people of the several colonies of New Hampshire, Massachusetts Bay, Rhode Island and Providence Plantations, Connecticut, New York, New Jersey, Pennsylvania, Newcastle, Kent, and Sussex on Delaware, Maryland, Virginia, North Carolina, and South Carolina, justly alarmed at these arbitrary proceedings of parliament and administration, have severally elected, constituted, and appointed deputies to meet and sit in general congress, in the city of Philadelphia, in order to obtain such establishment, as that their religion, laws, and liberties, may not be subverted: Whereupon, the deputies so appointed being now assembled, in a full and free representation of these colonies, taking into their most serious consideration, the best means of attaining the ends aforesaid, do in the first place, as Englishmen, their ancestors, in like cases, have usually done, for effecting and vindicating their rights and liberties, declare,

That the inhabitants of the English colonies in North America, by the immutable laws of nature, the principles of the English constitution, and the several charters or compacts, have the following rights:

Resolved, N. C. D. 1. That they are entitled to life, liberty, and property: and they have never ceded to any sovereign power whatever, a right to dispose of either without their consent.

Resolved, N. C. D. 2. That our ancestors, who first settled these colonies, were, at the time of their emigration from the mother country, entitled to all the rights, liberties, and immunities of free and natural born subjects, within the realm of England.

Resolved, N. C. D. 3. That by such emigration they by no means forfeited, surrendered, or lost any of those rights, but that they were, and their descendants now are, entitled to the exercise and enjoyment of all such of them, as their local and other circumstances enable them to exercise and enjoy.

Resolved, 4. That the foundation of English liberty and of all free government, is, a right in the people to participate in their legislative council: and as the English colonists are not represented, and from their local and other circumstances cannot properly be represented in the British parliament, they are entitled to a free and exclusive power of legislation in their several provincial legislatures, where their right of representation can alone be preserved, in all cases of taxation and internal polity, subject only to the negative of their sovereign, in such manner as has been heretofore used and accustomed. But from the necessity of the case, and a regard to the mutual interests of both countries, we cheerfully consent to the operation of such acts of the British parliament, as are *bona fide*, restrained to the regulation of our external commerce, for the purpose of securing the commercial advantages of the whole empire to the mother country, and the commercial benefits of its respective members; excluding every idea of taxation internal or external, for raising a revenue on the subjects in America without their consent.

Resolved, N. C. D. 5. That the respective colonies are entitled to the common law of England, and more especially to the great and inestimable privilege of being tried by their peers of the vicinage, according to the course of that law.

Resolved, 6. That they are entitled to the benefit of such of the English statutes, as existed at the time of their colonization; and which they have, by experience, respectively found to be applicable to their several local and other circumstances.

Resolved, N. C. D. 7. That these, his majesty's colonies, are likewise entitled to all the immunities and privileges granted and confirmed to them by royal charters, or secured by their several codes of provincial laws.

Resolved, N. C. D. 8. That they have a right peaceably to assemble, consider of their grievances, and petition the king; and that all prosecutions, prohibitory proclamations, and commitments for the same, are illegal.

Resolved, N. C. D. 9. That the keeping a standing army in these colonies, in time of peace, without the consent of the legislature of that colony in which such army is kept, is against law.

Resolved, N. C. D. 10. It is indispensably necessary to good government, and rendered essential by the English constitution, that the constituent branches of the legislature be independent of each other; that, therefore, the exercise of legislative power in several colonies, by a council appointed during pleasure, by the crown, is unconstitutional, dangerous, and destructive to the freedom of American legislation.

All and each of which, the aforesaid deputies, in behalf of themselves and their constituents, do claim, demand, and insist on, as their indubitable rights and liberties; which cannot be legally taken from them, altered, or abridged by any power whatever, without their own consent, by their representatives in their several provincial legislatures.

In the course of our inquiry, we find many infringements and violations of the foregoing rights, which, from an ardent desire that harmony and mutual intercourse of affection and interest may be restored, we pass over for the present, and proceed to state such acts and measures as have been adopted since the last war, which demonstrate a system formed to enslave America.

Resolved, N. C. D. That the following acts of parliament are infringements and violations of the rights of the colonists; and that the repeal of them is essentially necessary, in order to restore harmony between Great Britain and the American colonies, viz.:

The several acts of 4 Geo. III. ch. 15. and ch. 34.—5 Geo. III. ch. 25.—6 Geo. III. ch. 52.—7 Geo. III. ch. 41. and ch. 46.—8 Geo. III. ch. 22. which impose duties for the purpose of raising a revenue in America, extend the power of the admiralty courts beyond their ancient limits, deprive the American subject of trial by jury, authorize the judges, certificate to indemnify the prosecutor from damages, that he might otherwise be liable to, requiring oppressive security from a claimant of ships and goods seized, before he shall be allowed to defend his property, and are subversive of American rights.

Also, 12 Geo. III. ch. 24. entitled, "an act for the better securing his majesty's dock-yards, magazines, ships, ammunition, and stores," which declares a new offence in America, and deprives the American subject of a constitutional trial by a jury of the vicinage, by authorizing the trial of any person charged with the committing any offence described in the said act out of the realm, to be indicted and tried for the same in any shire or county within the realm.

Also, the three acts passed in the last session of parliament, for stopping the port and blocking up the harbor of Boston, for altering the charter and government of Massachusetts Bay, and that which is entitled, "an act for the better administration of justice, &c."

Also, the act passed in the same session for establishing the Roman Catholic religion in the province of Quebec, abolishing the equitable system of English laws, and erecting a tyranny there, to the great danger, from so total a dissimilarity of religion, law, and government, of the neighboring British colonies, by the assistance of whose blood and treasure the said country was conquered from France.

Also, the act passed in the same session for the better providing suitable quarters for officers and soldiers in his majesty's service in North America.

Also, that the keeping a standing army in several of these colonies, in time of peace, without the consent of the legislature of that colony in which such army is kept, is against law.

To these grievous acts and measures Americans cannot submit: but in hopes their fellow subjects in Great Britain will, on a revision of them, restore us to that state, in which both countries found happiness and prosperity, we have, for the present, only resolved to pursue the following peaceable measures: 1. To enter into a non-importation, non-consumption, and non-exportation agreement or association. 2. To prepare an address to the people of Great Britain, and a memorial to the inhabitants of British America: And 3. To prepare a loyal address to his majesty, agreeable to resolutions already entered into.

Oct. 20, 1774.

The association being copied, was read and signed at the table, and is as follows:

Non-Importation Covenant.

We, his majesty's most loyal subjects, the delegates of the several colonies of New Hampshire, Massachusetts Bay, Rhode Island, Connecticut, New York, New Jersey, Pennsylvania, the three lower counties of New Castle, Kent and Sussex, on Delaware, Maryland, Virginia, North Carolina, and South Carolina, deputed to represent them in a Continental Congress, held in the city of Philadelphia, on the 5th day of September, 1774, avowing our allegiance to his majesty, our affection and regard for our fellow-subjects in Great Britain and elsewhere, affected with the deepest anxiety, and most alarming apprehensions, at those grievances and distresses, with which his majesty's American subjects are oppressed; and having taken under our most serious deliberation, the state of the whole continent, find, that the present unhappy situation of our affairs is occasioned by a ruinous system of colony administration, adopted by the British ministry about the year 1763, evidently calculated for enslaving these colonies, and, with them, the British empire. In prosecution of which system, various acts of parliament have been passed, for raising a revenue in America, for depriving the American subjects, in many instances, of the constitutional trial by jury, exposing their lives to danger, by directing a new and illegal trial beyond the seas, for crimes alleged to have been committed in America: and in prosecution of the same system, several late, cruel and oppressive acts have been passed, respecting the town of Boston and the Massachusetts Bay, and also an act for extending the province of Quebec, so as to border on the western frontiers of these colonies, establishing an arbitrary government therein, and discouraging the settlement of British subjects in that wide extended country; thus, by the influence of evil principles and ancient prejudices, to dispose the inhabitants to act with hostility against the free Protestant colonies, whenever a wicked ministry shall choose to direct them.

To obtain redress of these grievances, which threaten destruction to the lives, liberty, and property of his majesty's subjects, in North America, we are of opinion, that a non-importation, non-consumption, and non-exportation agreement, faithfully adhered to, will prove the most speedy, effectual, and peaceable measure: and, therefore, we do, for ourselves, and the inhabitants of the several colonies, whom we represent, firmly agree and associate, under the sacred ties of virtue, honor, and love of our country, as follows:

1. That from and after the first day of December next, we will not import, into British America, from Great Britain or Ireland, any goods, wares or merchandise whatsoever, or from any other place, any such goods, wares or merchandise, as shall have been exported from Great Britain or Ireland; nor will we, after that day, import any East India tea from any part of the world; nor any molasses, syrups, paneles, coffee, or pimento, from the British plantations or from Dominica; nor wines from Madeira, or the Western Islands; nor foreign indigo.

2. We will neither import nor purchase, any slave imported after the first day of December next; after which time, we will wholly discontinue the slave trade, and will neither be concerned in it ourselves, nor will we hire our vessels, nor sell our commodities or manufactures to those who are concerned in it.

3. As a non-consumption agreement, strictly adhered to, will be an effectual security for the observation of the non-importation, we, as above, solemnly agree and associate, that from this day, we will not purchase or use

any tea, imported on account of the East India company, or any on which a duty hath been or shall be paid; and from and after the first day of March next, we will not purchase or use any East India tea whatever; nor will we, nor shall any person for or under us, purchase or use any of those goods, wares, or merchandise, we have agreed not to import, which we shall know, or have cause to suspect, were imported after the first day of December, except such as come under the rules and directions of the tenth article hereafter mentioned.

4. The earnest desire we have not to injure our fellow subjects in Great Britain, Ireland, or the West Indies, induces us to suspend a non-exportation, until the tenth day of September, 1775; at which time, if the said acts and parts of acts of the British parliament, hereinafter mentioned, are not repealed, we will not directly or indirectly, export any merchandise or commodity whatsoever to Great Britain, Ireland, or the West Indies, except rice to Europe.

5. Such as are merchants, and use the British and Irish trade, will give orders, as soon as possible, to their factors, agents, and correspondents, in Great Britain and Ireland, not to ship any goods to them, on any pretence whatsoever, as they cannot be received in America; and if any merchant, residing in Great Britain or Ireland, shall, directly or indirectly, ship any goods, wares or merchandise, for America, in order to break the said nonimportation agreement, or in any manner contravene the same, on such unworthy conduct being well attested, it ought to be made public; and, on the same being so done, we will not, from thenceforth, have any commercial connexion with such merchant.

6. That such as are owners of vessels will give positive orders to their captains or masters, not to receive on board their vessels any goods prohibited by the said non-importation agreement, on pain of immediate dismission from their service.

7. We will use our utmost endeavors to improve the breed of sheep, and increase their number to the greatest extent; and to that end, we will kill them as seldom as may be, especially those of the most profitable kind; nor will we export any to the West Indies or elsewhere; and those of us, who are or may become overstocked with, or can conveniently spare any sheep, will dispose of them to our neighbors, especially to the poorer sort, on moderate terms.

8. We will, in our several stations, encourage frugality, economy, and industry, and promote agriculture, arts, and the manufactures of this country, especially that of wool; and will discountenance and discourage every species of extravagance and dissipation, especially all horse-racing, and all kinds of gaming, cock-fighting, exhibitions of shows, plays, and other expensive diversions and entertainments; and on the death of any relation or friend, none of us, or any of our families, will go into any further mourning dress, than a black crape or ribbon on the arm or hat, for gentlemen, and a black ribbon or necklace for ladies, and we will discontinue the giving of gloves and scarves at funerals.

9. Such as are venders of goods or merchandise will not take advantage of the scarcity of goods, that may be occasioned by this association, but will sell the same at the rates we have been respectively accustomed to do for twelve months last past. And if any vender of goods or merchandise shall sell any such goods on higher terms, or shall, in any manner, or by any device whatsoever, violate or depart from this agreement, no person ought, nor will any of us deal with any such person, or his or her factor or agent, at any time thereafter, for any commodity whatever.

10. In case any merchant, trader, or other person, shall import any goods or merchandise, after the first day of December, and before the first day of February next, the same ought, forthwith, at the election of the owner, to be either re-shipped, or delivered up to the committee of the county or town wherein they shall be imported, to be stored at the risk of the importer, until the non-importation agreement shall cease, or be sold under the direction of the committee aforesaid; and in the last mentioned case, the owner or owners of such goods shall be reimbursed out of the sales, the first cost and charges; the profit, if any, to be applied towards relieving and employing such poor inhabitants of the town of Boston, as are immediate sufferers by the Boston port-bill; and a particular account of all goods so returned, stored, or sold, to be inserted in the public papers; and if any goods or merchandise shall be imported after the said first day of February, the same ought forthwith to be sent back again, without breaking any of the packages thereof.

11. That a committee be chosen in every county, city, and town, by those who are qualified to vote for representatives in the legislature, whose business it shall be, attentively to observe the conduct of all persons touching this association; and when it shall be made to appear, to the satisfaction of a majority of any such committee, that any person within the limits of their appointment, has violated this association, that such majority do, forthwith, cause the truth of the case to be published in the gazette; to the end, that all such foes to the rights of British America may be publicly known, and universally contemned as the enemies of American liberty; and thenceforth, we, respectively, will break off all dealings with him or her.

12. That the committees of correspondence, in the respective colonies, do frequently inspect the entries of their custom-houses, and inform each other, from time to time, of the true state thereof, and of every other material circumstance that may occur relative to this association.

13. That all manufactures of this country be sold at reasonable prices, so that no undue advantage be taken of a future scarcity of goods.

14. And we do further agree and resolve, that we will have no trade, commerce, dealings, or intercourse whatsoever, with any colony or province, in North America, which shall not accede to, or which shall hereafter violate this association, but will hold them as unworthy of the rights of freemen, and as inimical to the liberties of their country.

And we do solemnly bind ourselves and our constituents, under the ties aforesaid, to adhere to this association, until such parts of the several acts of parliament passed since the close of the last war, as impose or continue duties on tea, wine, molasses, syrups, paneles, coffee, sugar, pimento, indigo, foreign paper, glass, and painters' colors, imported into America, and extend the powers of the admiralty courts beyond their ancient limits, deprive the American subject of trial by jury, authorize the judge's certificate to indemnify the prosecutor from damages that he might otherwise be liable to, from a trial by his peers, require oppressive security from a claimant of ships or goods seized, before he shall be allowed to defend his property, are repealed—and until that part of the act of the 12th G. 3. ch. 24, entitled "an act for the better securing his majesty's dock-yards, magazines, ships, ammunition and stores," by which any persons charged with committing any of the offences therein described, in America, may be tried in any shire or county within the realm, is repealed—and until the four acts, passed the last session of parliament, viz.: that for stopping the port and blocking up the harbor of Boston—that for altering the charter and government of the Massachusetts Bay—and that which is entitled "an act for the better administration of justice, &c."—and that "for extending the limits of Quebec, &c." are repealed. And we recommend it to the provincial conventions, and to the committees in their respective colonies, to establish such further regulations as they may think proper, for carrying into execution this association.

The foregoing association being determined upon by the Congress, was ordered to be subscribed by the several members thereof; and thereupon, we have hereunto set our respective names accordingly.

IN CONGRESS, PHILADELPHIA, OCTOBER 24,

Signed, PEYTON RANDOLPH, *President.*

New Hampshire . . . . . . JOHN SULLIVAN,
  NATHANIEL FOLSOM.

Massachusetts Bay . . . . THOMAS CUSHING,
  SAMUEL ADAMS,
  JOHN ADAMS,
  ROBERT TREAT PAINE.

Rhode Island . . . . STEPHEN HOPKINS,
  SAMUEL WARD.

Connecticut . . . . ELIPHALET DYER,
  ROGER SHERMAN,
  SILAS DEANE.

New York . . . . ISAAC LOW,
  JOHN ALSOP,
  JOHN JAY,
  JAMES DUANE,
  WILLIAM FLOYD,

New York.........Henry Wisner,
                 S. Boerum,
                 Philip Livingston.

New Jersey........James Kinsey,
                  William Livingston,
                  Stephen Crane,
                  Richard Smith,
                  John De Hart.

Pennsylvania.......Joseph Galloway,
                   John Dickinson,
                   Charles Humphreys,
                   Thomas Mifflin,
                   Edward Biddle,
                   John Morton,
                   George Ross.

New Castle, &c.......Cæsar Rodney,
                     Thomas M'Kean,
                     George Read.

Maryland..........Matthew Tilghman,
                  Thomas Johnson,
                  William Paca,
                  Samuel Chase.

Virginia...........Richard Henry Lee,
                   George Washington,
                   P. Henry, Jr.,
                   Richard Bland,
                   Benjamin Harrison,
                   Edmund Pendleton.

North Carolina......William Hooper,
                    Joseph Hewes,
                    R. Caswell.

South Carolina......Henry Middleton,
                    Thomas Lynch,
                    Christopher Gadsden,
                    John Rutledge,
                    Edward Rutledge.

May 11, 1775.

Mr. Hancock laid before the Congress a letter from the Provincial Congress of Massachusetts Bay, together with certain resolutions formed by said Congress, and a copy of a letter, sent by said Congress to their agent in England, and an address to the inhabitants of Great Britain, on the late engagement between the troops under Gen. Gage, and the inhabitants of Massachusetts Bay; and also a number of depositions, duly attested, relative to the commencement of said hostilities, all which were read.

Ordered, That the secretary have the depositions and the address to the inhabitants of Great Britain published.

Resolved, *N. C. D.* That the Congress will, on Monday next, resolve itself into a committee of the whole, to take into consideration the state of America.

Ordered, That the letter from the Provincial Congress of Massachusetts Bay, be referred to that committee.

JUNE 2, 1775.

The president laid before the Congress a letter from the Provincial Convention of Massachusetts Bay, dated May 16, which was read, setting forth the difficulties they labor under for want of a regular form of government, and as they and the other colonies are now compelled to raise an army to defend themselves from the butcheries and devastations of their implacable enemies, which renders it still more necessary to have a regular established government, requesting the Congress to favor them with "explicit advice respecting the taking up and exercising the powers of civil government," and declaring their readiness to "submit to such a general plan as the Congress may direct for the colonies, or make it their great study to establish such a form of government there, as shall not only promote their advantage, but the union and interest of all America."

Ordered, To lie on the table for farther consideration.

Doct. Benjamin Church being directed by the convention of Massachusetts Bay, to confer with the Congress respecting such matters, as may be necessary to the defence of that colony, and particularly the state of the army therein,

Ordered, That he be introduced.

After he withdrew, an express arriving with despatches from Massachusetts Bay, the president laid before the Congress letters from the conventions of that colony, and New Hampshire, also from Gov. Trumbull, which were read.

JUNE 3, 1775.

The letter from the convention of Massachusetts, dated the 16th May, being again read,

Resolved, That a committee of five persons be chosen to consider the same, and report what in their opinion is the proper advice to be given to that convention.

The following persons were chosen by ballot, to compose that committee, viz.: Mr. J. Rutledge, Mr. Johnson, Mr. Jay, Mr. Wilson and Mr. Lee.

JUNE 7, 1775.

The committee appointed to prepare advice in answer to the letter from the convention of Massachusetts Bay, brought in their report, which was read, and ordered to lie on the table for consideration.

JUNE 9, 1775.

The report of the committee, on the letter from the convention of Massachusetts Bay, being again read, the Congress came to the following resolution:

Resolved, That no obedience being due to the act of parliament for altering the charter of the colony of Massachusetts Bay, nor to a governor, or a lieutenant governor, who will not observe the directions of, but endeavor to subvert that charter, the governor and lieutenant governor of that colony are to be considered as absent, and their offices vacant; and as there is no council there, and the inconveniences, arising from the suspension of the powers of government, are intolerable, especially at a time when Gen. Gage hath actually levied war, and is carrying on hostilities, against his majesty's peaceable and loyal subjects of that colony; that, in order to conform, as near as may be, to the spirit and substance of the charter, it be recommended to the provincial convention, to write letters to the inhabitants of the several places, which are entitled to representation in assembly, requesting them to choose such representatives, and that the assembly, when chosen, do elect councillors; and that such assembly, or council, exercise the powers of government, until a governor, of his majesty's appointment, will consent to govern the colony according to its charter.

Ordered, That the president transmit a copy of the above to the convention of Massachusetts Bay.

JUNE 14, 1775.

A letter from the convention of New York, dated 10th instant, respecting a vessel which is stopped there, on suspicion of having on board provisions for the army and navy at Boston, was read and referred to the delegates of Massachusetts Bay, Connecticut and New York.

JUNE 27, 1775.

A letter from the convention of Massachusetts Bay, received by express, was laid before the Congress, and read.

MISCELLANEOUS PAPERS.

Gov. Gage's Proclamation.

PROVINCE OF THE MASSACHUSETTS BAY.

By the Governor.

A PROCLAMATION.

WHEREAS, a number of persons unlawfully assembled at Cambridge, in the month of October last, calling themselves a Provincial Congress, did, in the most open and daring terms, assume to themselves the powers and authority of government, independent of, and repugnant to his majesty's government legally and constitutionally established within this province, and tending utterly to subvert the same; and did, amongst other unlawful proceedings, take upon themselves to resolve and direct a new and unconstitutional regulation of the militia, in high derogation of his majesty's royal prerogative; and also to elect and appoint Henry Gardner, Esq., of Stow, to be receiver general, in the room of Harrison Gray, Esq., then, and still, legally holding and executing that office; and also to order and direct the moneys granted to his majesty, to be paid into the hands of the said Henry Gardner, and not to the said Harrison Gray, Esq.; and further earnestly to recommend to the inhabitants of the province to oblige and compel the several constables and collectors to comply with and execute the said directions, contrary to their oaths, and against the plain and express rules and directions of the law; all which proceedings have a most dangerous tendency to ensnare his majesty's subjects, the inhabitants of this province, and draw them into perjuries, riots, sedition, treason and rebellion:

For the prevention of which evils, and the calamitous consequences thereof, I have thought it my duty to issue this proclamation, hereby earnestly exhorting, and in his majesty's name strictly prohibiting all his liege subjects within this province, from complying, in any degree, with the said requisitions, recommendations, directions, or resolves of the aforesaid unlawful assembly, as they regard his majesty's highest displeasure, and would avoid the pains and penalties of the law. And I do hereby charge and command all justices of the peace, sheriffs, constables, collectors, and other officers, in their several departments, to be vigilant and faithful in the execution and discharge of their duty in their respective offices, agreeable to the well-known established laws of the land; and to the utmost of their power, by all lawful ways and means, to discountenance, discourage and prevent a compliance with such dangerous resolves of the abovementioned, or any other unlawful assembly whatever.

Given at Boston, this 10th day of November, in the fifteenth year of the reign of his majesty George the third, by the grace of God, of Great Britain, France and Ireland, king, defender of the faith, &c., Anno Domini, 1774.

THOMAS GAGE.

By his Excellency's command,

THOMAS FLUCKER, *Secretary.*

God save the King.

————

The Committee of New York to the Provincial Congress.

NEW YORK, APRIL 19, 1775.

GENTLEMEN:—The following very interesting accounts were this day received by the snow General Johnson, Capt. Dean, in thirty-one days from England. The writer is a person of undoubted veracity, and has the best means of intelligence, who may be depended on, having for these twelve months past always furnished the most certain advices of the ministry's designs, &c. In consideration of which, and the present posture of affairs in America in general, but more particularly on account of the situation of your province, and the consequences to which it is more immediately liable, it is thought an indispensable duty to give you this late advice. It is unfeignedly wished that you may improve it to your own safety, as well as to the advantage of the whole continent.

We have the honor to be, with great respect,

Your obedient servants,

HENRY REMSEN, *Deputy Chairman.*

To the Hon. Provincial Congress.

————

Extract of Letters, &c.

LONDON, FEBRUARY 24, 1775.

Providence seems to have placed me here, in order to give you the earliest intelligence of the most interesting affairs, relative to the colonies.

To my great astonishment, I have now before me an act for blocking up the other colonies; and another called the black act, to prevent the fisheries. The whole nation seems to be deeply affected at such an enormous crime, which is supposed to be done at the request of the king and his creatures. God forbid, that you should be intimidated at this iniquitous law, which is calculated to ruin what was a mutual benefit to you and us. This must convince you what you are to expect, if you submit to the most shocking set of men that England can produce. You now see their humanity. Rouse up then with a just indignation, and exercise your militia. Watch your governor and council. The new assembly is to be composed of such creatures as will give up the people's rights, and join in the most horrid plot against them. What a melancholy reflection, that the riches and trade of a great nation should be abused and turned to the destruction of themselves and the colonies!

In short, the king is determined to be as absolute as the French king, and with the most obstinate head and bad heart, has set himself against the people, whom he will not see, keeping himself retired from his subjects, in pride and ignorance. He has discarded men of veracity from all places of profit and honor, and filled their offices with a set of the most abandoned villains on earth. These are they who advised him to break his oath with the people, for which they are despised by the nation. If you hold out a few months, England will rise and do you justice, as well as relieve themselves from those accursed tyrants, who want to corrupt you, and deprive you of both liberty and property.

There are two hundred and eighty-five members of parliament, who are all paid with the people's money to vote whatever Lord North proposes, and he has his lesson from eight more, who compose a club, that meets in the most private manner, in the night, at Mrs. Keens, near the palace, where they have a box, which contains the papers that pass between his majesty and them. The king overlooks their schemes and corrects them, as well as gives orders how to proceed for the future. Hutchinson is consulted, and to their shame, Governor Colden, Penn, and Martin, who have written such letters to Lord Dartmouth, that the king has appointed them to meet at New York, in order to join with your other lying spirits in betraying the colonies. To complete which villany, Lord North has made a motion in parliament, as if he intended to promote peace with the colonies; but it is to deceive them, and the people of England too. It is intended to defeat the salutary advice of the Congress, which does credit to British America!

Set the press immediately to work, and publish to the world the wicked designs of the king and his councillors; that you despise their slavish schemes, and are determined to preserve your laws and religion.

Encourage the brave people of Massachusetts Bay to act worthy of their noble ancestors!

I have the pleasure to assure you, that the noble lords with whom I have conversed, all join you in contempt of the junto here. You are desired to let the colonies know that there is a deep plot formed to divide them, and deceive the people into a compliance. But tell them that you want not their trade nor protection at the expense of your liberty.

You will see, by the papers, the treatment Lord Chatham's plan met with. Those lords, who advised the king to declare you rebels, and appointed

94

Messrs. Hancock, Adams, &c., &c., have gone so far as to say that Chatham shall fall a sacrifice to their designs, &c.

I know there is public virtue among you. I know your fondness for England will not let you believe the wicked designs that are meditating against you; but I do now, in the presence of God, warn you that the king has no good intentions towards you, but what you oblige him, by your own wisdom and virtue, to have. Take care of yourselves, and act as the wise and brave have done in all ages when oppressed by tyrants. Resist unto blood, all who attempt to betray you.

The parliament have registered Colden's and Penn's letters; look to them, and see for yourselves. Believe the court your worst enemies. Be much on your guard.

Yesterday, Doct. Fothergill and Mr. Barclay were so pressed in spirit, that they went to Lord North, and told him that the bill for prohibiting the fishery, was so horrid and inhuman an act, that the nation would rise and oppose it: and that if it did pass into a law, it would be a scandal to humanity, and perhaps occasion a revolt. They plead two hours with him, but to no purpose.

The bill is to be read a third time on Tuesday; so that in five days this horrid bill passes into a law, without any further consideration. Oh, America! Oh, England!

The ministry, in order to quiet the mob, ordered an inflammatory pamphlet to be burnt at Guildhall, which drew off the people, whilst the bill passed in parliament.

A report is sent into the city that the transports are stopped. This is to quiet the merchants. But the officers are gone down in private coaches, of other people, and America is to be divided and driven into compliance, before England is apprised of it.

Lord North has just given out that he will resign, and at the same time says that he fears nothing from the people, unless it be the breaking of his coach doors, or some such trifle, and no resistance of importance from the city, only a clamor, which he has often experienced. He expects that this manœuvre will quiet the people on both sides of the water.

Goods are shipped in the transports with the officers' baggage, marked *Rex*, and under the protection of the king's troops, who are to land them, and protect the trade.

North Carolina is to be a store house, it is said. Support the committee, and watch the officers of the customs, &c. Your friends are afraid that you will be surprised into compliance. The offers of peace were only to raise the stocks, which had fallen. They are now four per cent. higher on account of the report.

The council sat up all night, in order to find out ways and means to conquer Virginia, and procure tobacco. Great offers will be made to those who will raise it, &c.

Men of large fortunes are afraid to oppose government, least the bank should fail, which is said to be in danger.

The interest of the year 1774, is not paid.

Many of the people are your most hearty friends, but the king is your greatest enemy. Be not deceived by his low cunning; act wisely, and the wicked plot will break on the heads of those who want to destroy you.

The king is his own secretary; he gets up at six o'clock every morning, to send off his box, with remarks, on a bit of paper tied round each order: four of the ablest lawyers are constantly with him, whose business it is to advise and search for precedents, to screen his head, and throw the blame on the parliament.

Two millions have been squandered in bribery and corruption. The crown has nothing to fear but the hunger of the poor.

A steady adherence to the proceedings of the Congress will save England and America.

Beware of Gov. Penn, who has had offers made him to comply with the designs of the court.

Send this to Boston immediately. Mr. Hancock's lands are already divided among the officers.

Lord Dartmouth is your bitter enemy, and determined to destroy the liberties of America.

All the wise wish that you may attend to the advice of the Congress.

MARCH 1, 1775.

Part of the troops now ordered for embarkation here and Ireland, are to rendezvous at New York, to make it a place of arms, securing the defection of that province, from the general alliance in the cause of freedom and every thing that is dear to man; and to prevent the communication between Virginia, Maryland, and the other southern colonies, with New England; when Gen. Gage, with such assistance as he may get from New York, is to subdue those colonies by a garrison and place of arms, with the assistance of Quebec, to rule with a rod of iron all the slaves of America.

Without the concurrence of New York, this scheme can never be carried into execution, of which every gentleman and man of knowledge in this kingdom is fully convinced; therefore, on your virtue, in a great measure, it depends, whether America shall be free, or be reduced to the most abject and oppressive servitude, worse than that of Egyptian bondage, in which you must inevitably be involved, if you lend your aid to enslave your brethren in the other colonies.

I have to inform you that the bill for preventing the four colonies and provinces of New England from fishing, getting any provisions from the other colonies, or carrying on any commerce whatever to any part of the world, except to Great Britain, Ireland, or the British West Indies, will finally pass the House of Commons to-morrow, and is to take place the first of next July. You may also depend, that in a few days, another bill will be brought in to prohibit any of the other colonies from carrying on any trade whatever with each other, or to any other part of the world, except to Great

Britain, Ireland, or the British West Indies, which will probably take place in July also: therefore, you will act accordingly, and let this be publicly known.

LONDON, MARCH 1ST, 1775.

The measures of the ministry will, I hope, do more towards uniting the colonies, than any efforts of America itself. You will easily perceive their wicked intentions to divide, as well as their designs after that hoped for division. They have high hopes of success, from the last accounts from New York. I trust the people of that province will soon displace those rascally and treacherous tories in your assembly, who dare thus negatively encourage the system of despotism now adopted for your government. The wisdom of the Congress, and the firmness of the people, give the strongest assurances of future conduct. Several names are made use of here as authorities to warrant the defection of America. Pray print this short hint for the observation of the honest men among you. I need not endeavor to expose the baseness or folly of the present men in office, for they take care to do it themselves.

The foregoing were at first, intended only to be communicated to the inhabitants of Massachusetts Bay, but on more consideration, it was judged best to inform those of Connecticut also, leaving them to forward the account to Concord with the utmost despatch.

Joseph Hawley to Thomas Cushing.

NORTHAMPTON, FEB. 22, 1775.

DEAR SIR:—Since I left Cambridge, I have had many thoughts on the state of this province, and the continent; and suffer me to say, Sir, that the time is in fact arrived, when we are to drop all chimerical plans, and in our contemplations thoroughly to think down and pervade every step that is proposed for practice; to judge of its practicability, and, as far as possible, to view all its consequences. With this conviction, I have been most seriously contemplating the commission and most important trust of our committee of safety, and especially that branch of it which relates to their mustering the minute men and others of the militia, when they shall judge that the late acts of parliament, viz.: the regulation act, and the murder act, are attempted to be carried into execution by force. A most critical, most important, most arduous trust this. Here let me observe, that the soldiers, when thus mustered by the said committee, who have this power devolved on them by the representative body of the province, will suppose it is their duty to fight; they therefore, will only deliberate how to fight to advantage. They will not consider the question, whether or not the time is that they ought to fight;

they will suppose that the continent have devolved the resolution of that question upon this province, and that this province have devolved it on the committee of safety, and that the committee, by calling them, have decided it. They will judge, that if they should decline fighting when they are called for that intent, their honor and courage will be impeached. The soldier therefore, will probably, at all events, fall on. Thus, hostilities will be commenced; which we must suppose, will, thenceforward, continue, and be most vigorously pushed, until the fate of America be decided: hostilities in which we must have the vigorous and persevering assistance of the other colonies, or we must sink under them. Suffer me then to ask, whether it will not be the height of presumption to enter on such a scene with no other assurance or security of such effectual and continued aids as will be absolutely necessary, than what is contained in a resolution of about six lines, and they consisting of terms and expressions not the most definite, or of certain and precise meaning? The words used in the resolution to state the case wherein hostilities are to be commenced, are, in my opinion, by far too loose, to wit: "when the acts shall be attempted to be carried into execution by force," as well as the words made use to secure the aid of the colonies, to wit: "all America ought to support them in such opposition," not that they will actually support them, but a mere declaration that it would be reasonable and just that such support should be afforded. Is this a treaty offensive and defensive of sufficient precision to make us secure of the effectual aid of the other colonies in a war with Great Britain? Besides, by whom was this declaration or engagement, such as it is, made? Was it by delegates specially authorized and instructed to make an engagement of this sort? Who knows whether the respective constituent bodies will avow this declaration? Moreover, it ought to be well considered, with regard to all the other colonies, excepting Connecticut and Rhode Island, what situation they are in to fulfil an engagement of this sort, in case they were generally disposed to come into it. Do'nt we all say, that this province cannot levy, subsist, and pay an army sufficient to afford us any hopes of present resistance, without a legislature which the people will cheerfully submit to? Is not that precisely the case with all the other colonies, the two above mentioned excepted? Have they not as much to do to assume a new government, every one of them, in order to levy, subsist, and pay their respective quotas of an army, as we have? Nay, would not the success of an attempt of this sort be more precarious in every one of them than in this province, as their people cannot be supposed so thoroughly to apprehend the necessity of it as ours may be supposed to do? Are they oppressed and affected with the new measures as we are? Will not their governors obstruct and labor to embarrass every attempt of the kind as much as ours? Will they not have as many friends to government to assist them, as there are here? Can it, therefore, be much short of madness and infatuation in us, to enter on a scene of this sort in the present state of affairs? Nay, is it not obvious, therefore, that actual hostilities must be suspended, if possible, until the continent, by their representatives, shall, in the most explicit manner, in fact say, that the moment is actually arrived when the scene shall open? No one, I presume, will say, that it will be sound policy for us to enter on hostilities with only some prospects of such donations from the other colonies to support the war as have been made and are making for the support of the poor of Boston. Does it not infinitely import us, to admit these and many more considerations into our minds before we enter upon lasting, most important hostilities? When once the blow is struck it must be followed, and we must conquer, or all is lost forever. If we are not supported, perseveringly supported, by divers other colonies, can we expect any thing else, than, in a short time, to fall a prey to our enemies? May God, make us consider it. Should large numbers of men come voluntary into the province service, unless they should have been regularly raised and proper provision made for their subsistence, and magazines of ammunition provided by the colony from whence they come, will they do any more than just look on us, turn about, and hasten home as fast as they came? In order, therefore, for the necessary establishment of auxiliary troops, as I said before, must not the other colonies assume new forms of government as well as we? Is it to be supposed that all this can be done suddenly? We know, that according to the present respective constitutions, nothing of the sort above mentioned, to wit: the levying, subsisting, and paying of troops, can be done in a governmental way. When we shall have once made the hostile attack, we are, thenceforward, to look for nothing but fire and sword, until we have conquered or are ourselves vanquished. Therefore, if we, by order of our committee of safety, should begin the attack, and so bring on hostilities before the general express consent of the colonies that hostilities are altogether unavoidable, and that the time to commence them is absolutely arrived, and that we are actually ready, I conceive that there will be infinite hazard that the other governments will say, that we have unnecessarily and madly plunged into war, and therefore, must get out of the scrape as we can, and we shall have no other aid from them, only some warm people who will resort to us in a fit of zeal, and soon return home again as fast as they came, without affording us any real service, but will leave us in a worse state than we should have been if they had never come. I know your concern will be, that if we proceed in this deliberate way, the spirit of our people will evaporate and be lost. But let me assure you, that there is no danger of that. If I can make any judgment, all the danger is, on the other hand, that our people will rashly and headily rush into hostilities before they can be upheld and supported: they will consequently fail of success: the tide will then turn: a very low ebb will succeed the high tide of flood: they will then give all up: and the good cause will be lost forever.

I beg of you, therefore, as you love your country, to use your utmost influence with our committee of safety, that our people be not mustered, and that hostilities be not commenced, until we have the express, categorical decision of the continent, that the time is absolutely come that hostilities ought to begin, and that they will support us in continuing them. As to the courts, we must embarrass and retard them, by preventing suitors, jurors, witnesses, &c., going into them, by all ways and means, that I have not time now to explain. A sharp eye must be kept on them, that we may fully know the success of the attempts to establish the regulation so far as it respects the courts. Sir, I think it of much importance to do this: as you regard your own life and your usefulness to your country, you should most attentively watch all the steps and proceedings of the court now sitting at Boston. If they get a grand jury, then they will probably obtain indictments of high treason, and indictments will not be procured without a view and respect to arrests and commitments, convictions, hangings, drawings, and quarterings. What your chance will be I need not tell you.

I am, Sir, with most sincere regard,

Your most obedient humble servant,

JOSEPH HAWLEY.

Hon. Thomas Cushing.

Inhabitants of Montreal to the Committee of Safety.

MONTREAL, APRIL 28, 1775.

GENTLEMEN:—We have received your letter of the 21st of February, by Mr Brown, and see clearly the great injustice that has been done you. We deeply feel the sorrows and afflictions of our suffering brethren ; and sincerely wish it was in our power to afford you effectual relief; but alas! we are more the objects of pity and compassion than yourselves, who are now suffering under the heavy hand of power; deprived, as we are, of the common right of the miserable, to complain. You have numbers, strength, and a common cause to support you in your opposition : we are still more divided here, by our interests, than by our religion, language, and manners. The apprehension of evils to come upon us, in a short time, from the unlimited power of the governor, strikes all opposition dead: indeed, few in this colony dare vent their griefs ; but groan in silence, and dream of *lettres de cachet,* confiscations, and imprisonments ; offering up their fervent prayers to the throne of grace, to prosper your righteous cause, which alone will free us from those jealous fears and apprehensions that rob us of our peace.

In a word, were the British inhabitants of this widely extended province, united in their sentiments, we have neither numbers nor wealth sufficient to do you any essential service. We must, therefore, cast ourselves into the arms of our sister colonies, relying upon the wisdom, vigor, and firmness of the general Continental Congress for our protection, hoping they will entertain no animosity or resentment against us because we cannot join them in the ensuing general Congress, which, were we to attempt, the Canadians would join with the government to frustrate.

You will please to bear in mind, that not only those who hold the helm of government, but also, all those who make wealth or ambition the chief objects of their pursuit, are professedly your enemies; and would be glad to reduce you to the same abject state, with themselves: nevertheless, the bulk of the people, both English and Canadians, are of quite contrary sentiments; and wish well to your cause; but dare not stir a finger to help you; being of no more estimation in the political machine, than the sailors are, in shaping the course or working the ship in which they sail. They may mutter and swear, but must obey: however, should government handle them too roughly, and arbitrarily attempt to force them upon dangerous and disagreeable service, to which they have already shewn an irreconcilable aversion, they may, perhaps, dearly repent it.

The case is quite different with their noblesse, or gentry. The pre-eminence given to their religion, together with a participation of honors and offices in common with the English, not only flatters their natural pride and vanity, but is regarded by them, as a mark of distinction and merit, that lays open their way to fortune. Of liberty, or law, they have not the least notion.

As to the savages that dwell round about us, doubtless there are some to be found among them, who, for the sake of plunder, would murder, burn, and destroy; but we conceive that their chiefs know their own interests better, than to interfere as a nation, in this family quarrel: for let which side will, prevail, they are sure, in that case, to be the victims.

We desire to know, whether English delegates would be accepted under the above named limitations; namely, without entering into the general association for the non-importation of goods from Great Britain, or the non-exportation of the produce of this colony, and the Indian countries above: and beg to be informed in what manner we can be serviceable to your cause, without bringing down ruin upon our own heads.

It may not be amiss just to hint, that the idea the Canadians seem to have of this colony, at present is, that it is to be a French government, holding under the crown of Great Britain; from which they mean to exclude every Englishman, save the governor and lieutenant governor.

We heartily wish our abilities to serve you were equal to our wills, and pray Heaven to prosper your generous purpose; and are, with the utmost consideration and feeling for your distresses,

Gentlemen, your most obedient,

And very humble servants, and fellow sufferers,

THOMAS WALKER,
JOHN WELLES,
JAMES PRICE,
WILLIAM HAYWOOD.

P. S. It is our earnest request, that this letter may not be now published, for fear of bad consequences to the subscribers.

Mrs. Bowdoin to the Committee of Safety.

DORCHESTER, JUNE 4, 1775.

GENTLEMEN:—Mr. Bowdoin has just received the enclosed deposition, and being in a very weak state, desires me to inform you, that for some time past, the Falkland, sloop of war, commanded by Capt. Linzey, has been cruising about the islands called Elizabeth islands, near Martha's Vineyard: that the said sloop's boats have, divers times, landed armed men on the said islands, who have abused the inhabitants, stove their boats, and by force taken away a considerable part of their property, as may more fully appear by the said deposition.

It is humbly apprehended, if about one hundred armed men were properly posted on the said islands, they would be a sufficient force to defend the inhabitants, and protect their stocks of cattle and sheep, which are very considerable, and which have, hitherto, every year, furnished divers parts of this colony with fat sheep and cattle for provisions, and particularly with a large quantity of wool for our home manufactures.

I beg leave to make this representation, that you may take such measures as your wisdom shall dictate; and am, most respectfully, in Mr. Bowdoin's behalf, who is part owner of one of said islands,

Gentlemen, your most obedient humble servant,

ELIZABETH BOWDOIN.

To the honorable Committee of Safety.

Deposition of Elisha Nye.

MAY 31, 1775.

Elisha Nye, innholder, living on one of the Elizabeth islands, commonly called Naushan, and near to Tarpolin Cove, testifieth and saith, that some time about the 5th of May, the sloop of war called the Falkland, commanded by Capt. Linzey, came into the cove, and as soon as the vessel had come to anchor, the captain came on shore with his boat's crew, all armed, and came to the house, and said unto the deponent, "you need not be scared," upon which, he told him it was enough to scare any body to see so many men come on shore armed; and the women were all fled, and to where he knew not; upon which, Capt. Linzey told him to call them in, for he did not mean to hurt any body—upon which promise, I and my family were satisfied. Soon after that, the captain asked me to walk with him; which he complied with; and in the course of the walk, he demanded to know what stock I had, and added, to tell him right, for if I did not, he would take all that he met: upon which, I gave him the account. Then the captain told me, the deponent, if I sold any of them, he would take the remainder by force: upon which, I told him, if he were here when they were fit for market, he might have them, paying the price I used to have. Soon after, he went to Rhode Island, and returned back in a few days; after which, he used to pass and repass the island almost every day, mostly in company with the doctor of the ship, leaving down the fence repeatedly, which let the cattle often mix together, which I told the doctor was a great damage: the doctor's answer was, "then you may put it up yourselves, for I will not;" and he often talked in an abusive, insulting manner, that he, the doctor, would soon take what he wanted, without any pay.

On the 26th instant, a sloop came into the cove, with about twenty passengers, men, women, and children, in great distress for provisions, and made application to me for supplies. Capt. Linzey knowing that, his boat having boarded her, sent his boat on shore, and forbade my letting them have any. Then I advised them to apply to Capt. Linzey, and see if they could not prevail upon him to let them have some; accordingly they went; afterwards, the captain of the sloop told me, that he absolutely refused them, and said, " damn the dog that would let them have any! and if they were not gone immediately, he would sink them:" upon which, they set sail immediately without any supplies. And further, the deponent declareth, that the doctor came on shore, and said, that the captain's orders were, that I should go with him, the said doctor, and destroy all the boats belonging to the island. I told him I could not go upon such business as that; he said he would send me on board the ship if I did not go; upon which, I found I must comply, and accordingly went with him, and saw him, the doctor, stave three boats.

On the 29th, about eight o'clock, in the evening, he, the said doctor, came on shore, and told me he had come for my sheep, upon which, I told him they were out in the pasture, and I could not get them into the pen it being dark, but would fetch them in as early in the morning as he pleased; the answer from the doctor was, " damn you! what did you turn them out for?" the reason, I told him, was, that they had got out their own sheep, and did not say any thing about when they should want mine, and I thought it best the sheep should be let out to feed; upon which, the said doctor said to me, " damn you! go on board the ship and I'll see what they were turned out for;" I told him, I would not, but would go and try to get the sheep up; he said " well, damn you! make haste!" and swung his sword over my head,—but upon trial I found it so dark, I could not get them in; and, on my return, was informed that he, the doctor, had sent on board for more help to carry me and my brother on board the ship; upon which, with the abuses and threats I had received before, I thought it time to make my escape, which I did, to the main land, and begged the assistance of the people, who readily came to my assistance. When I returned, which was about three o'clock, in the morning, some of my family told me, they had been on shore, armed, and taken all my calves, being seven in number; two of the poorest and smallest, they sent on shore in the morning; the others, with four sheep they had some days before, they carried off without paying any thing for them. I do further declare, the abuses and threats I received, from Capt. Linzey and the doctor, were the occasion of my moving off the island, leaving my interest. And I declare, that I never refused Capt. Linzey, or any other person belonging to any ship of war, entertainment in my house, or a supply of provisions that I had on my farm, and could spare. And I further declare, that on the night of the 29th instant, the aforesaid doctor, as my wife informs me, came on shore and demanded my gun, with his sword in hand, which she delivered to him, and I have not seen it since, though it was the only weapon of defence that I had on the island.

The value of the sheep, calves, and gun, which they took from me, and the use of my horse and well, are as follow, viz.:

Four sheep,	£2 16 0
Three calves, four months old,	. 3 6 0
Four quarters of veal, sixty pounds, sold,	2 8 0
One gun taken out of my house by the doctor of the ship, of great value,	3 0 0
Riding my horse and use of my well,	. 3 0 0
	£15 6 0

ELISHA NYE.

BARNSTABLE, ss. MAY 31, 1775.

Sworn to, before

THOMAS SMITH, *Justice of the Peace.*

POPULATION OF MASSACHUSETTS, 1776.

Counties.	Whites.	Blacks.	Total.
Suffolk,	27,419	682	28,101
Essex,	50,903	1,049	51,952
Middlesex,	40,119	702	40,821
Hampshire,	34,315	245	34,560
Plymouth,	26,906	487	27,393
Barnstable,	15,344	171	15,515
Bristol,	26,656	583	27,241
York,	17,593	241	17,834
Dukes,	2,822	59	2,881
Nantucket,	4,412	133	4,545
Worcester,	46,331	432	46,763
Cumberland,	13,910	162	14,072
Lincoln,	18,563	85	18,648
Berkshire,	18,552	216	18,768
	343,845	5,249	349,094

WARLIKE STORES IN MASSACHUSETTS, 1774.

Returns of warlike stores were received from almost all the towns of the several counties of Massachusetts and Maine, except Dukes and Nantucket, April 14, 1775. The aggregate was as follows:

Fire-arms,	21,549
Pounds of powder,	17,444
Pounds of lead balls,	22,191
Number of flints,	144,699
Number of bayonets,	10,108
Number of pouches,	11,979

Aggregate of the Town Stocks.

Fire-arms,	68
Barrels of powder,	357
Pounds of lead balls,	66,781
Number of flints,	100,531

AN ACT

OF THE

GENERAL COURT OF MASSACHUSETTS,

TO CONFIRM AND ESTABLISH THE

RESOLVES OF THE SEVERAL PROVINCIAL CONGRESSES OF THIS COLONY,

JULY 20, 1775.

WHEREAS this oppressed colony has, for many months past, been deprived of the free exercise of its usual powers of government, which has necessarily occasioned the public business thereof to be conducted by Congresses; and as many matters of the greatest importance for the recovery and preservation of that liberty, which God, nature, and compact have given to this people, have been resolved, done, and transacted, by Provincial Congresses, some of which have not yet had their full effect: and whereas, the legality of such resolves, doings, and transactions, may hereafter be called in question, and may occasion much litigation, unless confirmed and established in some known constitutional manner:

Be it therefore enacted, by the council and house of representatives of this colony, in general court assembled, and by the authority of the same, that all and every [of] the resolves, doings, and transactions of the several Provincial Congresses of this colony, from and after the fourth day of October, one thousand seven hundred and seventy-four, to the twentieth day of July, one thousand seven hundred and seventy-five, be, and they hereby are confirmed and established, as lawful and valid, to all intents, constructions, and purposes whatsoever, as fully and effectually, as if the same resolves, doings, and transactions, had been done by any general court or assembly of this colony.

And be it further enacted, by the authority aforesaid, that whenever any person or persons shall be sued, or prosecuted, before any superior court of judicature, court of assize, and general gaol delivery, or before any inferior court of common pleas, or any court of general sessions of the peace, or before any single magistrate, for any thing done in obedience to, or in compliance with any of the resolves, doings, recommendations, or other proceedings of said Congresses, such person or persons shall and may give this act, and the record of the resolves, doings, and transactions of the several Provincial Congresses aforesaid, in evidence, under the general issue, and the same thus given in evidence, shall avail to all intents and purposes, as if the same were specially pleaded: any law, usage, or custom, to the contrary notwithstanding.

And be it further enacted, by the authority aforesaid, that the records of the resolves, doings, and transactions of the several Provincial Congresses aforesaid, be immediately lodged, and forever hereafter kept in the secretary's office of this colony, and that the secretary shall copy and authenticate all such records of said resolves, doings and transactions, as shall be demanded of him to be used in any of the courts aforesaid, which copies, so authenticated, shall be received as full evidence, in said courts, of all such resolves, doings, and transactions.

INDEX.

As the table of contents indicates the principal subjects of this volume, the index refers to the pages where the names of persons and places are mentioned.

Printed in the USA
CPSIA information can be obtained
at www.ICGtesting.com
LVHW041249300923
759526LV00004B/778